"[Matthew Hollis] creates stunning juxt[...] [...]ntext and text. A repossession of *The Waste Land* is the chief effect of reading his book. But the structure of the book is itself a work of art."
—Helen Vendler, *Times Literary Supplement*

"Hollis succeeds brilliantly in bringing the literary landscape of the 1920s to life. . . . [He] turns a complex process of literary composition into a rattling good story. His criticism is personally engaged . . . and wonderfully compelling as a result."　　　—Tristram Fane Saunders, *Sunday Telegraph*

"[An] impressive examination of artistic creation. Hollis is expert at blending biographical detail with literary criticism. . . . It's a testament to his own talent at dissecting his subject matter and infusing it with imaginative empathy that the reader comes away from his 'biography' ready to look at *The Waste Land* with fresh eyes."　　　—Alex Clark, *Guardian*

"[Hollis] examines, with amazing forensic diligence, the context and fraught composition of the most famous poem of the 20th century. The clarifying light in each case is exemplary. The celebrated 'difficulty' of [Eliot, Pound] and their work was revealed as perhaps not so difficult at all."
—William Boyd, *New Statesman*, Book of the Year

"[Hollis's] quest is for all the seeds of intellectual and emotional pressure that shaped the poem. Such is the energy and engagement of Hollis in this task that you find yourself rooting for the emergence of the poem along with Eliot and his supporters, willing it into life as the book progresses. . . . The evolution of those pages . . . [has] become folkloric among Eliot's readers, but still Hollis invests them with fresh life."　　　—Tim Adams, *Observer*

"With elegance, wit and . . . warmth, [Hollis] tells the story of *The Waste Land*'s difficult birth. . . . At times the book reads, delightfully, as a group biography of modernism's bright lights.
—Susannah Goldsborough, *Times* (UK)

"[A] rewarding literary dive into the alchemy of a classic, from Eliot's leap of courage to Pound's scorched-earth battle for respect with *Poetry* magazine in Chicago."   —Christopher Borrelli, *Chicago Tribune*

"[*The Waste Land*] brings to life the exciting, even overheated, creative environment in which the poem came into being. . . . Meticulously grounding his account in time and place and paying close attention to the interplay of poetic intuition and critical mind, Hollis succeeds in gripping our attention."
                                                          —Hilary Davies, *Literary Review*

"Illuminating. . . . Hollis blends rich characterization and historical background to create a vivid picture of the London literary scene. . . . Hollis's sharp prose sings and is poetic in its own right. . . . This fascinating and brilliantly researched history will delight Eliot's fans."   —*Publishers Weekly*, starred review

"An authoritative and beautifully written account of the peculiar alchemy that produced the most influential poem of the twentieth century. This is more than the story of T. S. Eliot's genius: Matthew Hollis reveals how the forces of friendship, love, despair, madness, and ambition shaped *The Waste Land*. Literary history at its finest."   —Heather Clark, author of *Red Comet*

"A great work of art takes on a life of its own. This is the strategy—equally artful and assessive—of Matthew Hollis's superb new study. . . . [Eliot's] *The Waste Land* helped to define modernism and lives on vividly into our present day. To tell the life story of this poem, Hollis tells the story of the poet, sometimes minute by minute, conversation by conversation. The moving result—as Whitman would say of his own sweeping poetry—is that 'who touches this [book] touches a man.'"
                    —David Baker, author of *Whale Fall* and professor of English at
                                                                      Denison University

THE WASTE LAND.

THE WASTE LAND.

A Biography of a Poem

//

MATTHEW HOLLIS

W. W. NORTON & COMPANY
Celebrating a Century of Independent Publishing

for Claire

There is always another one walking beside you
— *The Waste Land*

I think of a friend who, in the early days, was as much concerned with the encouragement and improvement of the work of unknown writers in whom he discerned talent, as with his own creative work; who formulated, for a generation of poets, the principles of good writing most needful for their time; who tried to bring these writers together for their reciprocal benefit; who, in the face of many obstacles, saw that their writings were published; saw that they were reviewed somewhere by critics who could appreciate them; organized or supported little magazines in which their work could appear – and incidentally, liked to give a good dinner to those who he thought could not afford it, and sometimes even supplied the more needy with articles of clothing out of his own meagre store. To him, several other authors, since famous, have owed a great deal.[1]

– T. S. ELIOT, 1949

Recollections? let some thesis-writer have the satisfaction of 'discovering' whether it was in 1920 or '21 that I went from Excideuil to meet a rucksacked Eliot. Days of walking – conversation? literary? le papier Fayard was then the burning topic. Who is there now for me to share a joke with? Am I too right 'about' the poet Thomas Stearns Eliot? or my friend 'the Possum'? Let him rest in peace. I can only repeat, but with the urgency of 50 years ago: READ HIM.[2]

– EZRA POUND, 1966

Contents.

Illustrations.

Plates

Morocco 1960.

Winters were becoming harder. Each year the chill reached deeper into his chest, each year the breathing tightened. Doctors urged for warmer climes, and in the biting cold of an English January he finally left London for Marrakesh. But the recuperation was not to go as planned. Two hundred miles to the south-west, the dogs of Agadir howled in unison and rats were driven up on to the streets; a column of fire shot into the sky.[3] The earthquake unleashed at that moment was so forceful that it would shake the foundations of his hotel more than a day's journey away, whipping up debris and dust clouds that threatened to suffocate his airways. His evacuation north through the night came too late: particles of rubble had entered his lungs and would trigger an attack of emphysema that would incapacitate him for months. T. S. Eliot had five years of life ahead of him, but he would spend those years in poor health. He told Ezra Pound that nowadays he had to put most of his energy into breathing.[4] But Pound faced trials of his own. Released after more than a decade's incarceration for treason, he expressed to Eliot his sense of a life in extreme failure: *sitting in my ruins*, he wrote, *a sick mouse on a rubble heap*.[5] He was disgraced by war crimes, discredited as man and poet, 'and heaven comes down like a net / and all my past follies'.[6] Eliot would cable in correction: 'I NEVER FORGET MY OWN GREAT DEBT TO YOU TO WHOM ALL LIVING POETS ARE INDEBTED STOP'.[7] And he would open his arms in empathy: 'I have known well enough states of mind similar to yours,' he wrote.[8] But Pound's state of mind was not stable. A judicial pronouncement of insanity may have been all that saved him from a death sentence in 1945; fifteen years later, he told a caller in a faltering voice, *you – find me – in fragments.*[9] For Eliot, in contrast, the foundations were secure. He had no more poems left to write, but his standing as the eminent poet of the age was assured. Decades ago, he had left behind the formative style with which he had made his reputation, but from North Africa in that winter of 1960, he found himself returning to the one piece that had become the most influential of them all. Struggling for breath, Eliot began to transcribe, from memory, to raise funds for a London library, his poem of four hundred lines.[10] In capital letters he penned its title, and beneath it he wrote '1922', and beneath that he signed his name. His hand faltered as he recalled the epigraph, but for twenty-three pages it moved fluently. As it did, something remarkable took place: he recollected a line that had been culled from the drafts of the poem four decades before. Then, he had excised it at the insistence of his wife, Vivien, for whom it had been too painful a portrait of their troubled marriage. Now, he restored the words that once had been considered so hurtful. *The ivory men make company between us.* In writing out the poem, he had returned in mind to the company of those who once had worked alongside him. To Vivien, who had tuned his ear and lent a voice of her own, and who, through her marriage to Eliot, had accelerated the conditions that would bring the poem into being. And to the more forensic reader besides: one who had cleared the undergrowth of the poem in order to uncover its heart; one whose own life lay in tatters, and who looked to Eliot for his salvation. To him, Eliot inked the dedication for the last time: *for Ezra Pound,* he wrote, and, below it, *il miglior fabbro.* The better craftsman.

Ez Po and Possum
Have picked all the blossom,
Let all the others
Run back to their mothers[11]

— EZRA POUND, 1935

Armistice.

The runner was breathless when he finally caught up with the 157th US Infantry Brigade on the furthest reach of the Western Front. It was 10.44 in the morning and he carried with him the news that the ceasefire brokered overnight would begin at eleven o'clock. Further runners were urgently dispatched to inform the other companies; but with no clear instruction on how to proceed in the sixteen minutes that remained, the Brigade Commander of the 157th took the decision that there would be no let-up in fighting until eleven. Private Henry Gunther was pinned with his company beneath a cover of fog on the rise of Côté-de-Romagne. The war had divided the loyalties of many of those fighting, but for Gunther it had been more divisive than most. A German-American from East Baltimore, his neighbourhood were people from the old country; when war broke out he found himself the subject of racial abuse. He cared more about his job in the National Bank of Baltimore, and about Olga, the girl he wanted to marry, than he did about the war, but he was drafted into the infantry regiment dubbed 'Baltimore's Own' for the Maryland men who served in it. A supply sergeant, he witnessed harrowing conditions at the front and wrote to a friend at home urging him to stay out of the conflict if he possibly could. An army censor reported his letter and Gunther was broken to the rank of private; his fiancée ended their engagement, and with it the last of his morale. In the final minutes of the war, he lay face down on the ground occupied by his unit, bayonet fixed to his rifle, preparing to advance. Shells exploded in the boggy ground around him, sending up founts of iron and mud. On the slope above him, two squadrons of German machine-gunners counted down the minutes; they knew the armistice was imminent and could not believe their eyes when Gunther's company rose and began to approach through the fog. Had they not received the message of ceasefire? The Germans fired a round of warning shots overhead and the advancing troops dropped to find cover. Gunther alone rose to his feet and continued his advance. Perhaps he was driven to avenge his demotion, or perhaps to prove himself to Olga – perhaps he had lost all sense of having anything left to salvage; whatever it was that urged him on, he ignored the call of his sergeant to stay down. A German gunner waved him back, but he would not turn, and was fired upon. Gunther was killed by a bullet to the temple. Sixty seconds later, the war to end all wars ended.[1]

Henry Gunther was the last of ten million soldiers to fall in the Great War: a sad, senseless end, his hometown newspaper remembered.[2] Six million civilians had also died, and the influenza that was to follow would kill tens of millions more. The world had never witnessed destruction on such a scale or such wastage of life, and with the signing of the armistice a search to comprehend the conflict would begin.

Up and down the length of the British Isles, towns and villages lay bereft of young men. The loss of 'pals battalions', where friends and neighbours were in service together, had wiped out the men of some communities almost entirely. Many who survived returned physically maimed and were unable to work; some wore masks to hide their terrible injuries, others were crippled by what was then known as shell shock. Those who were physically able came home to a landscape of rationing, recession and unemployment. Social patterns had changed in the workplace and at home; women had substituted for men in the factories and the fields. Labour disputes built towards the General Strike of 1926; in Ireland, the War of Independence was followed by a vicious civil war. As old empires crumbled across Europe, some gave way to modes of communism sweeping out of the east. New countries emerged within old borders, nation states replaced kingdoms. Terrorist bombings in the United States fuelled a 'Red Scare', leading to round-ups of subversives. The General Strike in Seattle of 1919 was denounced as a Bolshevik revolution, one of thousands of walkouts nationwide; race riots swept through the Midwest. The prohibition of alcoholic drinks polarised the national debate and financed organised crime, while agriculture began to collapse. The 'roaring' economy of the early 1920s would overheat on the road to the Great Depression. And the reparations inflicted on Germany by the victorious Allies, and the treaty that defined them, would cripple that country and dismay the world, laying the foundation for disaster. Civilisation and progress – watchwords of the pre-war era – seemed emptied of meaning, robbed of certainty or value.

T. S. Eliot had spent the months leading up to the armistice trying to enlist in the United States Army. A childhood hernia and tachycardia had made active duty impossible, though he felt sure that he had something to offer military intelligence and had pursued applications with the Navy and the Army. But on 11 November 1918, he had returned to his job at Lloyds Bank in London, his efforts to enlist, he said, having 'turned to red tape in my hands'.[3] As an American citizen (he would not become a British subject until 1927), the obligations upon him were not those of the Englishmen he had lived among since 1914. Then, he had felt unassimilated: 'I don't think that I should ever feel at home in England';[4] but as the war progressed, Eliot came to understand it through the eyes of those who fought in it, 'as something very sordid and disagreeable which must be put through'.[5]

Ezra Pound had spent Armistice Day wandering through London, in order, he said, to observe the effect of the ceasefire upon the city's people; but instead of gaining insight he caught a cold from loitering in the November rain.[6] 'I know that I am perched on the rotten shell of a crumbling empire,' he had told an English audience in 1913, 'but it isn't my empire, and I'm not legally responsible, and anyway the Germans will probably run it as well as you do.'[7] But as the conflict ground on and on, he had worried about Eliot persistently and went so far as petitioning the American embassy to spare his friend from service. 'If it was a war for civilisation (not merely for democracy)', he told the ambassador, 'it was folly to shoot or have shot one of the six or seven Americans capable of contributing to civilisation or understanding the word.'[8] The armistice that spared his friend from service might have afforded some relief, but instead it brought only friction and unease. He remarked to James Joyce that the returning troops were 'competition' with which he must now contend.[9] London had been the 'place of poesy',[10] but now he felt a growing disgust towards a country that had offered up so many of its young men for slaughter, as he would put it in 'Hugh Selwyn Mauberley', for 'an old bitch gone in the teeth, / For a botched civilization'.[11] He would repeatedly tap his Adam's apple and announce that this was where the English 'stopped short': in their failure to speak out, to engage their minds.

'Everyone's individual lives are so swallowed up in the one great tragedy', wrote Eliot, 'that one almost ceases to have personal experiences or emotions, and such as one has seem so unimportant!'[12] And yet with so many lost and disfigured, few lives were untouched, and Eliot's and Pound's were no exception.

Jean Verdenal was a medical student of twenty when he boarded in Paris with Eliot in 1910. The young men bonded over the verse of Jules Laforgue, and found in one another a brother-in-arts of a kind rare in English–American letters. Verdenal was killed on the battlefield at Gallipoli, attempting to dress the wounds of a fallen officer.[13] Eliot would dedicate his first book, *Prufrock and Other Observations*, 'To Jean Verdenal, 1889–1915', adding in time 'mort aux Dardanelles'.[14] And he would carry a grief that he was hesitant to unburden, one that would cast a shade across the initial years of his life in London. Only later would he admit to what he called a 'sentimental' sunset: 'the memory of a friend coming across the Luxembourg Gardens in the late afternoon, waving a branch of lilac, a friend who was later (so far as I could find out) to be mixed with the mud of Gallipoli'.[15]

Pound had lost an artistic 'brother' of his own. Henri Gaudier-Brzeska was twenty-one when he met the American poet at an exhibition at the Albert Hall in 1913: 'a well-made young wolf', recalled Pound, as he attempted to pronounce from the catalogue what he called the appalling assemblage of consonants that comprised the sculptor's name ('Brzxjk——', he slurred, 'Burrzisskzk——'; *Jaersh-ka*', corrected the sculptor himself from behind the pedestal with a voice of 'the gentlest fury'). Pound bought pieces at a sum that would have been ridiculous, he admitted, had Gaudier any market and he any income. 'At any rate,' said Pound, 'he was the best fun in the world.'[16] Gaudier-Brzeska was killed in the trenches south of Vimy Ridge, at Neuville-Saint-Vaast, one month after Jean Verdenal; 'a great spirit has been among us, and a great artist is gone.'[17] The loss would fire in Pound such undirected and retributive fury that he would make an attempt of his own to enlist.[18] His belief in England and America would be forever poisoned, the poet Charles Olson believed, by his wish to avenge the young man's death.[19] It would seed in Pound a despair to which he would return in his darkest times. 'The instinct to kill is not extinct or even decently weakened,' he wrote, chillingly, of the armistice. 'The instinct to kill is still wakenable in nearly all men.'[20]

In November 1918, in its first peacetime issue, the *Little Review* of New York ran an edition 'Devoted Chiefly to Ezra Pound' – sixty-four pages in which Pound was talisman: poet, translator, critic, polemicist, essayist, and author of unsigned articles. He was, it appeared, master of all he surveyed. In nine poems he stretched out across its pages, magnificent and domineering as the beast of his opening line: 'The black panther lies under his rose tree'.[21]

(Wyndham Lewis had once watched Pound approaching strangers 'as one might a panther': showing no fear, expecting attack.)[22] But appearances were not quite as they seemed. The address for the journal's so-called 'Foreign Office' was Pound's own Kensington flat, and its 'London Editor' none other than himself. The issue was in part a pretence, leading *Poetry* magazine in Chicago to sneer that the *Little Review* had fallen 'under the dictatorship of Ezra Pound'.[23] And the last of its showcased poems would preview a different kind of trouble, riddled with an anti-Semitism that was soon to deform Pound's thinking.[24] He had turned thirty-three with the armistice. He had published athletically: a dozen volumes of poetry, translation and plays, three critical books and two anthologies, almost two hundred reviews in two years. But it was in his role as a literary impresario that he had been more influential still. In the years before the war he had been kingmaker: aide to W. B. Yeats, envoy to Rabindranath Tagore, publisher to James Joyce and Wyndham Lewis, agent and editor to H. D. (Hilda Doolittle), Richard Aldington, Robert Frost. He was a cultural supremo 'booming' his writers, and when he recommended, others listened. For Ezra Pound did not make polite suggestions; instead he would 'pass on the benefit of his discoveries to others', Eliot noted diplomatically, forcefully and without ambiguity: a style, said Eliot, that could lend Pound the appearance of someone attempting to tell a deaf man that his house was on fire.[25]

Everything had been going Pound's way, observed Richard Aldington, but somehow Pound had 'muffed' it: whether through conceit, folly or plain bad manners, the literary crown to which he aspired had begun to slip from his grasp.[26] Many who had resisted his presence at the heart of literature seized the moment to push him to its fringes. Virginia Woolf admitted to having read fewer than ten words of Pound's but her conviction of his 'humbug' was unalterable.[27] For years he had advanced an army of artists, but in the wake of the armistice he was to tell Marianne Moore that his days of boosting American poets in London were now behind him.[28] To James Joyce he wrote that he seemed better at 'digging up corpses' (by which he meant translating) than tackling 'this bitched mess of modernity' (poetry).[29] And he was stymied by the recognition in his own work that he had been unable to find a more 'ample modus' than either formal or free verse could allow him. Eliot identified in Pound the 'temporary squatter' that made him a restless figure. 'Every room, even a big one, seemed too small for him,' he observed. 'In America, he would no doubt have always seemed on the point of going abroad; in London, he always seemed on the point of crossing the Channel.'[30]

As Pound began to look further afield, Eliot's gaze sharpened its focus upon London. Three years younger than Pound, he had no achievements to match his friend's. He had witnessed, under Pound's direction, the printing of 'The Love Song of J. Alfred Prufrock' in Chicago, 1915, after it had been dismissed in London as 'absolutely insane',[31] and had seen, with thanks again to Pound, the same poem open his debut collection of poems from the Egoist, two years later. But the reception of that book had been underwhelming, and left Eliot feeling that he was regarded merely as a satirist, and hardly as a poet at all. Armistice Day had brought an introduction that might change all of that. It was an invitation to dinner for the coming weekend in Richmond, on the Thames, with Leonard and Virginia Woolf at their newly established Hogarth Press – a first encounter that Virginia recorded in her diary with pin-point insight:

Mr Eliot is well expressed by his name – a polished, cultivated, elaborate young American, talking so slow, that each word seems to have special finish allotted it. But beneath the surface, it is fairly evident that he is very intellectual, intolerant, with strong views of his own, & a poetic creed. I am sorry to say that this sets up Ezra Pound & Wyndham Lewis as great poets, or in the current phrase 'very interesting' writers. He admires Mr Joyce immensely. He produced 3 or 4 poems for us to look at – the fruit of two years, since he works all day in a Bank, & in his reasonable way thinks regular work good for people of nervous constitutions. I became more or less conscious of a very intricate & highly organised framework of poetic belief; owing to his caution, & his excessive care in the use of language we did not discover much about it. I think he believes in 'living phrases' & their difference from dead ones; in writing with extreme care, in observing all syntax & grammar; & so making this new poetry flower on the stem of the oldest.[32]

Making this new poetry flower on the stem of the oldest. Of all the learned analyses that Eliot would go on to receive, was there ever a more intuitive description of his art than this? She did not expand upon the nervous constitution she had identified, for she could not yet know the depth to which Eliot's mental health had plunged; but she undoubtedly sensed the trouble within.

'It's only very dull people who feel that they have "more in their lives" now –' Eliot had written in the war; 'other people have too much.'[33]

Too much was a phrase that recurred again and again in his letters. His mind was too much filled with practical worry; his private anxieties were too much; too much effort might be taken out of him; his financial outlay was too much.[34] He needed release.

I have a lot of things to write about if the time ever comes when people will attend to them.[35]

Even the shade of 'the one great tragedy' could not disguise the unhappiness he felt at home. His marriage to Vivien Haigh-Wood in 1915, two months after they had met, had brought only strain and near constant illness; he had pledged his love to another woman, Emily Hale, barely two years before. In the wake of the marriage, Eliot felt dazed and numbed, and would say that he could not yet see the price he had paid.[36] By the war's end, the Eliots had been serially unwell with one physical ailment after another, and from the deterioration of Vivien's mental health that had begun to materialise in the first winter of their marriage. With the coming of the armistice, Pound knew that Eliot was 'in a bad way', and that he had been ordered by his doctor to have a complete break from the strain of writing.[37] Bank work by day, literary work by night: the combination had exhausted his mind and body. But it was the mental distress that he found most debilitating, unable to right the increasing imbalance in Vivien's erratic behaviour: 'I do not understand it,' he confided in his mother, 'and it worries me.'[38] Once, Vivien had been the anchor of Eliot's decision to make a life in England, but another presence had disturbed their union almost from the start: Bertrand Russell. Suspicion and doubt and wrongdoing had worked into the heart of the marriage and was a torment that he could not bear. As the world began to rise from its knees in the autumn of 1918, Eliot had begun sinking to his. He worried that his mind no longer acted as once it did, and acceded to Vivien's insistence upon a period of what she called *complete mental rest*.[39] He would suspend writing critical prose early in 1919, and sign off the last of his wartime poems. When the moment came to renew his art, it was with two poems that pointed to a new mode: more open and allusive in style, more expansive in line and gait, guided by the phrase and not the metronome of formality.

For more than a year, there would be no further poetry. Work pushed, family pressed, the scar of matrimony deepened. 'Horror and apprehension' – 'the old symptoms', as he would come to call them – would lock into his daily condition, and nowhere more so than in his splintered and whirling life with Vivien.[40]

'To her, the marriage brought no happiness,' wrote Eliot. 'To me, it brought the state of mind out of which came *The Waste Land*.'[41]

I.

At a particular date in a particular room, two authors, neither engaged in picking the other's pocket, decided that the dilution of *vers libre*, Amygism, Lee Masterism, general floppiness had gone too far and that some counter-current must be set going. Parallel situation centuries ago in China. Remedy prescribed 'Émaux et Camées' (or the Bay State Hymn Book). Rhyme and regular strophes.

Results: Poems in Mr Eliot's *second* volume, not contained in his first ('Prufrock', *Egoist*, 1917), also 'H. S. Mauberley'.

Divergence later.[1]

— EZRA POUND, 1932

I.

Rain came to London in torrents. The snow that followed would harden to ice as the month grew colder and the streets began to freeze. Vivien had woken on New Year's morning to a migraine; by the evening her condition had deteriorated. She lay prostrate in the darkness, listening to her husband talking in the lounge with Ezra Pound; the sound of their voices through the thin walls drove her to distraction.[1] The migraine endured for twenty-six hours: 'worse ever yet had', she would report. When Dorothy Pound called on her two days later, she would discover Vivien near exhaustion.[2] The visit of the family doctor brought neither comfort nor hope. 'Am losing confidence,' she wrote in her diary.[3]

Daily, Eliot commuted the four miles from Crawford Mansions, the Eliots' claustrophobic flat in London's Marylebone w1,[4] to an office building in EC3 that stretched between the City's Lombard and Threadneedle streets. There, between 9.15 and five o'clock with an hour for lunch, he worked in the Colonial and Foreign Department of Lloyds Bank: 'documentary bills, acceptances, and foreign exchange' was awarded to him, he said later, under the false pretences that he was a linguist.[5] It was an unrelenting workload that encompassed weekdays and Saturdays, and he said that he came to know no scenery but that of EC3.[6] When Aldous Huxley later visited, he found Eliot not on the ground floor, nor even on the floor beneath that, but sitting in 'a sub-sub-basement', in a row of co-workers, 'the most bank-clerky of all bank clerks'.[7] Eliot had been with the firm for less than two years, but in that time the methods of work had modernised unrecognisably. Telephones were now installed on every desk, photostats made duplicates in their hundreds, while addressographs stamped automated mailouts and telewriters sped handwritten memos between departments. Most notable of all were the typists – women who had largely replaced male clerks in the war – who were now ubiquitous in every echelon of business. It was a workplace that was instrumental and mechanised: 'in a word,' a colleague of Eliot's recalled, 'the epitome of modern banking and efficiency.'[8]

Eliot had found refuge in such efficiencies. A year-and-a-term of teaching in schools had left him worn thin: underpaid, endlessly preparing lessons, unable to pursue his writing – losing, he sensed, in every way.[9] The bank by contrast provided structure: it brought conventional hours, and gave him evenings in which to write; it also paid him £360 a year, more than twice his teaching salary, a development that pleased Eliot's father.[10] 'My Tom is getting along now and has been advanced at the bank so that he is independent of me,' wrote Henry ('Hal' to his friends) Eliot Snr in a new year letter from St Louis to his brother, adding: 'Wish I liked his wife, but I don't.'[11] It had been three and a half years since his son's marriage to Vivien and still the family had not met her. Hal had not approved of the union, nor of his son's decision to abandon an academic career for literature, nor, for that matter, the decision to leave America to settle in the old country. The diplomatic pilgrimage Eliot made to Missouri in the wake of his wedding in 1915 had done little to ease the tension: he was, he learned, to be marginalised from the family's estate in light of the marriage, and father and son parted in bitterness.[12] But if he hoped that the life he returned to with Vivien would offer consolation, he would be disappointed; it was becoming 'the most awful nightmare of anxiety that the mind of man could conceive'.[13] It would take a wall around his working life for Eliot to preserve his sanity. So when, on 8 January 1919, around about midday, a telegram arrived at Crawford Mansions from Eliot's mother – a telegram *most terrible* – Vivien knew better than to interrupt her husband at work and waited instead for his return that evening. Hal had died from a heart attack; he was seventy-five. 'A fearful day, & evening,' recorded Vivien in her diary.[14]

For four days Eliot could not find it in himself to acknowledge his mother's message; when he did he was able to write little more than that he loved her. He longed for her to sing him the songs he knew in childhood.[15] With his brother he could be candid: all was dreamlike, nothing seemed real, and yet he feared waking to find the pain intolerable.[16] As a silence descended between mother and son it would fall to Vivien to break what she described as the inadequacy of correspondence between them. She would relay her husband's profound shock and upset at the news, and convey the couple's own thoughts for Mrs Eliot herself: 'These days are very awful for Tom,' wrote Vivien, 'he would give anything to be with you now.'[17] A further week would pass before Eliot would commit his own feelings to paper. Little, very little, of what one feels can ever filter through to pen and ink, he wrote.[18] Should he, he asked, return to be at his mother's side in St Louis? No, do not come now, his brother Henry counselled, not while the family's plans were uncertain.[19] And so Eliot informed his mother that he would continue at the bank while it was short-handed and travel home to her when things became settled. When, a week later, he wrote to her again, he did not mention his father at all. He would not return to Missouri for more than a decade, and by that time his mother, too, was dead.

A service for Henry Ware Eliot Snr took place at the Unitarian church on the corner of Locust Street, where his own father had once been pastor.[20] He was born, died and cremated a citizen of St Louis, the city to which he gave a good part of his life. His ashes were laid under evergreen shade in Bellefontaine Cemetery near the broad banks of the Mississippi River, in a modest plot not far from that of the Prufrock family, close by his father, beside the grave of his infant daughter, in ground into which his wife would follow. Eliot wrote in later years: 'they all lie in Bellefontaine now.'[21]

Fourteen years would pass before Eliot visited his father's grave.[22] It was then that he confessed, 'I shall be haunted by my last sight of him until my last day.'[23]

//

One bedroom, one bathroom, a sitting room, a kitchen (sort of), plenty of steps and a view from the top of them. Number 1 Hatfield House, Great Titchfield Street, Fitzrovia, the top-floor flat adopted by Wyndham Lewis after his return from the war – the 'jolliest suite of rooms', said Herbert Read, with something not found on any floorplan. 'He had a girl there "to pour out the tea",' explained Read. 'I did not catch her name but she is a young poetess who has not yet published,' Iris Barry, whose affair with Lewis would be summarised by him in a whistle-stop story of that year: dinner, drinks, pregnancy in a taxi, and a refusal to marry him.[24] But it wasn't quite true that Barry was unpublished: Harold Monro had printed four pieces for his journal, *Poetry and Drama*, in the Christmas of 1914, and Pound, who had work of his own in the same issue, had spotted them.[25] He wrote to Barry in his self-appointed capacity as talent scout for London, so initiating an education-by-correspondence that led to her move from Birmingham to 'enrol' in an exclusive course at what Pound liked to call his 'Ezuversity' (he was prone to a splash of eponymy). (A typical tutorial: the whole of art can be divided into the need for *concision* and *construction* – concision, 'saying what you mean in the fewest and clearest words'; construction, 'an image, or enough images of concrete things arranged to stir the reader' – and the glue to bind them was the sensual pulse: 'one must have emotion or one's cadence and rhythms will be vapid and without any interest' – objects are the aim, not statements or conclusions.)[26] By then Pound had submitted her work to *Poetry* magazine in Chicago ('I enclose 14 brief poems by Iris Barry. I want you to print the lot'), and published it in the *Little Review*, for which he was the London editor.[27] He provided her with a reading list of writers to avoid: Wordsworth (a dull sheep), Byron (rotten), Kipling (debased), Yeats (sham Celticism); only with the Roman poets did we share genuine concerns, and he urged upon her the works of Catullus and Propertius, and if she couldn't find a decent translation of either, well then – in words that would have more significance for him than he knew – 'I suppose I shall have to rig up something.'[28]

It was as a life coach that Pound's attention went still deeper. By the time Barry arrived in London in February 1917, she knew precisely what her expenditure would be on heat and bus fares, that alcohol lamps were cheaper than electricity, and how to breakfast on a budget. She knew this because Pound had calculated it to the penny, and secured for her the best available room in Chelsea, with an open fireplace, a gas ring and wash cupboard on the stairs, an electric-metered light and 'a bawth with a penny in the slot geyser'.[29] He even found her a landlady who was accustomed to 'the ways of literature', meaning that she wouldn't suspect a single lady like Barry of fornication, provided she kept a shawl on the bed and called it a couch, and remembered to serve tea at weekends. And most important of all, he made introductions: a tea party with Eliot on her first Sunday, a soirée with Yeats on her first Monday, and in between he fed her dinner.[30]

First in an Italian restaurant on Old Compton Street, Soho, and then, when Zeppelins forced its closure, on to the New China Restaurant on Regent Street ('quite cheap . . . quite nourishing'), owned by the uncle of the notorious underworld boss Brilliant Billy Chang: a remarkable cast of talents would assemble for a weekly dinner through the war years and after.[31] There Iris Barry learned Pound's most important instruction of all – how, in conversation, to be always intimate, never personal.[32] There she set eyes on Wyndham Lewis, washed out, on leave from the front. There she saw Eliot, tall, lean, silent, formal as a bank clerk should be. There was May Sinclair, small, dark-eyed, crisply spoken, invariably dressed in raspberry pink. Ford Madox Ford (he had changed his name in 1919 from the Germanic 'Hueffer'), his voice booming from beneath his moustache on the subject of Victorian literature. Violet Hunt, loquacious, oblivious, sharp-tongued, telling how she peeled snails off the bust of Pound by Gaudier-Brzeska that she kept in the back garden (her parrot sounded only the words 'Ezra, Ezra').[33] Richard Aldington in military uniform looking every bit the country farmer, besides H. D., his haunted wife. Harriet Shaw Weaver, proprietor of *The Egoist*, upright like a bishop's daughter, arch hat and nervous air, and alongside her the Ovid Press in the form of John Rodker and his vermilion-haired wife, Mary Butts, authors and printers both. W. B. Yeats was an honoured guest, a lock of hair flopping into his soup. But by far the most essential and imposing of the regulars were Ezra and Dorothy Pound, who, Barry later wrote, never so much arrived as *entered*.

Into the restaurant with his clothes always seeming to fly round him, letting his ebony stick clatter to the floor, came Pound himself with his exuberant hair, pale cat-like face with the greenish cat-eyes, clearing his throat, making strange sounds and cries in his talking, but otherwise always quite formal and extremely polite. With him came Mrs Pound, carrying herself delicately with the air, always, of a young Victorian lady out skating, and a profile as clear and lovely as that of a porcelain Kuan-yin.[34]

In wartime the table talk was of air raids and literary squabble, the explosion at Alfred Mond's munitions yard; in peacetime: social reform and continuing squabble, Catullus, sculpture, Amy Lowell, translation out of the Orient, Keats, ragtime, the Ballets Russes, even a row of stone houses in Earl's Court guarded by a row of stone dogs. And whatever the year, whenever the occasion, whether with a debutante such as Barry or a statesman like Yeats, the talk of the poets never strayed far from the important matter of getting published.

In January 1919, Eliot had only one volume of poetry to his name: a slim collection comprising just a dozen poems in a modest print run of 500 copies. But these were no ordinary poems. *Prufrock and Other Observations* had been published in London in 1917 at the Egoist. Its lyrical intelligence ought to have set the literary world alight, but instead it had met mostly with condescension and a soured bemusement ('erudition is one thing, the dictionary another, and poetry different from either of them', typified the response).[35] Notices had been more forgiving in New York than they had in London, but the book had been published *solely* in Britain, and that had proven a hindrance to Eliot of two kinds. For one, he was an American poet who lacked an American readership; for another – and this was the more pressing concern – the lack of a US publisher left him unable to establish copyright in America, which was only conferred upon books manufactured in (and not merely imported into) that country. No American copyright, no American royalties, and Eliot could hardly earn money as an author if he had no US sales. And if he could not generate earnings from his writing then how could he face his family after all that had happened and call himself an author? By the turn of 1919, the quest had become urgent: he required an American book with an American publisher if for no other purpose than what he now didn't mind admitting were 'private reasons'.[36]

Four months had passed since Ezra Pound delivered a typescript of Eliot's to Alfred Knopf, New York, without so much as an acknowledgement of receipt.[37] The silence worried Eliot, as it did Pound, who had irons of his own in the publisher's fire. Pound had put before Knopf a selection of his own prose, *Instigations*, a sequel to his *Pavannes and Divisions* which the same publisher had issued in 1918. That book had been a colourful hybrid of prose and poetry, a manifesto for Pound's early art, and the first publication of 'A Retrospect', his revisitation of Imagism; it also located his sense of a tradition in troubadour and Elizabethan verse, and articulated his long-standing belief that humanity's hope for social improvement lay with the arts, and that artists were the antennae of the race.[38] It would be 'a miscellany of the outlandish',[39] as one review would call it, and that was an approach that similarly suited Eliot, who had not enough original verse for a full collection of poems, only what he called 'the overworked, distracted existence of the last two years', but which marked a pragmatic response to the dual challenge of finding an imprint and creating a copyright. 'This book is all I have to show for my claim,' he confessed: 'it would go toward making my parents contented with conditions – and towards satisfying them that I have not made a mess of my life, as they are inclined to believe.'[40] The day after he wrote this, Eliot's father died.

Eliot had been desperate to show some evidence that his chosen career was not a failure. Four and a half years had passed since he had left behind a promising academic career at Harvard University for the life of an unknown writer in Europe. His father had then deplored the decision, but even so trusted his son to make a success of himself. A single edition of twelve poems from an avant-garde London press had seemed a poor return to both men. By 1919, Eliot was a young man under pressure exhibiting an unusual patience. 'The only thing that matters is that these should be perfect in their kind,' he acknowledged of his poems that spring, 'so that each should be an event.'[41] (A poem does not *say* something, it *is* something, he would write in 1948.)[42] He was demonstrating the exacting approach to his poetry that he would maintain throughout his life; in time, he would say that the most important thing for a poet to do was to write as little as possible.[43] Even so, *some* tangible validation of his art was sorely needed, and with his father's passing Eliot was burdened with a debt he suddenly felt unable to repay. 'If I can think at the end of my life that I have been worthy to be his son I shall be happy,' he wrote in a letter to his mother.[44] He had failed in his father's lifetime: he must not fail within hers.[45]

But Eliot's hopes for literary preferment were about to be dashed, as were Pound's for his *Instigations*. At the end of January, Alfred Knopf replied that he was turning down both typescripts. Pound's last book had been far from a commercial success, and Knopf had no wish to follow on in kind, nor for that matter to sponsor the hybrid offered by Eliot, when what he really wished to see was an adequate volume of poetry. For both Pound and Eliot this was a significant blow. Knopf had been the publisher of Pound's last three books and of an anonymous booklet by Eliot on Pound: it seemed to make every sense for the publisher to move forward with both writers, but it wasn't to happen. Pound told his father wearily that Knopf had 'given out'; for the remainder of their working lives, they would have no further dealings.[46] But Eliot could not bear to share a similar disappointment with his mother, and had disclosed little more to his brother by February, save to say euphemistically that his typescript was yet to find a berth.[47] The rejection seemed all the more remarkable against the background of boom in new verse that the bigger houses of New York had published since the end of the war: Edgar Lee Masters and Amy Lowell with Macmillan; Sherwood Anderson with Huebsch; Holt, Rinehart and Winston, publisher of the young Robert Frost, would see the Pulitzer Prize for poetry shared between volumes by Carl Sandburg and Margaret Widdemer (the inaugural award had just gone to Eliot's St Louisan neighbour, Sara Teasdale). With avenues closing before them, Eliot and Pound now turned as one for assistance: to a lawyer, art collector, patron of the arts in New York, a man who would not only find a publisher in the US for both books, but would in time secure a publishing contract for *The Waste Land*.

'If there were more like you,' quipped Pound in 1915, 'we should get on with our renaissance.'[48] The 'you' was John Quinn, whom

Pound had identified as a prospective patron worth his attention. And get on with it they did: not only with Pound's advancement but with that of James Joyce and W. B. Yeats. Each would benefit from a tailor-made patronage by Quinn that included the funding of appointments and publications, the purchasing of typescripts, and literary and legal representation. Quinn was a collector of contemporary European painting and a corporate lawyer of Irish descent; he took a special interest in the old country and had assisted Yeats in the founding of the Abbey Theatre in Dublin. His republican sympathies earned him the friendship of Sir Roger Casement, who had been arrested by the British government three days before the Easter Rising in April 1916 and hanged four months later in Pentonville Prison for his efforts to import German munitions. Quinn's campaign for a posthumous pardon was unsuccessful, but then his own position was not without complication: he repudiated armed conflict, and reported to British intelligence on Irish revolutionary activity in the United States. He was a man in need of direction, suspected Pound, who took it upon himself to ensure that Quinn didn't fritter a single dollar further in supporting the outmoded and defunct, but would redirect his capital to where it was needed. From London, Pound undertook for Quinn a sweeping survey of everything discerning that came to his attention – what he called his 'encyclopedia Ezraica' – and it was in one such letter, in August 1915, that Pound first mentioned T. S. Eliot. 'I have more or less discovered him,' he boasted to Quinn – and with some justification.[49]

Eliot had arrived in London in 1914, knowing no one, with a sheaf of loose poems in his bag. 'The first recognition I received was from Mr Ezra Pound,' he said later.[50] It was an encouragement that proved decisive at a moment when a career in the academy awaited him. Pound got to work on finding a publisher. He sent 'Portrait of a Lady' to the New York periodical *Smart Set*, and then, when it was turned down, to the New Jersey magazine

Others, where it was accepted.[51] He sent 'Preludes' and 'Rhapsody on a Windy Night' to Wyndham Lewis, who took them for the second (and, as it turned out, final) instalment of his excoriating journal *Blast* in July 1915.[52] By then, the first and most important of his publications had been achieved: 'The Love Song of J. Alfred Prufrock' had appeared in *Poetry*, Chicago, in the summer of 1915, after six months of haranguing by Pound ('*Do* get on with that Eliot').[53]

When Pound tested a full collection of Eliot's work on his own London publisher, Elkin Mathews, he received only a grumble about the price of paper, and a request for a financial subsidy, and so took it instead to Harriet Weaver. '"The Egoist" is doing it,' he told John Quinn at the time, or rather *The Egoist* in name, as Pound had borrowed the printing cost and was to take on the publisher's risk himself. 'But Eliot don't know it, nor does anyone else save my wife, and Miss Weaver of the Egoist. & it is not for public knowledge.'[54] It would take four years to sell the print run; there would be no reprint.

Two years passed between the publication of 'Prufrock' the poem and *Prufrock* the book. But one critic hadn't been willing to wait. Arthur Waugh was a veteran literary reviewer for the *Daily Telegraph*, but it was in the *Quarterly Review* that he pronounced Eliot to be exemplary of a generation who had traded beauty for 'incoherent banalities', and in so doing had released a literary anarchy upon readers from which only the Georgians (corralled under the direction of one J. C. Squire) could save them.[55] In what was intended as a sermon to youth, Waugh warned readers repetitively of 'the banality of a premature decrepitude' (here he meant Eliot), and of 'wooden prose, cut into battens' (here he meant Pound), and likened his own literary duty to that of a Spartan father who knew that to make an exhibition of a delinquency was the best deterrent for any son. As it would transpire, this particular father's son would be undeterred. Evelyn Waugh would title one of his novels *A Handful of Dust* after a line of *The Waste Land*, and in another would have a character declaim it from a balcony megaphone; a third novel would recall the poem and its author once again.[56]

Arthur Waugh typified a stance echoed by the likes of *The Times*, who found the poems 'frequently inarticulate', barely above triviality ('they certainly have no relation to "poetry"'), and the Boston *Literary World*, which suggested that this young revolutionary would be better served 'on traditional lines'.[57] And for each condemnation there was a rebuttal by Pound. Eliot had abandoned beauty for strangeness, came the charge; quite the reverse, countered Pound, *his melody rushes out*. The craft was untidy; *you will hardly find such neatness* (Pound). The poems lacked emotion; *rubbish* – Pound fumed – *there is no intelligence without emotion*. Eliot was guilty of cleverness; Pound insisted on his genius.[58]

'Silly old Waugh', said Pound, relentless in Eliot's defence. 'His practice has been a distinctive cadence, a personal modus of arrangement, remote origins in Elizabethan English and in the modern French Masters, neither origin being sufficiently apparent to affect the personal quality.'[59] In three short phrases, Pound had distilled Eliot's craft: an original rhythm, an inventive form, a personal take on tradition.

A distinctive cadence. When Eliot said of Dante in 1929 that 'genuine poetry can communicate before it is understood', he would describe something close to a central nervous system for poetry: that a poem has a pre- or para-linguistic pulse – a pattern of emotive sound that suggests a tonal meaning before the words arrive.[60] He went on to call this the *auditory imagination*, a 'feeling for syllable and rhythm, penetrating far below the conscious levels of thought and feeling'.[61]

A personal modus of arrangement. A modern form: neither Victorian nor Georgian, Parnassian nor Symbolist, and not Imagiste or 'free verse' either, but a lineation and phrasing of his own, born of a studied craft. 'To put it briefly,' Eliot would advise younger poets in time, 'learn the rules before you start breaking them.'[62]

Remote origins, a personal quality. Tradition, but with an individual talent. 'Never attempt to do something that has been done, in your own language, as well as it can be done,' said Eliot, the result of which is mimicry; and 'never aim at novelty', the result of which is conventional vision; find a path between imitation and originality that will allow the only thing that can be said in the only way to say it.[63]

There was not a thing that was incoherent or banal about the craft that Eliot applied, as even a glance at just the opening three lines of 'The Love Song of J. Alfred Prufrock' would confirm.[64]

Let us gó then, yóu and Í,

Here began a formal metre: a trochaic tetrameter catalectic – a stressed–unstressed four-foot line, clipped of its final syllable. Propelling and directive as it is, no sooner do we tune our ear to it than it alters:

When the évening is spréad oút agáinst the sky

All that has been learned from the first line is cast out in a heartbeat. The delicacy of the unstressed pyrrhic that muffles the opening steps; the sturdy mid-line spondee stress spreading out over spread out.

Like a pátiént étherised upón a táble;

It has been said of this third line that upon reaching the word *etherised* the history of modern literature began, so surprising and juxtaposed and electrifying was its introduction. Here was *distanced intimacy* for sure – a chemical word from outside the emotional register of the poem registering emotively within it. It is from the pull and push of predictive rhythm that a line receives its charge:

and *etherised* was a dynamo, lighting a line of hexameter that was like no known hexameter.

And to think they called it free verse.

In 1929, after a reading of 'Ash-Wednesday' at the Oxford Poetry Club, an undergraduate asked Eliot: 'Please, sir, what do you mean by the line: "*Lady, three white leopards sat under a juniper tree*"?' Eliot looked at him and said: 'I mean, "*Lady, three white leopards sat under a juniper tree.*"'[65]

If you experience the cadence then you animate the image, and if you can do that then you have communed through your senses with the poem before it has been decoded by the brain phenomenologically. The rest – intention, allusion, tradition, context – is additional, and is something that happened around the event of the poem, but which is not the poem itself. The meaning of a poem is its sensory event: imagined pictures cast on received sounds.

'Mr Eliot is one of the very few who have brought in a personal rhythm, an identifiable quality of sound as well as of style': of this Ezra Pound was in no doubt. 'And at any rate, his book is the best thing in poetry since . . . (for the sake of peace I will leave that date to the imagination).'[66]

//

18 Crawford Mansions, Homer Row, Marylebone w1, was the compact, three-roomed apartment into which the Eliots had moved in the spring of 1916, a year after the property was built; it would remain their home until November 1920. Vivien said it was the tiniest flat imaginable: 'just a dining room – a drawing room – a large bedroom – a kitchen and a nice bathroom', a modest 700 square feet in all. She decorated the place herself, with wallpapers of black and white stripes in the hall and orange in the dining room, which doubled as Eliot's dressing room and the study from which he worked with his back to the fireplace.[67] Running hot

water meant that the property was a cut above the neighbourhood, while a small iron balcony accessed from the kitchen allowed just a little of the outside in. Vivien had taken to the place at first, and considered it the Eliots' 'remote tower', a parapet where neighbours were strangers and living was anonymous: she came to think of it as 'a wilderness'.[68]

The apartment overlooked the boisterous Laurie Arms (now Larrik) public house in what Vivien described as 'a little noisy corner, with slums and low streets and poor shops close around'.[69] The noise would bother the Eliots. When Osbert Sitwell visited the flat, he reported that the neighbours below were two 'actresses' who spent the evenings singing around the piano or playing the gramophone loudly or hollering down into the small hours to 'gentlemen friends' in the street below. Eliot when he complained was given a patient explanation by the landlord: 'Well, you see, Sir, it's the Artistic Temperament.' Osbert Sitwell would later say that in the calls of the 'actresses' and the response from the street he could hear the voices of *The Waste Land*.[70]

'It is rather noisy,' Eliot said despairingly in 1919, three years into their residency: the flat had become very dirty, in need of re-papering and paint, and the Eliots were fatigued from living out of just three rooms.[71] Neither the neighbourhood nor the neighbours were quite what they should like, he confided to his brother, but a good flat in a good part of town was beyond their current means.

The situation was given a quasi-imagined life by Eliot in a dialogue for the *Little Review*, in which an Eliot-like Eeldrop and a Pound-like Appleplex surveyed the street from their rooms above. Each had known 'evil neighbourhoods of noise' and 'evil neighbourhoods of silence', and preferred the silence as being the more evil of the two; but this imagined neighbourhood overlooked a police station, which, like the real pub of Eliot's Crawford Street, would periodically become the centre of excitement, bringing the residents onto the street to spectate at some dramatic row in their dressing gowns. At such moments,

> Eeldrop and Appleplex would break off their discourse, and rush out to mingle with the mob. Each pursued his own line of inquiry. Appleplex, who had the gift of an extraordinary address with the lower classes of both sexes, questioned the onlookers, and usually extracted full and inconsistent histories: Eeldrop preserved a more passive demeanor, listened to the conversation of the people among themselves, registered in his mind their oaths, their redundance of phrase, their various manners of spitting, and the cries of the victim from the hall of justice within.[72]

Eeldrop was a bank clerk, a theologian and a sceptic with a taste for mysticism; Appleplex was an anthropological criminologist, who studied human science and recorded it in a large notebook; together they smoked from the balcony, watching for acts of cruelty on which to focus, like crows eyeing carrion or the 'tyros' that Wyndham Lewis would invent in 1921, 'all their villainies in this seductive glow'.[73] Eliot said that the figures were little more than a 'useless celebration', but Pound, who had commissioned the work from Eliot, believed 'his two queer chaps are quite real'.[74]

Two miles south-west from the neighbourhood of Marylebone, across the plains of Hyde Park, Ezra Pound was certain that he had located the centre of literary activity. Kensington: Pound's home since 1909, and, since his marriage to Dorothy Shakespear in spring 1914, 5 Holland Place Chambers, Kensington w8, a gloomy and chilly three-roomed curiosity of architecture that Pound told Wyndham Lewis had been 'designed by an imbecile or an Eskimo'.[75] There was no bathroom, and the toilet was positioned beside the front door, so an improvised wash corner was erected once a geyser and gas had been installed in the largest room. That room was almost too dark to eat in, let alone write, so Pound set up a triangular writing table in the corner of the tight, 'eight by ten pentagonal room'[76] that was the reception, whose regular guests included Richard Aldington and H. D., whom Pound referred to as Faun and Dryad, and who lived in the flat next door with not even enough sugar to borrow.[77] 'Remember, I can't do a thing myself,' Dorothy had warned her husband-to-be: she hadn't learned to cook, and so meals were prepared by Pound ('he is an excellent cook' – Lewis) by gaslight in one corner of the dark main room.[78] 'Why do we stop here?' he would ask her from time to time. 'That I have often wondered myself,' would be her reply.[79]

'If anyone in America did do anything good, he, she or it would come here.'[80] London had been the heart of the matter ever since Pound had removed his pince-nez in a Kensington 'bun shop' in 1912 and informed Aldington and H. D. that they were Imagists.[81] And so it was still in 1919, he told his father, as he caught him up on the gossip. W. B. Yeats had asked him to be a godparent; Aldington was bored of army life now that the conflict was over; Wyndham Lewis was about to have an exhibition in Regent Street's Goupil Gallery. Pound himself had completed his prose book *Instigations*, and had taken the opportunity to restate that Lewis was one of the three writers 'In the Vortex' who were worthy of readership: he was 'the man with a leaping mind', and, with him, James Joyce, so far beyond his contemporaries that he was 'utterly out of their compass', and, with them both, T. S. Eliot, whose work (along with his own renditions of the Roman poet Sextus Propertius) he had just sent out for publication: 'Confound it, the fellow can write – we may as well sit up and take notice.'[82] But disturbing news of his friend had just arrived.

'Eliot's father just dead,' Pound wrote to his parents; Vivien had called by with the message. 'Dont know whether he will be going to America or not.'[83] The doubt troubled Pound, for without an emissary in the States he knew that Eliot's opportunity might founder, and he asked his father in Philadelphia to contact Alfred Knopf in New York for news.[84] Eliot, meanwhile, had been concerned for Pound: he had detected a shift in the reception of the man and his work, and he was worried.

> *He* is well known, exciting various reactions of harmony or irritation; but there is no tradition in English verse which might have prepared for the general acceptance of his work; and England in 1910 could have been no more ready for him than in 1890; and perhaps there is even less to respond to him in 1918 than in 1910.[85]

//

For some time the Woolfs had searched for a manual activity that might release Virginia from the relentless pressure of her writing; by 1915 it was decided that this activity could be printing.[86] But wishing and doing were different things, as they soon discovered that the printing trade was a closed shop for unionised labour: there were no apprenticeships available to people like them, and their aspirations to become publishers seemed thwarted before they had begun.

On a blustery March day in 1917, the Woolfs passed beneath the arches of the Holborn Viaduct where they found the Excelsior Printers' Supply Company, 41 Farringdon Street, whose windows were crammed with elegant machinery of every kind: hand presses, accompanied by all the cases, chases, sorts and furniture that any self-starting printer could need. 'We stared through the window at them,' recalled Leonard, 'rather like two hungry children gazing at buns and cakes in a baker shop window.'[87] They explained their predicament to the proprietor, who assured them cheerily that no apprenticeship was needed: he could sell them the equipment they required, including a pamphlet of instructions, 'Everyone his own printer'; they would be making books in no time.[88] The Woolfs purchased a small platen machine: a device large enough to print a single demy-octavo page some 8½ × 5½ inches, but small enough to be worked from their dining-room table, where it would be delivered one month later.[89]

'We unpacked it with enormous excitement,' recorded Virginia, 'set it on its stand – and discovered that it was smashed in half!' The mechanism had shattered in transit and would have to be repaired before they could begin. The scale of the task was not lost on Virginia: it would be 'the work of ages', she told her sister Vanessa Bell, especially if she continued to muddle the *h*s and *n*s as she had in distributing the sorts. 'I see that real printing will devour one's entire life.'[90]

A new press had acquired a new home: Hogarth House on Paradise Road in Richmond, then Surrey, now Greater London, just a few hundred yards from where the oldest standing bridge across the Thames arced into Alexander Pope's Twickenham. It was by far the nicest house in England, said Virginia.[91] The ground-floor drawing and dining rooms had light, high ceilings; there was a first floor with a bedroom for each of them and a cast-iron bath; four small bedrooms on the floor above, quarters for the servants and nurses, glimpsing the canopy of Kew Gardens; and the heart of the industrial hive: the basement, the vaulted roof under which the press worked amid the cellars and scullery, the household kitchen, and a door leading out to a high-walled garden. It was most likely here that the press began its tradition of using old galley proofs as toilet paper in the ramshackle loo.[92] Virginia was undergoing psychiatric care for depression when the Woolfs moved in during the spring of 1915. She had visions of sunlight on the bedroom wall quivering like gold water, and heard the voices of the dead while lying in her bed quite 'mad'.[93]

The Woolfs had purchased their press together with a range of sizes of Caslon Old Face roman and italic type – Long Primer (10pt), Small Pica (11pt) and English (14pt), to which they soon added a large, Double Great Primer (36pt) in Old Face Titling for the covers and the display. When Virginia ran out of sorts, she would travel to the Caslon foundry that had stood in Chiswell Street EC1 since 1737 to purchase whatever was needed: on one day, 1s 6d of lowercase 'h', other days a replacement of worn or frocked sorts. William Caslon's type had become so firmly established with printers that by his death in 1766 he was described as the most widely read man in the world, and his roman face was known as *the script of kings*: the thirteen colonies of the uniting states of America chose Caslon for the Declaration of Independence in 1776; almost two hundred years later, Eliot's Faber & Faber would launch the career of a young Seamus Heaney with it. The face was so dependable that it carried a printer's maxim: *when in doubt use Caslon*, which was soon adopted as a catchy marketing slogan. And it would become the first face of *The Waste Land*.

'My wife and I have started a small private Printing Press,' Leonard wrote to Eliot in October 1918, 'and we print and publish privately short works which would not otherwise find a publisher easily.'[94] Roger Fry had mentioned to them that Eliot might have some poems: could they take a look? Three or four were tentatively proffered by Eliot (the fruit of two years, noted Virginia), and on 29 January 1919 he returned the pages that had by then been set in proof, describing them as 'admirable' (in fact it carried setting errors missed by both the Woolfs and Eliot), and accepting an invitation to dine at the end of the week.[95] There they would discuss the cover stocks, which would be individually mixed papers emblazoned with a label denoting in bright red ink the title of the work, 'POEMS', and, beneath that, its author: 'T. S. ELIOT'.

//

The Paris Peace Conference had opened on 18 January, and the treaty that would be signed in Versailles that summer placed the blame for the war exclusively at the door of Germany and her allies. It would impose a schedule of punitive reparations – a 'Carthaginian Peace', warned John Maynard Keynes, that would enslave the German economy and begin ticking a future of conflict from which 'the clock cannot be set back'.[96] Nor could the clock be stopped in Britain and Ireland, where pressure from the regions and nations was mounting and the political centre struggled to hold. The general election of December 1918 had been the first in which women (over the age of thirty) and men (of twenty-one or over) had been permitted to vote, but it had been bitter and divisive; the governing Liberal Party was terminally weakened and the new Labour Party had become the opposition. It had been called a 'khaki election' for its demobbed electorate and the campaign for post-war reconstruction, but after the armistice unemployment had swept through the munition factories and port towns. Strikes erupted on the Clyde and the Lagan, and riots ensued; on 31 January 1919, tanks rolled onto the streets of Glasgow to face down vast crowds of protestors. In Dublin's Mansion House, Dáil Éireann, an Irish parliament, convened for its historic first session while its president, Éamon de Valera, was detained in England's Lincoln Gaol (he would be broken out by Michael Collins that February). Sinn Féin had won an electoral landslide, and on 21 January it would fulfil the Proclamation made during the rebellion of 1916 to declare an independent Irish Republic. Under driving rain that day, in Cranitch's field in the townland of Soloheadbeg, in a quarry north of Tipperary town, a horse and cart bearing gelignite was ambushed by a small group of the Irish Volunteers, who were acting without the authorisation of the nascent Irish government or their own military leadership. The two officers of the Royal Irish Constabulary escorting the cart were Catholics; both were shot dead. Their deaths at the hands of republican forces signalled the beginning of a vicious struggle between the IRA and the British government.

'There has been a great deal of pneumonic influenza about,' Eliot told his brother on 27 February, 'and if one of us got it he would have to go to a hospital.'[97] Eliot may have been neurotic about his health and Vivien's, but on this occasion his concern was justifiable. The influenza that had torn around the world in 1918 had arrived in London for a third time that winter. It had ridden with the war. From an army mess tent in Camp Funston, Kansas, it had spread in March 1918 to the Eastern seaboard where the US Army was mobilising for embarkation to Europe. It crossed the Atlantic with the troops, overrunning the ports of France by April, and reaching the Western Front shortly afterwards. Throughout the summer of 1918, troops invalided to their home countries carried the virus with them into the lives of their loved ones. A second strain rose in New England in September 1918: this time it swept west, with a greater virulence than before, killing two hundred thousand Americans in a single month, before spreading worldwide: East Africa, West Africa, South America, China, Russia, Iran and on to the Pacific countries. The crowds that gathered in European cities in November 1918 to celebrate Armistice Day accelerated the spread of the disease cruelly, as did the demobilisation that followed. The virus attacked indiscriminately and worked with ruthless speed: symptoms in the morning could lead to death by the evening, and it killed even the young and healthy. In France and Russia, almost half a million lives were taken; one to two million Iranians died; estimates of deaths in India would vary between twelve and seventeen million. Indigenous populations with little immunity were devastated: Western Samoa lost more than a quarter of its population. The War to End All Wars had killed upwards of twenty million combatants and civilians, but as many as five times that number would perish in the pandemic of 1918 and 1919.

In Marylebone, influenza reached right into the Eliot home, to Ellen Kellond, the Eliots' maid, who collapsed with fever early that February. Without an additional bedroom in which to be treated (the Eliots used their second bedroom as a dining room), Ellen was put to bed on the living-room couch, where she was nursed by Vivien for five days and nights: 'We thought she would die on

our sofa.'⁹⁸ The Eliots were convinced that they too would contract the virus. They had only just recovered from a bout of flu that
had laid them low before Christmas, but it was exhaustion rather
than influenza that each of them succumbed to that February.
Eliot was consigned by his doctor to a week's rest in bed, and slept
throughout the first two days, attended by Vivien, herself already
exhausted from her intensive care of Ellen.⁹⁹ She had been manag-
ing the housework and the cooking, and was also looking after her
mother in Hampstead, North London, who had been taken ill at
the same time. 'I have been and am still afraid of Vivien breaking
down,' Eliot told his own mother.¹⁰⁰

St Louis, where Eliot's mother and sisters resided, had watched
the second wave of influenza rolling out of New England, and had
taken precautions that would suppress the spread of the virus. But
Philadelphia, home to Ezra's parents Homer and Isabel Pound,
was closer to the epicentre and had precious little time to react;
worse: it had been fatally complacent. The city government and
the newspapers told citizens that 99 per cent of the clean-minded
and the calm would be spared, and only the fearful and unclean
would fall ill. The decision to permit the annual Liberty Loans
Parade on 28 September 1918 would ignite a devastating contagion
that would later be described as the deadliest parade in American
history. Homer sent his son clippings from the papers: it made for
reading, said Pound, that amounted to 'constant testimony to local
imbecility'.¹⁰¹ He reported on his own health: 'Am suffering from
cold contracted on Monday in observing the ceremonies of armistice,' he told his mother in November. 'Have not yet succumbed
to influenza.'¹⁰² And nor did he intend to, for Pound was writing
in the *Little Review* almost as if weak health was the submission
of a weak mind. Wisdom, he suggested, could travel through the
senses, an osmosis between body and soul, but it required a strong
body to do so.¹⁰³ But in London preparations for the second wave
of influenza had been little better than those in Philadelphia. The

government had issued few guidelines on prevention, and those that were published had sowed confusion: brush your teeth, said a Westminster official; eat porridge, advised the *Daily Express*. On the streets of Eliot's and Pound's Kensington in 1919, one in four deaths would be from influenza. By the time this third wave had rolled on, almost 250,000 Britons and 700,000 Americans were dead.

'I have simply had a sort of collapse,' Eliot told his brother Henry on 27 February.[104] Two days of continuous sleep were followed by a week confined to the flat as Eliot was released from the bank on doctor's orders; he was not 'fit' when he returned to work the next week, reported Vivien, who while he rested had been 'picked up' by three Canadian servicemen at the Elysée Galleries, Bayswater, and danced as she had never done since before the war.[105] The death of his father, the grind of daily bank work, the maid's influenza, Vivien's swings between fatigue and euphoria, the disappointment of Knopf's rejection: the strain had been overbearing – the result of what he told his mother were 'the trying events and worries of the past two months'.[106] His mind had been turning on Locust Street, his childhood home in St Louis, and Gloucester, Massachusetts, where the family would summer in a house overlooking the sea. And most of all he had been thinking on his father. He wished that his father might have taken more satisfaction from his children, but then he had never appreciated success in their terms, he reflected, only by his own, which were derived from a world of commerce into which none of his children had followed him. Eliot told Henry that, in spite of their affection for one another, he felt that their mother and father were lonely people and that father was the lonelier of the two. 'In my experience everyone except the fools seem to me warped or stunted.'[107] Their physical reserve had been crippling.

//

'St Louis affected me more deeply than any other environment has done,' said Eliot in 1930.[108]

Dark streets and mud ways, sickbeds and flooded cellars, fever at every turn: such was the frontier town to which Eliot's grandparents settled from New England in 1837.[109] Rev. William Greenleaf Eliot had come with his new wife, Abby Cranch, to found a Unitarian mission among families who had gambled with their lives to reach so far west and who lived accordingly – drinking hard, gambling to ruin, duelling to settle their debts.[110] Those who could owned slaves; those who could not aspired to such possession. Cholera killed thousands during the 1860s, and the city sewers were little improved by the time Thomas Stearns Eliot was born in 1888. Putrid air clung beneath the gas lamps, coal dust plumed from the factory flues to blanket the city in poisonous fog. This was the yellow smoke through which J. Alfred Prufrock would wander, rubbing its muzzle on the window-panes, lingering in pools and drains; the purple shadows of Sara Teasdale's 'St Louis Sunset'.[111] To Tennessee Williams it was 'St Pollution', its buildings the colour of dried blood; he said the city made him want to drink.[112] To Maya Angelou, it brought a childhood of crowded, soot-covered, choking buildings: 'a new kind of hot and a new kind of dirty'.[113] What the city lacked in clean water, Walt Whitman had written, it made up for in 'inexhaustible quantities of the best beer in the world'.[114] Brewing boomed, but it also brought crime. Politics became bedevilled by corruption and cronyism. To one journalist at the turn of the century this was 'the shamelessness of St Louis': a city of blackmail, kickbacks and extortion, of payrolls padded with non-existent workers – where the banks were bursting with 'boodle', the hospitals crammed with rats, and the hotels churned liquid mud from the taps: governance 'by the rascals, for the rich'. When St Louisans complained that the streetlamps were out, the mayor replied, 'You have the moon yet – ain't it?'[115]

Before Eliot had reached his first birthday, the city's first electric streetcar had made its inaugural run along Lindell Boulevard, so beginning a 'white flight' from the West End to the suburbs by the middle classes. Racial enclaves grew entrenched. On 29 February 1916, St Louis became the first American city to pass a residential ordinance by popular referendum decreeing that no persons were allowed to move into a neighbourhood in which 75 per cent of residents belonged to a race other than their own. The separation of communities defines the city to this day.

St Louis was never an ordinary town. The refugees who came in waves from Europe's 1848 revolutions carried with them a language of radical collectivism. The defence of the city during the Civil War was entrusted to Joseph Weydemeyer, former officer of the Prussian Army and declared communist, a friend and publisher to Karl Marx: like many in the Union Army, he thought the abolition of slavery a precondition of the emancipation of all men. Freedom flowed into the arts. By the 1890s, St Louis was so crowded with musical venues and musicians that Missouri native Scott Joplin had trouble securing work. He wrote 'The Entertainer' in the city, but it was his turn-of-the-century 'Maple Leaf Rag' that would sell a million sheets for the pianola rolls that played in parlours across America; he became the King of Ragtime, a music named for the ragpickers who scoured the city's refuse for salvage, and the first African American music to find acceptance in white society.[116] It was the sound of the city that a young Eliot heard emanating from the nearby honky-tonk bars, and one he would return to in *The Waste Land*. The city would long continue as a radical nursery for musicians. Josephine Baker was born and grew up there; Chuck Berry and Miles Davis were born on facing banks of the city's Mississippi River; so were the house guitarist of the Blue Note jazz label, Grant Green, and the soul singer Fontella Bass, whose producer Ike Turner would begin a career of his own in St Louis with Tina Turner.

Writers, too, found in the city a rich inspirational seam. When Marianne Moore said in 1962 that she could think of no city more cultured than her hometown she had in mind the artists who had lived and worked in the city.[117] Mark Twain (Sam Clemens) had worked 'a solid mile' of riverboats before the railways obliterated the trade.[118] The novelist Kate Chopin was born and died a St Louisan: she attended the elite women's society, the Wednesday Club, and knew Eliot's mother. So too did the poet Sara Teasdale, who attended the Mary Institute, founded by Eliot's grandfather next door to the family home on Locust Street.

The land was old before it was new. Cahokia, centre of the Mississippian culture, an eleventh-century city on the eastern bank, was the largest settlement on the continent, on a scale beyond even the London of Harold II, last Anglo-Saxon king of England. It was a mound dwelling, with as many as 120 man-made, ritual earthen piles, some towering to 100 feet, overlooking land that would later be named for King Louis IX of France; it would remain in the memory as the Mound City long after the levelling of its earth structures in the nineteenth century.

St Louis was a city closer to Chicago than to Nashville, but its rivers ran south, and so did its history, and 'A river,' wrote Eliot, 'a very big and powerful river, is the only natural force that can wholly determine the course of human peregrination.'[119] St Louis was cradled in the arms of not one but two such powerful waterways.

There's a saying, sometimes given to Mark Twain, that the Missouri River is 'too thick to drink, and too thin to plough'; even so, its vast watershed was home to fifty and more separate native cultures, as well as the roaming great bison, when Lewis and Clark began their colonising expedition from the city in 1804. They carried with them army rifles and handguns, trading where they could, ruthlessly imposing their will where they could not. The meandering, springtime swells of Eliot's youth have since been tamed by embankments and dams, but still today the river carries the name of 'Big Muddy' for the sediment swept off the hills of western Montana and carried through ten states before circling the northern perimeter of St Louis and emptying into the mighty Mississippi.

It was this second river that flowed with such force through the heart of the settlements on either bank of the settlement. The 'Old Man' of American rivers made a vast entrance upon the city: from its headwaters in Minnesota, it drew upon more than one million miles in the great basin between the Rocky and the Appalachian mountains before discharging into the Gulf of Mexico. For Mark Twain it was 'that lawless stream', for Eliot 'a treacherous and capricious dictator'.[120] He loved to watch it from the Eads Bridge in flood-time.[121] His grandfather, caught in the Great Flood of 1844, once stepped from a second-storey warehouse window onto the upper deck of a ferry boat in order to escape drowning.[122] And though he said his people were New Englanders, and though his adopted country became old England, Eliot felt an incommunicable bond with the big river. 'Missouri and the Mississippi have made a deeper impression on me than any other part of the world.'[123] Igor Stravinsky said that no meeting with Eliot was ever complete without him returning in conversation to the Mississippi.[124]

By 1861, St Louis was the slave trade's most northerly enclave, bordered to the south by the Confederacy and on all other sides by free states. Its people were heavily divided between Germanic Unionists in the city boroughs and Confederate settlers in the rural hinterland. People were compelled to declare themselves, recalled Eliot's father: 'Life long friends were separated; families were divided among themselves – children following father or mother according to preference or influence.'[125] When Eliot's grandfather preached against the 'vile traffic', parts of his congregation walked out.[126] 'The institution of slavery is the greatest obstacle,' he pronounced, 'perhaps the only great obstacle, by which our moral, social, and general advance as a people is hindered.'[127]

Missouri had experienced some of the most atrocious violence of the Civil War: and vengeful executions and impromptu massacres continued in the Ozarks long after the war had ended. On 27 September 1864, twenty-three unarmed Union soldiers on leave were captured on the North Missouri Railroad by an irregular Confederate force led by the notorious 'Bloody' Bill Anderson; they were stripped, shot and their bodies mutilated, their train set alight and sent flaming down the tracks. The Union reinforcements that went in pursuit were massacred at Centralia; it is said that the decisive shot was fired by a young Jesse James. No wonder that to the youth T. S. Eliot, it was 'to me, as a child, the beginning of the Wild West'.[128]

Ulysses S. Grant had been the commanding general in the Union Army; he made the city his marital home before the war ('we are not so intolerant in St Louis as we might be').[129] As President of the United States he sponsored the Fifteenth Amendment of the Constitution that prohibited any state from denying the right to vote based upon 'race, color, or previous condition of servitude'. But the former Confederate states responded with Jim Crow laws, and the parks of St Louis remained racially segregated in Eliot's day, while the few Black schools that managed to operate were often attacked and burned and white supremacism marched annually in the streets in the city's Veiled Prophet Parade.

On 6 April 1917, when Woodrow Wilson had taken the United States into the Great War, Ezra Pound gave an appreciable shrug: 'America is doing what she damn well ought to do, and what so far as I can see, she ought to have begun doing sooner.'[130] Eliot wondered how St Louis might take it all – what the different nationalities and social groups might feel. He could imagine, he told his mother, a mob rising to smash the windows of Tony Faust's elite oyster restaurant on Broadway and Elm Street, where Adolphus Busch and Eberhard Anheuser, owners of the powerful brewery, dined at its so-called 'millionaire's table' daily.[131] But 'the mob', as Eliot had termed them, would have more impoverished targets in their sights that summer, and would do far worse than break windows.

As the June temperatures rose across the city in 1917 so did the heat of labour disputes. When a predominantly white, emigrant workforce walked out from the Aluminum Ore Company in East St Louis, the owners hired strike-breakers from the South, many of whom were Black. On the evening of 1 July, a group of white men in a dark Model T Ford drove through the South End, firing indiscriminately into African American homes. The bell of the True Light Baptist Church on Tudor Avenue rang out a warning that triggered the dispatch of an unmarked police car, an identical dark Model T Ford that was mistaken in the lamplight for the shooters' own. The occupants were five plainclothes officers; Sergeant Samuel Coppedge and Detective Frank Wodley were killed when residents fired on their car. For three hot days and nights in July 1917, on the Illinois bank of the Mississippi, some of the worst racial atrocities in the country's history were perpetrated.

African American men from Missouri had been among the first sent to fight in Europe that year when the US joined the war; while they served their country abroad, their wives and children were being boarded up in their homes by white rioters and burned alive. Newspapers recorded escapees being thrown back into house fires. Those who fled were shot down from the railway tracks by snipers. A lynched man swung from a telephone pole on South 4th and East Broadway; bodies were thrown from the new Free Bridge; one woman witnessed a beheading. Gangs of white men and women and even children torched and clubbed and shot their way through the streets and homes of East St Louis while police and army looked on. No tally for the number of African American deaths has ever been agreed upon, but estimates of one to two hundred victims have been advanced, with some six thousand burned from their homes.[132] It became known as the Massacre at East St Louis: 'a pogrom', wrote *The Crisis* that autumn, and 'the shame of American democracy'; in the words of Marcus Garvey, 'one of the bloodiest outrages against mankind'.[133] By 20 July, the *St Louis Argos* had reported a mass evacuation of the few remaining Black families.[134] Eight hundred miles east, in the White House, President Wilson refused to condemn the violence.

Later, in 1950, when T. S. Eliot wrote how the Mississippi could sweep away lives, he told of its carrying off 'human bodies, cattle and houses' in Mark Twain's floodwater. But his source for those words had been his own *Four Quartets* that described something more brutal and graphic: 'Like the river with its cargo of dead negroes, cows and chicken coops, / The bitter apple, and the bite in the apple.'[135]

Less than three miles separated the riots from the Eliot family home, but it might have been three hundred. Eliot's mother and father were summering at Eastern Point, Massachusetts, on the day the violence began in 1917. Eliot wrote to them there from London to say that he had just played tennis with Pound.[136] In the letters of that summer, the Eliots passed no comment on events in East St Louis, but W. E. B. Du Bois, sent by *The Crisis*, would report the horror he found in the days that followed. In 1903 he had prophesied that 'the problem of the Twentieth Century is the problem of the color-line'.[137] Amid the rubble of East St Louis he sounded a warning for all America.

Eastward and westward storms are breaking – great, ugly whirlwinds of hatred and blood and cruelty. I will not believe them inevitable. I will not believe that all that was must be, that all the shameful drama of the past must be done again today before the sunlight sweeps the silver seas.[138]

//

Check trousers, thick overcoat, top hat, fur for neck, long coat or cloak for term, rough coat for country, and day dress for term and day dress for country:[139] Bertrand Russell had been hounding Vivien for the return of his possessions, and Eliot had become impatient. 'It is not the case that Vivien "won't reply",' he wrote brusquely to Russell on 3 February. 'I have taken the whole business of Marlow into my own hands, as she cannot have anything to do with this or with anything else that would interfere with the success of her doctor's treatment.' Eliot had called a meeting: 'I have a great deal to talk to you about.'[140] That conference was, on the face of it, to release Russell from the contract of a shared cottage at Marlow, in Buckinghamshire, although the 'great deal' to which Eliot alluded was not about real estate matters. But the interview with Russell didn't go quite to plan, or at least not to Eliot's plan. Rather than relinquish his hold, Russell had identified the cottage as a retreat for himself and his lover, Constance Malleson, telling her 'I fancy Eliot would like to be rid of it.'[141] His unexpected offer to take over the property wrongfooted Eliot, who swiftly embraced the proposal as a resolution to a situation that he had come to find unbearable. But on relaying the offer to Vivien, Eliot realised that he had underestimated her attachment to the place and how unprepared she was for the rupture of letting it go. She had worked hard at the house and at the rose garden, and looked to it to aid her recovery: 'I should be *wretched* without it,' she implored. 'I *do love it*.'[142] Eliot was left to back-pedal in his negotiation with Russell, and wrote again, implying that he had been so overrun with worry that Russell's proposition had taken him by surprise. 'So that I think after all we must go on as we are, and hope that there will be fewer misfortunes in the future.'[143] Between Vivien's claims and Russell's, Eliot's defeat was unmistakable.

Tired. Misunderstood. Tortured. Tortuous. Four words that opened the four stanzas of an 'ode' that Eliot completed early in 1919:

> When the bridegroom smoothed his hair
> There was blood upon the bed.[144]

The Eliots had followed their honeymoon in Eastbourne in the summer of 1915 with a second in the autumn in the same place, but it had not gone well.[145] Eliot had worn a truss since childhood, Vivien was menstruating. Her brother Maurice reported that Eliot slept in a seafront deckchair.[146] When Vivien carried home to London the soiled sheets for cleaning, the guest house accused the couple of theft. 'It seems their sort of pseudo-honeymoon at Eastbourne is being a ghastly failure,' Russell had reported at the time from his flat in Holborn. 'She is quite tired of him, & when I got here I found a desperate letter from her, in the lowest depths of despair & not far removed from suicide.'[147]

Eliot had been an 'extraordinarily silent' postgraduate student in Russell's seminars at Harvard when they met in the spring of 1914, but he made a remark on Heraclitus so good that Russell wished that he would make another.[148] On meeting him again in London that autumn, Russell had taken a growing interest in Eliot ('exquisite and listless'), and, in turn, Vivien ('light, a little vulgar, adventurous, full of life'), so much so that by the autumn of 1915, to ease their finances, he had taken the couple in to his flat in Bury Street, London's Bloomsbury.[149] 'I was fond of them both, and endeavoured to help them in their troubles,' he recalled, 'until I discovered that their troubles were what they enjoyed.'[150] Eliot returned the personal warmth, although his veiled portrait of Russell as 'Mr Apollinax', written at that time, recorded 'His pointed ears . . . He must be unbalanced,' and his laugh 'like an irresponsible foetus'. The sound of that laughter, sinking through sea water, sinking like the cries of the *Lusitania*, sinking beneath coral, like that of the old man of the sea, like the Phoenician Sailor:

> Where worried bodies of drowned men drift down in the
>   green silence,
> Dropping from fingers of surf.[151]

Russell responded that he would come to love Eliot, 'as if he were my son'; he told his then-lover, Lady Ottoline Morrell, that what he extended to the young couple was 'the purest philanthropy', perhaps even believing it himself.[152] But his feelings for Vivien were moving in another direction. He had begun to observe her, hawk-like, admiring in her an effervescence that among Eliot's friends had earned her the nickname of the River Girl; and he particularly admired her moments of what he regarded as a coquettish cruelty towards Eliot. 'I myself get very much interested.'[153] Vivien, in turn, was not unresponsive. 'He is all over me, is Bertie, and I simply love him.'[154]

Ottoline Morrell understood all too well where this was headed: she urged him to desist, warning that he risked the Eliots' marriage by entreating Vivien to fall in love with him.[155] But Russell's investment in Vivien had already outstripped friendship. He would dine with her when Eliot was away from town and he would pay for her dance lessons, and, according to Morrell, began sending Vivien 'silk undergarments'.[156]

For a year the flirtation continued, heating and cooling, rising to the brim and then falling back. Russell spoke in 1916 of the 'end of the readjustment', and soothed Ottoline that matters were to be put on a better footing, and that everything would be all right.[157] But Russell had misjudged feelings, and a crisis was coming.

In the autumn of 1917, the Eliots had been looking for a retreat in the country in which to spend their weekends, somewhere within easy reach of London, but rural enough to write in and to ease recovering nerves. Vivien had taken rooms at Sewhurst Farm on Abinger Common, in the Surrey Hills, as a base from which to house hunt: it was the last of sixteen places that she had tried, or so she told Eliot's mother.[158] But the site was almost certainly found not by Vivien but by Russell, who knew the farmers personally, and who may have stayed for a while at the neighbouring Lemon's Farm.[159]

On the weekend of 20 October 1917, baked in sunshine and blue skies, the Eliots took up lodgings at the farmhouse which was tucked into a picturesque hollow high on the Greensand Ridge of the Surrey Hills. A brook descended through the grounds on its way into the Tillingbourne, where it crossed under a sandstone cart track that climbed from the valley. Two footpaths branched around the farm: one banked south-west to Sewer's Copse, a second climbed south-east into the pine woods of High Ashes Hill and the birch forest beyond that opened onto the summit of Leith Hill.[160] The farmers, Alfred and Annie Marie Enticknap, didn't take boarders, but they were once gardeners at nearby Shiffolds to the poet R. C. Trevelyan, who was known to Eliot, and were happy to take in friends of his and spoil them with homemade butter, fresh eggs and fowl. It was, thought Eliot, an idyll – a 'fairy tale farm', wrote Vivien[161] – but what transpired there would initiate a living hell for Eliot.

The farm was more cut off than Vivien said she had expected: six miles from the nearest railway station, she told Mrs Eliot – in fact three, but far enough that Eliot would have to shorten his visits to allow for the longer commute to London. No sooner had he returned to Lloyds on that first weekend than a north-west wind blew in, sending temperatures plummeting towards freezing; it was then that Vivien was joined at the farm by Russell.

'At last I spent a night with her,' Russell confided to Constance Malleson, who had succeeded Morrell as Russell's lover.

> I intended to be (except perhaps on very rare occasions) on merely friendly terms with Mrs Eliot. But she was very glad that I had come back, and very kind and wanting much more than friendship. I thought I could manage it – I led her to expect more if we got a cottage –[162]

There had been a quality of loathsomeness about the night together, he said, that he found difficult to describe, but describe it he would to Malleson, on whose mercy he now fell. '*It was utter hell*,' he confessed: he felt imprisoned in his own egotism, sick with himself and the pain that he spread everywhere, and felt a devouring hunger within him that was, he admitted, 'ruthless & insatiable'.[163]

It was Vivien who had found the cottage in Marlow soon afterwards, in December 1917: a narrow, three-storey terrace and former post office with a neat walled garden in the street where Shelley once lived, Eliot would be heard to say.[164] It had been rented to restore the Eliots' fragile health, and had burdened their expenses hugely; but a solution to that had been found in Russell, who came in on the lease and also provided the furniture. It was an arrangement that promised something to them all. To Eliot, it offered a weekend retreat from his day job at Lloyds, his evening work for *The Egoist* and his twice-weekly lectures. For Vivien it would provide the rural recuperation that she had been seeking. For Russell it promised a writing sanctuary to finish his book, *Roads to Freedom*; with Eliot largely in London, he envisaged a working life there 'with Mrs E'.[165]

But arrangements had been disrupted almost at once when, in January 1918, a pacifist article by Russell appeared in *The Tribunal* warning of the imperial threat of American militarism, in a rousing echo of Karl Marx: 'All that we hold dear will be swallowed up in universal ruin.'[166] The revolution in Russia was less than a year old, and the British government was not about to tolerate Bolshevism in its own backyard. Russell was charged with interfering with the war effort, and sentenced to six months' incarceration in Brixton Prison, a deterrent that did not entirely have the desired effect: 'I found prison quite agreeable,' he recorded. 'I wrote a book.'[167] It was there in the summer of 1918 that he had decided to withdraw from the Marlow arrangement, leaving Eliot to find a replacement tenant for his share of the property, which he had done by the time of Russell's release in the middle of September.

Eliot may never have known for certain what transpired between Vivien and Russell, and it is unlikely that he ever confronted them. But then worse than knowledge may have been suspicion itself, which for Eliot would have grated against the pride of his well-made manners and his belief in respectability and composure. By the summer of 1918, with Russell still confined to Brixton Prison, Eliot appeared overcome by doubt. It was then that he made an unexpected call on Russell's mistress, Constance Malleson, who felt perplexed as to the motivation of his visit. She experienced the detached and 'cat-like' presence of his eyes observing her, and beneath them what she sensed as 'a curiously deep despair'.[168] Perhaps the call had been little more than a personal courtesy, or a promise fulfilled to Russell; but perhaps Eliot had come to find out exactly what Malleson knew.[169]

On 26 November 1918, a fortnight after the armistice, Russell took Vivien to dinner and told her that he was unlikely to renew contact for some time. The conversation passed off without disaster, he reported with relief, but it had been a heavy-handed manoeuvre that undoubtedly stirred in Vivien a sense of rejection.[170] She told Russell in January 1919 that she disliked fading intimacies and that she was breaking off contact entirely. Russell maintained that it was not a matter of any distress to him, and yet he continued to paw and peck at the Eliots' arrangements, demanding the return of items that were impractical to retrieve now that the house was let furnished. *But the coffee-grinder*, he badgered, *the tea-table*: these he wanted as soon as possible . . .[171]

Russell had been a cuckoo in the nest of the Eliots' short marriage. He had dazzled and spoiled and harried Vivien, and had taken something very precious in the form of the couple's fidelity to each other. The cottage at Marlow would cast a shadow over the marriage until Eliot was able to release himself from the rent entirely in the summer of 1920. By then, the events had triggered in Eliot a despair that was to reach a crisis while he was in the company of Ezra Pound in France in the summer of 1919.

II.

Eliot had followed the poems of *Prufrock* with a silence that lasted almost two years. By the spring of 1917 he was 'rather desperate', believing that he had dried up completely. But he discovered he could still compose in French, and that writing in a second language alleviated a pressure to take himself seriously; he had written five poems when the impulse to write in English returned. Edited and abetted by Pound, he began in 1917 a run of English poems in a 'French' style, drawing upon the formal example of Théophile Gautier's *Émaux et Camées*, a work from 1852 that would, for the next three years, become a model for both Eliot and Pound. Said Eliot later: 'We studied Gautier's poems and then we thought, "Have I anything to say in which this form will be useful?" And we experimented. The form gave the impetus to the content.'[1]

The form was battened down. Gone was the melodious expanse of the *Prufrock* poems, and in their place a tightened lyric tetrameter, in nimbly stitched quatrains, with end rhyme clasping shut every second and fourth line. By early 1919, Eliot had half a dozen pieces in final draft, and was finishing two more. Opening on *a cavernous waste shore*, 'Sweeney Erect', completed that February, was anything but cavernous. Like its predecessors in form, it emphasised technical precision above linear expanse, objective observation above personal declaration, and was delivered in a style that was a reaction to the perceived excess of Romanticism. It was a form given further impetus by the mode of drafting: Eliot had recently begun composing on a typewriter, which he said had the effect of shaking off all his sentences that he used to dote upon, and leaving him with a style that was 'short, staccato, like modern French prose'.[2] The typewriter had made for lucidity, he told a friend, but he wasn't sure that it encouraged subtlety. Amused with amusing, archly mischievous, it should have surprised no one that the work would be accused of cleverness: *l'art pour l'art* was, after all, a point of principle for the Parnassians who followed Gautier. But cleverness was not the only accusation that the work of this period would have to face. For the culmination of Eliot's French form was about to produce the poem that he said he liked the most of all of them, but which included the most repellent lines that Eliot would ever write.

Ezra Pound didn't much care for how the draft of 'Bleistein with a Cigar' had ended (the longer title was still to come); he didn't much care for how it opened, come to that. He marked 'Diptych' on the top corner of the first draft, indicating that he thought the poem should comprise not one part but two. And he targeted its second line – 'And Triton blew his wrinkled shell' – for sounding too little of Gautier and too much of Wordsworth: 'if you / "hotel" this / rhythm shd. be / weighted a bit, / I think', he wrote in the margin, and Eliot took up the suggestion. 'And Triton blew his wrinkled shell' became *Descending at a small hotel*, modernising the poem in a heartbeat. Pound then scored a double line between the second and third stanzas, marking 'OK. from here anyhow'. But it wasn't OK, not yet, and he further queried 'punctuation?', and prompted quotation marks ('for clarity?'), before making a directing intervention in the final stanza, which had opened with a question, 'Who clipped the lion's mane?', until Pound changed 'mane' to *wings*, deepening the mythic dimension of the piece.[3]

These were good, renovating and clarifying interventions by Pound. But about the lines that would become most notorious, he had been silent. For the draft contained three stanzas on the title character Bleistein, a 'Chicago Semite Viennese', described in the poem as bent-kneed, his palms outstretched, mired in an associative language of degradation: *lustreless, protrusive, protozoic slime, money in furs*. Other names signalled a diminishment: a salacious Lady Volupine (from the fox-like *vulpine*) 'entertains' a Sir Ferdinand Klein (German: *small*); but it was the name of Bleistein around which the poem's deepest disgust would be built, a name meaning 'leadstone', an element weak in its metallic character, toxic at critical levels. Bleistein's appearance in the poem included the following two lines:

> The rats are underneath the piles.
> The jew is underneath the lot.

What was Eliot thinking? He would not elucidate; but then he didn't believe that any writer held an executive position when it came to interpretation. 'The only legitimate meaning of a poem is the meaning which it has for any reader,' he would remark in 1927, 'not a meaning which it has primarily for the author.'⁴ Intention, in other words, is unimportant: all there is in the end is effect. It was a neat sidestep, but it left the lines exposed without an authorial voice to defend them. For some readers, no defence was required: the lines were a benign or even affirmative exploration of hatred, whose weapon was irony, whose subject was subjugation itself; other readers have felt that the reference was inoffensively particular: to *a* Jew, and not to *all*, a stroke of character and not therefore general to a people.

'Beauty is difficult,' wrote Pound in 'Canto LXXIV'.⁵ He had made the point once before, in 1914 with Wyndham Lewis in *Blast*. 'The Art-instinct is permanently primitive.' That had been statement seven, of their manifesto; statement eight read: 'In a chaos of imperfection, discord, etc., it finds the same stimulus as in Nature.'⁶ Namely, art born from a war-torn world could – *should* – find inspiration in subjects not previously thought beautiful. That poetry should be a meeting ground for beauty and not-beauty was a thought engaging Eliot in 1919. In his 'Tradition and the Individual Talent', written that year, he would identify in seventeenth-century literature 'an intensely strong attraction toward beauty and an equally intense fascination by the ugliness which is contrasted with it and which destroys it'.[7] Soon after, in the spring of 1920, he would write: 'The contemplation of the horrid or sordid or disgusting, by an artist, is the necessary and negative aspect of the impulse toward the pursuit of beauty.'[8] At the same time, he cautioned against a modern tendency for frivolity in literature by which 'the sensation of enjoying something ugly is more amusing than the worn out enjoyment of something beautiful'.[9] This was a calculated judgement for Eliot to make in this moment, for it was the very charge that critics were making against his poetry. 'He has forgotten his emotions, his values, his sense of beauty,' *The Times* was shortly to write of his poems.[10] But Eliot would persist, and would refine his pursuit to its most clear and elegant position in an essay on Matthew Arnold in 1933, stating: 'The essential advantage for a poet is not, to have a beautiful world with which to deal: it is to be able to see beneath both beauty and ugliness; to see the boredom, the horror, and the glory.'[11] Was such panoptical vision Eliot's achievement with Bleistein? Was its purpose an attempt to look beyond the superficiality of prejudice and scrutinise the horrific?

Few readers have thought so. Most have found it hard to pass beyond two insistent readings of the poem: that 'the jew' is lower than vermin, and that 'the jew' conspires behind all the negative tendencies in modernity. And compounding both readings is a further grievance: a lowercase 'j' that was not capitalised in print until 1963 and which has served only to deepen the wound of disrespect and prejudice.

Travelling on a tourist visit to London in 1911, Eliot recorded in a letter the sights that he had seen: the British Museum, the City, St Paul's and 'Whitechapel (note: Jews)'.[12] For the next decade and more he makes a small number of references in passing to someone or other's Jewish origin – 'an Irish Roman Catholic Jew!' or 'a Jewish lady in Whitechapel' or 'a small Jewish messenger boy' – observing rather than condemning – all made to family (with one exception to Pound), where Eliot had first encountered anti-Semitism. 'I have an instinctive antipathy to Jews,' wrote Eliot's mother in 1920, 'as I have to certain animals.'[13] Anti-Semitism had been a commonplace in his Missouri childhood home, and it was prevalent in England. On visiting the home counties in 1917, Vivien would describe 'horrible Jews in plush coats by the million'.[14] Dorothy Pound could likewise state that 'rich, stockbroking Jews are *not* nice company'.[15] In certain friendship groups and literary circles anti-Semitism was ubiquitous. G. K. Chesterton, Hilaire Belloc and Rupert Brooke were open in their prejudice, while John Maynard Keynes – who would become so admired by Eliot – complained of civilisation being trapped under the thumbs of 'impure' Jews.[16] Lytton Strachey wrote to Leonard Woolf to bemoan the 'placid, easy-going vulgarity of *your* race',[17] and Virginia, disparaging her husband's own family, said, 'I do not like the Jewish voice; I do not like the Jewish laugh.'[18] Leonard, when asked to weigh the matter of Eliot's prejudice, would say in 1967, 'I think T. S. Eliot was slightly anti-Semitic in the sort of vague way which is not uncommon,' adding, 'He would have denied it quite genuinely.'[19] Few in these circles spoke out expressly against the tide of what E. M. Forster would call 'this anti-Jew horror'. Writing on the eve of the Second World War, Forster warned of a danger that many had failed to challenge: 'To me, anti-Semitism is now the most shocking of all things. It is destroying much more than the Jews; it is assailing the human mind at its source.'[20]

Eliot and Pound depended upon Jewish figures to bring their work to print. In London, Leonard Woolf ran the Hogarth Press, John Rodker was starting the Ovid Press, Alida Monro managed the Poetry Bookshop and Sydney Schiff underwrote *Arts & Letters*: all these publishers were Jewish. In New York, Alfred Knopf's family were Polish Jews; Benjamin Huebsch, who published Joyce, was the son of Hungarian Jewish immigrants; Albert Boni and Horace Liveright, who would publish *The Waste Land*, were from Russian and German Jewish families respectively. Each of these men encountered exclusion and prejudice in publishing, but it was Liveright whom John Quinn singled out for a bilious stream of abuse in correspondence that overwhelmed many of his letters to Eliot and Pound. Ezra Pound was the one who corrected it. 'The by-you-so-scorned Liveright is the best of 'em,' he told Quinn in 1922. 'He is still young enough to think an author ought to be paid a living wage. NO elderly publisher even does think that.'[21] It wouldn't be the last time that he defended Liveright to Quinn, or the last time that Quinn raged against Jews. Eliot, too, absorbed a tide of racist ranting from Quinn: Liveright was a crook and vulgarian, a grubby publicist and a money grabber, and not – *not* – to be trusted. If Quinn's sentiments, articulated extensively over many letters across many years, tapped bigotries shared by Eliot, he did not show it. Not once. Until he did. In the winter of 1923, Quinn had written a letter which, even by his standards, represented a low in his racial bigotry. He told Eliot of the 'infested' streets and sidewalks of Broadway *with swarms of horrible looking Jews, low, squat, animal-like*.[22] By then, Liveright had reprinted *The Waste Land*, and had sold the first run, said Quinn, without advancing a cent in royalties. Eliot's veneer now cracked. 'I am sick of doing business with Jew publishers who will not carry out their part of the contract unless they are forced to.'[23] And there was more. 'I wish I could find a decent Christian publisher in New York who could be trusted not to slip and slide at every opportunity.'

'My own views are Liberal,'[24] Eliot would write in 1919, and yet it's difficult to read a subtle interrogation of prejudice into Bleistein, or admire an examination of ugliness. Instead it *is* ugly. Ugly to its core.

//

As for booze . . . Ezra Pound was once again taking aim at America that February . . . *personal liberty in that country had been done in.* On 16 January 1919, the Eighteenth Amendment of the US Constitution had been ratified, prohibiting the production, transportation and sale of alcohol in a belief that the removal of temptation would lead to the removal of poverty and vice. It would take a full year for the change in the law to come into effect, and would remain in force until 1933, when it became the first and only amendment in American history to ever be repealed in its entirety. But already Pound's antennae were twitching for an America that he thought was sleepwalking into disaster. Having always been 'free' (the scare quotes were Pound's), the country had lost any sense it once had of the value of individual liberty, or any feeling for the sheer ardour needed to maintain it. 'Having got rid, supposedly of Prussianism, oppression, tyranny,' he told his father, 'you are in for a worse era.'[25]

'Twas 1919 that brought down the Rum Trust –
LIGHT OF THE WORLD, our grand-dads took it neat.[26]

Smuggling and speakeasies and rum-running and bootlegging: a new age had brought a new language. Bill McCoy had grown up on the Delaware River, the son of a bricklayer, with a longing for the sea. His passion for sailing needed a subsidy, and so he began to smuggle. He became known as a gentleman crook, a self-styled 'honest lawbreaker', who, alone among traffickers, didn't water down his contraband liquor, earning the moniker 'the real McCoy'. He was at the Gloucester pier of Eliot's youth when he first laid eyes on a schooner called the *Arethusa*: she was elegance from keel to truck, he said, a craft that could ghost under full sail, and enter a harbour like an aristocratic lady gracing a room; he said he fell in love at first sight. He refitted her hold to carry five thousand cases in burlap wrapping, and mounted a Colt-Browning machine gun on the foredeck to stave off the pirates who patrolled for easy pickings. He saw himself as a swashbuckler against Prohibition, trading at the designated three miles offshore that constituted international waters, thereby allowing him to escape US law. This was the infamous 'rum row' – a stretch of water between the peninsulas of Montauk, New York, and Cape May, New Jersey – which became a floating distribution centre for the liquor that would irrigate the speakeasies of New York City. It became a settlement on the water, with floating bars, VIP tours and jazz musicians shipped in for ambience. A symbol of resistance in a puritanical age, a strike against Prohibition, a subject that would in time give Eliot the opening to *The Waste Land*.

//

If there had been an opinion maker in London, until now it had been Pound. In 1918, he had published well in excess of one hundred articles in what had been the most prolific publishing year of his life (more than six times the critical output of Eliot that year); and for the first half of 1919 his reviews would flow out in the *New Age* at a rate of four a month under the pseudonyms of William Atheling on music and B. H. Dias on fine art. But of literary reviews in his own name there were almost none, and of those that were signed there was little of Eliot's growing edge and rigour about them. Pound, who had been prophet to Imagism, assassin to Georgianism, reviver of Rome and the lost Langue d'Oc, traveller on the Silk Road and trader in the Occident and Orient – he who more than anyone else had been the modernising voice par excellence – was engaging in criticism that seemed thin, unfocused, rolled out aimlessly to order.

One piece alone in the *Little Review* announced itself that spring as though it might set itself apart. 'The Death of Vorticism' was a teasing title intended by Pound to showcase the movement's achievements and was anything but an elegy.[27] Vorticism attempted to represent the industrial world of objects in art, led by Pound in ink and by Wyndham Lewis in paint. But Lewis lay in End-sleigh Palace Hospital with double pneumonia, and there was no sign that what he had practised so dynamically in the arrange-ment of colour – what Pound had aptly named 'planes in relation' – had been adopted by younger artists.[28] Pound had intended to give one last and deserved spin of the vortex to its embattled art-ists, but with Lewis ill and Gaudier-Brzeska dead, what instead he appeared to honour were the wounded and the fallen. In 1914, *Blast* had anticipated a world made grotesque by the horror of a looming war; Lewis and Pound had seen it coming and as visionary art-ists would congratulate themselves ('VERY WELL ACTED BY YOU AND ME', Lewis had written in a short Vorticist play of 1914).[29] But the war that followed brought devastation on a scale that no print journal could reflect: the scale of the trauma was simply too vast. Vorticism had been a clarion call, of that there was no doubt; but as a herald it had been obliterated by the ferocity of the experience about which it warned. The astuteness of Pound's criticism was failing, while Eliot's only sharpened.

John Middleton Murry did not know Eliot personally, but he knew of his work. In 1917, he had listened transfixed to Katherine Mansfield as she read aloud 'The Love Song of J. Alfred Prufrock' at a party hosted by Ottoline Morrell at her Garsington Manor, in Oxfordshire; now that Murry had taken up restoration of the ailing journal *The Athenaeum*, he had decided that Eliot was the man to help him in his task. On 12 March 1919, he invited Eliot to become assistant editor, as he currently was at *The Egoist*, only this time at a salary of £500 per annum for two years, a sum generously above his earnings at the bank. It seemed the literary opportunity that Eliot had been craving: respectable, lucrative, a door to the respectable literary life that he had so wished to open for his fam-ily. But unexpectedly he turned down the post, telling his mother that he feared that the need to produce copy mechanically would exhaust the creativity he needed for his writing. It would never be his first interest, any more than finance was; but banking at least he could leave behind at the end of the day, whereas reviewing would be an endless companion. 'I could not turn it out mechanically and then go to my own work.'[30]

The setback to Murry's plans was immense. He could think of no one else in England whose literary judgement he might trust; and so he didn't: he went without any editorial assistance, and instead employed Eliot as a freelance critic, in a series of reviews that would delight Murry and expand considerably the literary standing of the journal. By April, Murry had enthused that he hoped their collaboration would not cease until the two men had 'restored criticism'.[31] Eliot would make three dozen contributions in a little over a year, and would regard them as his finest pieces to date, 'longer and better' than anything he had written before; and the *Observer* agreed: as a critic, he was now 'known to the world at large', unmatched in British or American letters.[32] His literary ascent had been sudden, and for a moment, Eliot's practised modesty slipped. 'I really think that I have far more *influence* on English letters than any other American has ever had,' he told his mother, 'unless it be Henry James.'[33] He said he *knew* a great many people, but there were a great many more who now wanted to know *him*.

In 1919 Eliot would double his critical output of each of the last three years in a series of articles that were no mere summaries of books under review, but ever more precise outlines on poetry itself.

Emotion. The Elizabethans' vice was rhetoric, but seldom did they let sentiment ruin their writing.[34]

Style. A writer should not adhere to a creed or a party in style, but be simply and solely themselves: an Individual.[35]

Material. Poe, Whitman and Hawthorne were the keys to American literature, but theirs were the works of an immature society.[36]

Audience. The mistake of a writer was the attempt to address a large readership, instead of a small one. 'The only better thing is to address the one hypothetical Intelligent Man who does not exist and who is the audience of the Artist.'[37]

Criticism. A reader must be enticed into a receptive mood and provided with *a personal point of view* if a critical book is to hold together.[38]

These were cornerstones for any young poet in thinking about how to write and of what to write and for whom to write. Eliot was just thirty-one, but already he expressed a veteran's foresight when he emphasised the need of writers to strike out on their own. To all writers Eliot now gave an ultimatum: hang together in groups and 'schools' as a footnote to fashion, or chance going it alone and risk oblivion, and maybe, just maybe, find a higher place beyond the vagaries of public taste. Refusal to distinguish oneself from the literary clique was to threaten writers if not quite with a literary grave then with a 'Bloomsburial' of their genius.[39] Aldous Huxley had been the target of those remarks, although with his tireless advocacy of peers and groupings – Imagist or Vorticist, of Joyce, Lewis and even himself – Eliot must have hoped that his friend Pound, the great gatherer of literature, was listening in. But Pound was already more exposed than even he knew, for he was about to strike out into the open, unflanked and alone, and with catastrophic effect.

//

'You will remember all the fuss about Ezra Pound's *Propertius*,' Eliot warned Robert Lowell in 1961: 'Keep the word translation out of it.'[40] The 'it' to which Eliot referred was *Imitations*, renderings by Lowell of renowned European poems into his own idiom, a work on the eve of publication at Faber & Faber that would come to mark a creative fusion of original writing and translation. Lowell had heeded Eliot's warning and withheld the word from the title, but he hadn't kept it from the introduction, and reviewers would seize on an approach to 'translation' that they found imperial and opportunist, a robbing of the graves of the great for self-advancement (reading for schoolboys in salt mines, mocked one review).[41] But in recasting existing work into modern idiom, there was in his approach, Lowell admitted, 'nothing new': he had taken Thomas Wyatt as his guide, he said, although he might also have added John Dryden, who had used the word 'imitation' almost three centuries before to describe a form of translating in which the writer 'assumes the liberty, not only to vary from the words and sense, but to forsake them both as he sees occasion; and taking only some general hints from the original, to run division on the groundwork, as he pleases'.[42]

In his rendition of the Latin of Sextus Propertius, published in the March of 1919, Ezra Pound had most certainly run the groundwork as he pleased. Sextus Propertius was a rebel and a hero to Ezra Pound. An Umbrian, and therefore an incomer to the citadel, he had ridden on the acclaim of his first collection of *Elegies*, circulated in Rome around the year 25 BCE. The work won him attention which, like his friends Virgil and Horace, brought him under the patronage of Gaius Cilnius Maecenas, minister of culture to Emperor Augustus. But an eminent place in the Augustan court was not without a price: patriotic homilies and political odes were among the tributes expected, thereby beginning for Propertius many years of cat-and-mouse evasion to elude propaganda and find the true subject of his work, a mistress he called Cynthia, in a move in which, wrote Pound, 'S. P. ceased to be the dupe of magniloquence'.[43] Instead he became a strategist, an outsider bending the centre to his favour: a model, thought Pound, for his own quest to construct not a single translation, but what he called *a composite character* – of Propertius certainly, but also 'something of Ovid', and the spirit of any young man of the time of Augustus, 'undeceived by imperial hog-wash'.[44] And it was this spirit of an independent youth in which Pound placed his investment.

'All ages are contemporaneous,' Pound had written in 1910. 'The future stirs already in the minds of the few.'[45]

If a single thought could capture Pound's approach to translation, if not all literature, it might be this remark from his first book of prose, *The Spirit of Romance*. It would anticipate his relation to Propertius exactly, in which the passage of time was not so much a river flowing in a single direction but a pool in which the past and the modern met and mingled freely. 'This is especially true of literature, where the real time is independent of the apparent,' he wrote, 'and where many dead men are our grand-children's contemporaries.' The thought that all literature happens at once was one on which Eliot was about to elucidate, but for Pound, this implied a unique relationship between a poet in one time and a translator in another: one not based upon deference or fidelity, and most certainly not upon textual pedantry, but something closer to collaboration – something like the mind of the poet voiced through the mouth of the translator. 'Tain't what a man sez, but wot he *means* that the traducer has got to bring over,' wrote Pound.[46] And the key to that transmission is not scholarship but something more akin to a personal presence, an ability in the translator to convey a temporary identity, to adopt a mask, and be both 'traducer' and poet at once. And that was exactly the art of the 'Homage', as Eliot would later express it: 'It is not a translation, it is a paraphrase, or still more truly (for the instructed) a *persona*.'[47]

'It's you,' Robert Lowell told Pound in the 1950s, but a 'you' refracted by modern light: 'You are a man writing in the Occident of the first World War – humorous, skeptical, shocked that such a thing could happen, *quia pauper amavi*.'[48] And that meant the tone could never be classical, nor quite modern, but awkwardly in between, resistant to description: in its design a way to defy the grasp of the academy, and in humour and irony to suck its thumb at authority. *And there is no high-road to the Muses*, the 'Homage to Sextus Propertius' insisted. And that was never a provocation that a self-respecting academy was ever likely to tolerate.

'Please punch my face in order to save my soul,' Pound told Harriet Monroe in 1913: in criticism, Pound expected the treatment he received to match that which he dispensed.[49] But with the publication by Monroe of four parts from 'Homage to Sextus Propertius' in the spring of 1919, what Pound would experience was no mere slap in the face. For no sooner had the passages appeared in *Poetry* magazine than a response was delivered, in the very next issue, by William Gardner Hale, a professor of Latin at the University of Chicago. *Undignified. Flippant. Incredibly ignorant. Unintelligible. Absurd.* Identifying as many as sixty 'errors' of translation in a mere four sections, Hale went to town on what he saw as fundamental incompetence. In his ignorance, Hale declared, Pound had confused the Latin verb *canes* (from *cano* or *canto*, to sing) with the noun *canes* (*canis*, dog), and compounded his error in coupling it with the neighbouring *nocturnaeque* (nocturnal); and so rather than giving Propertius' *you will sing . . . of midnight escapade*, Pound instead had returned the inadvertently comic *night dogs*.[50] 'For sheer magnificence of blundering this is unsurpassable,' Hale pronounced, although he did what he could to give that blunder a run for its money by citing an extended list of mishaps.[51] He concluded, 'If Mr Pound were a professor of Latin, there would be nothing left for him but suicide.'

'Cat-pisss and porcupines!!'[52] Pound exploded in response.

Hale had misunderstood the mode of the poetry, he protested, and wrote fiercely to Harriet Monroe exhorting her to let the readers of *Poetry* magazine know this to be the case. 'Allow me to say that I would long since have committed suicide had desisting made me a professor of latin,' he began.[53] And he continued:

Hale was the embodiment of a spirit (the 'high road') that kept the classics out of reach: so petty and pedantic and fixed in his reading that it left no room for the fluency of poetry, and it was Hale and not Pound who was exemplary of a deep disrespect to its subject. Pound's retort was a plausible one, but he had failed to make it clearly. His tone seemed petulant, juvenile even, when what he might have said is that the 'Homage' should have been understood in terms of what Dryden described as 'something new produced', as something which is 'almost the Creation of another hand', and as 'a Liberty to be allowed'.[54] Instead, he seemed caught unexpectedly on the back foot. Which is when something rare and remarkable happened to Ezra Pound: he lost his nerve. He did not send the letter he had drafted to *Poetry*; instead, he repeated the same retort, only this time privately to a friend, saying that Hale's own errors should sentence him to the fate he assigned to Pound ('He has NO claim to refrain from suicide if he errs in any point').[55] And he made the remark yet again, this time to his family: 'As Hale has nothing by his syntactical accuracy to stand on he had better lie down.'[56] He began a second letter to Harriet Monroe, but on this occasion in a briefer form for publication. 'The thing is no more a translation than my "Altaforte" is a translation,' he protested, in a reference to his celebrated reworking in 1909 of a poem by the troubadour Bertran de Born.[57] But Monroe did not print the letter, and Pound's voice went unheard. Silenced, he turned instead to A. R. Orage, editor of the *New Age*: 'There was never any question of translation, let alone literal translation. My job was to bring a dead man to life, to present a living figure.'[58] And to Felix Schelling, his former professor at Pennsylvania, Pound said again: 'No, I have not done a translation of Propertius. That fool in Chicago took the *Homage* for a translation.'[59] The floundering grew more tangible with each comment.

Harriet Monroe did not believe, as Pound charged her, that

her selective printing of just four of the poem's twelve parts constituted a mutilation ('the left foot, knee, thigh and right ear of my portrait of Propertius', said Pound), and as late as 1930 she would state that it was not she, but Pound, who had 'mutilated' Propertius through his excisions and additions.[60] Pound knew the attack to be 'unanswerable', said Monroe, one that could neither be forgiven nor recovered from.[61] And when, on 1 November 1919, after a silence of nearly seven months, Monroe replied to Pound's April letter, she chose to interpret his signature 'In final commiseration' as a formal resignation from the post of foreign editor to the journal, and with that Pound's formative connection with *Poetry* came to an end.[62] If that had been an act of subterfuge, it was not Monroe's only one. Professor Hale was a personal friend of hers: she had shared the translation with him before printing, and then encouraged him to write his attack upon it; Pound, it seemed, had been caught in an inexplicable 'sting' orchestrated by his own publisher and employer, and William Carlos Williams was not alone in raising his voice in anger to discredit *Poetry* as 'a ragbag'.[63] In 1920, he would lead a group of poets from that journal into the pages of *The Dial* in New York, an act that would send the circulation of Monroe's journal tumbling by more than a third.[64] E. E. Cummings and Marianne Moore would join Williams and Yeats in taking new work to *The Dial*. That Pound had been badly damaged, there can be no doubt; but so had *Poetry* magazine, and Harriet Monroe's reputation would never fully recover. 'Hale is a bleating ass and Harriet Monroe another,' summarised Pound.[65] She took extended leave from 1922, and was absent from her post when the rival *Dial* secured the coup of its era, in acquiring a poem that might otherwise have conceivably gone to *Poetry* magazine: *The Waste Land*.

Eliot himself would wade into the argument that autumn of 1919: 'It is one of the best things Mr Pound has done.' He announced: 'It is a new *persona*, a creation of a new character, recreating Propertius in himself, and himself in Propertius.'[66] But for Pound, Eliot's defence – six months after publication – was too little, too late. His state of mind had become so exacerbated that it seemed even his friend and literary ally could not do enough, and he told John Quinn that Eliot's response amounted to 'granite wreaths, leaden laurels'.[67]

Belittled by the academy, betrayed by his editorial peers, it wasn't clear where Ezra Pound could turn. He told Joyce of his 'complete stasis or constipation'.[68] The time had come for a new era in Pound's life, for a new idea, and, if nothing else, a new place to live. An exit was sorely needed, and at last it came. A friend had found the Pounds a room on the rue Sainte-Ursule, in Toulouse, which they would make their own for the next three months. From there they would travel to Bordeaux in the summer, and, in the autumn, to Paris. On 22 April, Dorothy and Ezra crossed the English Channel. 'Hope Eliot can also come out,' he told his father. 'Time I had a let up; time he had a let up.'[69] For the next five months the Pounds disappeared entirely from England – 'vanished', said Lewis, into 'a mist of recuperation and romance'.[70]

//

The collapse of Pound's arrangement with *Poetry* in Chicago had been as spectacular as it was painful, but it was just one of three such relationships that would end in 1919.

For two years, Pound had run the 'Foreign Office' of the New York journal the *Little Review*, founded in 1914 by Margaret Anderson with the purpose of rekindling what she saw as a dwindling enthusiasm for literary criticism. Her opening editorial became a manifesto for the fifteen years of the journal's life: 'criticism, after all, has only one synonym: appreciation'.[71] Modernising in outlook, anarchist in politics, it published poetry and polemics, and was unapologetically elitist: 'making no compromise with public taste', its masthead proclaimed proudly, 'the magazine that is read by those who write the others'. When Jane Heap became an editorial partner in 1917, Anderson relocated the journal from Chicago to 31 West 14th Street, Greenwich Village, New York City, from where she accepted a suggestion by Ezra Pound to engage him as an international talent scout: 'Why stop at New York?' he had asked her, 'London and Paris are quite interesting.'[72] Pound had seen in the journal an ethos that matched his own (Heap said of the *Little Review* that it was 'a trial-track for racers'), and he was in no doubt about the direction he wished the journal to go.[73] 'I want a place where I and T. S. Eliot can appear once a month (or once an "issue"), and where Joyce can appear when he likes, and where Wyndham Lewis can appear if he comes back from the war.'[74] The first of twenty-two issues under Pound's direction appeared in May 1917, carrying work from three of the four men ('a magazine is made with FOUR writers', Pound insisted in 1936).[75] From now on, poetry would be as important to the journal as criticism; the entirety of Eliot's Hogarth collection *Poems* (1919) would find its initial home in the review, as well as a sweep of new work from W. B. Yeats, beginning with 'The Wild Swans at Coole'.[76] But the crowning glory of Pound's tenure at the *Little Review* – and, as it turned out, the journal's undoing – would come with his serialisation of James Joyce's *Ulysses*.

The *Little Review* had encountered controversy before it encountered Joyce. An issue from 1917 was destroyed by the United States Postal Service as anti-war and obscene because of a story by Wyndham Lewis, in which a young girl is seduced by a disaffected soldier. When Pound agreed to serialise six thousand words from Joyce in March 1918, the journal was already under scrutiny. He couldn't have known the scale of the book that Joyce would go on to write: a work so vast that it would have required four years of monthly instalments to cover it. Nor could he have known that publishing Joyce would signal the beginning of the end for both the *Little Review* in New York and the London *Egoist*, and would trigger a dispute that, in 1921, would lead all the way to an American courtroom.

It was cold comfort, but the *Little Review* was not alone in its legal troubles. In London, beginning in the new year issue of 1919, Pound had serialised five instalments of *Ulysses* in his other venue, *The Egoist*, an act designed to give Joyce a readership on both sides of the Atlantic and, just as importantly, to establish his copyright (and therefore earnings) in each territory. In England the problem was the printers, who, under the ageing but still enforceable Obscene Publications Act 1857, were jointly liable with the publisher for any materials deemed by a court to be offensive; when the foreman printer read the pages he was typesetting, he downed tools and refused to continue for fear of prosecution. By the time the proprietor Harriet Shaw Weaver had found a printer willing to set what she called 'an unmutilated copy' in type it was too late: the financial threat to her publishing had become too great, and she announced that from now on there would be no further issues of the journal, only books.[77]

The Egoist had run monthly in journal form in London from 1914 to 1919 under the benefaction and direction of Weaver: 'a quiet little Quaker',[78] as Pound condescendingly described her, an ardent campaigner for social justice, communist and a voluntary social worker to boot. *The Egoist* succeeded the *New Freewoman*, a feminist monthly edited by Dora Marsden, whose actions in support of women's suffrage had included arrest for assaulting a policeman, derailing a public address by Winston Churchill, and being among the first of Britain's female university graduates. Pound had succeeded Rebecca West at the *New Freewoman* in 1913, and initially worked with Marsden in renaming and repositioning it as a literary–philosophical journal that believed the real force for social change lay in the ego's ability to think individually and not in the collectivist mantras that were emanating from the east. But the two editors quickly discovered that they were too individualist to combine upon a method: Marsden stopped reading her own contributors in order, she said, to maintain the purity of her ego for her editorials (result, said Pound = 'four pages of slosh on the forehead of every number').[79] She would be the target of Pound's patronising judgement, but Marsden had been brought up to stand up: the daughter of a single-parent seamstress in Manchester, survivor of an impoverished childhood, she was not about to be pushed around by international literary types of 'the gadding mind', who suffered from what she called 'cultural brain-rot'.[80] It wasn't a partnership built to last.

Eliot met Marsden only once and said that he 'frothed at the mouth with antipathy'.[81] But he and Pound would prosper not only under her stewardship but on the rafts provided by other literary women: *Poetry*, *Little Review*, *New Freewoman*, *The Egoist* – all were edited by women, as was the house of Shakespeare and Company, the publisher of *Ulysses*, and in time *The Dial*, too. It was a position about which the men struggled to be graceful. Pound longed for what he called a 'male review' and Eliot said that he did what he could to put *The Egoist* 'in Male hands' as assistant editor, 'as I distrust the Feminine in literature'.[82] And yet each man prospered incalculably in the employment of these pioneering women, and under no one more than Harriet Shaw Weaver herself, who, in taking control of *The Egoist*, brought H. D., Richard Aldington and Eliot onto her payroll, and Pound, too, though he divided his salary between Lewis and Joyce.[83] She published *A Portrait of the Artist as a Young Man* in winter 1917, then *Prufrock and Other Observations* that same summer, and a string of new voices: a young Robert Frost (Pound: 'Have just discovered another Amur'kn'), Amy Lowell, D. H. Lawrence,

F. S. Flint, William Carlos Williams's epic of alienated labour, 'The Wanderer', Charlotte Mew's 'The Fête', Marianne Moore's 'The Fish'.[84] But its crowning achievement – which was also its terminal disaster – would begin in 1919, with the serialisation of Joyce's *Ulysses*, and with the two-part printing of Eliot's essay, 'Tradition and the Individual Talent'. When it folded in December 1919, it was sustained by a mere four hundred subscribers. Not everyone was sad to see it go. Aldous Huxley called it 'the horrid little paper' filled by 'whatyoumay-callem-ists'.[85] But for Eliot and Pound, the announcement in July 1919 that *The Egoist* was to close was an unenviable blow. 'It robs Pound and me, of course, of any organ where we can express ourselves editorially or air any affair such as this of Joyce,' wrote Eliot.[86] And for Pound it would mark the third successive termination of employment, leaving him to reflect upon a year in which 'I deceased, descended, departed, excerpted and otherwise wholly severed official connection.'[87]

Huxley's whatyoumay-callem-ists were Imagistes, writers to whom Weaver and Marsden had offered a privileged platform. Rebecca West would introduce Pound's poems in 1913 with an overlooked description of the task in hand: 'Poetry should be burned to the bone by austere fires and washed white with rains of affliction,' she wrote: 'the poet should love nakedness and the thought of the skeleton under the flesh.'[88] Printed alongside her account were seven of Pound's poems from the period, including a reprinting from *Poetry* of what would become his most singular example of Imagist verse:

IN A STATION OF THE METRO.

The apparition   of these faces   in the crowd :
Petals   on a wet, black   bough .[89]

In 1911, Pound had stepped out of the Paris Métro at Concorde to see the face of a child, and the face of a woman, and then another face and another, striking, he thought, each beautiful. Day long, he had wondered how best to translate what the eye had seen into what the page might hold. In the end, he said, he found not words but *an equation* – or what he called *little splotches of colour* – a poem of a single picture painted across a metrical structure. It was a simple formula that obscured the complex ardour behind it. The poem began in the shape of thirty-nine lines that were destroyed by Pound for their lack of focus; six months later, the poem returned in a draft of half its original length; a further year would pass before it found the two-line, *hokku*-driven form that survives. There was nothing accidental about the process, and he was never in doubt about his goal. 'In a poem of this sort one is trying to record the precise instant when a thing outward and objective transforms itself, or darts into a thing inward and subjective.'[90] The work that followed showed Pound at his most delicate and lyrical, forging a unique meeting place of Western rhythm and Eastern sensibility. A lyric for Dorothy from the same time invited her with great poise to be in him as the eternal moods: not the sweep of grand romance, but prone to the real, and therefore lasting, toughness of life 'as transient things are', while a later epigraphic poem captured faultlessly his style of the period:

> And the days are not full enough
> And the nights are not full enough
> And life slips by like a field mouse
> Not shaking the grass.[91]

It was a method – the movement of the outward and objective towards the inward and subjective – that would be adopted by Pound and Eliot alike, though Eliot would find a different language for it when he came to express the idea in his essays of 1919, 'Tradition and the Individual Talent' and '*Hamlet*', when the expression he used was 'objective correlative'. That spring of 1919, Eliot posed the writer and literary hostess Brigit Patmore a question. 'Do you think it is necessary to subdue your personality to that of the person you are with, in order to understand them?'[92] It was a question for which he already had an answer: *no*, subduction was *not* a requirement, it was instead a case of being interested enough *to forget oneself*, which was a different quality altogether, he said. A need, in other words, to depersonalise.

//

Homer Pound had seen many things in life, but a double-decked owl was not among them. A month below the Pyrenees in Haute-Garonne and his son reported seeing two, marvelling at their remarkable optics; to that count of misidentifications he added five bald eagles of the 'dollar models'.[93] Ornithology was not his forte, but Pound's tone was relaxed and all was quiet as he enjoyed a month of rest. 'Nothing doing,' he told his father with an air of satisfaction.[94]

The Pounds had made the city of Toulouse their home that spring, the first of multiple civic disappointments 'steeped and soggy in boredom' that Pound would detail in eighteen articles that ran in the *New Age* that summer, a series that would tire long before the column ceased that November.[95] Nevertheless, the city became a comfortable base from which to travel for the next three months as Dorothy painted and Pound rattled off his journalistic commitments. Meanwhile he kept his literary affairs turning over in London and New York. He received an instalment of proofs from John Rodker of his handmade edition of poems, *Quia Pauper Amavi*, and learned from John Quinn that his essay collection *Instigations*, turned down by Knopf, might at last have found a berth with Horace Liveright in New York.[96] It was bits and pieces, but a rebuilding of sorts at a pace that suited him perfectly at that moment.

James Joyce had sent to Pound a draft of 'Sirens', his eleventh episode of *Ulysses*, for comment ahead of submission to *The Egoist* and the *Little Review*. *Hard to follow* had been Pound's first impression, *too long* his second, and he suggested to Joyce that the reader might benefit from a few more signposts and a little more focus: 'One *can* fahrt with less pomp & circumstance.'[97] He sensed that Joyce had placed himself under pressure to deliver the chapter and the hurry in his writing was discernible. 'If you want more time take it,' urged Pound, but Joyce had taken five months to write the chapter and was not pleased with what Pound had called a 'record of uncertainty'; he ignored the remarks as 'not legitimate'.[98]

Early on the morning of 24 July, Ezra and Dorothy left Toulouse and by the following evening had a new address to share with family:

Hotel Poujol

Excideuil

Dordogne

'It is a small village with lovely ruins,' Dorothy wrote on a postcard of the castle, 'of towers & a château, & this entrance gate.'[99] Ezra had been there once before, on a walking tour of 1912. He wrote then of the calm in encountering Excideuil after sunset, silhouetted, 'carefully fashioned' by fields, '& the great gentle tower // clear edged, / unascendable,' and,

> for no known reason
> these things wrought
> out a sort of perfect mood
> in things,[100]

'Poetry is a sort of inspired mathematics,' wrote Pound, 'which gives us equations, not for abstract figures, triangles, squares, and the like, but for the human emotions.'[101] It was a special kind of poet of whom Pound was thinking when he wrote these lines in

1910, one associated with the 'perfect mood' of Périgord into which Pound had settled. The troubadours wrote in Occitan, Provençal, between the early twelfth and mid-fourteenth centuries, in the days before the Black Death ravaged the continent. They composed not only the poetry of the court but its music, and included in their number women (trobairitz) as well as men, although what survived in manuscript was overwhelmingly written by the men, from whom we understand their tropes and codes.

A man is in nature. A man is in love. He is defined by his nature and his love, and is in service to each. It is a love separated by distance or by duty (in the case of the Crusades by both), and so he sings across space. His object is elevated, superior, above the fray; he cannot match it, so his love remains insatiable. But in singing of it he is made whole, made pure. And in singing he sings of intimacy: love of a love, love of ideals, love of the flesh, 'courtly' love. These are no homilies to the Catholic Church but heretical hymns, a stance on life that won the lasting admiration of the young Ezra Pound, student of medieval Provençal in upstate New York, who had placed its poetry at the centre of his first prose book, *The Spirit of Romance*, 1910.

Guilhem IX of Aquitaine, grandfather of Eleanor, is the first of the troubadour poets whose works survive, and a person of political as well as literary power who 'brought the song up out of Spain'.[102] Pound called him the 'great crusader, and most puissant prince', but he was a disastrous leader on the battlefield whose army was, but for six men, annihilated by the Turks at Heraclea in the Crusade of 1101.[103] His fame lay instead as 'a man of many energies', in Pound's gentle euphemism for the bedchamber ('He was, as the old book says, "of the greatest counts in the world, and he had his way with women"').[104]

If Guillaume was first, *finest* of all was Arnaut Daniel, the most delicate in thought, the most artful in craft, the perfect gift from the twelfth century.

Ieu sui Arnautz, q'amas l'aura	I am Arnaut who love the wind,
E chatz le lebre ab lo bou	And chase the hare with the ox.
E nadi contra suberna.	And swim against the torrent.

(trans. Pound)[105]

In these words alone, wrote Pound, Arnaut earned his fame; but it was for a single line that he held Arnaut in deepest affection, where, in a half-lit bedchamber, the poet's love reveals herself with greatest delicacy: *E quel remir contral lums de la lampa* ('And its glowing against the lamplight').[106]

Arnaut Daniel was, in Dante's tribute, *il miglior fabbro*, the better craftsman – a tribute that was to become Eliot's to Pound. He was every bit the model for the poet Pound wanted to be. Independence of thought, refinement of sensibility, attention to the character of the natural world, the pursuit of love over tyranny, one man fencing with the Catholic Church: 'a corresponding excellence'.[107] Pound cherished this poet of pioneering rhythm, inventive rhyme and distinctive vocabulary, a poet who eschewed courtly politics, who composed in the last moment in history that poetry was actually sung, when words and music were indivisible, and triumph lay in 'an art between literature and music'.[108] So it was the highest accolade when, in Excideuil that summer of 1919, Eliot would become 'Arnaut' in *The Cantos*. 'Hope Eliot will join us somewhere for a few weeks,' Pound had written wistfully to his parents on 30 May.[109] He asked Dorothy's mother at the same moment to forward the preface to the translations that he had prepared: 'Arnaut Daniel to T. S. Eliot 18 Crawford Mansions Crawford St. w1.'[110] It was a private recital of Arnaut for Eliot, and an overture to his friend to join him in the hills of Provence.[111]

//

As the pages of T. S. Eliot's *Poems* came off the press on Paradise Road, Richmond, 19 March 1919, Leonard Woolf was convinced that they marked 'a new note' in poetry. It was only the fourth publication of the fledgling Hogarth Press, and they printed 'rather fewer' than 250 copies, but they were pleased with the inking which marked 'our best work so far by a long way', said Virginia.[112] But just as the final touches were being put to the printing, the relationship between poet and publisher came under sudden strain. The first Sunday in April the Eliots had gone to dinner in Richmond with the Woolfs: 'sharp, narrow, & much of a stick', Virginia described Eliot in her diary; 'washed out, elderly & worn', she recorded of Vivien.[113] But the business had proceeded well enough over dinner: Eliot chose cover materials for his forthcoming book, while Leonard and Virginia asked him for a list of names and addresses of people they might inform of the imminent publication. Vivien wrote to Eliot's mother the next day to tell her that they were happy in the people they knew: 'Tom has a splendid social position here, and we belong to quite the most interesting set.'[114] Eliot followed up amiably on his review list by sending the Woolfs an invitation of his own to come to dinner at Crawford Mansions following its forthcoming redecoration at Easter. But when by early in May no reply had been received and no circular for the book issued, Vivien sensed trouble. Not for the first time, the Bloomsbury set, it seemed, had been talking, and not for the first time Mary Hutchinson, Bloomsbury hostess and cousin to Lytton Strachey, appeared to be at the centre of the intrigue.

Eliot had told her that he 'disliked' Virginia, or so it was reported to Virginia by Clive Bell, Vanessa's husband and Mary's lover.[115] Only it wasn't true: someone (most likely Bell himself) had been stirring the Bloomsbury pot, and by the time John Middleton Murry had stepped in to calm the tensions, damage had been done.[116] Murry assured Virginia that Eliot had nothing but praise for her, but she now mistrusted Eliot's motivations, which had the curious effect of piquing her interest in him even further. She resolved to 'draw the rat out from his hole', as she told Duncan

Grant, and to set a little bait of her own. She withheld a reply both to the dinner invitation and to the list of circulars, allowing the Eliots to fear that publication had been shelved at the last moment.[117] For Vivien this was too much: other journals had been denied her husband's poems so that Hogarth could have them, and now where were they? And what were they to do? People were expecting the book and its absence would be a humiliation to Tom, she said, and he should just go abroad to be rid of this dreadful company. Joyce was a lucky man to be out of such gossip, and as for Pound, well, she told Mary bluntly, *Pound was ruined by it.* 'See what he has become. A laughing stock. And his work all bad.' Only a hide as tough as Wyndham Lewis's could withstand such treatment. And it was a marker of the sudden increase in temperature that she threatened to terminate her friendship with Mary should she repeat any of this to Clive Bell and make the situation worse. She had seen Tom become ill with it all, she insisted, and it had to stop: 'He hates and loathes all sordid quarrelling and gossiping and intrigue and jealousy, *so much.*'[118]

Eliot, meanwhile, wrote to Leonard Woolf in an attempt to clear the air, and received a slightly curt reply ('it could not have been curter': Vivien) that the list of names for publicity had been misplaced and requesting that he provide another.[119] Woolf enclosed an advance copy of the publication both to prove the existence of the book itself, and to honour Eliot's request for an edition to send on to Sydney Schiff; there was no additional author copy for Eliot himself. 'Think of this sort of thing as going on continually in a society where everyone is very sensitive, very perceptive and very quick,' he told his cousin Eleanor Hinkley, 'and you will see that a dinner party demands more skill and exercises one's psychological gifts more than the best fencing match or duel.'[120] But a bout with your new publisher on the eve of publication was hardly an ideal beginning to the life of a book. Virginia, it seemed, couldn't help but descend to poisoned praise. 'Mr Eliot is an American of the highest culture,' she told a friend, 'so that his writing is almost unintelligible.'[121]

As the emotional temperature began to cool, Eliot was able to tell John Rodker in June that he thought the Woolf edition was 'very well done'.[122] The poems it contained were all from 1917 and 1918, each first published by Pound in the *Little Review*; more than any gathering they would bear the fruits of his management of Eliot's work. Not only did Pound give the poetry its life in print, but he worked on the draft typescripts, and nurtured the seed of Eliot's interest in the mid-nineteenth-century work of Théophile Gautier, whose inspiration seemingly provided almost everything else. Of the seven pieces that comprised the collection, four assumed the Gautier form (one, 'The Hippopotamus', went so far as to serve as a parody), while the remaining three were written in French as evidence of the effort that had helped Eliot to 'get started again'.[123]

Pound had delighted in discovering in Eliot a man who by 1914 had 'modernized himself *on his own*' (at last, he exclaimed, someone he didn't have to tell to wash his face and wipe his feet . . .), but redirecting that training through mid-nineteenth-century foreign-language form had not been without its challenges for either man.[124] 'Whispers of Immortality' was a scrappy and feeble affair in need of remodelling, Eliot confessed to Pound, too much in the shadow of Jules Laforgue.[125] He wondered about the title 'Try This on Your Piano', but Pound, bringing it back to the task in hand, suggested 'Night thoughts on Gautier', which seemed only to worsen the effect. Yet Pound had seen opportunity where Eliot had seen failure, and pushed his friend through five drafts until they arrived, or so he considered, 'nearer the desired epithalamium of force, clearness and bewtie'.[126] Of all the poems, this was the two men's most collaborative effort, from the micro level of articles and pronouns, to a trial of titles and entire stanzas. Pound introduced a partition, he challenged Eliot on his 'maccabre predilections', and he attempted to strike a balance in the poem's attention to eroticism and death. *Lust*, asked Eliot: 'Should I avoid using the word twice?' Pound thought so. 'Wash the whole with virol and leave in hypo,' he remarked: an invitation, presumably, for Eliot to sterilise the poem before he set it in photographic fixer.[127]

It wasn't the only such instruction by Pound, who likewise bristled at the sexual explication of 'Mr Eliot's Sunday Morning Service' ('menstrual' became the Poundian *mensual*, 'castrate' *enervate*), in a poem that Pound said was 'lacking syntactic symplycyty', as well, it seemed, as tact.[128]

Looser and lighter, the three pieces in French brought just such an ease. 'Le Spectateur' made mockery of literary London, while the two other poems – 'Mélange adultère de tout' ('Adulterous Mixture of Everything') and 'Lune de miel' ('Honeymoon') – heightened further the already sexually charged atmosphere of the book.

The pamphlet opened with 'Sweeney among the Nightingales', a poem which became a favourite of Eliot's, his choice, he once said, of those from the period of 1917–20.[129] It followed the ungovernable figure of Sweeney from Boston's South End where Eliot had once learned to box, and began with the animalistic Sweeney spreading his knees in a bordello and his ending mired in bird droppings. It was a poem intent on foreboding, Eliot said later, and indeed it would provide an atmosphere that he would return to in the opening scenes of *The Waste Land*; but even here, its presentiment seemed fully realised, where the nightingales were shorthand for prostitution, and where, in an epigraph from Aeschylus, Agamemnon is murdered in his bath by his wife (*Alas, I have been struck deep a mortal blow*). The Hogarth printing featured an additional epigraph that would appear only here and once afterwards, from *Edward III*, 'Why should I speak of the nightingale? The nightingale sings of adulterate wrong.'[130] Troubling themes and forces had coalesced: a predatory male, a prostituting woman, mariticide: all in a poem written in the wake of Vivien's relationship with

Russell. Katherine Mansfield would say that when she read Eliot at this time she saw a man torn open in self-examination: 'He is seeing why he fails and how he can separate himself from Sweeney through Sweeney.'[131] But it was a loathing, loathsome poem, and in its image of one 'Rachel *née* Rabinovitch', suspect and conspiratorial and tearing 'with murderous paws', he would once again revert to a derogatory and stereotyped portrait of a Jew.[132]

On May Day, a week before the release of *Poems*, one further piece, not collected in the Hogarth edition, appeared in a new journal called *Coterie*. 'A Cooking Egg' was a poem once again in 'French' form to which Pound had taken his blue pencil and struck out two stanzas entirely ('used before').[133] Eighteen months had passed since Eliot had read the poem at a literary soirée in London in December 1917, at which Aldous Huxley and Robert Graves ('big wigs', said Eliot) were fellow speakers, as were the Sitwells, Osbert and Edith ('Shitwells', he sniggered to Pound), and Pound's future nemesis Robert Nichols.[134]

I shall not want Capital in Heaven,
For I shall meet Sir Alfred Mond,
We two shall lie together, lapt
In a five per cent. Exchequer Bond.[135]

It was when Eliot reached these lines, according to Richard Aldington who was also present that evening, that 'there was a rumpus in the audience, and Lady Mond sailed indignantly out of the room'.[136] Alfred Mond was the Liberal MP for Swansea West, but he was also an industrialist, whose chemicals company Brunner Mond made munitions during the war, fifty tonnes of which, improperly stored in railway wagons, had exploded in January 1917, destroying his London factory at Crescent Wharf, West Ham, taking seventy-three lives and destroying nine hundred homes. A gasometer caught light across the water on Greenwich Peninsula, creating a vast fireball; the blast was heard for a hundred miles and blew out the windows in the Savoy Hotel on the Strand.[137] An inquiry critical of Mond was mothballed, and in 1926 he was permitted to oversee the creation of the giant chemical conglomerate ICI. For some, Mond was a war profiteer, whose German heritage raised questions about his loyalties: he became the centre of conspiracy rumours of gun batteries installed in his back garden and carrier pigeons sending intelligence to the Fatherland. But it was his position in Lloyd George's wartime government as First Commissioner for Works and Public Buildings that brought him to the attention of artists and architects alike. Lewis and Pound had identified his wife as a target of 'blasting' ('MAY WE HOPE FOR ART FROM LADY MOND?'), while Eliot's contrast of the financier with the Elizabethan national hero Sir Philip Sidney – a contrast between 'Capital' and 'Honour' – has been read as a resentment that the Monds were not only industrialists, but Jewish.[138]

Throughout the Hogarth *Poems* caricatures wearily reappear: predatory males, wanton females, unscrupulous outsiders, untrustworthy Jews, each one seemingly an expression of a paranoia darkening Eliot's mind in 1919, each one a symbol of an 'otherness' that he considered himself not to embody. Through such figures Eliot walked a line between misanthropy and bigotry, observing a piety to which his own religious upbringing seemed to offer neither enlightenment nor resistance. Eliot's Unitarianism might have brought tolerance, but to him it seemed only to offer a godless world, concerned, like both his Hippopotamus and his Sunday Morning Service, with petty vagaries, such as 'the religion of the blue sky, the grass and flowers'.[139]

After the expansive, experimental leap of *Prufrock and Other Observations* – their bold musicality and vocal dexterity, their nimble athleticism – these new poems seemed constrained in comparison, as conservative in form as the 'spectateur' that they mocked. Gone was the daring to disturb; in its place came a claustrophobic formality buttoned up in iambic tetrameter. This was thought that had yet to find its best expression in form and music. The review that appeared in *The Times* put it in starker terms. It described verse that was 'fatally impoverished of subject matter': hesitant, handicapped by inhibition to the point of paralysis, in short, 'very laboriously writing nothing'. And there was a moral repulsion besides, in which Eliot 'carries the game of perversity as far at least as anyone has ever carried it'. But poetry was a serious art, continued the review, too serious for such games, and the satirising Eliot was satirised: 'he is in danger of becoming silly.'[140] It was, acknowledged Virginia Woolf, 'a severe review' that in turn triggered a severe response.[141] The anonymous assessment that followed a week later in Middleton Murry's *Athenaeum* seemed a welcome riposte. It commended Eliot for possessing 'the rare gift of being able to weave, delicately and delightfully, an echo or even a line of the past into the pattern of his own poem'.[142] Here was a writer in search of something new, it surmised, something evolved from the inheritance of what had gone before. Instinctively, it understood Eliot's particular pathway to be one guided – to use his own terms – between tradition and individual talent. In fact, *so* closely had it anticipated the language of the essay that Eliot was shortly to publish, 'Tradition and the Individual Talent', that it was almost as if the reviewer had privileged access to the poet's own mind. Eliot was suspicious, and asked his publisher, Virginia, if she were the anonymous author. 'I have to confess that it was not I who reviewed your poems in *The Athenaeum*,' she replied, 'but my husband.'[143] If that were not awkward enough, the publisher's review of Eliot's output hinted at some dissatisfaction with it. 'Is this poetry?' it had asked, before concluding with an underwhelmed *yes*: it was, but it risked becoming a second-rate variety, 'the product of a Silver Age'.[144] In a tortuous turn, the 'rebuff' to *The Times* was a scam, and an ambivalent scam at that.

And that was all the meagre coverage Eliot's new collection would receive. Admittedly, it was barely more than a pamphlet

– what he called 'Woolf's small book' – and it had only half the print run of his debut, *Prufrock*; but the critical gulf in the level of interest between the two was undeniable.[145] Rate of sales aside (by November 140 of the 240 copies had sold), it had caused barely a ripple, backed by a fraudulent review. A whiff of corruption was beginning to surround Eliot in the eyes of some, not least William Carlos Williams. He had written of *Prufrock and Other Observations* that it was the work not of a radical but of 'a subtle conformist'; the charge then had seemed unfair for that dazzling first book, but it appeared to fit the Hogarth *Poems* of 1919, which seemed the more obvious European enterprise.[146] Eliot had 'fled the rigors of an American application', as Williams would later put it – he was 'a maimed man' – a European poet without any care for local culture. 'He should be branded for the worst possible influence in American letters.'[147]

//

Boni & Liveright had been swift to accept Pound's prose *Instigations* and would move quickly enough to bring it out in 1920. But the path into print for Eliot's first American book was altogether rockier. Horace Liveright now informed Quinn that he would be postponing a decision on Eliot's work for two or three months; he did not offer an explanation, although his request for a subsidy of $150 suggested he might have been wishing to test Eliot's financial resolve. It was, said Quinn, a 'damned impertinence' – he could think of no good reason for the delay and contacted yet another New York publisher, John Lane, offering him the personal subsidy that he had been so angered to be asked for by Liveright. But Lane did not embrace the proposal, writing that 'Mr Eliot's work is no doubt brilliant, but it is not exactly the kind of material we care to add to our list.'[148] In frustration, Quinn then reopened discussions with Alfred Knopf, using an additional typescript of poems and prose that Eliot had supplied in July. This time Knopf responded swiftly and affirmatively, and by August had committed not to a 'hybrid' edition of poetry and prose, but to a volume exclusively of poems. The breakthrough that Eliot had sought for so long had finally come. Knopf insisted that the book should not reuse the title *Prufrock*, which would undermine sales, but be simply and clearly presented as *Poems by T. S. Eliot*. Quinn negotiated a 12 per cent royalty (Pound's last book with Knopf had received only 10 per cent, he told Eliot indiscreetly), and a publication date of spring 1920. The process of finding an American home for Eliot's poetry had taken six months, but it was settled in time for Eliot's visit that summer to see Pound in France.

//

On 19 May, Eliot had been sent by the bank on a tour 'for some weeks' of the English provinces. Lytton Strachey teased him playfully that he might seize the opportunity to ingratiate himself with rural clergymen; the two had just enjoyed one another's company at Garsington and had followed with a dinner in London ('altogether not gay enough for my taste,' wrote Strachey to Dora Carrington. 'But by no means to be sniffed at').[149] Eliot replied stiffly that his thoughts were taken with matters more important than ever entered the heads of deans, such as how it was that steel could be bought more cheaply from America than Middlesbrough, or by the exchange rates of sterling and the rupee. He said that he had divided humankind into supermen, wireworms and termites, and that he was sojourning among the termites.[150] Eliot may have misjudged the tone, for Strachey told Mary Hutchinson that he found it a 'grim' letter from a man suffering from 'devitalisation'; rather ill, and rather American, was the description he gave Carrington.[151] Strachey was not yet familiar with the mannered style of Eliot's correspondence, which included a statement on prosody that might have been expected to tempt the playfully minded Strachey into engagement:

> Whether one writes a piece of work well or not seems to me a matter of crystallization – the good sentence, the good word, is only the final stage in the process. One can groan enough over the choice of a word, but there is something much more important to groan over first. It seems to me just the same in poetry – the words come easily enough, in comparison to the core of it – the tone – and nobody can help one in the least with that.[152]

London seemed to Eliot a place of disdain at that moment, from which he was glad to be away. Left behind, Vivien was feeling very much alone. She was struggling with her nerves, and had used her husband's travels to go into what she called 'a sort of retirement', partly in Marlow, from where she laboured back to London with yet more of Bertrand Russell's possessions.[153] There she had received from Ottoline Morrell a letter that upset her greatly, accusing her of 'a quick change etc. affair' – with Russell no doubt, but possibly having heard about a new flirtation that Vivien had begun with Mary Hutchinson's brother, James Strachey Barnes. 'Believe me it wasn't,' Vivien protested: she had suffered terribly over the collapse of her relationship with Bertie, she wrote; she would try never to see him again, though she was still fond of him – after all, he had been so generous to her, given more to her than he had anyone before her. Morrell had been Russell's lover at the moment that he had first taken an interest in Vivien, whose letter now could only have struck Morrell as tactless. She had dubbed Vivien 'a spoilt-kitten'; but, pleaded Vivien, couldn't Ottoline now see how 'beaten upon and worn' she had become by even the smallest amount of 'human intercourse'?[154]

Bertrand Russell waited until Eliot was absent on his tour to call by the Marylebone flat to collect the last of his possessions. Arriving earlier than expected, he found Vivien not yet dressed, leaving her to conduct their conversation through the bathroom door. She said that she had hoped that they might reach 'amicable relations', or at the very least take tea, but found him in short temper. She would make no further attempts at civility with him, she resolved. 'But it is strange how one does miss him! Isn't it hard to put him *quite* out of one's mind?'[155]

Such a spectacle, played out through a locked door, might have seemed like a drawing-room farce, were it not the source of such pain to Eliot. Russell was becoming, to Eliot, 'one of my lost illusions', who in 1953 would publish a story in which a Mr Ellerker and a Mr Quantox were competing rivals for Mrs Ellerker's attention. Quantox, who had 'a roving eye', would seduce Mrs Ellerker in the library; in time, she would be removed to an asylum – *the hapless victim*, recorded the story, *desolate and alone*. Russell entitled it, 'Satan in the Suburbs or Horrors Manufactured Here'; he later denied the affair.[156] 'He has done Evil,' Eliot would write in 1933.[157]

Eliot returned from his tour in June, for once making the final leg by motor car, which was not a journey without its perils. Travelling through the South Coast Plain, his car punctured and then broke down entirely. With almost no traffic on the empty roads, he was left to walk the remaining distance, passed only by a wagon of Boy Scouts, and pursued by a line of three ducks.[158]

//

The house overlooked the tidal Hards on Bosham Channel in the Chichester Harbour. Twice a day high water swept over the estuary to the sea wall directly beneath the front door. Since 1916, the Eliots had been coming to the South View, the detached Georgian cottage on Shore Road, run as a guest house by the 'bouncing kindly' Miss Kate Smith, whose cooking was excellent, and whose brother-in-law offered the guests daily weather forecasts that invariably predicted rain.[159]

Life in the village charmed the Eliots. Fishermen with ringed white beards played bowls on the green or quarrelled contentedly in the harbourside tavern (*Better to have been / A fisherman at Bosham* – Tennyson).[160] Through their deferential manner and the twang of their accent, these men reminded Eliot of childhood in Missouri and Massachusetts, but seemed to be remnants of a much older time. Bede had recorded the village surrounded by woods and sea; it was the site of a humble monastery, Bosanham, where a small band of brothers served in 'a life of humility and poverty', a life that Bede believed was quite lost upon the local inhabitants.[161] As if to test the point, it was at Bosham that King Canute is said to have attempted to demonstrate the limit of his omnipotence against the encroaching tide: 'Let all the world know that the power of kings is empty and worthless.'[162]

Eliot was not one to linger over naturalistic description (he told Conrad Aiken that the tide was either very much in or very much out), but he must have heard the arrival of the curlew, whose calls began to fill the estuary by the month's end, with whimbrel and redshank soon to follow.[163] He sailed from the old Raptackle barn on the quayside almost every day, regardless of the weather, not minding a bit if he took a soaking or a falling wind left him with a lengthy row back; he cycled, too, and walked the Sussex Downs, or picnicked with Vivien.

London friends rented in the area, none nearer than St John and Mary Hutchinson, whose summer home lay behind the shingle spit named Ella Nore in the mouth of the estuary at nearby West Wittering, reached by a donkey trap or via a curmudgeonly ferryman who sometimes could and sometimes couldn't be summoned from over the water at Itchenor.[164] The Hutchinsons' home, which they called Eleanor House, was serviced by a well, and decorated by Duncan Grant and Vanessa Bell, who lit it with lamps and candles, and furnished it with a copper bath – every bit the artist's retreat, though Bell complained that being open to the lane, it prevented guests from going about naked on the lawn.[165]

St John and Mary Hutchinson led a busy social life at their London home, River House, in Hammersmith. Mary ran her romantic life at a similar pace: Clive Bell, Vanessa's husband, was her longest-running entanglement, Aldous and Maria Huxley the most complex. Katherine Mansfield observed of Mary that she moved between the men at her parties like 'a spilt liqueur', and observed her with an eye on Robert Graves and an eyebrow on Eliot ('who grew paler and paler and more and more silent' as the evening wore on).[166] Virginia Woolf wondered if Eliot and Mary had become more than merely friends, and probed Ottoline Morrell on what she called 'the case of Mary Hutch. & Eliot', though Morrell seemingly had her hands full corresponding with Vivien and Russell.[167]

The atmosphere between the Eliots had been tense and scratchy on their arrival at Bosham that weekend of mid-June, and they didn't get along at all well. They walked around the peninsula the two miles down to the foreshore at Ferry Hard, but it was hot, and they were tired, and fell asleep in the ryegrass on a bank of tree mallows before they reached Eleanor House. Tom returned on the train to London, where Ellen Kellond, the Eliots' maid, had taken a fortnight's break, leaving him in sole charge of a Yorkshire terrier, with a shelf of hair overhanging its eyes, that had followed him home as a stray through Marylebone one day and whom they had subsequently named Dinah Brooks. Vivien remained in Bosham, and confided to Mary that she felt 'very dull and tired', and had a great longing to speak to her if she could summon the energy. 'But I must wake up first. Now, I am asleep all the time.'[168] With the passing days on the Sussex coast, her energies began to return. She bathed daily in the harbour, and met with Mary for walks and picnics, and, on one occasion, a soaking in the woods during a downpour. By month end, even the sudden rain couldn't suppress her lifting spirits: she was away from what she told Mary were the 'wars in town', and said that she never wanted to go back to London, where she knew both Eliot and Russell to be.[169]

After a week she did briefly return to the city, and found Eliot 'looking very ill'.[170] He was reluctantly entertaining an old Harvard roommate, Harold Peters; the two men had turned the Marylebone flat to a horrible mess. Eliot had exhausted himself guiding Peters across miles of the East End and Greenwich docks, a guest who had turned up 'so suddenly' that he had forced Eliot to forgo an invitation to Garsington with Virginia Woolf, arranged by Ottoline Morrell in order to ease tensions between poet and publisher.[171] 'Think of Virginia, Tom, & Ottoline! O think of it,' Vivien told Mary – but it wasn't to happen: Eliot was obliged to his guest, and could feel improved relations with his publisher slipping from his hands.[172]

Vivien sensed that her husband was now at the limit of his capacity, and that a breaking point was coming; Tom's return to her in Bosham on the coming weekend was a critical juncture for them both, she understood: 'we must MUST have a G O O D T I M E,' she told Mary in capital letters.[173] But a restorative sailing trip from Itchenor to Eleanor House didn't go quite as planned. With Mary and her guests Sacheverell and Osbert Sitwell aboard, the journey had begun well enough: Eliot took them out over the Bell Hole at Bosham Deeps (where Norsemen were said to have sunk the great stolen bell of Bosham church); with the tide making, they sailed effortlessly towards East Head, putting the boat up on the sands before the Ella Nore shingle spit before the Hutchinsons' house in good time for lunch. But Eliot had misjudged the tidal conditions. The new moon was just two days old and he'd breached at the height of a spring tide; by the time they had eaten at Mary's they returned to a falling tide and a headwind that would test even the most experienced sailors. They grounded on a sandbank in the estuary. Eliot snapped the boathook and Vivien jumped out to push, before they gave up and waded ashore, laying planks across the saltmarsh to prevent themselves from sinking. They abandoned the boat at anchor, no doubt to the fury of the ferryman at Itchenor from whom they had hired the craft, and left Mary to make the arrangements for its return. 'He thinks its friendly to ask people to clear up his muddles for him,' Vivien apologised.[174] Eliot had to be driven to the station to catch his London train: the sailing had, he admitted, been 'rather disastrous', and left the ferryman to be 'settled with'; yet to Vivien it had been 'pure joy' – 'glorious – but I'm never sure that anyone else sees things with my eyes'.[175] For once, Eliot may indeed have seen things with Vivien's eyes. The sight of her stripping off her stockings and jumping overboard in an effort to free their stricken craft seemed for a moment to wake something in Eliot's heart. *Vivien is splendid in a boat*, he wrote admiringly to his mother, as if the memory of the River Girl had been briefly woken.[176]

But then Vivien could handle a boat. On her penultimate day there, with Eliot in London, on the morning of 9 July, she took a dinghy out single-handed from Bosham harbour for a day's sailing with Mary. It was slack tide and windless when she cast off, and she had to row three and a half hard nautical miles to Eleanor House to collect Mary before the breeze rose sufficiently to fill the sail. From there she navigated the two of them up the rithes to Hayling Island, where she bathed and listened delighted as 'Mary told me her life'. She returned to Itchenor before sailing back alone to Bosham, exhausted but electrified by her day.[177] 'Mrs Eliot in a boat,' Lytton Strachey exclaimed, impressed, having heard the admiration expressed by Mary.[178] For a moment, all of her own, Vivien found her strength again and her serenity.

Wonderful impression of Bosham in the evening, last thing. Full moon, & only half dark at 10, & a mist. The water like glass.[179]

III.

The Pyrenean mountain town of Foix was furled in banners, swollen with crowds and musicians when the Pounds passed through on 22 June, the summer solstice, days before the celebrations to mark the signing of the Treaty of Versailles on 28 June. Their destination was the rock of Montségur, once the stronghold of the Cathars, a site ruined and rebuilt and ruined once more, where, in the shade of the equinox, Pound climbed with Dorothy. There are tales that connect the castle to the Holy Grail, but it is its alignment to the sun that compels most visitors. Yearly, on the morning of the summer solstice, light blazes through the old east windows and illuminates the ruins spectacularly. Pound arrived a day late for this event, but then his fascination wasn't so much with the sunrise but with the Cathars themselves – deistic Christians whose faith in twin gods of the spiritual and the physical worlds set them against the Catholic Church. At the foot of the hilltop castle lies the field of the burned. It is said that the *perfecti* – the Cathar adepts – went voluntarily into the flames, more than two hundred in number, rather than renounce their faith. An Occitan memorial marks the present day: *Als catars, als martirs pur amour crestian.* To the Cathars, to the martyrs of pure Christian love.

'A religion is damned', wrote Pound that summer, '. . . the day it burns its first heretic.'[1] Montségur had withstood a Crusade, but it couldn't survive the combined assault of the Catholic Church and the French crown, who in 1244 arrived with an army of ten thousand men to correct the ways of the heretics. Montségur, temple of the spirits of nature, the ward of the troubadour poets, was violently razed by the forces of orthodox religion. In Pound's mind, it became the setting for a series of historical, criss-crossing pathways that would run throughout *The Cantos*. A Cantabrian sun temple, 'Sacred to Helios'.[2] An alignment to 'the city of Dioce' otherwise known as the ancient and mythical Ecbatana in Persia.[3] 'An altar to Terminus', god of boundaries.[4] Mithras, born of rock, conqueror of bulls, sun god, before whom the sun knelt down, to begin – or is it to end? – the world: 'and in Mt Segur there is wind space and rain space / no more an altar to Mithras'.[5] Pound named such confluences 'snippets', and believed that in such fragments the wrongs and rights of history are illuminated. And this would be the method of *The Cantos*.

The sacrifice of the *perfecti* haunted him. 'Liberties as easily acquired have been as easily lost,' he wrote: the American people would squander theirs, trading liquor for the soda water of Prohibition.[6]

Time in waves, and waves in stone.

'And went after it all to Mount Segur, / after the end of all things.'[7]

//

No further reviews of Eliot's Hogarth pamphlet appeared, although 'Burbank' and 'Sweeney Erect' were reprinted in Sydney Schiff's *Art & Letters*, and the first parts of Pound's Propertius were rerun from *Poetry* magazine in the *New Age*.[8] With respectable journals printing their work, these should have felt like successful days for them both; but Eliot felt sidelined, and Pound had received the kind of attention for his Propertius that no writer would seek for themselves. In the early summer of 1919, it was no longer clear where either man's writing would go next.

But a new venture was offering a crack of light. John Rodker had started the Ovid Press and would present each man with a new publishing opportunity. On 1 June Eliot advised Rodker that to assemble a new edition of his poems, the contents of both *Prufrock* and the Hogarth *Poems* would be required, as well as the two pieces from *Art & Letters*, the *Little Review*'s 'Dans le Restaurant', *Coterie*'s 'A Cooking Egg', and, with an added note of mystery, 'one half-finished one'.[9] Pound, too, had a project for the new press: a broadsheet of *The Fourth Canto* – forty copies, foolscap, folded and then folded again to make a four-page quarto printing, 'set up and printed by John Rodker at his press'. *Privately* printed, Pound corrected the title-page proof.[10] Perhaps after Propertius, he was not quite ready to resume the public spectacle of print.

//

Remote, extreme, foreign: such was the mind of W. B. Yeats. Subtle, erudite, massive: that of James Joyce. The occasion of Eliot's remark was the English publication of Yeats's essays, *The Cutting of an Agate*, published in New York before the war, but not issued in London until earlier that spring of 1919.[11] Eliot used *The Athenaeum* to measure quite how far he had come to mistrust the work of Yeats, and to take the opportunity to 'boom' Joyce.[12] Yeats was no longer of this world, wrote Eliot, but a citizen of one inhabited by ghosts, mediums, leprechauns, sprites and seances – his senses were no longer earthed. Powerful feeling *is* crude, admittedly, but in Yeats it was crude *without* being powerful, wrote Eliot. Joyce, by contrast, harnessed power: Eliot had now seen the 'Scylla and Charybdis' section of *Ulysses*, and told John Quinn: 'I have lived on it ever since I read it.'[13] It seemed that Eliot was clearing a literary pathway, sweeping out the old to make room for the new.

The Cutting of an Agate was one of two books that Yeats published with Macmillan that spring. It had followed on from his volume of poetry, *The Wild Swans at Coole*, published that March in a print run of 1,500 copies for each book that was half as big again as Pound's publication with Elkin Mathews, and three times the printing that he and Eliot had been granted at the Egoist Press.[14] And for the two Americans, *The Wild Swans at Coole* had that most envious quality of all about it: it was published simultaneously in New York and in London. It would reprint within the year.

For Ezra Pound, Yeats was an avuncular figure whom he aided secretarially and editorially, printing his poems in the *Little Review*; it was with affection that Pound sent up a memory of overhearing the noise in the chimney at Stone Cottage, Sussex of 'Uncle William' composing his poem 'The Peacock' in 1913 ('that had made a great Peeeeacock / in the proide ov his oiye / had made a great peeeeeeecock in the . . . / made a great peacock / in the proide of his oyyee').[15] Eliot adopted an altogether more formal and cautious approach to Yeats, a man twenty years his senior, though Eliot considered him his contemporary.[16] He said that he never witnessed the arrogance attributed to the Irishman (on the death of Swinburne in 1909 Yeats announced that he was now 'King of the Cats'), and insisted that he never saw him meet other poets on any level other than equality.[17] And yet despite the respect, Eliot maintained a feline distance from Yeats, regarding his early work dimly, and scribbling in his preparatory notes for his notorious American lectures of 1932–3, *After Strange Gods*, that he was 'slow to develop – a sign of magnitude'.[18] But Eliot would come to admire the later work, and give the first memorial lecture for Yeats at the Abbey Theatre, in Dublin 1940, when he praised the impersonality of his mature years. No poet had shown a longer period of development, he would say: a charge that in the hands of another commentator would have appeared a slight, but which, in Eliot's, was sincere praise. In 1935 he would call him the greatest poet of his time.[19] At the same moment, Yeats dismissed Eliot's art as 'grey, cold, dry', the work of a bureaucrat; he would never let go of the belief – so painful to Eliot in 1919 – that he was a 'satirist rather than a poet'.[20] '[H]e and Tom are ← →,' Vivien would acknowledge in the winter of 1919. 'He hates Tom's poetry.'[21]

If Yeats *became* great, Thomas Hardy, by contrast, the second of the towering reputations, never made it to greatness, thought Eliot. That he was a minor poet was all Eliot ever said of the verse, but of his prose and personality Eliot would say that they were 'uncurbed'. Hardy wrote with 'extreme emotionalism', with decadence and self-absorption, and worst of all, was swamped by feeling, leaving nothing of substance with which to engage: 'Unless there is moral resistance and conflict there is no meaning.'[22] But for many readers, Hardy's poems *teemed* with meaning: demand for his wartime poems was such that his 1917 volume, *Moments of Vision*, was reprinted by Macmillan in 1919. Like many of Hardy's poems, his 'Going and Staying', published that November, fused private grief and public grievance: 'The silent bleed of a world decaying, / The moan of multitudes in woe / These were things we wished would go; / But they were staying.'[23] That the poem appeared in J. C. Squire's *London Mercury* said everything necessary to Eliot.

Hardy in return met Eliot's poems with suspicion, and wrote warily beside a stanza from 'The Love Song of J. Alfred Prufrock' in his notebooks, 'T. S. Eliot – a poet of the vers libre school.'[24] It was a school certain to fail in England, Hardy would tell Robert Graves in 1920: 'All we can do is to write on the old themes in the new style, but try to do a little better than those who went before us.'[25] For all their differences, what Hardy said here anticipated Eliot's own discoveries: as Thom Gunn would later remark, 'A work is not the same as its source'[26] – an appreciation that Eliot would make in discussing 'Gerontion', a poem of his own that he was about to circulate to friends. Even so, Eliot believed he was on a very different path from either Hardy or Yeats by the summer of 1919, and he didn't underestimate the task before him.

To communicate impressions is difficult; to communicate a co-ordinated system of impressions is more difficult; to theorize demands vast ingenuity, and to avoid theorizing requires vast honesty.[27]

//

In *The Athenaeum* that July, Eliot began to sketch a vocal technique that he would soon employ for the long poem he was contemplating. He dispensed with what he called the 'conversational' in poetry in favour of something more polyphonic: 'If we are to express ourselves, our variety of thoughts and feelings, on a variety of subjects with inevitable rightness, we must adapt our manner to the moment with infinite variations.'[28] Shakespeare was a master of rhetorical variance, wrote Eliot, quoting in quick succession three plays that would serve as source matter for his poem, among them a passage from *Antony and Cleopatra* in which Enobarbus describes Cleopatra in 'her infinite variety', and from which Eliot recorded in his review from just half a line: 'The barge she sat in . . .' The quote trailed off, the ellipsis Eliot's . . . as if this were a thought to be continued.[29]

//

Saturday 19 July was Peace Day. A vast crowd had begun to assemble in London from three o'clock that morning to celebrate the signing of the Versailles Treaty, taking up position along a seven-mile route that began and finished in Hyde Park. The fanfare of brass bands was heard along the route. Led by the Allied high command – General Pershing, Marshal Foch and Field Marshal Haig – a victory parade of fifteen thousand troops passed through Whitehall, where a new monument to the fallen by Edwin Lutyens had been unveiled, and where King George told the wounded that their scars inspired in their countrymen 'the warmest feelings of gratitude and respect'.[30]

Solid rivers of silent people, mute hordes of shabby workers: such were the bedraggled crowds described by Richard Aldington, who had each suffered the war in their way, unsure what it was they were celebrating.[31] The Woolfs' household staff watched from Vauxhall Bridge a procession that took two hours to pass – 'Generals & soldiers & tanks & nurses & bands'.[32] Virginia Woolf stood in the Trafalgar Square drizzle the day before, and described the gathering mass of people as sticky and torpid, like a cluster of drenched bees. 'There's something calculated and politic and insincere about these peace rejoicings,' she recorded in her diary; 'some thing got up to pacify & placate "the people".' But in Luton, Bedfordshire, the people could not be so easily pacified: servicemen angry at the lavish cost of the London parade rioted, and the town hall was burned to the ground. A summer rain fell on the nation's celebrations until evening. Virginia Woolf climbed Richmond Hill to take in the atmosphere. Fireworks struggled against the damp weather; some lit up the Star and Garter military hospital beneath, where lamed soldiers lay, backs to the crowd, smoking and waiting for the noise to pass.[33]

The Eliots had left London to its celebrations, and taken a Friday afternoon train to stay with Sydney and Violet Schiff at Eastbourne – 'very nice Jews', Eliot would tell his mother.[34] He seemed in no mood to celebrate. 'Tom is IM possible,' wrote Vivien to Mary Hutchinson, 'full of nerves, really not well, very bad cough, very morbid and grumpy', adding: 'I wish you had him!'[35] He was needled by what she called 'the money trouble', worried that the couple were once again living beyond their means, which provoked him to flashes of anger. Even so, Eliot adapted better to the company of his hosts than Vivien, who complained that she found them fatiguing and irritating, and said summarily of the weekend that it had been 'rather unsatisfactory'.[36] It was, as it turned out, a curious phrase for Vivien to have chosen: despite the stressed and spiky mood, the 'Peace weekend', as Vivien referred to it, had brought a temporary truce in the couple's fractious relations. In a letter the following month, Vivien confided in Mary that the weekend had quite unexpectedly rekindled a sexual intimacy with her husband. 'I had rather an affair with him, for one thing,' she confided. 'Don't you yourself find that staying in people's houses together is very conducive to reviving passions?'[37]

//

Richard Aldington had decided that at last the moment had come to introduce himself to T. S. Eliot. Several times he had stopped himself from writing in appreciation of Eliot's criticism in the hope of a personal meeting.[38] Although he had been neighbour and 'Imagiste' to Ezra Pound ('Unkil EZ') since 1912, and husband to H. D. since 1913, inexplicable as it seemed, the microcosm of London literary life had somehow contrived to keep Aldington and Eliot apart. Each would come and go at the dinners at the New China restaurant without their paths crossing, nor did they meet at Kensington when Eliot would come calling for Pound, nor did they meet at *The Egoist* when Eliot inherited the editorial role that Aldington vacated on enlisting in June 1916. When Aldington had demobilised in February 1919, he was already exhibiting the signs of a painful struggle with his wartime experience, and had nearly broken down under the strain of it. He was suffering from headaches, trench throat, insomnia, and pains in his arms and neck that had been explained to him as a form of delayed shell shock. Nursed by her new friend Bryher, H. D. had left London for Cornwall to have a child with the music critic Cecil Gray, and Aldington found himself without a place to live. The mansions of leafy West London stood empty because their wealthy owners didn't need use of them, he told Amy Lowell that autumn, and all the while thousands of demobilised soldiers like him had nowhere to call home. Discontent was widespread, labour was in disarray: it would take a half-decade and more for social conditions to resettle, he believed, if a revolution were to be escaped.[39] A profound and possibly suicidal pessimism swept over him and his work: he described himself as a man tormented and obsessed with what he called 'a vision of ruins', of a world dissolving; he issued melancholic collections with *The Egoist* and Elkin Mathews that year of 1919.[40]

Aldington never would be able to abide Eliot's verse: it was wilfully intellectual, he said, and was in fear of the very emotions that made poetry; he saw no shame in telling Eliot that he disliked his poetry profoundly. But he was in no doubt of the singular importance of his criticism.[41] Eliot possessed a gift not simply for *apprehension* and *analysis* but for the *dissociation of ideas* – a talent for poise and wit that made him 'not the best but the only modern writer of prose criticism in English'.[42] With their shared roots in European literature, Aldington saw in Eliot – and Pound – a common ground that he could share; and he was full of admiration for the words of Eliot's he read in *The Egoist* that July.

> We do not imitate, we are changed; and our work is the work of the changed man; we have not borrowed, we have been quickened, and we become bearers of a tradition.[43]

'In 1919 to admire his poetry was daring and revolutionary,' wrote Aldington, looking back in 1941.[44] And this, he said, had triggered a counter-attack by the guardians of the status quo to discredit Eliot. On more than one occasion, he stood up for both Eliot and Pound when their names were taken in vain – as they frequently were – at Harold Monro's dinners at the Poetry Bookshop. He never lost his affection for Pound, the man he called 'a small but persistent volcano in the dim levels of London literary society' and 'one of the problem children of modern poetry'.[45] But he had no answer for Yeats when asked, 'How do you account for Ezra?' – a man so distinguished in his art but so uncouth in life, said the Irishman; it was only later that a friend provided him with it: 'In real life Pound is himself – in his best poems he's always someone else.'[46] For a time, the relationship with Eliot would blossom along the same lines. Eliot would call upon his support more than once after the blooming of their friendship, which would reach its height during his breakdown and recuperation in Margate in the autumn of 1921. But Aldington would have struggles of his own over which Eliot could offer little help, and a time would come when he would round on his new friend with castigating force.

//

The Pounds had travelled south west to Montréjeau, and by the middle of July had reached the foot of the Pyrenees, where Dorothy sketched the mountain tops and Pound pondered the couple's next move. A lecture commitment in Newcastle ('the northern wilds') demanded their return to England that autumn (when the time came, more than seven hundred people would hear him speak on the troubadours), but Pound admitted to his father that he didn't in the least know where he would be or what he would do after his French sojourn had come to an end.[47] A fifth and sixth instalment of 'Homage to Sextus Propertius' ran in the *New Age* in London that July, and England, however unreceptive it appeared, remained the most likely base for him at least until the new year.[48] But his time away had nurtured peripatetic instincts: he told his mother that he now felt 'very much at home in Toulouse', and that he had an eye on other places besides: Venice, Verona and the Sirmio promontory on Lake Garda. And for a third time he uttered in his letters the fervent wish: 'Hope Eliot will get out next month.'[49] A few days later, Pound was at last able to confirm the good news with reasonable certainty: 'Eliot probably coming out in August.'[50]

In London, the Eliots returned from their 'Peace weekend' at Eastbourne to attend the first night of Manuel de Falla's

Three-Cornered Hat, performed by Leonid Massine and the Ballets Russes, with costume and stage sets by Picasso.[51] It would run for a week and be the talk of the town, and it seemed that half of literary London turned out for its opening: Jack and Mary Hutchinson were there with her brother James Barnes, as were Ottoline Morrell, Herbert Read, Richard Aldington, and figures from art circles including Nina Hamnett, Clive Bell and Viola Tree. The wealthy young socialite Nancy Cunard was there that evening, 'head whirling with the music', she wrote in her diary, 'longing' to see Eliot, who, to her disappointment, 'did not appear'.[52] But Eliot was there with the Sitwell siblings, and with Vivien, who felt unwell and looked *horrible*, she thought, and stayed home with a migraine when Eliot went to the performance for a second time the following evening with the Hutchinsons. Yet despite such society, Eliot like Pound was finding that life in England was not without its difficulty. 'London is something one has to fight very hard in, in order to survive,' he told his brother in July:

> Don't think that I find it easy to live over here. It is damned hard work to live with a foreign nation and cope with them – one is always coming up against differences of feeling that make one feel humiliated and lonely. One remains always a foreigner.[53]

There could be no assimilation for him, he said: he felt he was on constant dress parade, a strain from which he could never relax. He was very glad to be getting out of London, he told Mary Hutchinson. 'Perhaps I won't ever come back!'[54]

It was time for both Eliot and Pound to shake off the city for a while.

//

Eliot was finding it difficult to keep in front of him the things that he most wanted to do, he told John Quinn in July, and he lived under constant pressure to meet his daily needs.[55] Even so, he had managed to maintain his drive for publication in America, and had sent Quinn an additional typescript of *Athenaeum* columns and four poems, the titles of which he didn't specify, but which were probably 'Burbank', 'Sweeney Erect', 'A Cooking Egg' and 'Dans le Restaurant'. But he left out a poem that he was just about to circulate to friends.

It was almost certainly at a picnic at Itchenor woods on 6 July that Eliot first mentioned 'Gerontion' to Mary Hutchinson. 'Here is the poem for which you asked, out of politeness I dare say,' he wrote after returning to London on 9 July. 'I don't feel at all finally satisfied with it, so please don't let anyone see it, but let me have your candid opinion upon it when you will.'[56] Mary showed her husband St John, who must have disregarded Eliot's instruction, for on 14 July he carried the draft with him when he went to see Nancy Cunard at Turks Croft, her summer cottage of old low roofs near Crawley, Sussex.[57] The two of them wandered together, walking through what she called a respectable calm country (more sleep than dream), reading 'an amazing new poem by <u>Eliot</u>' that she described as 'very intense and good'.[58] The two of them devised pet names partly in light of it: he was to be the 'religious arithmetician', and she the 'romantic weevil' in an 'intricate' reference to a line late in the poem. The Hutchinsons, it seems, were not to be trusted as literary confidants, but Eliot had at least now had back from Sydney Schiff his comments on the draft, and thanked him for them on 16 July, telling him, in an echo of the poem's opening line, 'Here, *I* am an outsider.'[59] A few days later he told Mary that he thought everyone must make their own estimation of their power of assimilation.[60] Foreigner, outsider, assimilator: in the space of a fortnight, Eliot had spoken of each.

All of the English-language poems that Eliot had written since 1917 had relied for effect upon the control of the four 'French' feet; 'Gerontion' was different. Formal rhythm was now replaced by an open cadence that rolled across the measure and back in waves of loose pentameter. Nor did the new work have anything like the comfort of the rhyming refrains of the *Prufrock* poems: 'Gerontion' was out on its own, between styles, neither 'French' nor 'free' but something found by Eliot himself. 'The title means "little old man",' he said, and was a revision of 'Gerousia', the council of elders in ancient Greece that had given Eliot his first title.[61] By 1 June 1919, the poem was 'half-finished', and by early July had reached a level of completion that allowed Eliot to alert Wyndham Lewis to its presence for tentative inclusion in the third issue of *Blast*, then in preparation. He also mentioned it to John Rodker, saying that he would supply it for their planned publication together, once he knew that it was wanted.[62]

'Gerontion' was the first of Eliot's poems to be saturated in the Great War: the Siege of Antwerp, whose 'estaminet' cafe life had been so violently destroyed in the autumn of 1914; 'blistered' Brussels, abandoned to the Germans in August 1914 after the fall of the last forts on the River Meuse; the city of London, 'patched and peeled' under the air bombardment that had begun in May 1915. These would be the sites of the poem, as would the woman sifting the fire grate, sneezing at evening, like so many sufferers of influenza. It was not a commemoration of the kind conferred by the soldier poets upon the fallen; it was instead a memorial to the ageing, to the incapable, the non-combatant, those who were 'neither at the hot gates / Nor fought in the warm rain / Nor knee deep in the salt marsh, heaving a cutlass, / Bitten by flies'. It was resonant with the humiliating reparations that were Eliot's job at the bank to solicit, and with the treaty signed on 28 June 1919 at Versailles, in *a wilderness of mirrors*, the palace's Galerie des Glaces de Louis XIV, with its *contrived corridors* and *whispering ambitions*. Decrepitation, decay, lives without culture or belief: history was a collapsing roof, Europe fallen utterly. In the words of an essay Eliot was writing on Pound at the time: 'The present is no more than the present existence, the present significance, of the entire past.'[63] Its setting could only have been Europe in 1919, from the opening of its 'hot gates' to its finale of 'fractured atoms'. *The Times* had reported on 7 June that the physicist Ernest Rutherford had successfully 'disintegrated' the nucleus of nitrogen through a bombardment of radioactive alpha particles to emit fast protons: in plain language, he had split the nitrogen atom, launching humanity into the nuclear age. *After such knowledge*, asked Gerontion, *what forgiveness?*

Even so, the ending of the poem wasn't in place by midsummer:

> De Bailhache, Fresca, Mrs Cammel, whirled
> Beyond the circuit of the shuddering Bear
> In fractured atoms. We have saved a shilling against oblivion
> Even oblivious.
>
>   Tenants of an old man's house,
> Thoughts of a dry brain in a dry season.[64]

With their 'fractured atoms' the draft lines would anticipate those still to be written in *The Waste Land*, where 'saved' would become *shored*; 'a shilling', *fragments*; 'against oblivion', *against my ruins*. The shillings, with their distended line, would disappear from 'Gerontion' long before *The Waste Land* was written, but for the time being, Eliot just couldn't find his ending, and would wait for the eye of Ezra Pound.

'And of course you are unjust to Pound,' Eliot told Mary Hutchinson that July. 'One must learn to appreciate his "literary-appreciative" style as a medium for expressing something of his own.' *Literary-appreciative* was an exacting capture of Pound's passion for the writing of others. 'I daresay he seems to you derivative. But I can show you in the thing I enclose how I have borrowed from half a dozen sources.'[65] Among the borrowings to which he referred was undoubtedly 'The Dream of Gerontius', a poem by John Henry Newman written in 1865 after his conversion to Roman Catholicism, that follows a life through death into reawakening before God; 'a tiresome footling little Anglican parson', said Joyce, who had also become a discernible presence.[66] Eliot had admired the second episode of *Ulysses*, 'Nestor', when it was published in the *Little Review* in 1918, and more deeply still when he found himself proof-reading it for a printing in *The Egoist* in the new year of 1919. 'I am a struggler now at the end of my days,' Joyce had written, 'old as I am'.[67]

But something even more explicit had been borrowed, for Eliot had, in his words, 'lifted bodily' from an existing source: in this case from a 1905 biography of Edward FitzGerald by A. C. Benson.[68]

Here he sits, in a dry month, old and blind, being read to by a country boy, longing for rain. (Benson)

Here I am, an old man in a dry month,
Being read to by a boy, waiting for rain. (Eliot)[69]

'Immature poets imitate; mature poets steal.'[70] Eliot's words in 1920. He continued: 'Bad poets deface what they take, and good poets make it into something better, or at least something different.' Theft, in other words, is not really theft if fused with something unique of the borrower's own; at that moment it becomes a contributor to the greater conversation of literature.

Borrowing was not the poem's only controversy. For 'Gerontion' would become infamous for a solitary line, 'the jew squats on the window sill' (like 'Burbank', 'jew' was left in minuscule by Eliot until 1963) – a figure who may or may not be 'the owner' of the decaying house, depending upon a pair of succeeding and ambiguous commas that serve as a set of points to send readers in differing directions. Taken in one bearing, the Jew is the dispossessed of the poem, taking temporary shelter in the crumbling house owned by a refugee from Europe's war-torn cities; taken in another, the Jew is 'the owner', a slum landlord, a rackman: spawned and blistered and peeled in the same cities that may now be thought of as financial capitals. For other readers again, there can be no meaningful distinction in the ambiguity: read either way, 'the jew' is subject and object of ruin and decomposition, singled out in decrepitude, languishing in lowercase contempt; the mere presence of such a symbol is odious in itself.

As July progressed, Eliot had not found his ending, but then nor had he been able to work on the poem: both his ribbon and carbon copies were out of his hands, and on 6 August, with his walking tour with Pound imminent, he wrote to Mary to request that she urgently return hers.

> **Important**
>
> *Please* send *Gerontion* back to me at once. I leave Saturday night, and I must revise it in France, so *just* put it in an envelope and send it by return.[71]

//

At five o'clock on a sweltering[72] Saturday afternoon, 9 August, Vivien saw Eliot off from Waterloo for the midnight ferry at Southampton. It would dock at Le Havre at eight o'clock the following morning, but the stamping of passports took so long that Eliot missed his train to Paris and had to improvise an onward route, hitching along with a French couple aboard a local steamer to Trouville-sur-Mer in pursuit of an alternative connection. The overnight train pulled out from Paris Austerlitz at nine that evening: Eliot dashed – 'just caught it' – and settled in for a long and unhurried journey – even the express didn't travel much above forty-five miles per hour, but he didn't mind: he was excited and could hardly get himself to sleep.[73] At four in the morning, he pulled into Limoges and waited for an hour on the platform between trains; when he pulled out again, he found himself sharing a compartment with two French soldiers on leave who played the accordion relentlessly and urged Eliot to sing along. As daylight began to fill the carriage Eliot could see for the first time the rolling woodland of the Périgord. He arrived at half-past seven on the Monday morning, tired, hungry and hot, at the station stop of Périgueux, where he was met by Ezra Pound. The scent of garlic was in the air and he could hear the clatter of ox-carts and donkey hooves; he had travelled for more than thirty-six hours, but felt as though he had reached the South in one instant.[74]

Excideuil was a troubadour village on the River Loue, but as the town troubadour, Guiraut de Bornelh (or Borneil), had not met with the approval of Dante, he hadn't met with the approval of Pound either ('facile, diffuse, without distinction of style, without personality' – adding, to put the matter beyond doubt, 'over-praised').[75] But Bertran de Born, at nearby Hautefort, was a poet Pound did rate: it was with his 'Sestina: Altaforte'[76] in 1909 that Pound had been able to make a powerful first impression upon London, and it was he whom Dante had portrayed dramatically in the eighth circle of hell raising his severed head like a lantern. Bertran de Born had stood in opposition to the marauding Richard Coeur de Lion, whom he nicknamed *Oc-e-Non* (Richard Yes-and-No) in description of his rival's autocratic rule. Three times the castle at Excideuil had withstood the siege of Coeur de Lion.

> 'Here such a one walked.
> 'Here Coeur-de-Lion was slain.
> 'Here was good singing.
> 'Here one man hastened his step.
> 'Here one lay panting.'[77]

The castle, like de Born himself, stood to Pound for resistance and timelessness: everything he would come to see symbolised in a single block of limestone that he noticed embedded on the high parapet, carved with a wave pattern.

In July 1919, the Pounds had taken rooms in a pension that Ezra had first visited in 1912, with a hospitable proprietor, Mme Louise Poujol. Eliot fell asleep there at once, and woke at lunchtime to sit out with the Pounds in the hotel garden through the remainder of the afternoon. He seemed to them thin and discoloured, and they prepared for him a restorative course of 'sun, air & sulphur bath' in the mineral waters at nearby Brive.[78] As the days passed, Eliot improved. It was his first significant journey abroad since the war, though he couldn't help but see London's bombed-out sites reflected in the Roman ruins around him.[79] It was also the first time since 1915 that he had put real distance between himself and Vivien. Pound now stood in place of all his ambivalent English acquaintances: reader, guide, counsellor, friend. As they spoke of the old Occitanie – of the pilgrimages they were about to make – the two men must have felt like troubadours themselves, immersed in Provence, outsiders and rebels to most causes, talking the good fight. Pound would publish a quartet of 'Malatesta' *Cantos* in Eliot's *Criterion* in 1923, from which a draft typescript, subsequently cut, pictures Eliot and Pound and Dorothy there:

> As we had sat, three of us at Excideuil
> over Borneil's old bake-oven
> .. that was three years ago . . .
> on the roman mound
> level with the town spire,
> 'e poi gli affina' for you.[80]

E poi gli affina, 'and then purifies them': a homage handed down through history.

It was Arnaut's homage to the poet Guido Guinizelli, who 'vanished in the fire' (*Purgatorio*, 26.134); it was Dante's to Arnaut, *Poi s'ascose nel foco che gli affina* ('Then hid him in the fire that purifies them'), quoted by Eliot in *The Waste Land*; it was Pound's to Eliot, 'for you': a breaking of bread at the site of the old bakery that was said to belong to Guiraut de Bornelh's father.

By Saturday, Eliot felt sufficiently recovered to undertake the short walking tour he had prepared with Pound, and on 16 August, the two men left Dorothy at the hotel and set out on their journey. They covered thirteen miles to Thiviers that day, a hilltop climb from an old Roman road, where they took rooms for the night and from where Pound sent Dorothy a postcard to let her know that their first stop had been reached without incident. The next morning broke thick with mist. That day they went further than before: seventeen miles to Brantôme, which they reached by the afternoon; *pleasing*, wrote Pound simply in a second postcard to Dorothy. But there was nothing to please Eliot's feet, which were already a cause of concern. 'T. has 7 blisters,' wrote Pound. 'Will probably proceed by train tomorrow.' When Monday came it wasn't by train that they set off, but once more on foot, navigating the seven miles to Bourdeilles with Eliot's sore feet wrapped in *le papier Fayard* blister papers. Fewer than forty miles, but three days of climbs in hot weather: 'intensely' (Eliot), 'very very' (Dorothy).[81]

The walking tour ended at Bourdeilles, from where – despite Eliot's insistence that he was on foot the whole time[82] – the two men probably took advantage of the steam tramway that trundled the sixteen miles towards Périgueux in order to rest Eliot's tender feet. At the Place Francheville, beneath the shadow of the Tour Mataguerre, last of the city's walled defences, the friends would have parted. A tramway led Pound north and east to Dorothy and Excideuil for the couple's preparations for their final departure for Paris. 'Eliot went on to the Fonts de Gaume, & Les Eyzies grottes,'[83] reported Pound, although whether that was before or after he had made his defining visit to Périgueux cathedral Pound didn't reveal. What is known is that what took place at the cathedral would be a turning point in Eliot's life.

'St Front of Périgueux! St Front. What a cathedral,' repeated Pound – 'what a cathedral!'[84] The enormous Byzantine tower and the five soaring cupolas of the Basilique Saint-Front had left a dramatic impression upon his visit of 1912. He had marvelled at its 'domes of Byzant, & pattern of the east', and what he called the 'fine immoral music of its streets', and its 'whirl for dance'. A twelfth-century fire had consumed the site almost entirely, and it is said that the bells in the tower and its precious ornaments roasted in a conflagration that took with it a great many lives as a punishment for its people's sins. It was this moment, or probably a conflation with the Cathars going to their deaths, that Pound depicted in the eerie lines of a 1915 poem, 'Provincia Deserta':

> I have walked
> > into Périgord,
> I have seen the torch-flames, high-leaping,
> Painting the front of that church,
> And, under the dark, whirling laughter.[85]

It was a cathedral named, it is said, after the legendary St Front, sent by St Peter to preach in the lands of Aquitaine; although it was a successor, Paternus, who might have stirred Eliot's attention: he had been deposed as the Bishop of Périgueux in 361 CE for the Arian heresy that Jesus was begotten from God, and therefore a subordinate being unequal to Him. Paternus, along with the diocese of Arles, would be fiercely punished by St Hilary of Poitiers, the Nicene 'Hammer of Arians', who restored, in the words of one later history, 'the Ancient Faith' of a Jesus co-eternal with God the Father, and so 'procur'd the Condemnation of *Saturninus* Bifhop of *Arles*, who oppos'd this Defign, as well as Paternus, Bifhop of *Périgueux*'.[86] Other bishops who 'acknowledg'd their Fault' were pardoned, history records, but Paternus would make no such acknowledgement. To deny the Trinity was not only a folly, but a heresy, believed Hilary. 'To undertake such a thing is to embark upon the boundless, to dare the incomprehensible,' to attempt to speak of God with more refinement than He has provided us with. It is enough that He has given His nature through the Trinity of Father, Son and Holy Spirit. 'Whatever is sought over and above this is beyond the meaning of words, beyond the limits of perception, beyond the embrace of understanding.'[87] Hilary was writing in the fourth century in language that would resonate in the twentieth with Eliot's arrival at Trinitarianism in *Four Quartets*. But that was a journey Eliot was still to travel, and it must surely have been the vision of a man choosing condemnation over survival that would shake Eliot to his foundations.

In Périgueux, that summer, Eliot was a son separated from the love of a father in death and in life, and had yet to find the guidance of a holy spirit with which his joining of the Church of England in 1927 would allow him to commune. In the chronicles of the building before him, and in his walking conversations with Pound, Eliot could trace the accounts of martyrs and heretics alike who had gone into exile – or gone into the fire – for their convictions or their sins, people who had found a measure to live by and even to die for, who had found a family of higher calling. What had Eliot to offer compared to such commitment? Not the 'one great tragedy' of the war in which he was denied a part. Not the daily negotiations at the bank for a treaty that he considered immoral and unjust, and altogether 'a bad peace'.[88] Not the wedding vows, taken before God, that seemed to him to have turned to ashes in his hands. He found he had no direction, no ideological framework from which to respond. The Unitarianism of his childhood seemed to him a poor man's fuddle: a culture of humanitarianism, of ethical mind games rather than a passionate adherence to Incarnation, Heaven and Hell; in *The Athenaeum* that May he had dubbed it 'the Boston doubt'.[89] And in the absence of a religious conviction, his writing simply could not bear the weight: regarded merely for its satire and wit, it had yet to find the ground from which to respond to the intensity of the emotions he was experiencing. He was a son who had failed a father, bereft of the father who had failed a son.

The train that left Périgueux climbed past the ruined fortress at Mauzens before descending into the Vézère valley to cross the river that marked the entrance to the small town of Les Eyzies. There, the station hotel was plain but good, and only a short walk to the cave of Font de Gaume, a prominent headland rising above a canopy of holm oaks in the Beune valley. The recent discovery by a local schoolmaster of Magdalenian wall art had become a sensation: a treasury of polychromatic cave paintings dating back nineteen thousand years – bison, mammoths, ibex, woolly rhinoceros, a wolf, a lioness, a leaping horse, an antlered reindeer grooming the forehead of a doe. Many of its beasts were painted in an iron-rich ochre of heated sienna and umber deposits, that under the shadow and flicker of firelight would appear to turn the caves crimson. On the cave walls, under the shadow of this red rock, Eliot witnessed a connection between art and instinct that he would elucidate in an essay for *The Athenaeum* that autumn:

> And as it is certain that some study of primitive man furthers our understanding of civilized man, so it is certain that primitive art and poetry help our understanding of civilized art and poetry. Primitive art and poetry can even, through the studies and experiments of the artist or poet, revivify the contemporary activities. The maxim, Return to the sources, is a good one.[90]

The artist is conscious of both the civilised and the primitive mind, and is therefore the person best placed to understand how the primitive mind brings the clearest illumination of its own time, *and* how its understanding can be improved upon in the time of civilisation. In a review of Wyndham Lewis some months before,

Eliot had identified what he had called the thought of the modern in the energy of the caveman; but now he took the challenge a step further.[91] The duty of the poet should be no less than the following: to know everything that has been accomplished in art since the beginning, in order to understand what real accomplishment might be. In the cool air of the Font de Gaume cave, it was clear to Eliot what he had to do. To return to the sources, to know everything, to understand tradition in order to release contemporary talent. In the rock drawing of the Magdalenian draughtsmen he now saw the key to understanding the change in what he was about to call 'the mind of Europe'.[92]

Eliot must have spoken with animation to Pound of his experience in the caves on their reunion in Brive, for he sketched a map of the route from the station to the cave in case Pound should ever wish to find his way there and experience it himself. Pound never returned, but Eliot's encounter there lingered in his imagination and in a draft of 'Canto II', from Paris 1920 or 1921, he projected himself there, 'At les Eyzies, nameless drawer of panther':

> So I in a narrow cave, secret scratched on a wall,
> And the last reader, with handshake of departing sun[93]

And he would recall Eliot's presence there in lines written two decades later:

> so his eminence, the eminent Possum
> visited Dordogne cavernes[94]

Even if he had made the journey himself, it is doubtful that Pound would have come away agreeing with his friend on the need for an all-seeing poet. 'One can't read everything,'[95] he grumbled in an article of 1934: the art of poetry after all was discernment not comprehension, and it was not, despite Eliot's moment at the Font de Gaume, desirable or possible to digest it all. 'With one day's reading a man may have the key in his hands,' he wrote in the *Pisan Cantos*.[96] Contra Eliot, the poet *cannot* know it all, but should instead train the mind to hunt selectively, as the panther hunts selectively, taking no more than it needs to survive and prosper.

The cathedral and the cave had brought revelation to Eliot twice that summer, but he was still to experience one further encounter, and that was to take place at Excideuil castle. It was on a visit to the ruins there that Eliot faltered in the company of Pound.

The caretaker of the ruins was an elderly lady who occupied two small rooms on the castle grounds, beside a dilapidated well in the forecourt. Touched by her plight, Pound carried up to the castle from the town below a beam and a chain, and laid the former over the curbstone and tied the latter around it, and so enabled her to once again draw water from the ancient well. It had been no small task on his part: a climb so elevated that the castle courtyard was level with the tips of the nearby poplars and a distant church spire. The old lady gave thanks with what she could: some *tilleul* leaves from the linden tree from which to brew tea.[97] Pound remembered her as the Madame Pierre who returns in 'Canto CVII':

> as tenthril thru grill-work
> > wave pattern at Excideuil
> A spire level the well-curb,
> > Mme Pierre bought a lamb in that market.[98]

But it was neither the lady nor her well that left the deepest impression upon Pound, but the 'wave pattern' of small interlacing grooves carved into a parapet of the castle limestone. Pound was captivated by it. Again and again he came back to the wave stone image in *The Cantos*, interpreting it as a motif for time and timelessness in equal measure, a fluid connection between all places

– specifically, the ancient cultures of Provence, Greece and Rome interleaved with those of modern France, Britain and America. 'Canto LXXX':

> And the wave pattern runs in the stone
> on the high parapet (Excideuil)
> Mt Segur and the city of Dioce.[99]

To Pound, it was a symbol of eternal movement, and it should perhaps be no surprise that the stone that he and Eliot saw has itself since moved: 'the high parapet' on which Pound encountered the stone can no longer be found after dereliction and fire caused many of the castle's blocks to topple, and they were reassembled haphazardly. Today, a stone with a pattern of waves incised into it guards an outer archway to the chateau.

It was here, in August 1919, tracing the wave-like carvings, that Eliot told Pound, suddenly and unexpectedly, that he feared a life after death.[100]

Pound recorded the moment, in 'Canto XXIX', published in 1930, in a scene in which he pays Eliot the ultimate compliment in naming him 'Arnaut' – a compliment that by then Eliot had advanced in his dedication of *The Waste Land*.

> So Arnaut turned there
> Above him the wave pattern cut in the stone
> Spire-top alevel the well-curb
> And the tower about that, saying:
>   'I am afraid of the life after death.'
> and after a pause:
> 'Now, at last, I have shocked him.'[101]

And he had. Pound would return again and again to renew the moment in his writing. He would continue the conversation with Eliot in person, in Verona the following summer, sitting on the steps on the amphitheatre when Pound's Confucianism and Eliot's wakening Anglo-Catholicism met head on.[102] Confucius, Pound recorded in 'Canto XIII', 'said nothing of the "life after death"', and to him the investment in an afterlife was all but incomprehensible, whether by Eliot or the Cathars.[103]

And I, 'But this beats me,
'Beats me, I mean that I do not understand it,
This love of death that is in them.'[104]

But to Eliot a series of tracings had been overlaid one on another, for he had seen something else in the Provençal story of the *perfecti* who went willingly to the flames beneath Montségur in 1244: a purgatorial suffering. These were once a mysterious people, he wrote soon after his conversion to the Church of England in *Dante* (1929), who 'had a religion of their own which was thoroughly and painfully extinguished by the Inquisition'.[105] These were a people who understood, as Dante himself wrote in *La Vita Nuova* (1294), what Eliot now called *sublimation* and also called *the philosophy of disillusion*: 'not to expect more from *life* than it can give or more from *human* beings than they can give; to look to *death* for what life cannot give'.[106] As he would write many years later, in 'Little Gidding', as though resuming his talk with Pound:

Whatever we inherit from the fortunate
We have taken from the defeated
What they had to leave us – a symbol
A symbol perfected in death . . .[107]

The fire, the rock, the wave, a final breath. A surrender so elemental, so truly immense, that Eliot had fallen in the face of it.

'There are moments,' wrote Eliot in 1935, 'perhaps not known to everyone, when a man may be nearly crushed by the terrible awareness of his isolation from every other human being.'[108]

Marlow, he said, had been one such moment. There, he had

experienced what he called a 'dispossession by the dead',[109] an experience that he would have only once again in his life, in Périgord that summer.

> This sense of dispossession by the dead I have known twice, at
> Marlow and at Périgueux.

To say that Eliot's choice of words is enigmatic is to leave a great deal unsaid. What *did* he mean by them exactly, and what exactly happened at Marlow and at Périgueux to call them into being?

A dispossession was a casting out: a confiscation of occupancy, of property or land. It is traced in the Old Testament Deuteronomic word *yarash*: to seize, inherit or disinherit, drive out, to become impoverished or brought to ruin. But a dispossession was also an exorcism: a word to describe the purging of demons, as applied by the Catholic Church from as early as its second century: it is a removal *of* the bad *by* the good. But that wasn't exactly what Eliot had said. A dispossession not *of* the dead but *by* the dead: not an action undertaken *by* him, but one done *to* him. From what exactly was Eliot expelled, and by whom? His Unitarianism did not permit demons, nor have any call for exorcism; his church had nothing to say to him on the subject of dispossession, *nothing*. He was simply powerless in response.

Unitarianism, the religion of his father, and of his father's father, had not equipped him for the undertaking that he now faced. It left no room for refinement, for purgatory, it left no room for atonement. It had stripped him of a capacity to chart an independent morality. And through the quarrel of beliefs and values with his father, it had even stripped him of an independent income. Eliot knew that he wasn't to inherit from his father's estate as his siblings would: his marriage to Vivien had seen to that, and what inheritance was to come to him would do so in the form of a trust that would be restored to the family in the event of his death, so that it could not be bestowed by him upon her.[110] For a married man of thirty, living and working professionally a continent apart from his family, to have his financial arrangements manipulated in such a way was a humiliation. He felt isolated and expelled, cast out by the dead for both the actions he had taken and those he had failed to take. And that he called it a dispossession signalled at the depth of his devastation. The departed, it seemed, were calling him out.

What transfixed Eliot in this moment was not heaven and hell, but purgatory, the temporary suffering or expiation for the purpose of spiritual cleansing. 'In purgatory the torment of flame is deliberately and consciously accepted by the penitent,' he wrote in his 1929 *Dante*. And he made his own translation of the moment in the *Purgatorio* in which Dante is approached by souls from the flames:

> Then certain of them made towards me, so far as they could, but ever watchful not to come so far that they should *not be in the fire*.[111]

The emphasis was Eliot's own. The souls in purgatory suffer 'because they *wish to suffer*, for purgation', he wrote, because they wish to be in the fire, because 'in their suffering is hope'.

In such a moment of isolation, Eliot would write in years to come, he felt only pity for the man who found himself alone, as he had, 'alone with himself and his meanness and futility, alone without God'. For it is only in the moment that we are alone *with* God, he continued, that we can truly appreciate the awareness of what he called 'our *membership*'. To be without the company of God, Eliot would later write, is to be abandoned to the wilderness, to an endless seesaw between anarchy and tyranny: 'a seesaw which, in the secular world, I believe has no end'.[112]

By Friday 22 August, the Pounds were in Brive, where Eliot joined them, staying at the town's Grand Hôtel de Bordeaux, a renowned railway stopover for travelling dignitaries ('good', Eliot's Baedeker summarised austerely; 'a real hotel with stationary', Pound punned

– or possibly misspelled).[113] Through the heat of another Saturday, the two men walked again, this time east through to Malemort, 'so fine & sinister name'[114] (Pound), where the lords of Limousin put to the sword the army of Richard Coeur de Lion, two thousand strong by legend. The next day, on Sunday 24 August, after two weeks together, the poets parted company. The Pounds headed north that night on the sleeper to Orléans, reaching Paris at mid-week, where they treated themselves to a fortnight's stay at the Hôtel Elysée, on the Left Bank: 'a large room from which we see the Seine & Pont Royal and a corner of the Louvre & windows of rue de Rivoli, on the opposite side'.[115] Eliot headed north-east into Corrèze for his final week of walking; he was bearded and sunburnt and, for the first time in a long time, happy: 'melons, ceps, truffles, eggs, good wine and good cheese and cheerful people', he scribbled on a postcard to Lytton Strachey. 'It is a complete relief from London.'[116]

Indeed it must have been. In the three weeks that he had been away, he had found reclusion not possible for him in England. He had been made by his doctor to promise that while away he would not read or write, and it was with a wounded sense of grievance that Vivien confirmed to Mary Hutchinson that he had obeyed medical instruction: France had really swallowed him up, she wrote gloomily, the strain of their separation showing.[117]

'To the Lansdowne again,' Vivien noted in her diary. On the day that Eliot delivered himself into Pound's hands in Périgord, Vivien had returned herself to the same room of the same hotel in which the Eliots had spent their troubled honeymoon in 1915. She recorded that it was nice to be back, the faces friendly and familiar, and that she looked forward to a fortnight's rest accompanied by her friend May Pacy. But she was journeying through her life in reverse as Eliot was moving forward in his. Her brother Maurice joined her briefly: they had a roaring time dancing; but her return to London on 24 August quickly dispelled any hope that a recovery in her health had been effected. 'Now I am ill,' she wrote to Mary Hutchinson. 'I have got influenza: the minute I got back.' Once again she was prostrate, sneezing violently and with pulsing headaches. And then she wrote something more telling. 'In future I am going to simply wash my hands of Tom and refuse politely to explain him or interpret him or influence or direct him,' she wrote abruptly. 'I mean to have some sort of individual existence, and Tom must manage his own muddles.'[118] It seemed that changes were on the horizon.

As Eliot sailed across the English Channel he seemed a man altered by his travels, a man closing in on home and yet somehow just embarking on a journey. But any newfound sense of himself would quickly dissolve. On Sunday 31 August he was at home at Crawford Mansions. 'Very nice at first,' wrote Vivien in her diary, but 'depressed in the evening'.[119]

Eleven days later, the Pounds, too, returned to London.

IV.

'My trip was a complete success,' wrote Eliot of Périgord in September: 'I feel much better for it.'[1] But to Vivien he seemed dishevelled now that he had grown a beard, his mood more volatile than before. He had returned to London to find Vivien in bed with bronchitis, having concealed her illness in the hope of preserving his holiday. Rumours abounded that pets could transmit influenza (Yancia, a five-year-old Boston bulldog, had found national fame when she appeared masked on the second page of the *Seattle Star*),[2] and Vivien was worried about both her health and that of their dog, Dinah Brooks, who was confined to the flat.[3] Daily, she recorded the dog's deteriorating condition. Tuesday, worse. Wednesday, very ill indeed. Thursday, worse. Friday, 'Took Dinah to a vet, in a taxi with Tom. Nothing could be done. Put her to death at once.'[4] Saturday, 'Frightful day of misery.'[5]

The Eliots were back in Bosham that Saturday, 6 September. Vivien was almost too distressed to travel, but Eliot felt as sure as ever that what she needed most was to escape London. For the fifth time in three years they looked to the little Sussex harbour for their recuperation, only this time they hadn't given enough notice to secure their regular room in South View, and for ten days took interim accommodation until it became available. But if Vivien had hoped to draw strength from her husband's company she was soon disappointed. He stayed only for one night before returning to London, leaving her to manage an acute pain in her right side and a state of feeling 'very very nervous'.[6] Eliot felt he had little option. He had taken up a new position with the

Information Department at Lloyds on returning from France, in an imposing room with a large south window overlooking the Mansion House. For the next fortnight he stayed in London, establishing himself in his new role by day, and working by night on an essay on *Hamlet*. He was, too, covering the absence at *The Athenaeum* of John Middleton Murry, who had accompanied his wife Katherine Mansfield to Ospedaletti, on the Italian Riviera, for her treatment for pulmonary tuberculosis, diagnosed two years before.

Vivien bathed off the quay at Bosham and attempted sketching; she felt her spirits beginning to return with the good weather, marking her diary *perfect* and *perfect*, *glorious* and *glorious*.[7] When the weather broke mid-September so did Vivien's recovery. A stay with Mary Hutchinson overnight at Eleanor House left her washed out; the next day she sheltered from a storm in Mary's outhouse, which creaked like an old ship while the gale roared round and about. Eliot returned after a fortnight, and met Vivien in Chichester on the Saturday afternoon, 20 September, where she had been running errands for Mary, to whom she scribbled a tense and hasty pencil note. 'I feel you are right about T. & he must somehow be tamed,' it read. 'You dont know it but he is often very unkind to me, in that way, & often makes me wretched.' Vivien's anxiety at her husband's arrival was palpable, but may also have been motivated by actions of her own that may not have been regarded as entirely proper. She signed off her note with a cryptic trail: 'Don't tell Jack about Jim it would not do I assure you.'[8] Jack was Mary's husband, and the Jim she didn't want him to know about was James Strachey Barnes, Mary's brother, who worked in the Foreign Office, who would in time become infamous for his proselytising fascism – 'a queer bird', said Eliot, in whom Mary may have encouraged Vivien's interest.[9] When Vivien returned to London a fortnight later, she complained to Mary that she wanted to go shopping for a new outfit but 'I don't know what will please Jim most either!' And she went further, telling Mary, 'You must begin laying foundation stones for me with Jim,' and 'Meanwhile I have no underclothes.'[10] The gulf between Vivien and Eliot was widening, and his arrival in Chichester was not about to narrow it. He went out the same evening to see the landlady's brother-in-law, 'Capn',[11] leaving Vivien alone with her tiredness and nerves, and describing the evening in a now familiar phrase as 'rather unsatisfactory'.[12] But the Eliots had at least now moved into South View on the harbour, and the next day went slightly better: they blackberried after a picnic with the Hutchinsons, before he returned to London in the evening on the eight o'clock train.

Eliot's birthday, his thirty-first, arrived on 26 September; the couple spent it apart. He worked at the London bank all day, she struggled with head pain in Bosham. As the day wore on Vivien began to wish that they had spent it together, and became eager to leave behind an estuary that had now begun to turn wintry. But her headache had become a migraine and her face had swollen and she was menstruating painfully. She overheard that Mary Hutchinson had spoken of her own exhaustion following Vivien's overnight stay, and this proved too much. *She* expected to feel exhaustion herself but couldn't understand it in Mary, and she lashed out at her in a churlish note.[13] No sooner had she sent it than she regretted it: it was a 'silly' and 'unfortunate' letter,[14] she admitted, and one which she said drew from Mary in turn a 'nasty' response. Vivien called her 'little cat',[15] and spikily signed off her next letter, '"Your loving" Vivien', with inverted commas, and below that, 'The Woman's Friend' – and below that 'Damn you'.[16] But escaping Bosham was not as easy as Vivien had expected. A railway strike had begun on 26 September (the government had reneged on a wartime pay promise), and would last for nine days. 'Going home', she crossed out in her diary, and gave up on the effort for the rest of the weekend. By Monday she could bear Bosham no more, and hired a private car at thirty shillings for the ride: a wild drive with a man with false teeth. She cabled Eliot, but her message failed to reach him in time: he went to meet her train at London Bridge while she was driven by motor car to Putney; she waited there two hours for him, he waited for her at London Bridge for nearly four. By the time they converged at the flat, both were in tears. And she had left part of her luggage behind at Putney Bridge and part in Chichester.[17]

Tom was 'IMpossible', the weekends were 'rather unsatisfactory', and then came the unexpected intimacy of 'Peace weekend': the Eliots' time together in July and early August had been tumultuous. Between Eliot's bank tour in mid-May and Vivien's return from Bosham at the end of September – a stretch of some twenty weeks – the couple had spent only those three summer weeks together, with just two weeks either side: one, in June, when Eliot had been occupied with a 'furiously laboured' article, and another with the illness and death of their dog. There had been weekends where he would visit her in Bosham, and those where she would return to him in Marylebone, but even so the daily business of living and being together had been all but suspended for more than four months. Not that the Eliots were alone in their troubles. Mary's marriage to St John had come under strain that autumn: he was spending more time with Nancy Cunard than he should, and when Clive Bell departed suddenly for Paris in November, Mary felt abandoned. How sad that Clive was going to France, Vivien sympathised: was Mary going with him? She was, came the reply, which brought out a strange and worrying response from Vivien. 'I also have a gun-powder plot in preparation,' she wrote, 'but mine is not timed to go off until the New Year, so perhaps it will be a case of he who laughs last laughs loudest.'[18] The undated message from Vivien was most likely written in late October, a week or so before bonfire night: what exactly was her 'plot'? Was Mary's brother Jim her conspirator? She never disclosed; and that might have been the end of it, though Vivien's relationship with Jim maintained a charge for some time to come. In 1926, after the Eliots chanced upon Jim at a tennis club in Rome, Vivien sent Mary a wistful postcard saying that she had watched him watching world number one Suzanne Lenglen play 'but at a distance'; on the reverse of the card was a portrait of Benito Mussolini.[19] A dinner with Jim and the Hutchinsons at the Eliots' home in 1931 ended in disaster after Eliot accused Vivien of keeping secrets; her efforts to call Jim back went unheeded, and the 'gunpowder' plot failed to go off.[20]

//

'What else was to be expected?'[21] The day after the Pounds returned to London on 11 September, Eliot had scribbled a hasty note: he was to call by at their flat on Holland Place Chambers the next evening to show off his beard, and if his hosts were out, *n'importante*. What was expected was presumably the drafts that Pound had not yet seen but which Eliot had promised in France to deliver on his return: among them, 'Gerontion'. But the Pounds had found the journey back from Paris tiring, and had accepted an invitation to the country from the illustrator Edmund Dulac and left that morning before Eliot's note arrived.[22] His call that Saturday must have gone unanswered.

Eliot had abandoned in 'Gerontion' a draft epigraph from Dante in which a dead soul wanders dazed upon the earth – 'How my body stands in the world above, I have no knowledge.'[23] But Pound's attention passed straight to the opening lines. A. C. Benson had been among a litany of names that Pound had excoriated in 1914, and whether or not he had actually read the biography of Edward FitzGerald that Benson had written, he didn't a bit like the lines that Eliot had drawn from it:[24]

Here I am, an old man in a dry month,
Being read to by a boy, waiting for rain.

Pound ringed and partially deleted the first line, and took fright at the '*b – b – b*' consonants of the second and their accompanying prepositions, before turning his focus to the interior of the poem. From there he worked diligently, circling, underlining, cancelling and re-punctuating as he went. Eliot had just pencilled a new ending on the back of the draft that he was yet to incorporate, tearing up the *shillings* that had followed his *fractured atoms*, and replacing two lines with five:

[In fractured atoms.] Gull against the wind, in the windy straits
Of Belle Isle, or driven by the horn,
White feathers in the snow, the gulf claims,
And an old man driven by the trades
To a sleepy corner. Twitching with rheumatism
[. . . Thoughts of a dry brain in a dry season.]

Eliot had sailed the New England coast in childhood, only here he had transposed the setting north to Newfoundland and Labrador, and the last isle on the trade line between North America and Britain. The plume in the snow returned the draft to the war and to Périgord: the Order of the White Feather had been formed in 1914 to disgrace cowardice and pacifism; Gerontion had neither fought at the hot gates, nor gone into the flames like the Cathars. Pound gave these new lines his attention: not *driven* by the horn but *running*, he prompted, which Eliot duly accepted. He had pummelled at percussive syntax, and steered the poem away from repetition or refrain, urging upon it the kind of economy of phrasing that marked the work of each writer in recent years. He bracketed articles and conjunctives, and small linking phrases – *the* – *Think now* – *has many* – *She* – all sensitive and agile edits for what he had once called an 'absolute rhythm'. But Eliot was lengthening his stride, and Pound hadn't quite kept in step. The tight intensities of the 'French' style were moving behind Eliot now, and he was reaching for something more oblique and musical – a hovering intelligence and a departure from satire. 'Gerontion' spoke with a new seriousness that would clear the way for the poem that was to come next, and Eliot was beginning to resist the more controlling of Pound's clippings.

Asked later if old age may be taken to be a symbol for a declining civilisation, Eliot replied that he supposed it might, but that it was not an image that had been in his thoughts at the time. Instead he said that in the construction of the poem (and here he paused to spell out precisely what he meant by construction: what he called 'the mental operation of writing it') there had been no appearance of an 'intellectual generalisation', only mood, variation and associative memory. That may have been keeping his powder dry, but in doing so he rehearsed an increasingly familiar position that no reader should look to an author for meaning, whether or not it stands for a civilisation in decline. 'It may certainly be what the poem "means",' he commented, 'so long as that is not identified with what the author is supposed to have consciously meant when he wrote it.'[25] Meaning, in other words, lies at the discretion of the reader, and by the end of September, having been through Pound's hands, he had placed a final draft of the poem with two readers who for the moment were serving as his publishing gatekeepers: John Rodker at the Ovid Press in London, and John Quinn in New York, who would pass the poem on to Alfred Knopf.[26]

//

Eliot retained his beard deep into September. 'He looked perfectly awful, like one of those comic-strip caricatures of Southern hicks,' said Aldington, convinced that it would prejudice the upcoming introduction that he had arranged for Eliot with Bruce Richmond, the editor of the *Times Literary Supplement*.[27] In the event it didn't: Richmond invited Eliot to write a leading article for the paper on Ben Jonson, which would be published that November. In it, he would speak to the relationship of the present and the past, as he would in most of his work that autumn. To understand Jonson, he would write, we must see him not in seventeenth-century England, but as a contemporary in the London of our day: an act that, like the art itself, required a 'transfusion of the personality, or, in a deeper sense, the life, of the author into the character'.[28] But for now at least, Eliot was able to take a moment to look out from the mountain that he had climbed. 'This is the highest honour possible in the critical world of literature,' he told his mother, 'and we are pleased.'[29] But in fact he had already reached greater critical heights that month.

Two of Eliot's most influential essays were published that September: 'Tradition and the Individual Talent' in the first of two instalments in Harriet Weaver's *Egoist*, and 'Hamlet and His Problems', which had appeared at almost the same moment in *The Athenaeum*.

Tradition is not an inheritance but a labour, the work of our common culture.

Every poem has ancestors. As readers, we tend to reward poets for their differentiation from that which has gone before, whereas if instead we simply read without judgement we might find that the most individuating moments of our poets are those in which they are in communication with the past. To be in possession of this insight is to be in possession of 'the historical sense', which can open a portal that permits the poet to write not only from their own era but in a common existence with 'the whole of the literature of Europe from Homer'. To do that is not only to affect the literature of the present but – and this was Eliot's crucial point – to alter the literature of the *past*. An existing order is ever so slightly changed by the arrival of new work: what we learn from the new alters how we look at the old, and the whole of art readjusts – just fractionally – to admit a new presence and create a new order. In that moment, all work converges simultaneously in a moment that is both temporal and timeless: this is the thread of tradition that binds the endless community. 'No poet, no artist of any art, has his complete meaning alone,' and that's because the significance of contemporary art is co-dependent and interactive with the art of the past. Art never improves, but it is always aggregating, absorbing itself in what has come before, and this amalgamation brought Eliot to what he called 'the mind of Europe', an evolving consciousness from which nothing is ever lost, be it Shakespeare or Homer or, he wrote, in a private allusion to the Font de Gaume, 'the rock drawing of the Magdalenian draughtsmen'. We know more than the past because the past is what we know. And the channel for this – the pathway through which the poet can commune – would culminate the first instalment and be the subject of the second in November:

> What happens is a continual surrender of himself as he is at the moment to something which is more valuable. The progress of an artist is a continual self-sacrifice, a continual extinction of personality.[30]

Here at last was the critical concentration of all that Eliot had put before his audience. Everything was now converging in one place: the mind of Europe that lives equally in the caves of Font de Gaume as the trenches of the Great War. The mind of society that sacrifices the ego to serve with the termites in common good. The mind of the individual that accepts extinction, like the Cathars going into the flames. And in 'Hamlet and His Problems', an accompanying essay in *Athenaeum* that September, Eliot gave a name to the process of transference and extinction of self. He called it the *objective correlative*. It was a phrase that didn't seem to belong to the language of poetry, and that was surely the idea.

> The only way of expressing emotion in the form of art is by finding an 'objective correlative'; in other words, a set of objects, a situation, a chain of events which shall be the formula of that *particular* emotion; such that when the external facts, which must terminate in sensory experience, are given, the emotion is immediately evoked.[31]

//

'All religions are evil,' Pound had written in the months before Eliot's arrival in France. Whether or not a religion is founded upon sound ideals, it eventually resorts to *un*sound principles – will to power, speculation, sheer bluff, and, most evidently of all, an attempt to impose 'a thought-mould'; in that way, every religion becomes a 'kultur'.[32] Pound had protested that summer to the vicar of Kensington that his church bells were disturbing his silence; he made his complaint in the form of a letter written in Latin, which amused the vicar sufficiently that he pinned it to his church noticeboard. But Pound hadn't intended humour, and the invasiveness of religious ritual continued to irk him. A second article in *New Age* that autumn took aim at the warmongering of the Catholic Church during the Sixth Crusade ('May the gods save us from the horrors of an "age of Faith"!').[33] This was throwaway prose by Pound's standards, barely more than measuring out the words for his weekly column of regional pastiche for the *New Age*; it was augmented in the new year when he wrote that the two great obstacles to human fraternity were religion and nationality, and of these obstacles religion was the greater.[34] This may not have been the most discerning critique of organised religion, and Pound's comments in the *New Age* of 1919 had gone seemingly unnoticed by readers; but one among them had filed the pieces away as something to be dealt with, and in the autumn of 1920, G. K. Chesterton would do just that.

Pound returned from France that September with a pressing need to earn money. He secured work as theatre critic for the journal *Outlook*, a role that lasted for all of two issues before he was fired ('in the most caddish manner possible') for reasons he declined to share.[35] But if the search for an income was a challenge that autumn, Pound's work was at least finding publication. In October, Harriet Shaw Weaver at the Egoist Press published a new volume of his entitled *Quia Pauper Amavi*, named from the epigraph to his 'Homage to Sextus Propertius': 'Pauperibus vates ergo sum, quia pauper amavi' ('I am the poet of the poor, because I was poor when I loved') – as Pound clarified: 'Pauper refers to subject. I am the pauper.'[36] It gathered four long poems previously printed in the *Little Review*, *New Age* and *Poetry* in Chicago: the 'Langue d'Oc'–'Moeurs Contemporaines' diptych, 'Three Cantos' and, most importantly, the first complete printing of 'Homage to Sextus Propertius'. Weaver produced the edition well: 500 copies, set in Caslon type with drop caps, elegantly printed at the De la More Press in Hanover Square and priced at 6 s. Pound was pleased with it, telling John Quinn it was the 'best shaped book of verse I have had since Personae', his 1909 volume.[37] But it almost didn't happen at all, after Elkin Mathews had refused to publish an edition that included 'Sextus' and 'Moeurs Contemporaines', which he regarded as an unacceptable attack on any number of things, but most particularly upon the middle class; it was at this moment that Weaver stepped in.

The book shook very little critical response out of literary London: only Eliot wrote a review of it that autumn, in *Athenaeum*. 'The present volume of poems by Mr Pound is probably the most significant book that he has published.'[38] So began Eliot's review boldly. 'As to the Propertius there can be no doubt; it is one of the best things Mr Pound has done.' Eliot praised the 'historic method' of the author, having just written in *The Egoist* of 'the historic sense': most poets could manage their present existence and see the world immediately before them, but few could integrate with the past; that took an immense capacity of a kind that Pound possessed in abundance, although with a method that Eliot described euphemistically as 'difficult to pursue'. And here Eliot appeared to sow doubt into the review. The book demonstrated, he wrote, that there was design and purpose in Pound's creative workings, confirming that the good moments in his earlier writing were 'more than accidental'. But whoever had suggested that the good moments were accidental? Was this praise or a sideswipe? Pound was not sure: it was then that he told John Quinn that Eliot's review amounted to granite wreaths.[39] And he went a step further, writing to the journal's editor, John Middleton Murry, to say that although he was grateful for Eliot's remarks he remained puzzled to know 'whether T. S. E. has or has not found my "Homage to Propertius" enjoyable'.[40] The letter was printed, and Eliot was backed into a response that was also printed. 'As for his suspicion that I did not enjoy his Propertius, I did not think the question of public interest: *his non plebecula gaudet*' (these things do not delight people in general).[41] Eliot had sidestepped his friend's examination with a suggestion that such discussions were not for public airing, and his reluctance to be drawn into greater clarity was understandable. Eliot's gift was for critical insight, not cheerleading, and what he had skilfully opined was an astute distinction between translation and hybrid that might have saved Pound from his critical abuse had others read the Propertius poems in the same way. 'A new *persona*' was everything that needed to be said on the subject, and in doing so Eliot had not only reset the tone for the debate on the Propertius poems, he had respectfully out-manoeuvred Pound in correspondence.[42]

But Eliot seemed uncertain, too, about the inclusion of three

Cantos, which, on their first appearance in *Poetry* in 1917, he had described as 'a rag-bag' of reading and 'reticent autobiography'. Now he wrote that they were too early to appraise; they should be regarded not as achievement but as promise – and here Eliot was at his most perceptive – 'as showing what the consummation of Mr Pound's work could be: a final fusion of all his masks, a final concentration of the entire past upon the present'.[43] As a summary description of the vast project of *The Cantos* to come, Eliot's words might have made for an artful blurb, but they didn't please Pound, whose trust in his friend had seemingly been rocked so soon after their revelatory time in Périgord; that Pound voiced his misgivings in public said much about the vulnerable position that he found himself in. For Katherine Mansfield, the episode left both men on shaky ground. Pound was most certainly a cheat and a charlatan, she said, but Eliot's defence of his friend made him look silly, 'carrying cannon balls for the prestidigitator'.[44] And of Pound's further rebuff to Eliot in print, well, for that she reserved her most colourful description: 'that arch-snorter, that ludicrous old sea-lion Ezra blowing' *Quia Pauper Amavi* had set out on an uncertain path.[45]

Eliot may not yet have found his spiritual accompaniment that autumn, but in Pound he had certainly found spirted company. For Pound, as for Eliot, the walking tour had brought – in Pound's image from 'Canto XXIX' – a moment of turning. Just as Eliot was gathering the miscellany of experience and critical vision from which he would ultimately make *The Waste Land*, so too was Pound laying out a scrapbook of his own. It was in southern France that summer that he outlined the quest that he sensed was to be made from those bits and pieces before him. 'Once in a lifetime', he wrote in the *New Age* that August, 'a man may try – without rhetoric, without hankering after grandiose utterance – to straighten out his ideas on history, the rise of nations, the developments and atrophies of civilization.'[46] This sounded a little like Eliot's experience in the caves of Font de Gaume, but unlike Eliot's projected poem which was yet to be started, Pound was now bringing a fourth and fifth sequence into his.

'What do I mean by all this clattering rumble?' Pound had mused in an interim draft of 'Canto IV'.[47] That was a poem that would evolve across eight years from 1915 to 1923, but which would pause just long enough in October 1919 for John Rodker to publish at his new Ovid Press a version of forty copies on a single folded quarto sheet of Japanese vellum, decorated with an initial capital by Edward Wadsworth.[48] But Pound's work that autumn was the concentration of the experience of his French summer, which would bring him the fifth, sixth and seventh *Cantos*.

'Great bulk, huge mass, thesaurus', opened 'The Fifth Canto' in a reflexive allusion to the first four.[49] Pound had begun it on the eve of departing for Toulouse in April 1919, and had worked on it in Eliot's presence through the summer of 1919; on 6 October he told John Quinn that it was done.[50] With its ticking and fading clock and with its clutch upon 'the barb of time', the canto soaked itself in the bloody and murderous crimes of Renaissance Europe, and did so at the same moment that Pound published an article from France in which he professed to a growing hatred of violence, an increasing contempt for destruction, even of an empire's cherished monuments: he would not, he said, even lay a hand on, of all things, the Albert Memorial.[51]

//

Late in October, Eliot lectured to the Arts League of Service in a bustling Central Buildings, Westminster on the subject that occupied him that autumn: impersonality. It was necessary, he told his audience, for the poet to study the poetry of the past every bit as for the scientist to know the history of their subject. Both must affect 'a complete surrender' of themselves to their work, channelling their personality into their subject matter in such a way that outcomes seem all but impersonal, even though it would take a powerful force of personality to effect as much. The poet, like the scientist, should exhibit 'a trained sensibility'; but with a distinction: poetry is *not* in the end a science, and this is most apparent when we encounter the problem of writing about emotion. A reader cannot be expected to take interest in the *poet's* emotion, only in the expression of emotion through a form common to both reader and writer alike, namely the senses. This transfer of emotion from feeling to the senses Eliot called the 'objective equivalent' – another naming of the 'objective correlative' that he had outlined in 'Hamlet') – and in doing so he affirmed the theory for which he would become renowned, where through a knowledge of tradition and the impersonality of objects, a force of individuality can uncover an expression personal to the poet and understood by the reader:

> the great poet is prolonging the work of the people who preceded him, and laying out the work for those who follow him; the greater the poet, the more evident his hand in every line, and the more elusive his personality.[52]

Pound had just returned to London from a lecture of his own to the Literary and Philosophy Society of Newcastle: 714 people heard him speak on the troubadour poets of Provence.[53] He told his parents that his portrait had been finished by Wyndham Lewis and he hoped to have it photographed for them, and that Yeats and family were in town 'enveloped in celto-spiritist fog'.[54] But Eliot by contrast seemed free of such haze, his writing full of directive drive that autumn. So creatively had his criticism been developing that he now had a hope of producing 'a small book' to which he hoped to give the title *The Art of Poetry*. The Egoist Press went so far as to announce its publication for the spring before Eliot changed his mind. When the idea re-emerged in a new form with Methuen, it became the book that would occupy him through the summer of 1920, *The Sacred Wood*. In the meantime, he told John Quinn that he pressed on with his debut article for the *Times Literary Supplement* on Ben Jonson; but more significant still was what Eliot said next: 'When that is off I hope to get started on a poem that I have in mind.'[55]

Just at that moment there was a loss in the family. 'Aunty Emily died at 3 a.m,'[56] Vivien recorded in her diary of the same day, 5 November. The news came as a terrible shock: she had been with her aunt in Eastbourne in October, and found her well. When Eliot went to the Hutchinsons' party in Hammersmith the next evening, Vivien didn't come, but instead prepared funeral arrangements at her parents' house in Hampstead. The service was on the morning of 8 November. 'Terrible day & experience.'[57] Once again, the Eliots were returned to turmoil.

//

November the eleventh marked the first Remembrance Day. Among the records of that day, the report of the *Manchester Guardian*:

> The first stroke of eleven produced a magical effect.
> The tram cars glided into stillness, motors ceased to cough and fume, and stopped dead, and the mighty-limbed dray horses hunched back upon their loads and stopped also, seeming to do it of their own volition.
> Someone took off his hat, and with a nervous hesitancy the rest of the men bowed their heads also. Here and there an old soldier could be detected slipping unconsciously into the posture of 'attention'. An elderly woman, not far away, wiped her eyes, and

the man beside her looked white and stern. Everyone stood very still . . . The hush deepened. It had spread over the whole city and become so pronounced as to impress one with a sense of audibility. It was a silence which was almost pain . . . And the spirit of memory brooded over it all.[58]

//

If the friendship of Eliot and Pound had been tested by *Quia Pauper Amavi*, by the middle of November it was back on a firmer footing. Three times in a single week, the Pounds and the Eliots dined together.[59] It was after the third occasion, on 23 November, that Eliot and Vivien went to the Lyric Theatre, Hammersmith, for the Phoenix Society's revival of John Webster's *The Duchess of Malfi*.[60] By all accounts it was a rotten production. *The Times* reported the next day that, where suspense was required, the audience had instead responded with 'some tittering', while the critic William Archer was blunt: 'three hours of coarse and sanguinary melodrama'.[61] Rather than restore the original play from its ashes, the Phoenix Society had burned the piece to the ground, in a production that would keep the play off the stage for the next sixteen years. Eliot had recently praised Webster for his 'skill in dealing with horror', but even so he found the performance ridiculous and vogueish, criticising the performance of Catherine Nesbitt in the title role for a failure to 'transmit' the original lines of blank verse, but instead attempting to 'interpret' them.[62] And in keeping with his critical direction of 1919, what Eliot wrote next would be important for his own verse. 'Poetry is something which the actor cannot improve or "interpret",' he wrote; 'there is no such thing as the interpretation of poetry; poetry can only be transmitted.'[63] Nothing should come between the poem and its reader – not the personality of the poet nor the voice of the poet, and certainly not the voice of somebody else.

The ideal actor for a poetic drama, he continued, was one with no personal vanity at all.

Despite the shortcomings of the production, one moment in particular caught his attention, 'a scene which always haunted his imagination', Valerie Eliot revealed in a radio broadcast of 1971: when the duchess sits at her dressing table, combing her hair and talking into the void of a bedroom to a husband who has departed without her noticing.[64] For much of 1919, Eliot had been working on a poem that he called 'The Death of the Duchess':

'But I know you love me, it must be that you love me.'
Then I suppose they found her
As she turned
To interrogate the silence fixed behind her.[65]

It was not the only moment that seemingly examined the temperature of the Eliots' marriage: the opening passages of the poem had taken aim at the London suburb where Vivien's parents lived:

The inhabitants of Hampstead have silk hats
On Sunday afternoon go out to tea
On Saturday have tennis on the lawn, and tea
On Monday to the city, and then tea.

These lines, and the four that followed, would not survive Pound's censorship, but they would be repackaged for 'The Fire Sermon': a silk hat that would appear upon the head of a Bradford millionaire, while Hampstead would be transposed to Highgate, Richmond and Kew. The next four lines broke out of form:

But what is there for you and me
For me and you
What is there for us to do
Where the leaves meet in leafy Marylebone?

What indeed would autumn bring to the Eliots? Loneliness, love-lessness, fearfulness, the poem appeared to imply: *But it is terrible to be alone with another person.* And in ten lines towards the end of the poem, an even longer shadow would be cast.

> If I said 'I do not love you' we should breathe
> The hands relax, and the brush proceed?
> How terrible that it should be the same!
> In the morning, when they knock upon the door
> We should say: This and this is what we need
> And if it rains, the closed carriage at four.
> We should play a game of chess
> The ivory men make company between us
> We should play a game of chess
> Pressing lidless eyes and waiting for a knock upon the door.

It would be from these tortured, torturing lines that 'A Game of Chess' would soon draw for *The Waste Land*, in places word for word; other lines from the 'Duchess' would also find their way into the poem, but it was from this particular passage that Vivien would ask of her husband in 1921 what she had never asked before: to remove a line from his work.

> The ivory men make company between us.

That moment was still to come, and for now Eliot would simply leave this poem in typescript, unpublished, and draw down upon it, in time, stripped for parts. It was unkempt in places and undoubtedly needed tidying, and it was frequently rough in phrasing; yet its tone was compelling, its gaze was penetrating, and in its portrait of domestic devastation it was utterly harrowing.

'What hideous noise was that?' the terrified duchess asks in Webster's play, sensing that her death is near. 'What noise is that?' she repeats.[66]

'What is that noise?', Eliot will ask in *The Waste Land*. 'What is that noise now?'

'The Death of the Duchess' seems to have shadowed 'Gerontion' in its composition through 1919, and was probably given to Pound alongside it in September 1919; and although Eliot had found his ending to 'Gerontion' that autumn, for 'The Death of the Duchess' there would be no such neat conclusion. With his final lines in draft, Eliot may even have begun a passage in a new voice that he realised he simply couldn't finish.[67] Against the suspicion of Vivien's affair with Russell, the draft's last line of all, trailing into elliptical silence, seems a haunting and moving evocation of the mistrust within the Eliots' own marriage.

But I know, and I know she knew . . .

//

The second and final instalment of 'Tradition and the Individual Talent' ran in *The Egoist* in November with an opening note: 'Honest criticism and sensitive appreciation is directed not upon the poet but upon the poetry.'[68] Just as Pound had once likened the mind of poetry to the magnetisation of iron filings, so Eliot now pursued a likeness with platinum. When oxygen and sulphur dioxide are put together in a chamber nothing will happen; but adding platinum creates a reaction in the form of sulphuric trioxide.[69] The platinum, which remains unaltered by the combination, is a catalyst for its creation. The poet's mind is the platinum.

Eliot knew that his catalytic poet of depersonalised self had been expressed by others before him. He was aware that Keats, a century earlier, had rejected what he called Wordsworth's 'egotistical sublime', preferring the 'chameleon poet' over the one who claimed the authority of the speaking self ('it is not itself – it has no self – it is every thing and nothing – It has no character').[70] Keats, like Eliot, sought to overturn the conviction of the *Lyrical Ballads* that 'all good poetry is the spontaneous overflow of powerful feelings', and guided Eliot to one of the most important paragraphs in all of his prose:[71]

There is a great deal, in the writing of poetry, which must be conscious and deliberate. In fact, the bad poet is usually unconscious where he ought to be conscious, and conscious where he ought to be unconscious. Both errors tend to make him 'personal'. Poetry is not a turning loose of emotion, but an escape from emotion; it is not the expression of personality, but an escape from personality.

The passage would be among the most quoted of any Eliot would write, but it was incomplete, and the next sentence would bring a crucial if often unquoted addendum:

But, of course, only those who have personality and emotions know what it means to want to escape from these things.

In order to depersonalise, we must first have had the personal experience; in order to transmit emotion, we must rely not upon the personal history of the poet but upon the objects corralled and correlated for the poem.

The poet's mind is in fact a receptacle for seizing and storing up numberless feelings, phrases, images, which remain there until all the particles which can unite to form a new compound are present together.

For a theorist of depersonalisation, Eliot sounded remarkably like a man corralling his lived experience for the moment that his numberless feelings and phrases – his heap of broken images – would one day fuse into a poem. And with that, in the winter of 1919, the journal life of Harriet Shaw Weaver's *Egoist* came to an end.

//

Of all the subjects that came under the scrutiny of Eliot throughout 1919, it was perhaps John Donne whom he illuminated most brightly, and in a style that anticipated so much of *The Waste Land*. Celebrating 'the famous "Mundus Mare"' passage of 1619, Eliot wrote that Donne had distinguished his sermon with a rolling refrain, in which existence was likened to a sea that was *subject to stormes, and tempests*; that was *bottomlesse to any line*; that *hath ebbs and floods*, like those of the tidal prose used to convey his oratory. But just as illuminating as Donne's original prose was the language with which Eliot described it. Donne, wrote Eliot, had produced *a vivid figure of speech*; *an image developed at length*; a *reference to spiritual truth*; a life of *flows, storms and tempests*; he had given us a world with *no place of habitation, but a passage to our habitations*. Phrase on phrase, wave on wave, it was a literary style of analogy and refrain, wrote Eliot, that had been used once before by a master even greater than Donne: 'the method of the Fire-Sermon preached by the Buddha', an utterance as important as the Sermon on the Mount.[72] He would single out a translation by Henry Clarke Warren of 1896 from the Mahā-Vagga, where the Blessed One addresses the priests:

> All things, O priests, are on fire. And what, O priests, are all these things which are on fire?
>
> The eye, O priests, is on fire; forms are on fire; eye-consciousness is on fire; impressions received by the eye are on fire; And whatever sensation, pleasant, unpleasant, or indifferent, originates in dependence on impressions received by the eye, that also is on fire.[73]

Eliot had written of Donne as the most self-aware of writers: 'the artist as an Eye curiously, patiently watching himself as a man'.[74] How that expression might likewise have been applied to Eliot.

Every ship that sails on this sea must have some part of itself under water, Donne had written, just as some part of our hidden endeavours must also be expended; but that part of the ship by which we sail, the conscious part, like the conscious writer, is above water, and that part brings us closer to God. *And in this Sea, are we made fishers of men, of all men, of that which makes them men, their soules.*

Buddha's fire, Donne's sea. Eliot's waste land.

//

By December, Pound had completed *Cantos* V, VI and VII, 'each more incomprehensible than the one preceding it,' he told his father, 'dont know what's to be done about it'.[75] He told John Quinn that he was much distressed by his preoccupation with the twelfth century, which he admitted was 'very unfortunate from point of view of immediate impact on general public'.[76] The history of Provence that had been likened to the *Odyssey* in 'Canto VI' would continue into the seventh. Pound left a draft of 'Canto VII' with Eliot, who replied in a note that he was sorry to have missed his friend on a social call, but wanted him to know that he was absorbing the poem *slowly*.[77] 'Eleanor', the canto opened – daughter of troubadour William X, imprisoned in the Tower of London by her husband Henry Plantagenet '(she spoiled in a British climate)' – with a turn of swirling transitions now marking the style of *The Cantos* themselves. Here was Helen of Troy with Arnaut Daniel, here was Desmond FitzGerald, minister in the 1919 Sinn Féin government, 'the live man, out of lands and prisons', jailed for his part in the defence of the General Post Office in Dublin, 1916. It was the most engaged and elusive of *The Cantos* so far, at a height of fluency and lyric phrasing, finding metrical force in the movement of the physical world around him – *The sea runs in the beach-groove, shaking the floated pebbles* – in its way, as good as anything he would ever write in *The Cantos*. In phrasing, it seemed to share so much with Eliot, and at times it seemed hard to tell the two authors apart:

> We also made ghostly visits, and the stair
> That knew us, found us again on the turn of it,
> Knocking at empty rooms, seeking for buried beauty;[78]

To read 'Canto VII' across *The Waste Land* is to understand something of the confluence that existed between the minds of the two poets, something of their interests and their musical ear, something in the tone of their address. It's even possible to detect a tide washing from canto to waste land. Pound's opening with Eleanor of Aquitaine will be harmonised in Eliot's Mrs Equitone. Pound gives us Homer blind, Eliot blind Tiresias; Pound grants sea-surge, Eliot sea-wood, Pound Rome, Eliot Carthage; a rattle of old men in Pound is in Eliot an old man wrinkled; Pound's marble is narrow for seating, Eliot's will glow from the splendour of a burnished throne; Pound via Ovid: 'if there is no dust', Eliot will have a handful of dust; Pound hears chatter above the circus, Eliot clatter and chatter from a public bar; Pound's 'sightless narration' is Eliot's tarot card which Madame Sosostris is forbidden to see; Pound through Dante sounds out '*ciocco*', Eliot *Co co rico*. These from just the first stanza of the canto alone. 'People are inclined to think that we write our verses in collaboration as it is,' Eliot would tell Pound by 1923, 'or else that you write mine & I write yours.'[79] When Pound came to draft his 'Canto VIII' in 1922, he would begin it with a line from *The Waste Land*.[80]

As 1919 came to a close, Pound had written seven *Cantos* and published four. For almost the next two years, he would pause and set them aside; they were not yet his major work of the post-war period. That distinction would belong to the poem that he was about to write next.

//

Hugh Selwyn Mauberley – Pound's antihero – was a pre-modern poet in a modern age, a relic 'out of key with his time'.[81] His country was 'half savage', speaking in a mantra and a metre that was partly Gautier's and which was adopted, said Pound, against *the sluggishness and swishiness* of the British line.[82] 'He was done in Dec. & Jan.' said Pound: twelve sections and an envoi before Christmas; five sections added in the new year.[83] His name may have lain in a tale told by Basil Bunting, that Hugh Selwyn Mauberley was a hoax dreamed up by Pound and Eliot together one evening in London as 'an impossible poet' (the phrase belongs to Pound's later editor, James Laughlin) invented to lampoon his literary enemies with parodies in verse and prose; the project had to be abandoned after the identity of the invented poet was leaked.[84] It's a plausibly far-fetched story for a work fixated on forgery, whose very title is troublesome to pin down. For although the poem has been almost invariably printed under the title of 'Hugh Selwyn Mauberley', what Pound intended was probably the wording that appeared on the title page and boards of the Ovid Press edition of 1920, *Hugh Selwyn Mauberley by E.P.* – as if Mauberley were the subject, E.P. the author, and Ezra Pound, whose name appears nowhere in the edition, the publisher who had discovered them both. Then there was also a slippery 'subtitle', as Pound later described it, '(Life and Contacts)', bracketed, subsequently reversed for 'the actual order of the subject matter' – whatever that meant – a clarity which was most certainly not aided by the ambiguous single word '*MAUBERLEY*' appearing on the contents page in uppercase italics as neither title nor section, but a presence governing eighteen sections, some numbered, some titled, some numbered *and* titled, with an envoi between them.[85]

The epigraph had an edge of topicality: *The heat calls us into the shade*. Nemesianus, flourished third-century Rome, but no Roman: an outsider (and some say *imitator*), designated on his manuscripts *Carthaginiensis*, of Carthage – an allusion seemingly timed to respond to the vast attention that John Maynard Keynes was receiving for his book on the 'Carthaginian Peace' of Versailles that autumn.[86]

E.P., the initial letters on the initial poem: neither a title nor here an author, but a memorial; E.P., the representative of the writer Ezra Pound, to whom Mauberley has come to pay tribute: a figure who strove and failed *to resuscitate the dead art*, who *fished by obstinate isles* but who has already passed from the memory of men. As a literary disguise it seemed to some readers a barely veiled one. But Pound would separate himself in saying, 'Mauberley buries E.P. in the first poem; gets rid of all his troublesome energies.'[87]

The second section broadened the scorn towards a period bereft of literary subtlety:

The 'age demanded' chiefly a mould in plaster,
Made with no loss of time,
A prose kinema, not, not assuredly, alabaster
Or the 'sculpture' of rhyme.[88]

Then the poem turned to the Great War, to those who had died 'learning love of slaughter', *pro patria, non dulce non et decor*, who 'walked eye-deep in hell / believing in old men's lies', then returned home to old deceits and new infamies: 'Daring as never before, wastage as never before.'

It was then that came the clearest and most affecting elegy for the war dead that Pound would ever write. The section in its entirety:

v.

There died a myriad,
And of the best, among them,
For an old bitch gone in the teeth,
For a botched civilization,

Charm, smiling at the good mouth,
Quick eyes gone under earth's lid,

For two gross of broken statues,
For a few thousand battered books.[89]

A seventh section began with a line of Dante's (*Purgatorio* V, 134): 'Siena mi fe', disfecemi Maremma' ('Siena made me, Maremma undid me'), that Eliot would pick up with Highbury and Richmond and Kew for 'The Fire Sermon'. Other sections to other grounds – among them a literary critic who instructed Mauberley to 'give up verse, my boy, / There's nothing in it' (the model was Arnold Bennett, though it might equally have been J. C. Squire) – and an 'Envoi', ending:

Siftings on siftings in oblivion,
Till change hath broken down
All things save Beauty alone.[90]

(In the draft of 'Gerontion' that Pound had just edited: 'We have saved a shilling against oblivion.') And there, after twelve sections and an envoi, the typescript would briefly rest, until Pound completed it early in the new year.

'Of course, I'm no more Mauberley than Eliot is Prufrock,' said Pound of the question of autobiography, and he meant it: Mauberley was not Pound, but a projection of what Pound feared he would become if he were to do nothing about his situation. He called the poem 'mere surface', and to some degree he meant that too: the image being the surface, just as the mask is a surface, as it was for another of his personas, Propertius. But that Mauberley was intended as a literary soldier like Pound there can be little doubt, and Pound most certainly instructed his character for the front line. 'Shock troops. All right,' he would tell his old university professor. In 1919, he had told readers of the *New Age* that he abhorred violence; by 1922, he felt differently. 'There are things I quite definitely want to destroy,' he commented ominously, 'and which I think will have to [be] annihilated before civilization can exist.'[91]

//

For the Eliots, Christmas was as usual: the two of them in the flat with stockings and a small tree, though they found presents expensive and in short supply.[92] Vivien carried a gramophone from Marylebone to her parents' house in Hampstead for Christmas dinner, and came home again not having enjoyed her evening, any more than she enjoyed having them to the flat for new year.[93] Eliot looked for a change of his own, and travelled to friends in Wiltshire on Boxing Day, but the countryside helped little and the return train ran late through the pouring rain; Vivien remained behind, too exhausted to accompany him.[94] Even a boozy dinner party at the Hutchinsons' in Hammersmith failed to lift their spirits. Vivien felt that she looked awful, Osbert Sitwell and Duncan Grant were there as old acquaintances, but newer faces were also present: Iris Tree and her husband Curtis Moffat, as well as a young, aristocratic socialite who would make a profound impact upon the Eliots' marriage, Nancy Cunard. 'Glad this awful year is over,' were Vivien's final words of her 1919 diary. And then she added, 'Next probably worse.'[95] But Eliot had different hopes, and he shared them with his mother: his new year's resolution was, he told her, 'to write a long poem I have had on my mind for a long time'.[96]

//

'I wonder if America realises how terrible the condition of central Europe is,' Eliot wrote to his mother in the new year of 1920.[97] He could never *forget* – no, he crossed that out – he could never *quite put out of mind* Vienna, a capital of culture, a city on its knees, with food rioters ransacking and looting its streets that December, and a 'red riot' after the arrest of communist activists claimed eight lives the previous summer.[98] The Habsburg empire that in Eliot's mind symbolised the continuity of a European civilisation inherited from ancient Rome had just been dismantled by the peace treaty. 'I am all for empires,' he would write in 1924, 'especially the Austro-Hungarian Empire'; but now it seemed that the barbarians were the gatekeepers of Europe.[99] The future of Germany, the future of the world, he wrote, looked bleak. *Falling towers / Jerusalem Athens Alexandria / Vienna London.* 'They say that there is no hope unless the treaty is revised. I believe by the way that J. M. Keynes: *Economic Consequences of the Peace* is an important book, if you can get hold of it.'[100]

The book, published that December, had emerged from Keynes's attendance at the 1919 peace conference as chief representative of the British Treasury. A brilliant economist – a 'free mind', said Eliot in an obituary of 1946 – Keynes was a special adviser to the British government, but he had no authority at the negotiating table, and was horrified by the punitive direction in which the Allies were headed.[101] Germany was to be held solely accountable for the conflict, and would be required to pay compensation to the Allied states. Germany would be crushed, as once Carthage had been destroyed by Rome, when its walls were razed and its soil was said to have been sown with salt. Keynes resigned, warning that we had become numb to the consequences of our own actions: 'The greatest events outside our own direct experience and the most dreadful anticipations cannot move us.'[102]

Germany was to be disarmed, but it was also to be stripped of territory that would be reassigned to new or reborn nations such as Poland, or into Allied control. Its international empire and overseas accounts were confiscated, leaving a domestic economy in a dire state with no international reserves to draw on, and no feasible method of paying the costs imposed upon it. But Germany had been wounded in a less obvious way besides, in its sense of national pride. Although its naval fleet was commandeered, it was the loss of control of its great rivers that had the more tangible impact upon the national psyche. Rivers that rose or emptied in lands other than Germany were now considered international territory. The Rhine, the Danube, the Elbe, the Oder – Germany's four great waterways – were to be handed over to an international administration which, Keynes estimated, was little more than a pretext for wresting the river system of Germany out of German control. 'The events of the coming year', he wrote in autumn 1919, 'will not be shaped by the deliberate acts of statesmen, but by the hidden currents, flowing continually beneath the surface of political history, of which no one can predict the outcome.'[103] The destiny of Europe was out of anyone's hands, leaving us to chaos and worry – he quoted Shelley: 'In each human heart terror survives / The ruin it has gorged.' Never has the human spirit burned so dimly; 'We are at the dead season of our fortunes.'[104]

'Keynes' style is appalling,' wrote Pound that February, and the man himself quite simply 'an ass'.[105] Nevertheless, such was his standing that he couldn't be ignored, and so Pound issued him with an invitation to meet with his own economic thinker of choice, Major C. H. Douglas, an occasion which Pound parodied in 'Canto XXII', with Keynes as a 'Mr Bukos' pleading 'I am an orthodox / Economist' and Pound, in reply, exploding, 'Jesu Christo!'[106] Douglas was 'the real mind', he told John Quinn afterwards, a 'blessed relief from fabianism and "nationalisation"'.[107]

Pound had met Clifford Hugh Douglas through the offices of the *New Age*, where A. R. Orage had edited and serialised his book, *Economic Democracy*, throughout 1919. Pound saw in Douglas an anti-hero of a kind that he had come to identify with: an engineer, not an economist by training, a man of industry rather than of the academy, and therefore a figure outside the establishment and a natural ally to Pound.

'Every industry creates PRICES faster than it distributes the POWER TO BUY,' Douglas theorised.[108] Workers are not paid enough to be able to buy back the goods that they produce, and that's because the price of a good reflects not only its labour cost but also charges to the manufacturer of an external kind, such as interest on bank loans and wastage. As a result, labour is always unable to meet prices, which in turn creates a perpetual shortfall into which the government must intervene with a national dividend to supplement salaries in parity with prices. This Douglas called Social Credit, and it was, wrote Pound later, 'the doorway through which I came to economic curiosity'.[109] He dedicated 'Canto XXXVIII' to the problem: 'The mind of man was bewildered', he wrote, 'and the power to purchase can never / (under the present system) catch up with / prices at large.'[110] The culprit of this imbalance was not as the producer but the financier; 'Canto LXXI':

Every bank of discount is downright corruption
taxing the public for private individuals' gain.
        and if I say this in my will
the American people wd/ pronounce I died crazy.[111]

Pound would pose the question 'What is money for?' And he would answer: that the whole people shall be able to eat (*healthily*), that the whole people shall be housed (*decently*) and that the whole people shall be clothed (*adequate to the climate*).[112] Social Credit became an economic response to a moral question of which poetry could be the lasting document. 'An epic is a poem including history': so Pound opened a 1935 pamphlet entitled *Social Credit*, in the first of a two-point statement; the second: 'No one can understand history without understanding economics.'[113] There, in two short sentences, would be a model for *The Cantos*: the poem as social history seen through the lens of economics. It was a hymn to an earthly paradise that Pound would never stop believing was possible, if only finance could be made to serve society.

Pound raged at economic disparity, and that individuals should be allowed to profit in the transfer of wealth owned by the state on behalf of its people; in the *New Age* on 4 March 1920, for the first time he put a name to the focus of his ire. It was an angry name, a hateful name: one that signalled an acceleration down a path from which he would turn only too late. And it took a name that became racially tinted from the moment he advanced it. *Usury.*[114]

It has been said of Ezra Pound that this was the moment that anti-Semitism took hold of him. But Social Credit didn't make Pound anti-Semitic, it merely offered him an economic defence of an existing prejudice, of which there had been flashes before. Three times between 1912 and 1914 he had published offensive remarks, only to seek redemption: one he tried to mollify with praise, a second he revised out entirely on reprinting, and a third he corrected to clarify that it was not Jews but moneymakers who were the target of his ire. In those earlier days, Judaism didn't particularly receive special attention from a man whose approach to insult was to be as inclusive as possible. A reference in 1917 in the *Little Review*'s fictive series of imagined letters to the 'vigorous animality' of 'yidds, letts, finns, esthonians, cravats, niberians, alergians' brought upon its editors 'countless letters from Jews, Letts, Greeks, Finns, Irish, etc., protesting against Mr Pound's ignorance and indiscrimination' (Pound had concluded the letter praising each as the promise, the vitality and the sap of the nation).[115] But in the same journal in November 1918, at the very moment that others were embracing armistice, for the first time he brought the prejudice into verse, in a smear of a poem he would attempt neither to correct nor collect. In 'Upon the Harps of Judea', a noble but 'unbearable Jew' imposes his short, rotund and balding body upon his dining company, while a 'younger semite' companion 'slides' between restaurant tables and a 'smirking' daughter inveigles herself upon a wounded (defenceless?) 'Tommy'.[116] It was a poem without purpose, but it captured a strand of racial denigration that was present even before it was touched by the economics of Major Douglas.

More than once was Pound himself mistaken for being Jewish.

Wyndham Lewis had not yet met the American when one among a lunch party in 1910 'pronounced him a Jew'; so it was with some surprise that he was greeted by a red-bearded, blue-eyed 'nordic blond' that day. 'Most of those present felt that he was indeed a Jew, disguised in a tengallon hat, I later heard – a "red Jew" it was decided, a subtle blend, but a pukka Kosher.'[117] In 1917, Pound was told by his landlady that in a publicity photograph he bore a likeness to 'the good man of Nazareth', while a literary editor, on seeing the same photograph, lowered his voice to whisper: 'Il est Semite?' ('He was forcibly informed to the contrary,' Pound recorded.)[118]

That January of 1920 Pound told readers of the *New Age* that he considered himself fifteen parts English, 'racially', and that his sixteenth and remaining part was Celtic. Anglo-Saxon 'stock' (his phrase) was now said to be in a minority throughout the eastern and central states, where people of continental and mixed origin were in the majority: 'I am therefore accustomed to being an alien,' he wrote of his upbringing, 'and it is just as homelike for me to be an alien in one place as in another.'[119]

Intolerance in small-town Pennsylvania where Pound grew up was common towards Jews, Italians and foreigners, and was regularly represented in the local pages of the *Jenkintown Times-Chronicle* and *Public Spirit*. So when local proprietors announced in 1892 that they were no longer taking Jewish boarders at their Beechwood inn, one contemporary resident of Pound's hometown described the moment as little more than a materialisation of a prejudice that was everywhere, like the dust, ready to be kicked up at any moment.[120] But not so in the Pounds' household, which would be sublet by his parents Homer and Isabel to the Jewish Hospital Association, as reported publicly in the same paper, as was Homer's work with children in the Italian community of Philadelphia. Unlike the situation of his friend Eliot, whatever the root of what late in life Pound apologised for as his 'suburban prejudice', it was not inherited from his parents.

What Pound articulated was little different from that which was then known as 'American Nativism' – not, as the term might suggest, a concern for indigenous culture and peoples, but instead a colonial claim of the early settlers to the mantle of the 'first race'. It was a politics of paranoia among so-called 'Yankee' Protestant Americans of the nineteenth century towards the immigration of German and Irish Catholics and diasporic Jews. But by 1920, it was clear that Pound thought of himself as usurped twice over: too Anglo-Saxon for Americans, too American for the Anglo-Saxons. Despite his belief that he was equally alien everywhere, his patience was beginning to run out with his Anglo-Saxon roots. He could sense the clock ticking on his English stay.

//

The Eliots were shivering in their cramped Crawford Mansions flat that new year. Both were unwell, Eliot from bronchitis, Vivien from care of him. The burden of the additional *Athenaeum* business upon Eliot had become apparent, and it was hard to work in a run-down household. The writing of weekly articles, too, had taken its toll, and he told Sydney Schiff that he had come to feel that he was 'losing both the energy, and the power of sustained thought necessary for a longer piece of work'.[121]

'We had Abigail Eliot to tea,' wrote Vivien to Eliot's mother on 3 January 1920, with more than an ounce of provocation. 'She is the first of Tom's relations I have ever seen – it does seem strange, after 4½ years.'[122] Cousin Abigail was to spend the year in Oxford and the Eliots were not going to let an opportunity for Vivien's familial ingratiation to pass. Vivien had always longed to meet an Eliot, Tom reminded his mother a few days later: 'I believe she thinks every day about you.'[123] Eliot told a friend once that he had been brought to understand that there were 'Eliots, non-Eliots and foreigners'.[124] And to the family, Vivien was never to be counted among the Eliots of St Louis.

2635 Locust Street, a roomy, late nineteenth-century two-storey mansion with decorous eaves and a wooden porch two miles to the west of the Mississippi River. Hal, Eliot's father, had not wished to move from the property he built there, any more than Abigail, Eliot's grandmother, had wanted to leave the house her husband, William Greenleaf, had built 800 feet away at 2660 Washington Avenue. And so the family stayed on long after friends had moved west into the wealthier suburbs along the new tramlines. The family home stood on the fringe of an area of poverty and deprivation, on a plot that had been racially mixed in Greenleaf's time, in a neighbourhood peppered with saloons, brothels and heavy drinking – the perfect site, in other words, for the foundation of Greenleaf's Unitarian church.[125] 'We lived practically in a slum,' Eliot told Emily Hale, or at the very least, 'shabby to a degree approaching slumminess', he said in a later reminiscence.[126] This was Eliot's home for the first sixteen years of his life, before the family moved to the more salubrious Central West End.[127] It was lit by dim gas lamps, and by brighter Welsbach mantles which emitted an incandescent white light. On cold mornings, a tin bath was brought out from under Eliot's bed and filled by the maid from a kettle lit by the fire.[128] There was no alcohol and no smoking in the house, and sweets were to be shared or not to be had at all.[129] 'No one could say that the Eliots are much given to mirth and whimsicality,' Eliot told Emily.[130] *Tace et fac*, the family motto: Be quiet and do.

On a mound in the neighbouring schoolyard of the Mary Institute stood a large ailanthus tree of heaven, a scrub tree renowned for growing through concrete dereliction, and for its 'rank' odour ('The Dry Salvages').[131] A high wall separated the Eliots' back garden from the schoolyard, so that he grew up listening to the disembodied sound of unseen girls at play. There was a door in the wall and a key to fit it, and when the pupils left at the end of the school day, Eliot was given the run of the playground by his nurse Annie Dunn. But the high wall and the drift of children's voices instilled in him a sense of isolation from playmates that left him 'both conceited and timid; independent and helpless' – the bookish and withdrawn child that he pictured in his 1929 poem 'Animula': 'The pain of living and the drug of dreams / Curl up the small soul in the window seat / Behind the *Encyclopaedia Britannica*.'[132] He felt like an only child, partially mute. 'I never talked, for who was there to talk to? And I had no playmates.'[133]

Eliot's parents were in their mid-forties at his birth and seemed to him like 'ancestors'.[134] Hal had never considered himself the high-flyer that his own father had been. That man, the Rev. William Greenleaf Eliot, T. S. Eliot's grandfather, was a capable business-man who seemed destined for entrepreneurial life, had a Unitarian calling not taken him into the church. Greenleaf's achievements were intimidating: a graduate of Harvard Divinity School, he had been co-founder and the inaugural director of Washington University in St Louis in 1853, an institution that called itself the Eliot Seminary in his honour until Greenleaf put a stop to that, believing that secular scholarship should not be compromised by an association with his religious work. (George Washington would instead provide the eponym.) He founded nurseries, free and public schools, as well as Smith Academy where a young T. S. Eliot would study, and the Mary Institute. His mission was not mass literacy, remembered Eliot's mother, but the excellence of the few, a Platonic ideal that would influence T. S. Eliot's own thinking: 'One best was more than many good.'[135] Although he died before grandson Eliot was born, grandfather Greenleaf was 'still the head of the family', long after his death, sovereign of the household's 'law of Public Service' that was operant in three areas of religion, community and educa-tion: the church, the city and the university.[136]

Hal didn't follow his father into the church ('too much pudding choked the dog'), although his own achievements, hard won, were not negligible.[137] At the booming Hydraulic-Press Brick Company on the banks of the Mississippi he prospered greatly. As America's cities soared skyward so did Hal's rise through the company: by 1890, it was producing more pressed bricks than any company in the world (two hundred million of them across sites in eight states), and Hal was to be its next president.[138] T. S. Eliot retained shares in the company until 1948.

Hal had described his relationship with Greenleaf as one of 'reverential awe', believing his father to be infallible, but within his own household Hal was held in mixed affection by his children.[139] To the elder siblings, he was a man of sensibility and humour, who took pride in being family chess champion, and who drew faces for the children on their boiled eggs.[140] Scarlet fever in his own childhood had left him all but deaf, although a heightened sense of smell enabled him to delight them in identifying which daughter had dropped her handkerchief in the house by scent alone. But to the youngest child, Tom, devotion to his father was less assured; their relationship in adulthood would not survive Hal's decision to place his property in trust. As in the teachings of the family church, Eliot the Son felt forsaken by Eliot the Father.[141]

Charlotte Champe Stearns Eliot was an incomer from Baltimore, Maryland, who taught across four states before finding work at St Louis Normal School, where she met Hal, whom she married in 1868. She adopted the Greenleaf manner of corrective social responsibility (one of her ancestors had been a judge in the Salem witch trials), and was active in social work, and effective too: her campaigning for young offenders contributed to the passing of the 1901 Probation Act, which professionalised the responsibility of courts, police and the state towards children under sixteen.[142] She was also a literary woman, author of a pamphlet of poems and a biography of her father-in-law ('Written for my Children / "Lest they Forget"'"), and engaged in the elite literary Wednesday Club of St Louis. She took the same approach to poetry as to religion – namely that redemption lay in positive thinking and good deeds ('Ring out the doubts that like a cloud enfold us, / Ring in the faith that clearer vision brings!'), although her pronounced anti-Semitism was a poison that infected both her thinking and her deeds.[143] Eliot would aid her long poem *Savonarola: A Dramatic Poem* into book form in 1926, and introduce it besides. It was a long, cumbersome series of verses that were, as one reader recalled, not bad enough to be comic but just serious enough to be a bore.[144] Charlotte was admired and feared. Eliot told her that he felt that the two of them were alike more than they knew: anything good he had made in the world was something that they had made together, he said.[145] But privately, he admitted that such words were, in his term, a white-wash.[146] He never experienced feelings of closeness towards her, and confided to Emily Hale that he couldn't feel 'united' with his parents, nor could he ever have confided in them as he did her, 'remote' as they were to him. Instead he felt duty, obligation and a sense of role play: 'Sometimes one is just oneself, but for the most part one is being hustled about (as well as such a lazy idle fuddler as myself can be hustled) by one or another of a crowd of shadows.'[147]

Thomas Stearns was Charlotte's seventh child; she was forty-three. His upbringing was entrusted to Annie Dunn, a nursemaid of Irish parents from Co. Cork, who heated the bath water for Eliot each morning, and whose affectionate presence in the house warmed the space in the young boy's life that his mother left vacant. It was Annie, said Eliot later, who was his earliest influence, and the household figure to whom he was greatly attached.[148] She took him to school, and sometimes, at prayer times, to the small Catholic Church of Immaculate Conception on the corner of Jefferson Avenue and Locust Street (then Lucas Place), where he would delight in the colourful statues, the bright paper flowers and glowing lights, and swing on the miniature gates that latched to the end of the pews.[149] It was with Annie that he had his first conversations about the presence of God.[150] To a young boy of six and seven, her religion was the vivid entertainment that his family's Unitarianism was not. 'I was devoted to her,'[151] he recalled, and he liked to consider that he gave her the kind of run-around that children do ('Was ever a Nurse so put about!', he wrote in a squib of 1937).[152] It was with Annie that Eliot saw in a children's picture book images of fellow infants naked; there was something wrong with each of them, he told her: they weren't wearing trusses like the one he wore to support a childhood hernia.

Annie was required company when the young Eliot summered with the family at Gloucester, Massachusetts, on two acres acquired by his father in 1890, and built upon a few years later: a large, sturdy clapboard house known as The Downs, flanked on three sides by a pillared porch, nestled between the granite outcrops of the New England shoreline, Eastern Point. Every year, for fourteen years, the journey east was made in some style: in a gaslit Pullman carriage, with upper and lower sleeping berths and a modest drawing room.[153] High waters on the Mississippi would partly re-route the journey upriver into Illinois, but at all other times it was a modern crossing unrecognisable to the one made in reverse by Greenleaf fifty years before. It was at Eastern Point that Eliot learned to sail, accompanied by an instructor, named Skipper, and, for the most part, by Annie and his mother, to preserve the young boy from too much sunshine on warm days and too much chill on cold ones.[154] And it was here that he learned to listen in on what he came to describe as 'true narratives': the fishermen's tales overheard on the harbour, stories like poems that could 'be learnt by word of mouth from the men between trips', he remembered, 'as they lounged at the corner of Main Street and Duncan Street in Gloucester'.[155]

//

A 'good stiff punch'. That's what London's literary elite had taken to its midriff, or so Pound told his father of an article that appeared in French on New Year's Day 1920.[156] *L'Art libre*, a journal edited in Brussels by the young pacifist Paul Colin, had proclaimed a new path for Europe: antimilitarism over warmongering, humanity over nationhood, and, above all, a social commitment to the arts. It saw Belgium as 'a crossroads of the Occident', a place where international currents could meet,[157] and this was a territory that suited Pound down to the ground. 'L'Art seems glad to get my stuff, and I like the way they have translated the first article.'[158] Pound told his continental readers that the British literary establishment had grown old and insular, guarding its narrow island from European influence, while the turrets of academia repelled genuine discourse and criticism. Three writers almost alone were worth the trouble of continental readers, and he rehearsed the names that had become almost a mantra: James Joyce, Wyndham Lewis and the 'revolutionary' T. S. Eliot. Commending such writers had made him enemies in London, he said, and left him precious little time for his own writing, though taken as a quartet they constituted what Pound called 'the "opposition"': those brave enough to go without the favour of 'the episcopate of the corpses of official English literature'.[159] The remainder was mediocrity, and mediocrity, lest we underestimate it, was a destructive force that reduces everything to its own, devastating level.

But no one seemed to be listening to Pound any more. By February, Pound shared with readers of *Much Ado* magazine in St Louis that he now felt 'frozen out of everything'.[160] F. S. Flint, once a collaborator on Imagisme, had been among the first of his old allies to turn on him, in comments that now seemed prescient. 'The truth is', he had written in 1917 to Harriet Shaw Weaver, 'we are all tired of Mr Pound. His work has deteriorated from book to book; his manners have become more and more offensive; and we wish he would go back to America.' Flint dubbed Pound 'the sinister

Charlie Chaplin' of his generation. 'Those of us who were once associated with him are so no longer, for very good reasons, [and] detest him with the heartiest of loathings.'[161]

At the Richmond home of the Hogarth Press, Virginia and Leonard Woolf were barely over their winter illness before they resumed their busy programme of literary dinner parties. Among their new year guests was one John Collings Squire esquire and his wife, the novelist E. H. Anstruther (Eileen Harriet). Renowned drinkers (Squire was said to be responsible for the quip 'I am not so think as you drunk I am'), the Squires surprised the normally unshockable Woolfs by a volume of intake which left Mrs Squire slouched in the armchair ('a jelly fish', noted Virginia) 'like some natural function, performing automatically'.[162] Squire himself did little better, and spoke of patriotism in a way that made his hosts mildly nauseous. But on literature at least he was intelligible: he intended to position his new *London Mercury* in direct opposition to the hard sceptical, elite tone of *The Athenaeum*, which was, he told Virginia, *a frost of death* for all creative activity. And he was to be an unyielding champion of the Georgians, hostile to the 'disgusting insects' who were the moderns, 'scuttling about' in all their forms.[163]

The *London Mercury* had been launched under Squire's editorship as a monthly in the weeks before the closure of Harriet Weaver's *Egoist*. His tenure would last for fifteen influential years, and he published work by Robert Frost, W. B. Yeats, Siegfried Sassoon and Katherine Mansfield along the way. As literary editor of the *New Statesman* in 1917, Squire had regarded himself as a Fabian; he had lost his deposit in the 1918 general election as a Labour Party candidate for the true-blue seat of Cambridge University (a Manx cat would have stood a better chance, mused Woolf).[164] But with his ascent to the new *Mercury* (or *Murkury*, as Pound referred to it) his political views moved to the right. By the 1930s, he had – as had Pound and James Strachey Barnes – met with Benito

Mussolini, and would become an associate of Oswald Mosley as a founder of the notorious January Club of British fascists.[165] By then he had long been regarded as an odious figure in literary circles – 'fat, & consequential' said Woolf by 1924 – tending to a thiefdom of Georgian antiquity that was sentimental, nationalistic and, worse still, ubiquitous.[166] Through his editorial and critical work he curated a garden for British poetry of such tranquil abundancy that it became known as the 'Squirearchy'. But it was as a poet that Squire was anthologised in the Poetry Bookshop's hugely popular *Georgian Poetry* series. 'Now very quietly, and rather mournfully' his poem 'The House' had opened his selection in 1918, with six words that might have stood as an epithet for Georgian poetry itself, only for his poem to collapse into the kind of pale, iambic haze that had given Georgianism such a poor name: 'In clouds of hyacinth the sun retires,' and many thought his poetry should go the same way.[167] 'Ridiculous', Virginia Woolf said tersely; 'plain stupidity', Eliot thought, and he hoped to see the *Mercury* with its 'small clique of bad writers' fail.[168] The failure of the Georgians, said Eliot, was their self-sufficiency – they lacked the benefit of the pollination of other languages and therefore lacked a lineage – on which matter Eliot was unusually blunt: the word he used was 'inbred'.[169] Never to be outdone when it came to bluntness, Pound went one further: Georgians = dry dung; *London Mercury* = wet dung, he told William Carlos Williams in 1920.[170]

Named after the inaugural and highly popular 1911/12 anthology of that name, 'Georgian poetry' was a form that trusted in naivety, that affected simplicity and that conjured innocence. It was a work that was plainer than the ornate Victoriana before it, and could in the right hands be a discerning portrait of the human experience in the natural world. But many of its most able proponents had died in the war, and the hands that now carried it well were few. As a form, it seemed immature when set against the precision of the Imagists, and feeble-minded in the face of the horrors of war.

Robert Graves gave a demeaning list of its concerns: 'Nature and love and leisure and old age and childhood and animals and sleep and other uncontroversial subjects.'[171] The Georgians, said Richard Aldington, were 'in love with littleness'; it was, Ford Madox Ford summarised, the poetry of safety.[172]

But Squire would be a cannier opponent than Eliot and Pound supposed, for Eliot had returned from France in 1919 to find a letter inviting him to become a contributor to the *Mercury*. Eliot, who had by then publicly denounced Squire, replied diplomatically that he wasn't sure that he had room to take on another periodical and that he was trying to protect his time for a book; but he would be happy to talk about the possibility.[173] Eliot never wrote for the new *Mercury*, and nor would Pound, to whom Squire was 'a time-server', a booster of 'borrowed produce' and, best of all, 'a plague of potato bugs'.[174]

If the *London Mercury* took a divisive approach to the modernising and Georgian streams of writing, a second newcomer to the publishing scene attempted an ambitious union between the strands. *The Dial* had begun its print life in 1840, and was in a tired state when Scofield Thayer, a friend of Eliot's from Milton Academy, Massachusetts, became its editor in the summer of 1918, while James Sibley Watson took up the journal's presidency. Thayer and Watson wanted their publication to be eclectic, mixing both the modernising and the Mercurian writers: they hoped to be nondenominational. And they had something appealing to both camps: money – they were wealthy men from wealthy families who would privately subsidise the journal to the tune of almost $70,000, from a circulation of fewer than ten thousand copies. Eliot had been delighted to offer himself as a transatlantic correspondent at the time: 'Studies in European literature, by one on the SPOT! Reflections on American literature, by one NOT on the spot'.[175] The result, beginning in 1921, would be a column in the form of a 'London Letter' for US readers. And Pound would help too, provided that it didn't offer Squire 'an attempt to keep the aged corpses in evidence'.[176]

The new *Dial* was relaunched from 152 West 13th Street in Greenwich Village, New York, in January 1920, with something that neither the *London Mercury* nor *The Athenaeum* could match: for Scofield Thayer was not only a literary editor but also a collector of the visual arts, and he wanted his new journal to be a gallery in which to exhibit all that was good in print, on canvas and in other media. The January 1920 issue featured the work of sculptor Gaston Lachaise and painters Charles Demuth and Boardman Robinson, and would soon expand its coverage: Paul Cézanne that spring, Constantin Brâncuși, Marc Chagall, Henri Matisse and Pablo Picasso to follow. Critical prose came from Walter Pach and Arthur Symons, while emerging and established poets were granted space in equal measure: Evelyn Scott and Edna St Vincent Millay had just one collection between them, but their poems appeared alongside Pulitzer prize-winners Carl Sandburg and Edwin Arlington Robinson. But of all the introductions made in that January edition, none would make a more profound impact than the seven poems and four line drawings by an unknown twenty-five-year-old called E. E. Cummings, including one of the poems that would make him famous for his wry intelligence and typographic inventiveness, his spoofed homage to the late pioneer-showman, Buffalo Bill.[177] Cummings would publish a dozen poems with *The Dial* before the summer was out, and would do so in the company of Marianne Moore, Hart Crane, Ezra Pound, AE, Djuna Barnes; he typified the vanguard of a new style that seemed wholly at odds with the Squirearchy in London. Even so, there were future contributors who were not impressed: Eliot and Pound for two, who didn't hide their disappointment, each man summarising the production in the same word, *dull*.[178] And it was true that for all its commitment to the visual and poetic arts the issue was choked by less than interesting prose. But that balance was to change, and, despite its grumblers, *The Dial* had taken a first step to become among the most modernising journals of the era.

//

Work at the bank had become ever more demanding. Eliot had now been put in charge of settling all of the pre-war debts between Germany and Lloyds at a salary of £500 and with the help of various assistants.[179] It was important work, full of legal tangles, he told his mother, but heavy going, too, in its efforts to implement what he now quite openly called 'that appalling document the Peace Treaty'.[180] Strains outside the bank were also showing. With not one but two collections of poems imminent with the Ovid Press in London and Knopf in New York, Eliot was eyeing the literary community with caution. Getting noticed in print was no small matter. In London, Eliot knew, the debutant writer would always attract attention ('while he is unknown he has no enemies'), but an established writer needed the allegiance of the newspapers in order to remain visible. Pound and Lewis were now the only writers in London worth promoting, he believed: but Pound had not been able to maintain even the most basic literary alliances. His lack of tact had done him great harm, admitted Eliot: 'He is becoming forgotten,' he said. 'I am worried as to what is to become of him.'[181]

Pound had been photographed in shirt sleeves and necktie by Malcolm Arbuthnot for *Vanity Fair* that new year, as one of the 'Masters of English Prose Style'.[182] He had a look of a hunter about him, arms folded, watching for his moment, or was that the look of a man who was now the hunted? 1919 had witnessed the savaging of Pound the translator, and the dismissal of Pound the editor; the new year began with the razing of his critical prose. Alfred Knopf's edition of *Pavannes and Divisions* had been written off by the *New Republic* as 'a carefully enshrined series of trivialities, translations, annotated exits, beauty submerged in banalities, criticisms smothered in a mixture of snobbery and bad temper'.[183] Even supporters such as Conrad Aiken had dismissed it as 'without value'. ('Did he always write so badly?') It had seemed almost a relief when the reviews began to peter out.[184] But Harriet Monroe's *Poetry*, the slayer of 'Sextus', had not yet had its say. Now, in January 1920, a year and a half after publication, it savaged the book. Pound had lost any common touch he once had, the reviewer wrote; he had estranged himself from his readership to the point of provoking irritation, and the review poured scorn on his 'fierce little contempt against America', and mocked him accordingly: 'Look! he's throwing pebbles at our skyscrapers.'[185]

Nor would there be shelter for his poetry. In January the London *Observer* rounded on *Quia Pauper Amavi* with excoriating force. The publication showed Pound at his 'abominable worst', not least in its reprinting of the three 1917 *Cantos*, 'a ragbag without synthesis'. The review contained a string of epithets closer to libel than literary criticism: ineptitude, vulgarity, incompetence, tedium, cocksureness, perversity, the tatters of second-hand clothes – the 'queer compost' that made up the author's personality. 'Mr Pound is not, never has been and almost, I might hazard, never will be, a poet.'[186]

The hazarding 'I' was that of Robert Nichols, a poet younger in years than Ezra Pound but more old-fashioned in taste, who had once shared a publishing house, Elkin Mathews, with his antagonist. Nichols had been a combatant in the trenches, who had signed off the preface of his 1918 selection of war poems, *The Assault*, declaratively from 'The Western Front, January, 1918'. Strangely, the vocabulary of Nichols's poems came from preserved jars rather than from the battlefield of which he had actual experience: mist 'bedews' a soldier's tunic, clouds are 'melancholy', the gulls below them 'reiterant'.[187] In the diplomatic phrasing of T. Sturge Moore, his poems 'cannot be said to push beyond appearances'.[188] Even so, Chatto & Windus in London and Charles Dutton in New York would take up and reprint the work with enthusiasm, while Edward Marsh would include it in the Poetry Bookshop's anthology *Georgian Poetry*. At the time that Nichols was reviewing Pound's *Quia Pauper Amavi* with its challenging Latin title, the title page of his own most recent book seemed to belong to a church fete: *Invocation and Peace Celebration, Hymn for the British Peoples, Year of Our Lord Jesus Christ 1919*. That book had opened with a celebratory couplet that seemed to strike an unintended comic note: 'A hymn, a hymn for these our joys! / Peace is here: where is Alfred Noyes?'[189] (Princeton University was the answer, where Noyes taught English literature and from where he had composed patriotic English homilies for combatants at the Front.)

Nichols's review was incendiary and drew an explosive reaction. Wyndham Lewis called out the *Observer* for its 'suffocating and malignant rubbish', explaining in no uncertain terms that it was part of the same blind conservativism that Pound and his circle had to break through daily simply to find an imaginative space.[190] And nor did Pound sit on his hands, either. He wrote to the paper that Nichols had failed to understand the paradox of his Propertius: 'Are we to suppose that he was never ironical,' he questioned, and, turning to Nichols himself, said 'that he was as dull and humourless as the stock contributors to Mr Marsh's series of anthologies'.[191]

Nichols used a right of reply to rebuff what he called this 'Poundian nonsense', and repeated that what Pound displayed was 'ignorance, incompetence, and vulgarity'; but he offered nothing new of substance.[192]

Tempers were running high, and no one was emerging well from the encounter. The retort by Pound and by Lewis at least may have served to caution others, as there followed only one other caustic review, by John Gould Fletcher, a friend and fellow traveller in

Imagism who might have been a bankable supporter; yet he wrote in Harold Monro's *Chapbook* that the poems 'are almost valueless'.[193] But a truce on the publication of bad reviews is not the same as receiving a good review, and support remained desperately thin on the ground. Even friends weren't entirely sure how to help. Eliot's review in *The Athenaeum* had served only to cause a quarrel with Pound, and now Richard Aldington, that most loyal of friends, could be seen trying to bring every benefit of doubt to a review for *Poetry*: 'The writing is so elliptic, the thought so carefully hidden, that I cannot imagine what the poem is about,' he puzzled, adding limply, 'but it has delightful lines'.[194] Only May Sinclair was unequivocal in support. It was true that Pound had let off some squibs, she shrugged, and that one or two had hit respected persons in the eye. 'But in this immense and hospitable universe there is room, not only for magic in delight and terror, but for the clear hardness, the civilised polished beauty, the Augustan irony of Ezra Pound.'[195] For Augustan irony read Propertius: a seemingly rare moment of critical generosity. But there was surely now no breathing life back into the failing body of Sextus Propertius, and there was surely now no way back for Pound.

Ezra Pound brought 'Hugh Selwyn Mauberley' to a conclusion with five new poems in January. Like a variation on an aria, the pieces of the second part revisited the subject of the first, reaching back into the December poems for material and even drawing quotation from them. But these new lines were sharper than their predecessors, wiser, weathered in the skin, scolding of the febrile poet of Part I, a figure of 'no guts, balls, viscera', as Pound told Basil Bunting.[196] They turned a knife in the heart of the beleaguered H. S. Mauberley, belittling his craft and condemning his failure to make a memorable self-portrait – 'Not the full smile, / His art, but an art / In profile'. Intervention passes, posterity passes, a life of love slips by as the artist's assurance crumbles into 'non-esteem', and all roads lead to one destination: 'his final / Exclusion from the world of letters'. Mauberley in this final section drifts almost unnoted towards annihilation, and is left to construct his own epitaph: 'I was / And I no more exist; / Here drifted / An hedonist'. It was not so much a culmination as a dissipation: of energy and art, of hope. Mauberley's is a life not grasped, of love unconsummated; a shadow of the existence that his Roman or Provençal ancestors lived. Pale and unmissed, Mauberley slips off the face of a world he barely touched.[197]

'Hugh Selwyn Mauberley' had been Pound's most sustained experiment in a quatrain form that was now simply too rigid to contain the volume of history that Pound poured into it. 'In verse one can take any damn constant one likes, one can alliterate, or assone, or rhyme, or quant, or smack,' wrote Pound to Ford Madox Ford that year, 'only one MUST leave the other elements irregular.'[198] 'Hugh Selwyn Mauberley' achieved the strength and energy of such a balance more perfectly than Pound would ever be able to repeat. 'Thing is to cut a shape in time,' he said later of the poem: which it was, after a fashion.[199] But fashions can be cruel, and the poem would not sustain through time in the way that Eliot's work would, even though his friend would champion it. In March, Eliot told John Quinn of Pound: 'He has just finished a new long poem which I think has some very good things in it.'[200] But Pound knew where the limitations lay: thin, was how he described it to Thomas Hardy, and although W. B. Yeats had approved 'rather vigorously of parts of Mauberley', it had *only* been parts: the first five, in fact, but not the remaining thirteen.[201] For years he had pursued the 'French' quatrains, and encouraged Eliot to do the same, but never again would he return to them. The experiment of Gautier was over. It was, Pound knew, a failure: a good failure, in Mauberley's words 'the best, among them', but a failure nonetheless.

When Eliot called the poem 'the last stage of importance before *The Cantos*', he didn't in fact say as much as he might, for it was the last stage of *any* kind before *The Cantos*, the last landmark before the vast ocean. But when he added in 1928 that it was 'much the finest poem' of Pound's career to date, and that it was 'a great poem', he undoubtedly meant it. It was the high-water mark of Pound's craft to date, the result of hard work to effect great simplicity, a document of an epoch; 'It is, in the best sense of Arnold's worn phrase, a "criticism of life".'[202]

'Mauberley' was to have brought 'shock troops'. It had targets in sight, but it left them standing. What the poem saw collapse, in the end, was a social bond, a form of trust, if not a wishful dream: that a poet could exist in our society who would be talented enough to define the age in an age intelligent enough to listen. 'Humanity is malleable mud,' Pound would write of the poem in 1922, 'and the arts set the moulds it is later cast into.'[203] If so, then not this art, and not this mould. For 'Mauberley' would mark more than just the end of an engagement with literary form: it marked, also, for Ezra Pound, the end of an idea of England: an idea that literature could be a force of change, an idea of poetry as an unignorable conscience, an idea of a civilising culture. And in 1926, he underscored what his friends in 1920 could already sense when he confirmed, 'The sequence is so distinctly a farewell to London.'[204]

'Meliora speramus', Pound would say with resignation looking back from the summer of 1922: we hope for better things. By then 'Mauberley', like 'Propertius', had been reprinted detrimentally in extracted parts – 'mutilations', he called such extracts, and he had learned a lesson. When the moment came, he wouldn't permit the same mistake to be made for *The Waste Land*: no, he would howl *to high heaven* to ensure that was printed whole; he would say, 'Dragging my own corpse by the heels to arouse the blasted spectators.'[205] That moment would be seized with the kind of literary selflessness that had characterised Pound's entire career; with it, he would refound his belief in humanity's collective advancement through the aiding of another writer's work. 'Eliot's *Waste Land* is I think the justification of the "movement", of our modern experiment, since 1900,' he would write to a former professor in July 1922. 'It shd. be published this year.'[206]

V.

'I congratulate you on an admirable book,' Eliot told John Rodker, on 1 February.[1] Eliot's *Ara Vos Prec* had been printed on 10 December 1919 in a run of 264 artisan copies on handmade paper from the James Whatman mill in Maidstone, Kent: thirty signed by the author, the remainder numbered but for ten out-of-sequence copies destined for review. Every care had been taken with materials. Edward Wadsworth, friend and collaborator with Wyndham Lewis, provided the colophon and the ornamented initials that opened each poem with the flourish of a five-line drop. His work, together with Rodker's typesetting, was praised in the *Observer* as 'one of the most beautiful productions of the modern press'.[2] But closer inspection revealed a different story. The title page was poorly letter-spaced; the contents page departed from the contents in titles, spelling and running order; page numbers moved between fore-margin and gutter or were absent without any pattern; and the poems themselves moved between the head margin and the baseline vertically as though the forme had broken loose in the chase. Most disabling of all, the production was poorly inked by Rodker on worn Caslon type that made some letters partly illegible.[3] Despite his initial enthusiasm, Eliot would come to agree that the volume had been badly printed.

But the most startling error of all was not of Rodker's making, but Eliot's, and it lay in full view on the title page. 'Vos' had been spelled as 'Vus' after Eliot reproduced an error in the edition that he was working from. 'I don't know Provençal,' he confessed, 'and I was quoting from an Italian edition of Dante the editor of which apparently did not know Provençal either.'[4] It was a title taken from what he called 'the superb verses of Arnaut Daniel in his Provençal tongue' – or, more accurately, from a rendering of Arnaut Daniel by Dante in the *Purgatorio*:

'Ara vos prec, per aquella valor
   que vos guida al som de l'escalina,
   sovegna vos a temps de ma dolor.'
POI S'ASCOSE NEL FOCO CHE GLI AFFINA.[5]

Ara *now*, vos *you*, prec *pray*. When Eliot wrote that it was a title 'unintelligible to most people',[6] he may have included some translators, who have rarely agreed upon a phrasing. *Therefore I do implore you*; and *I pray you*; and *To you we pray*; and *Now I beg you*.[7] Thomas Okey's Temple Classics was the translation of the day: 'Now I pray you, by that Goodness which guideth you to the summit of the stairway.'[8] But Eliot himself, in a 1929 book on Dante, would make a translation of his own:

'And so I pray you, by that Virtue which leads you to the topmost of the stair – be mindful in due time of my pain.' Then dived he back into that fire which refines them.[9]

Eliot had made that topmost moment of the stair his own. The Cathars, Périgueux, the wave pattern at Excideuil: how the summer of 1919 must have returned to him when he retrieved that final line of Dante's diving back into the fire.

'It would seem that there is no such word as *Vus* in that language,' Eliot wrote dejectedly of his mistake.[10] After all the anticipation of a first full collection, he was left to correct each title by hand. He inscribed the fifth of his personal copies for his brother Henry; the third for Emily Hale. But the first of them was reserved for his wife, and he inscribed it stiffly on the front endpaper, 'Vivien Haigh Eliot / February 1920 / from her husband / T. S. Eliot'.[11] That formality and lack of ease may have been compounded by a further typo that had crept into the epigraph of the already charged 'Sweeney Among the Nightingales', where the 'adulterate wrong' of the Hogarth *Poems* 1919 had been mis-set as 'adulterous wrong': a humiliating correction to make by hand in Vivien's copy, but make it he did. It was after that that Eliot would excise the line from the epigraph for ever.

At last, he had what was by any standards a full-length collection: twenty-four poems across fifty-six pages, with a running order that placed the newest pieces first, then those from the Hogarth *Poems* (1919) and finally those from *Prufrock*: 'I always prefer people to like best what I have written most recently, & in that order backwards.'[12] Misspelled or otherwise, the title had partly served its purpose to be 'non-committal about the newness of the contents', for a closer inspection would reveal it to be little more than a gathering of *Prufrock* and Hogarth, where all but six of the pieces had been published; of the remainder, four had already appeared in journals, and only two were unpublished.[13] It was just such a familiarity with existing material that would contribute to the sense of fatigue with which the poems were to be received, for although the reviews were more numerous than for his Hogarth *Poems* (1919), they were barely more generous.

'What are we to make of him?' came the perplexed question from John Middleton Murry in *The Athenaeum*, for which he had reviewed all year: 'It seems that he is like the chameleon who changes colour infinitely, and every change is protective.'[14] *The Times* continued where its despair for the Hogarth edition left off: here was a poetry that was tired and bewildered, it announced, a grubby verse of 'endlessly recurring squalor' by an author 'fed up' with life – and if fed up, it posited, then 'why write verse about it; why not commit suicide?'[15] (Eliot could at least now join Pound in their critical invitations to self-harm.) The weary tone of reception was nowhere better expressed than in the *Observer*: 'The irony of things-as-they-are haunts the poet as it haunted his forerunner Laforgue,' it reported, 'and levies board-wages upon all his emotions.'[16]

There were better reviews to come, but they were still a year away, and for the moment the critical response was precisely the disheartening one that Eliot had predicted. 'Here I am considered by the ordinary Newspaper critic as a Wit or satirist,' he confided in his brother Henry in February, 'and in America I suppose I shall be thought merely disgusting.'[17]

Alfred Knopf's edition, *Poems*, was released in New York two weeks after *Ara Vos Prec* in London, at a price of $1.25. Its print run is unknown, but as trade pressings for poetry typically ran in batches of five hundred copies it would have been by any measure by far the most numerous of Eliot's printings. Unlike the Ovid Press edition, Knopf had given the title page some care, and this time the contents page married the contents, even if the cheap trade binding reminded one reviewer of an ugly schoolbook.[18] There were small changes from the London edition: *Prufrock*'s dedication to Jean Verdenal, absent from *Ara Vos Prec*, was restored; and while the Knopf edition repeated the principle of placing the recent poems first, Eliot had given a new attention to the texts and revised six of the poems, as well as the order in which they appeared.[19]

But there was one significant difference between the London and New York books that was not about production or revision. 'Ode', which had appeared in *Ara Vos Prec*, was certain to upset his mother with its rendering of menstruation and the marital bed. He had considered sending her a copy of the London book with the page torn out, suggesting that there had been a printer's error; his solution, in the end, was not to mention the Ovid edition at all, but to replace the poem in Knopf's edition with *Prufrock*'s 'Hysteria'. With that he lent his energies to other worries: 'Do you think that "Sweeney Erect" will shock her?'[20] he asked his brother Henry, and said that he was thinking continually of his wish to see her. Might she come to England in the summer, he wondered; might she finally meet Vivien? The desire to release such long-standing pain was almost overwhelming. 'Unless I can really *see* her again I shall never be happy.'

Cipher. That was the word Henry had used to describe the Knopf *Poems* to his mother – the book was written *in cipher*. It contained nothing sensual, wrote Henry, only the occasional expression of what he described to their mother as 'a horror of sensuality'.[21] But there was another word that came to define not only the Knopf edition, but all of Eliot's publishing to date. It was a word that a review of 1916 had warned would be the 'pitfall' of all new poetry – a word that had come up in two reviews of Eliot in 1919 already, but which from the early months of 1920 would become persistent.[22] 'Clever' (*Athenaeum,* February); 'cleverness' (*Times,* April); 'very, very clever' (*Oakland Tribune,* April); 'extraordinarily clever' (*Freeman,* June).[23] In fact the word was so variously deployed that in 1926, one critic decided to call time on it. 'Over and over again', Louise Morgan observed in *Outlook* magazine, the critics had repeated the charge that he was 'merely clever, very very clever', all brain and no heart; but, she wrote, this was to misunderstand the profound emotional quality of the work in this most misunderstood poet.[24] Even so, one critic in the 1930s would look back with hindsight on the time as 'the "clever" period' in Eliot's poems; there seemed to be no getting away from it.[25]

Now it was the turn of the American critics to be unimpressed. The *Prufrock* poems were worth the volume, wrote the *New York Evening Post,* in May, but the newer poems revealed an amateur ironist, a scholar rather than a maker.[26] The *Boston Evening Transcript* likened the experience of reading the poems to 'a room of foul air', stale with exotic perfume and the memory of lust.[27] *Poetry* magazine in Chicago had been home to 'The Love Song of J. Alfred Prufrock' and its view would surely matter. It wrote in June that the poems were in a class of their own, but the compliment was backhanded: their distinction was to be found in a labour of mystifying titles, coy complexities, line-consuming words and whimsical pathos. Readers were told that they would benefit from a dictionary, an encyclopedia and a martyr's spirit.[28]

Not that condemnation was entirely unanimous: one young writer, whom Eliot would one day publish at Faber & Faber, felt differently. E. E. Cummings was serving in the US ambulance corps in 1917 when he was arrested and imprisoned on suspicion of espionage (he had declined an opportunity to say that he hated Germans); his experiences of prison were reworked as an autobiographical novel, *The Enormous Room*, in 1922. But in 1920, he was still three years away from his debut collection of poems, though a rising star of Scofield Thayer and Sibley Watson's new *Dial*. But he was already starting out as a critic with an unusual turn of phrase. 'Not any of *Poems'* fifty-one pages fails to impress us with an overwhelming sense of technique,' he wrote. His reading of Eliot was first rate, even if the heightened language he deployed sometimes obscured the quality of his insight (he praised the volume as an 'uncorpulent collection of instupidities').[29] He wrote of a vocabulary that was *almost brutally tuned to attain distinctness*: that well described the hard-working ease for which Eliot was aiming. He wrote of *an extraordinarily tight orchestration of the shapes of sound*: that, too, well identified the intense sonic pressure under which the poems were operating. And he wrote of their cadence in his best phrase of all: *the delicate and careful murderings of established tempos by oral rhythms*; in other words, a spoken cadence weaving across the traditional rhythms of verse. Unexpectedly, Cummings had brilliantly illuminated the formal skill that lay beneath these supposedly post-free-verse poems.

//

Between Eliot and Quinn, an invitation had been wrung from Scofield Thayer for Pound to serve as correspondent for the revived

Dial. 'I don't suppose we can ever be precisely your "spiritual home",'³⁰ Thayer admitted to Pound, but would he be willing to set aside some time to identify new materials for the journal at an annual salary of $750 (£200)? Pound would. 'I have no objection to being your foreign editor or English agent, or whatever it is to be termed, IF we can start on some sort of basis that will not lead to constant misunderstandings.'³¹ Namely: realism about the content he would supply. America was *not* a free country, he wrote, and it made no sense for him to provide materials such as *Ulysses* that would only lead to the journal's suppression. Lewis would be writing very little, Hardy even less, while D. H. Lawrence was practically out of reach in Italy; Conrad was a question of price, Beerbohm, price, George Moore, price, price, price. Who did that leave? Yeats, essentially, but he would keep Thayer supplied with Yeats 'as fast as it is written'.³² And then of course there would be Eliot and himself, 'in homeopathic (very) doses'.³³ In no time at all the new *Dial* would be a 'live periodical'.³⁴ And so too might *The Athenaeum*, for which, unexpectedly, Pound had just been employed as the drama critic.³⁵ After losing his editorial position at *Poetry*, the *Little Review* and *The Egoist*, Pound was suddenly back in the thick of it. It seemed like a lifeline. And the person he had to thank for his positions with *The Dial* and *The Athenaeum* was Eliot.

//

The loss of Alsace-Lorraine in the west to France, of Northern Schleswig in Jutland to Denmark, and the ceding of swathes of East Prussia and Silesia to Poland and Czechoslovakia had had a devastating impact on the economy, the morale and the identity of Germany. Tens of thousands of square miles had been stripped away – entire rivers with it – one-tenth of all the land mass, and more than two million people. To the north, the port of Danzig, 98 per cent German, was now a Free City to which the new Polish

Republic had rights of access. To the south, Sudeten Germans didn't think of themselves as Czechs and resisted their incorporation in a state dominated by Slavs. As tensions grew, an effort was made to overthrow the Weimar government, led by the nationalist civil servant Wolfgang Kapp and Walther von Lüttwitz, the highest-ranking general in the German army. On 13 March, the elected government went into hiding, from where it called on the people to mobilise in the form of a general strike that brought the coup to its knees. Among the armed supporters of the coup had been the II Marine Brigade of Hermann Ehrhardt; the uprising had been the first time the brigade's new insignia had been seen in public. Two bent crosses of chiral clockwise symmetry. A swastika.

//

At the Hogarth Press in Richmond, Virginia Woolf was 'half blind' with corrections. She had finished setting a 445-line poem that had been with her since the previous summer, and on 2–3 March 1920, she and Leonard ran off 175 copies on the basement hand press; six weeks later they were bound.[36] But the production hadn't gone well (the wrong year was printed on the title page), and by late April Virginia was slaving over amendments to the finished copies that had to be inked by hand.[37] It was the first poetry publication by a talented young novelist called Hope Mirrlees; the work was *Paris: A Poem*, written in that city in the spring of 1919.

Within days of it rolling off the Hogarth Press, *The Times* had dismissed it as 'a futurist trick', spluttering and incoherent down to its title ('it is certainly not a "Poem"').[38] It was almost possible to forgive the reviewer their partial blindness – almost. It was a work that lacked a recognisable form, that traded the security of metre for a syncopated style, that failed to establish a lasting cadence, that employed rhyme haphazardly; and yet there was something about its wide-eyed peregrination through a night and day in Paris that was worthy of Baudelaire's *flâneur*. Only this time, for once, it was not the gaze of a man but a *flâneuse*, and this time, for once, it offered a woman's tapestry of impressions; and if that wasn't reason enough to engage with it then it was, in addition, and without doubt, a new note in English polyphony. Even a cursory glance by the *Times* reviewer across the English Channel would have crystallised its position as a bridge between new French literature and the modernising spirit in English poetry, as the reviewer of *The Athenaeum* noted two weeks later in aligning the poem with 'the idiom of the younger French poets' in its learning, wit, skill and accomplishment.[39] Therein, undoubtedly, lay a literary debt, for while Mirrlees was writing her own poem in Paris, she had become aware of the recent publication of Jean Cocteau's *Le Cap de Bonne-Espérance* – an extended fragmentary elegy to his friend the aviator and war hero Roland Garros – that might also have been read in French by Eliot, and was most certainly read by Pound, who would become a friend of its author and help it into translation for the *Little Review* in 1921.[40] Whatever the sequence of reading, Mirrlees, Cocteau, Eliot and Pound were at that moment responding to the forces around them in ways that bore common traits. They were reading the same journals, attending the same galleries, watching the same operas, meeting the same composers, and corresponding with the same creative artists. It would not be a surprise if, under such conditions, their works should bear what Eliot had recently called 'family features'.[41]

Paris: A Poem was a stablemate in the small Hogarth list only a year after Eliot's own *Poems*; he may have been aware of the book from the notice in *The Athenaeum* if he had missed *The Times*.[42] But such was the limitation on print run and distribution that Eliot would not have been likely to receive a courtesy copy or to have seen it in any bookshop, nor was the poem serialised in any journal that he might read; it would have been surprising to learn that he had sought it out. Certainly, he didn't possess a copy at home, but if he had, he would not have agreed with the reviewer of *The Times* that 'it does not belong to the art of poetry': that would have been to set it the wrong test, which was never one about belonging, but of quality.[43] By those terms, Eliot would go on to hold Mirrlees in high regard: a friendship would blossom between the poets in the years before and during the Second World War, when they sheltered together from the Blitz at the Mirrlees family home, and where Eliot would write the poems that became *Four Quartets*. She would also find friendship with Vivien, and say perceptively she saw in her the ghost of a woman who had seen a ghost.[44]

For Virginia Woolf, Mirrlees was over-dressed, over-elaborate and over-scented: 'That is I like her very much.'[45] She would come also to like her intelligence, as Eliot would, but with few backers to the edition, few reviews and few sales, attention was always going to be in short supply. 'Hope dribbles along,' Virginia recorded in the weeks after publication, 'but she is a negligible matter.'[46]

//

Katherine Mansfield had wanted to get to know Eliot personally ever since she had discovered 'The Love Song of J. Alfred Prufrock'. That poem was what she wished modern poetry to be, and she believed that Keats would have admired it as much as she did.[47] She imagined what meeting him would be like; the grey door of her mind's room kept on *opening and opening* as Eliot entered, although Vivien she couldn't see at all.[48] Then they met: Friday 14 May, dinner at the Hampstead home she shared with her husband, John Middleton Murry. 'They are just gone – and the whole room is *quivering*. John has gone downstairs to see them off. Mrs E's voice rises "Oh don't commiserate with Tom; he's *quite* happy."' It was extravagant of her to pass judgement so soon, she knew, 'but I dislike her so *immensely*. She really repels me. She makes me shiver with apprehension . . .' Every nervous, busybody part of Vivien had grated on her. Murry had dropped a spoon over dinner and Vivien had jumped to cry: 'I say you are noisy tonight – whats wrong.' She smoked idly on Mansfield's bedroom sofa, and shocked her in commenting invasively on how much the room had changed. This startled Mansfield: *however had she seen it before?* At a party of Murry's, came the answer, when she befriended (or was it inveigled?) him and he drank to overcome the state of nerves she left him in. And worst of all, worse than her repulsion towards this invasive lady, was the sight of Eliot, the 'Prufrock' poet, demeaning himself: 'leaning towards her, admiring, listening, making the most of her – really minding whether she disliked the country or not . . .' She felt an instinctive fondness for him, an instinctive sympathy. But Vivien . . . 'this teashop creature' . . .[49]

//

Pound had played his offer of employment from *The Dial* with a veteran's cool ('the Trial = I mean <u>The Dial</u>', he joked of his new employer to his father), but Eliot had noted 'a great effect in raising his spirits' now that he was once again employed.[50] From Italy, Pound engaged without delay, commissioning and cajoling new work for the journal from the writers he had discussed with Thayer. 'Remember they are two sets. / One lot wants all the cash it can get. / The other lot wants to publish as little as possible; it wants the Flaubertian luxury of producing only six books in a lifetime.'[51] Thayer was delighted with the submissions, and had even received the rare gift of a poem from Joyce.[52] Pound in turn was delighted to learn that efforts to partner with Squire and the *Mercury* had now been set aside as 'impractical'.[53] Further encouraging news would come his way in the form of an offer to reprint 'Canto IV' from the limited Ovid broadsheet (even if it needed a little dynamite under it to get it done, Pound told Homer);[54] but Thayer had made his first mistake with Pound, too: he had returned *Cantos* V–VII with the same submission, and though Pound said nothing of this immediately, the rejection of the new works – the sum total of all that he had unpublished – would begin to undermine the newly found trust.[55] And something even stranger took place with Boni & Liveright's *Instigations*, Pound's prose published on 25 April in a run of eight hundred copies. W. C. Blum, reviewing it in *The Dial* that autumn, would observe that what Pound wrote wasn't prose at all but 'funny oaths and insults'.[56] 'Who is Blum?? nom de Plum, nom de Blum?'[57] Pound asked Thayer of the mysterious writer: he was 'a wicked man' and his statements 'buncumb', so Pound would tell the *Little Review*.[58] Thayer would not answer, because 'Blum' was a pseudonym for his co-editor at *The Dial*, James Sibley Watson.

In London, Eliot's spirits were not in such good shape. He and Vivien had at last taken the decision to find a new home with more space for them both, but the search hadn't gone well. He told Pound that both he and she were near prostration, and with rents at three or four times what they were currently paying, the prospect of a swift move looked unlikely.[59] The move would happen, but it would occupy almost half a year of effort and worry.

//

Pound had been only too glad to leave London behind. On 26 April, he and Dorothy departed for Paris, and two days later had reached Venice, treating themselves to a room they said they couldn't afford at the elegant Hotel Pilsen-Manin, close by the Rialto Bridge.[60] The city seemed so quiet: the Grand Canal wasn't lit at night, and theirs was the only gondola to venture out on it. But Dorothy didn't take well to the air of the lagoon; by 10 May the couple had retreated to Verona, and ten days later they were in

Sirmione, which Pound had loved since his first visit in 1910. He had come to cherish the little town that stretched out into Lake Garda along a narrow promontory: he once likened it to living on the edge of a large sapphire that *certain damn fools* mistook for water.[61] Or at least that was his superficial explanation, for what really drew Pound to the place was its notable distinction as the hometown of Catullus. He liked to say that he slept on Catullus' 'parlour floor' (the Hotel Eden), and he liked to believe that here he could feel forgotten gods moving.[62] So instantly at home was he that he seemed almost to lose interest in reaching his intended destination, and tried instead to see if his destination would come to him. Trieste was the place he had in mind, and the man who lived there a writer with whom Pound had corresponded, edited and published since 1913, but not yet met. 'I wish you would spend a week here with me ("on me", as my guest, or whatever the phrase is),' Pound wrote to his man in Trieste. 'The place repays the train trip.'[63]

'O shite and onions!' James Joyce had been suffering the straits of his *damnable boredom* without a soul to talk to about *Ulysses*: 'When is this bloody state of affairs going to end?'[64] From the beginning, Pound had identified James Joyce as one of the few writers to have given a remarkable language to modern thought, a man who possessed the necessarily active chemical of the mind so valuable that it must be given its own 'court yard'.[65] And it wasn't only in prose that he believed that Joyce had achieved this rare feat. *Chamber Music*, a 1907 volume of poems, had demonstrated Joyce's ability to invert lyric rhythm across traditional metre, matched only by Pound's brilliant description of the achievement: *the cross run of the beat and the word, as of a stiff wind cutting the ripple-tops of bright water.*[66]

Trieste had become a confinement since Joyce's move there in 1904, and he sensed that Pound's invitation might be just what he needed to break the rut. But he couldn't afford *the clothes*, he said, and was wearing his son's old boots (too large) and his son's old suit (too small):[67] he had just two chapters of *Ulysses* left to write, but suspected Dublin was the place to finish them and not Trieste, nor Sirmione for that matter. Pound had set aside a gift of 1,000 lire, about enough to put Joyce and his family in two rooms for a fortnight. 'Take this stage of your journey now, and proceed to Ireland later,' he advised, and he added by way of a PS that clothing was emphatically *not* a requirement of Sirmione.[68] He prepared a welcome dinner, but Joyce didn't arrive for it: a thunderous storm blew in instead, and it seemed that the meeting of Pound and Joyce was not to take place after all. It was then, on 8 June 1920, that Joyce arrived in Sirmione, with his son Giorgio in tow, whom he brought along, he said, as 'a lightning conductor'.[69] Pound preserved the moment in 'Canto LXXVI': 'In fact a small rain storm . . . / as it were a mouse, out of cloud's mountain / recalling the arrival of Joyce et fils / at the haunt of Catullus.'[70]

The day following their meeting, Joyce told his Italian translator Carlo Linati that he was in Sirmione *col amico Pound*, and Pound told John Quinn of his equally pleasing company – stubborn and cantankerous, admittedly, but beneath the bluff exterior was to be seen a sensitive and delicate if exhausted genius.[71] The next day, Pound left for Paris, Joyce for Trieste, but the new companionship was not over. Joyce had gone back to Trieste to collect his family and few possessions, and would arrive to join the Pounds in the French capital on 9 July. He expected to stay for a week; it became his home for the next twenty years.

//

It was from Venice that Pound wrote the first of twelve weekly articles for the *New Age*, under the title 'Indiscretions; or, Une Revue de Deux Mondes';[72] by the time he reached the Eden pension at Sirmione, the first among them had been published in London. The series would run for three months, and by their completion in August, an unexpected portrait of the childhood and ancestry of Ezra Pound had been revealed. For his parents, it was just a little too revealing, and when they learned that their son planned to gather them in book form, they objected, and in a rare deviation from literary allegiance asked him instead to 'HAVE A HEART', and not revive all the stories that served only to belittle the family name.[73] He went ahead, even so.

'One hotel, one street, 47 saloons, and one newspaper.'[74] Hailey, Idaho, 1885, as Ezra Pound was born into it. A mining settlement and frontier town, tucked within a narrow plain through which the Big Wood River wound, beneath Red Devil Mountain, in the shadow of the Sawtooth Range. Hard-drinking, cattle-rustling, claim-jumping, gun-toting: Hailey was no place for faint hearts. There, in 1883, Homer Loomis Pound ran the Land Office, filing and assaying claims to ore – some of which were made in a friendly manner, some at the point of a gun. Hearing such tales, Homer had packed a revolver of his own as he set off from Wisconsin, only to have it confiscated by a cousin, saying 'Better not 'cause it might go off and hurt someone.'[75] He bought another on arrival, and took it into the mountains for practice: he missed five shots at a sedentary rabbit, and so on meeting a mountain lion didn't risk a final sixth but turned on his heels and fled back into town. (Mother 'always regretted that lion skin', said her son.) Five hundred dollars bought Homer a new-built house and the plot it stood upon on the corner of Second and Pine, three bedrooms and a music room, said to be the first in all of Hailey with interior plaster.[76]

Ezra's father's father Thaddeus Coleman Pound was born in a log cabin in Pennsylvania around 1832, give or take: the family weren't quite sure. Amassed and lost two fortunes by Ezra's time. Owned what Ezra described rather loosely as 'a few silver mines' in Hailey, which were prone to being 'jumped', and to where he had sent his lethargic son Homer to test both the honesty of his employees and the backbone of his offspring. Third fortune lost on his farm in Chippewa Falls, Wisconsin, reducing the length of cow's horns, and bottling sparkling spring water that he said would make him a millionaire but which Ezra said tasted 'only like water'.[77] Married into a family of horse thieves: good ones, and the nicest people in the territory, said an elderly lady in Oneida County, but horse thieves nonetheless. Died penniless but with state honours, after a spell in Congress for north-west Wisconsin: none too shabby for a man from a line of whalers, rustlers and lumbermen, with two great ancestors in between: the first, Captain Joseph Wadsworth, stole the Connecticut Charter in 1687; the second, to the enduring shame of great-nephew Ezra, the once popular poet Henry Wadsworth Longfellow, whose mission in poetry to build 'Some tower of song with lofty parapet' would later provide a target for Ezra's arrow-tipped Imagism.[78]

Hailey, Idaho. One hundred and ninety-nine nights below freezing. Where snow stayed till May, and the air at five thousand feet was too fine for Isabel Weston, newly wed to Homer, abandoned by two waves of servants on account of her high style; and so the Pounds packed up and headed back east through the blizzard – the Big Die-Up was its name, for the devastation it caused to ranching – behind the first rotary snow plough, the sickly, eighteen-month Ezra coughing all the way: 'and no one got any sleep in the sleeper', until the inventor of the rotary plough, whose day it was, stepped forward to administer a sugar lump soaked in kerosene oil, which sent the child to sleep.[79]

Isabel Weston Pound. Born 14th Street and Second Avenue, New York City, 1860, aspirational, athletic social climber: 'Early painting lessons, penchant for the pretty – horror of all realism in art. Belief in the pleasant.' Ezra could barely conceal a mockery of his mother in a letter of 1914 to his wife-to-be, Dorothy Shakespear. Would have liked to see her son in the diplomatic corps, he said spikily.

'Believes that I should be well clothed.'[80] Remote, bewildered, erect, immaculately turned out, remembered William Carlos Williams;[81] every evening, she would greet her husband returning from work at Jenkintown Station, Wyncote, Pennsylvania.

Homer Loomis Pound. Born 1858 in Chippewa country, north Wisconsin, and named for a peripatetic vigour that never materialised, for he would spend forty years as an assayer at the Philadelphia Mint. Quaker turned Presbyterian, social reformer in South Philadelphia's slums, founder of a College Settlement House for the poor. Devoted to his son, believing there was nothing that his boy didn't know; 'I've kept everything he's ever written, I guess.' Interviewed in 1928, Homer asked the journalist: 'Have you ever read any of his *Cantos*? Well, I must admit I can't make much out of some of them. Ezra told me unless I read Browning's "Sordello" I couldn't expect to understand *The Cantos*. So I waded through that. Ever read it? Well, I don't advise you to. I found it didn't help me much with Ezra's *Cantos* anyway.'[82]

A house in the suburb of Jenkintown, then a move south-east onto nearby Fernbrook Avenue, Wyncote, and a house of six bedrooms and three storeys that stands today, on a lot two hundred feet by fifty, with a playroom for young Ezra on the very top floor. This was the American suburb that in 1921 Pound told Thomas Hardy he emerged from: a place of no roots, and no centre, where his parents were foreigners merely by virtue of coming from out of state.[83]

Homer Loomis Pound, 'the naivest man who ever possessed sound sense',[84] or 'cents' for that matter, in the words of the old joke that had special family significance, with whom Ezra would conclude the twelfth and final instalment of his 'Indiscretions'. As a young boy he followed his father into work at the grand old Philadelphia Mint on the corner of Chestnut and Juniper, behind white marble frontage – the impression of its '"Greek temple" façade' not lost upon young Pound: a temple of money with a classical edifice.[85] In *The Cantos*, he recalled as a child watching the men of the smelting room, stripped bare to the waist, 'as I have seen them by shovels full / lit by gas flares',[86] working the old coins for recast as if they were sweeping litter. 'Things like that strike your imagination,' he recalled in 1962. 'You can go on for a long time on that.'[87] He watched, too, his father, raised beside a high shelf table, working under natural light like an alchemist in his cavern to measure to one-thousandths the proportion of golds in his cylindrical bottles; hours seated at his father's roller-top yellow desk with its two dozen drawers and cubby holes, its assortments of filament and ore, and government gold, and blank coin discs yet to be pressed into value. It seemed a conjuror's art. And with it came a parlour trick: for a visitor, Homer would weigh a small blank card on his measuring scales and ask his guest to sign it in pencil. Then he would weigh the card once again: in the difference, he said, was the weight of a man's name.[88]

//

'Hero, Prophet, Poet,' wrote Thomas Carlyle, 'many different names, in different times and places, do we give to Great Men.' Carlyle's lecture of 1840 had stated that it was through the actions of a few that the many advanced. Universal history was the history of great men, he believed, and while some are trapped by their time, 'the Poet is a heroic figure belonging to all ages': an endless contemporary, the voice of an era.[89]

> Such a man is what we call an *original* man; he comes to us at first hand. A messenger he, sent from the Infinite Unknown with tidings to us. We may call him Poet, Prophet, God; – in one way or other, we all feel that the words he utters are as no other man's words.[90]

To a younger Pound, this was heady stuff. He took to heart Carlyle's vision of the poet as the 'Hero-soul' living each day *direct from the inner facts of things*.[91] In 1911 he gave such a figure a name of his own, and called him 'over-man' – brother most certainly to the *Übermensch*, to the poet-hero, to Aristotle's magnanimous man.[92] When the strength of the body combines with the fortitude of will then a new kind of person is born, one who can combine superior strength with artistic endeavour to achieve greatness. This 'perfect creature' was a force in which to believe, wrote Pound – 'something beyond man, something important enough to be fed with the blood of hecatombs'.[93] It was a notion of a flawless organism that would find its place in Nazi Germany, and as the New or 'Super' Man of Mussolini's new Italy.

Boxer, fencer, master of the tennis court (Ford Madox Ford said he returned serve 'like a galvanised agile gibbon'),[94] Pound believed that the health as well as the fortune of a man lay in his own hands. And Eliot's poor health worried him: for the prospective voice of a generation, he spent an inordinate amount of time laid up, and was an unwelcome reminder to Pound of the physical fragility of the artist, a figure who can only respond with a forceful strength if art is to survive. It was for this reason that he wrote with such despair of the feebleness of H. S. Mauberley: 'Him of all men, unfit.' Eliot, he knew, mustn't be allowed unfitness. Following his new year 1920 visit to Crawford Mansions, Pound wrote of the 'osmosis of body and soul', noting that 'wisdom, if not of the senses, is at any rate via the senses'.[95] On introducing Eliot to John Quinn, Pound said of him, 'He has more entrails than might appear from his quiet exterior,' before adding, 'I think.'[96] Over many years, and throughout his correspondence, Pound returns to the word 'guts'. So-and-so is *the only person with guts enough*; someone else *has more invention, more guts*; someone else again suffers from an *Anemia of guts*; elsewhere he writes of *people who have some guts*; elsewhere again, *people not having the guts*.[97] Poems and projects and people have them or don't have them, but either way they are frequently described by Pound in relation to them. And Eliot surely needed them if he were to be a literary leader; if he were being robbed of them – either by his wife or by the grind of his daily work at the bank – then Pound was going to do something about that: Eliot had to be *taken off the wreckage*,[98] he told Quinn.

'No use blinking the fact that it is a crime against literature to let him waste eight hours vitality per diem in that bank.'[99] After that summer of 1919, and the critical prose of that autumn, Eliot's poetry should have been coming to fruition, but where was it? He had written nothing since finishing 'Gerontion' the previous September, and the incomplete 'The Death of the Duchess'. Work and home life seemed to be occupying the place of writing, and while it wasn't possible to buy him out of his marriage ('His wife hasn't a cent and is always cracking up, & needing doctors, & incapable of earning anything'), perhaps, with the right support, it might be possible to lure him away from the bank.

Tested on the matter, Eliot would share with Pound his earnings at the bank that summer – £500 ($2,000) including bonus – indicating that he thought he would need to secure half as much again if he were ever to risk leaving such steady employment.[100] It would take Pound some time to solve the problem, and in 1922 immediately after Eliot had finished *The Waste Land* he published his response – a circular seeking thirty subscribers, each to contribute £10 a year, to guarantee Eliot support enough to allow him to leave the bank and concentrate on literature. In the event, the scheme, which Pound called his *Bel Esprit*, would pose chronic and predictable embarrassment to Eliot: how could it not to such a proud, independently financed man? Lloyds Bank would be publicly named as the institution from which he was seeking release, thereby threatening the security of that income; but more devastating still, Eliot was portrayed as economically hapless, which was a message that mustn't be allowed to get as far as America in case it appeared to suggest that he had a family there who *should* be providing for his support. Pound might have known the anguish he would cause; but then, for all his intended kindness, for him the needs of literature would always triumph over the sensitivities of the individual.

//

Interest in *Hugh Selwyn Mauberley* was thin on the ground that summer, and Eliot was worried. He had asked Harold Monro to cover it for the *Chapbook*, but had received a dispiriting response. Monro said that he couldn't begin to see how he might review such a book for the ordinary public, and with no desire to condemn it (but no wish to praise it), he felt he could not be of assistance. Eliot suggested to Rodker *The Athenaeum* instead, but he knew that for a challenging work to be critically well received it must first have its path prepared by work that the critics *will* tolerate; 'Mauberley' wasn't it, he admitted, and 'the only hope of fame is posthumous'. Anything stronger from *The Times* would only be worse, he said. And indeed it was.

In July, the *Literary Supplement* conceded that the poems in this finely printed book had structure, rhythm and sincerity, 'but they are needlessly obscure', and 'esoteric', hellbent to appeal to only a small circle.[101] But then, what else was to be expected? There are always other voices. Except that this time there weren't. The round-up in *The Times* was all the attention that *Hugh Selwyn Mauberley* would get. The greatest original effort of Pound's career: he had aimed at a withering assault upon establishment Britain, its hyp-ocritical war, the slaughter of its young men in a futile cause, the failure of art to adequately respond to the trauma of the time, the unwillingness of a society to listen, the widening chasm between art and everyday life, the farewell to failure, to a bygone world: for all that effort, the reward would be four brief sentences in *The Times* that culminated in a hope that *his poems would be sweeter.* No word from *The Athenaeum* or the *Observer*, nothing from the

New Age or *New Statesman*; no interest from *Poetry* in Chicago, or *Smart Set* and *Others* in New York and New Jersey; no place in the *Little Review* and not in *The Egoist* and *Art & Letters* now they were a thing of the past, while *The Dial* had tied its hands in reprinting an extract as well as 'The Fourth Canto' that summer.[102] It was almost as if the book had never existed.

Reviewers would touch upon it again in the volume *Poems 1918–21* in which it was later reprinted, but the response would be little better. John Peale Bishop wrote then that there was nothing in 'Mauberley' that was as poignant as the poems of T. S. Eliot. Edmund Wilson made the same comparison, describing the poems as furious attempts to conceal simple reactions behind complicated riddles ('Pound merely paraphrases statements of obvious fact in a tortured pedantic jargon').[103] Edwin Muir grieved in equal measure for the 'laziness' of the readership and the wilfully 'cryptic' mode of Pound's writing that left 'Mauberley' destined to be ignored.[104]

Only one voice spoke to support the poem, and that was Maxwell Bodenheim, who wrote in 1922 that no one had better captured *the redundant propaganda, realistic horrors, and emotional revolts* of war and its poetry.[105] That was a comfort; but then Bodenheim's review was in the journal that employed Pound as its correspondent, *The Dial*. By the 1930s, F. R. Leavis had written despairingly that the poem had 'almost wholly escaped recognition', though undoubtedly it was, he believed, Pound's major achievement.[106] But by then the moment of the poem was more than a decade past, for a work that, as Pound said, had described the war-torn mood of the terrible year 1917.

It had almost been possible to feel the critical silence wash over him, as if the fortune that befell Mauberley, drifting and forgotten at sea, had finally come to be conferred upon Pound.

For a brief moment in the summer of 1920, it was hard to keep up with Pound's output. *Instigations* had appeared in New York

ABOVE Dorothy and Ezra Pound, during their engagement, *c*.1913.

ABOVE LEFT AND RIGHT 314 Second Avenue South, Hailey, Idaho, birthplace of Ezra Pound in 1885, now listed on the National Register of Historic Places; 2635 Locust Street, St Louis, Missouri, birthplace and childhood home of T. S. Eliot in 1888; a parking lot now occupies the space.

RIGHT T. S. Eliot and Vivien Eliot, 18 Crawford Mansions, in the first year of marriage, 1916.

LEFT T. S. Eliot in front of South View, Shore Road, Bosham, 1916.

BELOW T. S. Eliot, 18 Crawford Mansions, Marylebone, 1916.

ABOVE 'At last I spent a night with her', Sewhurst Farm, Abinger, Surrey, site of Vivien's encounter with Bertrand Russell, 1917.

BELOW 'One of the bloodiest outrages against mankind': Walnut Street, reduced to rubble in the East St Louis race riots, 1917.

LEFT Eliot's *Poems*, from the Hogarth Press, with marbled cover, probably by Vanessa Bell, 1919.

BELOW 'I am afraid of the life after death': Chateau at Excideuil, where Eliot confided his revelation to Pound, 1919.

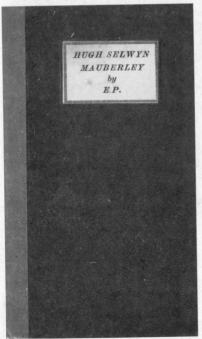

LEFT
Hugh Selwyn Mauberley by E.P., Ovid Press, London, 1920.

ABOVE The Albemarle, Cliftonville, advertisement c.1903.
BELOW Hôtel Pension Sainte-Luce, Lausanne, where Eliot wrote 'Death by Water' and 'What the Thunder Said'.

Lausanne, Pension Ste. Luce

'The state of mind out of which
came *The Waste Land*': the Eliots at
9 Clarence Gate Gardens, 1922.

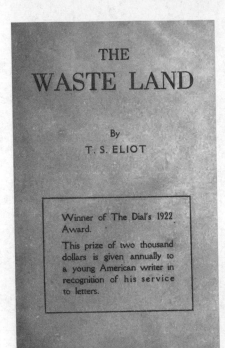

THE
WASTE LAND

By
T. S. ELIOT

Winner of The Dial's 1922
Award.

This prize of two thousand
dollars is given annually to
a young American writer in
recognition of his service
to letters.

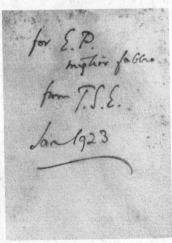

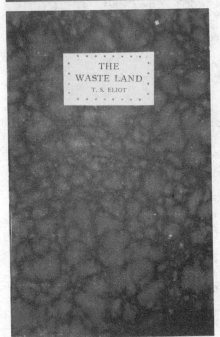

THE
WASTE LAND
T. S. ELIOT

in April, his 'Fourth Canto' was reprinted by *The Dial* in June at the moment that *Hugh Selwyn Mauberley* appeared with the Ovid Press in London. And there was yet another book: a retrospective of his early poems with Elkin Mathews in London, called *Umbra*. If 'Mauberley' had been Pound's farewell to London, then *Umbra* was his retrospective, his backward glance, a selection of early poems. It was the last of the eight collaborations with Elkin Mathews, who had been the primary publisher for Pound since his arrival in London in 1908. When Mathews died unexpectedly in 1921, the last plank in Pound's London publishing was washed away with him. For the next decade, Pound would publish almost exclusively in Paris, without a London partner. And things did not look very much better for him in New York. He wrote soberly in 1924: 'My American publishers do not exist.' He began to plan accordingly. 'I shall never again take any steps whatever to arrange publication of any of my work in either England or America,' he said at that time.[107] It would not be until 1928 that Pound would once again find a publisher in London, in a new venture that had recently hired a debutant director: the house of Faber & Gwyer, edited by T. S. Eliot.[108]

A small-press, limited printing like 'Mauberley' would never have been expected to garner much in the way of critical attention, but a full retrospective by an established publisher like Elkin Mathews could. So when *Umbra*, like 'Mauberley', went unnoted in the London papers it felt like a final blow. The *New Age* alone covered it, a journal friendly to Pound which might be counted upon for a good review: *individual and imaginative with distinction; fastidious vigour, a subtle form of strength.*[109] The review would be the last word on Pound's English residence: the next time he received note of his work in Britain, he would have left the country behind him.

//

Despite his complaints and exhaustion, Eliot's writing for *The Athenaeum* continued with two instalments of 'The Perfect Critic', whom Eliot revealed to be Aristotle: a figure capable of turning his mind to all matters, and thus a mind above the average man, able to look, as Matthew Arnold had, 'solely and steadfastly at the object'.

> The end of the enjoyment of poetry is a pure contemplation from which all the accidents of personal emotion are removed; thus we aim to see the object as it really is and find a meaning for the words of Arnold. And without a labour which is largely a labour of the intelligence, we are unable to attain that stage of vision *amor intellectualis Dei*.[110]

//

James Joyce arrived in Paris with his family on 8 or 9 July 1920, greeted by Pound, who directed him and his family to temporary lodgings he had found for them at a small hotel on 9 rue de l'Université, near the Hôtel Elysée at which he and Dorothy were staying. Pound would make introductions whose aim was to find a translator for a French edition of *A Portrait of the Artist*, and he settled on Madame Ludmila Bloch-Savitsky (soon to be John Rodker's mother-in-law), who would make a contract for the edition with Éditions de la Sirène. She would offer Joyce her apartment in the Bois de Boulogne, which would give him and his family a base in the city, rent free into the autumn.

The Pounds were back in London on 21 July after ten weeks of travels. From there Ezra saw to it that royalties owed to Joyce were paid, and no doubt was the force behind the generous subsistence payments by John Quinn and Harriet Shaw Weaver that would help Joyce to settle in Paris that summer. Pound attempted to find a publishing home for *Ulysses*, but both G. W. Huebsch, Joyce's American publisher, and Boni & Liveright in New York were apprehensive of a printing boycott. John Rodker had the idea for a workaround in which an edition would be printed in Paris and imported, in order to avoid any prosecution that could affect a book published in Britain. He duly went to Paris to meet with Joyce, offering to print on behalf of the Egoist Press. The arrangement wouldn't be necessary by then; Pound had prepared for Joyce the most important of all the introductions he would make in Paris.

In November 1919, at 8 rue Dupuytren in the Latin quarter, an English-language bookshop had opened. It was called Shakespeare and Company, and was no ordinary bookshop: it was also a curious lending library, for which no catalogue or card index existed, and from which loans were mostly recorded by memory. Lending was much easier than selling, its proprietor, Sylvia Beach, discovered – some authors borrowed more than others (Joyce kept certain books for years) – but somehow a business model emerged that kept it trading to become a remarkable centre for 'pilgrims from America',[III] some of whom were escaping prohibition and literary censorship. Paris was booming, and soon Everyone was in the city (Beach capitalised the 'e') – Joyce, Picasso, Stravinsky – well, not quite Everyone, she admitted, as Eliot was regrettably still in London – but certainly the literary cast of the time, gravitating to her English – and to Adrienne Monnier's French – bookshops of Saint-Germain. Djuna Barnes, F. Scott Fitzgerald, André Gide, Mina Loy, Ernest Hemingway, Paul Valéry, George Antheil, Nancy Cunard, Robert McAlmon and Bryher – all were callers and friends; Sherwood Anderson was found gazing fondly at his own book in the window, while Ezra Pound, a passing guest, put himself to good use by mending a cigarette case and a chair. Here was the centre of a literary community, the venue for readings and even a residence for guests.

It was at the house party of André Spire that Beach first shook hands with James Joyce in July 1920 – 'that is, he put his limp, boneless hand in my tough little paw', said Beach, 'if you can call that a handshake'.[112] What did she do? he asked her politely; she ran a bookshop, she replied. He took out a notebook and, holding it close to his eyes, recorded her address. The next day he came to see her.

Sylvia Beach had followed the serialisation of Joyce's *Ulysses* with wonder, but she had no idea how much she would also enjoy his company. She learned that languages were his 'favourite sport', and that he spoke 'at least nine' (they counted between them that day: English, Italian, French, German, Greek, Spanish, Dutch, Norwegian, Swedish, Danish – he counted 'the three Scandinavian tongues' as one – and Yiddish; he also knew some Hebrew.)[113] She learned, too, that he was frightened not only of thunderstorms but of dogs, that he couldn't afford clothes ('Joyce was always a little bit shabby'), and that he wondered how to keep his family of four in food and shoes and shelter. She learned too that he was desperate to finish *Ulysses*, and that she could provide an office that he would christen 'Stratford-on-Odéon' when in 1921 the shop moved to new premises on rue de l'Odéon. Though it was early days, Joyce and Beach had founded an extraordinary partnership that would produce remarkable results: another in a long line of warming fires that Ezra Pound – 'that busy Manager', as Lewis called him – had lit.[114]

//

The Eliots spent the August bank holiday weekend at Garsington Manor, Oxfordshire, where the Huxleys were also among the guests of Ottoline Morrell, a hostess of such blue blood, Virginia Woolf once commented, that she entered a room like the Cornish sea.[115] It was an occasion too far for Vivien: she collapsed on her return to London, for which Eliot blamed himself, having seen it coming and done nothing to prevent it. 'Vivien has broken down rather badly,' he explained to Sydney Schiff ahead of the Eliots' prospective visit to Eastbourne the following weekend, which was now in doubt. In the event, they went anyway, Eliot carrying the news from Leonard Woolf that the 250 or so copies of his 1919 Hogarth *Poems* had now sold out.[116] Wyndham Lewis was also a guest that weekend, and the two men discovered that their desire to visit France that month coincided, and could be simultaneous, if Eliot didn't mind staying on the coast with Lewis, who had work there. Eliot didn't mind a bit, and would bathe, he said, while Lewis worked, and they would travel by bicycle. But the news did not please the exhausted Vivien, weakened as she was, looking 'very tired and ill' when Eliot departed from Waterloo Station on Saturday 14 August, leaving her behind for a second summer on her own. A rare surviving letter between the couple – the earliest preserved – tells as much. Writing to him between stations at Nantes and Vannes in Brittany, she implored him to keep in touch.[117] 'Yesterday I felt so ill and despairing that I went to my room and cried and called yr. name,' she explained.[118] And she likened her numbered lives to those of a cat, though if she sensed which life she was on then she kept that information to herself.

In the small Hôtel Elysée, on the Left Bank of the Seine, Lewis and Eliot waited patiently for their introduction to James Joyce. Eliot carried with him a parcel for Joyce from Pound in London; he was not permitted to know what it contained, but it was too large for his suitcase and so was carried under his arm and upon his lap on two trains and a ferry. Lewis later told the story of the encounter.

Eliot had written to Joyce to invite him to receive the parcel from Pound, and to dine immediately afterwards. At six o'clock, Joyce arrived punctually at the hotel with his son Giorgio to collect the package that Eliot had placed ceremoniously in the middle of the room on a marble table footed by gilded eagle claws. Introductions were exchanged with bows and nods, before Joyce sat down and dangled his straw boater to wait on whatever was to come next. At this moment, Eliot stood up ceremoniously, and, pointing to the packet, announced that *this* was the package which he now delivered, thereby discharging his duties. Joyce played along, obligingly: 'Ah! Is this the parcel you mentioned in your note?' It was indeed, confirmed Eliot, resuming his seat. Now it was Joyce who stood to take up the package, but found it so exacting in its knots that he was unable to untie them. He asked if anyone present had a knife – 'You want a knife?' said Eliot. 'I have not got a knife, I think!' – and managed to locate instead a pair of nail scissors sharp enough for the occasion. The ties undone at last, Pound's gift was revealed. An old and slightly beaten pair of brown shoes. 'Oh!' said Joyce faintly, and sat down. 'Oh!' repeated Lewis. It was Eliot who broke the silence. *Dinner?*[119]

The choice of restaurant that evening would be Joyce's, who took upon himself the duty of host. He surveyed the evening's specials, and ordered on behalf of the table to please his diners; he chose a wine to complement the soup, and another for the subsequent courses, and despite his circumstances settled the bill before anyone else had thought to ask for it. From time to time, Eliot or Lewis would be permitted to buy a drink for themselves, but never for Joyce, and never when dining. For the table was Joyce's court, and it was there, reported Lewis, sampling the Château Latour he had selected, that he raised a toast to 'the band' – 'the literary band', Lewis corrected – 'a group, comprised within the critical folder of Ezra Pound – the young, the "New", group of writers assembled in Miss Weaver's *Egoist* just before and during the War'. It was a tribute made with a certain wrinkling of the nose (four people more dissimilar in every respect would be difficult to find, said Lewis), but it was a tribute nonetheless to the four young men of the moment, these contemporaries in arts, 'these four *Zeitgenossen!*'

'He does not take much notice of me!' protested Eliot mildly to Lewis one day in Paris, when they were contemplating how best to buy Joyce a beer without his refusing. Eliot saw in Joyce's generosity a flamboyance, but Lewis sensed something different: that the used shoes had been an embarrassment to the man's self-respect. The gift itself had been no more or less than the kind of consideration shown by Pound in Sirmione, when Joyce had pleaded to a lack of clothing; but the ceremony conducted by Eliot had been a humiliation that triggered in Joyce a counter-display of benevolence and wealth. However Joyce had taken the message, it seemed he hadn't taken kindly to its messenger. 'To the last Eliot was treated distantly,' said Lewis.[120]

//

Eliot returned from France determined to renew his search for a better place to live. More than ever, he wanted to be released from what he unexpectedly told his mother was 'the neighbourhood of prostitution'.[121] From now on, the hunt for a property would occupy his evenings, placing so much pressure on his literary work that he had to enlist the Pounds to help him to proofread Methuen's pages for *The Sacred Wood*, a task littered with time-consuming checks on foreign-language sources. Proof work, house-hunting, holiday and the bank – 'I want to get settled quietly and write some poetry,' but it was no wonder that Eliot hadn't.[122] He supposed that he wouldn't be settled into writing before November, but at least the urge was burning. 'I have several things I want to do,' he told his mother on 20 September, 'and I want a period of tranquility to do a poem that I have in mind.'[123]

//

G. K. Chesterton was a man who had tried many hats: critic, novelist, philosopher, theologian, even a poet of war ('But they that fought for England, / Following a falling star, / Alas, alas for England / They have their graves afar').[124] His was a literary style pinpointed by Eliot as 'first-rate journalistic balladry';[125] 'slop', in other words, said Pound.[126] Eliot observed in 1918 that although Chesterton's head swarmed with ideas, he saw no evidence that it contained any actual thought.[127] To him and Pound alike, Chesterton was a brute from a bygone age (and brute he was, six foot four in his shoes and twenty stone), best remembered for stating that 'poets have been mysteriously silent on the subject of cheese'.[128] In mockery, Pound transformed him into a cake of soap: 'Lo, how it gleams and glistens in the sun / Like the cheek of a Chesterton.'[129]

In September 1920, Chesterton was on the cusp of conversion to Catholicism. In a serialisation that month of his book *The New Jerusalem*, he finally responded to the articles in the *New Age* of the previous summer in which Pound had taken a half-hearted swipe at the Catholic Church. He called Pound a *vagabond* pursuing a *dim tribal tendency* and *blind aboriginal impulse* – a habitual language of ethnic offence that had already marked Chesterton as an anti-Semite: 'In plain words,' he wrote of Pound, 'this sort of theory is a blasphemy against the intellectual dignity of man.'[130] Pound would bat the assault aside. It was impossible to be annoyed by Mr Chesterton's calling him 'a Boche, a bungler, and a blasphemer', he wrote in reply, 'since Mr Chesterton has so long been engaged in trying to prove that no word means anything in particular, and that precision of language is undesirable.'[131] It was a witty and well-judged put-down that would have tickled Eliot at the time. But times would change, and in the years after Eliot had joined the Church of England in 1927 he would write that Chesterton's religious views (like Eliot, he had been brought up a Unitarian) placed him 'consistently on the side of the angels'.[132] Pound's spat with Chesterton in 1920 would be merely a warm-up for the disagreement he would have with Eliot in the 1930s. By then, Eliot and Pound had taken their disagreement over religion into print in a public and, for Eliot at least, distressing way.

In a lecture given in Virginia, in 1930, and later reprinted in *After Strange Gods* in 1934, Eliot made an incendiary remark.

The population should be homogeneous; where two or more cultures exist in the same place they are likely either to be fiercely self-conscious or both to become adulterate. What is still more important is unity of religious background; and reasons of race and religion combine to make any large number of free-thinking Jews undesirable.[133]

Eliot would be asked to explain this remark for years to come. He would tell a former Harvard student, J. V. Healy, in 1940 that by 'free-thinking' he had not intended a racial slur, but despair at the fading effects of a religion which its practitioners were unwilling to practise.[134] By the time Eliot clarified himself to Isaiah Berlin in 1952, a complete picture of the horror of Nazi concentration camps was before him: 'The sentence of which you complain (with justice) would never have appeared at all at that time, if I had been aware of what was going to happen, indeed had already begun, in Germany,' he wrote. 'I still do not understand why the word "race" occurs in the sentence, because my emphasis was on the adjective "freethinking".'[135] Another decade and another explanation, to a journalist in 1964: 'I did make the statement which you quote, but I have ever since regretted making it in that form, for it was not intended to be anti-semitic. What I had in mind was that I hoped there would be more co-operation between practising Christians and practising Jews, but I agree that the statement as it stands is regrettable.'[136] *After Strange Gods* would be the only substantial work of Eliot's that he chose to keep out of print.

Not unreasonable that Pound might have a bone to pick with Eliot, but this wasn't the bone he chose to pick. Reviewing *After*

Strange Gods, Pound took issue with Eliot's proposition that the weakness of the condition of literature was an effect of the weakness in the condition of religion. So began a correspondence in print that would be sustained in the pages of the *New English Weekly* for almost four months.

As Pound grew more waspish, Eliot grew more wounded. Economic injustice is what ruins lives and isolates people (Pound). It is a lack of religious engagement that prevents a cohesive society (Eliot). A Christian faith will eradicate the need for inequality (Eliot). A Christian Church enforces inequality (Pound).[137]

By the time the *New English Weekly* was moving into its fourth month of coverage, Eliot was determined to sign off. Someone had to sweep up after Ezra, and as it seemed he wouldn't stop flinging tomatoes Eliot was going to take his leave in the personal code of Brer Rabbit that the two used in their private correspondence.

> I am going to set round the chimbly and have a chaw terbacker with Miss Meadows and the gals; and then I am going away for a 4tnight where that ole Rabbot can't reach me with his letters nor even with his post cards.[138]

For all the outrage, what the two men expressed so publicly in *New English Weekly* was no more than a magnification of the differences already growing between them in 1920 that would take such sharp relief in the poetry to come: the hope for economic justice in *The Cantos*, the desire for spiritual direction in *The Waste Land*.

//

The search for a new flat had dragged on into October. 'We have been worried out of our wits,'[139] Eliot told his mother. 'I simply cannot any longer work where we are, or even rest. I have of course been unable to write, or even read and think, for some weeks.' The anticipated expense meant that the Eliots knew they might have to consider living without Ellen Kellond, their maid of four years, who accepted low wages and large responsibilities – including nursing the both of them – that no one else would; they hoped she would stay, but had to find a flat in which they could manage if she were to leave. As it was, the Eliots' immediate fears for Ellen were unfounded: she stayed with them until she married in 1926. Vivien described her then as her greatest and almost only friend of nine years.[140] Such was the intimacy with Ellen that, during a period in the winter of 1925 of enforced isolation in a nursing home, Vivien poured out her fears that her husband had abandoned her. 'You see, he no longer wants me and no longer cares for me,' wrote Vivien at the time. 'O Ellen what shall I do what shall I do.' Kept against her will, Vivien said that she was being tortured with neglect, cruelty and despair. 'I mean to take my life. At the first opportunity I shall do so. It is difficult here, but I shall find a way. This is the end.'[141] It may be that the distress of this episode hastened Ellen's departure from service three months later. Vivien said in 1928: 'She can never be replaced';[142] and she is forever etched into 'A Game of Chess' in *The Waste Land*. It was from Ellen's accounts that the Albert and Lil sequence was created – 'pure Ellen Kellond', was the description Eliot gave later to the passage.[143] When her husband William Sollory lost his job as a foreman in a metalworks in 1932, Eliot supported him financially, and sought legal advice on his behalf that led to the labour exchange making payments that it had previously denied. 'You have been a God send to me,' Sollory told Eliot; 'I only wish I could be of some service to you in return.'[144]

//

Every day, without missing a day, William Carlos Williams had written down something – *anything* – that came to mind, and that wasn't to be changed. For a year he did so, and then, after that year, he went back to the words he had written and went through them once more, adding a commentary below them.[145] They were 'wild flights', he said later, an embarrassment in retrospect, but in October 1920 they were published by the Four Seas Company of Boston as *Kora in Hell: Improvisations*.[146] On one level, he said he had wanted merely to 'sound off', to tell the world and his friends what he thought of them, and most particularly those in London, who were able to see 'no alternative but their own groove'.[147] But there was also a more nationally minded aim, to discover just what a modern American literature might look like, one that didn't adopt the style of the old masters but that might instead find a language and form adequate to the experience of a modernising America. Viewed that way, Eliot was easy pickings, engaged in no more than a rehash of European literature. Williams called him the 'archbishop of procurers to a lecherous antiquity', someone who looked backward, someone who had rejected America.[148] That was no surprise; but what he said of his old friend Ezra was certainly shocking. Williams published a personal letter he had received from Pound in 1917 ('you're such a devil for printin' one's private affairs' – Pound) which had challenged the grounds of Williams's Americanism.[149] Williams knew nothing of the prairies of the Sierra Nevada, Pound had written: WOT could he know of America? 'But I (der grosse Ich) have the virus, the bacillus of the land in my blood,' Pound continued, 'for nearly three bleating centuries.'[150] Williams did not like that, and he wasn't about to let anyone – friend or no friend – question his credentials for forging a new literature. It was Pound who was a rogue trader, misrepresenting American verse to Europe, passing off as American what was really European. 'E. P. is the best enemy United States verse has.'[151]

'You're a liar,' Pound snapped on 11 September 1920. His old friend was dissembling, and this was 'bilge, just sloppy inaccurate bilge'.[152] Williams had sat on his prescription backside (he was by employment a physician), while Pound had been fighting a troubadour's fight 'for honest clear statement in verse'. Pound never claimed to be writing 'US poetry', and didn't give a curse for international divisions. 'I don't care a fried – – – – about nationality,' he told Williams, who was nothing if not a hypocrite: a second-generation émigré ('Spanish, French, English, Danish' wrote Pound, though his parents grew up in the Caribbean), and Williams had all the benefit of 'the fresh flood of Europe' in his veins.[153] Pound and Eliot, by contrast, were old 'Yankees' despairing at the generational decay of their culture: they simply couldn't have stayed. 'There is a blood poison in America,' said Pound, moving the matter further onto troubled grounds. 'You don't need to fight the disease day and night; you never have had to. Eliot has it perhaps worse than I have – poor devil.' The blood poison was not named, but the inference was clear. It was immigration, and Pound gave voice to resentment at the erosion of Anglo-Saxon Protestant settler values, to which Pound might as well have added 'White'. 'The "race problem" begins where personal friendliness ceases,'[154] Pound had written in the *New Age* that summer with a pose of tolerance; but whatever his motivation then, his language was so addled with tropes about 'the old South', generational stereotypes and use of the n-word, that any effort to be progressive appeared undermined by many of its own assumptions.

//

Eliot and Pound's first articles for *The Dial* came at almost the same moment. Eliot's was the lead contribution that November,[155] and took for its theme poetic drama – one among several poetic forms, Eliot acknowledged, but the one most capable of *greater variation* and expressing *more varied types of society*. Its key lay not simply in shape, rhyme and rhythm, but also in the half-formed matter surrounding it – what he called the 'temper of the age' – the stimuli of the moment to which a public would respond. The task at hand, he wrote, is to seize the permanence of thought and feeling by *simplifying* it through actions and objects that an audience can understand. This requires the artist to meld form and temper into a 'precise statement of life which is at the same time a point of view, a world'. To be at once both a point of view *and* a world places a supreme stress upon an art: depersonalisation, he had said before, is the method of transfer from personal view to public world, but what material could possibly lend itself to such variety in form and temper? Entertainment could do that, he believed – entertainment subjected to a process that would transmute it into art. Few at the time agreed that popular culture could be the matter of art, but Eliot was now imagining culture beyond what was considered 'lower' and 'higher', in a way that would energise the long poem he was contemplating. 'Perhaps the music-hall comedian is the best material,' he wrote.

//

'*The Sacred Wood* is the most stimulating, the most intelligent, and the most original contribution to our critical literature during the last decade.'[156] By the time Richard Aldington wrote these words for the journal *Today*, in September 1921, the reception of Eliot's critical essays had already been assured. Published in November 1920, it carried eighteen pieces from 1919 and 1920: half taken from *The Athenaeum*, three of them new, and included among them his essays on Hamlet, Dante, 'Tradition and the Individual Talent', opening with 'The Perfect Critic'. The book's title, like the notes to *The Waste Land*, would draw from James Frazer's *The Golden Bough* – here, a competition among priests to be King of the Wood[157] in a seeming allusion to the competitive flavour of professional literary London. But in its preliminary material, the book would carry a more private reference besides.

An epigraph, taken from the *Satyricon* by Petronius, in a translation of the time, read, 'I am a poet,' he said, 'and one, I hope, of
no mean imagination, if one can reckon at all by crowns of honour, which gratitude can set even on unworthy heads.'[158] If there
was any doubt to whom Eliot was addressing these proud words,
the mystery would be clarified five pages later: FOR / H. W. E.
/ 'TACUIT ET FECIT'.[159] *He was silent and acted*: the Eliot family
motto, cast into the past tense.[160] The next time Eliot would draw
on Petronius and Frazer it would be for an epigraph and a note
to *The Waste Land*.

Very quickly it was clear that *The Sacred Wood* was to serve
in exactly the way Eliot had hoped, as a concentration of his
theory of impersonality. For it was on this that the first reviews
would focus, often going out of their way to summarise Eliot's
argument. One, a literary work is an object that arouses emotion; two, the poet manufactures an object that elicits feeling in
others rather than one that has given voice to his or her own
feelings; three, the success of that accomplishment is measured
in the reader's engagement with the object; four, in any assessment of that engagement, the critic must illuminate that emotion
without reliance upon emotions of their own. Some reviewers
produced allegories of their own. The *New Statesman* likened the
role of the poet to a dumb man expressing what he is feeling
by holding up objects one after another; it was not the object
itself that was the subject of his thoughts, but the emotions it
suggested to the reader. It was for criticism, wrote John Middleton Murry in the *New Republic*, to assay the degree of perfection
with which this act is performed and to describe the quality of
art that it produced. In so doing, Eliot had elevated criticism to
its rightful realm, wrote Marianne Moore in *The Dial*: *a genuine
achievement in criticism is an achievement in creation.*[161]

Not everyone concurred that the author had achieved his effect.
The Times thought Eliot's account was less disinterested than

he admitted – *perverted by malice*, no less – betraying a personal investment in a literature of detachment.[162] The result was a critical failure, thought *The Nation*.[163] More meticulous was his old friend Conrad Aiken, who questioned the notion that art could be impersonal or scientific, or even that Eliot himself was clear what he meant when he wrote in such terms. To understand art we must begin with its social function, and see it as a force in the community of life itself. Eliot, thought Aiken, was looking in the wrong place: 'life' should come first; Eliot's 'aesthetic' or 'science' second.[164]

But even for the critics who disagreed with the answer, the question asked of whether poetry should be personal or impersonal was now at the heart of discussion. From what material should the poet write? In what form should experience be transmitted? The answers were debatable, but as the *New Statesman* put it, whenever the question of modern poetry was raised, the name T. S. Eliot was now certain to come up.[165]

Why did it matter so deeply to Eliot to consolidate the link between poetry and criticism? Because they were interlocutory. Each engaged the other in a mutually supportive dialogue. Criticism was capable of energising poetry with the rigour it needed for deep development. Poetry, too, can do that for itself, but was slower to act than journalism. As Pound had observed in an article of that year,[166] even the most modest volume of poetry takes *infinite* time for its ideas to circulate. Criticism can simply get there faster, making its case quickly through the broader readership of prose. Later, Eliot would say that at the time of *The Sacred Wood* he still hadn't quite made up his mind what criticism was *for*; but he had: it was to enable the conditions in which to animate creative writing. Criticism is the chamber of poetry; how the room is arranged is the poem. Eliot had used his criticism of 1919 and 1920 to map the prospectus for the poetry he now wanted to write. One that was learned from the poetry of the past but written in a modern cadence. One that privileged the sensory response of the reader above the directive intent of the writer. One that altered the past as it altered the present. *A new poetry that flowers on the stem of the oldest. An original cadence. An inventive form. A distanced intimacy.* A music hall in which all that was missing was the discovery of cadence and tempo.

'The only criticism of poetry worth noticing is that of poets,' Eliot wrote in a letter of 1927. 'Theoretically, it does not matter at all whether the critic is a poet or not; it is merely true in experience that most of the best critics of poetry have been poets themselves.'[167] And why is the poet important to criticism? Because the poet is the artisan with the skill to manipulate the object through its necessary states of being. The poet is the smith at the poem's forge; the poem is the heated metal; criticism is the anvil over which the object is shaped; when it is cooled, it is for the reader to determine the sensory significance of the artefact.

It was perhaps this that Leonard Woolf meant, when he wrote in *The Athenaeum* that Eliot had produced something that can serve as a foundation for knowledge.[168]

//

John Quinn had offered financial assistance to aid Pound, but he wouldn't accept it, saying that given his plight it should be Eliot who was the first to be saved. *I want to get T. S. E. out of that bank.* And by that he meant to 'release his fading energy for writing; not increase his earnings while he is in the bank'. He didn't give a damn whether his friend made and spent three times what Pound did: he *had* to get him writing. He didn't underestimate the financial commitments that Eliot faced at home: 'If someone wd. murder or elope with his wife it wd. have the same effect as finding a few hundred £.'[169] But Pound's own finances were not all stable. So long as America continued to exclude him then his 'exile' had some reality to it. What work could he actually undertake there? He had no obvious base for lecturing in the universities, and editing promised thin returns. His work with *The Dial* was going well (he had just sent Thomas Hardy the invitation that would produce the poem 'Two Houses'), and two letters from 'The Island of Paris'[170] had been printed there; but surely he and Thayer had reached the natural threshold of their mutual tolerance, and anyway, as William Carlos Williams had pointed out, there was no longer enough of a contemporary American in Pound to think he could edit the poetry of contemporary America. London, for all its attractions, had become a place where he said he could hear only his own playing, and that was not a good place from which to write. He came to Europe to build a civilisation, but instead he felt as though he was administering opiates to a dying patient. 'There is a point at which self-inflicted discomfort becomes mere sadism.'[171] England, he said, seemed unlikely to provide 'the white hope'.[172]

//

In Shirehampton Public Hall, on the River Avon, beginning at ten minutes to eight, the programme of the local choral society promised a 'Grand Concert'. What it premiered that evening was a sonata for violin and piano by Ralph Vaughan Williams. It was a piece written on the eve of the Great War that seemed to pass elusively between the stations of pre-war peace and the horrors that followed, what a review called 'serene disregard of the fashions of today or of yesterday'.[173] The piece was called *The Lark Ascending*. Marie Hall was the violinist that December night, and she would reprise the part for the first orchestrated version in London's Queen's Hall the following summer. It was not a performance that would register in Pound's column as a music critic for the *New Age*, begun that autumn. His attentions had been captured by a different concert and a different performer: a young violinist from Ohio, who played from a haunting catalogue of her own at the Aeolian

Hall, in London's New Bond Street on 10 November. It was a programme to fall for: Handel's Sonata in D, Lalo's Symphonie Espagnole, Boulanger's Nocturne and Cortège, Pizzetti's Sonata in A.[174] And fall Ezra Pound would, when, in 1923, he met the soloist in person rehearsing in Paris. Her name was Olga Rudge, and she would dedicate the next fifty years of her life to Pound; but before then, on that November night in the Aeolian Hall, Pound limited himself to saying simply, 'Olga Rudge charmed one by the delicate firmness of her fiddling.'[175]

If there were a redeeming grace at that moment for Ezra Pound, then it had lain in his hearing. Just as Eliot was tuning up his ear for the composition he was about to begin, so Pound had opened his to an enlivening variety of forms. In the second of his Parisian letters for *The Dial* that November, he had praised the verses of Maurice Vlaminck for their ability to 'make a music for singing'.[176] And he had reminded Ford Madox Ford that summer of his paraphrasing of Dante: 'A poem is a composition of words set to music.'[177] Like Eliot, he was hearing in everything the interconnectedness of poetry and music.

Roland Hayes was the first Black artist to sing spirituals in a programme at Wigmore Hall in London. Pound had been in the audience the night of 28 October for his English debut, and wrote rapturously in the *New Age* of a recital in which, through the purity and clarity of rhythm and expression, Hayes had become the very embodiment of the lyric form: 'The *meaning* of the poem is in him.'[178] It was the variety of his vocal performance that was most arresting: from Southern spirituals to the Parisian opera of Massenet, to the graveside elegies of Paul Laurence Dunbar, not an ascending lark but the kept bird bruised and beating. *I know what the caged bird feels.*[179] Pound could think of no singer who employed 'so many different qualities of voice, from operatic delivery to a singing which is almost speech'. The tapestry of voice and genre was a shared pursuit for Pound and Eliot in the winter of 1920–1.

'The art of fitting words to tunes', wrote Pound in *The Dial*, 'is not to be confused with the art of making words which will be "musical" without tunes.'[180]

//

'*Note new address –* !' Vivien wrote on 17 November. 'Telephone. Pad[dington] 3331.'[181] Four months of flat-hunting had culminated in a long negotiation with an 'insane she-hyaena'[182] of a seller, who had spitefully cut off all the amenities so that Eliot would have to reconnect them. But at last, the Eliots were in.

An Edwardian mansion block inspired by art nouveau and Arts and Crafts influences, Clarence Gate Gardens, Glentworth Street was to be the Eliots' home for the next six years. 'It is a very nice flat,' a relieved Eliot wrote to his mother: only a little more expensive to rent than Crawford Mansions and with half as much floor space again. A corridor ran from the entrance through the spine of the flat and provided a sense of spaciousness that the Eliots had not previously known. Two bedrooms flanked a reasonable sitting room on one side of the corridor, while a box bedroom, bathroom and kitchen lay on the other, which led out to a small balcony at the back. It came with electricity, gas and anthracite stoves throughout, and a constant supply of hot water 'to *all* the building', stressed Eliot to his mother, as well as an aspect, which, for her pleasure, he translated into American: 'First floor (i.e. second floor, American style) and lift (elevator) also.'[183] They had moved less than half a mile north-west across the busy Marylebone Road, and were now just yards from the wrought iron gate that opened onto the boating lake and Clarence Bridge of Regent's Park. An extra room meant they were able to consider both an additional bedroom and a work space for Eliot, but the flat had one still more important advance on Crawford Mansions: it was quiet. For the first time, Eliot was in possession of two ingredients as valuable as any typewriter: he had space and he had quiet.

//

The body of the Unknown Soldier had been carried through the night to a makeshift chapel at Saint-Pol, in Northern France, and placed in a casket carved from an oak tree that had once grown in Hampton Court Palace. It travelled with a military entourage to Boulogne, from where it was conveyed across the Channel aboard HMS *Verdun*, flanked by an escort of six battleships. It docked at the Dover Marine Railway Station on 10 November, the eve of the second Remembrance Day, and was carefully transferred to the meticulously prepared Passenger Luggage Van 132, for an evening departure to Victoria Station. From there the *Daily Mail* recorded its journey:

> The train thundered through the dark, wet, moonless night. At the platforms by which it rushed could be seen groups of women watching and silent, many dressed in deep mourning. [...] In the London suburbs there were scores of homes with back doors flung wide, light flooding out, and in the garden, figures of men, women and children gazing at the great lighted train rushing past.[184]

The Unknown Soldier was laid to rest in Westminster Abbey on 11 November 1920. The procession that had approached the nave heard the cathedral choir sing 'I am the Resurrection and the Life', the signal for the Dean to conduct the service for the Burial of the Dead. The coffin was interred at twenty minutes past eleven in earth carried from the battlefield, bearing red roses and bay leaves from the King.[185]

In Dublin, in the early morning of Sunday 21 November 1920, Michael Collins sent execution squads across the city targeting

British intelligence operatives: fifteen people were killed, some in their beds, one or more in mistaken identity. The response of the Royal Irish Constabulary that day was one of the most shocking events of the War of Independence. Black and Tans drove a truck into a Gaelic football match at Croke Park, between Dublin and Tipperary, and began shooting into the crowd: fourteen were killed, including Jane Boyle, in the week before her wedding, and two boys, William Robinson and Jerome O'Leary, aged eleven and ten. Three men were executed in Dublin Castle that evening, taking the loss of life to thirty-two that day, a Sabbath that became known as Bloody Sunday. In the escalating violence that followed, a patrol of eighteen British auxiliaries was ambushed in Co. Cork a week later: all but one died. In reprisal, Black and Tans burned the city centre of Cork to the ground, shooting at firefighters and beating residents who were attempting to quell the blaze. Up to 350 properties were burned, and two thousand people left homeless or without work.

//

For all the esteem that *The Sacred Wood* would bring, by December Eliot said that he had grown tired of the book, and was anxious to move on to new work. 'I should more enjoy being praised if I were engaged on something which I thought better or more important.' He added, 'I think I shall be able to do so, soon.'[186] But first he would seek to clear his head from the exhaustion of the move, and take a week's holiday from the bank. He would return to Paris, alone, to the pension near the Panthéon, nestled between a poultry shop and a restaurant, where he had stayed on his first visit to Paris in October 1910. It was the place that he shared with Jean Verdenal, when Eliot once lobbed a sugar lump from his window into the garden below in order to get his attention.[187] Eliot and Verdenal had then been taken by the homely charm of the elderly proprietors, Monsieur Casaubon, who served afternoon tea in the garden from a silver pot, and Madame Casaubon, who presided each evening over dinner. Now, in 1920, he returned alone to find that the proprietors had passed away and left the running of the pension in the hands of their grandson.[188] Eliot might have been living among ghosts, he said. For Vivien he bought a drawing ('very cheap') by Raoul Dufy, and saw his brother-in-law Maurice, coincidentally in town, and he made new introductions besides. Without the kind of society that introduced him to new painters and poets, the experience of the city would have felt quite different. The memory of Verdenal was still raw, he told his mother. The word he chose to describe this sense was not without significance for the poem to come. *Desolate*, he wrote, the city would have felt *desolate*.[189]

//

As Eliot returned from Paris to the new flat in London, Pound was making his final arrangements for the journey in reverse. He was, he told his father vaguely just after Christmas, 'in some sort of trajectory toward Orange or Avignon'.[190] The Kensington flat at 5 Holland Park Chambers had been home to the Pounds since before the war, but now it was sublet to Agnes Bedford, a vocal coach and accompanist on *Five Troubadour Songs*, published that month ('full of misprints') by Boosey & Co., with piano arrangements by Bedford and texts in Provençal and Chaucerian English adapted by Pound.[191] Bedford had taken the apartment books and all, allowing Pound to leave his precious clavichord, a gift from Arnold Dolmetsch, in her safe hands. From now on, Bedford would be called upon to send on to Pound whichever of his books he felt he needed at the time. He was leaving London in unknown circumstances, as A. R. Orage announced in the *New Age*, 'perhaps for one year, perhaps for two, perhaps for good'.[192]

The move had been long in coming, but even so the abruptness of the news took Eliot by surprise. 'I infer that there is no prospect of seeing you,' Eliot wrote in a hurried note of 22 December. 'Your letter is extremely obscure, but it appears that you are going South. This is a blow. Please write and explain lucidly what your plans are and for how long.'[193] It was a blow indeed.

It had been Pound who identified a publisher for 'The Love Song of J. Alfred Prufrock', who subsidised the printing of *Prufrock and Other Observations* and found a home for its twelve poems in the literary journals of the day.

It was Pound who pre-published in the *Little Review* each of the seven pieces of the Hogarth *Poems* of 1919.

And it had been Pound who had taken his blue pencil to all but two of the additional pieces that made up *Ara Vos Prec* and the *Poems* of 1920.

Twenty-five poems had been published by Eliot since his arrival in London in 1914: Pound had a traceable hand in twenty-three, and may very well have contributed to them all.

It was Pound who had encouraged Eliot's commitment to England, who had reflected and directed Eliot's reading and thinking, fuelled the modernising fire and taken up arms in the field of criticism. Pound carried him over the threshold with 'Gerontion', and had, for four years as a near neighbour in West London, been the exclusive, unwavering champion of his art.

That man – editor, publisher, adviser, interlocutor, stimulator, supporter, conspirator in his dirty doggerel, Appleplex, Brer Rabbit, cohort, friend – that man was now leaving London behind for ever, and so ending his quotidian life with Eliot.

'If no more,' wrote Eliot, 'Farewell and Pleasure.'[194]

'We are in action of closing up,' said Pound enigmatically two days after Christmas.[195]

Soon after, he was gone.

II.

'Mr Eliot, may I ask a question?'
'Certainly.'
'Er – did you mean that poem seriously?'
Eliot looked non-plussed for a moment, and then said quietly,
'Well, if you think I did not mean it seriously, I have failed utterly.'

– OXFORD UNIVERSITY, 1928[1]

The Burial of the Dead.

'Banker, Critic, Poet': it was in that order that T. S. Eliot listed his occupation for a college alumni report of 1921; in the year ahead, his priorities would be reversed.[1] That New Year's Day, he wrote to Scofield Thayer, explaining that, with Vivien's father having been at the point of death for ten weeks (the surgeon had been so horrified by what he saw that, said Eliot, 'he wanted simply to sew him up and let him die in peace') he had not been able to write the 'London Letter' he had promised for *The Dial*; that, and the move to the new apartment, and the unexpected length of time it took to prepare *The Sacred Wood*, had created a block on his writing of a kind that he had not experienced in five years. He was at the bank six days a week, 9.30 to 5.00, and dividing everything else between evenings and Sundays, which meant that he couldn't possibly accept Thayer's offer to join Pound as a foreign editor for the journal. But he was able to offer some advice in business. He pressed upon Thayer the need not to rely on a subscription ('English people, with very few exceptions, are unused to *subscribing* to anything'), but to secure for the journal instead a physical presence on every bookstall and Underground station.[2] And he imparted advice of a more mercenary kind: on *no* account could Thayer hope to share his writers and readers with the *London Mercury*; for *The Dial* to succeed it would have to be prepared to 'cut the throat' of its rival by enticing away its writers, and that required more than merely financing its contributors: it meant seducing them with the promise of literary esteem. Thayer had already come to the same conclusion himself, and the presence of four drawings by

E. E. Cummings (one, a fawn rising onto to its hind legs before a nude woman) seemed to signal a clear divergence from the readership of the *Mercury*. But more likely still to have caught Eliot's eye was surely a description of Paris given by Ezra Pound in that issue. 'In a city the visual impressions succeed each other, overlap, overcross, they are cinematographic, but they are not a simple linear sequence,' he wrote. 'They are often a flood of nouns with verbal relations.'[3]

The Pounds had made the crossing to France early in the first week of the new year. On 10 January 1921, the *Paris Herald* printed a welcome to Ezra, 'just arrived in Paris from London', which seemed just the new beginning needed after a loveless departure from England. The Pounds spent ten days in the city before travelling south to Saint-Raphaël on the Côte d'Azur, where they would rest for the next three months. While Pound was only too pleased to leave his typewriter behind, Eliot was frustrated over his inability to settle at his. Vivien, too, was worried: Tom was so much better than he was at Christmas, she reassured Mrs Eliot, but he lived in constant distress that he could achieve so little writing. 'He gets tired with his long day at the Bank,' she reported, 'and feels more inclined for a quiet evening of reading, and early to bed, than to begin the real business of his life, and sit up late.'[4] But on the very week that Vivien would write those words to Charlotte, Eliot was indeed up late – and was, in Vivien's perceptive language, at last about to immerse himself in the real business of his life.

On the weekend of 22 January, Eliot finished the first piece of writing of any kind that he had managed for six months.[5] Prepared for *The Dial*'s American readership, it was the inaugural one of eight bimonthly reports from London, 'dealing with the literary life of the metropolis'.[6] The writing had come hard, he admitted, and the piece had been rewritten twice, but it was at least a breakthrough.[7] In it, Eliot labelled provincialism and dullness as 'the two stupidities' of British and American literary culture, and made some fairly provocative announcements besides. 'Culture is traditional, and loves novelty'; 'the General Reading Public knows no tradition, and loves staleness.' It was a salvo unlikely to win admirers: general readers were uncritical and therefore to be ignored, he had written, while cultured readers were snobs to be ridiculed. And ridiculed they most certainly would be, as Eliot focused his scorn upon what he defined as the 'Georgian' public: 'that offensive part of the middle class which believes itself superior to the rest of the middle class; and superior for precisely this reason that it believes itself to possess culture'.[8] It wasn't entirely apparent which readers might remain available for Eliot's attention, but one of them could have been Harold Monro, the man who had turned down Prufrock, and whose *Some Contemporary Poets: 1920*, published two months ago, Eliot now prepared to etherise under the critical knife.

Harold Monro had intended his book as a health check for contemporary poetry by one well placed for the job: he owned the Poetry Bookshop that had traded on Devonshire Street since before the war, and had been the founding editor of London's *Poetry Review* as an all-comers' showcase for poetry. But Monro wasn't quite where he thought he was: recently discharged from the army, he had fallen behind the curve, and didn't apprehend the fractious moment in poetry to which he had returned. He couldn't understand why the poets would no longer harmonise as once they had when he launched his anthology *Georgian Poets* in 1912, and he was in no mood to forgive petty squabbles. Old allies were brutally discarded. Poets he once published were written off as *turgid* (Lascelles Abercrombie), *facile* (Wilfrid Wilson Gibson), *insufficiently profound*, *specious* and *wearisome* (Robert Graves, John Drinkwater and D. H. Lawrence).[9] And that was merely the 'Georgians': more troublesome still were the modernisers. Neither Eliot's poetry nor his name had been considered worthy of inclusion, but Pound's had. Despite more than a dozen poetry collections to his name,

Pound was relegated by Monro to 'a mere experimenter in unusual rhythms' whose unfashionable obsession with archaic verse left him isolated and irascible, pelting his peers with paper darts.[10] It was, said Monro, simply bad manners for the poet content to scorn a botched civilisation, as Mauberley had, to make himself so comfortable as a permanent resident in its culture, which by now Pound no longer was.

Eliot was unimpressed. Criticism must work harder than this, he insisted, as readers were entitled to more insight than adjectives alone could bring, and what Monro had served up was mere middle-class smudge. There could be no literature without critical sense; and good criticism is the parent of good poetry.[11] And for once, Eliot did not stand alone in his critical opinion. Such was the outpouring of ill temper towards the book that Monro decided he had better lie low, and in January 1921 he left hurriedly for the Villa des Oliviers in France, illness the given reason, a flight duly honoured in the *Saturday Westminster Gazette* with 'Obituary Verses':

> Harold Monro
> Had got to go
> And (considering the kind of book he's been writing about his
>   friends lately)
> 'Tis better so.[12]

Monro, the last unifier in London's polarised poetic scene, had stepped out of the fray. *The Dial* had given up on its effort to be non-denominational. No one and no journal would now attempt to bring together the Georgian and the new poetries.

//

'It will be several months before I have any verse ready for publication,' Eliot told Scofield Thayer on 30 January, just after delivery of his first 'London Letter'.[13] Thayer was disappointed: 'Why no verse?' he responded, and served friendly notice that he felt this was a question that he hoped should never again need asking.[14] But Eliot hadn't said that there was *no* verse, only that it would take *time* in coming, and as January turned to February he did have a draft underway. At last, conditions for writing had altered. The noisy, overbearing surroundings of Crawford Mansions and the hours of flat-hunting were now behind him; the vigils for Vivien's father were over after he 'miraculously' stabilised and began a convalescence in Tunbridge Wells and Eastbourne. Vivien had relapsed after months of stress, and had taken to bed with a throat infection that had left her temporarily mute. Tired as he was – and he was: when Virginia Woolf saw him for lunch on Fleet Street she described him as 'pale, marmoreal Eliot' – he finally had peace.[15] And momentary as it would be, he had now found a place: one that was quiet and temperamentally stable, if only for a brief time, but long enough that he began to see the prospect of that longed-for period of tranquillity. The publication of *The Sacred Wood* had consolidated his critical reputation and removed any need to prove himself. His 'London Letter' had reawakened the ritual of writing. His visit to Paris had rekindled in him the energy of that pre-war time with Jean Verdenal and thrilled his sense of the *nouveau*; it had stimulated, as Pound had just written, filmic impressions overlapping, overcrossing, the flood of nouns and verbal relations.[16] He had spoken of hoping at last to be *able to get some work done*, 30 January, and before that of his wish to *settle down to work now*, 22 January. He had been anxious *to get on to new work*, December 1920; had wanted *to get to work on a poem he had in mind*, October 1920; sought a period of tranquillity *to do a poem that he had in mind*, September 1920; *to get settled quietly and write some poetry*, September again.[17] The straining verbs said it all: to get on, to get to, to do – a pressure he had experienced since November 1919, when he had first said that he *hoped to get started on a poem he had in mind*.[18] He had a lot of things to write about if the time ever

came when people would attend to them: December 1917. He had
lived through material for a score of long poems: January 1916.[19]

//

The Phoenix Society might have failed in their 1919 revival of *The
Duchess of Malfi*, but the production of Ben Jonson's *Volpone* brought
to the Hammersmith Lyric for two nights, 30 January and 1 February, played to a rapturous response. W. B. Yeats said he could think
of nothing else for hours after he left the theatre, Aldous Huxley
that he couldn't remember a production of such unmixed pleasure.[20] It was, Eliot would reflect in an article that summer for *The
Dial*, 'the most important theatrical event of the year in London':
a superbly executed demonstration of Jonson's unity of inspiration, terrifying in its directness, as bold as it was shocking.[21] But
the occasion was also significant for something that happened off
stage. Eliot had seen Wyndham Lewis at the theatre that evening,
and had hinted to him that something new was underway. 'Eliot,
like myself, seems to have been engaged in some obscure and intricate task of late,' Lewis told Violet Schiff in puzzlement, 'though
what *his* task has been I cannot say.'[22] He *hoped* that it was writing,
and said he intended to encourage Eliot in 'the writing of a poem
or two'; whatever it was, he sensed something unusual: 'It will be
music for some time to come, I hope.'

The 'music' was to materialise a few days later, when on 5 February, Lewis would meet again with Eliot, and this time he was
given sight of the 'intricate task' which had been occupying him.
'He is doing his article,' Lewis told Violet's husband Sydney, for
the 'paper in preparation' that would become his new journal, *The
Tyro*, financed by Schiff, to which Eliot had agreed to contribute.
But that wasn't the task in question. For Lewis had been permitted
to see something in draft that day that was far more significant
than the article. 'He also showed me a new long poem (in 4 parts)

which I think will be not only very good, but a new departure for him.'[23] Lewis did not reveal the title of the new long poem in four parts, but almost certainly it had one, and it is likely to have been the title that forms part of the poem today.

Eliot had found his way to his title long ago, at Harvard in 1913, where it had begun a five-line verse with its opening rite, 'I am the Resurrection and the Life'.[24] There he had left it, unpublished but stored, a lyric that would be preserved among the papers for *The Waste Land* gifted to John Quinn in 1922, and for a reason: eight years after its composition, in the wake of his father's death, it would seemingly provide the 'new long poem (in 4 parts)' with its first and most elegiac title, a service of rites from The Book of Common Prayer.

> *I held my tongue, and spake nothing: I kept silence, yea, even from good words; but it was pain and grief to me . . . My heart was hot within me; and while I was thus musing the fire kindled: . . . For I am a stranger with thee: and a sojourner, as all my fathers were . . . In the morning it is green, and groweth up: but in the evening it is cut down, dried up, and withered . . . he fleeth as it were a shadow, . . . In the midst of life we are in death: . . . dust to dust; . . . he is able to subdue all things to himself . . . O Father, to raise us from the death of sin unto the life of righteousness; . . . Come, ye blessed children of my father . . .*[25]

Eliot's typewriter had seen better days. It was a Corona, 'my wretched old one', that he had carried over in his suitcase from Harvard in 1914.[26] Since then seven years of essays and letters and poems had worn thin the mechanism, landing his heavily used vowels unevenly above the baseline. As he sat before it in the winter of 1921, he centred the carriage, and depressed the shift lock. The strikers swung up from the type basket, prompting the escapement forward, letter by letter: a title, concluded as were all his titles, with a terminal point.

THE BURIAL OF THE DEAD.

He rolled the platen twice for a two-line drop, and began to type the poem's opening. But it was not 'April is the cruellest month', the line that would become synonymous with the poem, but something altogether different.

In January 1921, Eliot had written to Maxwell Bodenheim to say he found life in England more comfortable than in America: 'I can get a drink of very bad liquor of any sort when I want it; which is important to me.'[27] Prohibition had been in force for a year in the United States, and was a subject on Eliot's mind that winter. In the essay he was writing for Lewis, 'The Romantic Englishman', he made a coded comparison between lives of the seventeenth century and those of the present day, speculating that our forebears were 'surrounded, indeed, by fewer prohibitions', or by 'the petrified product which the public school pours into our illimitable suburbs'.[28] It was a cause that was about to become the opening theme of the poem that had been so long in the planning. He typed:

First we had a couple of feelers down at Tom's place,
There was old Tom, boiled to the eyes, blind,[29]

The poem was to begin not with April or lilacs or with the spring rain that we know today, but with night-time, booze and brothels. Its voice was that of 'a nice guy – but rough', an unnamed guide who would direct a small crowd of companions through the back streets of an unnamed city ('Boston' was given by Valerie Eliot in 1971) in the draft's opening scenes.[30] Drinks were followed by dinner, then by a smoke and an adult 'show' at which the companions overstepped the permissible boundaries and found themselves ejected. More drink was taken, while one of the company tried for a way in at a boudoir to be told by its proprietor that she's not in business for guys like him, and indeed barely in business at all now, 'what with the damage done' by the new licensing laws. When a policeman interrupts the party in an alleyway for 'committing a

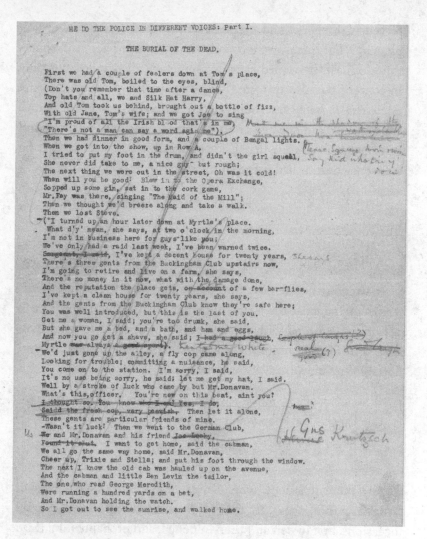

nuisance' (relieving themselves), arrest is avoided only by the chance arrival of the influential Mr Donavan, who takes the revellers onward in search of another club, running a hundred yards on a bet, and home.

It was knockabout stuff – bawdy, risqué in its subject and vernacular – fuelled by liquor and a slurring movement between popular songs in a continuous stanza of fifty-four lines. Undoubtedly it revved with energy and excitement, a soaked world of whirling pleasures, but there was, too, something wayward about it, something offbeat. It seemed scrawny, somehow, dishevelled not only in content but also in form. For one thing, he hadn't found the *distinctive cadence* that Pound had described as typical of Eliot's style, but instead hovered around a blank verse with just the kind of conversational tone that Eliot had said in a 1919 essay that he was set against. It had yet to think musically:

The next thing we were out in the street, Oh was it cold!

The vocalisation was rough, even ragged:

And now you go get a shave, she said; I had a good laugh,

It wouldn't be the last time that Eliot would tune in to such voices to dramatise the poem, but when next he did it would be in a London pub, and with the benefit of Vivien's ear to finesse his own. But for the meantime, the opening lines remained uncomfortable and unworn, awkward at the ear:

What's this, officer. You're new on this beat, aint you?
I thought so. You know who I am? Yes, I do,
Saidd the fresh cop, very peevish.

It isn't known exactly when Eliot produced the first page of typescript, but it appears that he revisited the draft on separate occasions, first in pen and then in pencil, and probably for a third time following that. His first pass was slight: he struck a *good laugh* for a *couple of laughs* and then reverted when he returned by pencil, before cancelling the phrase altogether. He trialled similar efforts in lines with the police officer: correcting first in ink and then cancelling as an afterthought in pencil; it seems he tried to break the single stanza into three at this time. The second edit, by pencil, was more determined, tightening the phrasing, deleting a line and several half-lines that seemed pernickety in their steps. And he reworked a name for its entrance into the German Club: *Joe Leahy* became *Heinie Krutzsch* became *Gus Krutzsch*. But he continued to struggle with the musical tone, ringing lines of song he'd taken from the 1908 musical *Fifty Miles from Boston* ('*I'm proud of all the Irish blood that's in me*'), and replacing them with two turn-of-the-century songs, each crossed out in favour of something closer to 'home': a ragtime tune called 'The Cubanola Glide', by Harry Von Tilzer of the Tin Pan Alley, who had in his time written music for the St Louis brewers Anheuser-Busch. Eliot struggled, too, with the speaking voices, and had repeated attempts at a conversation held at the bordello door, and finally struck out lines reprimanding the policeman. It seemed he knew the tone that he was after, but he hadn't teased out a memorable expression for it.

A second page was spooled into the typewriter's paper rest: four spaced asterisks marked a sub-section, and above those a folio number, '2'.[31] And below, there it came: a line that was to become among the most well known in literature, a frame so defining that generations of readers would commit it to heart.

April is the cruellest month

Only that wasn't the line, but part of it, for the full line would in fact read,

April is the cruellest month, breeding

It was a verb to make the difference: not a month of grow-ing or nourishing or nurturing as any other spring might expect, but *breeding*, as animals and bacteria breed, and in a moment of utmost cruelty. Its startling place at the line ending served as a supercharger, and would fuel the early engine of the poem through a chain of reacting echoes. *Breeding, mixing, stirring, covering, feeding*: so ended five of the first six lines, propelling the poem forward. It was a sequence of nouns with guardian adjectives: *cruellest* month, *dead* land, *dull* roots, *forgetful* snow, *little* life, *dried* tubers; only the spring rain countered the withered tone, like a memory of the once sweet downpour of Chaucer's 'Whan that Aprill with his shoures soote'.[32]

The 'Boston' lines had been plucky, if not wicked, but already from this second page it was clear how artificial an opening at 'Tom's place' would now be. For here, in this second section, lay the heart-work of the subject, and the emotional hard-wiring of the poem to come.

> April is the cruellest month, breeding
> Lilacs out of the dead land, mixing
> Memory and desire, stirring
> Dull roots with spring rain.
> Winter kept us warm, covering
> Earth in forgetful snow, feeding
> A little life with dried tubers.

A distinctive cadence. A personal modus of arrangement. Remote origins of a personal quality. Each of Pound's three tests for a poem was met in these seven lines. In form it was quite unlike anything else: neither Georgian (of course) nor Imagist either, nor resembling anything else of Eliot's, besides perhaps a partial likeness to the recent 'Gerontion'. Even the number of lines themselves was unusual – *seven* – not quatrains or the more familiar compliance of six or eight lines, but a tilt from the top that established a new timing from the outset. And then, mid-stanza, having anchored the septet, it tilted once more. *Summer surprised us.* The breath lengthened, the pace slowed, and it swept into an alliterative glide of swirling 's's and whirling 'w's, in a carousel of sound and childhood: *summer, shower, stopped, sunlight, winter, warm, when we were.*

The first of a busy cast of characters would take to the poem's stage: enter a Lithuanian who feels not Russian but German, in a symbol of warring Prussia; enter the reminiscence of Countess Marie Larisch von Moennich, the disgraced go-between in the doomed affair of the Archduke Rudolf, Crown Prince of Austria and his lover. In these twin characters alone lay the fall of two great empires, and, just as importantly, an *accent* for the poem. Like 'a set of snapshots' or sepia postcards spilled out upon a table, here were the first of the sensory signals that the Boston scene hadn't managed to convey – the 'object correlatives', as Eliot had come to call them – the symbols that he believed might serve to stir the emotive response of the reader: 'the faded poor souvenirs of passionate moments'.[33] Here, too, was the tone for the cameo chatter that would carry throughout the corridors of the poem: the overheard voices and glimpsed faces that bring only a 'partial realisation', characters that were to be drawn from music hall, comedy revue and cinema, who between them contained the possibility of combining to 'provide fragments of a possible English myth'.[34] This was an ancient idea that he had already observed in the works of Seneca: of members of a minstrel troupe 'rising in turn each to do his "number", or varying their recitations by a song or a little back-chat'.[35] But in Eliot's hands it had infused the technology of its day. The flicker of a moving picture, the jump of a gramophone needle, the rapid revolve akin to what Eliot always liked to call 'the wireless' (Stravinsky noted that Eliot had a fondness for such 'horse-drawn phrases' as 'the wireless').[36] It is not without reason that in 1945 the poem would be likened to the experience of listening to stations on a long-wave radio while tuning the dial between them.[37]

Another row of asterisks and another section. Ezekiel in the valley of dry bones, unable to decipher what stirs and what doesn't. A heap of broken images. (*And your altars shall be desolate, and your images shall be broken.*)[38] And for the first time, but not the last, a plunder from Eliot's earlier work: four lines chiselled from the rock of a 1915 poem, 'The Death of St Narcissus': *grey* it was then, now *red*, as the red-rock ochre of the caves of Font de Gaume, *Come in under the shadow of this red rock.*

A final part, a further line of asterisks marking a gateway. Here, a sailor's song from the doomed love story of *Tristan and Isolde*, Wagner (*Fresh blows the wind for home, my Irish child, where do you roam?*) rolling right into the hyacinth girl who, after a decade's silence, Eliot would tell Emily Hale was for her – his last romantic connection to America, a flower girl forgotten by the one who loves her, one who was neither living nor dead, the love of a ghost by a ghost. In 1930, Eliot would ask her to reread these lines as a measure of his love for her. 'I shall always write primarily for you.'[39]

Then Madame Sosostris and her wicked pack of cards foretasting the rise and fall of waters that would bring fertility and demise: 'Fear death by water,' she says.[40]

~~Terrible~~ city. No, that was not quite right, and returning the typewriter carriage to the start of the line, he retyped, in so doing finding in a flash what would be one of the poem's defining phrases. *Unreal City.*

He had almost reached the conclusion of the draft when, just four lines from the end, the typescript ribbon ran out of ink. Left with two faint lines he could barely read, Eliot changed the spool on his machine, and typed back over the top of the faded strokes, and in so doing he added a line:

You who were with me in the ships at Mylae!

Whether a spontaneous addition or a line left out at first by mistake, in its reference to the naval triumph of Rome over Carthage, an allusion to John Maynard Keynes and the Great War had been impressed into the poem.

Three pages of typescript, four parts, six stanzas, 130 lines. Too long, perhaps, and did the Boston beginning at 'Tom's place' read too much like a prologue? He would very soon return to take a look at that. But a draft – finally a draft – after all this time. 'The Burial of the Dead' was underway.

//

When an interviewer said in 1959 that he'd heard that Eliot composed on the typewriter, he received a qualified reply. 'Partly on the typewriter,' Eliot responded, and offered an insight into his recent play, *The Elder Statesman*, saying that it was initially produced in pencil on paper, before he transferred it to the machine.[41] 'In typing myself I make alterations,' he said, 'very considerable ones.' The early poems of the *Prufrock* years were mostly begun in manuscript and occasionally transferred to typescript (Conrad Aiken possessed a sheet produced by Eliot in splendid purple italic on a Blickensderfer). But for the poems of the 'French' style – the Hogarth, Ovid and Knopf editions – and for the period of *The Waste Land* – a run of five years and perhaps sixteen poems – Eliot appears to have altered his approach. In August 1916, he told Aiken that he was composing on the typewriter and enjoying lucidity and compression as a result.[42] Most likely, he was thinking of his prose when he wrote this, but it may not be a coincidence that from that moment no draft manuscripts at all survive until the pages of *The Waste Land* in 1921. Some papers may have been written and destroyed in the act of transfer onto the machine, a moment which, to Eliot, marked the end of their practical value; but the condition of some initial typescripts – many in states of reasonably heavy revision – suggests that at this time Eliot was making his first drafts directly onto the typewriter. Or at least that he was making his first *full* drafts on the typewriter, allowing for the possibility that fragmentary scraps or 'scattered lines', as he referred to them when writing to John Quinn, had provided a source from which to draw – what in Margate later in 1921 he gave another name to, when he called them 'rough' drafts. Two years after the publication of *The Waste Land*, he said of 'The Hollow Men' in 1924 that 'I compose on the typewriter,' and repeated the phrase word for word to a poet in 1927, adding: 'The nearest approach to a manuscript I ever have is the first draft with pencil corrections.'[43] That seemed an exact description for *The Waste Land*: a first full draft in typescript, sometimes from scattered lines that were destroyed once used, with corrections to the typescript made by hand, in pencil and in ink. Two years later he told the Bodleian: 'I work mostly on the typewriter from rough notes, which I usually destroy.'[44] His process was crystallised in the mid-1930s in a letter to a younger author:

> My practice is to start a passage with a few pencilled pages, and then when I get going I usually continue it on the typewriter, so that I should never have a complete pencilled manuscript of any poem of any length, and I never have any ink manuscripts at all, unless I prepare them especially.[45]

'As for verse,' he wrote to his brother at the same time, 'I usually make a few rough notes and then draft and redraft on the machine. Sometimes I start with a pencil and then when I have got going work straight on with the typewriter.'[46] He went still further in 1940 with the mother of Hope Mirrlees, saying that he could *only* think with a typewriter – so much so that there were occasions where he typed first and copied out in longhand second, indicating that 'my typing is equivalent to other people's handwriting, and my handwriting to other people's typing'.[47] The mechanical process of compilation aided the process of composition.

It was the typescripts, not the manuscript 'roughs', that were the precious object for Eliot. A single page took ardent effort to produce, as well as attention to preserve. Three sheets would be fed into the machine: two leaves sandwiching a carbon sheet. The top or 'ribbon' copy was always the most legible and would ideally be the one submitted to printers and publishers, but sometimes it was the clearer copy for annotating and would be the sheet that Eliot would share with friends. In that case, he would keep back the carbon copy for his records, and sometimes annotate that accordingly. Whether ribbon or carbon, copies were not for his friends to keep: an author needed them back for correction or submission, or else face the prospect of retyping from scratch. On occasion, a new copy would be necessary for just that reason, or because a redraft was sufficiently dramatic to require it. Friends may have clung on to pages longer than they should, and printers often recycled their setting copies once their job was complete: gaps in the record are the most likely explanations for 'missing' copies of typescript. Having both ribbon and carbon copies out with friends at the same time could speed the return of criticism, but it was also a risk, and may have caught Eliot out when he had no typescript of 'Gerontion' to take with him to France as both copies were in circulation. Where a typescript was annotated or revised for a second time, a different medium might be adopted: pencil in one instance, pen in another to distinguish a hierarchy of marking. But often a typescript was only as clean or as 'finished' as it needed to be for a reader or printer to follow, and was frequently a work in progress.

In 1968, when Eliot's bibliographer Donald Gallup became the first to document the rediscovered pages of *The Waste Land* in the New York Public Library, he recorded that many of the typescript pages were probably 'first draft'.[48] The bibliographer had been given only limited time to make his assessment before the archive was opened to the public, but nonetheless, his instinct had chimed with a remark made by Eliot only months after finishing the poem. In September 1922, he would tell John Quinn that 'the large[r] part is really typescript for which no manuscript except scattered lines, ever existed'.[49] Those that did exist were often destroyed by Eliot himself, as he had told the Bodleian, for reasons that were peculiar to Eliot's unusual mind. For some poets, drafting is not always progressive: some go back to go forward, preserving their drafts in order to reconnect to elements that might have been excised along the way. But Eliot's brain worked differently, and when he destroyed a manuscript he did so for one of two reasons: either because its content had been subsumed into a typescript, or because he wished it to continue to stir chemically in his mind. 'As a rule,' he told an interviewer of 1959, 'with me an unfinished thing is a thing that might as well be rubbed out.' Erasure was part of the process of making something new.

> It's better, if there's something good in it that I might make use of elsewhere, to leave it at the back of my mind than on paper in a drawer. If I leave it in a drawer it remains the same thing but if it's in the memory it becomes transformed into something else.[50]

Where manuscript roughs for *The Waste Land* survive it would be because their transformation had not been completed: they were neither absorbed yet into typescript nor rubbed out to create something new, but preserved on their way to a planned integration of the longer poem.

//

'Like a chapped office boy on a high stool': Eliot was tense at lunch with Virginia Woolf at the Cock Tavern on Fleet Street in the second week of February.[51] 'The critics say I am learned & cold,' he confided as they walked back along the Strand together. 'The truth is I am neither.' Coldness, she said, was a sore point with him. Once again, his tension had been stoked by the state of Vivien's health. She was confined to her bed, Wyndham Lewis said, when he and Eliot saw each other at *Volpone*. By 3 February, Eliot had explained to Mary Hutchinson that Vivien had been out too soon after experiencing an 'attack' and was now laid out, speechless with bronchial trouble. Eliot always believed that a remedy for Vivien lay in the countryside, and he expected her to repair there shortly; but her condition instead worsened, and she couldn't manage in the country on her own. Eliot told his mother that what Vivien was experiencing was a 'severe attack' of influenza: she was very weak and he had been unable to get to his writing.[52] By 13 February Vivien had left the flat, but not for the country: she had been installed in a nursing home at the very moment that her father was making a miraculous recovery and being discharged from his. For the next fortnight, at least, Eliot would have the flat to himself. He sent his mother a list. Would she let him know: 1. when she was coming to England; 2. her budget for board and lodging; 3. preferences for hotel; 4. preparations for food; 5. – and this would be the most important – whether she would consider taking a small furnished flat if the Eliots provided a cook. More than five years had passed since he had seen his mother, more than two since his father had died; it began to look as though the possibility of reunion with the former might at last be on the horizon. Might his mother finally be accepting of his marriage? Might his inheritance be restored? With that prospect before him, and with Vivien in care, Eliot would suspend his correspondence for the rest of the month in order to use the newfound quiet to immerse himself in writing of an altogether deeper significance.

//

The ruling by Justice McInerney on 21 February was swift and decisive. 'I think that this novel is unintelligible,' he told the New York Court of Special Sessions, 'and it seems to me like the work of a disordered mind.'[53] *Ulysses* had been convicted of obscenity after complaints about an episode of its 'Nausicaa' pages, in which a young girl called Gerty MacDowell leans back to watch a firework display, under the heated gaze of Leopold Bloom. ('And she was trembling in every limb from being bent so far back that he could see high up above her knee where no-one ever and she wasn't ashamed and he wasn't either.')[54] Or more accurately, it was the *Little Review* that had been convicted: its editors, Margaret Anderson and Jane Heap, were fined $50 each for violating section 1141 of the Penal Code in publishing obscenity, and forced to suspend serialisation. The next day, the *New York Times* reported the judgement with the headline: 'Improper novel costs woman $50', and the subhead 'woman's dress described', in a censored allusion to Gerty MacDowell's raised garments. The Great Red Scare was underway; Bolshevism was stirring the American workforce; one thousand arrest warrants for members of the Union of Russian Workers had been issued by the attorney general. The court held that sections of the story were 'harmful to the morals of the community' and the defence counsel John Quinn had failed to persuade it otherwise.[55] Serialisation had made Joyce's name better known, Ezra Pound believed, but 'the excuse for parts of *Ulysses* is the WHOLE of *Ulysses*'.[56] It was time to see the work published in its entirety.

A Game of Chess.

For two weeks Eliot wrote no letters but concentrated exclusively on his writing. Through the middle of February to the end of
March, he produced articles for *The Times* and *Chapbook*, and two
for Lewis's *Tyro*.[1] By the time he returned to his new long poem
the ribbon on his 'wretched old' Corona had faded slightly under
the load. But he had now a working title for the poem's second
section: it was to be called 'In the Cage', from the Sibyl of Cumae,
who had asked Apollo for immortality but not eternal youth.[2]
So withered by age had she become that her shrunken body was
trapped inside a two-handled *ampulla*, where she hung, wanting to
die. It was Eliot who had translated *ampulla* as 'cage', even though
he would have known that the Latin more closely translates to *bottle* or *flask* or *vessel*, and even though his own edition of Petronius'
Satyricon, from where it came, rendered the word as 'jar'.[3] Perhaps
he feared that the *ampulla* might magnify the focus on drinking
that 'Tom's place' had established; perhaps he was even beginning
to doubt the wisdom of that section as an opening passage for the
poem. Either way, the title of this second part of the poem was to
change – although when it did, the reference to the Sibyl would
not be lost for ever, but in time restored, when the whole poem –
by then a poem of five sections – would adopt the passage as its
final epigraph.[4]

'The barge she sat in, like a burnish'd throne'.[5] When Eliot had
referenced in 1919 Enobarbus' description of Cleopatra in 'her
infinite variety', he had trailed off the quotation with ellipsis as if
it were something he intended to return to. Now, it opened the

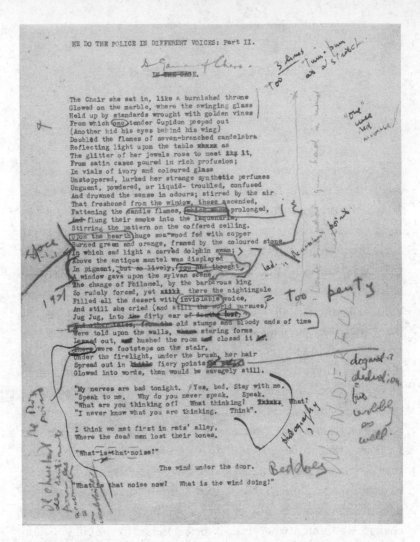

draft of the second part of his poem, where the barge had become a chair, and Cleopatra a figure of variety – an Egyptian queen, a Belladonna foreseen by Madame Sosostris, a woman framed below a painting of the brutal rape of Philomela by Tereus – terminating in Ophelia's 'Good night, ladies' – a figure whose death, like Cleopatra's, is marked upon the cards. These were lines more ornate and formal than anything that had gone before them in

'The Burial of the Dead' – griped by iambic pentameter, thickened by allusion, 'antique', even, to use the poem's own word, and quite unlike the sharp modernity of the first part. How did they belong, exactly, amid such contemporary lines? Littered as they were with rare and decorative ornaments, it seemed unclear how these lines could provide 'correlative' objects that were likely to be understood by the reader. Eliot, of course, may have intended exactly that: a disparate moment of a miscellaneous bill of the kind found in the music hall or the box of postcards that he had spilled out on the table of the first part. There is reason to think so, in fact, as before Eliot got very much further – and certainly before he reached a second page of the new typescript – he did something unexpected. It was an action to do with the title – and not the title for this part of the poem, 'In the Cage', which was soon to be retitled 'A Game of Chess', but one that would govern *both* parts of the poem written to date – a frame, as it were, for the whole. While the first sheet of 'In the Cage' was still in the typewriter, Eliot wound back the carriage wheel to the top of the paper and typed into the header:

HE DO THE POLICE IN DIFFERENT VOICES: Part II.

His source was a line from Dickens's *Our Mutual Friend*, but to the poem it promised what Eliot may always have intended – that 'infinite variety' of which Enobarbus had spoken: the vocal movement of the poem, its polyphony of speakers and its assortment of registers – a choir of 'different voices'. With the new title in place, Eliot wound down the sheet and continued with his draft of 'In the Cage'.

Vivien's treatment in the nursing home for suspected influenza had lasted no more than a fortnight; by the beginning of March she was recuperating at home. But then her condition suddenly worsened, until by mid-month she was in a dire state. As Eliot attempted to manage the visits of friends, he told Brigit Patmore that the doctors had never seen such a case, and had done nothing at all to help her. 'Vivien has been lying in the most dreadful agony with *neuritis* in every nerve, increasingly – arms, hands, legs, feet, back.'[6] *Dreadful* agony, *screaming* agony: he wasn't sure how much of it her body could take. 'In the Cage' records a similar desperation.

'My nerves are bad to-night. Yes, bad. Stay with me.
'Speak to me. Why do you never speak. Speak.

'Have you ever been in such incessant and extreme pain that you felt your sanity going, and that you no longer knew reality from delusion?' Eliot asked Patmore that March. 'That's the way she is.' 'Nerves' was the condition attributed to both Vivien and Eliot by doctors and friends, and even to each other: in Eliot's draft, 'nerves' seemed to express the fugue of a couple – or was it perhaps a single speaker speaking to themselves? – as well as tugging at lines from *The Tempest*: *Thy nerves are in their infancy again.*[7] And it was these same 'nerves' that carried the draft towards yet another tempest, the trenches of the Great War:

I think we are in rats' alley
Where the dead men lost their bones.

How subtly the fear and squalor of the conflict was admitted by Eliot in the poem at that moment, without being named directly. And it would surface still more clearly in a second page that followed, in a scene from a London pub at closing time, 'When Lil's husband was coming back out of the Transport Corps'.[8] By then, Eliot had returned not once but twice to *The Tempest*, first in a refrain of a line used already in 'The Burial of the Dead', 'Those are pearls that were his eyes, yes!', and then to beg the despairing question, 'What shall I do now? What shall I do?'[9]

Six times in the poem that followed Eliot would return to *The*

Tempest, six times to the same scene – Act One, Scene Two, in which a young prince receives the devastating news that his father has been drowned at sea:

> Full fathom five thy father lies.
>> Of his bones are coral made;
> Those are pearls that were his eyes;
>> Nothing of him that doth fade
> But doth suffer a sea-change
> Into something rich and strange.[10]

In Shakespeare's play, the young prince is tricked into grief: although he does not know it, his father is in fact alive and well and washed up on the same island; he will eventually find joy in reconciliation. But Eliot's poem will experience no such redemption, and will dwell instead on the image of a son tortured by the image of his father's body, dismantling and distributing, losing his bones like the men of rats' alley, collapsing and remaking under the metamorphic forces of the changing sea.

'*Splendid last lines*,' Vivien would write on reading the poem in May – and they were: the very last of them lifted from *Hamlet* verbatim – Ophelia's cry before her own drowning.[11] It was then, probably immediately upon completing his typed draft of 'In the Cage', that Eliot went back to the typescript of 'The Burial of the Dead' and wound its first page – the Boston scene – back into the typewriter once more. From there, he typed the same Dickensian title across its header, only this time slightly off-parallel to the existing text and in the lighter colour of ribbon ink used on the sheets of 'In the Cage' that he had just typed.

HE DO THE POLICE IN DIFFERENT VOICES: Part I.

The poem was now in two parts, with a governing title and two part titles, some 228 lines in length. It was by far the longest poem Eliot had written. And there was very much more to come.

It was Richard Aldington who had proposed to Harold Monro a special issue of *Chapbook* for an examination into the character of prose poetry; it was he who suggested Eliot for what he knew to be 'respectable and subtle' objections to the form that would make for an engaging debate.[12] Eliot accepted, saying that he thought such an enquiry might help to stimulate *the worn nerves and arthritic limbs of our diction*; it was probably at the compositional moment of 'In the Cage' that he wrote these words, and said that he proposed to respond in what he called *disconnected paragraphs* for *Chapbook* that March.

Eliot was interested in *intensity* as a distinguishing marker between poetry and prose, and he made a revealing statement. 'No long work can maintain the same high tension throughout.'[13] This was a distinguished thought, for it wasn't the view of many poets, Eliot admitted, and certainly not of Edgar Allan Poe, who had written that undue brevity was one challenge to writing, but 'undue length is yet more to be avoided'.[14] Intensity was the unity of feeling for Poe, and there could be no relaxation of tension at any length in order to achieve it; long or short, the intensity of a poem should be the same. Ezra Pound agreed in this with Poe: it was only through the precision of concentration that an author could energise their language. From the beginning Pound had stressed the need for a concentrated register: *direct treatment, no superfluity, the musical phrase* had been the three spears of the Imagist trident in 1913, and he had told Harriet Monroe soon after: 'The test of a writer is his ability for such concentration AND for his power to stay concentrated till he gets to the end of his poem, whether it is two lines or two hundred.'[15] But now Eliot was saying something quite different – something *fundamentally* different – about the working of a longer poem. In 1942, he would put the thought more clearly still:

In a poem of any length, there must be transitions between passages of greater and less intensity, to give a rhythm of fluctuating emotion essential to the musical structure of the whole.[16]

After 'modernising' themselves in like-minded ways, after a common valuation of tradition, after an interrogation of 'vers libre', after their defiant course against Georgians, the Squiredom and Mercurian poetry, after defending and promoting and expounding one another's art, after all of that: as each man cleared a way for his longest work – *The Waste Land* and *The Cantos* – Eliot and Pound were divided on a critical matter: the intensity with which a long poem may run. And now Eliot would make his most incisive – and, for the poem he was calling 'He Do the Police in Different Voices', his most important – statement of all:

I see no reason why a considerable variety of verse forms may not be employed within the limits of a single poem.[17]

There it was: the formal licence he had sought for poetry issued to himself in a single sentence. And he went on in the next breath to address the image and the textual eye, in what he called the impression received into the mind of the author: 'the rapid and unexpected combination of images apparently unrelated'.[18]

Right there was a second critical statement. Variety of form, combination of image: each licensed according to the requirement of the poem. And what animated both – what distinguished prose from poetry, finally, said Eliot – was a definite concession to what he called 'the desire for "play"'.

//

Dinner with the Woolfs at Hogarth House had overrun. Arriving late at Richmond Station afterwards, Eliot and Virginia discovered they had missed the train to Hammersmith, where they had tickets for the Phoenix Society production of Congreve's *Love for Love* at the Lyric Theatre. They shared a taxi instead, passing through the darkened market gardens that still flanked the river then. Virginia recorded the conversation in her diary.

> 'Missing trains is awful' I said. 'Yes. But humiliation is the worst thing in life' he replied. 'Are you as full of vices as I am?' I demanded. 'Full. Riddled with them.' 'We're not as good as Keats' I said. 'Yes we are' he replied. 'No; we dont write classics straight off as magnanimous people do.' 'We're trying something harder' he said.[19]

//

Conrad Aiken had reviewed *The Sacred Wood* – 'rather grudging', thought Eliot.[20] But then Aiken had just been very publicly hauled over the coals in *The Dial* for using, in Eliot's words to his mother, passages 'borrowed or stolen from me'. The work under scrutiny was *The House of Dust*, newly published in March by the Four Seas press of Boston, from which the critic Babette Deutsch had pulled out four passages and laid them against original lines by Eliot, concluding that they were 'obviously indebted'.[21] The review went so far as to credit Eliot as 'the "assisting artist"', saying that the flaw was not that Aiken had shared the same thoughts as Eliot, but that when the thought came he had lifted his eyebrows in the same way. Deutsch was just beginning her career as a young American poet with one collection to her name, but already she had proved herself an astute reader of Eliot's work. Her review of *Prufrock and Other Observations* in 1918 had stood above the fray, noting precisely that what gave Eliot's language its extraordinary charge was 'common words uncommonly used'.[22] Her response was more exacting than the vague pronouncements on beauty and rebellion that had emanated from the English journals, as was an observation that what defined Eliot's vision was a weary mind 'looking out upon a crowded personal experience with impartial irony'. Although she couldn't have known it, that was an uncannily accurate observation not only of a man but of a personal life. She could recognise Eliot in any costume and was certain she'd seen it beneath Aiken's.

The opportunity to review Aiken in *The Dial* had been offered to Eliot, but he wisely turned it down. He had been sent *The House of Dust* by Scofield Thayer in the autumn of 1920, and by the following day had 'glanced through' just enough to see an unwelcome likeness of himself.[23] He told Thayer that he, Eliot, was the workman called in to build the House, while Aiken had provided the Dust, and he swiftly directed Thayer to an overlapping passage that would serve to strain their personal friendship were he to review it. *The House of Dust* was the fourth in a series of book-length poems that Aiken called 'symphonies', in which the alienation of the city was a running motif. He had said that he was striving for an 'absolute music', not one based on a single dominant idea, but a polyphony where 'individual and crowd are used as contrasting themes with which one might play a species of counterpoint'.[24] If that sounded a little like a statement of Eliot's, then in a way it was, for parts of Aiken's work could read like a simulation of Eliot's past and imagined future. But influence doesn't always move in one direction only, and while Aiken's early debts to Eliot appeared incontrovertible, *The House of Dust* may have made a deeper mark on Eliot than he was willing to admit.

'Am I cuckoo in fancying that it cancels the debt I owed him?' Aiken asked an American editor after the publication of *The Waste Land*.[25] His own dues to Eliot had been acknowledged, but Aiken was certain that he could now detect what he called 'echoes or parodies' of his own work in his friend's. The violet hour, Madame Sosostris, the crowd of the unreal city, even the musical phrasing was like his own, he said. Aiken had already written about a tarot reading similar to one that Eliot had just drafted in 'The Burial of the Dead', as well as an under-sea passage of picked bones quite like the one that appeared in 'In the Cage'/'A Game of Chess'.[26] The first of Aiken's 'symphonies', *The Jig of Forslin* of 1916, had

suffered from an overexposure to 'The Love Song of J. Alfred Prufrock'; but there were moments in Aiken's book – which appeared
in its first London edition in the winter of 1921/2 – that seemed
to find an echo in *The Waste Land*: Eliot's (later) 'voices singing
out of empty cisterns' sounded surprisingly like Aiken's (earlier)
'voice crying from the cistern'.[27] Other allusions lay in other books:
Eliot's typist would smooth her hair with automatic hand, while
her lover descends the stair; in the second of Aiken's 'symphonies'
from 1918, *The Charnel Rose*, 'The eternal mistress lifts her hand,
/ To rearrange her hair, / For the deathless lover who climbs and
climbs the stair.'[28]

In *The House of Dust*, further parallels seemed apparent. 'We
crowd through the streets in a dazzle of pallid lamplight,' wrote
Aiken, then:

Good-night! Good-night! Good-night! We go our ways,
The rain runs over the pavement before our feet,[29]

Good night, Bill. Good night, Lou. Good night, George. Good
night . . . Eliot . . . *And each man kept his eyes before his feet* . . .
In yet another passage, a clock: a 'tower / Ticks with reverberant
coil and tolls the hour' (Aiken); 'towers / Tolling reminiscent bells,
that kept the hours' (Eliot).[30]

In the great scene of 'nerves' that Eliot had just written: 'What
are you thinking of? What thinking? What?' In *The House of Dust*:
'What are you thinking of?' Eliot, 1921: 'What shall we do tomorrow? / What shall we ever do?' Aiken, 1920: 'To-morrow – what?
And what of yesterday?' *and* 'What shall we talk of?'[31]

Not for the last time would Eliot find himself tangled in questions of originality or influence. But influence rarely travels in a
straight line and more often moves via a network, where there are
fields of common interest and nodes of mutual inspiration through
which writers and their poems pass. It's no surprise that peers of
the same generation, similar in their concerns, overlapping in their

reading matter, reacting at the same time to their time, might respond in similar terms. And for all his doubts about the derivation of parts of *The Waste Land*, Aiken would be one of the first to acknowledge its importance on publication, saying it was the best thing he had read in years.[32] But as Eliot's poem became a success, a sense of grievance would grow between the old Harvard friends; Aiken expressed it in a private letter of 1925:

> eliot is the cruellest poet, breeding
> lyrics under the driest dustpan, mixing
> memory and desire, stirring
> verb-roots with spring brain.
> aiken kept him safe, covering
> dearth with forgetful verbiage, needing
> no notes, no elaborate allusions or explanations,
> (for there was nothing to explain).[33]

//

At the end of March, Eliot completed the second of the two essays for Wyndham Lewis's *Tyro*. The first, 'The Romantic Englishman', had seemingly run in parallel with 'The Burial of the Dead's' brush with prohibition, and now this second essay, on Baudelaire, made reference to a firework display of 'Bengal lights', which had just made an appearance as a brand of cigarettes in the opening lines of 'The Burial of the Dead'. That was not the only reference to the draft on which he was working: the article ended, as had 'The Burial of the Dead', quoting a phrase of Baudelaire's: *Vous, hypocrite lecteur* . . .[34] There was in this moment a confluence in content between the verse and the prose, and there was, in addition, one further connecting spoke between the long poem and Eliot's writing for *The Tyro*.

It may have been in the week following his 5 February meeting with Lewis that Eliot began his 'Song for the Opherion' for *The*

Tyro, and it may have been in the final week of March that he completed it. Somewhere in between, Eliot produced not only the two articles, but this lyric of fifteen lines: two end-rhymed sextets and two envois, with a curious peninsula-like half-line to complete it. When, in April, the poem would be printed in the inaugural issue of the journal, it carried a revised and probably erroneous title, 'Song to the Opherian'. But about the pseudonym under which it appeared there could be no doubt: 'Gus Krutzsch' – a name that Eliot had pencilled into his typescript for the Boston scene in 'The Burial of the Dead'. Later, he would say that the poem had not been good enough to acknowledge under his own name, but at the time he may have had a more practical agreement with Lewis not to overload the new edition with work by a single writer, but to separate the authorship of the poem from prose published under his own name.[35]

Pound's assessment of the poem, when it came, was bleak.

The title, for one thing, simply wouldn't do, he thought, and he obliterated 'for the Opherion' in pencil on typescript, leaving visible only the word 'Song'. The early running of the poem didn't fare much better either. He singled out the third line – 'Perhaps it does not come to very much' – and scribbled beside it in jagged graphite, bracketed it for deletion, and, in case that were not clear enough, then took to ink and struck it out altogether, writing in the margin perhaps the most damning word in Pound's arsenal: 'georgian'.[36] It was an intervention of some radicalism: with it, the *abab* rhyme scheme was stripped out and the two sextet stanzas became instantly lopsided; in a stroke, Pound had run the poem formally aground. Then there was the provocative charge of Georgianism. Pound had once gone as far as challenging one proponent of Georgian poetry to a duel, and here he was now taking up arms against Eliot. And his intervention didn't stop there. Next, he turned his attention to two envois that Eliot had once hoped might clinch each stanza, rewriting the first and striking heavily through the second, which

Eliot himself had already dispensed with in *The Tyro*. Even so, what Eliot had once envisaged as a fourteen- or fifteen-line poem had become twelve, though Pound had doubts that even that much was worth preserving. 'The song, has only two lines which you can use in the body of the poem,' he told Eliot, and, later, 'I dare say the sweats with tears will wait.'[37] Those lines – 'When the surface of the blackened river / Is a face that sweats with tears?' – would find a meandering entry into *The Waste Land*, as the oil and tar with which the river sweats in 'The Fire Sermon'; they would, too, be among a number of lines to re-emerge in 1924 as 'The Wind Sprang Up at Four O'Clock'.[38] Forensic as he was, Pound may have overlooked for salvage lines that seemed exceptionally telling of Eliot's mental state that winter:

> This thought this ghost this pendulum in the head
> Swinging from life to death
> Bleeding between two lives[39]

But in their print life with 'Song', they would have only a brief time in *The Tyro* before being stripped for parts.

//

Wyndham Lewis had told John Quinn in 1920 that he felt he had not lived up to his own promise of the war years: he called himself 'a character of essay, and unfulfilment'.[40] But a new response was to begin now, he said, and his aim was nothing short of making these post-war years the first of '*complete* work'. His exhibition that opened at the Leicester Galleries in London in April was named 'Tyros and Portraits': he knew, as he told Agnes Bedford, Pound's musician-tenant in Kensington, that as a show it was not easy to like; but it came with the launch of its literary wing, his journal *The Tyro*.[41]

'We are at the beginning of a new epoch,' announced Lewis, slipping seamlessly back into manifesto mode. And his target was the 'tyros' of the journal's title: grotesques, grinning portraits of novice 'villainies' and simpleton 'interior broods' in which Lewis saw in humanity a regression to animalism of a kind that he had witnessed first hand in the trenches, under what he called the 'immense meaningless shadow' of the war.[42] There was no passage back across the chasm of the conflict to a time of innocence; equally, we had not yet reached a terrain beyond the void of an artistic no man's land. These were the in-between times of the tyros: these mannequins of conceit, this self-serving 'prettiness and fervour' and art-for-art's-sake of a kind to be found in Bloomsbury and Paris.[43] But we were children of change, Lewis believed, and we were not yet resigned: 'Europe grows more, not less, of one mind.'[44] Eliot did not agree with such a hopeful vision of the continent, but he was now happy to be conscripted into an avant-garde that turned its fire on the French nineteenth-century arts that he had only just stepped away from. Lewis was always at his best on the borders of satire and caricature, he said, and the *Tyros* might still prove to produce an energetic race.[45]

In 1914, *Blast* had called for 'MACHINES OF LIFE, a sort of LIVING plastic geometry', and what it began *The Tyro* would try to finish. Inevitably, for Lewis, that meant a continuing obsession with ageing targets – Clive Bell, Duncan Grant and Roger Fry – which even Pound thought was a waste of ammunition.[46] 'Cant see that TYRO is of interest outside Bloomsbury,' he told Lewis bluntly.[47] And in truth the journal felt narrow in its breadth, thin in its contributors (nine), and cramped in its production, and for all Lewis's campaign, and all Sydney Schiff's money, it would run for only one further issue.

//

The prospect of a general strike loomed that spring, as miners walked out for a second time in six months; Eliot expected the postal service to be stopped at any moment, and Lewis predicted the distribution of his *Tyro* to be halted as a result.[48] Two weeks later, the rail unions unexpectedly voted not to come out in solidarity with the miners in a moment that became known as 'Black Friday' for the bitter charge of disloyalty that went with it. Whatever else, this disorganised chaos was another step in the destruction of 'Europe', wrote Eliot. 'The whole of contemporary politics etc. oppresses me with a continuous physical horror like the feeling of growing madness in one's own brain,' he wrote.[49] The mind of Europe now seemed a place of torture complementary to his own, his language so like that which he used to describe Vivien's state only a month before. 'It is rather a horror to be sane in the midst of this; it is too dreadful, too huge, for one to have the comforting feeling of superiority. It goes too far for rage.' In the autumn of 1919 he had described himself as a liberal, now he sounded broken by rancour.[50] He had been observing the work of the French poet and polemicist Charles Maurras, whose 'three traditions'– '*classique, catholique, monarchique*' – had caught his attention back in October 1920, when he had written an appreciative letter that was published in *The Times*.[51] Maurras directed *Action Française*, a journal and political movement seeking restoration of a royal sovereign, a state religion, and exclusion from office of *les quatre États confédérés* – Jews, Protestants, freemasons and foreigners. Failure in the French legislative elections of 1919 had pushed the movement even further to the right, onto more anti-democratic grounds, from where Eliot watched, defending Maurras in print at the moment when he made his own conversion to Anglo-Catholicism in 1927. In time, he would appeal to Maurras for contributions to *The Criterion*. Now, in April 1921, he told Aldington, 'Having only contempt for every existing political party, and profound hatred for democracy, I feel the blackest gloom.'[52]

'It is true that I have started a poem,' Eliot wrote to John Quinn that spring.[53] Throughout March he had continued working on it, and early in April he explained to Schiff: 'My poem has still so much revision to undergo that I do not want to let anyone see it yet, and also I want to get more of it done – it should be much the longest I have ever written. I hope that by June it will be in something like final form. I have not had the freedom of mind.'[54] June was not an arbitrary date: Eliot had learned that it was the month that his family were coming from St Louis to stay.

//

The typist was floundering. No sooner had the apartment door opened than she had thrown her pages down on the floor, turned on her heel and vanished into the streets of Paris. Nine typists had failed in the attempt, Sylvia Beach reported; the eighth had threatened in despair to throw herself out of the window.[55] 'Circe', the fifteenth of the eighteen episodes of *Ulysses*, and the end-mark of section II, was finished at last, but it had almost not made it into typescript. Nine typists with nine ribbons on nine papers had left the draft in a shambles and Joyce at his apartment door in a state of high anxiety.[56] People were talking. He had overheard rumours that he was a cocaine addict. That he had broken down and was dying in New York. And most strangely of all, that he owned a chain of cinemas across Switzerland.[57] Where was Pound when his readership was needed? Three months of travelling south and still no sign, and it was too great a risk to post the pages while his address was unconfirmed. Since the prosecution of the *Little Review*, *Ulysses* no longer had a print outlet, and he feared that Benjamin Huebsch, his publisher in New York, would not take an interest, nor John Rodker, for that matter, in London. Paths to publication seemed to be blocked, and he said that he was struggling to keep his feet. He feared that the year spelled incessant trouble, and wrote out its digits as a doom-laden sum: 1 + 9 + 2 + 1 = 13.[58]

The omens did not read quite as Joyce thought. A week would pass and the Pounds would return to Paris, to a 'comfortable' two-room studio in the Hôtel Pas-de-Calais, 59 rue des Saints-Pères ('Vivien's old hotel,' Eliot would remark with pleasure) with a view of the Seine: 'slightly too expensive', but a home nonetheless for Ezra and Dorothy that would suffice until their move into the apartment at '70 *bis*' in December.[59] They had barely unpacked their cases before Joyce had brought over the pages from 'Circe' and, for good measure, a draft of what would become the sixteenth episode, 'Eumaeus'. That was a Saturday, the middle of the month. By the Wednesday, Pound had finished his reading.

'Circe' was 'Magnificent, a new Inferno in full sail', he told his parents; and to Agnes Bedford he said: 'enormous – megalo-scrumptious – mastodonic'.[60] Joyce had been told the same, and could feel his spirits renewed. Pound 'appears to be very excited', he told Harriet Shaw Weaver, and relayed the news that the typescripts were on their way to her from Pound, and asked her to pass them on to Eliot when she had finished.[61] It was a request that, very soon, would change the direction of the long poem Eliot was writing.

'Circe' was vast on every scale: it had taken eight drafts and six months, and was about as long in typescript as the first eight episodes combined. It would not only provide the book's memorable midnight hour amid the Nighttown brothels but summon almost every character in the novel into the service of the story. Each would undergo transformation, just as Circe had cast her mutable spells and turned Odysseus' men to swine on Aeaea. But it was in its style that the writing was so transformative: countless dreamlike spells conjured and broken, pages soaked in booze and 'snakes of river fog', raising memory and stirring trauma.[62] It was staged in the form of a playscript, freed from the shackles of a second-person speaker, disturbing the division between what can be said to take place and what might be fantasised, between the overtly expressed and the implicit. It was the whole novel and something entirely new besides: the heart of the book and at the same time a different rhythm beating against it. In these pages, Joyce had come to understand the potential for the novel as 'a kind of encyclopaedia'.[63]

But potential it would remain unless a publishing solution could be found. With no English or American publisher willing or able to take the legal risk, what options were left to him? Huebsch had indeed backed away from publication after John Quinn refused on Joyce's behalf to make any alterations to the text, and Boni & Liveright, next on Quinn's list, were equally cautious. Sylvia Beach witnessed the slump in Joyce's demeanour as he explained the position to her in the bookshop. It was a heavy blow, she wrote, one that hurt his pride: after seven years of relentless work, 'My book will never come out now.'[64]

'It occurred to me that something might be done,' said Beach decisively, 'and I asked: "Would you let Shakespeare and Company have the honor of bringing out your *Ulysses*?"'

Beach was a lender and a seller of books and a literary host par excellence, but she was no publisher; she was preparing to move premises to 12 rue de l'Odéon, 'a few steps down from the Boulevard Saint-Germain', near the church of Saint-Sulpice, and already had her hands more than full. Yet she understood the opportunity to bypass the censors by publishing from Paris, and she was determined to grasp it.

'He accepted my offer immediately and joyfully. I thought it rash of him to entrust his great *Ulysses* to such a funny little publisher. But he seemed delighted,' she recorded. 'And so was I.'

//

John Middleton Murry's attempt with Eliot to rescue *The Athe-naeum* had been a valiant one, but in February 1921 the journal had finally conceded to a dwindling readership and merged with *The Nation*. After *The Egoist* and the hamstringing of the *Little Review*, the closure of *The Athenaeum* marked the third of Eliot's publishing outlets to effectively dematerialise in a year, leaving *The Times* and the *London Mercury* as almost the sole literary forums in the capital. But even the survivors faced troubles: *The Times*'s insistence on the anonymity of its contributors left it unable to uphold any definite standard of criticism, said Eliot, while the *Mercury* suffered from the very reverse: the 'solemn trifling' of editor J. C. Squire was too much apparent in the 'mediocrity of the minds' brought to bear upon it.[65] Eliot now felt relief that he hadn't left the bank for the offer of the editorship that Murry had made him two years before – where would he be now if he had? Admittedly, the bank work was an encumbrance 'which breaks the concentration required for turning out a poem of any length'.[66] And that was now the urgent concern. With *The Sacred Wood* behind him, his commitments in prose were for the moment fulfilled: 'I am not anxious to produce another for a year or two,' he told Quinn in May, 'and meanwhile have a long poem in mind and partly on paper which I am wishful to finish.'

//

Dead to deadfish, that's how Pound described London that April, and while there were fools also to be found in Paris, he said, on the whole they were considerably less likely to get in one's way.[67] Eliot didn't agree. At the end of April he was finishing the second of his London letters for *The Dial*, a miscellany in which he made known his appreciation of the Phoenix Society's 'consummate' *Volpone* that had taken place in January and February, as well as Lewis's exhibition at the Leicester Galleries in the city.[68] But he worried over the state of criticism, and described as 'unanimous rubbish' the thought that a younger generation was taking up the form – which anyway was not the point, only that creativity will not flourish without criticism. Once again it was the music hall and the comic revue that Eliot turned to, praising England for having more of it than anywhere else, and at the same time asking that it should be treated with more seriousness. And he found room, also, to highlight the 'desuetude' of some of the churches inside the London Wall, which were due to be demolished in the district where he was forced to spend his days, in the 'dust and tumult of Lombard Street'. Among them was St Mary Woolnoth, on the corner of Lombard and King William streets, which would be saved from demolition, and which Eliot had preserved in the pages of 'In the Cage'/'A Game of Chess', where a crowd flowed from London Bridge, up the hill and down King William Street,

> To where Saint Mary Woolnoth kept the time,
> With a dead sound on the final stroke of nine.[69]

//

On the north bank of the River Liffey in Dublin, the Custom House was in flames. For more than a century, James Gandon's elegant building had survived, most recently as the offices of the Local Government Board, and the repository for the country's income tax records. It had been on the target list of the Irish Republican Army since 1918, but with the return of Éamon de Valera from a winter tour of the United States in 1920 it had become the symbolic target that the independence effort needed. A successful attack would cost the British government £2 million and more, it was calculated, but more importantly it would make the administration of Ireland from Whitehall all but impossible. Throughout the spring of 1921, informants were tapped and blueprints were leaked, as meticulous plans of the building were drawn up. An attack would require a republican force of 120, but Michael Collins feared heavy losses if more men and women weren't drafted in. Shortly before one o'clock in the afternoon, on 25 May, volunteers walked into the building carrying cans of paraffin. The janitor who telephoned the alarm was shot and killed. But word had reached the Royal Irish Constabulary, who were swift to mobilise a force of paramilitary auxiliaries, and with that the shooting began. The building blazed for five days; it was believed that the spread of the flames was made easier by sympathisers within the city's fire brigade. As many as seventy or eighty republican militants were arrested, but the profile of the cause had been raised internationally by the nightly scenes of this iconic British administrative centre in flames. Six weeks later, an uneasy ceasefire between the Irish Republican Army and the British government began.

//

'Circe' had reached London that spring, and not only 'Circe' but the later sequence of 'Oxen of the Sun', and 'Eumaeus', the fourteenth and sixteenth parts of *Ulysses*, had also found their way to Eliot via Harriet Shaw Weaver. Eliot had read the serialisation of *Ulysses* since it began in 1918, when he described it as 'volatile and heady', and had praised the element of the horrific that he found within it.[70] 'Both are terrifying,' he remarked at the time, comparing it to Wyndham Lewis's *Tarr*. 'That is the test of a new work of art.' When a work of art no longer terrifies us, he said, when what he called its 'attractive terror' has been diminished, then either our senses have been dulled or we were mistaken in our original reading, and he would say something similar in 1923, writing that the complete novel had given him 'all the surprise, delight, and terror that I can require'.[71]

On 9 May 1921, Eliot told John Quinn that he had liked Joyce on meeting him the previous summer, though cautioning that he was 'a handful', with a fanatic's conviction that everyone present should be in the service of his work. As it happened, in his case, the conviction was well placed: Eliot had been reading the latter part of *Ulysses* in typescript, and could report that it was 'truly magnificent'.[72] On 21 May, he returned the typescripts by registered post to Joyce personally, saying, in a slightly curious turn, that he was 'obliged for a taste of them'. There were one or two phrases in 'Circe' that he didn't get on with, and he listed them, but beyond that his criticism of the three chapters was negligible. 'I think they are superb – especially the Descent into Hell, which is stupendous.'[73] Eliot didn't offer any annotation, nor was he asked to; in fact, it wasn't quite clear why Joyce had wanted him to read it, beyond the fact that he knew Eliot to be an influential reader. 'But otherwise, I have nothing but admiration; in fact, I wish, for my own sake, that I had not read it.'

That statement has been given much attention ever since. *I wish, for my own sake, that I had not read it.* Why, for Eliot's sake, did he wish he hadn't read it? For some readers the plausible explanation was that Eliot would now draft the opening scene of 'The Burial of the Dead', as a prequel to April's cruellest month, based upon the nighttown pages of 'Circe' that he had just read, for which supporting overlaps in the two texts exist. More likely is that in his reading of 'Circe' Eliot had confirmed for himself what two passes of fiddly revisions to his typescript had already caused him to suspect: that his own scene in Boston was simply not good enough in the final analysis – not good enough when set against writing as 'stupendous' as Joyce's, not good enough to lead off his long poem, if he had any aspirations at all to produce a work of equal standing to *Ulysses*. Such a realisation would be a hard one for any writer of any genre, but most especially for one working in so concentrated a form as poetry, where every line is carefully weighted. To such a writer, to lose just one line might be a grievance; to lose fifty-four is a devastation. But it was probably at that moment that Eliot made his third return to the 'Tom's place' typescript and, having already made more than two dozen revisions, decided to abandon it and strike it out – all fifty-four lines, in broad pencil waves over the whole page. Or not quite the whole page: for there was one part of the typed leaf that he did not strike out, left, presumably, to retain the structure of the subsequent typescript: and that was the title, 'He Do the Police in Different Voices: Part I' and beneath that, 'The Burial of the Dead'. It seemed that, for now at least, those two elements of the title of the poem were there to stay; everything else was cancelled.

There may, in addition, have been a reason more personal than his reading of 'Circe' for Eliot to remove the section, as the pun of placing the opening drinks 'at Tom's place' might imply. In a theatre review written around this time Eliot had said that a man desires to see himself on stage, but in a projection: to be more admirable and forceful, to be more villainous and despicable.[74] Certainly, there may have been an element of self-reflection in the Tom's place sequence that appealed to Eliot, whose capacity to take a drink had not gone unnoticed in Bloomsbury. In winter 1923, Virginia Woolf would find him blurry-eyed and confused in the flat, before he left the room to be sick. 'After a long time, he came back, sank into the corner, & I saw him, ghastly pale, with his eyes shut, apparently in a stupor. When we left he was only just able to stand on his legs.'[75] But here, in the poem, the setting of the drinking may have had more than a projection to it. Although Eliot never expressly named the night out as taking place in Boston, it seems likely that he portrayed a Harvard crowd from Cambridge, where prohibition was particularly strict, and where his late father had hoped Eliot's academic career might flourish. For all the projection, a private message may have survived: one for Eliot's late father, a man who described syphilis as God's punishment for indecency, an infection for which he hoped there would be no cure.[76] In an attempt to stem the spread of venereal disease, the Missouri legislature had in 1872 introduced the regulation of prostitution, which to the Eliot family amounted to legalisation. Greenleaf had led the charge to repeal it: social evil should be treated like other crimes, he said, namely punishable by law.[77] An editorial in a St Louis newspaper once proposed Greenleaf for police commissioner on the grounds that 'forty-eight hours after Dr Eliot assumed the reins of the police department there would be no gambling houses in St Louis'.[78] It is reasonable to suppose that the revels of the poem so long in Eliot's mind would have appalled his father and grandfather alike. But upsetting his surviving mother would not have been something Eliot wished to do. If Mrs Eliot would have been shocked by the menstruation of 'Ode', then she would surely have been dismayed by these opening antics: bars, a brothel, urination in public, arrest – not what she would regard as suitable material for poetry. For Eliot's poem to begin with behaviour that was not only immoral but possibly illegal – a poem that he had invited her to anticipate, a poem he had told her was so long in mind – that could only come as a tremendous affront to his family.

Reuse, reuse, reuse: Eliot was nothing if not pragmatic. Like the discarded draft of 'Song', he would abandon but not forget the lines, and would in time return to them as a source for 'Sweeney Agonistes'. In the words of that poem, 'These fellows always get pinched in the end.'[79]

//

Eliot knew that with his family's imminent arrival in London, his hopes of finishing the poem by June were a mirage. He told Dorothy Pound that instead he would be ready for some mountain air by October, 'after I have finished a little poem which I am at present engaged upon'.[80] For the first time since the Pounds had left England in January, Eliot had secured a postal address for them, and he caught them up on his reading of *Ulysses*, saying that 'the unpublished manuscript is even finer stuff than the printed'. He said that he hoped Ezra had managed in the time away to produce a notable work of his own.

Vivien had been in bed for more than two months, Eliot explained to Dorothy, but he must have been counting only the continuous run at Clarence Gate Gardens, as she had also spent the month of February prostrate partly in a nursing home, partly in the flat. Such as it was, her recent improvement had been sufficient that by the second week of May she had left London for recuperation at the coast: Eastbourne, most likely, where her father was himself recovering from his operation. There she fell into familiar patterns of caring for him at the expense of her own recovery. Eliot described to Dorothy Pound how Vivien had finally got up from her own bed only to collapse at her father's: gastric flu was the diagnosis, but standing upright in anxious vigil had been the symptom, and had, he said improbably, without medical evidence, 'precipitated internal displacements'.[81] What he didn't mention to Dorothy, and therefore what Pound didn't yet know, was that Vivien had taken with her to the seaside, or received by post, a typescript of a second part of the 'little poem' on which he had been working, and upon which she would now report.

W O N D E R F U L, Vivien wrote in the margin beside 'My nerves are bad tonight'; *wonderful*, again beside the lines of knowing and seeing and remembering nothing; *& wonderful*, once more beside those of the streetwalker who will wear her hair down.[82] But Vivien was no cheerleader, and she had pertinent textual suggestions of her own to make. It was probably she rather than he who struck out the lethargic line about Lil's husband 'coming back out of the Transport Corps': *Discharge out of the army??* Eliot pencilled, in what was effectively an editorial query to his editor-of-the-moment, Vivien; no, 'demobbed', seven words reduced to one, for which the hand was Pound's (plausibly pencilled over Vivien's), but the ear and the English idiom Vivien's.[83] And she commented on the typescript elsewhere, too. 'No, ma'am, you needn't look so old fashioned at me': Eliot's line in draft; *If you don't like it you can get on with it*, Vivien had replaced assertively. Eliot's stiffened 'It's that medicine I took in order to bring it off' became Vivien's flowing *'It's that [them] pills I took to bring it off'*.

Not that she judged everything so perfectly. 'Something of that', Eliot's ladies had said in the draft; Somethin*k*, Vivien prompted, refining the ear; but Eliot explained in the margin *I want to avoid trying to show pronunciation by spelling*; Eliot and Vivien were speaking to one another through the draft. Beside *the hot water at ten* she prompted the improbable hot water *bottle!*, which was surely a picture of the Eliots' evenings, though a misstep here; and she had a thought that the publican's great acoustic – HURRY UP PLEASE IT'S TIME – was premature: *Perhaps better not so soon*, wrote Vivien in the margin, *Could you put this later*; Eliot would consider the comment, and transcribe it onto the carbon copy for further reflection.[84]

Vertically, in pencil, beside the first twenty-seven lines, Vivien wrote in the right-hand margin *Don't see what you had in mind here*. And she was right to do so: she had identified by far the most ritualised of all the sections of the draft to date – passages that possessed a formality of address beyond the iambic pentameter they were cloaked in that were ornate in tone as well as form – and distant too: *remote origins* without the necessary accompanying *personal quality*. Not only in the image of Philomel had the opening passage brought with it a brutal sexual violation: the section had carried the hint of frozen intimacy that culminated in four lines imported by Eliot from 'The Death of the Duchess', the estranging poem which he had shared with Pound in the autumn of 1919, and possibly with Vivien too. Further lines introduced from the same poem would conclude the scene of bad nerves, and beside those Vivien marked the more ambiguous, *Yes*. Was this an appreciation or an agreement? Or was it simply a recognition of having read the lines in the 'Duchess' poem once before? There they had lowered the temperature between the Malfi-like couple into an almost barren state. *But it is terrible to be alone with another person*, a 'call' line in that poem had run; *If it is terrible alone, it is sordid with one more*: the line with which it 'answered'. And shortly after the call-and-answer had come the intervention between the couple in the form of a game of chess, now repeated in the new poem, in which 'The ivory men make company between us'.[85]

It wasn't in this moment with 'In the Cage'/'A Game of Chess' that Vivien objected to this line, but object she did, and it is possible to speculate as to why. Ivory is cool before it is warmed by touch, and the chess pieces of the two poems stood in for absence: not of the poem's couple, who after all were present in the verses, but for that element of a relationship that introduces company of another kind. For it probably wasn't the thought that the lines might invite a portrayal of their marriage that troubled Vivien – after all, which partnerships around them were not straining under their own complications? – but the possibility that they hinted at the absence of generational company, of life without children. It was surely this that Vivien reflected upon most painfully when she asked for the removal of the lines: an atmosphere that Eliot would later describe for *The Family Reunion* in 'A man and a woman / Married, alone in a country house together, / For three years childless, learning the meaning / Of loneliness.'[86] When Eliot first wrote the line for 'The Death of the Duchess', the couple had been three years childless, almost four.

The line of 'ivory men' was the one that Eliot restored to the poem in Morocco in the winter of 1960. Asked why he had done so, he answered evasively that the line was originally omitted from the published poem 'for some reason or other' and left it at that.[87] But Valerie, Eliot's second wife, knew exactly how the line had come to be excised, and she knew this because her husband had written it down.[88] The fair copy of *The Waste Land* that Eliot produced in that Moroccan winter had been the last occasion that he had written out the poem, but it had not been the only occasion. Eliot also kept a humble ruled notebook that he called 'Valerie's Own Book', into which he made fair copies of those poems of his that he thought she particularly cared about following their marriage in 1957. Here too, in 1958, he wrote out *The Waste Land* by hand, as he had for the London Library; here too, he restored the omitted line, only this time he inked it with a forceful asterisk, and in the footer wrote by way of a legend: '*Line omitted from published text, at Vivien's insistence.*'[89] That was bold. Not *in deference to* or *out of respect for*, and not at Vivien's *request* either, but her *insistence*. Vivien had insisted upon the removal of the line because she didn't want her friends looking in upon a childless marriage.

Children were a matter that Eliot had been sensitive to in the past. A year after their wedding, he wrote defensively of a nine-month run of nerves, ailments and neuralgia that Vivien was experiencing: 'I may say that this was not a case of maternity in any degree,' he told Conrad Aiken. 'Most people imagine so unless I explain.'[90] And in a suppressed 1917 poem, it came in the form of an accusatory question, 'Est-ce qu'il n'a pas d'enfants?', *Has he no children?*, to which an answer followed: 'Il est eunuque, a s'entend.' *He is a eunuch, of course.*[91]

Children's voices had touched Eliot's premarital work but lightly, as something heard in a distant strain or a whimpering corner; but in the years that followed the honeymoon 'Ode' they would be encountered again and again as a witnessing presence.[92] Children would be at the gate in 'Ash-Wednesday' (1926–9), and seek a home in 'A Song for Simeon' (1928); they would form the whispers and small laughter of 'Marina' (1930) and would be the bodies who quickly tire in *The Rock* (c.1933); their voices were in the New Hampshire orchard between the time of blossom and fruit ('Landscapes', c.1934); they were the hidden laughter, buried beneath the leaves of 'Burnt Norton' (1935–6); and in their final form, their last and most haunted outing of all, in 'Little Gidding' (1941–2), they would become the undetected presence in the apple tree, half-heard but unknown because they were never looked for.[93] Three times children would rise in *The Waste Land*, twice more they would be cut from the drafts; but the most memorable of them survived in Vivien's correction of 'In the Cage'/'A Game of Chess'. 'You want to keep him at home, I suppose,' had been Eliot's faltering first effort; Vivien crossed that out decisively with what would become one of the poem's better-known lines. *What you get married for if you dont want to have children.*

'I think it must be dreadful to have children to think that you might pass on something of yourself,' Vivien said once: she thanked God that she hadn't, and had never wished to, since she was a girl.[94] She had grown up being told by her mother that mental instability was an inheritable condition, and had, from her middle teens, been medicated (bromide, probably) by the family doctors to suppress her polarising moods. In fact what she may have been experiencing as a teenager were hormonal fluctuations in the form of heavy and irregular menstrual cycles that still afflicted her in the early days of marriage, as Eliot's 'Hysteria' and 'Ode' appear to record. As an adult, she marked her periods in her diaries; some months she marked nothing else. By 1919, her cycle had become regular, though frequently accompanied by migraine.[95] That children remained a biological possibility, and even a desire, is traced in a remark that she posed to a friend and mother: 'What would you feel like if you were told you must not have children?'[96] A writer had once told her as much, insisting that the financial burden would be too great a burden for her husband: his writing came first, she was told, and motherhood must wait.[97]

There are clues that Eliot was good with children, and certainly that he could be charmed by them. In Paris in 1911, before he met Vivien, Eliot watched children playing with boats in the ponds of the Luxembourg Gardens, and marvelled at how in their hands the toy craft sailed right across the surface and through the fountain without upset.[98] In 1915, after Pound introduced him to the Dolmetsch family, he reported that he found their children extraordinary and said that he was wild to see them again.[99] There are even hints that this was a life that Eliot may have wanted for himself. His letters to Emily Hale are populated by an affectionate engagement with his friends' children. To her, he advertised frequently – perhaps even leadingly – their presence 'under my direction': at tea parties, birthday parties and at weekend stays, 'capering' around him and 'grumbusking' ('in the children's language grumbusking means "moving rapidly from place to place, like Genghis Khan" – thus I teach history').[100] He told her once, 'I confess that I very much enjoy the flattery of being liked by children and animals, and rather go out of my way to gain their approval.'[101] And after a visit from his nieces in 1931, he wrote most tellingly of all that he wished that he could see more of them, but felt a little baffled in their particular company: 'I feel towards them something of the affection I should like to have given to children of my own, but am too shy to express it very well.'[102]

The painful truth of the Eliots' marriage and their 'ivory men' may have been that Eliot after all might have wanted children; he simply hadn't wanted to have them with Vivien.[103]

We are tired children, he would draft for *The Rock* in 1934, *and can endure only a little light*.[104] In the typescript that had surely been through Vivien's hands:

> I was neither
> Living nor dead, and I knew nothing,
> Looking into the heart of light, the silence.[105]

From the seaside, in May 1921, Vivien folded the draft ready for the envelope. 'Make any of these alterations – or *none* if you prefer,' she scribbled on the back of the final page. 'Send me back this copy & let me have it.'[106] And there's every reason to think that this is exactly what Eliot did, for he had 'answered' her textual queries with marginal comments of his own, and had copied a selection of Vivien's annotations onto the carbon typescript that he retained, before folding up the ribbon copy once more, and – judging by the additional fold of the paper – posting it back to Vivien to help in her recuperation.

The Fire Sermon.

Seven decks, 700 feet in length, 25,000 gross tons, one Turkish bath, a surgeon, a postal service, a gymnasium and a library:[1] the SS *Adriatic* was among the largest and most luxurious liners ever to set out on the Atlantic. Since its maiden voyage in 1907, it had taken just over a week to make the crossing between New York and Southampton via Cherbourg, and it was on just such a journey that on 10 June 1921 Eliot's mother Charlotte, sister Marion and brother Henry arrived in England.[2] Their visit would be a turning point in the poet's life. For the next ten weeks Eliot's mother and sister occupied the flat at Clarence Gate Gardens; brother Henry took a room two stops along the Metropolitan line at 41 Gordon Square – the flat of James and Alix Strachey (who were in Vienna with Sigmund Freud), two doors up from Vanessa Bell and Duncan Grant. Vivien and Tom moved into the glass-roofed attic of 12 Wigmore Street, a mile to the south-east, a small flat rented by Lucy Thayer, sister of Scofield. It was, from the beginning, a tiring series of arrangements, and by early July, with Vivien's health having deteriorated once more, Eliot 'got her away'[3] to Itchenor, Sussex, allowing Henry to move into Wigmore Street with Tom. Barely had that happened than Vivien was summoned back in order to discuss an urgent offer that Eliot had received from Lady Rothermere to launch a new literary periodical that would in time become *The Criterion*. She returned to the cramped glass roof in Wigmore Street, which now included Henry – 'very confined and uncomfortable quarters for three people', said Eliot.[4] Tensions with Mrs Eliot were apparent from the beginning, and it hadn't helped that Vivien had to be presented, 'for their benefit', when medical advice sought to usher her away to the country. 'These new and yet old relationships involve immense tact and innumerable adjustments,' Eliot told Richard Aldington. 'One sees lots of things that one never saw before.'[5]

//

When Igor Stravinsky's ballet *Le Sacre du printemps* had first opened in Paris in 1913 the audience was so rebellious that police were called to restore order. The revival that opened in the Parisian winter of 1920–1 was choreographed by Léonide Massine and made its London appearance at the Princes Theatre as *The Rite of Spring* on 27 June 1921. It would provide Eliot with the outstanding element in the long-prepared tapestry of his poem. On the face of it, the production was a failure, he said, because it hadn't been able to unite the music with the dance. 'In art there should be interpenetration and metamorphosis,'[6] and the production had achieved neither, leaving the music and ballet as two divisible arts. For the fusion of ancient and modern something particular needed to take place: 'a revelation of that vanished mind of which our mind is a continuation'. This was his experience with the Magdalenian cave art at the Font de Gaume: the memory of the tribe, our modern roots from origin, tradition and the individual talent. But the ballet wasn't that, and seemed so locked in its own ritual that it was simply unable to break into the present. The music, in contrast, had achieved a modern art of its own. From the moment the opening bassoon began to climb through its Lithuanian folk melody like ivy it pulled achingly upon the root of the past; from the moment it found its percussive explosion it ignited into the modern. Stravinsky had found in the great Russian plains of his imagination a soundtrack for modernity. He had metamorphosed the rhythm of the Great Steppes into 'the scream of the motor horn, the rattle of machinery, the grind of wheels, the beating of iron and steel, the roar of the underground railway, and the other barbaric cries of modern life'. It was too new and strange to please many listeners, Eliot understood, but to him it was thrilling: *the sound of horns and motors*, he was about to write in the long poem. And he called Stravinsky 'our two months' lion' for the impact the run had in London. Stravinsky had succeeded in isolating the cries of modern life 'and to transform these despairing noises into music'. And there – right there in that moment for Eliot – was the final piece of the jigsaw puzzle that would become *The Waste Land*. His long poem had identified its subject matter; it had found its motivations in Eliot's daily life; it had grasped the multiplicity of voices, the variety of the music hall, the moving images of the cinema; and now it had the 'auditory imagination' within its hearing – not only the lyric melody of ragtime and dance, but the music of the primitive imagination played on modern instruments.

//

Marianne Moore had written in *The Dial* that March that Eliot's poems were 'troutlike'[7] (praise, in her language), which in turn had drawn an appreciative letter from Eliot, who said that he would like to try to get her poems published in England if at all possible. It wasn't possible, she said, she wasn't ready, and felt she had further to go before a collection of poems could make its appearance.[8] So Eliot was delighted but surprised when he learned that Harriet Shaw Weaver was bringing out Moore's English debut at the Egoist Press that summer. String-tied, print-decorated covers, it was an elegant piece of printing and typographic work. There was only one problem: Moore didn't know about it, and it most certainly did not have her permission. The Egoist volume had been assembled in the hope of advancing her reputation by her admirers in London, H. D. and Bryher, but Moore didn't want her reputation advanced, at least not until she had material sufficient to back such a claim, and she had told them as much; she was furious that this had been 'put over' her head.[9] She appreciated the unstinting care taken with the production, and didn't mind the simple title, *Poems* (although *Observations* would have been her choice), but she simply didn't want these poems appearing now, and some of them not ever, and as a publication it couldn't possibly be to her advantage. She told Eliot that although she understood it to be the tribute of a friend's affection, to her it was little more than a testimony to how little she had accomplished as a poet.[10] And in one sense, she never really changed her attitude towards the release of her work. In 1934, she found herself rekindling the conversation with Eliot, this time for a prospective edition at Faber & Faber with him as publisher. At that moment she was moved to decline, as she had been before, telling him that 'I have not yet quite enough for a book'.[11] Her ferocious standards and personal modesty engendered an unusually illuminating exchange between a poet and their prospective publisher over a matter of unceasing importance to poets: the question of just exactly when it is that a collection of poems is 'enough'. 'The point at which one has "enough" for a book (of verse) is not a quantitative matter alone,' replied Eliot; 'it's a question of form.'

> One only has not enough, when one feels that the poems written require the cooperation of certain poems not yet written, in order to be themselves quite.[12]

It was a brilliant materialisation of the immaterial: to anticipate how what is present might depend for its completion upon something not yet in existence. With that answer, Eliot laid a standard which many deliberating poets have followed. And as for Moore's particular case, while he didn't wish to badger her, he believed that she most certainly had 'enough'. From that moment, and for the rest of their working lives, Moore and Eliot would publish together in London at Faber & Faber.

//

Eliot's lens on London continued from what he called the 'fine hot rainless spring' into the early summer. Albert Einstein had arrived from America on 8 June, and laid a wreath on Isaac Newton's grave in Westminster Abbey on 13 June. In between, the scientist had attended a reception in his honour at the Royal Astronomical Society, Eliot recorded in the third of his letters for *The Dial*.¹³ That Bernard Shaw had been invited to meet Einstein did not escape Eliot's attention, and he recorded with just a hint of mischief that Einstein had made no comment on that subject. J. C. Squire had also been in the news, as had the discovery of a new strand of influenza that left a bitter taste and dryness in the mouth.

The Dial seemed to be flourishing in New York now, and while the *Little Review* limped on from its defeat in court, in London the condition was one of literary drought. *Art & Letters* and *The Athenaeum* had gone, and *The Egoist* was now exclusively a publisher of books alone. Squire's *London Mercury* was in serious danger of becoming the centre of activity. Eliot knew that the capital needed a literary journal of its own, and had come to feel that he must be the one now to drive it forward. He sounded Scofield Thayer on a prospective partnership. Together, they wondered if they could interest Lady Rothermere in establishing a journal with an international platform, comprising *The Dial* in America and a new magazine edited by Eliot in London. It was a bold idea, but one she would not take up, and by the beginning of August she had decided to restrict her contribution to an English review: the *London Quarterly* it might have been called, until the suggestion of *The Criterion*.¹⁴

Eliot was meanwhile reading John Dryden for the third of his articles for *The Times*. *Annus Mirabilis*, Dryden's long poem on the renewal of London, had used the elegiac quatrains that Eliot was about to adopt for himself; he praised too the 'genius' of Pope's heroic couplets that Eliot was similarly about to take up in his own poem. Shakespeare, Jonson, the music hall, the demolition of city churches, Baudelaire, Dryden: every matter that Eliot looked to came from the poetry of cities and, in particular, from London. Sure enough, the opening setting of his long poem had been elsewhere, but already that sequence had lost its place in the poem, while the chambers and churches and bridges and boozers had all moved in upon the unreal city on which he was about to expand. 'What is needed of art is a simplification of current life into something rich and strange,' he wrote in 'London Letter', in doing so returning once again to Ariel's song from *The Tempest*.[15] He had sketched five lines of manuscript, as either a rough for the present typescript or a memo to be incorporated in what that autumn would become 'Dirge' and 'Death by Water'. In other news, he wrote, octopus and poisonous jellyfish had been found at Margate.[16]

//

Ezra Pound peeled himself from the pillar he was leaning on and bowed: 'Sooner than might have been expected.' The young man before him in the Parisian street was E. E. Cummings, an introduction that Scofield Thayer had been attempting to effect without success, but which had happened in the event quite naturally. He was a gymnastic personality, said Cummings of Pound afterwards, but timorous and subtle with it – 'or in other words somebody, and intricate'.[17] Less elusive had been an introduction by Thayer to the literary court of Gertrude Stein. On Saturday evenings her salon would gather in her Left Bank studio apartment at 27 rue de Fleurus: Picasso and Braque and Matisse were among the regulars, Apollinaire and Picabia too; and then there was the raft of resident Americans, to which she gave Pound a wary welcome, but they hadn't taken well to each other. He was 'a village explainer', she explained, 'excellent if you were a village, but if you were not, not'.[18]

He couldn't forgive her for putting it 'all over' him in conversation, said Thayer;[19] she couldn't forgive him for breaking her chair. Ernest Hemingway suspected that Stein had given him the seat knowing that it would break.[20]

Pound took to life on the Left Bank. He liked to dine at an Alsatian restaurant called Emile, beside the famous Bal Bullier dance hall. There he would relax and hold court with all who would listen. He was 'the merriest spirit of the party', said one regular. A 'supreme' dancer, Sisley Huddleston wrote in 1920s Paris: 'Whoever has not seen Ezra Pound, ignoring all the rules of tango and of fox-trot, kicking up fantastic heels in a highly personal Charleston, closing his eyes as his toes nimbly scattered right and left, has missed one of the spectacles which reconcile us to life.'[21] The Australian artist Stella Bowen remembered his style from wartime London as 'highly personal and very violent' – springing up and down, swaying from side to side.[22] Caresse Crosby took him to hear a band of Martinique players at the Boule Blanche in 1930. He eyed the dancefloor scornfully, saying, 'These people don't know a thing about rhythm,' and began tapping out one of his own:

> Suddenly unable to sit still a minute longer he leapt to the floor
> and seized the tiny Martiniquaise vendor of cigarettes in his arms,
> packets flying, then head back, eyes closed, chin out, he began a sort
> of voodoo prance, his tiny partner held glued against his piston-
> pumping knees.[23]

As the tempo grew, a crowd swelled around the two dancers to crescendo, remembered Crosby. 'Ezra opened his eyes, flicked the cigarette girl aside like an extinguished match and collapsed into the chair beside me.'

Pound was flourishing, though some of his encounters were not without risk. Jean Cocteau had genius, Pound would say, but their friendship was nearly his undoing after a dinner in Pound's honour almost turned into his last.[24] Robert Desnos had sworn death to Cocteau, and joined the occasion believing the Frenchman would be an invited guest. When Cocteau didn't appear, Desnos lunged with a knife at Pound instead and had to be wrestled out of the restaurant into the Place de l'Odéon outside.[25]

These were new and daring days, and just as Pound needed. Paris was vibrant, pioneering and modern, and everything that London was once but had failed to sustain, and brought Pound an assured new lease of life. 'I actually believe he cooked better in Paris,' said Lewis.[26]

//

Eliot told Richard Aldington that he found his mother 'terrifyingly energetic for seventy-seven'. He travelled with her to Warwick for the weekend of 9 July, from where she headed onward to Stratford with Marion while he returned to London. But it was the variety of energy rather than the level that Eliot had begun to find terrifying that summer. 'Anxieties of several kinds' had overtaken him, he told Aldington: one undoubtedly had been the prospectus for the new journal with Lady Rothermere, but by far the deeper and more serious anguish was a familial one: 'the strain of accommodating myself to people who in many ways are now strangers to me'.[27] He admitted that he had not expected to do any work while his family stayed, but by mid-July he was falling behind on even basic correspondence.[28]

Vivien, however, on 20 July, said something rather different: she noted that, despite his fatigue, Eliot had been busily finishing off 'various things' ahead of joining her on a much-needed retreat to Itchenor.[29] Almost certainly he was writing the first half of the fourth of his 'London Letters', in which he reported on Stravinsky's June appearance; he probably covered the second half of the letter on his return: George Bernard Shaw's *The Shewing-Up of*

Blanco Posnet which would run through July and August at the Queen's Theatre on Shaftesbury Avenue. So anxious was he to be away from the strain of family that it seemed even to filter into the 'London Letter' he was drafting: 'One knows, oneself, that there are times when it is desirable to be seen and times when it is felicitous to vanish.'[30]

It was a sudden and great release that Eliot and Vivien experienced when they broke free from the family on 22 July for Chichester Harbour. 'My mind has left me,' Vivien told Scofield Thayer, 'and I am becoming gradually insane.'[31] Once, when the two had been on the verge of courtship, Thayer had invited her to drown her sorrows with him; now she reminded him of his offer. 'I am ready at any moment,' she said.

The Hutchinsons were away from Eleanor House, at nearby West Wittering, and so Eliot had no visitors to receive, wrote no letters that survive, had no immediate dealings with Lady Rothermere, and had seemingly left in London his 'wretched old' Corona typewriter, suspending any work on the 'London Letter'. It was, just at that moment, only Vivien and himself, and ten days without interruption or distraction. It was surely in these moments, with the tides making north along the estuary to Bosham Hards, or in walking south to the shingle spits of Ella Nore and East Head, that Eliot began to turn his mind to the next instalment of the long poem. Perhaps he even produced some scattered lines or rough manuscript in Itchenor; perhaps it was there that he found a title for the lines to come, in the flaming eye of Mahā-Vagga, from which was pronounced 'The Fire Sermon'.

//

If 'In the Cage'/'A Game of Chess' had seemed ceremonial in its opening lines, the draft of 'The Fire Sermon' would raise the formal register higher still. For seventy lines, it gathered itself in

THE FIRE SERMON.

7.

Admonished by the sun's inclining ray,
~~And swift approaches of the thievish day,~~
The white-armed Fresca blinks, and yawns, and gapes,
Aroused from dreams of love and pleasant rapes.
Electric summons of the busy bell
Brings brisk Amanda to destroy the spell;
With coarsened hand, and hard plebeian tread,
Who draws the curtain round the lacquered bed,
Depositing thereby a polished tray
Of soothing chocolate, or stimulating tea.

Leaving the bubbling beverage to cool,
Fresca slips softly to the needful stool,
Where the pathetic tale of Richardson
Eases her labour till the deed is done.
Then slipping back between the conscious sheets,
Explores a ~~page of ribbon~~ as she eats.   *the Daily Mirror*
Her hands caress the egg's well-rounded dome,
She sinks in revery, till the letters come.
Their ~~hobbled~~ contents at a glance devours,
Then to reply devotes her practic'd powers.

"My dear, how are you? I'm unwell today,
And have been, since I saw you at the play.
I hope that nothing mars your gaity,
And things go better with you, than with me.
I went last night - more out of dull despair -
To Lady Kleinwurm's party - who was there?
Oh, Lady Kleinwurm's monde - no one that mattered -
Somebody sang, and Lady Kleinwurm chattered.
What are you reading? anything that's new?
I have a clever book by Giraudoux.
Clever, I think, is all. I've much to say -
But cannot say it that is just my way -
When shall we meet tell me all your manoeuvers;
And all about yourself and your new lovers -
And when to Paris? I must make an end,
My dear, believe me, your devoted
                              friend".

This ended, to the steaming bath she moves,
Her tresses fanned by little flutt'ring Loves;
Odours, confected by the cunning French,
Disguise the good old hearty female stench.

artful

---

iambic pentameter, this time finished off with lines in couplets echoing the mock-heroic majesty of Alexander Pope's *The Rape of the Lock*. The white-armed Fresca of 'Gerontion' had returned as the wanton and obsessive subject of this sequence. From her waking to her morning toilet, every action of her day is described and ridiculed: her literary aspiration ('She may as well write poetry, as count sheep'). Her social pretension ('Not quite an adult, and still less a child'). Her diminution to a vessel of sexual and scatological function (a 'strolling slattern in a tawdry gown, / A doorstep dunged by every dog in town').[32] No doubt Eliot's aim was one of period style: a satire in an eighteenth-century mode, where scurrilous form was understood – such popular entertainments as he had been praising in his criticism. No doubt his aim was also to achieve a kind of humour, on which he had just written in praise of the English comedic style and the valuable place of the comedy revue. And he had also just written of poetic drama as the form that best expressed the varied types of society. In his critical prose, Eliot had foreshadowed the intention to bring both humour and drama into his poetry, but now that it had arrived it simply didn't fit the manner of the poem. These were prurient, damning and lustful reductions without clear motivation. Intolerance had dragged 'Bleistein' and 'Gerontion' into a mire, and it threatened to do the same here. As a literary trope it didn't work; as an evocation of personality it was repellent. As Gertrude Stein had told Ernest Hemingway of one of his short stories at almost that moment: it was *inaccrochable* – a work that could not be exhibited because the indecency of content prevented it.[33] There was no point in an *inaccrochable* art, she told him: it was non-transmissible, and therefore a non-starter.

It was a relief when the draft broke in with a new metre and a new moment, casting back for tone and rhythms already moulded in the first two parts of the poem. A rat returning through the vegetation; *The Tempest* returning for a fifth and sixth time, 'Musing upon the king my brother's wreck / And on the king my father's death before him' – and 'This music crept by me upon the waters'; Philomela and Tereus, returning, twit twit twit *So rudely forc'd*; the Unreal City returning.[34] And then the promised elegiac quatrains of John Dryden: seventeen of them, narrating the typist and her 'young man carbuncular', as told by Tiresias.

Tiresias, seer of Thebes, lived seven generations with prophecy granted by Zeus, could understand the language of birds, could divine the future from fire or smoke.

Tiresias, changed into female form for seven years, after beating with his stick two mating snakes to the displeasure of Hera; restored to male form encountering the same and this time letting them lie.

Tiresias, blinded by Athena (Callimachus) after he stumbled upon her bathing naked, or by Hera (Hesiod) for impiety after stumbling into her dispute with Zeus as to whether woman or man best understood sexual pleasure.

Tiresias, death by water poisoned in the tainted spring of Tilphussa.

Tiresias, 'the most important personage in the poem', said Eliot, in a somewhat wilful misdirection for his notes of the summer of 1922; never the *most* important, but a person of importance nonetheless through which are funnelled some of the multiple voices of the poem; said Eliot: 'uniting all the rest'.[35] This would matter more to the poem once the descriptive working title 'He Do the Police in Different Voices' had been abandoned, and it would offer a key indicator for it: for the poem was not to be a collage of various voices spliced together, but a single voice speaking variously, to create, as Pound said of the poem in 1924, 'an emotional unit'.[36] In reading Seneca, Eliot would imagine something similar, saying that 'the plays were written to be declaimed, probably by a single speaker'.[37] And in 1939, responding to a radio reading of *The Waste Land* which had been cast for four voices, Eliot said that he had a strong dislike of dividing 'poems which were conceived in terms of one voice'. He said that it was a pity that poets hadn't learned more from choral work: 'And by choral work I do not mean simply verse to be spoken by a number of people in unison, but by an orchestration of a number of different voices speaking singly in turn.'[38] Not a Greek chorus, then, but a harmony found in consecutive and sometimes discordant parts. And not a series of unrelated images, either, but a coordinated catalogue of visions that had given a title to the section: the blazing eye of prophecy, the seer, the prophet and the Buddha.

//

The rehabilitation of Ezra Pound in *The Dial* continued throughout the summer when in August Scofield Thayer gave a first outing in print to the fifth, sixth and seventh *Cantos*.[39] Meanwhile, the Pounds had at last found a studio apartment to rent in Montparnasse, across the Luxembourg Gardens; they would wait for four months for the tenants to vacate. Agnes Bedford was in town to work with Pound on his proposed opera, *Le Testament de Villon*, and he had taken up the bassoon – 'good for the lungs', he told his mother, and Dorothy agreed, admiring the finer noises amid the 'queer' ones. 'He will be a soloist always,' she told Mrs Pound ruefully.[40]

//

When Eliot returned with Vivien from Itchenor at the beginning of August it was to consecutive weekend visits to Ottoline Morrell's manor house at Garsington: first with his mother, and then the following weekend with his brother. His visits to Garsington were never so regular (he hadn't been for a year), but impressing upon his family the kind of circles in which he moved must have been of some importance. The performance was exhausting, but it would at least be the last of the common activities as the Eliot family began to prepare for their return to America.

On Saturday 20 August, ten weeks after their arrival, Charlotte, Marion and Henry sailed from the port of Liverpool aboard the RMS *Cedric* for New York.[41] Tom and Vivien were not only exhausted but depressed. It had been six years since Eliot had seen his mother: his father had died and had his ashes scattered at Bellefontaine Cemetery in that time, and neither his decision to marry Vivien nor her place by his side had been accepted by the family. The visit of Mrs Eliot had been the hope to change all that; but it simply hadn't transpired. More had been riding on his mother's visit than perhaps even he knew. In the shadow of his father's death, he had yearned for her, longed for reconciliation, for a reunion with his childhood days, for an endorsement of his literary and married life; but he was granted none of these things. In seeing her off on Saturday 20 August, there had been no bonding, no forgiveness, no promise of a new start. Reunion never seemed further away, and Eliot may have experienced a return of the sense of abandonment he knew as a child. He said that he felt *engrossed* by her departure, and told Sydney Schiff that 'the reaction from the strain of it has been paralysing'.[42]

For the first time, Mrs Eliot had observed first hand the relationship between Vivien and her son. There was love between them evidently, she said, even devotion, but it came at a cost to her Tom. Vivien expected so much of him, *demanded* so much of him: 'I think he is afraid of her,'[43] she told Henry. She had tried to remain above the fray of the comings and goings of Vivien's health, but had been drawn in nonetheless to something that she probably didn't understand – who among them could say that they did? 'She likes the role of invalid,' Henry interpreted her as saying, and that, together with a desire to be petted and fussed over, she unconsciously encouraged her own breakdowns. It was hard to tell what was physical and what mental, but Henry was in little doubt that her predicament was essentially pathological, and said that had she a will to be well then she could be well. 'She needs something to take her mind off herself,' he said, 'something to absorb her entire attention.'[44] Bootstraps, was what she should reach for.

To Vivien and Tom, Mrs Eliot had not done enough to show concern, and when two days had passed between Vivien's return from Itchenor and Charlotte's bedside visit to her at Wigmore

Street, she felt Tom's 'beautiful attitude of affection' towards her slip.[45] Vivien had found the atmosphere around Mrs Eliot an 'emotionless condition', a cause of great strain from which she said she wanted to break out to scream and dance.[46] Immediately, a migraine overcame her ('Vivien always recites some account of her migraines': Henry to his mother) that lasted until the following Tuesday.[47] She worried that in Charlotte's eyes her behaviour had been demonstrative, expressive, too wild, like that of an animal and 'no lady'; but she had felt stunned, *perfectly stunned* throughout the visit, and simply couldn't manage to rein herself in any longer, ending in what she described as a fit. 'Good-bye Henry,' she had said. 'And *be personal*, you must be personal, or else it's no good. Nothing's any good.'[48]

For ten weeks, Eliot had found himself in the eye of the storm between Charlotte's reserve and Vivien's extraversion; to each he had preserved his beautiful attitude of affection. It had taken every ounce of his 'prepared faces', as he once called them to Igor Stravinsky, and the effort had simply overwhelmed him.

No sooner had his family departed than Eliot attempted to renew his literary friendships, but his strength was barely up to it. On the Monday, he met Richard Aldington for lunch at the Cock Tavern in Fleet Street, and on the Tuesday, Dorothy Pound, newly arrived from Paris, for dinner at the Kensington Palace Hotel.[49] He was desperate to revive his fading effort on the poem if only he could summon the energy. He had told Mary Hutchinson that he wouldn't be able to return to Itchenor any time soon: he must stay in London partly to save expense, but also 'to tackle a special piece of work'.[50] By this he may have meant the preparations for the new journal with Lady Rothermere that he was keeping secret from friends until the arrangements had been finalised; but he may also have meant by this 'The Fire Sermon', which he wasn't far from typing out.

The Eliots couldn't bring themselves even to look in on Clarence

Gate Gardens until three days after the family's departure. It was then that Vivien had discovered an envelope that Henry had left behind, containing a cheque. She was quite overcome: 'It is *terrible* that you should be so generous,' she wrote at once. But there was a further surprise. 'And the typewriter? What does that mean please? You can hardly have mistaken them *in* (as Tom insists) the circumstances. But whatever it means, you are shown up as an angel. A bloody angel, as they say over here.'[51] Henry had exchanged his typewriter with Eliot's: one Corona for another, only Henry's was newer and in better working order, and would carry Eliot through the next two years.[52] Eliot was most painfully touched: he was glad to see the back of the machine he called 'my wretched old one', which had been in use since at least 1913 and had long since needed to be retired. He told Henry that he hoped this old machine wouldn't fall to pieces: 'I have the same feeling whenever I look at it or use it.'[53]

It took a further week for the Eliots to find the motivation to move back into their flat from Wigmore Street. Clarence Gate Gardens seemed desolate without his mother, he told her, but it wasn't true; both flats now seemed equally unbearable, and wishing to be in neither, they lingered on at Wigmore Street 'morosely'.[54] They couldn't even bring themselves to go out for the alcohol they needed and then bickered in the evening for going without. Finally, on the last weekend of August, they packed their suitcases and made the journey a mile north-east across the Marylebone Road to reclaim their home.

//

'I am feeling completely exhausted,' wrote Eliot to Mary Hutchinson on 1 September 1921. 'The departure of my family laid us both out – and have had some splitting headaches.'[55] To Richard Aldington he addressed the first letter on the typewriter that Henry had left him, but a new machine couldn't bring change to the old themes as he wrote of the Eliots' continuing illness.[56] Workloads pressed in on him. In addition to his daily routine at the bank, he wrote a 'London Letter' for *The Dial* and for the *Times Literary Supplement* struggled with a review 'unsatisfactory to myself'[57] of metaphysical poetry in which he described the decline of literature after Alexander Pope, a moment when English verse had 'gone to pieces'.[58] *Gone to pieces* was the very thing that Pound would soon tell Scofield Thayer that Eliot had done.[59]

By the end of September, Eliot's health had broken down completely. He told his brother that he had been feeling nervous and shaky and had very little self-control, and that he had overdrawn his nervous energy.[60] He could no longer manage his work at the bank, but they had been 'very kind', he said, and granted him a leave of absence, which was to take place under a medical regimen of rest, diet and repair. It was not an insignificant grant of leave: not a week or two, but three complete months.

For the first time since January, Ezra Pound was in London ('the bassoon slumbers') for a week's stay with his mother-in-law, Olivia Shakespear, in Kensington. He was meeting with Arthur Griffith, founder of Sinn Féin, who was also in town with an Irish delegation discussing terms with the British government that would lead to the signing of the Anglo-Irish Treaty in December: for an 'illuminating' hour Griffith listened to Pound advancing a case for Social Credit before telling him that it wasn't possible to move people with 'a cold thing, like economics'.[61] Paris had made Pound no less forgiving towards the English, who continued in his opinion to terminate 'below the cervical ganglion', but he saw Ford ('about as usual'), Yeats ('somnolent') and Lewis ('painting better than I had expected'), and on 12 October he called on Eliot at Clarence Gate Gardens to find him in an enfeebled state.[62] 'Eliot has been ordered away for 3 months rest,' he reported to his parents. 'It is high time.'

Eliot's psychological stability had been more dependent upon his parents than he cared to admit. The loss of his father had intensified a need for reconciliation with his mother that had, after two years of planning for her visit, simply failed to materialise, bringing no closeness or forgiveness. Her departure had left his crisis unresolved; worse, he now felt estranged, also, for he had no choice but to resign himself to the idea that there would be no compensation, no redemption in his familial purgatory, no amends for his father through his mother. 'It did not seem right or inevitable,' he said of his family's departure. 'We cannot reconcile ourselves to it.'[63] Neither right nor inevitable, but there it was, plainly before him. 'The rule of conduct was simply pleasing mother,' Eliot would write in time in *The Family Reunion*. She hadn't been pleased by Eliot's life on seeing it close up, any more than his father had approved from a distance. Like the lost prince Hamlet, fatherless, appeasing a mother with whom he could not connect, Eliot felt undermined and undone. 'And now,' wrote Mrs Eliot to Henry, 'as I always expected, he is the one to break down.'[64]

'I have seen the specialist (said to be the best in London) who made his tests and said that I must go away *at once* for three months, <quite> alone and away from anyone, not exert my mind at all, and follow his strict rules for every hour of the day,' Eliot informed Richard Aldington at the beginning of October.[65] A diagnosis of any kind must have seemed like progress of sorts, but it brought with it accompanying worries for Eliot. He said that he dreaded the solitude of being among strangers, and anticipated a period 'of great depression', particularly at first, which he had heard would be the hardest phase of all. But he would try.[66]

On 13 October, the day after meeting Pound, Eliot had decided on a destination.

'I am going to Margate tomorrow, and expect to stay at least a month,' he told Aldington.[67] Vivien would come too, at least until he was settled in; she wasn't supposed to but he couldn't bear to face this entirely alone.

'It is very terrifying to stop after having gone on for so long,' he told Henry.[68]

//

A hunter's moon hung low over Margate for the Eliots' arrival. The fine, rainless spring recorded in the 'London Letter' had turned to heatwave that summer. In London, Kew Gardens baked under the hottest October ever known, while in Kent, the thermometers held at a steady seventy-five through the first week of the month.[69] Margate had long boasted 'even more temperature' than any other seaside resort, and was soaking in ten hours of sunshine daily.[70] But now drought had struck the county of Kent: the grasses of Thanet were parched and scorched, its countryside a patchwork of yellow and brown, dried tubers. Autumn continued as if summer would never end: the desert year, it would come to be known.[71]

The holiday trade had long ended, and in the quiet left behind the local newspaper reported day-to-day business. A former sergeant, crippled in combat, had been found guilty of the petty theft of a rolled gold watch.[72] A Ramsgate trawler had landed an anchor and chain 'of ancient pattern'. On Marine Parade, the star turn in the boxing bout had seen better days. Curley Walker had been bantamweight champion during the war, but his reputation hadn't recovered since he headbutted an opponent in London's New Cross. More and more, Curley Walker's rivals seemed to escape his swing; his loss in twenty rounds at Margate was the midpoint in a run of eleven straight defeats.

Eliot told Richard Aldington that from 14 October he could be found at the Albemarle Hotel, Cliftonville, above Margate, and that he expected to stay for at least a month.[73] No one besides the bank had that address, and Aldington himself wasn't to give it up under any circumstances. Would he be good enough to take in their cat (a good mouser), acquired to replace dear Dinah Brooks? And would St John Hutchinson take over his column in *The Dial*? Eliot tied up as many loose ends as he could. The summer had been an exceptional struggle, but for the first time since the armistice, Eliot had largely spent it with Vivien. There had been no French trips with Lewis or Pound, as there had in 1919 and 1920, and for all the tension and strain with Vivien, Eliot could not bear the prospect of beginning his recovery alone. He thought that he might even ask her to join him on the continent, should he find the treatment there that he had heard about from Ottoline Morrell. More than at any moment in their troubled marriage, Eliot was reliant upon his wife for his stability and security. The family visit had failed to repair the years of damage; Pound was once again abroad and to all intents out of reach; the gratitude lavished upon Richard Aldington for 'an immense support' was out of proportion to the two men's connection, and underlined quite how vulnerable Eliot now seemed. Vivien had never been so needed; but at that moment she appeared intent on a flirtatious correspondence with Scofield Thayer, who had moved on from a summer in Paris, to the Frisian island of Sylt, in northern Germany, and was now in Vienna, a patient of Sigmund Freud. 'Tom has had rather a serious breakdown,' Vivien reported, adding, 'I have not nearly finished my own nervous breakdown yet.' He had stopped all work for three months to go away, she reported: *she* rather wanted to go somewhere too, just like Tom, she told Thayer; it didn't much matter where, 'but I must escape from England or it will smother me. Have been trying to escape for five–six years!' Six years had been the length of the Eliots' marriage. 'I may appear in Vienna,' she trailed.[74]

The Albemarle was, by Cliftonville standards, a modest hotel: a step above bed and breakfast, but well below the large, exclusive accommodation that had developed there in the late nineteenth century.

The grand 1868 Cliftonville Hotel offered three hundred rooms for well-to-do families and attic space for their entourage of nannies and personal servants; it had its own orchestra, and so noteworthy were its guests that a list of resident 'fashionables' would be printed each week in the local newspaper. Beside it stood the magnificent Queen's Highcliffe, second only to the Cliftonville in splendour, with its eight-course dinner for those wearing evening dress and a ballroom for four hundred dancers; it was from the windows of this hotel that John Betjeman looked out on the dark terrace as Britain braced for German invasion in 1940, its fairy lights dimmed as something to be fought for.[75] A narrow fissure descended to the beach, known to the fishermen who cut it as Devil's Gap, and across it, nestled into the south-east corner of the green at 41–3 Eastern Esplanade, was the Grand, opened in 1904 as the Hydro for its luxurious Turkish and Russian baths offering electric, thermal, seaweed and brine treatments. Of all the Cliftonville establishments that surrounded the green, the Grand felt itself the most exclusive, and advertised unblushingly for 'visitors of a class who have hitherto been inclined to look askance at the town'.[76] And next door but one to the Grand, on the broadest thoroughfare of Cliftonville, stood the Albemarle Hotel, 'newly furnished in the modern style' under the proprietorship of Walter Beazley, a four-storey double-fronted terrace before which, every evening, a lamplighter wicked the lanterns of the promenade.[77]

J. M. W. Turner sought out the unrestricted light and skies that were 'the loveliest in all Europe', but the early Victorians came 'escaping from a chrysalis state in London to flutter as a butterfly at Margate', and whether for holiday or convalescence they made the most of the town's entertainment.[78] The Winter Gardens opened on Fort Green in 1911, close by the five-storey Hotel Metropole: it carried a municipal orchestra that treated audiences of up to 4,500 to famous arias and classical favourites, and was close enough to London to entice Covent Garden's visiting stars of the moment – Anna Pavlova and Nellie Melba among them. On the day the Eliots arrived, the Gardens was preparing for the Christmas season with what the local paper described as 'first-class concert parties, a course of lectures, bands at the weekends, and dance'.[79] The Parade Cinema opposite the pier proudly advertised itself as 'the only place of entertainment in Thanet fitted with a "SLIDING ROOF"' – a retractable covering kept open when the films were not running, allowing fresh air and sunlight, 'the best of all disinfectants', to flood the auditorium: tip-stalls at 6d, a back row of doubles for couples at 1s.[80] On Monday 24 October, for six days only, Charlie Chaplin's *The Kid*, the 'Great Million Dollar Six Reel Production he took a year to make', screened daily at 2.45, 6.30 and 8.35. ('The egregious merit of Chaplin', Eliot would write in 1923, 'is that he has escaped in his own way from the realism of the cinema and invented a *rhythm*.')[81]

By the time of the armistice, variety and vaudeville shows were replacing classical concerts, and down on Marine Terrace in the south bay a more profound metamorphosis was taking place. The Hall-by-the-Sea had opened there in 1865 in a space vacated by a railway terminal. It was then a roofed corridor within which a music hall and ballroom were housed, to which were added a skating rink and a Ferris wheel, and then a circus arena in which the proprietor kept his faded lions. By 1919 it had found a new owner in John Henry Iles, and a new model in the amusement parks that he built in Pittsburgh and elsewhere in North America. The relaunched attraction housed a menagerie and a zoo, and a miniature railway puttering through ornamental gardens, and state-of-the-art mechanical rides: the Joy Wheel, the Whip and the boating River Caves. But its main attraction was the rollercoaster known as the Scenic Railway, whose mile-long wooden boards rose high into the Margate skyline, and whose thrill-screams would become almost as much a part of the local soundscape as the cry of the gulls. The ride drew half a million visitors in its first three months. It had opened in 1921, and carried a name that surely had been noted by Eliot: Dreamland. For years to come, it would be known as the Heartbeat of Margate.

Times were changing on Margate Sands. Bathing had been segregated until the decade before the war: men and women separated by a fifty-yard division, and by a policeman who patrolled an exclusion zone. Only in 1919 had bathing machines begun to give way to cabins and tents, but even so some bathers still insisted upon the machines – a wheeled, horse-drawn hut driven into three feet of sea water so that its inhabitant could bathe with discretion. Modesty was respectability, and so men sported jackets and a collar and tie and wilted under heat; women wore their beach dresses full length. The donkeys, it was said, carried angels by day and spirits by night: holidaymakers in the sunshine, smugglers' contraband in the dark.

Seven, eight, nine hours a day, the Eliots soaked in sunshine; by Tuesday of their first week Margate was basking under clear blue skies and seventy-three degrees. Eliot spent most of his days in the open air, some of the time resting in the hotel, trying to rid his mind of the swarming life of London that had left him feeling so rushed and tired.[82] He would tell Sydney Schiff, towards the end of his stay, that he rather dreaded returning to the city: it was possible to become dependent on sea or mountains to provide a sense of security.

The Eliots had taken well to the White Room of the Albemarle: such a nice, comfortable and inexpensive little hotel, said Vivien. They took their meals in, 'en pension', for which they paid £1 1s daily, with an extra shilling for breakfast and an extra shilling again for the bath. By the second week, Vivien was able to discern quite a change in her husband. 'Tom is getting on *amazingly*,' she told Violet Schiff. 'It is not quite a fortnight yet, but he looks already younger, and fatter and nicer.'[83] Walking west from the hotel would take Eliot down the Fort Lower Promenade into the town, across the crescent, jettied bay to Nayland Rock shelter where he could sit and watch the movement of the tide, and the locals working the beach for whelks or fishing off the pier with a simple line and hook. Tram cars clattered noisily between the station behind the shelter and the hotels on Cliftonville's heights. Walking east, he could clear the town entirely for the scotched brown cliffs overlooking Foreness Point while the long late summer lasted. But conditions had begun to turn. Sunshine warmed the cooling air, but when a depression blew in on strong winds from Ireland, the temperatures dropped so much that for the first time in a week the Eliots warmed up in a hot bath.

Eliot had been reflecting on a conversation with Ottoline Morrell. Exactly a decade had passed since her first visit to see specialist doctors in Lausanne, on the shores of Lac Léman, Switzerland. She had returned again in 1912 and 1913, by which time she was under the care of a young Swiss doctor called Roger Vittoz. Julian Huxley had been a patient of the same doctor, Eliot learned from Ottoline, and might also be able to provide a reference. Eliot had been instructed by his London doctors not to tax himself with writing, but now took up his pen: Ottoline had strongly advised him to go, he explained to Huxley on 26 October, but he knew nothing of Vittoz, and Switzerland was expensive and he must be sure of the benefit of treatment: could Huxley provide an evaluation of the doctor's worth? And even suggest a moderately inexpensive pension in which he might stay?[84]

Vivien continued to witness an improvement in Eliot's demeanour. 'I have started Tom well,' she told Mary Hutchinson after a fortnight, 'and he shows great improvement already. He looks younger and better looking.'[85] He even seemed well enough to be left to his recuperation, and on Friday 28 October, Vivien returned to London. Eliot moved into sole occupancy of Room 6, at half the daily price (10s 6d) of their previous accommodation. The Albemarle had served them well, Vivien wrote to Mary as she departed:

'marvellously comfortable and inexpensive', and something of the flavour of the town had entered pleasantly into the Eliots' consciousness: 'Margate is rather queer, and we don't dislike it.'

For two weeks, Eliot had honoured the terms of his reclusion. He had broken the embargo on correspondence only once, and then to make the necessary enquiry with Julian Huxley about Dr Vittoz. But that Saturday, 29 October, in Vivien's absence, he sent off a postcard to Richard Aldington deploring the state of reviewing in *The Times*, and in particular remembering the mauling of Pound's *Mauberley* in the *Supplement* the previous summer ('needlessly obscure . . . an esoteric volume'), an event from fifteen months before, and yet still he told Aldington, 'I am quite distressed about E. P.'[86] He wrote two open letters to the newspaper, only one of which was published, to his annoyance; but the letters alone signalled a critical re-engagement that now typically preceded his verse. It may have been that day that Eliot received a 'very full and satisfactory' reply from Huxley, and for the first time in his stay, his hotel bill recorded that he made a telephone call, most likely to Vivien, now back at Clarence Gate Gardens, in order to share the contents of the letter he had received. Huxley had commended Vittoz unreservedly, leaving Eliot to conclude, 'He sounds just the man I want.' The search for a solution had seemed endless, but at last he may have found a therapeutic response he had been looking for.

'I shall go to Vittoz.'[87]

//

The thirtieth of October was Pound's thirty-sixth birthday, but in his mind it was a date of mightier significance, for it was also the day that James Joyce completed *Ulysses*. Pound declared the moment Year 1 p.s.U', postscriptum *Ulysses*: 'Here was the JOB DONE and finished, the diagnosis and cure was here.'[88] He would say that it marked the end of the Christian Era, and the beginning of another: not *The Cantos*, as it would turn out, but quite a different poem altogether, whose opening drafts were now just days away from being placed in Pound's hands.[89]

//

For an evening, a day and a morning, Atlantic rain swept into Margate, soaking the dry soil. The weather had cooled dramatically, and struggled now to climb above ten degrees centigrade (fifty degrees Fahrenheit); Eliot took baths almost daily to warm up from the long, cold hours he now spent sitting in the shelter at Nayland Rock, on the far western cove of the town beach.[90] His decision to go to Switzerland was now made, but he waited for the clinic to confirm arrangements, and told his brother that he thought he might have to remain in Kent for several weeks longer ('Very good sea air, and quiet').[91] That Friday, 4 November, he made a telephone call so expensive at 4s 6d (almost half the rental of his room) that it could only have been a long-distance connection, to the clinic of Dr Vittoz or to the pension at which he would stay, the Hôtel Sainte-Luce, recommended by Ottoline Morrell, just north of the Gare de Lausanne. By Sunday, he was still awaiting a reply from the clinic to his telegram about his treatment, but if all seemed acceptable he would leave for Switzerland the following week. Only a few days before, Dr Vittoz was merely a recommendation; now Eliot was staking his recovery on him. He wrote to Richard Aldington, Sunday 6 November, to offer him the Eliots' flat, rent free, for a period of six weeks.

> My idea is to consult, and perhaps stay some time under, Vittoz, who is said to be the best mental specialist in Europe – now that I have a unique opportunity for doing so. I am satisfied, since being here, that my 'nerves' are a very mild affair, due, not to overwork, but

to an *aboulie* and emotional derangement which has been a lifelong affliction. Nothing wrong with my mind.[92]

Aboulie was the hallmark phrase of Dr Vittoz. His *Traitement des Psychonévroses par la Rééducation du Controle Cérébral* had been a publishing event when it was first issued in Paris in 1911, and in an English translation in London the same year. It had gone into a third edition by the time Eliot acquired his French-language copy in 1921. That he used the specific term with Aldington suggests that he may already have had his copy in his hands in Margate when he wrote his letter of 6 November. Eliot didn't possess the English edition, but if he had he would have seen the word translated as 'lack of will'; it was one of many sections marked by Eliot, and it contained a touchstone sentence: 'Que l'absence de volonté est plus apparente que réelle.' *The want of will is more apparent than real.*[93]

Eliot may have returned to 'The Fire Sermon' early on in his stay, but most likely he waited for Vivien's departure on Friday 28 October, explaining, as she did that week, that 'it is so difficult to write with people about'.[94] Possibly, he carried on in Margate where he had left off in Itchenor and London, continuing in blank verse but with a loosened rhyme scheme. He had been practising scales on the mandolin that Vivien had given him in Margate, he'd told Sydney Schiff.

> O City, City, I have heard + hear
> The pleasant whining of ~~the~~ [no, *a*] mandoline
> ~~Outside~~ [no, *Beside*] a public bar in lower Thames Street
> And a clatter + a chatter ~~in the bar~~ from within[95]

He decided to reverse the order of the second and third lines, perhaps seeking a departure from the end rhyme that he had established thus far. Then,

> Where fishmen lounge + loafe + spit at noon

He partly struck that out and had another go.

Where fishmen lounge at noon, where the walls
at noon *time*, where the walls
at noon time, *out* where the walls

– not *out*.

Where fishmen lounge at noon time, *there* the walls
Of Magnus Martyr stood, + stand, + hold
Their joyful splendour of Corinthian white + gold

And not *Their joyful* splendour either: *Inviolable* splendour?
No, he had that already in 'A Game of Chess'. *Inexplicable?* Yes.
And *splendour? music?* Splendour was right. *Inexplicable splendour
of Corinthian white + gold.* Nor were these lines quite in the right
order. The *fishmen* should come before the *clatter*; no, the *clatter*
should come before the *public bar*. Round and round went the carousel of the draft, but at least he was back in the activity of the
poem.

Beneath the lines 'O City, City', he ruled off the page in a clean
stroke, and began another sketch of the city, this time in twelve
lines of terza rima. 'London, the swarming creatures [no, *life*] that
you breed.'[96]

A second line required a jumpstart: 'Among half stunned' (no) –
'*Striving* half stunned' (no) – '*Scampering* half stunned', '*Huddled,
dazed*' (no, *no*) – 'Huddled, *stunned* . . .

Bollocks[97]

. . . Pound would write in shorthand in blunt black ink when he
was given the chance. It was a dense and tortuous rough draft that
would not survive its brief life in typescript once Pound had struck
through the entire passage of terza rima. But that exchange was
still to come, and in Margate Eliot continued onto a second leaf,

with some further London lines in pencil, this time with eyes on the lower Thames of Greenwich Reach and the Isle of Dogs. 'The river sweats / Oil + tar' . . .

O O hin hein heinh[98]

– he drew a wavy pencil line through this and found instead a consonantal phrasing that would come to capture the section:

Weialala leia
Wallala leialala

Götterdämmerung. Once again, Eliot was returning to the sources: Wagner, reprised from 'The Burial of the Dead', only this time his song of the Rhine daughters, a river no longer under German control, that Eliot in a mental leap had transferred to the Thames. It was a complete section of some twenty-six lines that with only minor amendment would survive into the finished poem as an interval between the elegiac stanzas.

A third leaf of manuscript. And still London, still the song of the Thames daughters:

'Highbury bore me. Highbury's children
Played under green trees and in the dusty Park.
~~We~~/Mine were humble people + conservative
As neither the rich nor the working class know.[99]

These and six further lines were struck by Eliot. 'Type out this anyhow,' commanded Pound that winter, but Eliot had already found the form of these lines, returning to the elegiac quatrains of the typist sequence:

'Trams and dusty trees.
Highbury bore me. Richmond + Kew
Undid me. ~~Beyond~~ By Richmond I raised my knees
Stretched on the floor of a perilous canoe'.

The draft continued to the foot of the page: *My feet were at Moorgate, My feet* are *at Moorgate, and my heart / Under my feet.*

Eliot turned over the same leaf and continued drafting on the back. Not the humble people of Highbury, he reflected, but those before his eyes at that moment. In summer, the jetty creaked under a tide of holidaymakers, but in autumn it returned to the locals, where the hard up fished with a simple line for a catch to put on the family plate, or scoured the surf for lugworms and crabs to sell for bait. *I sketch the people, after a fashion*, he told Sydney Schiff.[100]

'~~I was to be grateful.~~ On Margate sands
~~There were many others.~~ I can connect
Nothing with nothing. ~~He had~~
I still feel the pressure of dirty hand[101]

Then a second pass at the lines that have become so famous:

'On Margate Sands.
I can connect
   Nothing with nothing.
The broken finger nails of dirty hands.
My people ~~are plain~~ humble people, who expect
n/Nothing'.

And there it was. The connection of nothing with nothing that would for so many come to define a recognisable spirit of *The Waste Land*, the elegiac quatrains loosened in their grip, *abcabc*. Nothing would come of nothing, Cordelia had been told by her father, as perhaps Eliot felt he'd been told by his, as he brought the draft to its climax. He may have been yet to grasp the opening to 'The Fire Sermon' – that was still to undergo Pound's intervention – but he most surely had its ending:

To Carthage   then   I came.[102]

First the Rhine, now Roman Carthage – once again, a Keynesian
warning:

> Burning burning   burning   burning
> O Lord thou pluckest me out
> O Lord thou pluckest
>
> burning

//

Eliot's month in Margate didn't produce only rough drafts for
the long poem. There were two single – and apparently discrete –
poems that he also drafted on that second fortnight in the town.
For all the literary distance that he had travelled since the Hogarth
Poems of 1919, it was in some ways a surprise to find him return
to something like the 'French' form of the late war years, but so
he did, in both pieces. 'Dirge', a song, was the flightier of the two
poems, in two variable tetrametric stanzas, six lines by ten; 'Elegy',
the second, was the more formal, locked stiffly into *abcb* quatrains.
There was a proximity to them that was more than metric: they
were written on backing pages of the same leaf, for which there
should have been no need: new poems take new leaves, unless no
leaves are to be had, which is perhaps the situation that Eliot found
himself in that day in the Nayland Rock shelter.

'Dirge' was seemingly the first to be written. Once again Eliot
had returned to the same song in the same scene of the same play,
Ariel's dirge in *The Tempest*: *Full fathom five thy father lies.*[103] But
here, in Eliot's hands, it was given a horrific twist:

> Full fathom five your Bleistein lies
> Under the flatfish and the squids.
> Graves' Disease in a dead{ man's
>   { jew's eyes!
> Where the crabs have ~~nibb~~ eat the lids.[104]

Again he was reaching towards anti-Jewish tropes. A Jew's-eye was proverbially an object of prized value, but for all the wrong reasons: it could be a medieval torture to extract monies from defaulting Jews.

Such an annihilation would be systematic to the poem: a drowned body, picked at and lidless, gold teeth, lower once again than the rats, low where the lobsters *scratch scratch scratch*. But Eliot now had deliberated on a variant: which was it to be, a dead jew (again the lower case) or a dead man (the universal case)? Perhaps this time he would move beyond the trappings of 'Bleistein' and 'Gerontion' and universalise the experience: this time he surely meant 'man' – *a* man, *any* man and therefore *all* men. Or perhaps he meant a quite specific man: after all, as it was, the line read like the thinnest of exchanged veils: Shakespeare's word 'father' had become Eliot's word 'Bleistein', and Eliot may very well have had in mind a symbol of the same, a projection of his father as the figure dead to him, as the 'other', as the one outside of him – in Eliot's Unitarian upbringing, everything represented by the 'Jew'. After all, the original sequence in Shakespeare leads to a personal bereavement: a bereft and grieving son, imagining the death of a father, imaging as does 'Dirge' the sea-change, rich and strange into new atomic matter. Such an amalgam reading of the Jew-father wouldn't lessen anti-Semitic offence, but it might inform our understanding of his motivation. So which was it to be, a Jew or a man? It would take a month or two for Eliot to resolve, but when, in Lausanne that winter, he made a fair copy of the poem in manuscript, he would choose which. Jew. Shamefully he picked Jew.

That Eliot may have had his father in mind may also be inferred from the lines marked 'Elegy' on the verso leaf of 'Dirge'. Here, Eliot's revival of the 'French' form was more arch, more traditional, but then he was dressing for elegiac attire:

How steadfastly I should have mourned
The sinking of so dear a head!
~~But~~/Were't not for dreams ~~the~~/a dream restores
The ~~very~~ always inconvenient dead.[105]

Again the drowning, again the dead, and once again the purgatorial shade:

God, in a rolling of fire
Pursues by day my errant feet.
~~The~~ His flames of ~~pity horror passion~~ anger and ~~of ire~~ desire
~~a~~/Approach me with consuming heat.

This sounded not unlike the surrender of the *perfecti*, recalling
Eliot's encounter at Périgueux in 1919, as if he now adopted a
sustained effort to find the indirect address to his father that he
had sought for so long. Yet here the effort seemed forced, too
rigid in its armour to let the emotion out: as if the lines were
serving duty rather than the poet's heart. But then it may not
have been complete: the manuscript, little more than a fragment,
with its pencilled title squeezed into the corner, kept perhaps
more as a piece of mental filing than as a crowning of a final
draft.

There's reason to think that both poems might have been
imagined as part of a trilogy from that time. Another piece may
have been produced in typescript before he wrote either, and
before he left for Margate. Called 'Exequy', a funeral rite, it was
a highly ritualised memorial ode. Seven lines, a heptastich, again
tetrameter, this time an inventive *abbcaca* pattern. Here, too, it was
as if Eliot could not break through the distance between the personal experience locked within him and his desire for an objective,
public expression of it. This time, the poem carried lines from the
Purgatorio, from which Eliot had typed one and then replaced it by
hand with another: *be mindful in due time of my pain*, and, *in thought*

I see my past madness.[106] The first came from the same sequence as *Ara vos prec*, and would be quoted by Eliot in his 1922 Notes to *The Waste Land*; the second from four lines before, Arnaut Daniel's famed introduction: *I am Arnaut that weep and go a-singing*. These lines were ingrained upon Eliot in 1919, that winter of his father's death, and that summer of dispossession. It was as though Eliot was now connecting all levels of his recent experience but failing to find a form to record them in verse memorable enough to sustain the longer poem.

When the pages of *The Waste Land* that Eliot sent John Quinn in gratitude for his help with publication were lost – or at least thought lost by Eliot – he said he couldn't remember much about the incidental pieces that he excluded from the body of the final poem, but he had a name for them: he called them 'short poems' and 'Waste Land lyrics', and used a yet more telling word besides, 'interludes'. His specific reference when he said this was to the 'Song' that had appeared in *Tyro*, but most likely he may also have included any or all of 'Dirge', 'Elegy' and 'Exequy' when in 1946 he wrote: 'It may or may not have been one of those included as interludes in the first draft of *The Waste Land*. It is impossible to settle this point now. I preserved no copies of those Waste Land lyrics.'[107] Extraordinary as it seemed, at least some of these poems may have been intended as accompanying texts to the poem, even as interludes between the major parts of the long poem: a testimony to how focused Eliot was at that moment on his notion of the music hall, the comic revue and the popular variety show. Their introduction would have been a disaster, tangling the ground of the final poem with literary weeds, but for a moment at least in the winter of 1921–2, it appears that this was the course of action that Eliot was considering. It would take the wisdom of Ezra Pound to prevent it.

//

The eleventh of November was the first time that poppies served to commemorate Remembrance Day. In Margate, red paper flowers were sold along the pier; some blew in cartwheels across the sands.

> I have done a rough draft of part of part III, but do not know whether it will do, and must wait for Vivien's opinion as to whether it is printable. I have done this while sitting in a shelter on the front – as I am out all day except when taking rest. But I have written only some fifty lines, and have read nothing, literally – I sketch the people, after a fashion, and practise scales on the mandoline.[108]

It was most likely this day, Friday 11 November – though possibly the Friday before – that Eliot had written to Sydney Schiff. In his letter he had written something else of tantalising relevance to the long poem in progress. 'I should have liked to hear from you, but of course did not expect to, knowing that you had much to do and bad health and worries.' This remark deserves a little reflection, and might have appeared little more than a courtesy were it not for its placement immediately before the sentence outlining the 'part of part III'. That Eliot could mention a 'part III' at all without reference to a larger work suggests that he expected Schiff to understand exactly what it was a part in relation to – information that Schiff could have gathered in the course of a conversation, but more likely from being in temporary possession of the typescripts of parts I or II – or conceivably of an early typescript of part III. There is no evidence to corroborate that such an early third-part typescript was ever created; conversely, it would be entirely possible that Eliot had left drafts of the first two parts with his friend before he went to Margate. 'I enjoyed Sunday very much and am *very* grateful to you for encouragement,' Eliot wrote to Schiff in his week in London following his return from Margate.[109] The Sunday in question was 13 November, the day he travelled back from Kent, and the encouragement is not clarified: an encouragement towards Lausanne, perhaps, but more probably an encouragement in discussion of the long poem. Specifically, it may be that Eliot had lent Schiff the (now missing) carbon of 'The Burial of the Dead' and it was this that he took back that Sunday, and this that, on the Tuesday of that week, 15 November, he may subsequently have lent to Wyndham Lewis for comment.

In London, Vivien learned from Bertrand Russell of the imminent arrival of his first son (he would be named after Joseph Conrad). The mother was not Constance Malleson, but Dora Black, whom Russell had married in September while she was seven months pregnant with their child. Vivien must have relayed the news to Eliot during their phone call on Saturday 29 October, for he offered a Mr Apollinaxian blessing of sorts: he was quite sure that the baby would have pointed ears that would sharpen in time. Vivien shared with Russell Eliot's own predicament just as she had with Thayer. 'Tom is having a bad nervous – or so called – breakdown,' she confided. 'In a short time I hope he will go to Switzerland, to see Dr Vittoz.'[110] Vivien had vowed to be done with Russell, but it seemed she wanted the moment of her husband's collapse to be shared with both Thayer and Russell, the two men who, in her mind, had been – or were still – rivals for her affection.

//

Eliot was convinced that in *aboulie* he had identified the source of his disturbance. He had heavily marked his copy of Vittoz's book accordingly, including what may have stood in Eliot's understanding as a description of his own condition:

> Toute idée, tout acte de volonté éveille dans l'esprit du malade une sensation de crainte; il prévoit la stérilité de l'effort, le doute l'étreint et le paralyse. C'est la peur du vouloir qui le rend aboulique, car tout effort est douloureux, tout acte angoissant. (Every idea, every act of will causes a sensation of fear in the mind of the sufferer, he

foresees that all effort is in vain, and he is paralyzed and fettered by doubt. It is the fear of using his will that deprives him of the power of doing so, for every effort is painful, and every action causes great distress.)[111]

He marked special attention to 'Ouïe' ('Hearing'):

On constate en effet une hyperexcitabilité qui rend le malade sensible au plus léger bruit, cause très fréquente de l'insomnie. (There is, in fact, often an excessive excitability which makes the sufferer aware of the slightest noise, and is very frequently a cause of insomnia.)[112]

Throughout his copy, Eliot marked phrases in French that seemingly create an insight into the conditions that concerned him – in English translation: *Half-awake – the physiological life of man – insanity and purely mental illnesses – hysteria – a case of arrested development – complete submission to treatment – apathy, fatigue, want of interest in life – chronic symptoms as a result of even very slight mental shock – greater fatigue in the morning than in the evening – undue excitement – a fit subject for rest cures – the slightest change in habits or the smallest task may bring on an attack of great distress – want of will is more apparent than real . . . it is more a question of want of its use.*

And then there were the descriptions of physical pain that Eliot marked: digestion, genital-urinary, noise, insomnia, a feeling that the head will burst, a feeling that an iron band is gradually tightening round the head, a painful contracting of muscles (beside which he annotated 'handwriting'), and a contracting of the oesophagus, stomach and intestines (besides which, 'constipation').

Finally, he marked Vittoz's recommended responses: passages demanding a concentration on something definite, another on the resisting of self-examination. And beside 'La volonté', a passage which says that the will is a component force of every human being's life, he wrote a tentative question in the margin: 'Each person has a definite "quantity"?'

Someone, surely Eliot, bookmarked his copy at three sections of special interest. The first marked 'Symptômes de la periode d'état' ('Symptoms of the chronic state'), a section that records a neurological deterioration from instability to a loss of control in which sufferers grow ever more conscious of the state of their brain, and ever more anxious and fearful in response. The second, 'Effet psychique du controle des actes' ('Psychic effect of control over the actions'), describes how mastery over daily activity restores a calmness of being. Each of these two sections would have caught Eliot's attention, but of most concern of all would be the third and last bookmark, 'Concentration sur l'idée' ('Concentration on an idea'), in which the patient must learn to focus without distraction upon the object of attention, learning to dispel any thoughts that are irrelevant. It would be hard to overstate the coincidence of this thought as Eliot tackled the completion of his long poem in Lausanne that winter: Vittoz would encourage the concentration; the poem would be the idea.[113]

//

It was bitterly cold in Margate as Eliot at last prepared to depart: days of low forties, nights of frost and freeze. Snow swept over the south coast, dragging a squall of hail and thunder over Kent. On Sunday 13 November, he settled his final bill with the Albemarle Hotel, and caught the train to London. It was probably then that he saw Sydney Schiff en route back to Clarence Gate Gardens, and following a month away and a fortnight of solitude, he was glad of the company.[114] On Tuesday that week, he saw Wyndham Lewis, and probably passed him the same typescript that he had just taken back from Schiff: Lewis had been the first to set eyes on 'The Burial of the Dead' in February, but he hadn't yet been asked for a critical reading (Eliot would shortly send him a chasing post-card from Switzerland). Now back in the flat, and without Lloyds work to distract him, Eliot had time to type out 'The Fire Sermon', or at least partly: 193 lines across five leaves were produced – by far the longest of the parts to date – into which he inserted a dozen lines from 'London, the swarming life' that he had drafted in pen-cil in Margate. But he had not the time to type – or had not yet accepted the inclusion of – the remaining pages of Margate man-uscript that would conclude that section of the poem; instead, he packed them – three leaves, four pages – together with 'Dirge' and 'Elegy' – with the assortment of typescript pages for the poem that he intended to return to. On Wednesday, he saw Mary Hutchin-son, and passed her what he called 'a farewell note'[115] ('*Au bonheur!*') and told Harold Monro that he was on the eve of leaving for Laus-anne; he said the same to Glenway Wescott, whom he didn't know personally, but in whom, in an act of uncharacteristic disclosure, he confided that he'd had 'a nervous breakdown'.[116] And he even found time to tease Richard Aldington on his dislike of Eliot's poetry, saying that he expected him 'to abhor the poem on which I have been working and which I am taking away with me!'[117] Suddenly, in this last moment before departure, Eliot seemed determined to open himself to a new level of scrutiny, both of his wellbeing and of his verse.

'We leave London tomorrow morning.'

Death by Water.

At the Hôtel Pas-de-Calais, 59 rue des Saints-Pères, the Eliots checked into the pension that the Pounds had made their home until only a few weeks before. It would be just the second time that the two men had seen one another that year, but there would be an unexpected edge to the reunion. Pound had published an article in the New York *Little Review* in July in which he had referred sneeringly to Eliot as the 'Dean of English criticism'; it had taken until now for Eliot's subscription copy to reach England. Pound had told the journal editors that his contribution was 'my own declaration of independence' – but an independence from what exactly – from London, or from Eliot and his friends?[1] He ridiculed his old Imagist comrade Richard Aldington, whose serious-minded review of James Joyce in the *English Review* he called 'the funniest thing that has appeared in England for some time'.[2] But more particularly he appeared to signal an independence from Eliot, and feelings may have been hurt. 'Have they sent you the *Little Review* (quarterly) in which Ezra (in an otherwise irritating attempted-funny article) speaks of me as the "Dean of English Letters"?' Eliot asked Aldington on the eve of departure for Paris. 'He refers to you also in a common condemnation.'[3]

In *The Tyro* that April, Eliot had written in his essay on Baudelaire that 'All first-rate poetry is occupied with morality'.[4] Pound didn't care for that statement one bit, and found it aloof: he sensed that Eliot was now more concerned with appealing to the academy – or, worse, to God – than to poetry. He attributed to Eliot a remark that 'the greatest poets have been concerned with moral values', but that wasn't exactly what had been said: Eliot had written of poetry, not poets, and of morality, not moral values. Nevertheless, Eliot's article had prised open a discursive door that Pound would kick wide. 'This red-herring is justifiable on the grounds of extreme mental or physical exhaustion,' he announced in the *Little Review*, but justifiable on no other.[5] The greatest poets have equally been concerned with eating breakfast and taking a walk and . . . Eliot's statement, in other words, described nothing of significance. When Pound drafted his article in May, he hadn't seen Eliot for five months, but he was aware of the mental and physical distress that his friend was in, and his remarks cut close to the bone. He had encouraged Eliot never to be the battering ram (that was Pound's job), nor the explosives expert (that was Lewis's), but to try for a more subversive method in 'sapping the foundations' instead: as a literary heist, Pound was to go through the front door and Eliot was to go around the back. His task was to produce a criticism that was revolutionary, but instead all Eliot seemed to be serving up was parsimony. That Eliot's was a style of good manners was partly the result of Pound's direction, and those manners had won him acclaim: 'He is now respected by the Times Lit. Sup.,' Pound would say wearily. 'But his criticisms no longer arouse my interest.'[6] It was *buncomb* that poetry needed a moral code: that was the kind of dutiful fluff a writer said because he believed he *ought* to (and Eliot was nothing if not dutiful); when duty enters, pleasure departs: a truth in art as in love. A writer had to please himself alone if an artwork were to *live*, and not cower to the political or moral fashions of the day.[7]

Eliot, as it happened, would have agreed, and indeed had anticipated Pound on the point when in 1919 he had written that 'the best work, the only work that in the end counts, is written for oneself'.[8] In 1957 he would put the idea this way: 'The first voice is the voice of the poet talking to himself – or to nobody.'[9] But objectivity wasn't exactly in Pound's mind at that moment.

Primness needed puncture, and Pound was the man with the sharpest pin.

> The work of art is not a means.
> The work of art is an end.[10]

The review left Eliot in such a waspish mood that, for all the amicability of their Margate correspondence, he turned upon Aldington. H. D. had christened her new collection *Hymen* (a title that wasn't at all pleasing to Eliot), and he told Aldington that he found his wife's book riven with 'a neurotic carnality which I dislike'.[11] But he didn't say only that, he said 'morally': *morally*, he found a neurotic carnality which he disliked, as though a dislike of carnality was itself a *moral* position. It was Pound who had levelled the charge of morality at Eliot, and now it was Eliot who in turn sent it ricocheting onto Aldington. Aldington was a proud husband and had described H. D. as the greatest living exponent of *vers libre*.[12] Eliot was sorry but he couldn't agree: the new book was below par, lacking in vitality and sorely in need of an editor: 'fatiguingly monotonous and lacking in the element of surprise' was the ribbon he wrapped it in.[13] Eliot's personal reliance upon Aldington that autumn had not been inconsiderable, and his remarks on H. D. would not be forgiven. In the time to come Aldington would produce some of the most vociferous and most personal assaults on Eliot that anyone would make.

Walking back one afternoon in 1925 to his cottage in Padworth, Berkshire, Aldington collapsed by the roadside, believing his heart was giving out; in fact, it was a nervous exhaustion that left him prostrate for weeks. For some years, 'moods of depression' had swept over him unchecked, and the breakdown he experienced seemed to alter not only his outlook but his personality. In his criticism of others, Aldington had become unforgiving, to say the least. Robert Graves went as far as to call him the 'hangman of letters', bent on the gloomy destruction of his literary peers.[14] It was a damaging energy that Eliot would feel the weight of, charged by Aldington with not returning to others the support and help that he had himself received from the likes of Pound and Aldington.[15] Jibes escalated, and in 1930 resentment boiled over when Aldington wrote what Eliot described as a 'cruel and unkind lampoon' of his marriage with Vivien, in which her mental deterioration was met only by a coldness and sense of legal obligation.[16] 'I'm going mad, I'm going mad, I'm going mad,' Aldington would report her saying to a chilly and impassive Eliot.[17] He spoofed Eliot with Pound as 'Cibber' and 'Cholmp' perambulating the streets of London together, deliberating over the fate of the marriage to Vivien.

'You ought to do something about it,' Cholmp urged. 'What I mean is, haven't eether of you got any sense?'

'A situation so complicated . . .' Cibber murmured.

'But you can't go on like this. You're driving each other crazy.'

'Ye-es,' said Cibber.

'Well, can't you do *something*?'

'What is there to be said, what is there to be done?' Cibber retorted languidly.

'Well, you can't go on like this, can you?'

'No-o, no-o, probably not.'

'Then you'll have to do something.'

'Ye-es, ye-es, no doubt.'

'Well, what are you going to do?'

Cibber raised his arms slightly, and let them fall limp against his sides with the mute eloquence of despair. Cholmp restrained his impatience.[18]

Geoffrey Faber would call it 'a bitter and indeed a malevolent attack on Eliot', and it grew only worse.[19] Aldington would say in an essay of the 1930s that Eliot was deficient of all emotions except 'disgust, despair and suicidal impulse'.[20] And Eliot would accurately anticipate his response to *The Waste Land* when he said that Aldington would not be in favour of it. 'After that the only thing for us all to do now is to go Home and commit suicide as painfully as possible,' Aldington would write.[21]

Eliot would cut contact with Aldington after the attack on his marriage. But he knew, too, that he hadn't taken care with the man equivalent to the care he had received from him. He had been, he admitted, the first to give offence, and on more than one occasion had been clumsy and tactless. 'I hurt his feelings once or twice very deeply indeed.'[22] Aldington, like Pound, couldn't understand why Eliot did not look after his friends better than he did.

All things considered, Pound thought that Eliot seemed well when he saw him – or at least *fairly* well, as he qualified to Scofield Thayer.[23] Not bad for a man in the middle of a breakdown, travelling for therapy with a wife who seemed to be as busy engaging the attentions of her husband's peers as her husband himself, and whose friend and ally had just accused him of literary 'buncomb' in print.

Eliot emptied his briefcase before Pound.

For the first time, he gave Pound sight of 'The Burial of the Dead', leaving him the ribbon copy for his attention while Eliot was in Lausanne. (The carbon – if ever there was one – may still have been in London with Wyndham Lewis.)

He also left Pound 'A Game of Chess' in the ribbon copy that was Vivien's, and that still carried her markings *wonderful & wonderful*; the carbon copy he kept with him for carrying to Lausanne, with Vivien's remarks transcribed.

And he left with Pound the new, unblemished copy of 'The Fire Sermon' in typescript: this time the carbon copy, retaining the ribbon to take with him to Lausanne; he may also have left the Margate manuscript pages then, although it's more likely that he gave these to Pound on his return from Switzerland when he assembled the poem in full for the first time. With that done, he left Pound to his studio renovations.

The few days in Paris together were very perfect, said Vivien. But her husband's departure for Lausanne, probably on 21 November, would leave her disorientated. 'It was only after I saw him climb into that dreadful Swiss train, and me left on the platform, at 9.20 in the evening, that I felt someone had taken a broomstick and knocked me on the head.'[24] She found no company to replace her husband. The Pounds were busy with their studio, and in December, they became further occupied with Dorothy's hospitalisation for an abscess on her left forefinger. At the same moment, Vivien had a chance encounter in a Parisian post office with Roger Fry, who appeared alarmed to see her and anxious to escape her company. No one, it seemed, had time for her or wished for her presence. She said she felt thrown, pained and *absolutely* alone'. No one and nowhere seemed real to her, not even Eliot. Everything and everyone was forgotten. She began to make arrangements to visit an unidentified person to whom she obliquely referred as 'the man from Cologne'; but when the Deutschmark briefly stabilised in December Vivien's prospective costs doubled suddenly: he would come to visit her in Paris instead. 'The man from Cologne arrives tomorrow – will stay with me,' she told Mary Hutchinson. 'After that I don't know.' What was she thinking, exactly, and who was this mysterious man from Cologne? She wouldn't reveal, though it's possible that Cologne was little more than a cover for Vienna to prevent the name of Scofield Thayer finding its way back to Eliot. 'About Tom –' she told Mary, '*I don't know* I don't know.'

After '9 months of restaurants', Dorothy and Ezra Pound were now decorating and making furniture for their new apartment, a mile to the south of Vivien, down the busy boulevard Raspail.[25] 'The Pounds have a most exquisite Studio (with two rooms) not far from here!' Vivien noted with envy. 'Only £75 a year.'[26] (She didn't care at all for her own compact upper room, by comparison, nor the meals taken *en pension* to save money.) 70 *bis* rue

Notre-Dame-des-Champs, close to the south-west corner of the Luxembourg Gardens, was insulated from the street noise by 'two rows of building' via an alley that opened onto a pavilion courtyard of small trees and a crumbling statue of Diana and the hound.[27] Curtains hung over an entrance to the glass-fronted studio itself: a small single room, as described by Dorothy, which 'has a little room off it, a littler one up a staircase (the latter in the studio) and then a cupboardy kind of place across the hall where we shall have some kind of cooking apparatus.'[28] The little room was a former kitchenette that they decided to use as a box room; the littler room up the curling staircase became the bedroom, and the cupboardy kind of place a dressing room. They cooked on a gas stove in the main space – what Pound sketched in a letter to his parents as the 'conservatory kitchen'.[29] All around was decorated with evidence of Pound's physical prowess: his fencing foils hung above the bookcases, his tennis racket beside them, and near them a pair of boxing gloves with which he liked to pummel any guests who were willing to spar. From the untreated wood of packing cases, Pound made a low tea table, crimson painted, that he called his Chinese dining table. (Joyce said on inspection: a cobbler should stick to his last.)[30] From London, he shipped his triangular typing table. He crammed the few free spaces with artworks by Dorothy and Gaudier-Brzeska, and, given pride of place, the suitcase-sized clavichord that Pound had commissioned from Arnold Dolmetsch in London with money that Yeats had given him on his wedding. A subsequent resident would describe the place as 'a little country cottage set down in the middle of Paris', but to Pound it was 'magnificently large'.[31] There was even room for a cat.

With the street came history. Victor Hugo had lived at number twenty-seven, Pierre-Auguste Renoir once had a workshop at thirty-four, John Singer Sargent at neighbouring seventy-three, James McNeill Whistler at eighty-six. As many as half a dozen painters of note had lived in the apartment itself before Pound, and directly above him lived the poet Ralph Cheever Dunning of Detroit, an opium addict, said to have been christened by Ford Madox Ford for his reclusive lifestyle as 'the living Buddha of Montparnasse'. Dunning very rarely spoke and was never, ever seen to eat, and his spartan apartment had just a single chair, a stove, a bookcase and a cot. Back in 1910 he had published a slim collection of poems with Bodley Head in London, and had spent the next decade trying to perfect a second book, under the encouragement and championing of his new neighbour, Pound. Briefly and unexpectedly, and with Pound's help, he would be the toast of Parisian conversation when in 1925 he was awarded *Poetry* magazine's Helen Haire Nevinson Prize; but by 1930 Dunning was dead from tuberculosis, brought on by malnutrition, and the small gathering of work he left behind ignored thereafter.[32]

Most important of all the neighbours and visitors to 70 *bis* would be a young writer without a book to his name, who moved in at number 113 and who was filing columns for the *Toronto Star* when he met Pound at Shakespeare and Company, early in 1922. When Wyndham Lewis visited from London for the first time, the two men were producing such a noise from within the studio that no one answered the bell; he pushed open the door and found them in mid boxing bout. 'A splendidly built young man, stripped to the waist, and with a torso of dazzling white, was standing not far from me,' Lewis recalled. 'He was tall, handsome, and serene, and was repelling with his boxing gloves a hectic assault of Ezra's. After a final swing at the dazzling solar plexus Pound fell back upon his settee.'[33] The young man was Ernest Hemingway, and with Pound he would get on like a house on fire: he had 'a terrific wallop', Hemingway would acknowledge, 'and when he gets too tough I dump him on the floor'.[34] He became a regular caller, and said of the studio that it was as poor as Gertrude Stein's studio was rich.[35] And he became protective of Pound, who helped him into the world of print just as Eliot had once been helped in London. He told Pound that he was, quite simply, the *only* living poet; he said that the best of his writing would last as long as there was literature. In 1925, in a small and irregular Parisian journal, he paid tribute to Pound in tones that would anticipate those of Eliot's to come. Hemingway would describe, as would Eliot, a poet – a major poet – devoting but a small share of his time to himself and a lion's share to others. For his friends, said Hemingway and Eliot alike, Pound was both advocate and defence. He found publishers for their writing, review coverage for their books, journals to carry their work; he found audiences for their music and buyers for their art. When they were hungry he fed them, when they were threadbare he clothed them. He witnessed their wills and he loaned his own money, and encouraged in each of them a fortitude for life. 'And in the end,' said Hemingway, 'a few of them refrain from knifing him at the first opportunity.'[36]

//

To most visitors the vast Alpine lake on the shore of Ouchy carried the name Lake Geneva, or Genfersee in German, but to the French speakers in Lausanne and the Vaud it was Lac Léman: a stretch of water so vast that it takes a decade for the Rhone waters that enter near Villeneuve in the east to empty in the south-west through the city of Geneva. The wind that whipped out of the north-east brought such a chill that it had been given a name: *la Bise*, 'the kiss' from out of the Alps. Lausanne and Ouchy, on the north bank of the lake, were spared the worst by the shelter of the Jura mountains, but once the cold air found open water it would accelerate to whip up the surface of Léman and scour the southern windward shores with frozen spray that transformed trees to ice sculpture. *La Bise* was known to freeze tears. And when it grew colder still it became *la Bise noire*, so terrible to one clergyman traveller in 1870 that he saw in it 'the likeness of evil spirits'.[37] On some days, a *seiche*, or standing wave, would swing rhythmically from shore to shore, and when backed by *la Bise*, a surge five or six feet in height could roll eerily across the surface. On rarer days, when *la Bise* was all but stilled and its frigid air was colder than the water below, the lake would smoke with a phantom fog.

It was still dark when Eliot's early-morning train from Paris pulled into the Gare de Lausanne.[38] A pall of fog hung over the town and the thermometer had only just begun to climb above freezing, but to reach his hotel Eliot had only to cross the Place de la Gare, and climb the one-hundred-and-some yards up the curling rue du Petit-Chêne that rose towards the banks and post office at Église Saint-François. His hotel, on the corner of avenue Sainte-Luce, faced the old town uphill to the north, but the southern aspect, elevated in generous grounds, looked back across the station from which Eliot had arrived. From his hotel room on the second storey he could see, through the lifting fog, the mile down to the waters of Lac Léman at neighbouring Ouchy; a clear day brought sight of the French Alps, although Eliot would be blessed with only a few of those. Hôtel Pension Sainte-Luce was an early nineteenth-century villa built on an old vineyard. It cost half the daily rate of the upmarket Hôtel Continental just below it, although to take meals *en pension*, as Eliot did ('the food is *excellent*'), was to double the room rate.[39] Of the pension's thirty rooms one was special, and Eliot had it: it was the room in which Ottoline Morrell had stayed, as he reported to her contentedly: 'I am here, in your room (so they tell me) and under Vittoz.'[40]

The walk to the clinic took ten minutes: across the place de la Gare, 300 metres along the broad avenue d'Ouchy, until he reached the Villa Cimerose, a turn-of-the-century villa on the corner at avenue des Tilleuls 2.[41] Here lived Roger and Jeanne Vittoz, married in Paris in 1905, no children, surrounded by lime trees, dappled by a copper beech in the garden. This wasn't a sanitorium in recuperative grounds – no long lawns for patients to perambulate, no verandas with an aspect – but a small practice run from the family home, on the corner of the main road where the trams rattled down to the lake.

Here, Eliot knew, was the place of Ottoline Morrell and Julian Huxley's recovery from symptoms that he recognised in himself; Huxley had described a 'calamitous state when any mental effort, and any attempt to reach a decision, even in trivial matters, becomes a source of anguish'; Morrell had said simply that, at the time, she felt as though 'all my emotions are dead'.[42]

Ottoline Morrell was making a fifth visit to Lausanne when she met Vittoz in 1913.[43] She had suffered from two years of doubt and trial and worry, and had said her time with the doctor had been infinitely precious; she described his extraordinary poise, and goodness, and how he had enabled her to be calm but *actif* in mind. 'He taught his patients a system of mental control and concentration, and a kind of organisation of the mind, which had a great effect on steadying and developing me,' she recorded in her memoirs. 'I found it an enormous help then and always.' Part of the treatment was in teaching patients how to remove destructive thoughts by eliminating letters from words and numbers from sequences; her daughter would tease her as she stared into space: 'There is Mummy eliminating,' she would say.[44]

When Julian Huxley suffered a breakdown in 1919, his wife was bewildered and frightened by his condition: it was she who took him to Vittoz, in sessions recalled by her husband.

> His method was to propose some simple subject on which to concentrate, such as visualising a circle or a square, or solving an easy mathematical problem, and to test the validity of my efforts with the side of his hand on my forehead, whereby he claimed that he could feel and estimate the special brain-pulse accompanying genuine concentration. Gradually more complex subjects for concentration were propounded and the exercises became easier to

carry out. I thus got a little more control over my depression, but it was a dreary summer for us all.[45]

Eliot desperately wanted to attain just such control over his condition, and he had travelled a long way to take it. As he climbed the stairs to the doctor's front door, he must have wondered if his journey would be worthwhile.

Patients came to Vittoz with a spectrum of conditions. Some displayed milder behaviour, feeling that simple life events were beyond their control; in more profound cases, others had withdrawn entirely from social engagement, feeling their own personality to be detestable.[46]

Sessions were short: thirty minutes of contact daily, with the rest of the time given over to prescribed physical and mental exercise that included concentration upon specific parts of the anatomy, such as hands or feet or keeping an arm aloft, in order to perfect a mental control over it. Conscious thought was to master the unconscious, and Vittoz had, like Carl Jung in Zurich, dispensed with the hypnosis practised by Freud in Vienna because he believed it disabled the mental and physical activism that he saw as a necessary part of any recovery. This Vittoz called 'brain control', for which he believed he was able to detect vibrations in the head – pulses or waves emitted from the brain – by placing his hands on the patient's cranium. Such tremors marked a process of recovery in which the patient regained control over the immediate environment, which in turn aided memory, the loss of which was frequently a symptom in his patients. Reception of stimuli, concentration upon them, conscious action upon them: these were the tenets of Roger Vittoz. To be in touch with all that was around us; to pursue an idea without distraction. Vittoz's practice shared some elements with Taoism: to admit stimulation and not combat it, to accept an impulse and not react to it, to intercept thought and create a quarantine for emotion. He likened the process to the tuning of a mental piano, or of being conductor of the mind's orchestra, bringing each of its parts into harmony.

Vittoz encouraged self-examination. He spoke of *gnothi seauton* (know thyself), but with a Christian tint, and Eliot would not have missed the allegorical allusion to healing and self-reliance in the stories of the New Testament. He may have detected that Vittoz was a religious man, and in their praise for self-discipline, individual courage and regard for others, the doctor's nostrums may have echoed his grandfather's Unitarian church. The emphasis on willpower sounded much like Christian teachings: resistance to temptation, control over the body and mind, righteous behaviour, the discipline of a code.

Temperatures lowered to freezing that first week in Lausanne. Rain fell, turning to snow at night, and by the middle of the second week the thermometer struggled to rise above zero at all. Only a few days[47] into his treatment and the change in Eliot was pronounced. On 30 November, he told Ottoline Morrell that he had been put rapidly through the primary exercises by Vittoz and felt a confidence in him that he had not encountered before. Diagnosis had been swift: it was not a case of *nerves* – Eliot had never believed in nerves, or nor did Vittoz, he now reported – but a failure to fully master brain control. He understood that such a swift effect might prove to be illusory, but he felt committed to the routine. The transformation was already remarkable. 'At moments,' he wrote, 'I feel more calm than I have for many many years' – and then he added, 'since childhood'.[48]

//

Only once did Eliot leave Lausanne that month, as far as we know: on a visit to Berne, where he purchased a copy of Hermann Hesse's 1920 *Blick ins Chaos* in German, which he signed and dated, 'T. S. Eliot Berne Dec. 1921'.[49] He saw in the essays a seriousness which, he told the author, had simply not yet become apparent in English literature;[50] and he saw also a prophecy in what Hesse had called 'the Downfall of Europe':

> Es zeigt sich, daß Europa müde ist, es zeigt sich, daß es heimkehren, daß es ausruhen, daß es umgeschaffen, umgeboren werden will.
> (Europe is tired, it shows itself in that Europe wants to turn homeward, in that Europe wants rest, in that Europe wants to be recreated, reborn.)[51]

But Europe was struggling in its rebirth.

In Athens, it was clear now that the war with Turkey in Anatolia was heading for disaster.

In Vienna, Scofield Thayer had been caught up in riots, and almost stripped of his fur coat and gold watch.[52]

In London, David Lloyd George signed the Anglo-Irish Treaty with Arthur Griffith and Michael Collins. Crown troops were to leave Ireland, which would become a self-governing dominion of the British Empire, an Irish Free State with a British monarch at its head; Northern Ireland could withdraw from the Free State should it choose. Griffith and Collins were plenipotentiaries, but not everything they negotiated found support at home, especially the oath of allegiance to the British king. Splits widened; civil war ensued in June; within weeks, Collins had been shot and killed by anti-Treaty forces.

And the hand of London could be felt further afield.

In Jerusalem, Mandatory Palestine, unrest had marked the fourth anniversary of the Balfour Declaration of a Jewish homeland in Palestine. Blame for the Jaffa Riots that had left almost one hundred dead in May had been laid at the door of Arabs by the Haycraft Commission. Zionism pressed for advantage, a Supreme Muslim Council was established: 'the Conflict', as it was becoming known, was gaining momentum.

In Alexandria, scarred by race riots, martial law was imposed by the British administration in May.

Downfall would be seen in the wearing out of symbols, warned Hesse, in the devaluation of the spirit, in the internal despair of an inward generation. Europe was on the road to chaos, *am Abgrund entlang*, reeling on the edge of abyss.[53]

Jerusalem Athens Alexandria Vienna London.

Falling towers. Unreal.

In Paris, Ezra Pound called at Vivien's hotel. He hadn't neglected her, at least not entirely, though he continued to be busy with the refurbishing of the studio at 70 *bis*, and by now had constructed what he called two armchairs (rigid, uncomfortable, block-panelled thrones), a kitchen table, a Chinese dining table, a wash stand and shelving, and could finally dine at home. 'See end approaching,'[54] he told his parents, although to Scofield Thayer he conceded that for the time being he remained in the middle of a chain of 'plumbers, gasistes, fumistes, stovistes'.[55]

The pension was comfortable and the town very quiet, Eliot told Mary Hutchinson, except when children descended from the Cité or the Bourg on scooters over the cobbles.[56] It was mostly banks and chocolates shops, he said, but there was also a very good book-shop, Librairie Payot & Cie, on the rue de Bourg, which had traded on the same spot for almost half a century[57] and which still trades today; there he purchased a French-language copy of Baedeker's 1911 *Switzerland*.[58]

That the treatment of the first week had allowed little time for anything else suggests the poem was almost certainly set aside by Eliot for a period. But by the second weekend he was, if not writing, at least preparing the ground to do so, as he scribbled an abrupt postcard to Wyndham Lewis from the pension Sainte-Luce: 'I wish you wd. send me the criticism you said you would write, please. I shall be here till Christmas. Good doctor.'[59] The criticism sought was most likely comments on 'The Burial of the Dead' now that Eliot was once again ready to review the poem in draft.

'Je n'ai rien écris depuis longtemps,' Eliot wrote to Jacques Rivière in Paris on 5 December: *I have written nothing for a long time.*[60] Only a month had passed since the fifty lines in Margate and the pair of poems that accompanied them; it must have seemed longer to Eliot, or it could be that he was thinking in prose, remembering his promise to Rivière of a contribution to his journal *La Nouvelle Revue Française.* No article, not even a short one, would be possible for the next two months, and Eliot explained why: he shared the news that he was under the direction of a renowned doctor (*un célèbre médecin*) until Christmas at least: *un traitement de psychasthénie.* Psychasthenia wasn't a term much used by Vittoz himself (he deployed it only twice in his *Traitement*), but was associated instead with Pierre Janet to describe an obsessive-compulsive condition of anxious self-scrutiny, resulting in an inability to direct thought and speech: *not* neurasthenia, therefore, *not* a mechanical weakness of the nerves, and *not* a failure of the body's electrical impulses either, but a disorder of the mind. The neurasthenic had no feeling except for their personality, Vittoz had written, a personality from which they are desperate to escape but cannot.[61] Poetry, Eliot had written, is an escape from personality. *But, of course, only those who have personality and emotions know what it means to want to escape from these things.*

'It is a commonplace that some forms of illness are extremely favourable, not only to religious illumination, but to artistic and literary composition,' Eliot would write in 1931. 'A piece of writing, meditated apparently without progress for months or years, may suddenly take shape and word; and in this state long passages may be produced which require little or no retouch.' At this moment, the writer – like the patient of *aboulie* – has the sense of being a receptor, not a maker. 'You may call it communication with the Divine, or you may call it a temporary crystallisation of the mind.'[62] Whatever name it goes under, in Lausanne that month Eliot would have the most profound experience in working on the closing sections of the long poem. And when, later in the month, he would set down the last part of all, 'What the Thunder Said', he would complete it almost whole, with barely any correction.

More than likely, when Eliot returned to the poem in Lausanne he began by reviewing what he had most recently written: 'The Fire Sermon', for which he carried the ribbon copy, and for which he now drafted an 'apostrophe' for the Fresca sequence.[63] On distinctive quad-ruled paper that he had borrowed from Pound, Eliot produced a heavily worked pencil manuscript of seventeen lines in couplets, a portrait of a patron of the arts, Lady Katzegg, beginning with Venus Anadyomene. Pound had included a poem of that title by Arthur Rimbaud in his *Instigations* (1920), reprinted from the *Little Review*, whether or not the two men mentioned the poem while Eliot was in Paris.[64] That Eliot was still at this moment expanding upon a section that he soon excised said much about how he was struggling with 'The Fire Sermon', which now existed in five leaves of typescript, and four leaves of subsequent manuscript, and was still growing. The word 'breeding' appeared in the 'apostrophe', as it had in opening the 'Burial of the Dead': 'Thus art ennobles even wealth and birth, / And breeding raises prostrate art from earth.'[65] None of this felt quite right for the moment, and some kind of editorial or creative intervention was badly needed. The section seemed distended and disjointed, which wasn't helped by its various states of draft work. What the section required was to be brought fully into typescript now, but Eliot had no typewriter with him in Lausanne, and that would therefore have to wait. Pound would be able to offer a steer from the pages left with him when Eliot returned to Paris, surely he would.

//

'Death by Water' would be the title of the fourth section. Like the lines of the Venus Anadyomene, when Eliot came to begin the

Part IV. Death by Water.

The sailor, attentive to the chart or to the sheets,
A concentrated will against the tempest and the tide,
Retains, even ashore, in public bars or streets
Something inhuman, clean and dignified.

Even the drunken ruffian who descends
Illicit backstreet stairs, to reappear,
For the derision of his sober friends,
Staggering, or limping with a comic gonorrhea,

From his trade with wind and sea and snow, as they
Are, he is, with "much seen and much endured,"
Foolish, impersonal, innocent or gay,
Liking to be shaved, combed, scented, manicured.

*   *   *   *   *   *

"Kingfisher weather, with a light fair breeze,
Full canvas, and the eight sails drawing well.
He beat around the cape and laid our course
From the Dry Salvages to the eastern banks.
A porpoise snored upon the phosphorescent swell,
A triton rang the final warning bell
Astern, and the sea rolled, asleep.
Three knots, four knots, at dawn; at eight o'clock
And through the forenoon watch, the wind declined;

fourth section in Lausanne, he must surely have done so in part in a pencil rough that he later discarded; certainly the fair copy he would return with to Paris could not have been a first draft, so fluent – almost flawless – was it in its penmanship of the ninety-three lines and four leaves.

Most determinedly it had a sense of place and title: 'Part IV', wrote Eliot, 'Death by Water'; but part IV of what, exactly? Of 'He

Do the Police in Different Voices', as 'The Burial of the Dead' and 'A Game of Chess' had been its first two parts? If so, then why hadn't 'The Fire Sermon' been associated with either the police title or a part number? It appeared that the poem was now moving clearly away from the anchor of the Dickensian title, and this was to be a fourth, free-standing part in a larger poem.

Again, as had the second and third sections, the draft began in formality: again quatrains, again *abab* rhymed, again the tempestuous seas that, symbolically, had swallowed his father whole; only this time they brought with them what seemed a personal reflection on his treatment with Vittoz to overcome *aboulie*:

> The sailor, attentive to the chart and to the sheets.
> A concentrated will against the tempest and the tide,[66]

Quickly the mode dispersed into the travels of a schooner moving out beyond the eastern banks of the Cape and the Dry Salvages to open sea and danger. 'Thereafter everything went wrong.' Drinking water was contaminated, the gaff jaws jammed, the garboard-strake leaking, the crew gonorrhoeal. At last they caught up with the running codfish, and it was there that the trouble deepened. The vessel was blown scudding before a gale, into the roar of a running sea, into a deafening wind:

> and no one dared
> To look into anothers face, or speak
> In the horror of the illimitable scream
> Of a whole world about us.[67]

No longer in control of their destiny, the crew were subjected to the tempest around them, 'Frightened beyond fear, horrified past horror', facing into annihilation –

> – Something which we knew must be a dawn –
> A different darkness, flowed above the clouds,

And dead ahead we saw, where sky and sea should meet,
A line, a white line, a long white line,
~~Toward which we~~ A wall, a barrier, towards which we drove.[68]

– into the void of common silence:

And if <u>Another</u> knows, I know I know not,
Who only know that there is no more noise now.

It was a masterful draft: ninety-three lines, uneven perhaps, but sturdy in storyline and broad in its horizon. It drew so assuredly upon Eliot's childhood experience from the seas before the house that his father built in Gloucester, and did so with elemental force in a gripping passage, concluding with ten lines that Eliot had translated from the French of his own poem: the ending of 'Dans le Restaurant', from the 1919 Hogarth *Poems*: 'Le repassant aux étapes de sa vie antérieure' – which might then have translated into something like *Returning through the stages of his life before*, but to which Eliot now gave a subtle slant: 'He passed the stages of his age and youth'. The restoration of a life with his father was softened in the new line, but it was still detectable; and no longer was he *repassant*, pulled back through, but instead he now passed the stages in a movement away, forgetting both the profit and the loss.

Eliot had returned the poem to the drowned father and the grieving prince. It was the same drive that had introduced the refrain 'Those are pearls'; it had produced 'Dirge', which he likewise brought into an inked fair copy in Lausanne; it had provided the moment for Madame Sosostris to turn the tarot card and forewarn 'fear death by water', and so assign the fate of Phlebas, 'the drowned Phoenician Sailor', with whom finally Eliot now concluded his draft.[69] There is no such card as the drowned sailor in any tarot pack: this was a fortune told in particular to the poem.

//

In Paris, Pound had received advance copies from Boni & Liveright of the retrospective of his London work: *Poems 1918–21, Including Three Portraits and Four Cantos*. The portraits were the homages to Propertius, the Langue d'Oc and Mauberley, the cantos four to seven; it was to serve the audience in New York a little like the way the Ovid Press had in London with *Quia Pauper Amavi*. It was an erratic setting, cramped in places, without adhering to any typographic consistency, but it was eye-catching too, which had become a mark of all of Horace Liveright's work as a publisher, and it pleased Pound: 'Liveright has printed them with all the pomps.'[70] It seemed inevitable at this stage that Pound would get poor reviews, and so he did, with even his allies struggling to support him. Maxwell Bodenheim couldn't help but draw attention in *The Dial* to 'the massive isolation' between Pound and his peers: contemporaries who felt insulted by him, younger writers who lacked the sophistication to appreciate him.'[71] John Peale Bishop wrote in *Vanity Fair* that Pound had never stayed in one place long enough to build a constituency for his talents.[72] It took Harriet Monroe (who else?) to summarise the sense of disappointment in *Poetry*. Imprisoned in a library of 'mental easy-shares', year on year Pound's work had become increasingly narrow and reductive. 'It has lost its freshness and become secondary, deriving from books of the past instead of life of the present, and refining often to trivial excess.'[73] It was a damning epitaph on the post-war years. 'A youthful fire rather than an enduring light . . .'

Horace Liveright would stand by Pound where others hadn't. Their partnership still had another three books to run, culminating in the magisterial 1926 volume, *Personae*, that remains in print to this day. It was, at that moment in the winter of 1921–2, a bold new beginning between Horace Liveright and Ezra Pound. 'Liveright has sailed for YURUP,' Pound told his father with enthusiasm on Christmas Day.[74] It would be a visit that would have dramatic consequences not only for Pound, and for his Parisian neighbour,

James Joyce, but also for Eliot, who returned from Lausanne to a dinner that would change the course of both his poem and his life.

//

Eliot had been a month in Lausanne with such remarkable effect that by the middle of December he had begun to make arrangements for his departure. He expected to leave Switzerland at Christmas and rejoin Vivien at the Hôtel Pas-de-Calais, Paris, where they would stay until the middle of January.[75] 'The great thing I am trying to learn is how to use all my energy without waste,' he told Henry in the middle of the month, 'to be *calm* when there is nothing to be gained by worry, and to concentrate without effort.' Efficiency, perspective, control: the treatment with Vittoz was working dramatically. He had never been taught *mental* hygiene, he told his brother, and nor had the family ('so we are a seedy lot'). In that letter Eliot had underlined four words: *shameful, calm, thinking, talk*.[76] Henry had just written sympathetically to his mother about his brother's breakdown. Tom had been going on his nerves during their stay in London that summer, he wrote: overworked and almost permanently separated from his craving – 'poetical composition' – which had induced 'a frantic state of mind'. Vivien had drained off the last of it, said Henry, and Eliot had been left as an empty man behind his masks. 'To me he seemed like a man playing a part.'[77] Now, Eliot was able to report a change to Henry. 'I am very much better, and not miserable here,' he summarised. 'I am certainly well enough to be working on a poem!'

Unlike the draft labelled 'Part IV. Death by Water', this new, fifth part had no title, and no clear sense of numbered sequence in the poem, only folio numbers to show the order of the pages. It began simply, without fanfare, below the header in hurried pencil, with little by the way of hesitation or correction. In fact, 'The whole

After the torchlight red on sweaty faces
After the frosty silence in the gardens
After the agony in stony places
The shouting & the crying
Prisons and palaces and reverberation
Of thunder of spring over distant mountains
He who was living is now dead,
We who were living are now dying
With a little patience

Here is no water but only rock
Rock and no water and the sandy road
The road winding above among the mountains
Which are mountains of rock without water
If there were water we should stop and drink
Amongst the rock one cannot stop or think
The sweat is dry and the feet are in the sand
If there were only water amongst the rock
Dead mountain mouth of carious teeth that cannot spit
Here one can neither stand nor lie nor sit
There is not even silence in the mountains
But dry sterile thunder and no rain
There is not even solitude in the mountains
But red sullen faces sneer and snarl
From doors of mudcracked houses

section was written at one sitting,' Eliot said later, 'and never altered.'[78]

The draft began by returning to an earlier work, an untitled poem from Eliot's Harvard time or just after, beginning 'After the turning of the inspired days', from which he would draw his opening: 'After the torchlight red on sweaty faces'.[79] *After, After, After*: three times came the elegiac refrain, to be followed with a mesmerising couplet, *He who was living is now dead* and *We who were living are now dying*, so reversing the Order for the Burial of the Dead.[80] Eliot told Ford Madox Ford that there were about thirty good lines in the whole of the long poem ('The rest is ephemeral'), and these were lines evoking rock and water with which he continued onto a second leaf from his pension below the Alpine mountains – in the dead mountains, in this decayed hole among the mountains, under the sterile thunder, where there is neither silence nor solitude, but the continual spiritual presence of another, of 'one more member' than could be counted:[81]

> Who is the third who walks ^always^ besides you?
> When I count, there are only you and I together
> But when I look ahead up the white road
> There is always another ^one^ walking ^~~there~~^ beside you
> Gliding wrapt in a brown mantle, hooded
> I do not know whether a man or ^a^ woman
> – But who is that on the other side of you?[82]

London had been at the heart of 'The Fire Sermon', but now it was just one of the five unreal cities and their *tumbling, falling towers* that carried fluently onto a third leaf, with their tolling reminiscent bells.[83] The poem seemed to pour out, unhesitant. A child on a bridge above a dried-up river, suffering from water on the brain, was the only stanza in the entire part that Eliot struck out.

Everything now – the sum of all that Eliot had gathered towards him – seemed to reach an elevated level in this draft. The arid places of April had become the stony place of imminent thunder, the drowned father with pearls for eyes was now dead as the living are now dying, the deep elemental images of water and rock had fused in the prison and palace and silence and solitude of the mountains under which he wrote, the primitive in the rock, the faces in the rock; the eerie company of the other beside you, always another walking beside you, friend or father or spiritual ghost, the dissolving cities and the memory of bells.

Co co rico the cockerel crows, in a flash of lightning that wakes into the thunderous Sanskrit of the Upanishads – in a summary by Pound in 1924:

> *Datta* – Give.
> *Dayadhvam* – Sympathise.
> *Damyata* – Control.
> and *Shantih* – Peace.

'I don't care a damn where which influence crossed what other,' Pound wrote then of the referential trails that criss-crossed the final poem, but these four words of Sanskrit alone were worthy of cross-examination.[84] Give, sympathise, control: the first three, taken from Brahma's *Da*, *Da*, *Da* in the Hindu Brihadaranyaka scripture, were also healing of a kind administered by Dr Vittoz, whose expert hands were those to which the 'boat' of those lines responded.

Datta, give alms and relief, be charitable, do not keep for yourself more than you need, do not appropriate or confiscate.

Dayadhvam, sympathise with others and yourself, be compassionate, shun cruelty, seek mercy.

Damyata, control the self, restrain oneself, subdue the senses.

These three could be understood without translation from the emotive tone of the surrounding passages, said Pound; they were the booming voice of God. But of the fourth: 'Let it go that *shantih* means Peace; I think one does need to be told that.' A prayer for peace to mark the beginning or the end of ritual, *the Peace which passeth understanding*, as Eliot would notate, a formal ending, he said; but it surely was not a prayer to mark redemption.[85] Instead, at the very end of the poem, the poet lingers, fishing while the world about disassembles, wondering whether to set their lands in order. And into that void poured the poem's great and final collapse of cascading imagery and fleeting phrases, like a cine-reel of a disappearing Europe: London Bridge collapsing into the tradition of Arnaut Daniel's 'Ara vos prec', collapsing into Dante's *Purgatorio*, collapsing into the Vigil of Venus in Latin Rome, collapsing into the Aquitaine prince and his ruined tower, collapsing into Elizabethan drama – that great driver of the poem – 'mad againe'. *These fragments I have spelt into* – no, he would quickly alter that – *These fragments I have shored against my ruins.*

Peace in ruin, peace in horror, peace in madness.

Datta. Dayadhvam, damyata.

Shantih   shantih   shantih.[86]

//

By the time that another week had passed, Eliot was becoming sufficiently strong to express a growing boredom. He began to think that Lausanne was a dull place now that he was 'feeling much better', and he wouldn't stay longer than he had to: its chief recommendation, he told Sydney Waterlow, was its cast of international characters, which he listed like the entourage of his long poem: 'American countesses, Russian princesses, Rumanians, Greeks and Scandinavians, Czecho counts, Belgian punks etc.' But as a haven in which to master his cognitive direction, Lausanne had passed every test. 'I have been losing power of concentration and attention, as well as becoming a prey to habitual worry and dread of the future,' he explained: the net result had been wasting more energy than he used, and wearing himself out. 'And I *think* I am getting over that.' For the first time that week temperatures climbed above freezing, and under blue skies would rise to a balmy thirteen degrees centigrade, but Eliot had little time left to enjoy the new weather, for he would soon be leaving: south, perhaps, or back to Vivien in Paris, to be decided. 'I am trying to finish a poem

– about 800 or 1000 lines. *Je ne sais pas si ça tient*,'[87] he wrote. *I do not know if it holds.*

Eliot spent Christmas Day alone. He wrote to Alfred Knopf about his contract, and sent a letter and Christmas cable to his mother in which he mentioned again the improvement in his levels of concentration and energy: 'I am working at a poem too,'[88] he told her. He had finished his treatment with Dr Roger Vittoz clear minded and in control of events, and had written in excess of two hundred lines of the poem in less than a month. For once the bitter *Bise* was chased off the lake waters at Ouchy as the *Föhn* blew strongly from the south-west. Warm wet weather soaked the town. On New Year's Eve, as Eliot prepared to return to Paris, for the first time in his stay a rainbow arced over Lac Léman.

What the Thunder Said.

'I have a hunch that I'll like the five days in Paris with Ezra Pound,' Horace Liveright told Lucille, his wife, as he sailed for France.[1] Two years had passed since he had published Pound's essays, *Instigations*; *Poems 1918–21*, his selection of verse, was just out. In a short time, the two men had fostered a witty and frank publishing relationship (Liveright: 'Do you suppose I like to go along losing money on you miserable highbrows?'; Pound: 'Horace . . . is a pearl among publishers'), but they had not yet met.[2] Pound admired the gung-ho style of publishing ('LIVERIGHT HAS BEEN KNOWN to send cheques abroad'), and sensed a commitment to real literary development: his was a list like no one else's in New York or London, there was no doubt about it: Liveright was 'going toward the light not from it'.[3] For each of Liveright's days in Paris (he would eventually spend six there), Pound offered to be his personal guide to the artistic and musical figures of the city, introducing him to Picasso, Morand and Brâncuşi, to Igor Stravinsky and Erik Satie, although the publisher's inability to speak French left him unable to exchange a word with any of them. But he was reunited with Djuna Barnes, who had arrived from New York in 1921 on a commission with *McCall's* fashion journal, and whom he would soon publish.[4] He had, Pound said with assurance, seen the right people, and in case of any doubt clarified precisely who he meant by that: 'He saw Joyce and Eliot with me.'[5]

Liveright's approach to publishing was one of 'reckless splendour', author Sherwood Anderson remembered: a man who, if he believed in you, would gamble on you, a chancer at a time of gentlemen publishers from the established families.[6] Bennett Cerf, vice-president at Boni & Liveright, recalled an era of middle-aged men with gold watch chains straining across their portly bellies, who thought it vulgar to chase after a book, let alone to advertise one; to them Liveright was an upstart, who seduced authors and pioneered a grubby style of eye-catching marketing with heavy display type and ornamental borders that shocked polite publishing.[7] Liveright was simply not one of them: he was not one of the old families, he was not a conservative and, more troublesome still, he was not a Christian but a Jew.

Horace Liveright and Albert Boni founded their press in 1917 in three small rooms on West 40th Street, New York City. 'Albert, with all your socialist connections, why can't you get Lenin to do a book for us?' Liveright had nagged his partner at the time. 'Sure,' Boni had quipped, 'he'll stop the Revolution to write a book for Boni & Liveright.'[8] While he didn't quite do that, Vladimir Lenin did provide Liveright with an introduction to John Reed's *Ten Days that Shook the World* ('Unreservedly I recommend it to the workers of the world'), published in the spring of 1919.[9] The book became a national bestseller, moving nine thousand copies in three months, and underwriting the company for the next two years.[10] It became a handbook for revolutionaries in the United States, and, following the shipyard strike in Seattle in 1919, the focus for the 'red scare' that gripped the United States. By then, Boni & Liveright had already fallen under the watchful eye of the Military Intelligence Branch: the company's publishing of Leon Trotsky was by March 1918 technically considered aiding an enemy of the Allies, and strictly against the war effort.[11] To the authorities, Horace Liveright was not only a Jew but a socialist Jew; to Pound, he was the man to open doors that had slammed shut on him. *The Cantos* would recall with affection a night in a bar in Paris together in that new year of 1922, when they were warmly bid welcome: '*Entrez donc, mais entrez, / c'est la maison de tout le monde.*' Come in then, come on in, this is everyone's house. This is the house of the world.[12]

Eliot arrived in Paris from Lausanne around 2 January.[13] It was probably the day after arrival that he showed Pound his new pages of manuscript. And it was probably that same evening that the two men went on to what would emerge as a historic dinner with Horace Liveright and James Joyce. Liveright had earned himself a name for hard drinking and harder hangovers in New York, which was a reputation that would have put Eliot at his ease (Eliot once warned Pound that he could drink him 'under the table before breakfast'), and no doubt with James Joyce as well, whose 'unaffected love of alcohol' (Lewis's description) had been noted in Parisian circles since his arrival in July 1920.[14] Alone among them, Pound was the one who moderated his intake, believing drinking to be an unnecessary pause in his conversation.

By the end of the dinner, Liveright had made an arrangement with each of the three writers.

To Ezra Pound, Liveright would give employment as a European scout at an annual salary of $500, which he called 'a little arrangement' to take care of Pound's rent for two years.[15] In return, Pound would translate whatever French-language books he discovered, in a contract, drawn up the next day by Pound, which included a clause that Liveright would not demand of him 'the translation of any work that Mr Pound considers a disgrace to humanity or too imbecile to be borne'.[16]

To James Joyce, Liveright would offer US publication of *Ulysses*, for an advance of $1,000, to happen as swiftly as was practicable. It was a bold offer given the outcome of the trial in New York less than a year ago, and that Sylvia Beach's edition in Paris was all but printed. It may have been an offer *too* bold for both parties on reflection, for Liveright quickly sought counsel from John Quinn on the matter, while Joyce considered his own position. Pound couldn't understand the hiatus that followed: Liveright had offered '1000 bones' but Joyce had hesitated. 'Why the hell he didn't nail it AT once I don't know'[17] – the terms were reasonable, the risk was all the publisher's. Pound shrugged; at least it was no longer his problem: 'Joyce is off my hands.'

To T. S. Eliot, just as remarkably, Liveright offered a publication deal for the long poem 'sight unseen': $150 (£35) and a royalty of 15 per cent against the unfinished draft. Indeed, such was the impression that Pound – and perhaps Eliot, too – had made upon Liveright that he left Paris for London not even knowing the title of the poem he was offering to buy (it still didn't have one), but having made his commitment nonetheless. For Eliot, it was a moment like none he had experienced. After the subsidised edition of *Prufrock* by the Egoist, after the limited print runs of Hogarth and Ovid, after the trials and rejections of Alfred Knopf, here was a publisher in New York – *Pound's* publisher in New York, no less – trusting sufficiently in his work to invest in a poem that he had not seen, nor Eliot completed, but to which Eliot had already given everything. For the first time, Eliot's poetry was wanted by a trade house, without hesitation or question. Pound detected the relief in Eliot: he seemed 'so mountany gay', quipped Pound. 'May your erection never grow less.'[18] All that there was left to do now was to finish the poem.

//

Whether it was the day of the dinner or the one either side of it, Pound would have begun by returning the drafts given to him by Eliot as he passed through Paris in November: the ribbon copies of 'The Burial of the Dead' and 'A Game of Chess', and the carbon copy of 'The Fire Sermon'. Eliot would have given him in return the new Lausanne manuscripts of 'Death by Water' and 'What the Thunder Said', as well as the manuscript fair copy of 'Dirge'; he seems also to have given Pound the ribbon copy of 'The Fire Sermon' for a second look.

Pound didn't mark the first page of 'The Burial of the Dead' – the fifty-four lines cancelled by Eliot from the Boston night out – but he probably saw it, as without that page neither the 'Burial' title nor two-part 'Police' title would have been present, and it's likely that Eliot would have left the page temporarily in situ as a placeholder to guide his friend's reading. It's possible, too, that he would have taken the opportunity to seek a first and last opinion on whether to salvage the section that he had already cancelled: if so, the answer would be no. Upon the new beginning, 'April is the cruellest month', Pound's touch was light. Here and there he ringed lines that may have seemed too Romantic to him – *forgetful snow*, and *there you feel free* and *I look in vain* (Eliot changed the latter) – and he bracketed the *Unreal city* on the next page as a line of its own, which Eliot duly followed. More controversial were four lines he marked for removal: the first was the line most emblematic of the loss of Eliot's father, *Those are pearls that were his eyes. Look!*, which he may have preferred for its subsequent appearance in 'A Game of Chess', not yet appreciating the central motif that it would become. He also struck out a line referring to John the Divine (Eliot concurred) and the couplet on St Mary Woolnoth, writing in the margin that the lines were reminiscent of William Blake's, and 'too often used'. (Eliot retained the passage but in a revised form). And beside the line with which Eliot had simply been unable to make up his mind –

Sighs, short and infrequent, were ~~expired~~, ~~exhaled expired exhaled~~.[19]

Pound would simply annotate that this was *J. J.* – James Joyce.

Joyce aside, this was a respectful edit by Ezra Pound. 'The Burial of the Dead' would have been returned to Eliot with a clear sense that, once the opening lines from Tom's place were removed, the remaining seventy-six lines were in a sturdy enough condition to open the poem.

'A Game of Chess' was a different matter. From the beginning, Pound railed against its traditional form.

The <u>Chair</u> she <u>sat</u> in, <u>like</u> a <u>burni</u>shed <u>throne</u>
Glowed <u>on</u> the <u>marble, where</u> the <u>swinging glass</u>
Held <u>up</u> by <u>stan</u>dards <u>wrought</u> with <u>go</u>lden <u>vines</u>[20]

'Too tum-pum', Pound wrote of the opening lines, and, later, 'too penty', meaning pentameter – too rigid. Eliot duly removed the twin syllables of 'swinging' in line two, thereby reeling in the line from five to four feet, which was not a revolution, but just enough to jolt the logjam of the regular iambic pentameter. And he showed the revised second and third line to his friend, with 'golden' subdued to 'fruited':

The Chair she sat in, like a burnished throne,
Glowed on the marble, where the glass
Sustained by standards wrought with fruited vines[21]

OK, Pound would ink heavily in reply to Eliot's revision, but even so, he would take apart the stanza of the Belladonna's dressing room that Vivien had said she couldn't understand.[22] He wrote that parts were *dogmatic* in deduction and *wobbly as well*, and Eliot would remove altogether the line that Pound said contained *the weakest point*. Pound didn't want to see Romanticism, and he didn't want realism either, marking 'photography' and 'photo' against the nerves passages as if they were somehow too realistic to be art. And he most certainly did not want anachronism. He ringed 'the closed carriage' at four as a 'Blot' between '1922 & Lil' of the pub scene, and just to clear up any doubt, dated the lines he thought dated: '(1880)'. It was no good clothing a modern poem in nineteenth-century attire, he told Eliot, who suggested 'a closed car' in replacement, explaining 'I cant use taxi more than once': **OK**, Pound inked heavily once more.

Pound's comments to date had been isolated and incisive: single words and on occasion full lines pulled out for revision or removal where he felt they lacked fusion or modernity. But for the blue-ink carbon pages of 'The Fire Sermon' he took a more interventionist stance. He disliked the Fresca couplets that provided the first seventy-two lines. He challenged the inclusion of the woman's toilet habits, and the need to degrade her, but he appealed also at a macro level to the tone – 'Too loose', he marked; 'rhyme drags it out to diffuseness' – the trick of Pope had been *not* to let his couplets become diffuse, he told his friend, and here was Eliot squandering the precious store of energy that his first two parts had generated.[23] It was a relief to Pound when he encountered the lines of the rat creeping softly through the vegetation – *Echt*, he wrote in the margin, at last, something real and genuine to work with. But he thought the *Twit twit twit* returned the poem too soon to Philomela and Tereus and he was in no doubt whatsoever that the dozen lines of London, the swarming life, written in Margate, should be expelled altogether. But it was the long sequence of the typist's seventeen quatrains to which Pound most busily took his pencil, querying and circling and bracketing and cancelling as he went. *Verse not interesting enough as verse to warrant so much of it.* That told Eliot. *Not good.* So did that. *Inversions not warranted.* And *Too easy.* And too *Personal* and too tentative in mealy words of Eliot's such as 'perhaps'. As he had with Fresca's morning toilet – and as he had in places with Joyce's *Ulysses* – Pound tempered Eliot's more scatological instincts, and firmed up any hint of indecisiveness – ridiculing 'perhaps' (*Perhaps be damned*) and 'may' (*make up yr. mind*) – either we know our mind or don't, there's no *may* or *perhaps* about it.[24]

//

As Eliot took back the pages of the first three parts of the long poem, it seems that he replaced the marked carbon copy of 'The Fire Sermon' with the black ribbon copy he had taken to Lausanne, on which he had made half a dozen and more revisions, including cuts to the lines of 'London, the swarming life' and, most notably, the insertion of the new 'apostrophe' lines of manuscript of Venus Anadyomene. It may have been then, or the previous November, that he left Pound with the rough pages from Margate in order to guide his reading of the section. Pound didn't like to work from manuscript: *Type out this anyhow*, he commanded beside a cancelled passage, before conceding *OK* and *echt* in a thick green pencil beside the lines on Highbury, Richmond and Kew. But Eliot also gave Pound first sight of the manuscripts of 'Death by Water' and 'What the Thunder Said': ninety-three lines in fair copy, 117 in first draft, as well as the fair copy of 'Dirge'. And that wasn't all: 'Elegy' went through Pound's hands in typescript at some moment that winter, as did 'Song for the Opherion' and 'Exequy'. All in all, in excess of three hundred lines.

Pound was busy with Horace Liveright on 4 January, typing up his own contract of employment and seeing Liveright off to London for the next leg of his European tour. It may have been on 5 January that he inked Eliot's Lausanne manuscript of 'Death by Water' dismissively, *Bad – but cant attack until I get typescript*, making no other marks on this, nor upon 'What the Thunder Said', except to ink in its header *OK from here on I think*. Upon 'Dirge', he inked a single word only, *doubtful*. It was clear that Eliot was not going to receive anything of interest from Pound until he had turned his Lausanne manuscript into typescript.

The typescripts of 'Song for the Opherion' and 'Exequy' had already received pencil comments by Pound when he added inked marking that January (it may have been then that he wrote 'georgian' so damningly in the margin of 'Song'); but it was Pound's second reading of the 'The Fire Sermon' – this time from the black ribbon copy – that would have held the greatest importance to Eliot. That it *was* the second reading was made clear by Pound himself, who wrote on it *vide other copy* in reference to markings made previously on the blue carbon.[25] And now, in reading the draft once again, he was confirmed in his doubt about those first seventy-two lines that he'd previously marked as 'too loose'. This time he struck them through, all of them, from line two to seventy-two, and reaffirmed the conclusion he had already made that it was with the lines of the rat creeping through the vegetation that the section became *OK*, and was to be *STET.* On seeing once again Eliot's effort to rescue the lines on the swarming life of London, Pound's patience (but not his humour) may have left him, as he reached for the expletive:

B—ll—s.[26]

Between his two edits, Pound had let only four of the eighteen stanzas on the typescript pass as acceptable; coupled with his suggestion to keep only one of the first seventy-two lines, it wasn't apparent to Eliot quite how much of the 'The Fire Sermon' was to be left standing. The Margate roughs were still to be typed and might offer an answer, but even so it was clear that there was work still for Eliot to do on the opening and the closing sections.

Eliot had more than two hundred lines of manuscript to type up before Pound would review them, and that meant making use of Pound's typewriter, as the most convenient machine to hand. Like Eliot, Pound used a Corona typewriter, only his was rather different: it was a Corona 3 portable model on which the platen carriage folded neatly over the keyboard after locking the escapement throwout; from there it fitted into a compact handled case, which made it the choice of travelling writers. Hemingway so loved the model gifted to him for his birthday in 1921 that he wrote an ode to it.[27] It was manufactured at pica pitch, meaning that it produced ten characters per inch, making its running text noticeably wider than the condensed elite twelve pitch of Eliot's own Corona model in London. Some machines boasted an 'automatic reverse', ensuring that it was, in the words of the manual, 'unnecessary for the operator to pay any attention to the ribbon save to replace it when it has been in use so long that its ink is exhausted'.[28] Even so, Pound may have done well to pay just a little more attention than he had of late, as by the time Eliot came to type his drafts, Pound's purple ribbon was badly faded. Conceivably, Eliot sat at the typing table at 70 *bis* while Pound was out on errands; more likely he took advantage of its portability and removed it to his hotel a few streets away. Either way, it was certainly the machine that he used to bring 'Death by Water' and 'What the Thunder Said' into typescript that month on his friend's grainy foolscap paper, gathering the poem now into nineteen pages of loose typescript, including the cancelled leaf of the Boston episode that may have been preserved for working titles alone, with some rough manuscript pages still to be typed.

It isn't known exactly on what date Eliot produced those typescript pages on Pound's machine or when exactly Pound read them.[29] Probably it was 9 January, after he had made a visit to Jacques Rivière on the sixth and an unsuccessful attempt to call upon André Gide on the seventh in Auteuil (he had left for Brussels), and after Pound had used the typewriter himself for correspondence on 8 January, when he told his parents 'Eliot here, with a new poem in semi-existence.'[30]

The marked typescript of the new 'Death by Water' that Pound returned to Eliot after that read less like an edit than a redacted document. The opening lines and much of the first page were cancelled almost wholesale.

'The sailor, attentive to the chart and to the sheets / A concentrated will against the tempest and the tide' was reduced by

Pound simply to 'The sailor', in a stroke removing from the section the overcoming of *aboulie* set against the tempestuous tide of the father.[31] The first dozen lines of the page were bracketed – presumably for removal or repositioning – and then the next twelve or more fared even worse under a relentless pattern of cancellation. Full lines became half-lines or no lines at all under Pound's blunt graphite; by the time he reached the third page of four he had left only one line uncancelled, intentionally or not: *In the horror of the illimitable scream* – which, at that moment, may have been something Eliot felt moved towards. Only the final twelve lines of the typescript were left standing, ten of those being Eliot's reworking into English of the French lines of 'Dans le Restaurant', Phlebas the Phoenician. As much as 90 per cent of the draft had been marked for discarding: 'Death by Water' lay in ruins.

'What the Thunder Said' was a different story altogether. These four pages of typescript Pound touched very lightly, marking up almost nothing beyond typing errors he'd spotted from the manuscript. He didn't care for Eliot's resolution of a single phrase – *there is (are) only you and I* (he thought it should be *it is* only you and I) – but that was just about his only reconstruction on a four-page typescript of which he left the final page unmarked.[32] It was not only the best part of the poem, but the part that justified the whole, Eliot would tell Bertrand Russell in 1923, and Pound agreed.[33] *Give, sympathise, control, peace*: instinctively, Pound understood the motivation of the section, its focusing of the whole of the other four parts, and its consummation of them all. Eliot was so close now to completion of the entire work: it needed simply restraint and constraint. Its antique and extended features had to be cut away or cut back to allow the more dynamic modern poem to appear; its formal grip needed to be loosened to speak more clearly from its own time. Eliot could reach that point soon, very soon, and Pound encouraged his friend to finish the poem there and then in Paris, and get it published (he suggested *The Dial*) without further delay.[34] But by then Eliot's commitments may have begun to move against him: he was due back at Lloyds in the middle of January, and the moment of return to London was approaching.

In practical terms, 'The Burial of the Dead' was all but finished: the opening Boston lines were categorically not to be restored, but instead Eliot would allow the section to begin with 'April'. In doing this, he knew that the poem was guaranteed a dynamic start: he had sensed that for himself, but Pound had now confirmed it.

'A Game of Chess' would need some minor correction: a breaking out of its formal harness, wherever it could, to keep the kinetic energy of the poem live.

But it wasn't clear what Eliot should do with 'The Fire Sermon' now that Pound had effectively dismantled it. Neither the opening nor the ending was fit for purpose, and although the Margate fragments were still to be added, Eliot hadn't had an opportunity to type those on Pound's machine and it seemed now that their production would have to wait for his return to London. But he had an idea for a new opening to the section: just nine lines, in fact, to replace Fresca's seventy. He turned over the first of the typescript pages that Pound had struck out, and then he turned it upside down as well: *The rivers tent is broken*, he wrote in pencil; (*Sweet Thames etc.*). The et cetera was from the 'Prothalamion', a refrain of Edmund Spenser's that had celebrated the betrothal of Thames daughters, but it had also carried what Spenser had called the 'vndersong'[35] of a disenchanted poet. Eliot wrote this with Vivien, once 'the river girl', about to leave for Lyons; in Eliot's new lines, *the nymphs are departed*. And then, in addition to the nine roughed out in pencil, he began a tenth line, a fragment, for which he wrote just three words:

By the waters[36]

Perhaps, when Eliot wrote this, he was hurried, and the compression was nothing more than a shorthand, like the et cetera

of Sweet Thames, like the exiled rivers of Babylon, to be expanded in typescript: *By the waters of Leman I sat down and wept* . . .
Léman, to which he had arrived in pieces and left with some
semblance of unity. Léman, beside which he had unburdened
himself. Léman, where he had discovered *the hand expert with
sail and oar*. Léman, where he had learned to quarantine the feeling of rejection by a father and mother, and the state of mind
of a disintegrating marriage. Léman, the mistress waters, beside
which he had concluded his longest poem, a work that had been
a year in the writing and nurtured even longer in the mind. *They
have forgotten thee, O Sion*, he had written that past summer in
The Dial, as if anticipating this very moment. He knew, all right,
the line to come but just may not have wanted to write it in that
moment, like a line that he could not cross, a sign that he had
come as far now as he could.

By the waters

The last new words of the poem that Eliot would write.

//

'I have so much to tell you and complain,' Vivien wrote to Mary
Hutchinson as Eliot packed his bags for London, but she would
return in a fortnight and convey it personally: 'I would rather talk
it than write it.'[37] Had Eliot been uncaring on his return, or was
there a new security about his state of mind that appeared to leave
him less in need of her? Perhaps he seemed lost to the poem and
to Pound in those two weeks in Paris; even so, he made a small
shopping list of skin ointments to purchase for Vivien on the back
of the typescript of 'Death by Water'; few other details of their
time there survive.[38] Why, after six weeks apart, would the Eliots
not wish to travel home together? Why, after all the loneliness of
Paris, would Vivien seek out that moment to travel in the opposite

direction, not to London but to Lyons? But that was what would now happen, in the middle of January: Eliot to the north-west, Vivien to the south-east.

In the days that followed his return to London on 14 January, Eliot received news from Mary Hutchinson that was seemingly not easy for him to digest. 'I am very much disturbed by your note. I had wondered – you must tell me all about it, because we can't leave things like this.'[39] Mary may have intended only to complain at the mistreatment by Scofield Thayer of her husband, St John, whose 'London Letter', deputising for Eliot, had with some embarrassment been rejected by *The Dial*. Equally, time enough had passed that she could have seen Vivien on her return to London: was it news of this kind that she wished to impart? Had Vivien told Mary something different about Thayer? Whether it was Thayer or someone else, just what *had* transpired with the man from Cologne, if anything at all? It would be at this moment, in London, late January, that Eliot, who had been 'so mountany gay' in Paris, would tell Pound that he was now 'excessively depressed', and, in the very next sentence, 'V. sends you her love and says that if she had realised how bloody England is she would not have returned.'[40]

//

'Eliot's poem is very important,' Ezra Pound told Scofield Thayer early in February, 'almost enough to make everyone else shut up shop' – before adding characteristically, 'I haven't done so.'[41] And he hadn't, for Pound had completed his Eighth Canto, and, as Eliot departed Paris, had sent a draft of it not to the man he'd worked with so closely that fortnight, but to Ford Madox Ford in Sussex, asking him to go through it 'with a red, blood-red, green, blue, or other pencil and scratch what is too awful'.[42] It seemed telling that, at the moment of his great collaboration on Eliot's poem, Pound would not seek Eliot's opinion in return. Perhaps it was Pound's sense of selflessness that left him unwilling to disturb Eliot, but whatever the reason, Pound confided in Ford that it was so difficult to find good criticism, 'and one goes blind, deaf after a time'. *The Cantos* and *The Waste Land* could have been in mutual co-operative partnership that month, but Pound hadn't let it happen. He had prepared fifteen or more versions of an eighth canto without Eliot's attention, 'all worse or less or more'. In its theme, it was the most oceanic canto, funnelling throughout 'the long course of the seas', a voyage he had permitted himself in his poem but had not permitted Eliot in 'Death by Water', but instead had so stringently cut back.

> Water cutting under the keel,
> Sea-break from stern forrards,
>> wake running off from the bow,[43]

A curve of common names and images appeared in the canto as in Eliot's poem – Tiresias, Triton, a tower, one-eyed, a porpoise.

>> When they brought the boy I said:
> 'He has a god in him,
>> though I do not know which god,'
> And they kicked me into the fore-stays,
> And I was frightened,[44]

And I was frightened, used twice by Eliot, in the drafts Pound had just read.

> If you will lean over the rock,
> the coral face under wave-tinge,

The rock, the coral, the tempest, the wave pattern: Eliot could be seen in it all, despite Pound's peculiar insistence to John Quinn that his canto was 'not in the least *à la* Eliot'.[45] *Then quiet water*, Pound would conclude, 'splashing in rock-hollows and sand-hollows / In the wave-runs by the half-dune.'[46]

The Cantos had never read so fluently, bringing to Pound, in Paris then, a moment of reckoning. 'Some one has got to make the plunge, decide whether the Epic, or wottell of cosmographic volcano is extinct or not,' he told Ford. 'Mauberley' had failed, 'Propertius' had failed, the early lyrics and the 'French' form were distinctively modes of the past to him now. Surely this was the moment for him to make a commitment. 'It will take me another thirty years at least.'[47] But now, without exception, the epic of *The Cantos* would become the form of Pound's creative composition for the remainder of his life.

//

'Eliot as you perhaps know is back from Switzerland,' Wyndham Lewis reported to Ottoline Morrell on 22 January. 'I saw him the other day.'[48] Back in London and back in bed, Eliot had influenza again, this time for ten days, which no doubt was not what Lloyds had hoped for after their three-month grant of leave. As it would turn out, the recuperation gave Eliot the time to make the final creative decisions he needed. Said Lewis: 'He has written a particularly fine poem.'

'He Do the Police in Different Voices' had been a title in interim service to the poem. It had signalled the dramatic cast that Eliot had conceived in the first two parts: old Tom, Mr Donavan, the hyacinth girl, Madame Sosostris, the Belladonna, Albert and Lil; but it had made decreasing sense for the fire sermon that Tiresias directed, or the sequence at sea, or the thunderous tones of the prophetic lines that closed the poem. Most likely it had ceased as a possibility soon after those later sections were written. What title *could* possibly serve for the vast tract of territory over which Eliot's poem now stretched? It couldn't be one taken from the constituent parts, as that would be to privilege one section above

THE   WASTE   LAND.

By

T.S.Eliot.

"Did he live his life again in every detail of desire, temptation, and surrender during that supreme moment of complete
knowledge?   He cried in a whisper at some image, at some vision, - he cried out twice, a cry that was no more than a
breath -
        'The horror! the Horror!'"
                                        CONRAD.

another and so unbalance the work. It had to be something new.
But what? And then, around the middle of January, only a few
days after returning from Paris, Eliot believed that he had found
it. He wound a sheet of paper into his Corona typewriter and
tried it out on a title page.

THE WASTE LAND.

By

T. S. Eliot.

Three words, not two, as he would find himself pointing out with frequency, beginning with Ezra Pound himself. 'Not "Waste Land", please, but "The Waste Land",' he would tell his friend that summer; and 'not "The Wasteland" but "The Waste Land",' he would subsequently correct a translator; and '*not Waste Lands*' either, come to that (to Lady Rothermere).[49] Three words, one definite article.

The title, said Eliot, had been drawn from a recently published book by Jessie L. Weston, *From Ritual to Romance,* where among the many quests for the Grail had been 'the restoration to fruitfulness of a Waste Land'.[50] It may not have been the first time that he had encountered the aridity and the Grail. Eliot may also have remembered Tennyson's 'Morte d'Arthur' ('an agony / Of lamentation, like a wind, that shrills / All night in a waste land, where no one comes, / Or hath come, since the making of the world')[51] or Thomas Malory's description of a barren place without corn or grass or fruit, of water without fish, scarred by pestilence and harm: 'the waste land, for that dolorous stroke'.[52] An issue of *Poetry* magazine from 1913 had conceivably, though doubtfully, lodged in his recall: it contained a poem called 'Waste Land' by Madison Cawein (which may have been a misprint for 'Wasteland'), the pool-hall poet of Louisville known as 'the Kentucky Keats'.[53] In truth, the derivation didn't matter as much as the application, for it was most certainly well applied to Eliot's poem. *Waste* tapped the grief within – what Pound had written of despairingly in 'Mauberley' as 'wastage as never before' – the lives of countless millions lost to war.[54] It said all that Eliot needed to say about the falling towers of Europe, of desolate terrain uncultivated, of loss without profit, of excess and refuse, the ravage of the body by disease or decay, the mind in drink or immorality. It also marked a more personal place in the relationship between father and son, husband and wife. It spoke to Eliot's sense of the submarine sections of the poem more than might first be apparent: the expanse of ocean that Edmund Waller had called the 'Worlds great Waste', and Dryden the 'wat'ry Waste', the *mundus mare* ('so the world is a sea') for which *land* is not only a terrestrial noun but also a nautical verb – to surface, to disembark, go ashore, take bearings and survey.[55] Most certainly, Eliot had found his title.

An epigraph was taken from Joseph Conrad's *Heart of Darkness*, a work beginning, 'The sea-reach of the Thames stretched before us like the beginning of an interminable waterway,' and which might have lent so much to the poem had Eliot allowed it: its *mysterious life of the wilderness*, its *streams of death in life, cut off from the comprehension of our surroundings, from the heart of an impenetrable darkness*.[56] Eliot hadn't alighted on any of these passages, but on one that sees in the dying face of 'Mistah' Kurtz his pride and power, but also the expression 'of craven terror – of an intense and hopeless despair'.

> Did he live his life again in every detail of desire, temptation, and surrender during that supreme moment of complete knowledge?
> He cried in a whisper at some image, at some vision, – he cried out twice, a cry that was no more than a breath –
> 'The horror! The horror!'[57]

Desire. Temptation. Surrender. Complete knowledge. Each of these concepts had occupied Eliot's criticism as he prepared himself for the poem, into the heart of light. The passage was, Eliot told Pound, 'somewhat elucidative', and in no place more so than its final cry, *The horror! The horror!*, which was a condition that had stalked Eliot perennially. Twice already he had written it into the poem only for Pound to expunge it: *In the horror of the illimitable scream* and *horrified past horror*.[58] It was present in the intimacy of

'The Death of St Narcissus', and was a subject on which Eliot had praised John Webster for his capacity with *a network of tentacular roots reaching down to the deepest terrors and desires.*[59] Contemporary politics, he had written in 1921, oppressed him with a *continuous physical horror.*[60] Perhaps no word better stood for the dispossession, the *aboulie*, the anomie, the intimacy that Eliot struggled with in his marriage and himself: 'a horror of sensuality' that Henry Eliot had read across the work and no doubt into his brother's life.[61] Perhaps few words spoke so deeply to Eliot, because the horror was the route to redemption. He wrote in 1930:

> So far as we are human, what we do must be either evil or good;
> so far as we do evil or good, we are human; and it is better, in a
> paradoxical way, to do evil than to do nothing: at least, we exist. It
> is true to say that the glory of man is his capacity for salvation; it is
> equally true to say that his glory is his capacity for damnation.[62]

Eliot had found the most appropriate epigraph he could – one that was *somewhat elucidative* – the perfect balance in what an epigraph should be. But Pound didn't agree. 'I doubt if Conrad is weighty enough to stand the citation,'[63] he told Eliot. Did Pound mean Conrad's name or the passage itself was lacking weight, Eliot attempted to clarify. Pound conceded: who was he to begrudge Conrad his laurel crown? Eliot could keep it. But the doubt had been sown, and Eliot began the search that would lead him full circle: back to the presence of the *Satyricon* of Petronius that had been lost when the draft of 'In the Cage' had been retitled 'A Game of Chess'. In the event, the *Satyricon* would bring less to the poem than would *Heart of Darkness*, but then Pound's hesitation was explicable: why give away the laurel of a contemporary poem to another contemporary writer? Why not draw upon the tradition or on nothing at all?

Behind the new title page was a new typescript, produced in London on Eliot's new Corona around 20 January, and posted shortly after to Pound in Paris for final review. 'The Burial of the Dead' and 'A Game of Chess' were now as trim as they would be. 'The Fire Sermon' was much improved with its new opening replacing the Fresca couplets; its over-extended sequence of seventeen quatrains with Tiresias and the typist had been reduced to ten, without any loss to impact and with plenty of gain. 'What the Thunder Said' was left respectfully untouched, being the remarkable and momentary performance that it was. Only 'Death by Water' was now in doubt, a sequence which had arrived with Pound at ninety-three lines in length and left his hands at ten lines – or twelve, depending on his marking – but which Eliot was now planning to cut in its entirety. He told Scofield Thayer on 20 January that he presently had 'a poem of about 450 lines, in four parts', suggesting that he had already let go mentally of that section from the poem, and asked Pound that same week whether he agreed that he had *better omit Phlebas also???*[64] 'I DO advise keeping Phlebas,' Pound replied. 'In fact I more'n advise. Phlebas is an integral part of the poem; the card pack introduces him, the drowned phoen. sailor. and he is needed ABSoloootly where he is.'[65] That was clear, but in case it wasn't Pound inked in the margin of his letter *must stay in*. And stay it would, providing in its short ten lines something of the kind of interlude between sections that Eliot was about to discuss with Pound. And that brought with it exactly the kind of transition that Eliot had been striving for when he had written that spring that no long work could maintain the same high tension throughout[66] – there simply *had* to be variation, he believed, and this was the route to it. In fact, *so* much did he like the variation of the short fourth part in a five-part poem that he would reuse the model again when he came to write the poems that made up *Four Quartets*.

//

Eliot and Pound's work to complete the poem was almost done, but at the last moment their efforts ran into a problem. Horace Liveright, who had been charming literary circles in London ever since he left Paris, had received from Pound an assessment of the poem's length, and had written in response, 'I'm disappointed that Eliot's material is so short. Can't he add anything?'[67] It was an enquiry that would at the eleventh hour send Eliot into a spin, fearing that he might be about to default on the conditions of the offer of publication. Rapidly, even desperately, he calculated the permutations for a published book, and he came up with an unlikely solution. Quite against the tide of the edit that he and Pound had been making, Eliot now began adding to the typescript. He looked again at the satellite poems that had surrounded the drafting of *The Waste Land*: these could be interleaved as what he would later call 'interludes'[68] between the four sections ('Death by Water' had momentarily been dropped). Looked at as Eliot did, three 'interludes' promised everything of the long poem that he had asked of it: a variety bill like a music hall programme with interim relief between acts. Seemingly, from clues in Pound's responses, the interleaving trio that Eliot had intended was 'Song', 'Exequy' and 'Dirge', but those same responses tell us something different from Eliot's recollection: that the three 'remaining superfluities' as Pound called them were, at that point, placed 'at the end' of the typescript – 'the last three'. Asking whether anything would be lacking if they were removed, Pound answered his own question: 'I dont think it wd.' Better to *leave 'em, abolish 'em altogether*, he told Eliot: the 'Song' had only two lines worth preserving, 'Exequy' didn't hold with the rest, and 'Dirge' made no advance on earlier 'stuff'.

> The thing now runs from April . . . to shantih without break. That is 19 pages, and let us say the longest poem in the Englisch langwidge. Dont try to bust all records by prolonging it three pages further.[69]

With this, Pound had given the first confirmation that the Boston scene in 'The Burial of the Dead' had definitely been removed from consideration, but its absence only increased the pressure to bulk up the typescript still further. Pound continued: if 'the remaining super-fluities' *must* be retained, Eliot should run them at the beginning, and not the end. But therein lay yet another challenge, for Eliot, in a desperate bid to expand, was about to make an improbable suggestion.

'Do you advise printing Gerontion as prelude in book or pamphlet form?' he asked.[70]

Pound was shocked. 'Gerontion' had an existing print life of two years' standing in *Ara Vos Prec* and Knopf's *Poems*, and it was not a credible idea to introduce *The Waste Land* with a move of this kind. 'I do not advise printing Gerontion as preface. One dont miss it AT all as the thing now stands. To be more lucid still, let me say that I advise you NOT to print Gerontion as prelude.'[71] The message was clear – but a yet stranger request was to come.

Quite separately, as an aside in Paris, in order to commemorate the editorial partnership on the poem, Pound had composed what he called three 'squibs' – skits he referred to as 'an bloody impertinence' – among them one he had called 'Sage Homme', referring to himself as the wise man of the title:

These are the Poems of Eliot
By the Uranian Muse begot;
A Man their Mother was,
A Muse their Sire.

How did the printed Infancies result
From Nuptuals thus doubly difficult?

If you must needs enquire
Know diligent Reader
That on each Occasion
Ezra performed the caesarean Operation.[72]

Dont use 'em with Waste Land, he instructed Eliot, at least half-seriously, perhaps sensing the magpie-like way in which Eliot's mind was moving. But Eliot was grasping for anything now that would bulk the load, and he went right ahead and asked Pound if he might use these ten lines nonetheless in italics in the front matter. Surely Pound would stand by his first insistence and once again say no; but he didn't, he acquiesced. *Do as you like,* came the alarming response from Paris.

The poem that Eliot had worked on for a year, and carried in his mind for much longer, stood on the brink of a disastrous turn, almost wrecked at the very last moment by an act of literary filibustering. It had found a title (and, briefly, an epigraph) and at the same moment that it was progressing towards its trimmest shape, it was being distorted by the prospect of publication, and for a moment the poem that Eliot was about to call *The Waste Land* looked in his imagination suddenly like this:

> (1) Sage Home by E. P. – (2) Gerontion – (3) The Burial of the Dead – (4) A Game of Chess – (5) The Fire Sermon – (6) What the Thunder Said – (7–9, in order unknown) Song – Exequy – Dirge.

Don't print the first two, urged Pound at this eleventh hour; don't print the last three either. And *DO* restore 'Death by Water', *ABSoloootly.* Hold the line, Pound urged in the face of this last-minute wobble, hold the line.

And that's exactly what Eliot did.

//

'MUCH improved,' Pound wrote with thoughtful affirmation on 24 January.[73]

'Criticisms accepted so far as understood,' Eliot saluted by return.[74]

'Three times through the sieve by Pound as well as myself': that's what Eliot told Scofield Thayer that the poem had experienced.[75] The process had begun in November 1921, when Eliot first left his pages with Pound in Paris – that was the first sift. It blossomed in the fortnight there together in early January, when the men worked face to face – that was the second. But it had also continued in correspondence later that same month when Eliot returned to London. It had been an act of perceptive and selfless direction on Pound's part, but it had also been a studious and modest hearing on Eliot's. It is doubtful if anyone else could have inhabited Eliot's imaginative space as well as Pound did then, to accept the precepts of his approach, to know the possibilities of his talent, and to judge exactly how far to stretch him to his limits without snapping confidence or belief. In return, it is doubtful if anyone other than Eliot could have listened with such dedicated disinterest or act without ego in such service to the poem as to accept the scale of revision that was proposed to him.

Something truly exceptional had taken place between Eliot, Pound and *The Waste Land*, something truly rare. It wasn't that a good poem had been made a better poem through being well edited: that isn't what happened in Paris and London that winter. Instead, the common focus of Eliot and Pound transformed those pages into a poem for the first time. For what Eliot came back with from Lausanne wasn't yet a poem, or if it was to be called that then it needed to be qualified, as Eliot later did when he said it was 'a sprawling chaotic poem'.[76] Admittedly, it contained everything at that moment that the poem needed to exist (everything but its title and a beginning to 'The Fire Sermon'), but its pieces were still provisional, and had yet to be assembled in such a way as to make the most distinctive object from it. Like a sculpture half-emerging from its marble, the 'poem' that Eliot brought back from Switzerland was neither defined nor discrete – it was still a miscellany of parts, still a hinterland rather than the island it was forming. It had yet to become what Pound would say of it in 1924 when he called it 'an emotional unit'.[77] What Pound and Eliot achieved together in Paris and London didn't make it a *better* poem; it *made The Waste Land* a poem for the first time.

Like Eliot's example of the catalysing platinum, a transformation had taken place, a metamorphosis that was particular to the chemical minds of the two men. They had found a way for the poem to exist within them both at the same moment, possessed by neither but possessing of both. In that instant the poem was neither 'Eliot's' composition nor 'Pound's' editorial, but a common project, equally imagined, inhabiting each man simultaneously and fully.[78] The poem had become an event occurring in both men in unison, in creator and critic, in poet and reader, in two halves of a combining mind. Pound did not of course share the same life experience as Eliot – not with his father or with Vivien, not with Bertrand Russell, not with dispossession or the bank or any other of the influences on Eliot's life; but he understood how to experience the force of those feelings in the poem in which they were converging, and, crucially, he understood how to transmute them into an experience that others might comprehend.

Ezra Pound had, in Eliot's judgement of 1938, 'done so much to turn *The Waste Land* from a jumble of good and bad passages into a poem'.[79] But that's not to say that without Pound the pages would not have become *The Waste Land*. And nor is it to suppose that the drafts that Eliot left behind are the only alternative to what that final poem might have been. Such are the materials that Eliot would certainly have achieved something spectacular on his own, but probably not here, and not this spectacle. More likely he would have reached a different poem: one that was longer, more various in its voices, more formal and pernickety, more unkind in its consideration for others. One that was more obviously attuned to the experiences of Eliot's own life; one that was less mysterious in its transposition.

Pound's work on the poem that winter had been inspirational. He had dramatically stripped back the draft, clearing out all that he considered to be excess, explication or autobiography, leaving behind a shorter, sturdier and altogether stranger poem. His encouragement to strip out the Fresca lines, to pare back the typist's quatrains, and to shrewdly unstitch the piece from Eliot's surrounding work were instrumental decisions in the success of a final draft in which he had persuaded his friend not to clutter his typescript but entrust the work to stand confidently on its own. He may have misjudged the epigraph, and the decision to reduce 'Death by Water' so dramatically was more open to debate: powerful passages had been sacrificed, but 'the emotional unit' of the poem had been strengthened.[80]

In the event, Pound had been an editor to the poem in three ways. He had helped it at the level of the line, guiding it through intricate decisions about phonemes, words, phrases and whole passages – a mechanic in its engine room fine-tuning its performance. He had also aided it from above, defining its limits, melding the shape that it makes today – the poem of five parts that it is, and not the poem of eight or nine that it might have been. But beyond his micro and macro work on the text, he had achieved something more fundamental still. Pound had enabled Eliot in life – he had stood behind him from arrival in London in 1914, and encouraged in Eliot the belief that he was a poet capable of a work as significant as the poem he had now produced. Pound had encouraged the conditions in Eliot for that most intangible but essential of editorial arts: confidence.

'I think it is the best I have ever done, and Pound thinks so too.'[81] So said Eliot that summer.

Pound, of course, would be typically blunter. 'Complimenti,

you bitch,' he wrote in January. 'I am wracked by the seven jealousies.'[82]

And for a moment, for a brief moment, it seemed almost possible to imagine Eliot beaming.

London 1960.

Eliot couldn't accept the despair in which Pound held his own work and life. On the eve of his departure to Morocco, in January 1960, he wrote in an effort to comfort his friend that there was so much in his own life that he could not bear to think about: *The Waste Land* was an exception, he said. The advice from his doctor 'to get out of Europe' had been a disaster: his evacuation following the earthquake of Agadir had left him bed bound in London, receiving treatment for a fortnight.[1] As he began to make a recovery in the summer of 1960, he turned back to Pound's plight, and urged him to remember that he retained the genius he'd always had, only now he could count something additional: he could count knowledge and the practice of a lifetime's campaign.[2] It might be forgivable in older age to believe that one has nothing more to say and that there's nobody who would want to hear it if one did, but that was an impulse to which neither of them should submit. 'There's always something that one can do, and do better than anyone else,' he told his friend in 1961, and then he cut to the chase.[3] 'Damn it, you're still the biggest man in the poetry world, and have had the greatest influence on poetry of anyone in this century.'

Assuredly, Pound had proved the greatest influence on Eliot's poetry, and on *The Waste Land* most of all; but that influence hadn't stopped with the completion of the poem: it had continued in an effort to find it publication.

In 1922, Pound had secured from Horace Liveright an offer to publish *The Waste Land* in New York, but an American edition was just the first of four pieces that Eliot wished to put in place.

He also wanted to see the poem with a book publisher in Britain and, if possible, to appear in journal publication on both sides of the Atlantic in order to reach the widest audience and serve as an advertisement for the poem. *The Dial* was the natural place with which to begin, and on 20 January Eliot told Scofield Thayer that he would shortly have ready 'a poem of about 450 lines, in four parts' that could be divided between four issues, now that 'Death by Water' had for the moment been dropped.[4] He would like to know what *The Dial* could offer for such a poem. A fixed rate, would be the answer – $10 a page for a cast-off eleven pages, plus a little bit extra for Eliot thrown in: $150 (£35), sight unseen.[5] But it wasn't enough. It was rumoured that Thayer had paid George Moore three times that sum for a short story, and Eliot wasn't about to let his poem go for 'only £30–£35' – 'It is out of the question.'[6] On 8 March 1922, Eliot cabled a reply:

CANNOT ACCEPT UNDER !8!56 POUNDS = ELIOT +7

The telegram had been mangled in transmission, and Thayer didn't interpret it kindly. 'I have received from you a wire as follows, "Cannot accept under 856 pounds – Eliot". I presume there is some error upon the part of the telegraphic service.'[8] Thayer prided himself on paying all contributors – known and unknown – 'at the same rates', and he wasn't about to tear that up for a work he hadn't even read. But Eliot had intended £50, not £856, telling Ezra Pound: 'I would take £50 and no less.'[9] Pound understood this was a moment to step in. 'I am afraid Eliot has merely gone to pieces again,'[10] he told Thayer: *abuleia*, he explained, a physical inertia had left his friend paralysed in his literary progress, and Thayer should take the opportunity to get behind him. The poem was in its way every bit as good as *Ulysses*, Pound assured him, and not only ought the journal to snap it up but it should confer upon Eliot the lucrative new Dial Award – $2,000 (£475) – created in 1921 to honour annually a 'service to letters', and serve God or the Devil in any measure that suited the artist, the journal had announced the previous summer.[11] 'Three months off and he got that poem done,' Pound boasted. 'I think he is being in that bank is the greatest waste now going on in letters, ANYWHERE.'[12]

Flu had laid out Eliot and Vivien simultaneously and successively since they returned to London.[13] Once again Vivien's condition deteriorated, once again she entered a nursing home: 'She must be made to sleep.'[14] Eliot anticipated that he would be alone in the flat for weeks that winter of 1922: precisely the space he needed to manage the poem. On 26 February he wrote to Maurice Firuski, proprietor of the small Massachusetts press Dunster House on the advice of Conrad Aiken. 'I have now ready a poem,' he wrote: 435 lines which, with spacing *essential to the sense*, would require 475 book lines, spanning twenty-eight to thirty-two pages. The poem was once again in five parts with 'Death by Water' restored, and Eliot had now replaced the Conrad epigraph with the Sibyl of Cumae.[15] 'It is, I think, much the best poem I have ever written, and I think it would make a much more distinct impression and attract much more attention if published as a book.'[16] What would Firuski be prepared to offer? One hundred dollars would be the response; once again, it was not enough.[17]

While negotiations for journal publication with *The Dial* stalled, Eliot was making preparations of his own for English publication. 'I have undertaken the task of finding and selecting the contributors for a modest quarterly review,' he told T. Sturge Moore that spring. 'I shall make its aim the maintenance of critical standards and the concentration of intelligent critical opinion.'[18] The name of that journal was suggested by Vivien in June – *The Criterion* (Eliot would tell Pound teasingly that he was thinking of calling it *The Possum*) and by midsummer he had decided that its inaugural issue would carry the first two sections of *The Waste Land*, 'and the rest in the second number'.[19]

Imperfect as they were, Eliot was in possession of offers for book and journal publication in New York, and now he also had a London venue in *The Criterion*. His negotiations had become sophisticated, and Virginia Woolf said of him that spring that he had 'grown supple as an eel'.[20] Three pieces of his publishing puzzle were now in place, or, if not in place then at least in his own hands, but he lacked the last of those pieces: an English book publisher, and in March 1922, he offered the poem to the Hogarth Press. 'He has written a poem of 40 pages, which we are to print in the autumn,' Virginia recorded in her diary. 'This is his best work, he says. He is pleased with it; takes heart, I think, from the thought of that safe in his desk.'[21] But the strain of his situation must have been showing, for there was something off in his demeanour, she recorded. She reported a rumour circulating in Bloomsbury that Eliot was now applying violet powder to his face in order to make him look 'cadaverous'; she described his mood as 'slightly malevolent', and said that she wasn't sure that he did not also paint his lips.[22] By then she and Leonard had at last been given an encounter with the poem. Eliot had come to dinner at Hogarth House in June 1922, and read it aloud – or not so much read but 'sang it & chanted it rhythmed it', she recorded. It had tensity, symmetry, a great beauty and force of phrase, she said, adding in caution: 'What connects it together, I'm not so sure.'[23] When Eliot rushed away after dinner he didn't leave time for answers; but an impression had been made and the Woolfs would go ahead with publication. 'The Waste Land, it is called; & Mary Hutch, who has heard it more quietly, interprets it to be Tom's autobiography – a melancholy one.'[24] Production would take longer than Virginia and Leonard anticipated: the British book edition of *The Waste Land* did not appear until the autumn of 1923.

Eliot was not alone in his strained behaviour that spring of 1922. Margaret Anderson at the ailing *Little Review* had received a note purportedly from Dorothy Pound, informing her of the distressing news of her husband's unexpected death, and including photographs of a death mask that had been cast from the late poet's face by the sculptor Nancy Cox-McCormack.[25] The editors suspected a 'hoax', and told their readers so, refusing to publish the photographs they had been sent.[26] Pound was indeed alive and well and holidaying in Siena, and was furious that his ruse had been rumbled: he had been seeking 'a little repose', and considered his demise an effective way to go about it; but in refusing to play along the journal had 'bungled' it.[27] It seemed as though nothing, not even his literary death, lay any longer in Pound's own hands.

Death masks aside, Pound's efforts to rescue Eliot quickened. He repeated for readers of the *New Age* that March what he had told Thayer privately, that Eliot's employment in the bank was the greatest waste in contemporary literature; and he was more candid still: Eliot had experienced 'complete physical breakdown', Pound unblushingly told his readers, and during leave from the bank had produced what he called 'a very important sequence of poems'.[28] But Eliot was not grateful for the attention: he told Richard Aldington that although he appreciated the motives, the situation was a tiring embarrassment.[29] He was concerned that such public pronouncements by Pound might make him the subject of gossip; they might damage his position at Lloyds, and leave him with neither the bank nor the maintenance subscription that Pound was calling Bel Esprit.

In Paris, Sylvia Beach had finished printing *Ulysses*. She sent one copy, bound, to Eliot in London, that April, who had already acquired uncut sheets and was delighted to be spared making up the edition himself.[30] He would call the book 'the most important expression which the present age has found'.[31] Meanwhile, efforts to publish his own work were barely advancing. Still Eliot didn't feel in a position to commit to the offer from Liveright, even without an improvement from Dunster. Now it was Alfred Knopf's turn. He learned from Eliot that he had a poem of 450 lines primed for a small book of thirty pages: 'It is, I think, a good one.'[32] A neglected clause in his contract for the 1920 *Poems* gave Knopf first refusal on the next two books, and Eliot now enacted it. He hoped that Knopf might improve upon Liveright's offer of $150 at 15 per cent and an autumn publication. 'I am anxious to get the poem published as soon as possible,' he said in April, adding in May, 'on account of copyright'.[33] But Eliot was not leaving Knopf with enough time: he wished to see his four streams of book and journal publications converge at the same moment in the autumn, and Knopf's list for the fall was already confirmed; Knopf was left with no option but to pass.[34]

Meanwhile, negotiations with Scofield Thayer had completely broken down. Pound began enquiries with *The Dial*'s cross-town neighbour, *Vanity Fair*, to find out what they might pay for Eliot's poem; the enquiry would ultimately lead nowhere, but then Pound was using news of an editorial meeting in London that summer with John Peale Bishop, its recently departed editor, to pressure *The Dial* into action.[35] It had not gone unnoted that in the *New Age* that spring Pound had conferred upon *The Waste Land* the status of 'permanent value' – not bad for an unpublished poem; and he had also been working his private channels of influence among writers, telling William Carlos Williams that the poem was 'a masterpiece; one of the most important 19 pages in English'.[36] Neither the editors of *The Dial* nor *Vanity Fair*, nor any of the four publishers engaged in discussion that spring had actually read the poem, but they were being played off against one another skilfully by Eliot and Pound in an effort to stimulate interest. The poem had achieved a reputation even before it was read, and word of it was travelling. Aldous Huxley had also alerted Bishop to the existence of Eliot's poem, warning that it was promised to *The Dial*; so Bishop telephoned a contact there, Gilbert Seldes, and asked about his intentions. The enquiry came as something of a surprise to Seldes, who knew nothing of the poem, and who cabled Scofield Thayer in Vienna to clarify the picture, receiving in return his colleague's enigmatic response: 'ELIOT REFUSA THAYER'.[37] Seldes, sensing that something of value was slipping away, was not prepared to concede just yet: publication in *The Dial*, he told Bishop, was 'problematical but probable'.[38] But to Thayer it was not probable; he remained entrenched in his position that the journal had capped fees and could not make exceptions.

The strain of uncertainty was telling upon Eliot. His brain had run down, he told Richard Aldington, and he wrote to Ottoline Morrell that he felt another breakdown was impending.[39] With negotiations on the poem unresolved, and with his preparations for *The Criterion* adding to his stresses, Eliot felt like a man exposed and misunderstood that summer. He was upset not only that the proposed advance didn't recognise the work put into the poem, but also, as he revealed to Aldington that summer, it failed to acknowledge something stranger: 'the vast amount of verse, which in comparison with most writers, I refrained from writing'.[40] That was a new kind of thought for any publisher to be expected to absorb: that they might reward a writer for a discernment that made their work valuable in its rarity: that in effect they might reward a writer *not* to write. Eliot said that he was aware that the larger part of literary London stood against him, and that there were, in his words, 'a great many jackals swarming about waiting for my bones'.[41] It was time to find some security and complete arrangements with Horace Liveright.

When Boni & Liveright's contract arrived in June it was not at all what Eliot was expecting. With four publishers in the fray, Eliot was only in a position to grant Liveright North American volume rights – in other words, permission to make a book (alone) in the US (alone) – but the contract that Eliot was asked to sign was, he said, tantamount to conceding world rights, thereby preventing the possibility of any deals with *The Dial*, *The Criterion* or the Hogarth Press.[42] Liveright had been the only publisher involved when he made his offer over dinner in Paris that January, and a request for world rights was not an unreasonable one to make, even if it was a little slow to be formalised in a contract five months later. But Eliot had since complicated the picture through his wish for multiple printings, and now he cabled John Quinn to ask for his support in ironing out the growing tangle. Quinn was happy to help: he too had heard about the poem from Pound, and was only too pleased to remind Eliot that he was under no obligation to Horace Liveright.

Vivien's health continued to worsen. Her temperature had frequently risen above 100°F that spring, and by the summer she was diagnosed with colitis.[43] She wrote to Pound with an exhaustive list of symptoms and of 'increasing mental incapacity'.[44] The pressure on Eliot to provide for her grew and grew. Richard Aldington told him that he had become 'bitter and hypercritical'.[45] Eliot pleaded with Pound that he didn't want personal favours of the kind that Bel Esprit was projecting. 'Sometimes I simply want to escape from the whole thing and run away,' he told Ottoline Morrell.[46] When the *Liverpool Daily Post and Echo* reported falsely that Eliot was benefitting from the scheme to the tune of £800, Eliot sued for a correction and apology.[47] He received both. But he wanted more. He wanted to know the source of the allegation, and he believed it was Richard Aldington, to whom he wrote leadingly in a typed letter peppered with capitals and underlinings: both men *knew* 'FROM what source it is likely TO have emanated'.[48] Aldington was not involved, but the friendship was at breaking point: he told Eliot that indiscreet friends were far more dangerous than open enemies.[49]

Ezra Pound pressed Eliot for a typescript of the poem that he could sell to *The Dial*, but Eliot said that he couldn't give up those pages just yet: he had just sent a copy to John Quinn for delivery to Boni & Liveright, and he needed to retain the other one himself.[50] When John Quinn finally received a typescript of *The Waste Land* in July, he told Eliot what he hadn't wanted to hear: that it would benefit from adding 'four or five more poems to it'.[51] As Pound put it, 'Liveright wanted a longer volume and the notes were the only available unpublished matter.'[52]

It could have been at his reading of the poem at Hogarth House on 18 June that the idea of notes to *The Waste Land* first arose as a way of elucidating the poem. Clive Bell attributed the prompt to Roger Fry ('It may be,' Eliot agreed in 1963).[53] Eliot himself would suggest in the 1950s that the annotations began as a form of citation – preventative references for 'spiking the guns of critics' that were expanded upon when it seemed that, in book form, the poem was to be 'inconveniently short'.[54] But there is no evidence of such a tiered expansion, and it seems more likely that they were written in a concentrated effort that summer for the sole purpose of fulfilling Liveright's demand for a longer extent. On 19 July, Eliot told John Quinn that he would 'rush forward' with his work on them, but it wasn't until 31 August that anyone acknowledged having seen them.[55] Then, Gilbert Seldes told his colleagues at *The Dial* they were 'exceedingly interesting and add much to the poem', continuing, 'but don't become interested in them because we simply cannot have them'.[56]

Pound didn't agree about the value of the new notes, and encouraged readers to do as he did – namely, to read without them. 'The poem is there for the reader,' he wrote. 'The notes are for some other species of fauna.'[57] He was characteristically precise in his evaluation: the notes relied upon the poem, but not the poem upon the notes. They were not a sixth section to the poem but something more like a satellite, launched from it, but moving in a quasi-independent orbit. Eliot was probably keeping a card or two up his sleeve when he said with mischievous solemnity, in 1937, 'The notes to the *Waste Land* should be taken at their face value,' and yet his own patience with their value would run out in time.[58] He would call them a 'remarkable exposition of bogus scholarship' and would make a confession in 1956: 'I have sometimes thought of getting rid of these notes; but now they can never be unstuck.'[59] And they can't. For all Eliot's ambivalence, the notes are now forever fused with the poem.

It was Scofield Thayer's business partner, James Sibley Watson, who revived Pound's thought about the Dial Award. 'Eliot seems in a conciliatory mood,' he told Thayer on 12 August, having at last received a typescript of *The Waste Land* from Pound that month.[60] 'The poem is <better than> not so bad. Shall I try to persuade him to sell us the poem at our regular rate with the award in view?'[61] The pieces were falling into place. *The Dial* could protect their payment system by giving the award to Eliot, and in so doing allow all parties to maintain their dignity. *The Dial* would cover Liveright's advance of $150 in return for first publication of the poem, and there would be a considerable sweetener: Eliot would be given the Dial Award, the announcement of which might serve to generate publicity for Liveright's book, which was to follow the journal's first publication. Everybody would be a winner, or so it seemed. But only a few days passed before Eliot had a change of heart. The prize hadn't actually been offered, but merely floated: a float was not a certainty, he told Watson, and he couldn't possibly trouble John Quinn or Horace Liveright to alter the contract, not unless the award of the prize was to form the basis of the agreement, an entanglement that he anticipated the journal might find awkward. Eliot's action was either one of selfless respect to Quinn and Liveright, or it was calculated brinkmanship; he wrote to Watson: 'Let us hope that on a future occasion, if I survive to write another poem, no such difficulty will arise.'[62] But just so that no one was in any doubt where they stood, Eliot let John Quinn know that he had turned down 'an attractive proposal'[63] from *The Dial* that he had not wanted to trouble him or Liveright with ('particularly yourself'): he could not go into details, he said, but nonetheless shared with Quinn three paragraphs on the matter.

On 7 September, Quinn wrote to say that, despite Eliot's apparent protest, he, Liveright and Seldes had met in his New York office that morning, and drafted an agreement. This was everything Eliot had hoped for; so overwhelmed by Quinn's assistance[64] was he that he would gift him the typescripts and manuscripts of the poem and its accompanying pages that he and Pound and Vivien had worked upon so carefully together. But it was Gilbert Seldes at *The Dial* who had found a scheme to suit all parties. *The Dial* would publish first, 'about October 20th', in a text without the notes, and would give Eliot both the Dial Award and a standard fee; it would purchase the first 350 copies of Liveright's numbered print run to give away to subscribers of their journal.[65] Neither it nor Boni & Liveright would seek international rights, leaving Eliot free to publish in *The Criterion* and with the Hogarth Press in England. For Liveright, the deal was a stroke of genius: he had a firm sale for one-third of the first printing, allowing the book to wash its face commercially whatever happened; he would have to go second in the publishing queue that December or January, but when he did so he would have the added value of presenting the unpublished notes, advertised for him with a banner in *The Dial*, and the award to generate publicity.[66] For *The Dial*, conversely, this had become an expensive proposition: $150 paid to Eliot, a purchase order of perhaps $350 to Liveright, and then the small matter of the $2,000 award. But in return, they had confirmed their part in the publishing story of *The Waste Land*, and what price would history put upon that? They would be the first publisher of the poem anywhere in the world. Or almost anywhere: Eliot had retained rights in Great Britain and, in London, his journal, *The Criterion*, would, as it happened, pip *The Dial* to the post by just a few days. 'So everything is all right,' said Quinn, reflecting Eliot's own feeling.[67]

'Perhaps not even you can imagine with what emotions I saw *The Waste Land* go out into the world,' Vivien told Sydney Schiff the week that *The Criterion* was published, mid-October, 1922. 'It has become a part of me (or I of it) this last year. It was a terrible thing, somehow, when the time came at last for it to be published.'[68] A month later, with *The Dial* in print and the Boni & Liveright edition imminent, Eliot told Richard Aldington that the poem was a thing of the past, as far as he was concerned, and that he was now looking forward to a new form and style.[69] It was a remarkable resignation – or perhaps separation – from the poem in the moment of publication.

When an early notice praised the poem at the expense of Pound, Eliot felt overcome with despair. He was grateful for good notices, of course, but no praise was worth the humiliation of Pound. 'I am infinitely in his debt as a poet, as well as a personal friend,' he told Gilbert Seldes. 'I sincerely consider Ezra Pound the most important living poet in the English language.'[70] It isn't known how many of his personal copies from Boni & Liveright Eliot inscribed as gifts. But one – numbered 458 of 1,000 – carries a neat inscription in ink that would go on to have a permanent association with the poem:

> for E. P.
> miglior fabbro
> from T. S. E.
> Jan 1923[71]

Today, the page on which Eliot wrote those words bears a little foxing where mildew has ingressed into the upper and outer edge of the paper. It is said that in Italy, during the Second World War, knowing his capture from an invading German army might be imminent, and believing that his last possessions were to be stripped from him, Ezra Pound asked Dorothy to bury this copy in the earth where he stood, that no one – no army and no government – could ever take it from him.[72]

//

In the years that followed publication of *The Waste Land*, Eliot and Pound's worlds began to move apart. Eliot finally left the bank and joined Faber and Gwyer as editor of *The Criterion*, the journal it had acquired from Lady Rothermere. From there, he began to build one of the most respected literary lists in the English language; his and Pound's were the first books he brought to it. He adopted British citizenship, and joined the Church of England. As his standing grew, so did his fame: 'The Hollow Men', 'The Journey of the Magi' and 'Ash-Wednesday' followed *The Waste Land* and achieved for him a literary celebrity that would be his throughout the remainder of his life.

Pound's world began to unravel. He outgrew Paris and left for Italy with Dorothy, and with Olga Rudge, now his mistress, in tow; he fathered children with both women. His advocacy for Social Credit dragged him deeper and deeper into a hatred for usury. He became manic and unpredictable; his daughter, Maria, spoke of him 'visibly fighting a wasp nest in his brain'.[73] He began to date his letters by the fascist calendar, and would have an admiring audience with Benito Mussolini.

Vivien's health only deteriorated. In the spring of 1923, she and Eliot alike were convinced that she was on the point of death.[74] She was diagnosed with *Streptococcus fecalis*, and even contemplated suicide. 'Hell', Eliot told Pound at the time, it was hell.[75] The burden of unhappiness became more than Eliot could bear. His mother died in 1929, and he renewed a friendship with Emily Hale soon after. The lecture series he undertook three years later marked his first visit to the US since his humiliating pilgrimage to his family as a newly-wed in 1915. When he sailed from Southampton in the autumn of 1932 he parted from Vivien for ever: his absence would last nine months, and during his time in the US he would serve upon her a deed of separation. The life in England to which he returned would become ever more covert. As Vivien sought a reunion, he began to keep his whereabouts secret; but at public events he was vulnerable, and when in 1935 she cornered him at a book exhibition, he offered a formal handshake as if meeting her for the first time: 'How do you *do*,' he said, and signed the print editions she was carrying.[76] In the years that followed, Vivien would be found by the police wandering confused through the streets of Paddington in the small hours of the morning. Together with her brother Maurice, Eliot signed a reception order for her committal. She became a resident patient at Northumberland House psychiatric hospital in Finsbury Park in 1938, and died there eight years later.

'I was never quite a whole man,' Eliot told Emily Hale. 'The agony forced some genuine poetry out of me, certainly, which would never have been written if I had been happy: in that respect perhaps I may be said to have had the life I needed.'[77] Soon after his marriage to Vivien the harm of it was clear to him, but he came to see that it was a commitment he must 'expiate' for the rest of his life.[78] His feelings for Emily were not responsible for that, he assured her: even had she not existed, the marriage would have been the painful failure that it was.[79] He had felt 'unfitted' to the life of American academia, and found in Vivien someone who could not or would not emigrate, allowing him to cut all ties to home.[80] But their seventeen years together had been bitter.[81] In the time that followed Vivien's death, he had tried to steel himself to the thought that feeling was dead, that his heart was dead, that his life would be one of celibacy through to old age: 'I had done *The Waste Land*, and I thought my life was done.'[82] But Emily, 'friend, blood shaking my heart' had stirred in him 'the awful daring of a moment's surrender'. These lines from the poem were for her, he said, as he embarked on a romantic correspondence with her that he would sustain until his wife's death in 1947.

Eliot had longed for Vivien to die, he confessed, although he knew such a longing was sinful.[83] When the moment of her death came, he realised that he had lost not only Vivien but Emily too, for he discovered that he was not in fact in love with her at all, but with the apparitional life that he hadn't lived, or as he put it more callously in directions to his executors, with 'the love of a ghost for a ghost'.[84] He told Emily:

> That, in fact, was the real shock. That I am my past, and the whole of it, whether I like it or not; and that I meet myself face to face as a stranger whom I have got to live with, and make the best of, whether I like him or not; and while I still love you, and all those whom I love in various relations and degrees, as much as ever, it is this previously unknown man whom I, and they, will have to get to know.[85]

In 1930, Eliot made a startling confession. He told Emily that in the time before they renewed their friendship he had tried to have a love affair with a young and wealthy society woman, who was living apart from her husband, and who had made for herself a notorious reputation. Nancy Cunard had travelled to England in the early summer of 1922 from Fontainebleau, France; by the beginning of September she was back in Paris. But for June and July, she was staying at Eddington Mill, near Hungerford. In her scrapbook from that time, she placed a *carte du jour* from the Restaurant de la Tour Eiffel, on Percy Street, Soho: a printed menu with a Wyndham Lewis drawing on the front of what appears to be Ezra Pound and James Joyce dining with an unidentified woman.[86] There is no date beside it, though it comes between clippings dated 13 June (a *Times* review of Eliot) and holiday photographs from September.[87] It may have been a souvenir of an evening that Nancy would describe in a poem of 1965 on hearing on the radio of Eliot's death. In it, she said that they had coincided at a ball on a summer night of 1922, and had for *perhaps two hours on end and maybe more* been lost in conversation. When she proposed 'a tryst' for the following night, he accepted. They took a private room at

Restaurant Eiffel Tower, in what was known as the Wyndham Lewis Room, and had excused themselves from a dinner engagement with the Hutchinsons to be alone; they drank gin in the upstairs room, served by the restaurant's veteran Viennese waiter, Joe. The summer of 1922 would be one of the coldest on record,[88] and Cunard described them huddling together:

> So, by the little gas fire, on the floor, we lengthily sat.
> Our talk, it seemed to be going on so long,
> That Joe, the Tower's Austrian waiter, came up to see,
> Found us by that heat (cold evening) as close as could be:
> 'Want anything?' said Joe, smiling at me.
> 'More gin, Joe, please, make it doubles same as before.'[89]

Of dinner, Nancy said that she remembered little, only that the two of them were together. *And then?* she asked in her poem; the answer was discreet.

> Not every life-moment's recalled, though all of that night certainly
> is . . .

'It was over almost before it begun,' Eliot told Emily Hale, 'and it left a taste of ashes which I can never forget.'[90] It was the first occasion of adultery in his life, and it would be the last. 'I learned something, about the world and about myself,' he told Emily, 'and then I escaped finally from the influence of Bertie Russell.' Nancy returned to France that summer, and then to Venice. There, 'drunk a little', on vermouth *bianco*, surrounded by evening crowds and bells and *traghetti*, she said of Eliot, 'I loved him so, but . . .' her boozy letter trailed off; it was to Ezra Pound, who may have coded the encounter into *The Cantos* in a moment forever linked to the timeless wave-stone and to Eliot:[91]

> Nancy where art thou?
> Whither go all the vair and the cisclatons

and the wave pattern runs in the stone
on the high parapet (Excideuil)[92]

Pound may not have been the only one to know: Vivien, too, may have learned of it. In 1926, she would complain that Eliot had banished her to a care home and locked her out of London. 'Would this kind of thing happen to *Nancy?*' she asked bitterly. 'Why can't I even have the freedom & respect which is accorded to Nancy the *real* tart?'[93]

Never again would Eliot and Pound work together in the way they had on *The Waste Land*. Eliot would seek Pound's critical advice only once more and only briefly, asking of 'The Hollow Men' in 1925, 'Is it too bad to print?'[94] For the next four decades, their established roles would be reversed. Eliot would try to bring Pound within his sphere of influence, and keep him from his worst instincts. He would offer him a publishing home at Faber & Faber and a life-long editorial relationship – one that Pound would accept, but one throughout which he would squall and scratch at Eliot, like an animal unable to overcome ill-treatment.

'There did come a point, of course,' Eliot wrote, 'at which difference of outlook and belief became too wide.'[95] Pound's wartime broadcasts on Radio Rome formed the breaking point. He would say that Hitler was a martyr, comparable to Joan of Arc; he would later be hunted down and arrested by the Allies. Detained in a military camp in Pisa, he spent three weeks in a steel cage, six feet by six, exposed to blazing heat, which may have triggered his mental collapse – in words from *The Cantos*, 'when the raft broke and the waters went over me'.[96] It would take a presidential pardon to secure his release in 1958 from St Elizabeths Hospital for the criminally insane. Eliot was among those who campaigned to set him free.

Pound attempted a redemptive path back to Eliot, but he could barely lift his fingers to the typewriter. 'Now that I am wrecked, and have struggled three days to write a page to you,' he told Eliot. 'I am trying to repudiate 30 years of injustice to you' – saying, 'you doing real criticism and me playing a tin penny whistle.'[97] He turned once more to *The Waste Land*:

> From time's wreckage shored,
>   these fragments shored against ruin,[98]

Eliot was having none of it. 'What the hell is your offence and whom, if anybody, have you offended? If so be that there are any ruins I should like you to be as comfortable as possible.'[99] But Pound knew the ruins to be real, and his writing to be over, even if the spirit remained:

> A blown husk that is finished
>   but the light sings eternal
> a pale flare over marshes
>   where the salt hay whispers to the tide's change[100]

In 1922, Pound had vowed that he had 'the crust' to achieve a poem in 100 or 120 cantos; when he died half a century later, the poem he had written comprised 120 numbered and fragmented cantos.[101] And yet they were a 'botch', he said with a world-weary dismay: he knew too little about too many things.[102] Worse had been his folly in life. He sought what he called a 'verbal formula' to combat the 'rise of brutality' around him, he said – 'To be men not destroyers'.[103] This was to be the last word from *The Cantos*. He would find no such formula. Any good he had done had been spoiled by bad intentions, he said – 'And of man seeking good, / doing evil'.[104] 'But the worst mistake I made was that stupid, sub-urban prejudice of anti-Semitism' – 'idiocies', he called them.[105] If that was a turn – a sincere and repentant turn – then for many it came too little and too late.

'My old head just won't do any more work.'[106]

His final fragment from the sequence, written in August 1959, stops achingly:

> I cannot make it flow thru.
> A little light, like a rushlight
>   to lead back to splendour.[107]

There would be no more splendour, only silence. A pall descended upon him in which he stopped speaking; it lasted until the end of his life. 'I did not enter silence,' he remarked in a rare interview. 'Silence captured me.'[108] He was emptied now, gone somehow, a shell surrounded by people he could no longer hear. In notes made for a final, 117th canto, he wrote:

> That I lost my center
>   fighting the world.[109]

Eliot sent a cable that became mangled in transmission:

YOUR CRITICISM HAS ALWAYS BEEN IMMENSELY HELPFUL STOP YOUR OWN ACHIEVEMENT EPOCH MACHINGEN [MAKING] STOP[110]

He wrote by letter the same day. The cable's sentiment was all right as it goes, but its brevity simplified complex feelings, and Eliot had known well enough states of mind similar to Pound's.

To tell a man what he has achieved in the world, how big his own work is, all he has done for other people and for the world at large, civilisation, society etc etc. doesn't reach to the heart of the doubt, disgust, despair etc. from which the victim is suffereing [sic]. He knows all that and yet feels himself an utter failure. I got <have been> that way too.[111]

'I should have listened to the Possum,' Pound confided to his daughter towards the end of his life.[112]

In one moment, at least, he had. He had listened for the poem that Eliot heard within himself in 1921, and he tuned it to the poem he thought ought to be heard in public. The risk of ruin was high, but Pound had succeeded in steering the poem to the better version of itself, and Eliot never forgot it. In Paris, he had placed before Pound a sprawling chaotic poem, he said, that left Pound's hands reduced to half its size in the form which now survives today. It had, Eliot believed, been an intervention that stood as irrefutable evidence of his friend's critical genius.[113]

In the years ahead, *The Waste Land* would be called many things by many people. None would put it more clearly than Ezra Pound, who said all that should be said before the work is left with the reader's own judgement. And he said it in just four words.

'A damn good poem.'[114]

//

'a complete expression of this poet's vision of modern life . . . We know of no other modern poet who can more adequately and movingly reveal to us the inextricable tangle of the sordid and the beautiful that make up life.'

Times Literary Supplement (26 October 1922)[1]

'the finest poem of this generation'

New York Tribune (5 November 1922)[2]

'[*The Waste Land*] may be nonsense as a whole, but is certainly a sporting attempt to turn accident into substance.'

New York Evening Post (11 November 1922)[3]

'Mr Eliot's work is marked by an intense cerebral quality and a compact music that has practically established a movement among the younger men.'

New York Times Book Review (26 November 1922)[4]

'The poem is – in spite of its lack of structural unity – simply one triumph after another.'

Dial (December 1922)[5]

'remarkably disconnected, confused'

Nation (6 December 1922)[6]

'a pompous parade of erudition'

Freeman (17 January 1923)[7]

'Mr Eliot has failed to convince many readers that he has a soul'

New York Evening Post Literary Review (20 January 1923)[8]

'"The Waste Land" seems to me as near to Poetry as our generation is at present capable of reaching.'

Chapbook (February 1923)[9]

'one of the most moving and original poems of our time'

New Republic (7 February 1923)[10]

'the greatest poem so far written in contemporary literature'

Chicago Daily News (14 February 1923)[11]

'There is a new kind of literature abroad in the land, whose only obvious fault is that no one can understand it . . . It is rumoured that *The Waste Land* was written as a hoax.'

Time (23 March 1923)[12]

'A grunt would serve equally well'

London Mercury (October 1923)[13]

'The thing is a mad medley . . . so much waste paper.'

Manchester Guardian (31 October 1923)[14]

Acknowledgements.

I am deeply indebted to Clare Reihill, trustee of the Estate of T. S. Eliot, and to archivist Nancy Fulford and trustee Judith Hooper for their exceptional support and assistance throughout the preparation of this book. I am also grateful to Mary de Rachewiltz, trustee of the Ezra Pound Literary Property Trust, and to Declan Spring and Christopher Wait at New Directions for their enabling and generous access to materials.

My special gratitude to John Haffenden for his generous insight and advice, to Anthony Cuda, similarly, for his, and to the Eliot scholars from whom I have benefitted in working with at Fabers: Archie Burnett, Jim McCue, Christopher Ricks, Ronald Schuchard and Valerie Eliot herself. For their help with queries during my research I am grateful to Tim Dee, John Kelly, Bernard O'Donoghue and Hannah Sullivan.

I am grateful to the following institutions and individuals for their tireless assistance: British Library, London and Boston Spa (Trudy Southern); Cornell University, Division of Rare and Manuscript Collections, Ithaca, New York (Caitlin Holton, Natalie Kelsey); Emory University, Stuart A. Rose Manuscript, Archives, and Rare Book Library, Robert A. Woodruff Library, Atlanta, Georgia (Kathy Shoemaker); Faber & Faber, London (Robert Brown, Jane Kirby); Harvard University, Houghton Library, Cambridge, Massachusetts (James Capobianco, Mary Haegert, Sara Powell); Indiana University, Lilly Library, Bloomington (Joe McManis, Kristen S. Wilkins); McMaster University Library, Hamilton, Ontario (Bev Bayzat, Christopher Long, Rick Stapleton, Sheila Turcon, Bridget Whittle); New York Public Library, Henry W. and Albert A. Berg Collection of English and American Literature (Emma Davidson, Andrea Felder, Thomas Lisanti, Carolyn Vega); W. W. Norton, New York; Princeton University Library, Department of Special Collections, New Jersey (Emma Sarconi); University at Buffalo, the Poetry Collection, New York (Alison Fraser, James Maynard); University of California Berkeley, Bancroft Library (Dean Smith); University of California Santa Cruz, Special Collections and Archives, McHenry Library (Luisa Haddad); University of Chicago Library, Hanna Holborn Gray Special Collections

Research Center (Catherine Uecker); University of Oxford, Bodleian Special Collections, Weston Library (Angie Goodgame, Oliver House); University of Pennsylvania, Kislak Center for Special Collections, Rare Books and Manuscripts, Philadelphia (David McKnight); University of Texas, Harry Ransom Center, Austin (Steve Ennis, Elizabeth Garver, Rick Watson, Kristen Wilson); University of Toledo Libraries, Ward M. Canaday Center for Special Collections, Toledo, Ohio (Tamara Jones, Sara Mouch); University of Tulsa, Department of Special Collections and University Archives McFarlin Library, Tulsa, Oklahoma (Kelsey Hildebrand); University of Virginia, Albert and Shirley Small Special Collections Library, Charlottesville (Rebecca Bultman); Washington University in St Louis, Department of Special Collections, John M. Olin Library, Washington University Libraries, St Louis, Missouri (Joel Minor, Sonya Rooney); Yale University, Beinecke Rare Book and Manuscript Library, New Haven, Connecticut (Mary Ellen Budney, Nancy Kuhl, Sara Powell, Yasmin Ramadan).

I am also grateful to Dorking Museum and Heritage Centre, Surrey (Erica Chambers, Sue Tombs); Friends of Guildford Museum, Surrey (Matthew Alexander, Nicholas Bale); Surrey History Centre, Woking (Rose Anker); and Tanhurst Estate, Surrey (Colin Grimes). My thanks to Margate Museum (Ian Dickie), and to English Heritage (Rachel Morrison), and to Betty Miller, at Marble Hill Park, Armistice Day, 2021.

Merci aux Archives de la Ville de Lausanne (Jean-Jacques Eggler); Archives Hotelières Suisses (Rudolf Christa); Hôtel Élite Lausanne (Joel Iunius, Marcel Zufferey); Institut des Humanités en Médecine (Centre Hospitalier Universitaire Vaudois avec Université de Lausanne) (Magdalena Czartoryjska Meier); Musée Historique Lausanne (Mélina Ith, Sarah Liman Moeri).

My heartfelt thanks to Neil Belton for commissioning this work in 2012, and for his selfless editing and personal support beyond the page.

Alex Bowler at Faber & Faber was a discerning reader and the most supportive of publishers. Many colleagues at Fabers have given the book their time: Rachel Alexander, Mitzi Angel, Lizzie Bishop, Alex Bradshaw, Aisling Brennan, Louise Brice, Kate Burton, Mary Cannam, Rali Chorbadzhiyska, Jane Feaver, Katie Hall, Paul Keegan, Jamie Keenan, Krys Kujawinska, Julian Loose, Hannah Marshall, Belinda Matthews, Stephen Page, Lavinia Singer, Hannah Styles and Becky Taylor, as well as Sara Talbot and each of the beloved reps in Sam Brown's team. Anne Owen steered the text with expert hand and Kate Ward gave it elegance in design.

Robert Davies was sensitive in his copy edit, as was Sam Matthews in her typesetting and textual management. Anne Riley proofread and Paula Clarke

Bain originated the Index; Beth Dufour managed permissions in the text and Amanda Russell in the images.

Jill Bialosky at W. W. Norton provided impeccable advice and unswerving commitment, and my thanks are also due to her colleagues Steve Colca, Yang Kim, Elizabeth Riley, Gina Savoy and Drew Weitman.

I am grateful to Sarah Chalfant at the Wylie Agency, who created a space in which to research and write, and to Jessica Bullock, Ruby Hamilton, Luke Ingram, Rebecca Nagel and Alba Ziegler-Bailey.

To Rosie Alison and Susanna White at Oxford Films.

To Juliet Nicolson and Eleanor House.

Hurry up please, John Clegg, its time.

My loving thanks to Claire, James, Rose, Simon and Beowulf.

Notes on Sources.

Return to the sources, Eliot instructed. I have attempted to follow that directive in my original research for this book, while acknowledging that I do so in the debt of a great many researchers who have come before me, many of whom have given a lifetime's dedication to their study, and on whose shoulders my own work undoubtedly stands. Although I quote only from primary sources in this book, I have attempted to acknowledge those works that have directly or indirectly informed my thinking in the pages that follow, and hope that any accidental omissions or oversights do not cause unintended offence.

ARCHIVES

Draft works of manuscript and typescript are drawn from the archives listed below, although one source in particular requires special mention: the pages of *The Waste Land*, kindly rephotographed in colour for me by the Berg Collection of the New York Public Library, and first published in Valerie Eliot's edition of 1971, *The Waste Land: A Facsimile and Transcript of the Original Drafts Including the Annotations of Ezra Pound*, reissued in colour for the poem's centenary in 2022. Also of critical importance to my work have been the notebook and loose leaves of Eliot's early poems, again in the Berg Collection, published in an annotated edition by Christopher Ricks as *Inventions of the March Hare* (1996). Manuscript fair copies of *The Waste Land* held by the Eliot Estate and the Harry Ransom Center have proved an invaluable resource, as have the latter archive's copy of the Boni & Liveright edition of *The Waste Land*, gifted by Eliot to Pound, as well as Pound's draft typescripts and proofs held there for his 'Hugh Selwyn Mauberley'.

POETRY AND PROSE

Texts of the published poetry and prose are taken from those journals contemporary to the authors in which they first appeared. Where relevant, I have included in the citation the first reprinting of the work in a collected edition. These sources are given in full below and in shortened form in the notes.

Readers seeking current editions of the poetry might begin with Eliot's *The Waste Land and Other Poems* (first published in 1940), *Selected Poems* (1948) or *Collected Poems 1909–1962* (1963); Eliot's prose is available as *Selected Essays* (1932).

Readers of Pound's early verse should seek out *Personae: Collected Shorter Poems* (1926), while *Selected Poems 1908–1969* (1975/7) covers the arc of his career, as does his mighty *The Cantos* (Fourth Edition, 1987); his prose is available as *Literary Essays* (1954).

Annotated and compendium editions of the works of both writers offer an invaluable resource for readers and scholarship. Eliot readers are blessed with *The Poems of T. S. Eliot* (ed. Christopher Ricks and Jim McCue, 2 vols, 2015) and *The Complete Prose of T. S. Eliot: The Critical Edition* (ed. Ron Schuchard et al., 8 vols, 2014–19); *The Collected Prose of T. S. Eliot* (ed. Archie Burnett) will be issued by Faber & Faber in 2023.

Pound's writings are gathered as *Ezra Pound's Poetry and Prose: Contributions to Periodicals* (ed. Lea Baechler, Walton A. Litz and James Logenbach, 11 vols, 1991), accessible digitally via the Ezra Pound Society, which also hosts the Cantos Project online.

Donald Gallup provides an irreplaceable publication record of both writers.

LETTERS

Many of the letters consulted for this study are to be found in the archives cited, but a great number were drawn from published editions, and it is to the work of these editors that my own work must pay its greatest debt.

Eliot's letters written before 1941 are mostly drawn from the volumes of edited correspondence begun with Valerie Eliot and Hugh Haughton's edition of 1988 and scrupulously advanced since 2009 by general editor John Haffenden. Letters later than 1941, as well as some before, including those to Emily Hale, were consulted from archive sources given below.

Pound's letters are similarly taken from published and archive sources also given below.

BIOGRAPHY

Although I have not drawn upon existing biographical studies in my research, I would like to acknowledge the enormous contribution to both scholarship and readership made by many biographers before me. For more on Eliot's life I would encourage readers to consult works by Peter Ackroyd, Robert Crawford and Lyndall Gordon, and for Pound, those by Humphrey Carpenter, David Moody and Charles Norman; Peter Ackroyd and David Moody have written on both poets. Ann Pasternak Slater has enriched our knowledge of Vivien Eliot.

DATING THE DRAFTS

Eliot didn't date his draft pages of *The Waste Land*, and so following the publication of Valerie Eliot's facsimile of 1971 there began guided attempts by scholars to do precisely that.

Evidencing the dates commenced with the realisation that the poem had been prepared on more than one typewriter. Grover Smith (1972) and Hugh Kenner (1973) correctly identified the presence of three machines involved in the production of the typescripts, assigning certain sections of the poem to certain machines, as did Lyndall Gordon (1974), who was the first to compare the watermarked paper stocks against the machines used. Each scholar arrived independently at the conclusion that the earliest passage of the poem to be composed was its third part, 'The Fire Sermon'. Later examinations corrected those hypotheses: Peter Barry (1979) thought that 'The Fire Sermon' was the second piece composed, after the Boston night out in 'The Burial of the Dead' but before 'April is the cruellest month'; David A. Moody (1979) postulated a chronology much closer to the order of the finished poem, while S. Krishnamoorthy Aithal (1980) and Ronald Bush (1983) contributed alternative readings of their own. There matters rested until a comprehensive investigation by Lawrence Rainey (2005) deepened our understanding of events. Rainey compared the paper of Eliot's undated drafts with the various stocks of his letters, most of which were dated. On the supposition that Eliot worked systematically through reams of paper (exhausting one entirely before beginning other), he was able to surmise a timeline that brought the undated draft poems into the frame of dated letters of matching stock. He offered a revised and convincing account of the three typewriters: that the first machine was brought to England by Eliot from Harvard in 1914; that the second was the machine gifted by his brother Henry, left behind after the family's visit in 1921; and that the third was probably not Eliot's machine at all, but Ezra Pound's, from Paris in 1922. With that proposition in place, Rainey was able to demonstrate with reasonable certainty that each machine related to specific periods of use, and that the five parts of the poem were composed in the order in which they appeared in the first publication of the poem in 1922. While I have sometimes drawn differing conclusions in my research as to the exact order of composition of the poem (not least that Eliot didn't always draw down on his paper stocks systematically), it is nonetheless the case that Lawrence Rainey's invaluable work – as well as that of his predecessors – has provided a foundation for my book.

I — ARCHIVE SOURCES

Beinecke   Beinecke Rare Book and Manuscript Library, Yale University, New Haven, CT:
DCGP: Donald Clifford Gallup Papers, YCAL MSS 838
DSTP: Dial/Scofield Thayer Papers, YCAL MSS 34
EPP: Ezra Pound Papers, YCAL MSS 43
ORP: Olga Rudge Papers, YCAL MSS 54
WBEPP: William Bird Ezra Pound Papers, YCAL MSS 178

Berg   Henry W. and Albert A. Berg Collection of English and American Literature, New York Public Library:
BDP: Babette Deutsch Papers, MssCol 778
JQP: John Quinn Papers, MssCol 2513
TSECP: T. S. Eliot Collection of Papers:
[Notebook]: 'Complete poems of T. S. Eliot'. Holograph with the author's MS corrections. Final 2 pp are holograph copies of poems by Tristan Corbiere. Bound, n.d.
[Poems]: '[Poems]'. Holograph, typescript, and typescript (carbon), incomplete, with the author's MS corrections, n.d. (34 pp, 28 pp)
[Waste Land]: 'Waste land, The'. Typescript with the author's MS corrections. 18 pp include author's drafts and revisions, n.d.

Berkeley   Bancroft Library, University of California, Berkeley

BL   British Library, London:
SP: Schiff Papers, Add. MS 52919
TH: Edward (Ted) James Hughes Papers: 'Introduction to a Reading of *The Waste Land*, Palace Theatre, Sept 25 88', Speeches, Eulogies and biographical pieces, Add. MS 88918/6/11, fos. 44–8

Bodleian   Bodleian Special Collections, Weston Library, University of Oxford:
AVHE/D1–4: Archive of Vivienne Haigh Eliot/Diaries, 4 vols: 1. 1914, MS.Eng.Misc.e.876; 2. 1919, MS.Eng.Misc.f.532; 3. 1934, MS.Eng.Misc.e.877; 4. 1935, MS.Eng.Misc.e.878
MT: Mary Trevelyan, 'The Pope of Russell Square', unpublished TS, Dep. c. 969
PTEL: Papers of T. E. Lawrence and A. W. Lawrence, MS. Eng. d. 3341
WTSE: Works of T. S. Eliot, 'Manuscript and typescript drafts of "The rock", with related correspondence, 1933–1934' MS. Don. d. 44

Buffalo   Poetry Collection, University at Buffalo, NY

Cambridge   EPHB: Eliot, Papers of the Hayward Bequest of T. S. Eliot Material, GBR/0272/HB/B/16, Archive Centre, King's College, University of Cambridge

Chicago   HMP: Harriet Monroe Papers, Hanna Holborn Gray Special Collections Research Center, University of Chicago Library

Cornell   Division of Rare and Manuscript Collections, Cornell University, Ithaca, NY

Dorking   Dorking Museum, Surrey

Eliot Estate	Estate of T. S. Eliot, London:
	EVE: Valerie Eliot, 'The Waste Land: Broadcast Script', 2 Nov.
	1971, BBC Radio 3 (7 Nov. 1971)
	HWE: Henry Ware Eliot, 'Excerpts from Manuscripts of various
	lectures given by T. S. Eliot in America, 1932–1933, which T. S. E.
	allowed me to read while we were at Randolph, N. H. in June, 1933'
	VOB1–2: 'Valerie's Own Book of Poems by T. S. Eliot', manuscript
	notebook, 2 vols
Emory	Stuart A. Rose Manuscript, Archives, and Rare Book Library,
	Robert A. Woodruff Library, Emory University, Atlanta, GA
Faber	Faber & Faber, London
Hamilton	SpArc Special Collections and Archives, Hamilton College,
	Clinton, NY
Houghton	Houghton Library, Harvard University, Cambridge, MA:
	JRF: Jeanne Robert Foster letters from Ezra Pound and other
	papers, MS Am. 1635
	TSEAP: T. S. Eliot Additional Papers, MS Am. 1691.14
	TSEMP: T. S. Eliot Miscellaneous Papers, MS Am. 1691.3
	TSEP: T. S. Eliot Papers, MS Am. 1691
Kislak	Kislak Center for Special Collections, Rare Books and Manuscripts,
	University of Pennsylvania:
	CGC: Carl Gatter Collection on Ezra Pound, Ms. Coll. 182
	EPRC: Ezra Pound Research Collection, Ms. Coll. 183
Lausanne MH	Musée Historique Lausanne, Vaud
Lausanne Vd	Ville de Lausanne, Vaud
Lilly	Lilly Library, Indiana University, Bloomington
McHenry	Special Collections and Archives, McHenry Library University of
	California, Santa Cruz
McMaster	McMaster University Library, Hamilton, Ontario:
	BRA: Bertrand Russell Archives
	LCM: Lady Constance Malleson fonds
Margate	Margate Museum, Kent
NA	National Archives, Kew, Surrey
Norton	W. W. Norton, New York
Princeton	Manuscripts Division, Department of Special Collections, Princeton
	University Library, Princeton, NJ:
	EHL: Emily Hale Letters from T. S. Eliot, C0686
	TSEC: T. S. Eliot Collection, C0896
RAA	Royal Academy of Arts, London
Texas	Harry Ransom Center, University of Texas:
	EPC: Ezra Pound Collection, MS-03308
	EPL: Ezra Pound Library, LI-10962, PS 3509 L43 W3 1922 PND
	FSFC: F. S. Flint Collection, MS-1423
	JRP: John Rodker Papers
	MHP: Mary Hutchinson Papers

Texas (*cont.*)	NCC: Nancy Cunard Collection:
	NCC/D1–3: Diaries 1919, 3 vols: 1. Apr.–June 1919, b. 22, f. 8; 2.
	June–Aug. 1919, b. 23, f. 1; 3, Aug.–Dec. 1919, b. 23, f. 2;
	NCC/S1–3: Scrapbooks 1913–29, 3 vols: 1. 1913–21, b. 26, f. 1; 2.
	1919–29, b. 26, f. 2; 3. 1921–7, b. 26, f. 3
	OMC: Ottoline Morrell Collection
	OSC: Osbert Sitwell Collection
	TSEC: T. S. Eliot Collection, 'The Waste Land', handwritten copy,
	signed, made for an auction benefitting the London Library, 1960,
	T. S. Eliot Collection, Series I, b. 3, f. 15
Toledo	EPP: Ward M. Ezra Pound Papers, *The Cantos* (MSS-057), b. 1, f. 1,
	Center for Special Collections, University of Toledo Libraries, OH
Tulsa	JHEC: John Hamilton Edwards Collection of Ezra Pound,
	'Criticism of Hugh Selwyn Mauberley', author typescript, 1951,
	Department of Special Collections and University Archives
	McFarlin Library, University of Tulsa, OK
Virginia	DSC: David Schwab Collection of T. S. Eliot Manuscripts 1918–
	1933, MSS 7556, Special Collections, Albert and Shirley Small
	Special Collections Library, University of Virginia, Charlottesville
Washington	WGEPP: William Greenleaf Eliot Personal Papers, 1829–1937
	(WUA00068), Series 6, b. 1, f. 5, Department of Special Collections,
	John M. Olin Library, Washington University Libraries,
	Washington University in St Louis, MO

Books by T. S. Eliot

ALAL	*American Literature and the American Language*, St Louis, MO: Washington University, 1953
Animula	*Animula*, The Ariel Poems, No. 23, London: Faber & Faber, 1929
ASG	*After Strange Gods*, London: Faber & Faber, 1934
AVP	*Ara Vos Prec*, London: Ovid Press, 1920
CC	*To Criticise the Critic*, London: Faber & Faber, 1965
CP1936	*Collected Poems 1909–1935*, London: Faber & Faber, 1936
Dante	*Dante*, London: Faber & Faber, 1929
DS	*The Dry Salvages*, London: Faber & Faber, 1941
EE	*Elizabethan Essays*, London: Faber & Faber, 1934
EED	*Essays on Elizabethan Drama*, New York: Harcourt, Brace & Co., 1932
EPMP	*Ezra Pound: His Metric and Poetry*, New York: Knopf, 1917 [1918]
FLA	*For Lancelot Andrewes: Essays on Style and Order*, London: Faber & Gwyer, 1928
FPV	*From Poe to Valéry*, New York: Harcourt Brace, 1948
FR	*The Family Reunion*, London: Faber & Faber, 1939
FU	*The Family Reunion*, London: Faber & Faber/New York: Harcourt, Brace & Co., 1939
HJD	*Homage to John Dryden: Three Essays on Poetry of the Seventeenth Century*, London: Hogarth Press, 1924
ICS	*The Idea of a Christian Society*, London: Faber & Faber, 1939
KEPB	*Knowledge and Experience in the Philosophy of F. H. Bradley*, London: Faber & Faber, 1964/New York: Farrar, Straus & Company, 1964
LG	*Little Gidding*, London: Faber & Faber, 1942
Marina	*Marina*, London: Faber & Faber, 1930
MP	*The Music of Poetry*, Glasgow: Jackson, Son & Co., 1942
OPP	*On Poetry and Poets*, London: Faber & Faber, 1957
P1919	*Poems*, London: Hogarth Press, 1919
P1920	*Poems*, New York: Knopf, 1920
P1925	*Poems 1909–1925*, London: Faber & Gwyer, 1925
POO	*Prufrock and Other Observations*, London: Egoist, 1917
Rock	*The Rock: A Pageant Play*, London: Faber & Faber, 1934
SA	*Sweeney Agonistes: Fragments of an Aristophanic Melodrama*, London: Faber & Faber, 1932
SE	*Selected Essays: 1917–1932*, London: Faber & Faber, 1932; 3rd English edition, London and Boston: Faber & Faber, 1951
SS	*A Song for Simeon*, London: Faber & Faber, 1928
SW	*The Sacred Wood: Essays on Poetry and Criticism*, London: Methuen & Co., 1920
TWL1922	*The Waste Land*, New York: Boni & Liveright, 1922
TWL1923	*The Waste Land*, London: Hogarth, 1923

TWLF   *The Waste Land: A Facsimile and Transcript of the Original Drafts* (ed. Val-
        erie Eliot), London: Faber & Faber/New York: Harcourt, Brace,
        Jovanovich, 1971 (see *Annotated editions*, below)
UPUC   *The Use of Poetry and the Use of Criticism: Studies in the Relation of Criticism
        to Poetry in England*, London: Faber & Faber, 1933
WM   *Words for Music*, Bryn Mawr, PA: [Bryn Mawr], 1934

Articles by T. S. Eliot

Eliot, T. S., 'Address' (at the Centennial Celebration of the Mary Institute),
    From Mary to You: Centennial, 1859–1959, St Louis, MO: Mary Institute,
    1959, 133–6
——, 'American Literature', *Athenaeum*, 4643 (25 Apr. 1919), 236–7
——, 'Andrew Marvell', *Times Literary Supplement*, 1002 (31 Mar. 1921),
    201–2
——, 'Ben Jonson', *Times Literary Supplement*, 930 (13 Nov. 1919), 637–8
——, 'A Commentary', *Criterion*, XIII. 52 (Apr. 1934), 451–4
——, 'A Commentary', *Criterion*, XIV. 57 (July 1935), 610–13
——, 'Contemporanea. A review, in part, of *Tarr*, by P. Lewis, Wyndham,
    and *The People's Palace*, by Sacheverell Sitwell', *Egoist*, 5 (June–July 1918),
    84
——, 'Criticism in England', *Athenaeum*, 4650 (13 June 1919), 456–7
——, 'Dante as a "Spiritual Leader"', *Athenaeum*, 4692 (2 Apr. 1920), 441–2
——, 'Dramatis Personae', *Criterion*, I. 3 (Apr. 1923), 303–6
——, '"The Duchess of Malfi" at the Lyric: and Poetic Drama', *Art & Letters*,
    III. 1 (Winter 1920), 36–9
——, 'The Education of Taste', *Athenaeum*, 4652 (27 June 1919), 61
——, 'Eeldrop and Appleplex – I', *Little Review*, IV. 1 (May 1917), 7–11
——, 'Ezra Pound', *Poetry* (Chicago), LXVIII. 6 (Sept. 1946), 326–38
——, 'A Foreign Mind', *Athenaeum*, 4653 (4 July 1919), 552–3
——, 'A French Romantic', *Times Literary Supplement*, 980 (28 Oct. 1920),
    703
——, 'G. K. Chesterton', *Tablet*, 167 (20 June 1936), 785
——, 'Hamlet and His Problems', *Athenaeum*, 4665 (26 Sept. 1919), 940–1
——, 'In Memory of Henry James', *Egoist*, 5 (Jan. 1918), 1–2
——, 'The Influence of Landscape upon the Poet', *Dædalus*, 89 (Spring
    1960), 420–2
——, 'Introduction', in *The Adventures of Huckleberry Finn* (Mark Twain),
    London: Cresset Press/New York: Chanticleer, 1950, vii–xvi
——, 'Introduction', in *Charles Baudelaire: Intimate Journals* (tr. Christopher
    Isherwood), London: Blackamore Press, 1930, 7–26

——, 'Introduction', in *Pascal's Pensées* (tr. W. F. Trotter), London: Dent/New York: Dutton, 1931, vii–xix

——, 'Introduction', in *Seneca his Tenne Tragedies Translated into English, Edited by Thomas Newton Anno 1581*, vol. 1, London: Constable/New York: Knopf, 1927

——, 'John Maynard Keynes', *New English Weekly*, 29 (16 May 1946), 47–8

——, 'Kipling Redivivus', *Athenaeum*, 4645 (9 May 1919), 297–8

——, 'Leadership and Letters', *Milton Bulletin*, XII. 1 (Feb. 1949), 3–16

——, 'The Lesson of Baudelaire', *Tyro*, 1 ([Spring 1921]), [4]

——, 'Literature and the Modern World', *The Teaching Church Review: A Journal for Students of Religion*, 5 (Feb. 1935), 11–15; rep. *American Prefaces*, Iowa City, IA: I. 2 (Nov. 1935), 19–22

——, 'London Letter: March, 1921', *Dial*, LXX. 4 (Apr. 1921), 448–53

——, 'London Letter: May, 1921', *Dial*, LXX. 6 (June 1921), 686–91

——, 'London Letter: July, 1921', *Dial*, LXXI. 2 (Aug. 1921), 213–17

——, 'London Letter: September, 1921', *Dial*, LXXI. 4 (Oct. 1921), 452–5

——, 'The Metaphysical Poets', *Times Literary Supplement*, 1031 (20 Oct. 1921), 669–70

——, 'The Method of Mr Pound', *Athenaeum*, 4669 (24 Oct. 1919), 1065–6

——, 'Mr Pound and his Poetry', *Athenaeum*, XCIII, 4671 (7 Nov. 1919), 1163

——, 'Mr T. S. Eliot's Quandaries', *New English Weekly*, IV (12 Apr. 1934), 662–3

——, 'Modern Tendencies in Poetry', *Shama'a*, 1 (Apr. 1920), 9–18

——, 'The New Elizabethans and the Old', *Athenaeum*, 4640 (4 Apr. 1919), 134–6

——, 'A Note on Ezra Pound', *To-Day*, 4 (Sept. 1918), 3–9

——, 'Observations', *Egoist*, 5 (May 1918), 69–70

——, 'On a Recent Piece of Criticism', *Purpose*, X. 2 (Apr./June 1938), 90–4

——, 'The Perfect Critic [I]', *Athenaeum*, 4706 (9 July 1920), 40–1

——, 'The Perfect Critic, II', *Athenaeum*, 4708 (23 July 1920), 102–4

——, 'Philip Massinger', *Times Literary Supplement*, 958 (27 May 1920), 325–6

——, 'The Poetic Drama', *Athenaeum*, 4698 (14 May 1920), 635–6

——, 'The Poetry of W. B. Yeats', *Purpose*, 12 (July/Dec. 1940), 115–27

——, 'The Possibility of a Poetic Drama', *Dial*, LXIX. 5 (Nov. 1920), 441–7

——, 'The Post Georgians', *Athenaeum*, 4641 (11 Apr. 1919), 171–2

——, 'The Preacher as Artist', *Athenaeum*, 4674 (28 Nov. 1919), 1252–3

Eliot, T. S., 'Prose and Verse', *The Chapbook*, 22 (Apr. 1921), 3–10

——, [unsigned], 'Publisher's Preface', in James B. Connolly, *Fisherman of the Banks*, London: Faber & Gwyer, 1928, vii–viii

——, 'Reflections on Contemporary Poetry [IV]', *Egoist*, 6 (July 1919), 39–40

——, ['Richard Aldington'], Alister Kershaw and Frédéric-Jacques Temple (eds), *Richard Aldington: An Intimate Portrait*, Carbondale and Edwardsville: Southern Illinois University Press, 1965, 24–5

——, 'The Romantic Englishman, the Comic Spirit, and the Function of Criticism', *Tyro*, 1 ([Spring 1921]), [4]

——, 'A Romantic Patrician', *Athenaeum*, 4644 (2 May 1919), 265–7

——, 'A Sceptical Patrician', *Athenaeum*, 4647 (23 May 1919), 361–2

——, 'Syllabus for a Tutorial Class in Modern English Literature', London: University of London Press, 1918

——, 'Tarr', *Egoist*, 5 (Sept. 1918), 105–6

——, 'The Three Voices of Poetry', Annual Lecture of the National Book League, Cambridge: Cambridge University Press, 1953

——, 'Thomas Stearns Eliot', *Harvard College Class of 1910, Secretary's Fourth Report*, Cambridge, MA: Crimson Printing Co., 1921, 107–8

——, 'Thomas Stearns Eliot', *Harvard College Class of 1910, Twenty-Fifth Anniversary Report*, Cambridge, MA: Crimson Printing Co., 1935, 219–21

——, 'To the Editor of the *Transatlantic Review*', *Transatlantic Review*, 1 (Jan. 1924), 95–6

——, 'Tradition and the Individual Talent [I]', *Egoist*, VI. 4 (Sept. 1919), 54–5

——, 'Tradition and the Individual Talent – II', *Egoist*, VI. 5 ([Nov./] Dec. 1919), 72–3

——, '*Ulysses*, Order, and Myth', *Dial*, LXXV. 5 (Nov. 1923), 480–3

——, 'The Use of Poetry', *New English Weekly*, V (14 June 1934), 215

——, 'Verse Pleasant and Unpleasant', *Egoist*, 5 (Mar. 1918), 43–4

——, 'War-paint and Feathers', *Athenaeum*, 4668 (17 Oct. 1919), 1036

——, 'Whether Rostand Had Something about Him', *Athenaeum*, 4656 (25 July 1919), 665–6

——, 'Why Mr Russell Is a Christian', *Criterion*, VI. 2 (Aug. 1927), 177–9

Annotated editions

Collected Prose   *The Collected Prose of T. S. Eliot* (ed. Archie Burnett), London: Faber & Faber, 2023

Complete Prose 1–8 *The Complete Prose of T. S. Eliot: The Critical Edition* (general
ed. Ronald Schuchard), 8 vols, Baltimore, MD: Johns Hopkins
University Press/London: Faber & Faber, 2014–19

IMH *Inventions of the March Hare: Poems 1909–1917* (ed. Christopher
Ricks), London: Faber & Faber, 1996

PTSE 1–2 *The Poems of T. S. Eliot* (ed. Christopher Ricks and Jim McCue),
2 vols, London: Faber & Faber, 2015

TWLF *The Waste Land: A Facsimile and Transcript of the Original Drafts*
(ed. Valerie Eliot), London: Faber & Faber/New York: Harcourt,
Brace, Jovanovich, 1971 (as *TWLF 1971* where pagination is
to be distinguished from *TWLF 2022*, centenary edition in full
colour, London: Faber & Faber/New York: W. W. Norton, 2022)

Books by Ezra Pound

ABC *ABC of Reading*, London: George Routledge, 1934; new edition, London:
Faber & Faber, 1951, 1960

Cantos *Cantos*, fourth collected edition, London: Faber & Faber, 1987 (thir-
teenth printing, including Pound's English translation of 'Canto LXXII',
repaginated after p. 441, New York: New Directions, 1995 [1996])

Canzoni *Canzoni*, London: Elkin Mathews, 1911

Cathay *Cathay: Translations for the Most Part from the Chinese of Rihaku, from
the Notes of the Late Ernest Fenollosa, and the Decipherings of the Professors
Mori and Ariga*, London: Elkin Mathews, 1915

CNPJ *Certain Noble Plays of Japan*, Churchtown, Dundrum: 1916

DFC *Drafts and Fragments of Cantos CX to CXVII*, New York: New Directions,
1969/London: Faber & Faber, 1970

DRL *Diptych Rome–London*, New York: New Directions, 1958

DTC *A Draft of XXX Cantos*, Paris: Hours, 1930; revised edition, London:
Faber & Faber, 1933

Exultations *Exultations*, London: Elkin Mathews, 1909

FC *The Fourth Canto*, London: Ovid, 1919

FTS *Five Troubadour Songs: With the Original Provençal Words and English
Words Adapted from Chaucer, Arranged by Agnes Bedford*, London: Boosey
& Co., 1920

GB *Gaudier-Brzeska: A Memoir*, London: John Lane, Bodley Head, 1916

GK *Guide to Kulchur*, London: Faber & Faber/New York: New Directions,
1938

HSM *Hugh Selwyn Mauberley*, London: Ovid, 1920

Instigations *Instigations*, New York: Boni & Liveright, 1920

L 1916 *Lustra*, London: Elkin Mathews, 1916

L 1917 *Lustra, with Earlier Poems*, New York: Alfred Knopf, 1917

LE *Literary Essays* (ed. T. S. Eliot), London: Faber & Faber, 1954

NA *'Noh' or Accomplishment: A Study of the Classical Stage of Japan by Ernest
Fenollosa and Ezra Pound*, London: Macmillan & Co., 1916 [1917]

P*1909*   *Personae*, London: Elkin Mathews, 1909
P*1921*   *Poems 1918–1921*, New York: Boni & Liveright, 1921
P*1926*   *Personae*, New York: Boni & Liveright, 1926
PC*1948*   *The Pisan Cantos*, New York: New Directions, 1948/London: Faber & Faber, 1949
PC*2015*   *Posthumous Cantos* (ed. Massimo Bacigalupo), Manchester: Carcanet, 2015
PD*1918*   *Pavannes and Divisions*, New York: Knopf, 1918
PD*1958*   *Pavannes and Divagations*, New York: New Directions, 1958
QPA   *Quia Pauper Amavi*, London: The Egoist, 1919
Ripostes *Ripostes*, London: Stephen Swift & Co., 1912
SC   *Social Credit: An Impact*, London: Stanley Nott, 1935
SP*1928*   *Selected Poems* (ed. T. S. Eliot), London: Faber & Gwyer, 1928
SP*1949*   *Selected Poems* (ed. T. S. Eliot), London: Faber & Faber, 1949
SP*1975*   *Selected Poems 1908–1959*, London: Faber & Faber, 1975; revised edition, London: Faber & Faber, 1977
SR   *The Spirit of Romance*, London: Dent, 1910
Umbra   *Umbra: Early Poems*, London: Elkin Mathews, 1920
VC   *A Visiting Card*, London: Peter Russell, 1952 (trans. John Drummond from *Cara da Vista*, Rome: Edizioni di Lettere d'Oggi, 1942)
WMF   *What is Money For?* London: Great Britain Publications, 1939; rep. London: Peter Russell, 1952
WTSF   *A Walking Tour in Southern France: Ezra Pound among the Troubadours* (ed. Richard Sieburth), New York: New Directions, 1992

Articles by Ezra Pound

Pound, Ezra, 'Arnaut Daniel (Razo)', *Art & Letters*, III. 2 (Spring 1920), 44–9
——, 'Books Current – Joyce', *Future*, II. 6 (May 1918), 161–3
——, 'Briefer Mention', *Dial*, LXX. 1. (Jan. 1921), 110
——, 'C. H. Douglas, Etc.', *Little Magazine*, I. 2 (Feb./Mar. 1934), 16
——, 'A Communication', *1924: A Magazine of the Arts*, 3 (Sept./Nov. 1924), 97–8
——, 'Credit and the Fine Arts . . . A Practical Application', *New Age*, XXX. 22 (30 Mar. 1922), 284–5
——, 'The Crusades: A Reply to Mr Chesterton', *Daily Telegraph* (17 Sept. 1920), 12
——, 'De Gourmont: A Distinction (Followed by Notes)', *Little Review*, V. 10–11 (Feb./Mar. 1919), 1–19
——, 'The Death of Vorticism', *Little Review*, 10/11 (Feb./Mar. 1919), 45, 48
——, 'Dramedy', *Athenaeum*, 4688 (5 Mar. 1920), 315
——, 'Drunken Helots and Mr Eliot', *Egoist*, IV (June 1917), 72–4

——, 'For T. S. E.', *Sewanee Review*, LXXIV. 1 (Winter [1965/]1966), 109

——, 'Harold Monro', *Criterion*, XI. XLV (July 1932), 581–92

——, 'Historical Survey', *Little Review* ('Brancusi Number'), VIII. 1 (Autumn 1921), 39–42

——, 'How I Began', *T. P.'s Weekly*, XXI. 552 (6 June 1913), 707

——, 'Imaginary Letters – IV (Walter Villerant to Mrs Bland Burn)', *Little Review*, IV. 5 (Sept. 1917), 21

——, 'In Explication', *Little Review*, V. 4 (Aug. 1918), 5–9

——, 'Indiscretions; or, Une Revue de Deux Mondes – I', *New Age*, 1446, XXVII. 4 (27 May 1920), 56–7

——, 'Indiscretions; or, Une Revue de Deux Mondes – II', *New Age*, 1447, XXVII. 5 (3 June 1920), 76–7

——, 'Indiscretions; or, Une Revue de Deux Mondes – III', *New Age*, 1448, XXVII. 6 (10 June 1920), 91–2

——, 'Indiscretions; or, Une Revue de Deux Mondes – VII', *New Age*, 1452, XXVII. 10 (8 July 1920), 156–7

——, 'Indiscretions; or, Une Revue de Deux Mondes – IX', *New Age*, 1454, XXVII. 12 (22 July 1920), 187–8

——, 'Indiscretions; or, Une Revue de Deux Mondes – X', *New Age*, 1455, XXVII. 13 (29 July 1920), 204

——, 'Indiscretions; or, Une Revue de Deux Mondes – XII', *New Age*, 1457, XXVII. 15 (12 Aug. 1920), 236–7

——, 'The Island of Paris: A Letter, October 1920', *Dial*, LXIX. 5 (Nov. 1920), 515–18

——, 'The Island of Paris: A Letter, November 1920', *Dial*, LXIX. 6 (Dec. 1920), 635–9

——, 'A Letter from London', *Much Ado*, X. 5 (2 Feb. 1920), 1

——, 'The Little Review Calendar', *Little Review*, VII. 2 (Spring 1922), 2

——, 'List of Books: Comment by Ezra Pound', *Little Review*, IV. 4 (Aug. 1917), 11

——, 'Londres et ses environs: Un petit guide pour l'étranger bien intention-né', *L'Art libre*, II. 1 (1 Jan. 1920), 2–3; 'London and its Environs. A Short Guide for the Well-Meaning Foreigner', tr. Archie Henderson, 'Pound's Contributions to *L'Art Libre* (1920)', *Paideuma: Modern and Contemporary Poetry and Poetics*, 13. 2 (Fall 1984), 271–83

——, 'Mr Eliot's Looseness', *New English Weekly*, V. 4 (10 May 1934), 95–6

——, 'Mr Eliot's Quandaries', *New English Weekly*, IV (29 Mar. 1934), 558–9

——, 'Mr Pound and his Poetry', *Athenaeum*, 4670 (31 Oct. 1919), 1132

—— ('William Atheling'), 'Music', *New Age*, XVIII. 4 (25 Nov. 1920), 44

—— ('William Atheling'), 'Music', *New Age*, XVIII. 8 (23 Dec. 1920), 92–3

Pound, Ezra, 'The New Sculpture', *Egoist*, I. 4 (16 Feb. 1914), 67–8

——, 'Pastiche. The Regional. I', *New Age*, XXV. 7 (12 June 1919), 124

——, 'Pastiche. The Regional. II', *New Age*, XXV. 9 (26 June 1919), 156

——, 'Pastiche. The Regional. VIII[–IX] [*i.e.* VII]', *New Age*, XXV. 17 (21 Aug. 1919), 284

——, 'Pastiche. The Regional. XVIII', *New Age*, XXVI. 3 (20 Nov. 1919), 48

——, 'Prologomena' [sic], *Poetry Review*, I. 2 (Feb. 1912), 72–6

——, 'Propertius and Mr Pound', *Observer* (25 Jan. 1920), 5

——, 'Small Magazines', *English Journal*, XIX. 9 (Nov. 1930), 689–704

——, 'T. S. Eliot', *Poetry* (Chicago), X. 5 (Aug. 1917), 264–71

——, 'T. S. Eliot', *We Moderns: Gotham Book Mart 1920–1940* (ed. Frances Stelo and Kay Steele), New York: Gotham Book Mart, 1939, 24–5

——, '"Tarr", by Wyndham Lewis', *Little Review*, IV. 11 (Mar. 1918), 35

——, 'The Revolt of Intelligence – V', *New Age*, XXVI. 10 (8 Jan. 1920), 153–4

——, 'The Revolt of Intelligence – VI', *New Age*, XXV. 11 (15 Jan. 1920), 176–7

——, 'The Revolt of Intelligence – VIII', *New Age*, XXVI. 18 (4 Mar. 1920), 287–8

——, 'Through Alien Eyes, I', *New Age*, XII. 11 (16 Jan. 1913), 252

——, 'Troubadours: Their Sorts and Conditions', *Quarterly Review*, CCXIX. 437 (Oct. 1913), 426–40

——, 'Vers Libre and Arnold Dolmetsch', *Egoist*, IV. 6 (July 1917), 90–1

——, 'Vorticism', *Fortnightly Review*, XCVI. 573 (1 Sept. 1914), 461–71

Annotated editions

DFFN   *Drafts and Fragments: Facsimile Notebooks 1958–1959*, New York: Glenn Horowitz, Bookseller, 2010

EPPP1–11 *Ezra Pound's Poetry and Prose: Contributions to Periodicals* (ed. Lea Baechler, Walton A. Litz and James Logenbach), 11 vols, New York: Garland, 1991

PT   *Poems and Translations* (ed. Richard Sieburth), New York: Library of America, 2003

SPT   *Selected Poems and Translations* (ed. Richard Sieburth), New York: New Directions, 2010/London: Faber & Faber, 2011

VETC   *Variorum Edition of 'Three Cantos': A Prototype* (ed. Richard Taylor), Bayreuth: Boomerang – Norbert Aas, 1991

List of correspondents

AAK	Alfred A. Knopf	FSF	F. S. Flint
AB	Agnes Bedford	GB	George Boyle
ACH	Alice Corbin Henderson	GF	Geoffrey Faber
AF	Angel Flores	GC	Godfrey Childe
AFD	Albert Frank-Duquesne	GS	Gilbert Seldes
AG	Alyse Gregory	GW	Glenway Wescott
AH	Aldous Huxley	GZ	Gregor Ziemer
AL	Amy Lowell	HAM	H. A. Moe
APGG	André (Paul Guillaume) Gide	HC	Harry Crosby
ARO	A. R. Orage	HEM	Harold Edward Monro
BB	Basil Bunting	HG	Horace Gregory
BGB	B. G. Brooks	HGJ	Howell G. Jenkins
BP	Brigit Patmore	HH	Hermann Hesse
BR	Bertrand Russell	HHS	H. H. Shakespear (DP's father)
CA	Conrad Aiken	HL	Horace Liveright
CB	Clive Bell	HLM	H. L. Mencken
CCA	Claude Colleer Abbott	HLP	Homer Loomis Pound (EP's
CG	Charles Guenther		father)
CL	Carlo Linati	HM	Harriet Monroe
CM	Constance Malleson	HR	Herbert Read
CN	Charles Norman	HRC	Harry Ransom Center
CWE	Charlotte Ware Eliot, TSE's	HRCW	Harold Raymond (Chatto &
	mother		Windus)
DC	Dora Carrington	HSW	Harriet Shaw Weaver
DG	Donald Gallup	HW	Hugh Walpole
DHW	Daniel H. Woodward	HWE	Henry Ware Eliot (TSE's
DI	David Ignatow		brother)
DJCG	Duncan (James Corrowr)	HWES	Henry ('Hal') Ware Eliot Snr
	Grant		(TSE's father)
DP	Dorothy Pound	IB	Isaiah Berlin
EEC	E. E. Cummings	ISC	Iris Sylvia Crump (Iris Barry)
EH	Emily Hale	JCS	J. C. Squire
EHH	Eleanor Holmes Hinkley	JE	Jonathan Edwards
EK	Ellen Kellond	JF	John Freeman
ELM	Emily Lina Mirrlees	JG	Joy Grant
EMH	Ernest (Miller) Hemingway	JH	Julian Huxley
EP	Ezra Pound	JHW	J. H. Woods
E/RCC	Edward/Rebecca Clarke Cum-	JJ	James Joyce
	mings	JK	John Keats
FB	Frank Budgen	JMM	John Middleton Murry
FES	Felix E. Schelling	JQ	John Quinn

JR	John Rodker	RCS	Richard Cobden-Sanderson
JRF	Jean Robert Foster	RF	Roger Fry
JSW	James Sibley Watson	RL	Robert Lowell
JV	Jean Verdenal	RNL	Robert N. Linscott
JVH	J. V. Healy	RS	Robert Sencourt
KA	Kenneth Allott	RW	Richard Woodhouse
LL	Lucille Liveright	SB	Sylvia Beach
LS	Lytton Strachey	SHS	Stephen Harold Spender
LW	Leonard Woolf	SN	Stanley Nott
MA	Margaret Anderson	SOF	Seán O'Faoláin
MB	Maxwell Bodenheim	SS	Sydney Schiff (Stephen
MC	Marguerite Caetani		Hudson)
MdR	Mary de Rachewiltz	ST	Scofield Thayer
MEB	Mary (Ethel) Barnard	SW	Sydney Waterlow
MF	Maurice Firuski	TEC	Thomas E. Connolly
MG	Michael Goldman	TEL	T. E. Lawrence
MH	Mary Hutchinson	TES	Theodora Eliot Smith (TSE's
MHW	Maurice Haigh-Wood		niece)
MLD	Margaret Llewelyn Davies	TH	Thomas Hardy
MLH	Mary Lilian Harmsworth	THB	Thomas H. Benton
	(Lady Rothermere)	TLE	Thomas Lamb Eliot (TSE's
MM	Marianne Moore		uncle)
MMC	Mary Moore Cross	TSE	T. S. Eliot
MS	May Sinclair	TSM	T. Sturge Moore
MsF	Miss Fredman	VB	Vanessa Bell
MUC	Master, University College,	VD	Violet Dickinson
	Oxford	VHE	Vivien Haigh Eliot
MWC	Marquis W. Childs	VS	Violet Schiff
NRF	La Nouvelle Revue Française	VW	Virginia Woolf
	(Jacques Rivière)	WBY	W. B. Yeats
OM	Ottoline Morrell	WCW	William Carlos Williams
OS	Olivia Shakespear (DP's moth-	WFS	William Force Stead
	er)	WGH	W. G. Hale
PG	Patricia Gruber	WHDR	W. H. D. Rouse
PMJ	P. M. Jack	WL	Wyndham Lewis
PWR	P. W. Robertson	WS	William Sollory
RA	Richard Aldington	WWH	W. Wilbur Hatfield

Letters from T. S. Eliot

TSEL *1–9* *The Letters of T. S. Eliot* (ed. Valerie Eliot, Hugh Haughton and John
Haffenden), 9 vols (incl. revised edition of vol. 1), London: Faber &
Faber, 2009–21; especially vol. 1, *1898–1922* (ed. Valerie Eliot and Hugh
Haughton), revised edition, London: Faber & Faber, 2009

Letters from Ezra Pound

EPSL   *Letters of Ezra Pound 1907–1941* (ed. D. D. Paige), New York: Harcourt Brace, 1950; rep. as *Selected Letters of Ezra Pound*, New York: New Directions/London: Faber & Faber, 1971; references to the original and repaginated British edition of 1951 – *Letters of Ezra Pound 1907–1941* (ed. D. D. Paige), London: Faber & Faber, 1951 – are given in brackets at the end of the citation

EPLC   *Pound/Cummings: The Correspondence of Ezra Pound and E. E. Cummings* (ed. Barry Ahearn), Ann Arbor, MI: University of Michigan Press, 1996

EPLD   *Pound, Thayer, Watson, and The Dial: A Story in Letters* (ed. Walter Sutton), Gainesville: University of Florida Press, 1994

EPLF   *Pound/Ford: The Story of a Literary Friendship: The Correspondence between Ezra Pound and Ford Madox Ford and Their Writings about Each Other* (ed. Brita Linberg-Seyersted), London: Faber & Faber, 1982

EPLH   *The Letters of Ezra Pound to Alice Corbin Henderson* (ed. Ira B. Nadel), Austin: University of Texas Press, 1993

EPLJJ   *Pound/Joyce: The Letters of Ezra Pound to James Joyce with Pound's Essay on Joyce* (ed. Forrest Read), London: Faber & Faber, 1967

EPLJL   *Ezra Pound and James Laughlin: Selected Letters* (ed. David M. Gordon), New York: W. W. Norton, 1994

EPLWL   *Pound/Lewis: The Letters of Ezra Pound and Wyndham Lewis* (ed. Timothy Materer), London: Faber & Faber, 1985

EPLLR   *Pound/The Little Review: The Letters of Ezra Pound to Margaret Anderson* (ed. Thomas L. Scott and Melvin J. Friedman with Jackson R. Bryer), London: Faber & Faber, 1988

EPLN   *One Must Not Go Altogether with the Tide: The Letters of Ezra Pound and Stanley Nott* (ed. Miranda B. Hickman), Montreal: McGill-Queen's University Press, 2011

EPLP   *Ezra Pound to His Parents: Letters 1895–1929* (ed. Mary de Rachewiltz, A. David Moody and Joanna Moody), Oxford: Oxford University Press, 2010

EPLQ   *The Selected Letters of Ezra Pound to John Quinn, 1915–1924* (ed. Timothy Materer), Durham, NC: Duke University Press, 1991

EPLS   *Ezra Pound and Dorothy Shakespear: Their Letters 1909–1914* (ed. Omar Pound and A. Walton Litz), London: Faber & Faber, 1984, 1985

EPLW   *Pound/Williams: Selected Letters of Ezra Pound and William Carlos Williams* (ed. Hugh Witemeyer), New York: New Directions, 1996

EPLZ   *Pound/Zukofsky: Selected Letters of Ezra Pound and Louis Zukofsky* (ed. Barry Ahearn), London: Faber & Faber, 1987

Other correspondence

AHL   Aldous Huxley, *Letters of Aldous Huxley* (ed. Grover Smith), London: Chatto & Windus, 1969

BRSL1–2   Bertrand Russell, *Selected Letters*, 2 vols (ed. Nicholas Griffin), Boston: Houghton Mifflin, 1992

CASL   Conrad Aiken, *Selected Letters of Conrad Aiken* (ed. Joseph Killorin), New Haven, CT: Yale University Press, 1978

EECSL   E. E. Cummings, *Selected Letters* (ed. F. W. Dupee and George Stade), London: André Deutsch, 1972

EMHL*1–5*   Ernest (Miller) Hemingway, *The Letters of Ernest Hemingway*, 5 vols (general ed. Sandra Spanier), Cambridge: Cambridge University Press, 2011–20

ESSL   Edith Sitwell, *Selected Letters 1919–1964* (ed. John Lehmann and Derek Parker), New York: Vanguard, 1970

HCL   Hart Crane, *The Letters of Hart Crane 1916–1932* (ed. Brom Weber), New York: Heritage House, 1952

JJL   James Joyce, *Letters of James Joyce* (ed. Stuart Gilbert), London: Faber & Faber/New York: Viking, 1957

JJL*1–3*   James Joyce, *Letters of James Joyce* (ed. Stuart Gilbert and Richard Ellmann), new edition, 3 vols, London: Faber & Faber/New York: Viking, 1966–7

JJSL   *James Joyce, Selected Letters* (ed. Richard Ellmann), London: Faber & Faber, 1975

JKL   *Letters of John Keats* (ed. Robert Gittings), Oxford: Oxford University Press, 1970

JMMLM   John Middleton Murry, *Letters of John Middleton Murry to Katherine Mansfield* (ed. C. A. Hankin), London: Constable, 1983

KMCL*1–5*   Katherine Mansfield, *Collected Letters*, 5 vols (ed. Vincent O'Sullivan and Margaret Scott), Oxford: Clarendon Press, 1984–2008

LSL   Lytton Strachey, *The Letters of Lytton Strachey* (ed. Paul Levy), New York: Farrar, Straus & Giroux, 2005

LWL   Leonard Woolf, *Letters of Leonard Woolf* (ed. Frederic Spotts), New York: Harcourt Brace Jovanovich, 1989

MMSL   Marianne Moore, *Selected Letters of Marianne Moore* (ed. Bonnie Costello, Celeste Goodridge and Christanne Miller), New York: Knopf, 1997

RAAL   Richard Aldington, *An Autobiography in Letters* (ed. Norman T. Gates), University Park, PA: Penn State University Press, 1992

RLL   Robert Lowell, *The Letters of Robert Lowell* (ed. Saskia Hamilton), London: Faber & Faber, 2005

VBSL   Vanessa Bell, *The Selected Letters of Vanessa Bell* (ed. Regina Marler), New York: Pantheon, 1993

VWD*1–5*   Virginia Woolf, *The Diary of Virginia Woolf* (ed. Anne Olivier Bell and Andrew McNeillie), 5 vols, London: Hogarth Press, 1977–84

VWL*1–6*   Virginia Woolf, *The Letters of Virginia Woolf* (ed. Nigel Nicolson, asst. Joanne Trautmann), 6 vols, London: Hogarth Press, 1975–80

WBYL   W. B. Yeats, *The Letters of W. B. Yeats* (ed. Allan Wade), London: Rupert Hart-Davis, 1954

WCWSL   William Carlos Williams, *The Selected Letters of William Carlos Williams* (ed. John C. Thirlwall), New York: New Directions, 1957

WLL   Wyndham Lewis, *The Letters of Wyndham Lewis* (ed. W. K. Rose), New York: New Directions, 1963

Bibliographies

Bonnell, F. W. and F. C. Bonnell, *Conrad Aiken: A Bibliography* (*1902–1978*), San Marino, CA: Huntington Library, 1982

Cloud, Gerald W., *John Rodker's Ovid Press: A Bibliographical History*, New Castle, DE: Oak Knoll, 2010

Edwards, John, *A Preliminary Checklist of the Writings of Ezra Pound*, New Haven, CT: Kirgo, 1953

Gallup, Donald, *Ezra Pound: A Bibliography*, Charlottesville, VA: University Press of Virginia, 1983

——, *T. S. Eliot: A Bibliography*, London: Faber & Faber, 1969

Hanneman, Audre, *Ernest Hemingway: A Comprehensive Bibliography*, Princeton, NJ: Princeton University Press, 1967

Morrow, Bradford and Bernard Lafourcade, *A Bibliography of the Writings of Wyndham Lewis*, Santa Barbara, CA: Black Sparrow, 1978

Pound, Omar S. and Philip Grover, *Wyndham Lewis: A Descriptive Bibliography*, Folkestone: Dawson Archon, 1978

Sackton, Alexander, *The T. S. Eliot Collection of the University of Texas at Austin*, Austin: University of Texas at Austin, 1975

Slocum, John J. and Herbert Cahoon, *A Bibliography of James Joyce*, London: Rupert Hart-Davis, 1957

Turcon, Sheila, 'A Bibliography of Constance Malleson', *Russell: The Journal of Bertrand Russell Studies* n.s. 32 (Winter 2012–13), 175–90

Wade, Allan, *A Bibliography of the Writings of W. B. Yeats*, third edition (ed. Russell K. Alspach), London: Rupert Hart-Davis, 1968

Woolmer, J. Howard, *A Checklist of the Hogarth Press 1917–1946*, Revere, PA: Woolmer/Brotherson, 1986

——, *The Poetry Bookshop 1912–1935: A Bibliography*, Revere, PA: Woolmer/Brotherson, 1988

Other works

Ackroyd, Peter, *Ezra Pound and His World*, London: Scribner, 1980

——, *T. S. Eliot*, London: Hamish Hamilton, 1984

Aiken, Conrad, 'The Anatomy of Melancholy', *New Republic* (7 Feb. 1923), 294–5

——, *The Charnel Rose; Senlin: A Biography; and Other Poems*, Boston: Four Seas Co., 1918

——, *The House of Dust: A Symphony*, Boston: Four Seas Co., 1920

Aiken, Conrad, *The Jig of Forslin: A Symphony*, Boston: Four Seas Co., 1916/ London: Martin Secker, 1921 [1922]

——, '"Our Age Has Been and Will Continue to Be His Age": T. S. Eliot', *Life* (15 Jan. 1965), 92–3

——, 'A Pointless Pointillist', *Dial*, LXV. 775 (19 Oct. 1918), 306–7

——, *Scepticisms: Notes on Contemporary Poetry*, New York: Alfred Knopf, 1919

——, 'The Scientific Critic', *Freeman*, 2 (2 Mar. 1921), 593–4

——, *Ushant: An Essay*, New York: Duell, Sloan and Pearce, 1952

Aithal, S. Krishnamoorthy, 'The Typewriters in the Making of "The Waste Land"', *Studies in Bibliography*, 33 (1980), 191–3

Aldington, Richard, 'A Book for Literary Philosophers', *Poetry* (Chicago), XVI. 4 (July 1920), 213–16

——, *Ezra Pound and T. S. Eliot: A Lecture*, London: Peacock Press, 1954

——, *Images*, London: Egoist, 1919

——, *Life for Life's Sake*, New York: Viking, 1941/London: Cassell, 1968

——, 'The Sacred Wood', *Today*, 8. 4 (Sept. 1921), 191–3

——, *Stepping Heavenward: A Record*, London: Chatto & Windus, 1931

Alexander, Michael, *The Poetic Achievement of Ezra Pound*, London: Faber & Faber, 1979

Anderson, Galusha, *The Story of a Border City During the Civil War*, Boston: Little, Brown, 1908

Anderson, Margaret, 'Announcement', *Little Review*, I. 1 (Mar. 1914), 5

——, 'Judicial Opinion (Our Suppressed October Issue)', *Little Review*, IV. 8 (Dec. 1917), 46–9

——, *My Thirty Years' War: An Autobiography*, New York: Covici, Friede, 1930

——, '"Ulysses" in Court', *Little Review*, VII. 4 (Jan.–Mar. 1921), 22–5

Anderson, Sherwood, *Sherwood Anderson's Memoirs: A Critical Edition* (ed. Ray Lewis White), Chapel Hill, NC: University of North Carolina Press, 1969

Angelou, Maya, *I Know Why the Caged Bird Sings*, New York: Random House, 1969/London: Virago, 1984

Arbuthnot, Malcolm, 'Masters of English Prose Style', *Vanity Fair*, 13. 5 (Feb. 1920), 38

Archer, William, 'John Webster', *Nineteenth Century*, LXXXVII (Jan. 1920), 126

Bachelier, Samanthé, 'Hidden History: The Whitewashing of the 1917 East St Louis Riot', *Confluence*, IX. 1 (Fall/Winter 2018), 16–25

Baedeker, Karl, *Northern France from Belgium and the English Channel to the Loire Excluding Paris and its Environs: Handbook for Travellers*, fifth edition, Leipzig: Baedeker, 1909

——, *Southern France including Corsica: Handbook for Travellers*, sixth revised edition, Leipzig: Baedeker, 1914

——, *Switzerland and the Adjacent Portions of Italy, Savoy, and Tyrol: Handbook for Travellers*, twenty-fourth edition, Leipzig: Baedeker, 1911

——, *Switzerland Together with Chamonix and the Italian Lakes: Handbook for Travellers*, twenty-sixth edition, Leipzig: Baedeker, 1922

Barnes, David, 'Fascist Aesthetics: Ezra Pound's Cultural Negotiations in 1930s Italy', *Journal of Modern Literature*, XXXIV. 1 (Fall 2010), 19–35

Barnes, Djuna, *A Book*, New York: Boni & Liveright, 1923

Barnes, James Strachey, *Half a Life*, London: Eyre & Spottiswoode, 1933

——, *Half a Life Left*, New York: Coward McCann, 1937

Barry, Iris, 'The Ezra Pound Period', *Bookman* (Oct. 1931), 159–71

Barry, Peter, 'The *Waste Land* Manuscript: Picking Up the Pieces – In Order', *Forum for Modern Language Studies*, XV. 3 (July 1979), 237–48

Beach, Joseph Warren, 'Conrad Aiken and T. S. Eliot: Echoes and Overtones', *PMLA*, LXIX. 4 (Sept. 1954), 753–62

Beach, Sylvia, *Shakespeare and Company*, New York: Harcourt Brace, 1959/ London: Faber & Faber, 1960

Beare, Robert L, 'Notes on the Text of T. S. Eliot: Variants from Russell Square', *Studies in Bibliography*, IX (1957), 21–49

Bede, *Ecclesiastical History of the English People* (tr. Leo Sherley-Price, rev. R. E. Latham, 1955, 1968), London: Penguin, 1990

Behr, Caroline, *T. S. Eliot: A Chronology of His Life and Works*, London: Macmillan, 1983

Bell, Clive, *Old Friends*, New York: Harcourt, Brace & Co., 1957

——, 'Plus de Jazz', *New Republic* (21 Sept. 1921), 92–6

Bell, Robert, 'Bertrand Russell and the Eliots', *American Scholar*, 52. 3 (Summer 1983), 309–25

Benson, A. C., *Edward Fitzgerald*, London: Macmillan, 1905

Berryman, Jo Brantley, *Circe's Craft: Hugh Selwyn Mauberley*, Ann Arbor, MI: UMI Research Press, 1983

Betjeman, John, *New Bats in Old Belfries*, London: John Murray, 1945

Binyon, Laurence (tr.), *The Divine Comedy*, 1947, rep. London: Agenda, 1979

Bishop, John Peale, 'The Intelligence of Poets', *Vanity Fair*, XVII (Jan. 1922), 13–14

Blum, W. C., *see* Watson, James Sibley

Boaz, Mildred Meyer, 'Musical and Poetic Analogues in T. S. Eliot's *The Waste Land* and Igor Stravinsky's *The Rite of Spring*', *Centennial Review*, 24. 2 (Spring 1980), 218–31

Bodenheim, Maxwell, 'The Isolation of Carved Metal', *Dial*, LXXII. 1 (Jan. 1922), 87–91

Bogan, Louise, *Achievement in American Poetry 1900–1950*, Chicago: Henry Regnery, 1951

Bolgan, Anne C., *What the Thunder Really Said: A Retrospective Essay on the Making of The Waste Land*, Montreal: McGill-Queen's University Press, 1973

Bollier, E. P., 'T. S. Eliot's "Lost" Ode of Dejection', *Bucknell Review*, XVI. 1 (Mar. 1968), 1–17

Booth, Allyson, *Reading The Waste Land from the Bottom Up*, New York: Palgrave Macmillan, 2015

Bowen, Stella, *Drawn from Life*, 1941, rep. London: Virago, 1984

Boyle, George (ed.), *Twixt Lombard Street and Cornhill: Designed, Written and Illustrated by the Staff of Lloyds Bank Limited*, London: privately printed, 1930

Bradbrook, M. C., *T. S. Eliot: The Making of 'The Waste Land'* (ed. Ian Scott-Kilvert), Harlow: Longman, 1972

Bradford, Sarah, *Splendours and Miseries: A Life of Sacheverell Sitwell*, New York: Farrar, Straus & Giroux, 1993

Braithwaite, William Stanley ('W. S. B.'), 'A Scorner of the Ordinary Substance of Human Nature', *Boston Evening Transcript* (14 Apr. 1920), II, 6

Bressan, Eloisa, 'Reading *A Walking Tour in Southern France*: A Geographical Approach', *Make It New*, II. 1 (June 2015), 77–86

——, 'Regionalism and Mythmaking: A Map for Ezra Pound's Walking Tour in Southern France of 1919', *Make It New*, II. 4 (Mar. 2016), 44–55

Brooker, Jewel Spears, 'Dialectical Collaboration: Editing *The Waste Land*', in *The Cambridge Companion to The Waste Land* (ed. Gabrielle McIntire), New York: Cambridge University Press, 2015

—— (ed.), *T. S. Eliot: The Contemporary Reviews*, Cambridge: Cambridge University Press, 2004

Brooks, Cleanth, 'The Waste Land: An Analysis', in *T. S. Eliot: A Study of His Writings by Several Hands* (ed. B. Rajan), London: Dennis Dobson, 1947, 7–36

Bryher, *The Heart to Artemis: A Writer's Memoirs*, New York: Harcourt Brace, 1962

Bush, Ronald, *The Genesis of Ezra Pound's Cantos*, Princeton, NJ: Princeton University Press, 1976

——, *T. S. Eliot: A Study in Character and Style*, New York: Oxford University Press, 1983

C.P., *see* Powell, Charles

Carlyle, Thomas, *On Heroes, Hero-Worship, and the Heroic in History*, New York: Wiley & Halstead, 1840

Carpenter, Humphrey, *A Serious Character: A Life of Ezra Pound*, London: Faber & Faber, 1988

Carpenter, Margaret Haley, *Sara Teasdale: A Biography*, second edition, New York: Schulte, 1960

Carpenter, Martha C., 'Oedipal Conflict through Mythical Allusion in T. S. Eliot's "Sweeney Erect"', *Yeats Eliot Review*, 14. 3 (Winter 1997), 26–33

Carson, Anne Conover, *Olga Rudge and Ezra Pound: 'What Thou Lovest Well . . .'*, New Haven, CT: Yale University Press, 2001

Casillo, Robert, 'Anti-Semitism, Castration, and Usury in Ezra Pound', *Criticism*, 25. 3 (Summer 1983), 239–65

——, 'Damage Control in the Pound Industry: Response to Dasenbrock', *American Literary History*, 1. 1 (Spring 1989), 240–3

——, *The Genealogy of Demons: Anti-Semitism, Fascism, and the Myths of Ezra Pound*, Evanston, IL: Northwestern University Press, 1988

Cawein, Madison, *Minions of the Moon: A Little Book of Song and Story*, Cincinnati, OH: Stewart & Kidd, 1913

Cerf, Bennett, *At Random: The Reminiscences of Bennett Cerf*, New York: Random House, 1977

Chesterton, G. K., *Alarms and Discursions*, London: Methuen, 1910

——, *The Ballad of St Barbara and Other Verses*, London: Cecil Palmer, 1922

——, *The New Jerusalem*, London: Hodder & Stoughton, 1920

Chiari, Joseph, *T. S. Eliot: A Memoir*, London: Enitharmon, 1982

Childs, Donald J., *Modernism and Eugenics: Woolf, Eliot, Yeats and the Culture of Degeneration*, Cambridge: Cambridge University Press, 2001

Chinitz, David, 'T. S. Eliot and the Cultural Divide', *PMLA*, 110. 2 (Mar. 1995), 236–47

——, *T. S. Eliot and the Cultural Divide*, Chicago: University of Chicago Press, 2003

Clark, Ronald W., *The Life of Bertrand Russell*, London: Jonathan Cape/Weidenfeld & Nicolson, 1975

Clegg, John, 'Some Investigation and Digression into Lines 139–167 of *The Waste Land*', *PN Review 242*, 44. 6 (July/Aug. 2018)

Clutton-Brock, Arthur [unsigned], 'Not Here, O Apollo', *Times Literary Supplement*, 908 (12 June 1919), 322

Cocteau, Jean, *Le Cap de Bonne-Espérance*, Paris: Éditions de la Sirène, 1919; 'The Cape of Good Hope' (tr. Jean Hugo), *Little Review*, VIII. 1 (Autumn 1921), 43–96

Colin, Paul, 'Fin d'année', *L'Art libre*, 19 (1919), 211

Connolly, Cyril, 'Major Poet: The Influence of Mr Eliot', *Sunday Times* (3 May 1936), 8

Connolly, James B., *Fisherman of the Banks*, London: Faber & Gwyer, 1928

Connolly, Thomas E., 'Further Notes on Mauberley', *Accent*, 16 (Winter 1956), 59

Conrad, Joseph, 'The Heart of Darkness', *Blackwood's Magazine*, CLXV (Feb. 1899), 193–220; CLXV (Mar. 1899), 479–502; CLXV (Apr. 1899), 634–57, rep. in *Youth: A Narrative and Two Other Stories*, Edinburgh: Blackwood, 1902, 49–182

Cook, Eleanor, 'T. S. Eliot and the Carthaginian Peace', *ELH*, 46. 2 (Summer 1979), 341–55

Cookson, William, *A Guide to the Cantos of Ezra Pound*, 1985, revised edition, London: Anvil, 1985, 2001

Corona Typewriter Company, *How to Use Corona, the Personal Writing Machine*, Groton, NY: Corona Typewriter Co., n.d. [*c.*1920]

Cory, Daniel, 'Ezra Pound: A Memoir', *Encounter*, 30. 5 (May 1968), 30–9

Cox-McCormack, Nancy, 'Ezra Pound in the Paris Years' (ed. Lawrence S. Rainey), *Sewanee Review*, 102. 1 (Winter 1994), 93–112

Crawford, Fred D., 'Conrad Aiken's Cancelled Debt to T. S. Eliot', *Journal of Modern Literature*, 7. 3 (Sept. 1979), 416–32

Crawford, Robert, *Young Eliot: From St Louis to The Waste Land*, London: Jonathan Cape, 2015

——, *Eliot After The Waste Land*, London: Jonathan Cape, 2022

Crosby, Caresse, *The Passionate Years*, New York: Dial, 1953

Cuda, Anthony, 'Coda: The Waste Land's Afterlife: The Poem's Reception in the Twentieth Century and Beyond', in *The Cambridge Companion to The Waste Land* (ed. Gabrielle McIntire), New York: Cambridge University Press, 2015, 194–210

——, 'Evenings at the Phoenix Society: Eliot and the Independent London Theater', in *The Edinburgh Companion to T. S. Eliot and the Arts* (ed. Frances Dickey and John D. Morgenstern), Edinburgh: Edinburgh University Press, 2016, 202–24

——, 'The Poet and the Pressure Chamber: Eliot's Life', in *A Companion to T. S. Eliot* (ed. David E. Chinitz), Chichester: Wiley-Blackwell, 2009, 3–14

——, 'T. S. Eliot', in *A Companion to Modernist Poetry* (ed. David E. Chinitz and Gail McDonald), Chichester: Wiley, 2014, 450–63

——, 'Who Stood over Eliot's Shoulder?', *Modern Language Quarterly*, 66. 3 (Sept. 2005), 329–64

Cunard, Nancy, *Selected Poems* (ed. Sandeep Parmar), Manchester: Carcanet, 2016

Cummings, E. E., 'T. S. Eliot', *Dial*, LVIII. 6 (June 1920), 781–4

Cuoco, Lorin and William H. Gass (eds), *Literary St Louis: A Guide*, St Louis, MO: Missouri Historical Press, 2000

Dante Alighieri, *The Divine Comedy, 1: The Inferno* (ed. Herman Oelsner, tr. J. A. Carlyle, series ed. Israel Gollancz), London: Temple Classics, Dent, 1900

——, *The Divine Comedy, 2: The Purgatorio* (ed. Herman Oelsner, tr. Thomas Okey, series ed. Israel Gollancz), London: Temple Classics, Dent, 1901

——, *The Divine Comedy, 3: The Paradiso* (ed. Herman Oelsner, tr. Philip H. Wicksteed, series ed. Israel Gollancz), London: Temple Classics, Dent, 1899

Dardis, Tom, *Firebrand: The Life of Horace Liveright*, New York: Random House, 1995

Darroch, Sandra Jobson, *Ottoline: The Life of Lady Ottoline Morrell*, London: Cassell, 1976

Dasenbrock, Reed Way, 'Pound's Demonology', *American Literary History*, 1. 1 (Spring 1989), 231–9

Davie, Donald, *Ezra Pound*, New York: Viking, 1975

Day, Robert A., 'The "City Man" in *The Waste Land*: The Geography of Reminiscence', *PMLA*, 80. 3 (June 1965), 285–91

Dempsey, James, *The Tortured Life of Scofield Thayer*, Gainesville: University Press of Florida, 2014

Deutsch, Babette, 'Another Impressionist', *New Republic*, XIV (16 Feb. 1918), 89

——, 'Orchestral Poetry', *Dial*, LXX. 3 (Mar. 1921), 343–6

——, 'The Season for Song – A Page on the Poets – T. S. Eliot's Weird and Brilliant Book', *New York Evening Post* (29 May 1920)

Dickey, Frances, 'May the Record Speak: The Correspondence of T. S. Eliot and Emily Hale', *Twentieth-Century Literature*, 66. 4 (Dec. 2020), 431–62

—— and John Whittier-Ferguson, 'Joint Property, Divided Correspondents: The T. S. Eliot–Emily Hale Letters', *Modernism/modernity*, 5. 4 (29 Jan. 2021)

Donoghue, Dennis, 'Three Presences: Yeats, Eliot, Pound', *Hudson Review*, LXII. 4 (Winter 2010), 563–82

Doolittle, Hilda ('H. D.'), *End to Torment: A Memoir of Ezra Pound*, New York: New Directions, 1979

——, *Hymen*, New York: Henry Holt, 1921

Douglas, C. H., *Economic Democracy*, London: Cecil Palmer, 1920

Drew, Elizabeth, *T. S. Eliot: The Design of His Poetry*, New York: Scribner, 1949

Drury, John, 'World's Greatest Poem', *Chicago Daily News* (14 Feb. 1923), 15

Dryden, John (tr.), *Ovid's Epistles: With his Amours*, London: Printed for C. Bathurst, T. Davies, W. Strahan, W. Clarke, and R. Collins, T. Becket, T. Cadell, G. Robinson and S. Bladon, 1776

—— (tr.), *The Works of Virgil*, vol. 3, London: Printed for Jacob Tonson, 1721

Du Bois, W. E. B., *Darkwater: Voices from within the Veil*, New York: Harcourt, Brace & Co., 1920

——, *The Souls of the Black Folk: Essays and Sketches*, Chicago: A. C. McClurg, 1903

—— and Martha Gruening, 'The Massacre of East St Louis', *Crisis*, 14. 5 (Sept. 1917), 219–38

Du Pin, Louis Ellies, *A New History of Ecclesiastical Writers: Containing an Account of the Authors of the Several Books of the Old and New Testament: of the Lives and Writings of the Primitive Fathers . . . Also a Compendious History of the Councils, with Chronological Tables of the Whole . . . The Second Edition, Corrected. [The Editor's Preface Signed: W.W., i.e. William Wotton]*, vol. 2, London: Abel Swalle and Tim Childe, 1693

Duff, J. Wight and Arnold M. Duff (tr.), *Minor Latin Poets*, Cambridge, MA: Harvard University Press, 1934

Dunbar, Paul Laurence, *Lyrics of the Hearthside*, New York: Dodd, Mead, 1899

Durrell, Lawrence, 'The Other Eliot' (1965), in *From the Elephant's Back: Collected Essays and Travel Writings*, Edmonton: University of Alberta Press, 2015, 257–70

Edel, Leon, 'Abulia and the Journey to Lausanne', in *The Stuff of Sleep and Dreams: Experiments in Literary Psychology*, London: Chatto & Windus/New York: Harper & Row, 1982

Egleston, Charles (ed.), *The House of Boni & Liveright, 1917–1933: A Documentary Volume, Dictionary of Literary Biography*, vol. 288, Farmington Hills, MI: Thomson Gale, 2004

Eliot, Charlotte C., *Easter Songs*, Boston: James H. West, 1899

——, *Savonarola: A Dramatic Poem*, London: Cobden-Sanderson, 1926

——, *William Greenleaf Eliot: Minister, Educator, Philanthropist*, Boston: Houghton, Mifflin, 1904

Ellmann, Richard, 'The First Waste Land – I', *New York Review of Books* (18 Nov. 1971), 10–16

——, *James Joyce*, 1959, revised edition, New York: Oxford University Press, 1982

Emery-Peck, Jennifer Sorensen, 'Tom and Vivien Eliot Do Narrative in Different Voices: Mixing Genres in *The Waste Land's* Pub', *Narrative*, 16. 3 (Oct. 2008), 331–58

Empson, William, 'My God, Man, There's Bears On It', *Essays in Criticism*, XXII. 4 (Oct. 1972), 417–29

——, 'The Style of the Master', in *T. S. Eliot: A Symposium* (ed. Richard March and Tambimuttu), Chicago: Henry Regnery, 1949, 35–7

——, *Using Biography*, London: Chatto & Windus, 1984

Erkkila, Betsy (ed.), *Ezra Pound: The Contemporary Reviews*, Cambridge: Cambridge University Press, 2011

Espey, John J., *Ezra Pound's Mauberley*, London: Faber & Faber, 1955

——, 'Towards Propertius', *Paideuma: Modern and Contemporary Poetry and Poetics*, 1. 1 (Spring/Summer 1972), 63–74

Feldman, Matthew, 'The "Pound Case" in Historical Perspective: An Archival Overview', *Journal of Modern Literature*, 35. 2 (Winter 2012), 83–97

Ferkiss, Victor C., 'Ezra Pound and American Fascism', *Journal of Politics*, 17. 2 (May 1955), 173–97

Ferrari, Emanuele, 'Stravinsky and Eliot at the Mirror', *Journal of Modern Education Review*, 5. 4 (Apr. 2015), 335–50

Fitts, Dudley, 'It's Fidelity to the Spirit That Counts', *New York Times Book Review* (12 Nov. 1961), 5–6

Fleissner, Robert F., 'Dust Unto Dust: The "Handful of Dust" in *The Waste Land* – from Aiken's *House . . .*', *Journal of Modern Literature*, 22. 1 (Fall 1988), 183–6

Fletcher, John Gould, 'Some Contemporary Poets', *Chapbook: A Monthly Miscellany*, 11 (May 1920), 23–5

Flint, F. S., 'Imagisme', *Poetry* (Chicago), I. 6 (Mar. 1913), 198–200

Flory, Wendy Stallard, *The American Ezra Pound*, New Haven, CT: Yale University Press, 1989

——, *Ezra Pound and the Cantos: A Record of Struggle*, New Haven, CT: Yale University Press, 1980

Fogelman, Bruce, *Shapes of Power: The Development of Ezra Pound's Poetic Sequence*, Ann Arbor, MI: UMI Research Press, 1988

Ford, Ford Madox ('Ford Madox Hueffer'), 'Impressionism – Some Speculations', *Poetry* (Chicago), II. 5 (Aug. 1913), 177–87

——, *Return to Yesterday: Reminiscences 1894–1914*, London: Gollancz/New York: Liveright, 1931

Ford, Mark, 'Ezra Pound and the Drafts of *The Waste Land*', British Library, 13 Dec. 2016

Forster, E. M., *Two Cheers for Democracy*, London: Edward Arnold, 1951

Foster, R. F., *W. B. Yeats: A Life – I. The Apprentice Mage*, Oxford: Oxford University Press, 1997

Fox, C. J., 'Lewis Lairs', *Lewisletter*, 5 (Oct. 1975), 5–6

Frazer, *The Golden Bough: A Study on Comparative Religion*, 2 vols, London/New York: Macmillan, 1890

French, A. L., '"Olympian Apathein": Pound's *Hugh Selwyn Mauberley* and Modern Poetry', *Essays in Criticism*, XV. 4 (Oct. 1965), 428–45

Froula, Christine, 'Eliot's Grail Quest, or, The Lover, the Police, and *The Waste Land*', *Yale Review*, 78. 2 (Winter 1989), 235–53

Gallup, Donald, 'The Eliots, and the T. S. Eliot Collection at Harvard', *Harvard Library Bulletin*, XXXVI. 3 (Summer 1988), 233–47

——, 'The "Lost" Manuscripts of T. S. Eliot', *Times Literary Supplement*, 3480 (7 Nov. 1968), 1237–40

——, *T. S. Eliot and Ezra Pound: Collaborators in Letters*, New Haven: Henry W. Wenning /C. A. Stonehill, 1970

Gardner, Helen, *The Art of T. S. Eliot*, London: Cresset, 1949

——, '*The Waste Land*' *1972*, Manchester: Manchester University Press, 1972

——, '*The Waste Land*: Paris 1922', in *Eliot in His Time: Essays on the Occasion of the Fiftieth Anniversary of The Waste Land* (ed. Walton A. Litz), Princeton, NJ: Princeton University Press, 1973, 67–94

Garvey, Marcus, *The Marcus Garvey and Universal Negro Improvement Association Papers*, vol. 1, 1826–August 1919 (ed. Robert A. Hill), Berkeley and Los Angeles: University of California Press, 1983

——, *Philosophy and Opinions* (ed. Amy Jacques Garvey), second edition, London: Frank Cass, 1967

Gavaghan, Michael, *The Story of the British Unknown Warrior*, Preston: M&L Publications, 1995; fourth edition, Le Touquet, 2006

Geary, Matthew, *T. S. Eliot and the Mother*, New York/Abingdon: Routledge, 2001

Gilmer, Walker, *Horace Liveright: Publisher of the Twenties*, New York: David Lewis, 1970

Gittings, Robert, *The Older Hardy*, London: Heinemann, 1978

Glinert, Ed, *A Literary Guide to London*, London: Penguin, 2000

Gold, Matthew K., 'The Expert Hand and the Obedient Heart: Dr Vittoz, T. S. Eliot, and the Therapeutic Possibilities of *The Waste Land*', *Journal of Modern Literature*, XXIII. 3–4 (Summer 2000), 519–33

Goldstein, Bill, *The World Broke in Two: Virginia Woolf, T. S. Eliot, D. H. Lawrence, E. M. Forster, and the Year that Changed Literature*, New York: Henry Holt, 2017

Gordon, John, 'T. S. Eliot's Head and Heart', *ELH*, 62. 4 (Winter 1995), 979–1000

Gordon, Lyndall, *Eliot's Early Years*, Oxford: Oxford University Press, 1977

——, *Eliot's New Life*, Oxford: Oxford University Press, 1988

——, *The Hyacinth Girl: T. S. Eliot's Hidden Muse*, London: Little Brown, New York: W. W. Norton, 2022

——, *The Imperfect Life of T. S. Eliot*, London: Vintage, 1998; revised edition, 2012

——, 'The Waste Land Manuscript', *American Literature*, 45. 4 (Jan. 1974), 557–70

Gorman, Herbert, *James Joyce: A Definitive Biography*, London: Bodley Head, 1949

Grant, Joy, *Harold Monro and the Poetry Bookshop*, London: Routledge & Kegan Paul, 1967

Grant, Michael (ed.), *T. S. Eliot: The Critical Heritage*, 2 vols, London: Routledge & Kegan Paul, 1982

Graves, Robert, *Goodbye to All That*, London: Jonathan Cape, 1929

——, 'Lawrence Vindicated', *New Republic* (21 Mar. 1955), 16

—— with Laura Riding, *A Survey of Modernist Poetry*, London: Heinemann, 1927 (reissued as *The Common Asphodel*, Manchester: Carcanet, 1949)

Gregory, Horace and Marya Zaturenska, *A History of American Poetry, 1900–1940*, New York: Harcourt Brace, 1940

Grieve, Thomas F., *Ezra Pound's Early Poetry and Poetics*, Columbia: University of Missouri Press, 1997

——, 'Pound's Other Homage: *Hugh Selwyn Mauberley*', *Paideuma: Modern and Contemporary Poetry and Poetics*, 27. 1 (Spring 1998), 9–30

Grigson, Geoffrey, 'Recollections of Wyndham Lewis', *Listener*, 57 (16 May 1957), 786

Grover, Philip (ed.), *Ezra Pound, the London Years: 1908–1920*, New York: AMS, 1978

Gunn, Thom, *The Occasions of Poetry*, London: Faber & Faber, 1982

H. D., *see* Doolittle, Hilda

Haffenden, John, '"Literary Dowsing": Valerie Eliot Edits *The Waste Land*', *T. S. Eliot Studies Annual*, 2. 1 (2018), 133–50

——, 'Vivien Eliot and *The Waste Land*: The Forgotten Fragments', *PN Review 175*, 3. 5 (May–June 2007), 18–23

Hale, W. G., 'Pegasus Impounded', *Poetry* (Chicago), XIV. 1 (Apr. 1919), 52–5

Hall, Donald, 'Ezra Pound: The Art of Poetry No. 5', *Paris Review*, 28 (Summer/Fall 1962), 22–51

——, *Remembering Poets: Reminiscences and Opinions – Dylan Thomas, Robert Frost, T. S. Eliot, Ezra Pound*, New York: Harper & Row, 1979

——, 'T. S. Eliot, The Art of Poetry No. 1', *Paris Review*, 21 (Spring–Summer 1959), 47–70

Hamilton, Ian, *Robert Lowell: A Biography*, New York: Random House, 1982/London: Faber & Faber, 1983

Hardy, Thomas, *Late Lyrics and Earlier, with Many Other Verses*, London: Macmillan, 1922

——, *Moments of Vision and Miscellaneous Verses*, London: Macmillan, 1917

Hargrove, Nancy Duvall, *T. S. Eliot's Parisian Year*, Gainesville: University Press of Florida, 2009

Harris, Amanda Jeremin, 'T. S. Eliot's Mental Hygiene', *Journal of Modern Literature*, XXIX. 4 (Summer 2006), 44–56

Hartley, Marsden, 'Breakfast Resumé', *Little Review*, V. 7 (Nov. 1918), 46–50

Harwood, John, *Eliot to Derrida: The Poverty of Interpretation*, Basingstoke: Macmillan, 1995

Hastings, Michael, *Tom and Viv*, Harmondsworth: Penguin, 1984

Heap, Jane ('jh'), 'The "Art Season"', *Little Review*, VIII. 2 (Spring 1922), 60

——, 'The Episode Continued', *Little Review* (*'Devoted Chiefly to Ezra Pound . . .'*), V. 7 (Nov. 1918), 36

——, 'Lost: A Renaissance', *Little Review*, XII. 2 (May 1929), 5

Hemingway, Ernest, 'Homage to Ezra', *This Quarter*, I. 1 (Spring [May] 1925), 221–5; rep. *Ezra Pound: A Collection of Essays* (ed. Peter Russell), London/New York: Peter Nevill, 1950, 73–8

——, 'A Note on Ezra Pound', *The Cantos of Ezra Pound: Some Testimonies*, New York: Farrar & Rinehart, 1933, 13; rep. *Ezra Pound Perspectives: Essays in Honor of his Eightieth Birthday* (ed. Noel Stock), Chicago: Henry Regnery, 1965, 151

——, *A Moveable Feast*, New York: Scribner, 1964

——, *Three Stories & Ten Poems*, Paris: Contact, 1923

Henderson, Archie, 'Pound's Contributions to L'Art Libre (1920)', *Paideuma: Modern and Contemporary Poetry and Poetics*, 13. 2 (Fall 1984), 271–83

Hesse, Hermann, 'Die Brüder Karamasow oder Der Untergang Europas', *Blick ins Chaos: Drei Aufsätze*, Bern: Verlag Seldwyla, 1–20; 'The Brothers Karamasov or The Downfall of Europe' (tr. Stephen Hudson [Sydney Schiff], *Dial*, LXXII. 6 (June 1922), 607–18

Hewson, Marc, '"her style is quite her own": Recovering the Feminine in *The Waste Land*', *Yeats Eliot Review*, 18. 4 (April 2002), 14–23

Hicks, Granville, *John Reed: The Making of a Revolutionary*, New York: Macmillan, 1936

Hilary of Poitiers, St, *The Trinity* (*c.356–9*), Book 2, 5, *The Faith of the Early Fathers: A Source-book of Theological and Historical Passages from the Christian Writings of the Pre-Nicene and Nicene Eras* (tr. William A. Jurgens), vol. 1, Collegeville, MN: Liturgical Press, 1970

Hitchens, Christopher, *Unacknowledged Legislation: Writers in the Public Sphere*, London: Verso, 2000

Holroyd, Michael, *Lytton Strachey: A Critical Biography*, 2 vols, New York: Holt, Rinehart & Winston, 1967–8

Hooley, Daniel M., 'Pound's Propertius, Again', *MLN: Comparative Literature*, 100. 5 (Dec. 1985), 1025–44

Howarth, Herbert, *Notes on Some Figures behind T. S. Eliot*, Boston: Houghton Mifflin, 1964

Huddleston, Sisley, *Bohemian Literary and Social Life in Paris*, London: Harrap, 1928 (published in the US as *Paris Salons, Cafés, Studios*, Philadelphia, PA: Lippincott, 1928)

Hueffer, Ford Madox, *see* Ford, Ford Madox

Hughes, Ted, *A Dancer to God: Tributes to T. S. Eliot*, London: Faber & Faber, 1992

Huntingdon, Henry of, *The History of the English People 1000–1154* (tr. Diana Greenway, 1996), Oxford: Oxford University Press, 2009

Hutchins, Patricia, 'Ezra Pound and Thomas Hardy', *Southern Review*, IV. 1 (Winter 1968), 91–104

——, *Ezra Pound's Kensington: An Exploration 1885–1913*, London: Faber & Faber, 1965

Hutton, Clare, *Serial Encounters: Ulysses and the Little Review*, Oxford: Oxford University Press, 2019

Huxley, Aldous, '*Volpone*: Ben Jonson's Play Performed by the Phoenix', *Westminster Gazette* (2 Feb. 1921), 6

Huxley, Julian, *Memories*, New York: Harper & Row, 1970

Jackson, Kevin, *Constellation of Genius: 1922: Modernism and All That Jazz*, London: Hutchinson, 2012

jh, *see* Heap, Jane

Johnson, Walter, *The Broken Heart of America: St Louis and the Violent History of the United States*, New York: Basic Books, 2020

Jordan, Heather Bryant, '*Ara Vos Prec*: A Rescued Volume', *Text*, VII (1994), 349–64

Josephson, Matthew, *Life among the Surrealists*, New York: Holt, Rinehart & Winston, 1962

Joyce, James, *Chamber Music*, London: Elkin Mathews, 1907

——, *Dubliners*, London: Grant Richards, 1914

——, *Exiles*, London: Jonathan Cape, 1918

——, *Pomes Penyeach*, Paris: Shakespeare & Co., 1927, revised edition, London: Faber & Faber, 1966

——, *A Portrait of the Artist as a Young Man*, London: H. W. Huebsch, 1916

——, *Ulysses*, Paris: Shakespeare & Co., 1922, rep. London: Penguin, 1992

——, 'Ulysses, II', *Little Review*, IV. 12 (Apr. 1918), 32–45; rep. 'Ulysses – Episode II', *Egoist*, VI. 1 (Jan.–Feb. 1919), 11–14

Joyce, James, 'Ulysses, Episode XIII (Continued)', *Little Review*, VII. 2 (July–Aug. 1920), 42–58

Julius, Anthony, *T. S. Eliot, Anti-Semitism, and Literary Form*, new edition, London: Thames and Hudson, 2003

Keegan, Paul, 'Emily of Fire and Violence', *London Review of Books*, 42. 20 (22 Oct. 2020), 7–16

Kelly, John, 'Eliot and Yeats', *Essays in Honour of Eamonn Cantwell, Yeats Annual*, 20 (2016), 179–227

Kennedy, Sarah, *T. S. Eliot and the Dynamic Imagination*, Cambridge: Cambridge University Press, 2018

Kenner, Hugh, *The Invisible Poet: T. S. Eliot*, New York: MacDowell Obolensky, 1959

——, *The Poetry of Ezra Pound*, London: Faber & Faber, 1951; new edition, Lincoln: University of Nebraska Press, 1985

——, *The Pound Era: The Age of Ezra Pound, T. S. Eliot, James Joyce and Wyndham Lewis*, Berkeley: University of California Press, 1971/London: Faber & Faber, 1972

——, 'The Urban Apocalypse', *Eliot in His Time: Essays on the Occasion of the Fiftieth Anniversary of The Waste Land* (ed. A. Walton Litz), Princeton, NJ: Princeton University Press, 1973

Keynes, John Maynard, *Collected Works*, vol. 10, *Essays in Biography*, London: Macmillan, 1933, rep. Cambridge: Cambridge University Press, 1972, 2010

——, *The Economic Consequences of the Peace*, London: Macmillan, 1919, 1920

Kimball, Roger, 'A Craving for Reality: T. S. Eliot Today', *New Criterion*, XVIII. 2 (Oct. 1999), 18–26

Kineke, Sheila, 'T. S. Eliot, Marianne Moore, and the Gendered Operations of Literary Scholarship', *Journal of Modern Literature*, XXI. 1 (Fall 1997), 121–36

King, Michael J., 'An A B C of E. P.'s Library', *Library Chronicle of the University of Texas*, n.s., 17 (1981), 30–45

Kirkpatrick, Robin (tr.), *The Divine Comedy*, London: Penguin, 2012

Klaidman, Stephen, *Sydney and Violet: Their Life With T. S. Eliot, Proust, Joyce, and the Excruciatingly Irascible Wyndham Lewis*, New York: Anchor, 2015

Knight, G. Wilson, 'Thoughts on *The Waste Land*', *Denver Quarterly*, 7. 2 (Summer 1972), 1–13

——, '*The Waste Land*', *Times Literary Supplement*, 3646 (14 Jan. 1972), 40

Knoll, Robert E., *Storm over The Waste Land*, Chicago: Scott, Foresman & Co., 1964

Koestenbaum, Wayne, '*The Waste Land*: T. S. Eliot's and Ezra Pound's Collaboration on Hysteria', *Twentieth Century Literature*, 34. 2 (Summer 1988), 113–39

Kritikos, Dean, 'The Home Front *Waste Land*: Williams, Zukofsky, and Epistemology after Eliot', *War, Literature and the Arts: An International Journal of the Humanities*, 27. 1 (2015), 1–20

L.W., *see* Woolf, Leonard

Laughlin, James, *Pound as Wuz: Essays and Lectures on Ezra Pound*, Saint Paul, MN: Graywolf, 1987

Leavell, Linda, *Holding On Upside Down: The Life and Work of Marianne Moore*, London: Faber & Faber, 2013

Leavis, F. R., *New Bearings in English Poetry: A Study of the Contemporary Situation*, 1932, rep. London: Penguin, 1972

Lee, Hermione, *Virginia Woolf*, London: Chatto & Windus, 1996

Lees, Francis Noel, 'Mr Eliot's Sunday Morning *Satura*: Petronius and *The Waste Land*', *Sewanee Review*, 74. 1 (Winter 1966), 339–48

Lehmann, John, *Thrown to the Woolfs*, London: Weidenfeld & Nicolson, 1978

Lenin, V. I. ('N. Lenin'), 'Foreword', in *Ten Days that Shook the World* (John Reed), New York: Boni & Liveright, 1919, v

Lensing, George S., 'Hart Crane's Tunnel from *The Waste Land*', *Ariel: A Review of International Literature*, 6. 3 (July 1975), 20–35

Lewis, Wyndham, *Blasting and Bombardiering: An Autobiography 1914–1926*, London: Eyre & Spottiswoode, 1937; revised edition, London: John Calder, 1967, 1982

——, 'The Children of the New Epoch', *Tyro*, 1 (Apr. 1921), 3

——, 'Early London Environment', in *T. S. Eliot: A Symposium* (ed. Richard March and Tambimuttu), Chicago: Henry Regnery, 1949; third edition, London: Frank Cass, 1965

——, 'Enemy of the Stars', *Blast*, I (20 June 1914), 55

——, 'Ezra: The Portrait of a Personality', *Quarterly Review of Literature*, V. 2 (Dec. 1949), 136–44

——, *The Jews: Are They Human?* London: Allen & Unwin, 1939

——, 'Long Live the Vortex!', *Blast*, 1 (20 June 1914), 7–8

——, *Men Without Art*, London: Cassell & Co., 1934

——, 'Mr Ezra Pound', *Observer* (18 Jan. 1920), 5

——, 'Note on Tyros', *Tyro*, 1 (Apr. 1921), 2

——, *One-Way Song*, London: Faber & Faber, 1933

——, 'Paris Versus the World', *Dial*, LXXI. 1 (1921), 22–7

——, 'Roger Fry's Role of Continental Mediator', *Tyro*, 1 (Apr. 1921), 3

——, *Self Condemned*, London: Methuen, 1954

——, *Tarr*, New York: Alfred A. Knopf/London: Egoist, 1918

——, 'Vortices and Notes: Relativism and Picasso's Latest Work', *Blast*, 1 (20 June 1914), 139–40

Lewis, Wyndham, 'The War Baby', *Art & Letters*, 2. 1 (Winter 1918), 14–41

——, R. Aldington, [M.] Arbuthnot, L. Atkinson, Gaudier Brzeska, J. Dismorr, C. Hamilton, E. Pound, W. Roberts, H. Saunders and E. Wadsworth, 'Manifesto [II]', *Blast*, 1 (20 June 1914), 30–43

Litz, A. Walton, *Eliot in His Time: Essays on the Occasion of the Fiftieth Anniversary of The Waste Land*, Princeton, NJ: Princeton University Press, 1973

Longfellow, Henry Wadsworth (tr.), *The Divine Comedy of Dante Alighieri*, vol. 2, *Purgatorio*, Boston: Ticknor and Fields, 1867

——, *Selected Poems* (ed. Lawrence Buell), London: Penguin, 1988

Lynd, Robert, 'Buried Alive', *Nation*, 18 (4 Dec. 1920), supplement, 359–60

MacCarthy, Desmond, 'New Poets III: T. S. Eliot', *New Statesman* (8 Jan. 1921), 418–20

McCue, Jim, 'Editing Eliot', *Essays in Criticism*, LVI. 1 (Jan. 2006), 1–27

——, 'Vivien Eliot in the Words of TSE', *Review of English Studies*, 68. 283 (Feb. 2017), 123–64

—— and Christopher Ricks, 'Masterpiece in the Making: "The Waste Land" and "the miscellaneous poems which were considered for it"', *Times Literary Supplement* (9 Oct. 2015), 15–17

McGann, Jerome, 'Ezra Pound and Evil', *London Review of Books*, 10. 13 (7 July 1988), 16–17

McIntire, Gabrielle (ed.), *The Cambridge Companion to The Waste Land*, New York: Cambridge University Press, 2015

McKechnie, Gordon, 'Ezra Pound and T. S. Eliot at Excideuil', *Make it New: The Ezra Pound Society Magazine*, 4. 3 (Dec. 2017), 59–96

McLuhan, Marshall, 'Pound, Eliot, and the Rhetoric of *The Waste Land*', *New Literary History*, 10. 3 (Spring 1979), 557–80

MacNeice, Louis, 'Eliot and the Adolescent', in *T. S. Eliot: A Symposium* (ed. Tambimuttu and Richard March), Chicago: Henry Regnery, 1949, 146–51

——, *The Poetry of W. B. Yeats*, 1941, rep. London: Faber & Faber, 1962

McRae, Shannon, '"Glowed into Words": Vivien Eliot, Philomela, and the Poet's Tortured Corpse', *Twentieth Century Literature*, 49. 2 (Summer 2003), 193–218

Maddrey, Joseph, *Simply Eliot*, New York: Simply Charly, 2018

Malleson, Constance, *After Ten Years: A Personal Record*, London: Jonathan Cape, 1931

Malory, Thomas, *Le morte d'Arthur*, 2 vols, London: Dent, 1906

March, Richard and Tambimuttu (eds), *T. S. Eliot: A Symposium*, Chicago: Henry Regnery, 1949

Marsden, Dora, 'The Lean Kind', *New Freewoman*, I. 1 (15 June 1913), 1

——, 'Views and Comments', *New Freewoman*, I. 3 (15 July 1913), 44

Marsh, Edward (ed.), *Georgian Poetry 1916–17*, London: Poetry Bookshop, 1917

Martin, Jay (ed.), *A Collection of Critical Essays on 'The Waste Land'*, Englewood Cliffs, NJ: Prentice Hall, 1968

Martin, Mildred (ed.), *A Half-Century of Eliot Criticism: An Annotated Bibliography of Books and Articles in English, 1916–1965*, Lewisburg, PA: Bucknell University Press, 1972

Marx, Karl and Friedrich Engels, *Manifest der Kommunistischen Partei*, London: J. E. Burghard, 1848; *Manifesto of the Communist Party: Authorized English Translation*, tr. Samuel Moore, ed. Frederick Engels, London: William Reeves, 1888

Matthews, T. S., *Great Tom: Notes towards the Definition of T. S. Eliot*, New York: Harper & Row/London: Weidenfeld & Nicolson, 1974

Matthiessen, F. O., *The Achievement of T. S. Eliot: An Essay on the Nature of Poetry*, 1935, third edition, New York: Oxford University Press, 1958

Maxwell, Gavin, *The Rocks Remain*, London: Longmans, 1963; rep. Harmondsworth: Penguin, 1974

Menard, Louis, 'The Pound Error: The Elusive Master of Allusion', *New Yorker* (9 and 16 June 2008)

Mencken, H. L., [untitled notice], *Smart Set*, LXII (Aug. 1920), 143

Meyers, Jeffrey, *The Enemy: A Biography of Wyndham Lewis*, Boston: Routledge & Kegan Paul, 1980

——, 'New Light on Iris Barry', *Paideuma: Modern and Contemporary Poetry and Poetics*, 13. 2 (Fall 1984), 285–9

Mikriammos, Philippe, 'Ezra Pound in Paris (1921–1924): A Cure of Youthfulness', *Paideuma: Modern and Contemporary Poetry and Poetics*, 14. 2/3 (Fall/Winter 1985), 385–93

Miller, Jr, James E., *T. S. Eliot: The Making of an American Poet*, University Park: Pennsylvania State University Press, 2005

——, *T. S. Eliot's Personal Waste Land: Exorcism of the Demons*, University Park: Pennsylvania State University Press, 1977

—— and Irvin Ehrenpreis, 'Mr Eliot's Motives', *New York Review of Books* (4 May 1978)

Mirrlees, Hope, 'The Mysterious Mr Eliot', BBC One, 3 Jan. 1971

——, *Paris: A Poem*, London: Hogarth Press, 1920; rep. London: Faber & Faber, 2020

Miyake, Akiko, 'A Note on So-shu', *Paideuma: Modern and Contemporary Poetry and Poetics*, 6. 3 (Winter 1977), 325–8

Mizener, Arthur, 'To Meet Mr Eliot', *Sewanee Review*, LXV (Winter 1957), 34–49; rep. in *T. S. Eliot: A Collection of Critical Essays* (ed. Hugh Kenner), Englewood Cliffs, NJ: Prentice Hall, 1962, 21

Model Printing Press Company, *How to Print*, revised edition, London: Model Printing Press Co., 1902

Monk, Ray, *Bertrand Russell: The Spirit of Solitude, 1872–1921*, New York: Free Press, 1996

Monro, Harold, 'Notes for a Study of *The Waste Land*: An Imaginary Dialogue with T. S. Eliot', *Chapbook*, 34 (Feb. 1923), 20–4

——, *Some Contemporary Poets (1920)*, London: Leonard Parsons, 1920

Monroe, Harriet, 'Ezra Pound', *Poetry* (Chicago), XXVI (May 1925), 90–7

——, 'An International Episode', *Poetry* (Chicago), XIII. 1 (Oct. 1918), 94

——, 'Miss Monroe *Re* Ezra Pound' [letter to the editor W. Wilbur Hatfield, 22 Nov. 1930], *English Journal*, XX. 1 (Jan. 1931), 86–7

——, *A Poet's Life: Seventy Years in a Changing World*, New York: Macmillan, 1938

Montieth, Charles, 'Eliot in the Office', *Grand Street*, 9. 3 (Spring 1990), 90–100

Moody, A. David, 'Bel Esprit and the Malatesta Cantos: A Post-*Waste Land* Conjunction of Pound and Eliot', in *Ezra Pound and Europe* (ed. Richard Taylor and Claus Melchior), Amsterdam/Atlanta, GA: Rodopi, 1993, 79–91

——, *Ezra Pound: Poet, A Portrait of the Man and His Work*, 3 vols, Oxford: Oxford University Press, 2007–15

——, *Thomas Stearns Eliot: Poet*, Cambridge: Cambridge University Press, 1979, second edition, 1994

Moore, Don D., 'John Webster in the Modern Theatre', *Educational Theatre Journal*, 17. 4 (Dec. 1965), 314–21

Moore, Marianne, 'The Sacred Wood', *Dial*, LXX. 3 (Mar. 1921), 336–9

Moore, T. Sturge, *Some Soldier Poets*, London: Grant Richards, 1919/New York: Harcourt, 1920

Morgan, Louise, 'The Poetry of Mr Eliot', *Outlook*, 57 (20 Feb. 1926), 135–6

Morley, Frank, 'A Few Recollections of Eliot', *Sewanee Review*, 74. 1 (Winter 1966), 110–33

Morrell, Ottoline, *Ottoline: The Early Memoirs of Lady Ottoline Morrell* (ed. Robert Gathorne-Hardy), London: Faber & Faber, 1963

——, *Ottoline at Garsington: Memoirs of Lady Ottoline Morrell 1915–1918* (ed. Robert Gathorne-Hardy), London: Faber & Faber, 1974

Muir, Edwin, 'Recent Verse', *New Age*, XXVII. 12 (22 July 1920), 186–7

——, 'Recent Verse', *New Age*, XXXI. 23 (5 Oct. 1922), 288

Muirhead, Findlay (ed.), *London and its Environs*, second edition, London: Macmillan, 1922

Murray, Nicholas, *Bloomsbury and the Poets*, Kinnerton: Rack, 2014

Murry, John Middleton, 'The Eternal Footman', *Athenaeum*, 4686 (20 Feb. 1920), 239

Nadel, Ira B. (ed.), *The Cambridge Companion to Ezra Pound*, Cambridge: Cambridge University Press, 1999

Nichols, Robert, *The Assault and Other War Poems from 'Ardours and Endurances'*, London: Chatto & Windus, 1918

——, *Invocation and Peace Celebration, Hymn for the British Peoples*, London: Hendersons, 1919

——, 'An Ironist', *Observer* (18 Apr. 1920), 7

——, 'Mr Nichols Writes', *Observer* (25 Jan. 1920), 5

——, 'Poetry and Mr Pound', *Observer* (11 Jan. 1920), 6

Nicolson, Juliet, *The Great Silence: 1918–1920, Living in the Shadow of the Great War*, London: John Murray, 2009

Norman, Charles, *The Case of Ezra Pound*, New York: Funk and Wagnalls, 1968

——, *E. E. Cummings: The Magic-Maker*, New York: Duell, Sloan and Pearce, 1958, revised edition, 1964

——, *Ezra Pound*, London: Macmillan, 1960

North, Michael (ed.), *The Waste Land: A Norton Critical Edition*, New York: W. W. Norton, 2001

O'Donoghue, Bernard, *The Courtly Love Tradition*, Manchester: Manchester University Press, 1982

Olson, Charles, *Charles Olson and Ezra Pound: An Encounter at St Elizabeths* (ed. Catherine Seelye), New York: Grossman, 1975

Orage, A. R. ('R. H. C.'), 'Readers and Writers', *New Age*, XXVIII. 11 (13 Jan. 1921), 126–7

Ovid, *Art of Love. Cosmetics. Remedies for Love. Ibis. Walnut-tree. Sea Fishing. Consolation* (tr. J. H. Mozley; rev. G. P. Goold), Cambridge, MA: Harvard University Press, 1929

Patteson, Richard F., 'An Additional Source for "The Waste Land"', *Notes and Queries*, 23. 7 (July 1976), 300–1

Pearson, John, *Façades: Edith, Osbert and Sacheverell Sitwell*, London: Macmillan, 1978 (published in the US as *The Sitwells: A Family's Biography*, New York: Harcourt Brace, 1979)

Perinot, Claudio, 'Jean Verdenal, an Extraordinary Young Man: T. S. Eliot's mort aux Dardanelles', *South Atlantic Review*, 76. 3 (Summer 2011), 33–50

Perry, Seamus, *The Connell Guide to T. S. Eliot's The Waste Land*, London: Connell, 2014

Persico, Joseph E., *11th Month, 11th Day, 11th Hour: Armistice Day 1918, World War I and its Violent Climax*, New York: Random House, 2004

Peter, John, 'A New Interpretation of *The Waste Land*', *Essays in Criticism*, II. 3 (July 1952), 242–66; rep. with Postscript, *Essays in Criticism*, XIX. 2 (Apr. 1969), 140–75

Petronius, *Satyricon* (tr. Michael Heseltine), London: William Heinemann, 1913

——, *Trimalchio's Banquet* (tr. Michael J. Ryan), London/Newcastle: Walter Scott Publishing, n.d. [1892, rep. 1905, 1914]

Poe, Edgar Allan, 'Twice-Told Tales. By Nathaniel Hawthorne', *Graham's Magazine*, 20. 5 (1842), 298–9

Powell, Charles, 'The Waste Land', *Manchester Guardian* (31 Oct. 1923), 7

Power, Arthur, *Conversations with James Joyce* (ed. Clive Hart), London: Millington, 1974

Pratt, William, 'Eliot at Oxford: From Philosopher to Poet and Critic', *Soundings*, 78 (1995), 321–37

Propertius, *Elegies* (tr. G. P. Goold), Cambridge, MA: Harvard University Press, 1990

Quigley, Megan, '#MeToo, Eliot, and Modernist Scholarship', *Modernism/modernity*, 5.2 (28 Sept. 2020)

——, 'Reading "The Waste Land" with the #MeToo Generation', *Modernism/modernity*, 4. 1 (4 Mar. 2019)

R.H.C., *see* Orage, A. R.

Rachewiltz, Mary de, *Discretions: A Memoir by Ezra Pound's Daughter*, London: Faber & Faber, 1971

Raine, Craig, *T. S. Eliot*, New York: Oxford University Press, 2006

Rainey, Lawrence, 'Eliot among the Typists: Writing *The Waste Land*', *Modernism/modernity*, 12. 1 (Jan. 2005), 27–84; rep. as 'With Automatic Hand', in *Revisiting The Waste Land*, 1–70

——, *Ezra Pound and the Monument of Culture: Text, History, and the Malatesta Cantos*, Chicago: Chicago University Press, 1991

——, 'The Price of Modernism: Reconsidering the Publication of *The Waste Land*', *Critical Quarterly*, 31. 4 (Dec. 1989), 21–47; rep. as 'The Price of Modernism: Publishing *The Waste Land*', in *Revisiting The Waste Land*, 71–101

——, *Revisiting The Waste Land*, New Haven, CT: Yale University Press, 2005

—— (ed.), *The Annotated Waste Land with Eliot's Contemporary Prose*, second edition, New Haven, CT: Yale University Press, 2005, 2006

Rajan, B. (ed.), *T. S. Eliot: A Study of his Writings by Several Hands*, London: Dennis Dobson, 1947, 1971

Rascoe, Burton, 'A Bookman's Day Book – Thursday, October 26', *New York Tribune* (5 Nov. 1922), V, 8

Read, Herbert, *The Contrary Experience: Autobiographies*, New York: Horizon Press, 1963, 1973

——, 'T. S. E. – A Memoir', in *T. S. Eliot: The Man and His Work* (ed. Allen Tate), New York: Dell, 1966, 11–37

Reck, Michael, 'A Conversation between Ezra Pound and Allen Ginsberg', *Evergreen Review*, 12. 55 (June 1968), 27–9

——, Theodore Weiss, Alfred Kazin and Oliver Taplin, 'An Exchange on Ezra Pound', *New York Review of Books* (9 Oct. 1986)

Reed, John, *Ten Days that Shook the World*, New York: Boni & Liveright, 1919

Regnery, Henry, 'Eliot, Pound and Lewis: A Creative Friendship', *Modern Age* (Spring 1972), 146–59

Reid, B. R., *The Man from New York: John Quinn and His Friends*, New York: Oxford University Press, 1968

Ricks, Christopher, 'To Criticize the Critic', *Essays in Criticism*, 69. 4, 467–79

——, *Decisions and Revisions in T. S. Eliot*, London: British Library, 1993

——, *T. S. Eliot and Prejudice*, London, 1988

Rudwick, Eliot M., 'Fifty Years of Race Relations in East St Louis: The Breaking Down of White Supremacy', *Midcontinent American Studies Journal*, 6. 1 (Spring 1965), 3–15

Russell, Bertrand, *Autobiography*, 3 vols, London: George Allen & Unwin, 1967–8

——, 'The German Peace Offer', *Tribunal*, 90 (3 Jan. 1918), 1

——, *Satan in the Suburbs and Other Stories*, London: Bodley Head, 1953

Russell, Peter (ed.), *Ezra Pound: A Collection of Essays*, London/New York: Peter Nevill, 1950

Ruthven, K. K., *A Guide to Ezra Pound's Personae (1926)*, Berkeley: University of California Press, 1969

Schachtel, Ernest, *Metamorphosis*, New York: Basic Books, 1959

Schaum, Melita, '"Just Looking": Class, Desire, and the Consuming Vision in T. S. Eliot's "In the Department Store"', *Journal of Modern Literature*, XXIII. 2 (Winter 1999–2000), 335–60

Schimmel, Paul, '"In My End Is My Beginning": T.S. Eliot's *The Waste Land* and After', *British Journal of Psychotherapy*, 18. 3 (2002), 381–99

Schuchard, Ronald, 'Burbank with a Baedeker, Eliot with a Cigar: American Intellectuals, Anti-Semitism, and the Idea of Culture', *Modernism/modernity*, 10. 1 (Jan. 2003), 1–26

——, *Eliot's Dark Angel: Intersections of Life and Art*, New York: Oxford University Press, 1999

Schultz, Robert, 'A Detailed Chronology of Ezra Pound's London Years, 1908–1920: Part Two: 1915–1920', *Paideuma: Modern and Contemporary Poetry and Poetics*, 2/3 (Fall/Winter 1983), 357–73

Schwartz, Delmore, 'T. S. Eliot as the International Hero', *Partisan Review*, 12.2 (1945), 199–206

Scott, Peter Dale, 'Pound in "The Waste Land", Eliot in *The Cantos*', *Paideuma: Modern and Contemporary Poetry and Poetics*, 19. 3 (Winter 1990), 99–114

Scott, Robert Ian, 'The Waste Land Eliot Didn't Write', *Times Literary Supplement* (8 Dec. 1995)

Scourfield, J. H. D., 'Nemesianus, Marcus Aurelius Olympius', in *The Oxford Classical Dictionary* (ed. Simon Hornblower and Antony Spawforth), third edition, Oxford: Oxford University Press, 1996

Seldes, Gilbert, 'T. S. Eliot', *Nation* (6 Dec. 1922), 614–16

Sencourt, Robert, *T. S. Eliot: A Memoir* (ed. Donald Adamson), London: Garnstone, 1971

Seybold, Matt, 'Astride the Dark Horse: T. S. Eliot and the Lloyds Bank Intelligence Department', *T. S. Eliot Studies Annual* (2017), 131–55

Seymour-Jones, Carole, *Painted Shadow: A Life of Vivienne Eliot*, London: Constable, 2001

Shapiro, Karl, *The Poetry Wreck: Selected Essays 1950–1970*, New York: Random House, 1975

Simpson, Louis, *Three on the Tower: The Lives and Works of Ezra Pound, T. S. Eliot and William Carlos Williams*, New York: William Morrow, 1975

Sinclair, May, 'The Reputation of Mr Pound', *North American Review*, CCXI (May 1920), 658–8

Sitton, Robert, *The Lady in the Dark: Iris Barry and the Art of Film*, New York: Columbia University Press, 2014

Sitwell, Osbert, *Laughter in the Next Room*, London: Macmillan, 1949

Sitwell, Sacheverell, *For Want of the Golden City*, New York: John Day, 1973

Slater, Ann Pasternak, *The Fall of a Sparrow: Vivien Eliot's Life and Writings*, London: Faber & Faber, 2020

Sloane, Patricia, 'Searching for a Statue of a Girl: Freud's *Delusion and Dream* and T. S. Eliot's "Le Figlia che Piange"', *Modern Schoolman*, LXXXV (Mar. 1988), 237–51

Smith, Grover, 'The Fascination of *Hamlet*', *T. S. Eliot and the Use of Memory*, Lewisburg, PA: Bucknell University Press, 1996

——, 'The Making of *The Waste Land*', *Mosaic: An Interdisciplinary Critical Journal*, 6. 1 (Fall 1972), 127–41

——, *T. S. Eliot's Poetry and Plays: A Study in Sources and Meaning*, Chicago: University of Chicago Press, 1956

——, *The Waste Land*, London: George Allen & Unwin, 1983

Smith, Janet Adam, 'Tom Possum and the Roberts Family', *Southern Review*, 21 (Oct. 1985), 1060

Sorum, Eve, 'Psychology, Psychoanalysis, and New Subjectivities', in *The Cambridge Companion to The Waste Land* (ed. Gabrielle McIntire), Cambridge: Cambridge University Press, 2015, 162–77

Southam, B. C., *A Student's Guide to the Selected Poems of T. S. Eliot*, sixth edition, London: Faber & Faber, 1994

Spalding, Francis, *Duncan Grant*, London: Chatto & Windus, 1997

Spanos, William V., 'The Modulating Voice of *Hugh Selwyn Mauberley*', *Wisconsin Studies in Contemporary Literature*, 6. 1 (Winter–Spring 1965), 73–96

Spender, Stephen, *Eliot*, London: Fontana, 1975

——, *New Selected Journals 1939–1995* (ed. Lara Feigel and John Sutherland with Natasha Spender), London: Faber & Faber, 2012

——, 'Remembering Eliot', in *T. S. Eliot: The Man and His Work* (ed. Allen Tate), London: Chatto & Windus, 1967, 38–64

Spenser, Edmund, *The Shorter Poems* (ed. Richard A. McCabe), London: Penguin, 1999

Squire, J. C., 'The Man Who Wrote Free Verse', *London Mercury*, X. 56 (June 1924), 128

——, 'Poetry', *London Mercury*, VIII. 48 (Oct. 1922), 655–7

Stead, William Force, *The House on the Wold and other Poems*, London: Cobden-Sanderson, 1930

——, 'Some Personal Impressions of T. S. Eliot', *Alumnae Journal of Trinity College* [Washington, DC], 38. 2 (Winter 1965), 59–66

Steffens, Lincoln, *The Shame of the Cities*, New York: McClure, Phillips & Co., 1904

Stein, Gertrude, *The Autobiography of Alice B. Toklas*, New York: Harcourt Brace, 1933

Stock, Noel, *The Life of Ezra Pound*, London: Kegan Paul, 1970; rep. Harmondsworth: Penguin, 1974

—— (ed.), *Ezra Pound Perspectives: Essays in Honor of His Eightieth Birthday*, Chicago: Henry Regnery, 1965

Stockton, Sharon, 'T. S. Eliot and the Rape of God', *Texas Studies in Literature and Language*, 39. 4 (Winter 1997)

Stough, Christina C., 'The Skirmish of Pound and Eliot in *The New English Weekly*: A Glimpse at Their Later Literary Relationship', *Journal of Modern Literature*, 10. 2 (June 1983), 231–46

Stravinsky, Igor, 'Memories of T. S. Eliot', *Esquire*, 64. 2. 381 (1 Aug. 1965), 92–3

Strobel, Marion, 'Perilous Leaping', *Poetry* (Chicago), XVI. 3 (June 1920), 157–9

Sullivan, Hannah, *The Work of Revision*, Cambridge, MA: Harvard University Press, 2013

Sullivan, J. P., *Ezra Pound and Sextus Propertius: A Study in Creative Translation*, London: Faber & Faber/Austin: University of Texas Press, 1964

Sutton, Walter, 'Mauberley, *The Waste Land* and the Problem of Unified Form', *Contemporary Literature*, 9. 1 (Winter 1968), 15–35

Svarny, Erik, '*The Men of 1914*': T. S. Eliot and Early Modernism, Milton Keynes: Open University Press, 1988

Swanton, Michael (tr. and ed.), *The Anglo-Saxon Chronicles*, London: Phoenix, 2000

Swayne, George Carless, 'An Early Stroll to Zermatt', *Fraser's Magazine*, II. 8 (Aug. 1870), 243–50

Swift, Daniel, *The Bughouse: The Poetry, Politics and Madness of Ezra Pound*, London: Harvill Secker, 2017

Tate, Allen (ed.), *T. S. Eliot: The Man and His Work*, London: Chatto & Windus, 1967

Teasdale, Sara, *Flame and Shadow*, New York: Macmillan, 1920

Tennyson, Alfred Lord, *Becket*, London: Macmillan, 1885

——, *Poems*, 2 vols, Boston: William D. Ticknor, 1842

Thorn Jr, Henry C., *History of 3 13th US Infantry*, New York: Wynkoop Hallenbeck Crawford, 1920

Townsend, John Wilson, 'Madison Cawein', *Register of Kentucky State Historical Society*, 22. 64 (Jan. 1924), 80–5

Traversi, Derek, *T. S. Eliot: The Longer Poems*, London: Bodley Head, 1976

Trevelyan, Mary and Erica Wagner, *Mary & Mr Eliot: A Sort of Love Story*, London: Faber & Faber, 2022

Trombold, Chris Buttram, 'Alimentary Eliot: Digestive References and Metaphors in T. S. Eliot's Writings', *English Language Notes*, 34. 2 (Dec. 1996), 45–59

——, 'The Bodily Biography of T. S. Eliot [Part I]', *Yeats Eliot Review*, 15. 1 (Fall 1997), 2–9, 36–44

——, 'The Bodily Biography of T. S. Eliot: Part II', *Yeats Eliot Review*, 15. 2 (Spring 1998), 27–44

——, 'Earlier Versions of Eliot's Early Verse: The Newly-Published Drafts in the Berg Collection', *Journal of Modern Literature*, 21. 1 (Summer 1997), 89–108

Trosman, Harry, 'T. S. Eliot and *The Waste Land*: Psychopathological Antecedents and Transformations', *Archives of General Psychiatry*, 30. 5 (May 1974), 709–17

Trotzky, Leon, *The Bolsheviki and World Peace* (tr. Thomas Seltzer), New York: Boni & Liveright, 1918

Turcon, Sheila, 'Russell's Homes: Russell Chambers, Other London Flats, and Country Homes (1911–1923)', *Bertrand Russell Society Bulletin*, 150 (Fall 2014), 30–4

Twain, Mark, *The Adventures of Huckleberry Finn*, 1884/5, London: Cresset Press/New York: Chanticleer, 1950

——, *Life on the Mississippi*, Boston: James R. Osgood & Co., 1883

Ullyot, Jonathan, *The Medieval Presence in Modernist Literature: The Quest to Fail*, Cambridge: Cambridge University Press, 2015

Unger, Leonard, 'T. S. E. on *The Waste Land*', *Mosaic: An Interdisciplinary Critical Journal*, 6. 1 (Fall 1972), 157–65

Untermeyer, Louis, 'Disillusion vs. Dogma', *Freeman*, 6 (17 Jan. 1923), 453

——, 'Ezra Pound – Proseur', *New Republic*, XVI (17 Aug. 1918), 83–4

——, 'Irony De Luxe', *Freeman*, 1 (30 July 1920), 381–2

Vendler, Helen, 'The Most Famous Modern Poem – What Was Left In and What Was Cut Out', *New York Times*, Sunday Book Review (7 Nov. 1971), 1

Vittoz, Dr Roger, *Traitement des Psychonévroses par la Rééducation du Contrôle Cérébral*, 1911, Paris: Librairie J.-B. Baillière et Fils, 1930; *Treatment of Neurasthenia by Teaching of Brain Control* (tr. H. B. Brooke), London: Longmans, Green and Co., 1911, second edition, 1913

W. S. B., *see* Braithwaite, William Stanley

Warren, Henry Clarke, *Buddhism in Translations*, Cambridge, MA: Harvard University Press, 1896

Water, Frederic F. Van de, *The Real McCoy*, Garden City, NY: Doubleday, Doran & Co., 1931

Watson, George, 'Quest for a Frenchman', *Sewanee Review*, 84. 3 (July–Sept. 1976), 465–75

Watson, James Sibley ('W. C. Blum'), 'Super Schoolmaster', *Dial*, LXIX. 4 (Oct. 1920), 422–3

Waugh, Arthur, 'The New Poetry', *Quarterly Review*, 226 (Oct. 1916), 386

Waugh, Evelyn, *Brideshead Revisited*, London: Chapman and Hall, 1945

——, *A Handful of Dust*, London: Chapman and Hall, 1934

——, *Unconditional Surrender*, London: Chapman and Hall, 1961

Weaver, Harriet Shaw, 'Notice to Readers', *Egoist*, VI. 5 (Dec. 1919), 6

Wees, William C., 'Ezra Pound as a Vorticist', *Wisconsin Studies in Contemporary Literature*, 6. 1 (Winter–Spring 1965), 56–72

Weinstein, Noah, 'The Juvenile Court Concept in Missouri: Its Historical Development – the Need for New Legislation', *Washington University Law Quarterly*, 1957. 1 (Feb. 1957), 17–56

West, Rebecca, 'Imagisme', *New Freewoman*, I. 5 (15 Aug. 1913), 86

Weston, Jessie, *From Ritual to Romance*, Cambridge: Cambridge University Press, 1920

Whitman, Walt, *Specimen Days & Collect*, Philadelphia, PA: Rees Welsch & Co., 1882

Wilhelm, J. J., *The American Roots of Ezra Pound*, New York: Garland, 1985

——, *Ezra Pound in London and Paris (1908–1925)*, University Park: Pennsylvania State University Press, 1990

——, *Ezra Pound the Tragic Years (1925–1972)*, University Park: Pennsylvania State University Press, 1994

——, *The Later Cantos of Ezra Pound*, New York: Walker & Co., 1977

——, 'Nancy Cunard: A Sometime Flame, A Stalwart Friend', *Paideuma: Modern and Contemporary Poetry and Poetics*, 19. 1/2 (Spring/Fall 1990), 201–21

——, 'On the Trail of the "One" Crawfordsville Incident or, The Poet in Hoosierland', *Paideuma: Modern and Contemporary Poetry and Poetics*, 13. 1 (Spring 1984), 11–47

Williams, Dominic, 'Circulating Antisemitism: The Men of 1914', in *Modernist Group Dynamics: The Poetics and Politics of Friendship* (ed. Fabio A. Durão and Dominic Williams), Newcastle: Cambridge Scholars Publishing, 2008, 43–68

Williams, Ellen, *Harriet Monroe and the Poetry Renaissance: The First Ten Years of Poetry, 1912–22*, Urbana: University of Illinois Press, 1977

Williams, Tennessee, 'Facts About Me', *Tennessee Williams: Reading from His Works*, Caedmon Records, 1952

Williams, William Carlos, *Autobiography*, New York: New Directions, 1951

——, 'Belly Music', *Others* (July 1919), 27–31

——, *I Wanted to Write a Poem*, Boston: Beacon, 1958/London: Jonathan Cape, 1967

——, *Kora in Hell: Improvisations*, Boston: Four Seas Co., 1920

——, 'Prologue', *Little Review*, VI. 1 (May 1919), 76–8

——, *Spring and All*, Paris: Contact, 1923

Wilson, Edmund, 'The First Waste Land – II', *New York Review of Books* (18 Nov. 1971)

——, 'Mr Pound's Patchwork', *New Republic*, 30 (19 Apr. 1922), 232–3

——, 'The Poetry of Drouth', *Dial*, LXXIII. 6 (Dec. 1922), 611–16

Wood, David, from *T. S. Eliot between Two Worlds*, London/Boston: Routledge Kegan Paul, 1973

Woodward, Daniel H., 'Notes on the Publishing History and Text of *The Waste Land*', *Papers of the Bibliographical Society of America*, 58. 3 (1964), 252–69

Woolf, Leonard ('L. W.'), 'Back to Aristotle', *Athenaeum*, 4729 (17 Dec. 1920), 834–5

——, *Beginning Again: An Autobiography of the Years 1911 to 1918*, London: Hogarth Press, 1964

——, *Downhill All the Way: An Autobiography of the Years 1919 to 1945*, London: Hogarth Press, 1967

—— [unsigned], 'Is This Poetry?', *Athenaeum*, 4651 (20 June 1919), 491

——, *Sowing: An Autobiography of the Years 1880 to 1904*, London: Hogarth Press, 1960

Wordsworth, William and Samuel Taylor Coleridge, *Lyrical Ballads, with Other Poems*, I, second edition, London: Printed for T. N. Longman and O. Rees, 1800

Worthen, John, *T. S. Eliot: A Short Biography*, London: Haus, 2009

Worthen, William B., 'Eliot's *Ulysses*', *Twentieth Century Literature*, 27. 2 (Summer 1981), 166–77

Wylie, Elinor, 'Mr Eliot's Slug-Horn', *New York Evening Post Literary Review* (20 Jan. 1923), 396

Yeats, W. B., *The Cutting of the Agate*, New York: Macmillan, 1912/London: Macmillan, 1919

——, *Essays and Introductions*, Dublin: Gill and Macmillan, 1961

——, *The Wild Swans at Coole, Other Verses and a Play in Verse*, Dundrum: Cuala, 1917; *The Wild Swans at Coole*, London/New York: Macmillan, 1919

—— (ed.), *Irish Fairy Tales*, London: T. Fisher Unwin, 1892

—— (ed.), *The Oxford Book of Modern Verse 1892–1936*, Oxford: Clarendon Press, 1936

Notes.

FRONTMATTER.

1 TSE, 'Leadership and Letters', 7.
2 EP, 'For T. S. E.', 109; rep. Tate, 89.
3 Agadir earthquake, 29 Feb. 1960: Maxwell, 16–25.
4 TSE–EP, 29 Jan. 1960, Beinecke EPP, [Series I,] b. 15, f. 674.
5 EP's 'order dismissing indictment' was made by Chief Judge Bolitha J. Laws on 18 April 1958 (TSE sent a telegram: 'CONGRATULATIONS AND JOYFUL GREETINGS = POSSUM AND VALERIE', 21 Apr. 1958, Beinecke EPP, b. 15, f. 673); EP–TSE, 15 Sept. 1959, Beinecke EPP, b. 15, f. 673.
6 EP–TSE, 15 Sept. 1959, Beinecke EPP, b. 15, f. 673.
7 TSE–EP, telegram 30 Oct. 1959 (transmitted 31 Oct. 1959), Beinecke EPP, b. 15, f. 673, and Eliot Estate.
8 TSE–EP, 28 Dec. 1959, Beinecke EPP, Box 15, f. 673.
9 Hall, *Remembering Poets*, 114.
10 TSE, *TWL*, Texas TSEC.
11 EP, 'Song fer the Muses' Garden', EP–TSE, 28 Mar. 1935, *EPSL*, 272 (361).

ARMISTICE.

1 See Thorn, 50; Persico, 134–6, 350–1; see also Richard Rubin, 'Where the Great War Ended', *New York Times,* Travel (28 Dec. 2014), 1; Jacques Kelly, 'Henry Gunther: the Baltimorean who was the last U.S. battlefield death in World War I', *Baltimore Sun* (31 Mar. 2017); Christina Tkacik, 'The heroic, perplexing tale of the Baltimore man who was the last killed in WWI – minutes before Armistice', *Baltimore Sun* (9 Nov. 2018); Christopher Klein, 'The Last Official Death of WWI Was a Man Who Sought Redemption', history.com (9 Nov. 2018; updated 5 June 2019).
2 Dan Rodricks, 'The Sad, Senseless End of Henry Gunther', *Baltimore Sun* (11 Nov. 2008).
3 TSE–JQ, 13 Nov. 1918, *TSEL1*, 299.
4 TSE–EHH, 14 Oct. 1914, *TSEL1*, 66.
5 TSE–HWES, 13 June 1917, *TSEL1*, 203.
6 EP–JQ, 15 Nov. 1918, *EPSL*, 141 (201).
7 EP, 'Through Alien Eyes, I', 252.
8 EP–JQ, 11 Sept. 1918, *TSEL1*, xxviii.

9   EP–JJ, 22 Nov. 1918, *EPLJJ*, 145.

10 EP–WCW, 3 Feb. 1909, *EPSL*, 7 (41).

11 EP, 'V', *HSM*, 13.

12 TSE–HWES, 23 Dec. 1917, *TSEL1*, 242.

13 See Perinot, 44; for more on Eliot's pre-war friendships in Paris see Hargrove. Some critics have speculated that the relationship with Jean Verdenal was a sexually intimate one (see James E. Miller), and that Verdenal may have been represented in *TWL* by the figure of the hyacinth girl (see G. Wilson Knight), a notion apparently contradicted by the unsealing in 2019 of Eliot's letters to Emily Hale, to whom he wrote on 3 Nov. 1930 (Princeton EHL, b. 1, f. 1): 'And I want to ask you please, to re-read the hyacinth lines in <Part I.> The Waste Land, and the lines toward the very end beginning "friend, blood shaking my heart" (where *we* ~~of course~~ means privately of course *I*) and compare them with Pipit on the one hand and Ash Wednesday on the other, and see if they do not convince you that my love for you has steadily grown into something finer and finer. And I shall always write primarily for you.'

14 TSE, *POO*, 5; *P1925*, 7.

15 TSE, 'A Commentary', *Criterion*, XIII (Apr. 1934), 451–4.

16 EP, *GB*, 44, 46, 49.

17 EP, *GB*, 17, also 136.

18 EP–WL, [Aug. 1917], *EPLWL*, 93.

19 Olson, 45; see also EP, 'Canto XVI', *Cantos*, 71 (71): 'And Henri Gaudier went to it, / and they killed him, / And killed a good deal of sculpture'.

20 EP, 'The Revolt of Intelligence – VI', 177.

21 EP, 'Cantus Planus', *Little Review* ('Devoted Chiefly to Ezra Pound . . .'), V. 7 (Nov. 1918), 1.

22 Lewis, 'Ezra', 137.

23 Monroe, 'An International Episode', 94; rep. *Little Review*, 34.

24 EP, 'Upon the Harps of Judea', *Little Review* ('Devoted Chiefly to Ezra Pound . . .'), V. 7 (Nov. 1918), 6; also EP, 'Imaginary Letters – IV', 21; also jh, 'The Episode Continued', 36.

25 TSE, 'Introduction', *LE*, xii.

26 Aldington, *Life for Life's Sake*, 199.

27 VW–RF, [18 Nov. 1918], *VWL2*, 296.

28 EP–MM, 1 Feb. 1919, *EPSL*, 148 (210).

29 EP–JJ, 12 Dec. 1918, *EPLJJ*, 148–9.

30 TSE, 'Ezra Pound', 327; rep. 'Ezra Pound by T. S. Eliot', Peter Russell, *Ezra Pound*, 26.

31 CA–JG, 31 Oct. 1962, Joy Grant, 101.

32 VW, 15 Nov. [1918], *VWD1*, 218–19.

33 TSE–HWES, 23 Dec. 1917, *TSEL1*, 242.

34 TSE–CA, 10 Jan. 1916, *TSEL1*, 137; TSE–BR, Monday [17 Jan. 1916], *TSEL1*, 142; TSE–CWE, 29 Mar. 1919, *TSEL1*, 331; TSE–HWE, 14 Sept. 1919, *TSEL1*, 395; TSE–JQ, 9 May 1921, *TSEL1*, 557; also VHE–MH, [16 July 1919], TSEL 381; see also VHE–CWE, 28 June 1917, *TSEL1*, 206;

VHE–CWE, 11 Mar. 1918, *TSEL1*, 255; VHE–TSE, 20 Aug. [1920], *TSEL1*, 493; VHE–CWE, 25 Jan. 1921, *TSEL1*, 537; VHE–MH, [13? 20? Dec. 1921], *TSEL1*, 618.

35 TSE–HWES, 23 Dec. 1917, *TSEL1*, 242.
36 TSE–EH, 3 Nov. 1930, Princeton EHL, b. 1, f. 1.
37 EP–JQ, 18 Dec. 1918, *TSEL1*, xxviii.
38 TSE–CWE, 22 Dec. 1918, *TSEL1*, 310.
39 VHE–CWE, 15 Dec. [1918], *TSEL1*, 309.
40 TSE–JQ, 7 Sept. 1922, *TSEL1*, 750.
41 TSE, 'Directions to my Executors', 25 Nov. 1960, Houghton TSEP.

PART I.

1 EP, 'Harold Monro', *Criterion*, XI. XLV (July 1932), [581–92], 590.

I.

1 VHE, 1 Jan. 1919, Bodleian AVHE/D2, 6r: the poet and novelist Frederic Manning was also present.
2 VHE, 3 Jan. 1919, Bodleian AVHE/D2, 6v.
3 VHE, 9 Jan. 1919, Bodleian AVHE/D2, 8r.
4 18 Crawford Mansions, Crawford Street (Homer Row), Marylebone w1 (now w1h 4jp), where the Eliots lived between [16] Mar. 1916 and [8] Nov. 1920.
5 TSE, 'Thomas Stearns Eliot' (1921), 108; (1935), 219.
6 TSE–GB, 18 Sept. 1930, *TSEL5*, 321.
7 Aldous Huxley, in Spender, 'Remembering Eliot', 59.
8 Boyle, [70].
9 TSE–HWE, 5 Nov. 1916, *TSEL1*, 173.
10 TSE–CWE, 8 Dec. 1918, *TSEL1*, 306.
11 HWES–TLE, 3 Jan. 1919, *TSEL1*, 314.
12 For an account of TSE's 1915 visit see Sencourt, 51–2.
13 TSE–HWE, 6 Sept. 1916, *TSEL1*, 166.
14 VHE, 8 Jan. 1919, Bodleian AVHE/D2, 7v.
15 TSE–CWE, 12 Jan. 1919, *TSEL1*, 316.
16 TSE–HWE, 12 Jan. 1919, *TSEL1*, 316.
17 VHE–CWE, 12 Jan. 1919, *TSEL1*, 317.
18 TSE–CWE, 19 Jan. 1919, *TSEL1*, 317.
19 TSE–HWE, 12 Jan. 1919, *TSEL1*, 316.
20 The service took place on 9 Jan. 1919, at the Unitarian Church of the Messiah, 508 North Garrison Avenue, at the corner of Locust and Garrison Streets, St Louis, Missouri.
21 Henry Ware Eliot Snr was cremated and his ashes laid at Lot 3128, Block 32–3, Bellefontaine Cemetery, St Louis, MO, 10 Jan. 1919; TSE–MWC, 8 Aug. 1930, *TSEL5*, 282–3.

22 TSE visited St Louis on 16 Jan. 1933.

23 TSE–EH, 7 Feb. 1933, Princeton EHL, b. 4, f. 3.

24 Read, 26 Oct. 1918, *Contrary Experience*, 139; Lewis, 'The War Baby', 14–41; Barry had two children with Lewis, who said 'I have no children, though some, I believe, are attributed to me. I have work to do.' (Grigson, 786.)

25 Iris Barry, 'Ocean', 'Flirtation', 'Cauchemar', 'Nightfall', *Poetry and Drama*, II. 8 (Dec. 1914), 356–7.

26 EP–ISC, 27 July 1916, *EPSL*, 90–1 (141–2).

27 EP–HM, [n.d. 1916], Chicago, in Fogelman, 200n.; in the event, HM took eight poems for *Poetry* (Chicago), VIII. 4 (July 1916), 187–90, while EP published six in *Little Review*, IV. 4 (Aug. 1917), 17–19; the same issue carried a single sentence review by EP of TSE's *POO*: 'The book-buyer can not do better.' (EP, 'List of Books', 11.)

28 EP–ISC, 27 July 1916, *EPSL*, 91 (142).

29 EP–ISC, 31 Jan. 1917, Buffalo, Box 741, f. 42.

30 Tea party at Serafina Astafieva's new Russian Dancing Academy on the King's Road, 18 Feb. 1917, which would inspire TSE's portrait of Astafieva as 'Grishkin' of 'friendly bust' and 'pnueumatic bliss' in 'Whispers of Immortality'.

31 The New China Restaurant was at 107 Regent Street (Muirhead, 20); EP–ISC, 14 Feb. 1917, Buffalo, b. 741, f. 49.

32 Meyers, 'New Light on Iris Barry', 287.

33 Glinert, 404.

34 Iris Barry, 165.

35 Hartley, 47.

36 TSE–JQ, 6 Jan. 1919, *TSEL1*, 315.

37 TSE–JQ, 8 Sept. 1918, *TSEL1*, 283.

38 EP, 'In Explication', 8; rep. 'Henry James', *Instigations*, 109.

39 Mencken, 143.

40 TSE–JQ, 6 Jan. 1919, *TSEL1*, 315.

41 TSE–JHW, 21 Apr. 1919, *TSEL1*, 338–9.

42 TSE, *FPV*, 23.

43 TSE recorded in Empson, 'The Style of the Master', 35.

44 TSE–CWE, 19 Jan. 1919, *TSEL1*, 318.

45 TSE–JQ, 26 Jan. 1919, *TSEL1*, 319.

46 EP–HLP, 25 Mar. 1919, *EPLP*, 438.

47 TSE–HWE, 27 Feb. 1919, *TSEL1*, 324.

48 EP–JQ, postmark 9 Mar. 1915, *EPLQ*, 20.

49 EP–JQ, postmark 11 Aug. 1915, *EPLQ*, 31, 37.

50 TSE, ['biographical note'], TSE–AFD, 5 Nov. 1945; see 'An Autobiographical Sketch', *The Poems of T. S. Eliot*, 2, xi; 'Autobiographical summary', *The Complete Prose of T. S. Eliot*, 6, 698–9.

51 TSE, 'Portrait of a Lady', *Others*, I. 3 (Sept. 1915), 35–40; reprinted in *Others: An Anthology of the New Verse* (ed. Alfred Kreymborg), New York: Alfred Knopf, [25 Mar.] 1916, the first appearance in book form in the US of TSE's poetry.

52 TSE, 'Poems: 'Preludes [I–IV]', 'Rhapsody of a Windy Night', *Blast*, 2 (July 1915), 48–51.

53 TSE, 'The Love Song of J. Alfred Prufrock', *Poetry* (Chicago), VI. 3 (June 1915), 130–5; EP–HM, 10 Apr. 1915, *EPSL*, 57 (101).

54 EP–JQ, 11 Apr. 1917, Berg JQP; Gallup, *T. S. Eliot and Ezra Pound*, 8.

55 Arthur Waugh, 226.

56 Evelyn Waugh, *A Handful of Dust*, London: Chapman and Hall, 1934; *Brideshead Revisited*, London: Chapman and Hall, 1945; *Unconditional Surrender*, London: Chapman and Hall, 1961.

57 Unsigned, *Times Literary Supplement*, 805 (21 June 1917), 299; unsigned, *Literary World*, LXXXIII (5 July 1917), 107.

58 EP, 'T. S. Eliot' (1917), 264–71; rep. *Instigations*, 196–202.

59 EP, 'Drunken Helots and Mr Eliot', 72–4.

60 TSE, *Dante*, 8.

61 TSE, 'Matthew Arnold (March 3, 1933)', *UPUC*, 118–19.

62 TSE, [A speech by T. S. Eliot] (27 Apr. 1960), Transcripts of annual dinner speeches, Royal Academy of Arts, RAA/SEC/25/5/11; see 'Royal Academy Speech (1960)', *The Poems of T. S. Eliot*, 1, 1227; 'Speech at the Royal Academy of Arts dinner', *The Complete Prose of T. S. Eliot*, 8, 392–3.

63 TSE, [A speech by T. S. Eliot] (27 Apr. 1960).

64 TSE, 'The Love Song of J. Alfred Prufrock', *Poetry* (Chicago), VI. 3 (June 1915), 130–5.

65 Spender, 'Remembering Eliot', 42.

66 EP, 'T. S. Eliot' (1917), 271; rep. *Instigations*, 202.

67 VHE–HWE, 1 June 1916, *TSEL1*, 153.

68 VHE–MH, Tuesday [Dec? 1917], *TSEL1*, 239.

69 VHE–CWE, 28 June 1917, *TSEL1*, 207.

70 Osbert Sitwell, 'T. S. Eliot', Texas OSC, b. 14, f. 1, b. 24, f. 1; *TSEL1*, 334n.

71 TSE–HWE, 6 Apr. 1919, *TSEL1*, 334.

72 TSE, 'Eeldrop and Appleplex – I', 7–8.

73 Lewis, 'Note on Tyros', 2.

74 TSE–WL, 26 Sept. 1923, Cornell; *WLL*, 135; *TSEL2*, 223; TSE told John Quinn they were 'crude stuff' (TSE–JQ, 9 July 1919, *TSEL1*, 373; EP–JQ, 1 Apr. 1917, Berg JQP.

75 Lewis, *Self Condemned*, 6.

76 EP–WCW, 11 Sept. 1920, *EPSL*, 158 (223).

77 EP–DS, 3 Mar. 1914, *EPLS*, 314–15.

78 DS–EP, 9 Mar. [1914], *EPLS*, 321; Lewis, *Blasting and Bombardiering*, 277.

79 Lewis, *Self Condemned*, 6.

80 EP–HLP, 10 Jan. 1919, *EPLP*, 432–3.

81 Aldington, *Life for Life's Sake*, 122.

82 EP, '"Tarr", by Wyndham Lewis', 35 (rep. *Instigations*, 215); EP 'Books Current', 161–3 (rep. *Instigations*, 205); EP, 'T. S. Eliot' (1917), 271 (rep. *Instigations*, 202).

83 EP–HLP, 10 Jan. 1919, *EPLP*, 433; VHE, 10 Jan. 1919, Bodleian AVHE/D2, 8r.

84 EP–IWP, 23 Jan. 1919, *EPLP*, 434.

85 TSE, 'A Note on Ezra Pound', 3.

86 Virginia Woolf, 25 Jan. 1915, *VWD1*, 28; also VW–MLD, 22 Feb. [1915], *VWL2*, 59.

87 Leonard Woolf, *Beginning Again*, 234.

88 *How to Print* (rev. edn), London: Model Printing Press Co., 1902, 60pp; an advertisement from the Company at the time encourages prospective buyers to 'Send for our Illustrated Pamphlet "HOW TO PRINT", containing an abridged history of the Art of Printing, Instructions in Printing, Catalogue of Type, &c. Post free, 7d.'; it carries the banner, 'Everyone his own printer' and states that the machine 'Can be worked by a child of 10'; see also Lee, 815n9.

89 The Excelsior Printers' Supply Company took over the Model Printing Press Company based in neighbouring 16/20 Farringdon Avenue after it became insolvent in 1906. When Excelsior registered as a limited company in 1916 it continued to manufacture 'Model' presses built on the previous company's design in Walthamstow by Peter Hooker. It seems reasonable to suppose that they sold this as their own-brand entry-level machine, and may have done so to Leonard and Virginia Woolf in 1917. The bill, recorded by Leonard, came to £19. 5s. 5d.

90 VW–VB, 26 Apr. [1917], *VWL2*, 150.

91 VW–MLD, 22 Feb. [1915], *VWL2*, 60.

92 When the Press moved to Tavistock Square in 1924, the Woolfs would transfer their machinery setting to that building's basement, locating their printing press in a former scullery and their offices in the kitchen, and where a ramshackle lavatory was stocked with galley proofs to use as toilet paper; Lehmann, 10.

93 Virginia Woolf, 9 Jan. 1924, *VWD2*, 283.

94 LW–TSE, 19 Oct. 1918, *TSEL1*, 285.

95 Virginia Woolf, 15 Nov. 1918, *VWD2*, 219; TSE–VW, 29 Jan. 1919, *TSEL1*, 320.

96 Keynes, *Economic Consequences of Peace*, 32–3.

97 TSE–HWE, 27 Feb. 1919, *TSEL1*, 323.

98 VHE–CWE, 7 Apr. 1919, *TSEL1*, 335–6.

99 TSE–HWE, 27 Feb. 1919, *TSEL1*, 322.

100 TSE–CWE, 27 Feb. 1919, *TSEL1*, 324.

101 EP–HLP, 6 Nov. 1918, *EPLP*, 425.

102 EP–IWP, 15 Nov. 1918, *EPLP*, 425.

103 EP, 'De Gourmont', 2.

104 TSE–HWE, 27 Feb. 1919, *TSEL1*, 324.

105 VHE, 3 Mar. 1919, Bodleian AVHE/D2, 21r; 2 Mar. 1919, Bodleian AVHE/D2, 21r.

106 TSE–CWE, 27 Feb. [1919], *TSEL1*, 324.

107 TSE–HWE, 27 Feb. 1927, *TSEL1*, 324.

108 TSE–MWC, 8 Aug. 1930, *TSEL5*, 281.

109 Charlotte Eliot, *William Greenleaf Eliot*, 38.

110 Sencourt, 15.

111 Teasdale, 'Sunset: St Louis', *Flame and Shadow*, 22–3.

112 Tennessee Williams; see also Cuoco, 196.

113 Angelou, 57.

114 Whitman, 135.

115 Steffens, 'Tweed Days in St Louis', *McClure's Magazine* (Oct. 1902), collected in Steffens, 31–2, 38, 64, 103; Henry Ziegenhein was city mayor 1897–1901 responsible for the quip about the street lighting.

116 Scott Joplin moved into St Louis in 1901 from Sedalia, MO, a few hours along Interstate 70.

117 MM–CG, 1962, in Cuoco, 239.

118 Twain, *Life on the Mississippi*, 254–5.

119 TSE, 'Introduction', in Twain, *The Adventures of Huckleberry Finn*, xii.

120 Twain, *Life on the Mississippi*, 302; TSE, 'Introduction', in Twain, *Adventures of Huckleberry Finn*, xii.

121 TSE–MWC, 8 Aug. 1930, *TSEL5*, 281.

122 Henry Ware Eliot Snr, 'A Brief Autobiography', Washington WGEPP, fo. 3.

123 TSE–MWC, 8 Aug. 1930, *TSEL5*, 282.

124 Stravinsky, 92–3.

125 Henry Ware Eliot Snr, 'A Brief Autobiography', Washington WGEPP, fo. 44.

126 WGE in Charlotte Eliot, *William Greenleaf Eliot*, 131.

127 WGE–THB, 13 Jan. 1849, in Charlotte Eliot, *William Greenleaf Eliot*, 144.

128 TSE, 'American Literature and the American Language', *ALAL*, 3–24; rep. *CC*, [43–60] 44.

129 Ulysses S. Grant, in Galusha Anderson, 100.

130 EP–HLP, 23 Aug. 1917, *EPLP*, 401–2.

131 TSE–CWE, 11 Apr. 1917, *TSEL1*, 193.

132 Du Bois and Gruening, 219.

133 Du Bois and Gruening, 219; 'Editorial' (unsigned), *Crisis*, 14. 5 (Sept. 1917), 215–16; Garvey, 'Speech by Marcus Garvey, July 8, 1917', *The Marcus Garvey and Universal Negro Improvement Association Papers*, I, 213.

134 'Negroes Leaving East St Louis', *St Louis Argos*, VI. 14 (20 July 1917), 1.

135 TSE, 'Introduction', in Twain, *The Adventures of Huckleberry Finn*, xiii.

136 TSE–CWE, 1 July 1917, *TSEL1*, 208.

137 Du Bois, 'The Forethought', *Souls of the Black Folk*, vii.

138 Du Bois, 'The Souls of the White Folk', *Darkwater*, 51–2.

139 TSE–BR, 26 Mar. 1919, *TSEL1*, 330.

140 TSE–BR, 3 Feb. 1919, *TSEL1*, 320–1.

141 BR–CM, 6 Feb. 1919, McMaster BRA, b. 6.66; also Turcon, 32.

142 VHE–OM, [Dec. 1919], *TSEL1*, 423.

143 TSE–BR, 14 Feb. 1919, *TSEL1*, 322.

144 TSE, 'Ode', *AVP*, 30.

145 The Eliots married on 26 June 1915; their first honeymoon took place at the Lansdowne Hotel, Eastbourne, c.26 June–2 July 1915; the second at a guest-house, 8 Hartingdon Mansions, Eastbourne, c.4–16 Sept. 1915.

146 The honeymoon is dramatised in Michael Hastings' *Tom and Viv*, Act I, Part 1, 61, which may be taken from interviews that Hastings conducted with Maurice Haigh-Wood in 1980; in what may be a blurring of two events, Haigh-Wood also recalled Eliot sleeping in a deckchair in the hallway at Russell's Bury Street flat.

147 BR–OM, 9 Sept. 1915, Texas OMC, b. 25, f. 5.

148 Russell, *Autobiography*, I, 212.

149 Russell, July 1915, *Autobiography*, II, 54; also Morrell, *Ottoline at Garsington*, 57; Aldous Huxley similarly used the word 'vulgar' to describe Vivien, AH–JH, 22 June 1918, *AHL*, 156; Russell lived at 34 Russell Chambers, Bury Street, London WC.

150 Russell, *Autobiography*, II, 19.

151 TSE, 'Mr Apollinax', *POO*, 35–6; *AVP*, 52; *P1920*, 58; the 'veil' was lifted by Louis Untermeyer, 'Irony De Luxe', 381–2.

152 Russell, [*c.*10 Nov. 1915] *Autobiography*, II, 55; BR–OM, 10 Sept. 1915, *TSEL1*, 126n.

153 Spender, *Eliot*, 49–50; Russell, [*c.*10 Nov. 1915] *Autobiography*, II, 56.

154 VHE–ST, 2 Aug. 1915, *TSEL1*, 120.

155 OM–BR, 9 Sept. 1915, *TSEL1*, 126n.

156 Morrell, *Ottoline at Garsington*, 120.

157 BR–OM, Mon. night [Sept. 1916] *Autobiography*, II, 74.

158 VHE–CWE, 22 Oct. 1917, *TSEL1*, 224–7.

159 Russell stayed at Lemon's Farm in 1918 and possibly earlier on the site of Lemon's Croft, Beechwood House, which may be the location described by Constance Malleson in 'Lemons Cottage, Abinger Common, Nr: Dorking', n.d. [*c.*1918], unfinished TS, McMaster LCM, b. 6.74, f. 2.

160 TSE–CWE, 24 Oct. 1917, *TSEL1*, 227.

161 VHE–CWE, 22 Oct. 1917, *TSEL1*, 227.

162 BR–CM, 30 Oct. 1917, McMaster BRA, b. 6.65.

163 BR–CM, 25 Oct. 1917, McMaster BRA, b. 6.65; *BRSL2*, 129n.

164 31 West Street, Marlow, Buckinghamshire; TSE–CWE, 9 June 1918, *TSEL1*, 266.

165 BR–CM, 6 Jan. 1918, in Monk, 516; *TSEL1*, 266n.

166 Russell, 'The German Peace Offer', 1; rep. *Autobiography*, II, 106; Marx and Engels, *Manifest der Kommunistischen Partei*, 5; Marx and Engels, *Manifesto of the Communist Party*, 10.

167 Russell, *Autobiography*, II, 29–30.

168 Malleson, 126–7.

169 Schuchard, *Eliot's Dark Angel*, 124.

170 BR–CM, 27 Nov. 1918, McMaster BRA, b. 6.65.

171 VHE's letter to BR, now lost, is recorded by Constance Malleson: 'I do hope that you aren't very distressed about Mrs Eliot. I really don't know what to say about her letter – except that I'm distressed if *you* are.' (CM–BR, 19 Jan. 1919, McMaster BRA, b. 6.62); in an unpublished typescript in the McMaster archives, Phyllis Urch has annotated the letter with a footnote: 'Mrs Eliot had written Russell saying that she disliked fading intimacies and therefore intended breaking off all friendship with him.' Phyllis Urch (ed.), 'Letters to Bertrand Russell from Constance Malleson 1916–1969', unpublished TS, fo. 309, McMaster, Boxes 6.62–6.63; I am grateful to Sheila Turcon for her transcription; BR–TSE, 19 Mar. 1919, *TSEL1*, 330n.

II.

1 TSE, in Hall, 'T. S. Eliot', 56.
2 TSE–CA, 21 Aug. 1916, *TSEL1*, 158.
3 TSE, 'Bleistein with a Cigar', TS1, Berg TSECP, [Poems].
4 TSE–CCA, 13 Oct. 1927, *TSEL3*, 752; also TSE, 'The Modern Mind', *UPUC*, 130.
5 EP, 'Canto LXXIV', *Cantos*, 458–60 (464–6).
6 Lewis, *et al.*, 'Manifesto [II]', 33.
7 TSE, 'Tradition and the Individual Talent – II', 72.
8 TSE, 'Dante as a "Spiritual Leader"', 441–2.
9 TSE, 'Modern Tendencies in Poetry', 17.
10 Clutton-Brock, 322.
11 TSE, 'Matthew Arnold', *UPUC*, 106.
12 TSE–EHH, 26 Apr. [1911], *TSEL1*, 19.
13 TSE–EHH, 26 July 1914, *TSEL1*, 55; TSE–HWE, 13 June 1917, *TSEL1*, 242;
   TSE–EHH, 23 July 1917, *TSEL1*, 211; also TSE–EHH, 21 Mars [Mar. 1915],
   TSEL1, 100; TSE–EP, 31 Oct. 1917, *TSEL1*, 230; TSE–CWE, 3 July 1920,
   TSEL1 476; TSE–CWE, 9 Aug. 1920, *TSEL1* 488; CWE–TSE: 1 Aug. 1920,
   TSEL1, 482.
14 VHE–MH, 9 Oct. [1917], *TSEL1*, 222.
15 DP–EP, [25 Sept. 1913], *EPLS*, 261.
16 Keynes, 'Einstein', *Collected Works*, 382–4.
17 LS–LW, 20 June 1905, *LSL*, 68.
18 Virginia Woolf, 4 Jan. 1915, *VWD1*, 6.
19 LW–MG, 30 Aug. 1967, *LWL*, 559.
20 Forster, 26.
21 EP–JQ, 27 July 1922, Berg JQP; see also Dardis, 95.
22 JQ–TSE, 26 Feb. 1923, Berg JQP; also *TSEL2*, 71n.
23 TSE–JQ, 12 Mar. 1923, *TSEL2*, 71.
24 TSE–JQ, 28 Sept. 1919, *TSEL1*, 401.
25 EP–HWE, 2 Feb. 1919, *EPLP*, 436.
26 EP, 'A Canticle . . . (Special to H. T. of St Louis)', *Much Ado*, X. 3 (1 Jan. 1920), 1.
27 EP, 'The Death of Vorticism', 45, 48.
28 EP, *GB*, 101.
29 Lewis, 'Enemy of the Stars', 55.
30 TSE–CWE, 29 Mar. 1919, *TSEL1*, 331.
31 JMM–TSE, [*c.* Apr. 1919], *TSEL1*, 340n.
32 TSE–JQ, 25 May 1919, *TSEL1*, 354; Nichols, 'An Ironist', 7.
33 TSE–CWE, 29 Mar. 1919, *TSEL1*, 331.
34 TSE, 'The New Elizabethans and the Old', 134–6.
35 TSE, 'A Romantic Patrician', 265–7; rep. 'A Romantic Aristocrat', *SW*, 22–8.
36 TSE, 'American Literature', 236–7.
37 TSE, 'Kipling Redivivus', 297–8.
38 TSE, 'Criticism in England', 456–7.
39 TSE, 'The Post Georgians', 171–2.
40 TSE–RL, 1 June 1961, Houghton.

41 Fitts, 5–6.

42 RL–SHS, 14 Nov. 1961, *RLL*, 392; Dryden, 'The Preface', *Ovid's Epistles*, [xvii].

43 EP–FES, 8 July 1922, *EPSL*, 178 (246).

44 EP–ARO [? Apr. 1919], *EPSL*, 150 (212).

45 EP, *SR*, vi.

46 EP–WHDR, 18 Mar. 1935, *EPSL*, 271 (360).

47 TSE, 'Introduction', in EP, *SP1928*, 19.

48 RL–EP, 20 Mar. [1954], *RLL*, 222.

49 EP, quoted in HM–WCW, 7 Apr. 1913, Monroe, *A Poet's Life*, 272.

50 EP: 'Obviously crowned lovers at unknown doors, / Night dogs, the marks of a
    drunken scurry,' *QPA*, 35; *cf.* Propertius, *Elegies* (trans. G. P. Goold), Loeb Clas-
    sical Library, Cambridge, MA: Harvard University Press, 1990, 228–9, Book III,
    ll. 47–8: 'quippe coronatos alienum ad limen amantes / nocturnaeque canes ebria
    signa fugae' (228); 'For you will sing of garlanded lovers at another's threshold
    and the tipsy tokens of midnight escapade' (229).

51 W. G. Hale, 52–5.

52 EP–HM, 14 Apr. 1919, Chicago HMP.

53 EP–WGH, [n.d.] unsent, enclosure in EP–MS, 19 Mar. 1920, May Sinclair
    Papers, Ms. Coll. 184, Kislak; see also Carpenter, 340.

54 Dryden, 'The Preface', *Ovid's Epistles*, [xx], [xxii].

55 EP–ARO, [? Apr. 1919], *EPSL*, 149 (211).

56 EP–HWP, [? Apr. 1919], *EPLP*, 440.

57 EP, 'Sestina: Altaforte', *English Review*, II. 3 (June 1909), 419–20; EP–HM, 14
    Apr. 1919, Harriet Monroe Papers, Chicago.

58 EP–ARO, [? Apr.] 1919, *EPSL*, 148–9 (211).

59 EP–FES, 8–9 July 1922, *EPSL*, 178 (245).

60 EP–HM, Dec. 1918, Chicago HMP; EP, 'Small Magazines', 691.

61 Monroe, 'Miss Monroe *Re* Ezra Pound', 86–7.

62 HM–EP, 1 Nov. 1919, Beinecke EPP, b. 35, f. 1459.

63 WCW, 'Belly Music', *Others* (July 1919), 27–31.

64 Ellen Williams, 296.

65 EP–HWP, [?Apr. 1919], *EPLP*, 439–40.

66 TSE, 'The Method of Mr Pound', 1065–6.

67 EP–JQ, 25 Oct. 1919, *EPSL*, 151 (213).

68 EP–JJ, 30 May 1919, *EPLJJ*, 156.

69 EP–HLP, [?Apr. 1919], *EPLP*, 441.

70 WL–JQ, 3 Sept. 1919, *WLL*, 111.

71 Margaret Anderson, 'Announcement', 5.

72 EP–MA, [29 Nov. 1916], *EPLLR*, 4.

73 jh, 'Lost', 5.

74 EP–MA, [26 Jan. 1917], *EPLLR*, 6.

75 EP–SN, '24 Maggio, Anno XIV' [24 May 1936], *EPLN*, 215.

76 TSE, 'Poems' ('Le directeur', 'Mélange adultère de tout', 'Lune de miel', 'The
    Hippopotamus'), *Little Review*, IV, 3 (July 1917), 8–11; 'Four Poems' ('Sweeney
    among the Nightingales', 'Whispers of Immortality', 'Dans le restaurant', 'Mr

Eliot's Morning Service'), *Little Review*, V, 5 (Sept. 1918), 10–14; W. B. Yeats, 'The Wild Swans at Coole', *Little Review*, IV. 2 (June 1917), 9.

77 Weaver, 6.

78 EP–JQ, 26 Feb. 1916, *EPLQ*, 60.

79 EP–ACH, *EPLH*, 5 May 1916, 138.

80 Marsden, 'The Lean Kind', 1; 'Views and Comments', 44.

81 TSE–EP, 9 July 1919, *TSEL1*, 375.

82 EP–JQ, 26 Aug. 1915, *EPLQ*, 41; TSE–HWES, 31 Oct. 1917, *TSEL1*, 228.

83 EP–JQ, 26 Feb. 1916, *EPLQ*, 60.

84 EP–ACH, Mar. 1913, *EPSL*, 14 (49).

85 AH–JH, 3 Aug. 1917, *AHL*, 132.

86 TSE–JQ, 9 July 1919, *TSEL1*, 375.

87 EP–JQ, 31 Oct. 1920, *EPLQ*, 198.

88 West, 86.

89 EP, 'In a Station of the Metro', *Poetry* (Chicago), II. 1 (Apr. 1913), 1–12; rep. *New Freewoman*, I. 5 (15 Aug. 1913), 87–8; rep. in 'How I Began', 707.

90 EP, 'Vorticism', 465–7; an earlier version appeared in 'How I Began', 707.

91 EP, 'Δώρια' [Doria], *Poetry Review*, I. 2 (Feb. 1912), [77–81] 78, rep. *Ripostes*, 42; EP 'And the days are not full enough', retrospective epigraph for *Lustra*, in *P1926*, 80.

92 TSE–BP, [Apr. 1919?], *TSEL1*, 332–3.

93 EP–HLP, 30 May 1919, *EPLP*, 442; I am grateful to Tim Dee for the suggestion that what Pound may have observed were long-eared owls, and either ospreys or short-toed eagles.

94 EP–HLP, 30 May 1919, *EPLP*, 441.

95 EP, 'Pastiche. The Regional. II', 156.

96 EP–HLP, 30 May 1919, *EPLP*, 441–2.

97 EP–JJ, 10 June 1919, *EPLJJ*, 157–8.

98 EP–JJ, 10 June 1919, *EPLJJ*, 159; JJ–HSW, 20 July 1919, *EPLJJ*, 160.

99 DP–HHS, 'Friday', postmarked 25 July [1919], Ezra Pound Collection, Hamilton (n.n., ID 216).

100 EP, 'Provincia Deserta', *Poetry* (Chicago), V. 6 (Mar. 1915), [251–4], 252, rep. *L1916*, 62, *L1917*, 67; EP, 'Excideuil', 'Walking Tour' [1912] Beinecke EPP, [Series IV. Manuscripts], b. 103, f. 4328–30, *WTSF*, 26.

101 EP, *SR*, 5.

102 EP, 'Canto VIII', as 'Malatesta Cantos. (Cantos IX to XII of a Long Poem) – IX', *Criterion*, I. 4 (July 1923), 366, rep. as 'Canto VIII', *Cantos*, 32 (32).

103 EP, *SR*, 35.

104 EP, 'Troubadours', 426, rep. *PD1918*, 166.

105 EP, *SR*, 30.

106 EP, *SR*, 27–8.

107 EP, *SR*, 13.

108 EP, 'Arnaut Daniel: II', *Instigations*, 296.

109 EP–HLP, 30 May 1919, *EPLP*, 441.

110 EP–OS, 29 May 1919, Ezra Pound Collection, Hamilton (60, ID 230).

111 EP, 'Arnaut Daniel: Razo', 44–9; rep. *Instigations*, 286–95.

112 Leonard Woolf, *Beginning Again*, 241, 243; Virginia Woolf, 19 Mar. 1919, *VWD2*, 257.

113 Virginia Woolf, 10 Apr. 1919, *VWD1*, 262.

114 VHE–CWE, 7 Apr. 1919, *TSEL1*, 336.

115 Virginia Woolf, 2 Apr. 1919, *VWD2*, 261.

116 Lee, 440.

117 VW–DJCG, 17 Apr. 1919, *VWL2*, 350.

118 VHE–MH, [8 May? 1919], *TSEL1*, 344–5.

119 VHE–MH, [10 May 1919], *TSEL1*, 346.

120 TSE–EHH, 17 June 1919, *TSEL1*, 364.

121 VE–VD, [8? May. 1919], *VWL2*, 355.

122 TSE–JR, 1 June 1919, *TSEL1*, 358.

123 TSE, in Hall, 'T. S. Eliot', 56.

124 EP–HM, 30 Sept. 1914, *EPSL*, 40.

125 TSE, 'Whispers of Immortality', TS[1] (ribbon), Berg TSECP, [Poems]: TSE's
comments to EP given in footer; EP's suggested re-title given on recto, with
perceived influences ('Webster / Don[n]e / Gautier') given on verso.

126 TSE, 'Try This on Your Piano' / 'Whispers of Immortality', TS[3] (ribbon), Berg
TSECP, [Poems]; EP, undated [1917], TS accompanying TSE, 'Try This on
Your Piano' / 'Whispers of Immortality', TS[3] (carbon), Berg TSECP, [Poems];
see *IMH*, 371; *The Poems of T. S. Eliot*, 2, 351.

127 EP, undated [1917], TS accompanying TSE, 'Try This on Your Piano' / 'Whispers of Immortality', TS[3] (carbon), Berg TSECP, [Poems].

128 TSE, 'Mr Eliot's Sunday Morning Service', TS, Berg TSECP, [Poems].

129 TSE, introducing 'Sweeney Among the Nightingales', Harvard, 13 May 1947.

130 TSE, 'Sweeney Among the Nightingales', *P1919*, [5].

131 KM–JMM, 19 Nov. 1919, *KMCL3*, 104.

132 TSE, 'Sweeney Among the Nightingales', *P1919*, [5]; see Julius, 86–7.

133 EP's cancellation in TSE, ['A Cooking Egg'], TS (ribbon), Berg TSECP, [Poems].

134 TSE–EP, 31 Oct. 1917, *TSEL1*, 230; see also AH–JH, 13 Dec. [1917], *AHL*,
141; LS–CB, 31 Dec. 1917, *LSL*, 380.

135 TSE, 'A Cooking Egg', *Coterie*, 1 (May Day 1919), 44, rep. rev. *AVP*, 24; *P1920*,
22.

136 Aldington, *Life for Life's Sake*, 204.

137 'London's explosion was at Silvertown', *New York Times* (29 Jan. 1917), 3.

138 Lewis, 'Long Live the Vortex!', 8; see Julius, 136–9.

139 TSE, *ICS*, 71.

140 Clutton-Brock, 322.

141 Virginia Woolf, 14 June 1920, *VWD1*, 281.

142 Unsigned [Leonard Woolf], 'Is This Poetry?', *Athenaeum*, 4651 (20 June 1919),
491.

143 VW–TSE, 28 July [1920], *VWL2*, 437.

144 [Leonard Woolf], 'Is This Poetry?', 491.

145 TSE–JR, 17 May 1919, *TSEL1*, 350.

146 William Carlos Williams, 'Prologue', 76–7; rep. *Kora in Hell*, 26.

147 WCW–HG, 5 May 1944, *WCWSL*, 224–6.

148 JQ–TSE, 26 Aug. 1919, *TSEL1*, 389–92.

149 LS–DC, 14 May 1919, *LSL*, 433.

150 TSE–LS, 1 June 1919, *TSEL1*, 357.

151 LS–MH, 15 May 1919, *LSL*, 434.

152 TSE–LS, 1 June 1919, *LSL*, 446–7, *TSEL1*, 357, Holroyd, II, 775.

153 VHE–OM, [4? June 1919], *TSEL1*, 359.

154 Morrell, *Ottoline at Garsington*, 96.

155 VHE–OM, [4? June] 1919, *TSEL1*, 359.

156 Bertrand Russell, *Satan in the Suburbs*, 39; BR–RS, 28 May 1968, Robert Bell, 113.

157 TSE–OM, 14 Mar. 1933, *TSEL6*, 562–3.

158 TSE–MH, Tuesday [10 June 1919], *TSEL1*, 360–1.

159 TSE–EHH, 5 Sept. 1916, *TSEL1*, 161.

160 Tennyson, *Becket*, 111.

161 Bede, IV. 13, 226.

162 Henry of Huntingdon, II. 17, 18.

163 TSE–CA, 21 Aug. 1916, *TSEL1*, 159.

164 See Mary Hutchinson, 'T. S. Eliot', unpublished biographical sketch, Texas MHP, b. 1, f. 2, fos. [1]–4.

165 VB–VW, 'Sunday' [22 Aug. 1915], *VBSL*, 186.

166 KM–OM, [?24 June 1917], *KMCL1*, 312.

167 Virginia Woolf, 16 May 1919, *VWD1*, 272.

168 VHE–MH, Tuesday [17 June 1919], Texas MHP, b. 12, f. 7.

169 VHE–MH, Thursday [19 June 1919], Texas MHP, b. 12, f. 7.

170 VHE, 21 June 1919, Bodleian AVHE/D2, 48v.

171 TSE–OM, Monday [23 June 1919], *TSEL1*, 365.

172 VHE–MH, Tuesday [17 June 1919], Texas MHP, b. 12, f. 7.

173 VHE–MH, 'Tuesday' [17 June 1919], Texas MHP, b. 12, f. 7.

174 VHE–MH, 'Wednesday' [2 July 1919], Texas MHP, b. 12, f. 7.

175 TSE–CWE, 29 June 1919, *TSEL1*, 367; TSE–MH, Tuesday [1 July 1919], *TSEL1*, 369.

176 TSE–CWE, 29 June 1919, *TSEL1*, 367.

177 VHE, 9 July 1919, Bodleian AVHE/D2, 53r.

178 LS–MH, 17 July 1919, *LSL*, 448.

179 VHE, 10 July 1919, Bodleian AVHE/D2, 53v.

III.

1 EP, 'Pastiche. The Regional. VIII[–IX] [*i.e.* VII]', 284.

2 EP, 'Canto LXXXVII', *Cantos*, 588 (594).

3 EP, 'Canto LXXX', *Cantos*, 530 (536); EP, 'Canto LXXIV', *Cantos*, 439 (445): 'yet say this to the Possum: a bang, not a whimper, / To build the city of Dioce whose terraces are the colour of stars.'

4 EP, 'Canto XLVIII', *Cantos*, 243 (243).

5 EP, 'Canto LXXVI', *Cantos*, 466 (472).

6 EP, 'Pastiche. The Regional. VIII[–IX] [*i.e.* VII]', 284.

7 EP, 'Canto XXIII', *Cantos*, 109 (109).

8 TSE, 'Burbank with a Baedeker: Bleistein with a Cigar', 'Sweeney Erect', *Art & Letters*, II. 3 (Summer 1919), 103–5; EP, 'Homage to Sextus Propertius, I', *New Age*, XXV. 8 (19 June 1919), 132–3, rep. from *Poetry* (Chicago), XIII. 6 (Mar. 1919).

9 TSE–JR, 1 June 1919, *TSEL1*, 358.

10 EP, The Fourth Canto: proof, Beinecke EPP, [Series IV. Manuscripts,] b. 70, f. 3123.

11 Yeats, *The Cutting of an Agate*.

12 TSE, 'A Foreign Mind', 552–3.

13 TSE–JQ, 9 July 1919; *TSEL1*, 375.

14 Yeats, *The Wild Swans at Coole*.

15 EP, 'Canto LXXXIII', *Yale Poetry Review*, 6 (1947), 3–8; *Cantos*, 547–8 (553–64).

16 TSE, 'Lecture Notes for English 26: English Literature from 1890 to the Present Day', Houghton TSEAP; see *The Complete Prose of T. S. Eliot*, 4, 774.

17 See Foster, 616n.; Wilde, 153–4, 159–62; Yeats, 'Seanchan the Bard and the King of the Cats', *Irish Fairy Tales*, 141–50; TSE, 'The Poetry of W. B. Yeats', 115–27, rep. as 'Yeats', *OPP*, 252–62.

18 TSE, 'Lecture Notes for English 26: English Literature from 1890 to the Present Day', Houghton TSEAP; see *The Complete Prose of T. S. Eliot*, 4, 774.

19 TSE, 'The Poetry of W. B. Yeats', 115–27; 'A Commentary', *Criterion*, XIV (July 1935), 610–13.

20 Yeats, 'Introduction', *Oxford Book of Modern Verse*, xxi–ii; Yeats assigned more pages to Edith Sitwell (19pp) than he did to Eliot (13pp) and Pound (7pp).

21 VHE–OM, [Dec. 1919], *TSEL1*, 423.

22 TSE, *ASG*, 55.

23 Hardy, 'Going and Staying', *London Mercury*, I. 1 (Nov. 1919), rep. *Late Lyrics and Earlier*, 26.

24 Hardy, Literary Notebook II, Dorset County Museum, see Gittings, 193.

25 Hardy, in Graves, *Goodbye to All That*, 378–9.

26 Gunn, 90n.

27 TSE, 'The Education of Taste', 61.

28 TSE, 'Whether Rostand Had Something about Him', 665–6.

29 *Antony and Cleopatra*, 2.2.198, 2.2.242.

30 King George V, letter, *Daily Express* (19 July 1919).

31 Aldington, *Life for Life's Sake*, 206.

32 Virginia Woolf, 19 July 1919, *VWD1*, 292.

33 Virginia Woolf, 20 July 1919, *VWD1*, 294.

34 TSE–CWE, 9 Aug. 1920, *TSEL1*, 488.

35 VHE–MH, 16 July 1919, *TSEL1*, 381.

36 VHE, 20 July 1919, Bodleian AVHE/D2, 56r.

37 VHE–MH, Wednesday, [25? Aug. 1920; i.e. 27 Aug. 1919], *TSEL1*, 495.

38 RA–TSE, 18 July 1919, *RAAL*, 50.

39 RA–AL, 11 Oct. 1919, *RAAL*, 53.

40 Aldington, 'London (May 1915)', *Images* (1910–1915), London: Poetry Book-shop, 1915, 30; rep. *Images Old and New*, Boston, MA: Four Seas, 1916, 47; rep. *Images*, London: Egoist, 1919, [39–40] 40.

41 RA–TSE, 18 July 1919, *RAAL*, 50.

42 RA–TSE, 18 July 1919, *RAAL*, 50.

43 TSE, 'Reflections on Contemporary Poetry [IV]', 39.

44 Aldington, *Life for Life's Sake*, 201.

45 Aldington, *Life for Life's Sake*, 96, 94 (also 100).

46 Aldington, *Life for Life's Sake*, 95; *Ezra Pound and T. S. Eliot*, 11.

47 EP–IWP, 16 July 1919, *EPLP*, 443; *EPLP*, 451n.; EP–HLP, 13 July 1919, *EPLP*, 442.

48 EP, 'Homage to Sextus Propertius, II [i.e. IV]', 'Difference to Opinion' (1919), *New Age*, XXV. 10 (3 July 1919), 170; 'Homage to Sextus Propertius, IV [i.e. VIII]', *New Age*, XXV. 14 (31 July 1919), 231.

49 EP–IWP, 16 July 1919, *EPLP*, 443.

50 EP–IWP, 21 July 1919, *EPLP*, 444.

51 The premiere of *The Three-Cornered Hat* took place at the Alhambra Theatre, London, 22 July 1919, commissioned by Sergei Diaghilev of the Ballets Russes and choreographed by Léonide Massine, to music by Manuel de Falla.

52 Nancy Cunard, 22 July 1919, Texas NCD2.

53 TSE–HWE, 2 July 1919, *TSEL1*, 377–8.

54 TSE–MH, 9 July 1919, *TSEL1*, 387.

55 TSE–JQ, 9 July 1919, *TSEL1*, 373–5.

56 TSE–MH, Wednesday [9? July? 1919], *TSEL1*, 371.

57 Nancy Cunard, 10 July 1919, Texas NCD2.

58 Nancy Cunard, 14 July 1919, Texas NCD2.

59 TSE–SS, 16 July 1919, *TSEL1*, 380.

60 TSE–MH, [11? July 1919]. *TSEL1*, 377.

61 TSE, Eliot Estate HWE, [2].

62 TSE–JR, 9 July 1919, *TSEL1*, 372.

63 TSE, 'The Method of Mr Pound', 1065–6.

64 TSE, 'Gerontion', TS[1], Berg TSECP, [Poems].

65 TSE–MH, [9? July? 1919], *TSEL1*, 372.

66 JJ–HSW, 1 May 1935, *JJL*, 366.

67 Joyce, 'Ulysses, II', 43–4; rep. 'Ulysses – Episode II', 14.

68 TSE, 'On a Recent Piece of Criticism', 90–4.

69 Benson, 142; TSE, 'Gerontion' TS1–2, Berg TSECP, [Poems], rep. *P1920*.

70 TSE, 'Philip Massinger', 325–6.

71 TSE–MH, 6 Aug. 1919, *TSEL1*, 387.

72 VHE, 9 Aug. 1919, Bodleian AVHE/D2, 61r.

73 TSE–CWE, 3 Sept. 1919, *TSEL1*, 392–3; Baedeker, *Northern France*, xvii.

74 TSE–CWE, 14 Oct. 1919, *TSEL1*, 406–7.

75 EP, *SR*, 44–5.

76 EP, 'Sestina: Altaforte', *English Review*, II. 3 (June 1909), 419–20; rep. *Exulta-tions*, 14–15.

77 EP, 'Provincia Deserta', *Poetry* (Chicago), V. 6 (Mar. 1915), [251–4], 253, rep. *L1916*, 62, *L1917*, 67–8.

78 EP–JQ, 6 Aug. 1919, *TSEL1*, 384n.

79 TSE–CWE, 14 Oct. 1919, *TSEL1*, 406–7.

80 EP, 'Canto IX' ['Malatesta Canto'], TS1, Beinecke EPP, b. 70, f. 3138–43 (see also Moody, 'Bel Esprit and the Malatesta Cantos', 81); rev. as 'Malatesta Cantos. (Cantos IX to XII of a Long Poem)', *Criterion*, I. 4 (July 1923), 363–84.

81 DS–HHS, 15 Aug. 1919, Ezra Pound Collection, Hamilton (n.n., ID 218).

82 TSE–LS, [25? Aug. 1919], *TSEL1*, 388.

83 EP–HLP/IWP, 22 Aug. 1919, *EPLP*, 446.

84 EP, 'Périgueux', Beinecke EPP, b. 103, f. 4328–30; *WTSF*, 19.

85 EP, 'Poems: Provincia Deserta', *Poetry* (Chicago), V. 6 (Mar. 1915) [251–7] 252; rep. *L1916*, 62, *L1917*, 62.

86 Du Pin, 65.

87 St Hilary of Poitiers, 374.

88 TSE–CWE, 2 Oct. 1919, *TSEL1*, 404.

89 TSE, 'A Sceptical Patrician', 361.

90 TSE, 'War-paint and Feathers', 1036.

91 TSE, 'Tarr', 106.

92 TSE, 'Tradition and the Individual Talent [I]', 55.

93 EP, 'And So shu stirred in the sea', *PC2015*, 27.

94 EP, 'a quando?', *PC2015*, 129.

95 EP, 'Mr Eliot's Looseness', 95–6.

96 EP, 'Canto LXXIV', *PC1948*, 5 (10); *Cantos*, 441 (447).

97 Kenner, *The Pound Era*, 336.

98 EP, 'Canto CVII', *Cantos*, 772 (778).

99 EP, 'from Canto LXXX', *Poetry* (Chicago), LXVIII. 6 (Sept. 1946), [310–21] 313; *Cantos*, 524 (530).

100 Eliot and Pound visited the chateau between 12–15 or 20–21 August, most likely the first of these dates since there is no evidence that Eliot returned to Excideuil after Les Eyzies on 19/20 August and from where he probably went straight on to rendezvous with the Pounds at Brive.

101 EP, 'Canto XXIX', *Hound & Horn*, III. 3 (Apr./June 1930), [358–75] 366; rep. *DTC* (London 1933, 150).

102 EP, 'Another Canto' [Canto XII], 'Two Cantos', *Transatlantic Review*, I. 1 (Jan. 1924), [10–14], 13; rep. *Cantos*, 53 (53); 'Canto XXI', *Cantos*, 98 (98); 'Canto LXXVIII', *Cantos*, 481 (487).

103 EP, 'One Canto' [Canto XIII], 'Two Cantos', *Transatlantic Review*, I. 1 (Jan. 1924), [10–14] 11; rep. 'Canto XIII', *Cantos*, 59 (59).

104 EP, 'Canto XXIX', *Hound & Horn*, III. 3 (Apr./June 1930), [358–75] 366; rep. *DTC* (London 1933, 150).

105 TSE, *Dante*, 60.

106 TSE, *Dante*, 61.

107 TSE, *LG*, 13.

108 TSE, 'Literature and the Modern World', 13.

109 TSE–WFS, 9 Aug. 1930, *TSEL5*, 287.
110 TSE–JQ, 26 Apr. 1923, *TSEL2*, 116.
111 TSE, *Dante*, 33.
112 TSE, 'Literature and the Modern World', 11–15.
113 Baedeker, *Southern France*, 89; EP–HLP/IWP, 22 Aug. 1919, *EPLP*, 446.
114 EP, 'Brive', Beinecke EPP, b. 103, f. 4328–30; *WTSF*, 35.
115 EP–HLP, 3 Sept. [1919], *EPLP*, 447.
116 TSE–LS, [25? Aug. 1919], *TSEL1*, 388.
117 VHE–MH, 31 Aug. 1919, *TSEL1*, 392n.
118 VHE–MH, Wednesday, [25? Aug. 1920; i.e. 27 Aug. 1919], *TSEL1*, 496.
119 VHE, 31 Aug. 1919, Bodleian AVHE/D2, 66v.

IV.

1 TSE–SS, Sunday [14 Sept. 1919], *TSEL1*, 396; also TSE–CWE, 3 Sept. 1919, *TSEL1*, 392.
2 'This Seattle Dog Wears Flu Mask', *Seattle Star* (2 Nov. 1918), 2; subsequent stories included 'Pasadena "Flu" Mask Law Wide In Scope; Dogs, Cars Don 'Em', *Los Angeles Evening Express* (20 Jan. 1919), 13; 'Umpires had it Soft – These Players Couldn't Bite 'Em', *Richmond Palladium and Sun-Telegram* (Indiana) (10 Feb. 1919), 12.
3 TSE–CWE, 3 Sept. 1919, *TSEL1*, 393.
4 VHE, 2–5 Sept. 1919, Bodleian AVHE/D2, 67r–v.
5 VHE, 6 Sept. 1919, Bodleian AVHE/D2, 68r.
6 VHE, 7 Sept. 1919, Bodleian AVHE/D2, 68r.
7 VHE, 9–12 Sept. 1919, Bodleian AVHE/D2, 68v–69v.
8 VHE–MH, [?20 Sept. 1919], Texas MHP, b. 12, f. 7.
9 TSE–HWE, 7 Jan. 1947, *TSEL8*, 439.
10 VHE–MH, Friday night [3 Oct. 1919], *TSEL1*, 406.
11 TSE–EHH, 5 Sept. 1916, *TSEL1*, 161–2.
12 VHE, 20 Sept. 1919, Bodleian AVHE/D2, 71v.
13 VHE–MH, 26 Sept. 1919, *TSEL1*, 398–9.
14 VHE–MH, [3 Oct. 1919], *TSEL1*, 406.
15 VHE–MH, 29 Oct. [1919], *TSEL1*, 410–11.
16 VHE–MH, Wednesday eve [?1 Oct. 1919], Texas MHP, b. 12, f. 7.
17 VHE, 29 Sept. 1919, Bodleian AVHE/D2, 73v; VHE–MH, 3 Oct. 1919, *TSEL1*, 405–6.
18 VHE–MH, n.d. [?17–22 Oct. 1919], Texas MHP, b. 12, f. 7.
19 VHE–MH, 12 May [1926], Texas MHP, b. 12, f. 7.
20 VHE–MII, 2 June 1931, *TSEL5*, 581.
21 TSE–EP [12? Sept. 1919], *TSEL1*, 395.
22 EP–HLP, 15 Sept. 1919, *EPLP*, 448.
23 TSE, 'Gerontion', TS[1], Berg TSECP, [Poems]; Dante, 'Canto XXXIII', *The Divine Comedy, 1. The Inferno*, 121–3, 378 (tr. 379).
24 *Blast*, 1 (20 June 1914), 21.

25 TSE–SOF, 21 Feb. 1944.
26 TSE–JQ, 28 Sept. 1919, *TSEL1*, 400.
27 Aldington, *Life for Life's Sake*, 269.
28 TSE, 'Ben Jonson', 637–8.
29 TSE–CWE, 2 Oct. 1919, *TSEL1*, 404.
30 TSE, 'Tradition and the Individual Talent [I]', *Egoist*, VI. 4 (Sept. 1919), [54–5] 55.
31 TSE, 'Hamlet and His Problems, *Athenaeum*, 4665 (26 Sept. 1919), 940–1.
32 EP, 'Pastiche: The Regional – I', 124.
33 EP, 'Pastiche: The Regional – XVIII', 48.
34 EP, 'The Revolt of Intelligence – VI', 176.
35 EP–JQ, 25 Oct. 1919, *EPSL*, 151 (213).
36 Ovid, *Ars amatoria* (II. 165), *Art of Love. Cosmetics. Remedies for Love. Ibis.
    Walnut-tree. Sea Fishing. Consolation* (trans. J. H. Mozley; rev. G. P. Goold),
    Loeb Classical Library 232, Cambridge, MA: Harvard University Press, 1929,
    77; EP–HLP, [late Oct. 1919], *EPLP*, 450.
37 EP–JQ, 2 Dec. 1918, Berg JQP; *VETC*, 17.
38 TSE, 'The Method of Mr Pound', 1065–6.
39 EP–JQ, 25 Oct. 1919, *EPSL*, 151 (213).
40 EP, 'Mr Pound and his Poetry', 1132.
41 TSE, 'Mr Pound and his Poetry', 1163.
42 TSE, 'The Method of Mr Pound', 1065–6.
43 TSE, 'A Note on Ezra Pound', 3–9.
44 KM–JMM, 28 Oct. 1919, *KMCL3*, 54.
45 KM–JMM, 4 Nov. 1919, *KMCL3*, 70.
46 EP, 'Pastiche. The Regional. VIII[–IX] [i.e. VII]', 284.
47 EP, '[Canto] IV', *PC2015*, 21.
48 EP, *FC*; rep. *Dial*, LXVIII. 6 (June 1920), 689–92; *P1918*, 73–7.
49 EP, 'Three Cantos: The Fifth Canto', *Dial*, LXXI. 2 (Aug. 1921), 198–201;
    P1918, 78–82.
50 EP–HLP, [? Apr. 1919], *EPLP*, 441; EP–JQ, 6 Oct. 1921, Berg JQP.
51 EP, 'Pastiche. The Regional. VIII[–IX] [i.e. VII]', 284.
52 TSE's lecture at Central Buildings, Westminster, 28 Oct. 1919, was part of the
    ALS's series 'Modern Tendencies in Art', and was published as 'Modern Ten-
    dencies in Poetry', 9–18.
53 *EPLP*, 451n.
54 EP–IWP, [2 Nov. 1919], *EPLP*, 451.
55 TSE–JQ, 5 Nov. 1919, *TSEL1*, 413.
56 VHE, 5 Nov. 1919, Bodleian AVHE/D2, 82v.
57 VHE, 8 Nov. 1919, Bodleian AVHE/D2, 83v.
58 'The First Two-Minute Silence in London', *Manchester Guardian* (12 Nov. 1919).
59 VHE, 17, 21, 23 Nov. 1919, Bodleian AVHE/D2, 86r, 87r, 87v.
60 Don D. Moore, 314.
61 Archer, 126.
62 TSE, 'Syllabus for a Tutorial Class in Modern English Literature'.
63 TSE, '*The Duchess of Malfi* at the Lyric', 37.

64 Valerie Eliot, 'The Waste Land', broadcast script, 4.
65 TSE, 'The Death of the Duchess', TS1, Berg TSECP, Waste Land.
66 Webster, *The Duchess of Malfi*, IV. 2.
67 Eliot may have intended the penultimate line, 'I am steward of her revenue', to have been voiced by the Duchess's conduit in the play, Antonio.
68 TSE, 'Tradition and the Individual Talent – II', 72–3.
69 Eliot had initially described sulphurous acid as the chemical product of this reaction, but was corrected in letters beginning in 1926; see TSE–PWR, 9 July 1926, *TSEL3*, 212–13 and 212n.
70 JK–RW, 27 Oct. 1918, *JKL*, 157.
71 'Preface', Wordsworth and Coleridge, xiv.
72 TSE, 'The Preacher as Artist', 1252–3.
73 Warren, 'The Fire-Sermon', Mahā-Vagga (I. 211), 352.
74 TSE, 'The Preacher as Artist', 1252–3.
75 EP–HLP, 13 Dec. 1919, *EPLP*, 455.
76 EP–JQ, 24 Nov. 1919, *EPLQ*, 179.
77 TSE–EP, postmark 2 Dec. 1919, *TSEL1*, 421.
78 EP, 'Three Cantos: The Seventh Canto', *Dial*, LXXI. 2 (Aug. 1921), [198–208] 205; rep. *P1921*, 87–90.
79 TSE–EP, [27 May? 1923], *TSEL2*, 141.
80 'These fragments you have shelved (shored)': EP, 'Canto IX' ['Malatesta Canto'], TS1, Beinecke EPP, b. 70, f. 3138–43; rev. excluding the line as 'Malatesta Cantos. (Cantos IX to XII of a Long Poem)', *Criterion*, I. 4 (July 1923), 363–84; rev. including the line as 'Canto VIII', *DTC*, 32; *Cantos*, 28 (28); TSE would insist on removal of the line for the *Criterion* printing.
81 EP, 'Ode pour l'élection de son sépulchre', *HSM*, 9; rep. 'H. S. Mauberly' [sic], *Dial*, LXIX. 3 (Sept. 1920), [283–7] 283.
82 EP–FES, 8–9 July [1922], *EPSL*, 181 (249).
83 EP–ST, 7 June 1920, *EPLD*, 39l ; 'Hugh Selwyn Mauberley', MS [TS] and galleys, Texas JRP, b. 9. f. 5.
84 Laughlin, 173.
85 EP–JL, in preparing *DRL*, 1958; *PT*, 1308n., *SPT*, 301.
86 imitator: Scourfield, 1033; 'Vocat asetus in umbram' ('The heat calls us to the shade'): Nemesianus, *Ecologae* IV. 38, Duff and Duff, 480 (481).
87 EP–TEC, cited in Thomas E. Connolly, 59.
88 EP, 'II', *HSM*, 10.
89 EP, 'II', *HSM*, 13.
90 EP–FMF, 30 July 1920, *EPLF*, 35–7; EP, 'Envoi (1919)', *HSM*, 21.
91 EP–FES, 8–9 July [1922], *EPSL*, 180 (248); EP–FES, 8–9 July [1922], *EPSL*, 181 (249).
92 TSE–CWE, 6 Jan. 1920, *TSEL1*, 427.
93 VHE, 30–1 Dec. 1919, Bodleian AVHE/D2, 96v–97r.
94 TSE–SS, 12 Jan. 1920, *TSEL1*, 430; VHE, 28 Dec. 1919, Bodleian AVHE/D2, 96r.
95 VHE, 31 Dec. 1919, Bodleian AVHE/D2, 97r.

96 TSE–CWE, [Postmark 18 Dec. 1919], *TSEL 1*, 424.

97 TSE–CWE, 6 Jan. 1920, *TSEL 1*, 427–8.

98 '8 Killed, 66 Injured in Vienna Red Riot', *New York Times*, 17 June 1919, 19.

99 TSE, 'To the Editor of the *Transatlantic Review*', 95–6.

100 TSE–CWE, 6 Jan. 1920, *TSEL 1*, 428.

101 TSE, 'John Maynard Keynes', 47–8.

102 Keynes, *The Economic Consequences of the Peace*, 278.

103 Keynes, *The Economic Consequences of the Peace*, 100, 278.

104 Percy Bysshe Shelley, *Prometheus Unbound*, Act I, ll. 619–20 (Keynes follows the 1820 text *ruin* which was a corruption of the MS *ravin*, restored by Mary Shelley in her 1839 edition based on PBS's own errata); Keynes, *The Economic Consequences of the Peace*, 278.

105 EP–JQ, 21 Feb. 1920, *EPLQ*, 185.

106 EP, 'Canto XXII', *Dial*, LXXXIV.2 (Feb. 1928), 113–17; *Cantos*, 102 (102).

107 EP–HLP, 22 Feb. 1920, *EPLP*, 461; EP–JQ, 21 Feb. 1920, *EPLQ*, 185.

108 EP, 'C. H. Douglas, Etc.', 16.

109 Douglas, 6; EP, *VC*, 13.

110 EP, 'Canto Thirty-Eight', *New English Weekly*, III. 24 (28 Sept. 1933), 564–5; *Cantos*, 190 (190): 'and the power to purchase can never / (under the present system) catch up with / prices at large'.

111 EP, 'Canto LXXI' (trans. Giovanni Cecchetti), *PN*, 5 (Jan. 1955), 9–10; *Cantos*, 416 (416).

112 See EP, *WMF*.

113 EP, *SC*, 21; also EP, *ABC*, 46.

114 EP, 'The Revolt of Intelligence – VIII', 287–8.

115 EP, 'Imaginary Letters – IV', 21; jh, 'The Episode Continued', 36.

116 EP, 'Upon the Harps of Judea', *Little Review* ('Devoted Chiefly to Ezra Pound . . .'), V. 7 (Nov. 1918), 6.

117 Lewis, *Blasting and Bombardiering*, 273–4.

118 EP–MA, [29 June 1917], *EPLLR*, 85.

119 EP, 'The Revolt of Intelligence – V', 153.

120 Edward Hicks Parry, 11 Feb. 1973, Kislak CGC, b. 2, f. 51; the letter forms a discussion on 'suburban prejudice' in Carpenter 19–25 and Moody, *Ezra Pound*, I, 10–11, and also Wilhelm, *The American Roots of Ezra Pound*, 73–5.

121 TSE–SS, 12 Jan. 1920, *TSEL 1*, 431.

122 VHE–CWE, 5 Jan. 1920, *TSEL 1*, 426.

123 TSE–CWE, 6 Jan. 1920, *TSEL 1*, 428.

124 TSE to MT, 2 Apr. 1951, Bodleian MT.

125 TSE–MWC, 8 Aug. 1930, *TSEL 5*, 281.

126 TSE–EH, 7 Sept. 1931, Princeton EHL, b. 2, f. 2; TSE, 'The Influence of Landscape upon the Poet', *Dædalus*, 89 (Spring 1960), 420– 2.

127 The Eliots moved in 1905 to 4446 Westminster Place, although TSE lived there for only a year.

128 Stravinsky, 92–3.

129 Matthews, 11–12.

130 TSE–EH, 6 Nov. 1944, Princeton EHL, b. 12, f. 5.
131 TSE, 'Address' (at the Centennial Celebration of the Mary Institute), *From Mary to You: Centennial, 1859–1959*, St Louis, MO: Mary Institute, 1959, 133–6; 'In the rank ailanthus of the April dooryard': TSE, *DS*, 7.
132 TSE–EH, 7 Sept. 1931, Princeton EHL, b. 2, f. 2; TSE, *Animula*.
133 TSE–EH, 7 Sept. 1931, Princeton EHL, b. 2, f. 2.
134 Mary Trevelyan [Nov. 1949], Bodleian MT.
135 Charlotte C. Eliot, *William Greenleaf Eliot*, 101.
136 TSE, *ALAL*, rep. *TCC*, 44.
137 Henry Ware Eliot Snr, 'A Brief Autobiography', Washington WGEPP, fo. 46.
138 'The Clayworking Plants of St Louis', *Brick* (May 1904), 235–9.
139 Henry Ware Eliot Snr, 'A Brief Autobiography', Washington WGEPP, fo. 25.
140 Morley, 110–33; rep. Tate, 108–9.
141 Empson, 'My God, man, there's bears on it', 198.
142 In an historical review of the Missouri justice system, St Louis County Circuit Judge Noah Weinstein credited the 1901 Probation Act as 'the first positive legislation in Missouri in the general direction of our modern conception of juvenile court legislation'; Noah Weinstein, 'The Juvenile Court Concept in Missouri: Its Historical Development – The Need for New Legislation', *Washington University Law Quarterly*, Feb. 1957, [17–56] 24.
143 Charlotte C. Eliot, *William Greenleaf Eliot*, v; 'Ring, Easter Bells!', *Easter Songs*, 9.
144 Charlotte C. Eliot, *Savonarola*; Matthews, 9.
145 TSE–CWE, 27 Aug. 1927, *TSEL3*, 648.
146 TSE–EH, 27 Jan. 1931, Princeton EHL, b. 1, f. 2.
147 TSE–EH, 2 Apr. 1935; TSE–EH, 19 Feb. 1936, Princeton EHL, b. 6, f. 6.
148 TSE–MWC, 8 Aug. 1930, *TSEL5*, 281.
149 TSE–EH, 6 Nov. 1944, Princeton EHL, b. 12, f. 5.
150 TSE, 'Why Mr Russell Is a Christian', 177–9.
151 Janet Adam Smith, 1060.
152 TSE, 'The Jim Jum Bears are at their Tricks', TS[1], Houghton TSEMP, see *The Poems of T. S. Eliot*, 1, 302–3.
153 The Eliots summered at The Downs between 1896 and 1909; earlier visits had them based at Hawthorne Inn, Wonson's Point.
154 Matthews, 17–19.
155 TSE, 'Publisher's Preface', vii–viii.
156 EP–HLP, 14 Jan. 1920, *EPLP*, 457.
157 Colin, 211.
158 EP–HLP, 21 Jan. 1920, *EPLP*, 460.
159 EP, 'Londres et Ses Environs', 2–3; 'London and its Environs' (trans. Henderson), 278.
160 EP, 'A Letter from London', 1.
161 FSF–HSW, 21 Feb. 1917, Texas FSFC.
162 Virginia Woolf, 31 Jan. 1920, *VWD2*, 15.
163 J. C. Squire, 'The Man Who Wrote Free Verse', 128.

164 Virginia Woolf, 21 Apr. 1918, *VWD1*, 143; in the 1918 general election, Squire gained 641 votes, 11 per cent, and lost his £150 candidate's deposit.

165 EP–WCW, 11 Sept. 1920, *EPSL*, 158.

166 Virginia Woolf, 12 Mar. 1924, *VWD2*, 297.

167 J. C. Squire, 'A House', Marsh, 25.

168 Virginia Woolf, 3 Jan. 1918, *VWD1*, 95; TSE–RA, 3 Oct. 1921, *TSEL1*, 587; TSE–JQ, 25 Jan. 1920, *TSEL1*, 435.

169 TSE, 'Verse Pleasant and Unpleasant', 43.

170 EP–WCW, 11 Sept. 1920, *EPSL*, 158 (222).

171 Graves with Riding, 118–19 (112–13).

172 Aldington, *Life for Life's Sake*, 100; Ford Madox Hueffer [Ford], 'Impressionism – Some Speculations', 182.

173 TSE–JCS, 10 Sept. 1919, *TSEL1*, 394.

174 EP–ST, 24 Mar. 1920, *EPLD*, 15; EP, 'Historical Survey', 39.

175 TSE–ST, 30 June 1918, *TSEL1*, 269.

176 EP–ST, 25 Jan. 1920, *EPLD*, 11.

177 E. E. Cummings, 'Seven Poems', *Dial*, LXVIII. 1 (Jan. 1920), 22–6.

178 TSE–CWE, 26 Jan. 1920, *TSEL1*, 436; EP–HW, 30 June 1920, *EPSL*, 154 (218).

179 TSE–CWE, 15 Feb. 1920, *TSEL1*, 444.

180 TSE–CWE, 21 [i.e. 22] Feb. 1920, *TSEL1*, 446.

181 TSE–JQ, 25 Jan. 1920, *TSEL1*, 435.

182 Arbuthnot, 38.

183 Untermeyer, 'Ezra Pound – Proseur', 83–4.

184 Aiken, 'A Pointless Pointillist', 306–7.

185 Carnevali, 211–21.

186 Nichols, 'Poetry and Mr Pound', 6.

187 Nichols, *The Assault and Other War Poems from 'Ardours and Endurances'*, xi, 56, 58, 70.

188 T. Sturge Moore, 32.

189 Nichols, 'Invocation', *Invocation and Peace Celebration, Hymn for the British Peoples*, 5.

190 Lewis, 'Mr Ezra Pound', 5.

191 EP, 'Propertius and Mr Pound', 5.

192 Nichols, 'Mr Nichols writes', 5.

193 Fletcher, 23–5.

194 Aldington, 'A Book for Literary Philosophers', 215.

195 Sinclair, 658–8.

196 EP–BB, c.May 1935, Beinecke EPP, b. 6, f. 280.

197 EP, *HSM*, 22, 26, 27.

198 EP–FMF, 30 July 1920, *EPLF*, 35.

199 EP–MEB, 23 Feb. 1934, *EPSL*, 254 (339).

200 TSE–JQ, 26 Mar. 1920, *TSEL1*, 459.

201 EP–TH, [?Feb. 1921], in Hutchins, 'Ezra Pound and Thomas Hardy', 91–104; EP–HLP, 1 Sept. 1920, *EPLP*, 470; WBY–EP, 23 Aug. 1920, ALS Yale (I am grateful to John Kelly for this letter).

202 TSE, 'Introduction', *SP1928*, vii, xv, xxiv; *SP1949*, 7, 13, 20.
203 EP–FES, 8–9 July [1922], *EPSL*, 181 (249).
204 EP, 'Hugh Selwyn Mauberley', *P1926*, 185.
205 EP–HM, Jan. 1931, *EPSL*, 230 (310).
206 EP–FES, 8–9 July [1922], *EPSL*, 180 (248).

V.

1 TSE–JR, 1 Feb. 1920, *TSEL1*, 438.
2 Robert Nichols, 'An Ironist', 7.
3 Beare, 30.
4 TSE–DG, 21 Feb. 1936, Gallup, *T. S. Eliot*, 26.
5 Dante, 'Canto XXVI', ll. 145–8, *The Divine Comedy: The Purgatorio*, 330.
6 TSE–JR, 3 Oct. 1919, *TSEL1*, 405.
7 'Therefore I do implore you': Longfellow, *The Divine Comedy of Dante Alighieri*, 170n.; 'I pray you': Binyon, 326; 'To you we pray': Jordan, 349; 'Now I beg you': Kirkpatrick, 588n.
8 Dante, 'Canto XXVI', ll. 145–8, *The Divine Comedy: The Purgatorio*, 331.
9 TSE, *Dante*, 34.
10 TSE–DG, 21 Feb. 1936, Gallup, *T. S. Eliot*, 26.
11 Cloud, 72, 74.
12 TSE–VW, 12 Nov. 1935, *TSEL7*, 827.
13 TSE–JR, 3 Oct. 1919, *TSEL1*, 405.
14 John Middleton Murry, 239.
15 Unsigned, 'A New Byronism', *Times Literary Supplement*, 948 (18 Mar. 1920), 184.
16 Nichols, 'An Ironist', 7.
17 TSE–HWE, 15 Feb. 1920, *TSEL1*, 441.
18 Deutsch, 'The Season for Song', *New York Evening Post* (29 May 1920), Berg BDP, b. 10, f. 3 (date uncertain; given in Brooker, 40).
19 Beare, 30–1.
20 TSE–HWE, 15 Feb. 1920, *TSEL1*, 441.
21 HWE–CWE, 27 Apr. 1920, *TSEL1*, 467n.
22 Arthur Waugh, 386; also William Carlos Williams, 'Prologue', 76–8; Leonard Woolf (unsigned), 'Is This Poetry?', 491.
23 John Middleton Murry, 239; unsigned, 'A New Byronism', *Times Literary Supplement*, 948 (18 Mar. 1920), 184; unsigned, 'Some Recent Verse', *OT*, 4 Apr. 1920, 7; Untermeyer, 'Irony de Luxe', 381–2.
24 Morgan, 135–6.
25 Cyril Connolly, 8.
26 Deutsch, 'The Season for Song', *New York Evening Post* (29 May 1920), Berg BDP, b. 10, f. 3 (date uncertain; given in Brooker, 40).
27 'W. S. B.', Braithwaite, 6.
28 Strobel, 157–9.
29 Cummings, 'T. S. Eliot', 781–4.

30 ST–EP, 8 Mar. 1920, *EPLD*, 13.
31 EP–ST, 24 Mar. 1920, *EPLD*, 15.
32 EP–ST, 24 Mar. 1920, *EPLD*, 17.
33 EP–TEL, 20 Apr. 1920, Bodleian PTEL, f. 1214.
34 EP–ST, 24 Mar. 1920, *EPLD*, 15.
35 EP, 'Dramedy', 315, the first in a weekly theatre column.
36 Virginia Woolf, 18 June 1919, *VWD1*, 282; 6 Mar. 1920, *VWD2*, 22; 20 Apr. 1920, *VWD2*, 32.
37 Virginia Woolf, 24 Apr. 1920, *VWD2*, 33.
38 Unsigned, 'Paris: A Poem by Hope Mirrlees', *Times Literary Supplement* (6 May 1920), 286.
39 Unsigned, 'List of New Books', *Athenaeum*, 4699 (21 May 1920), 686.
40 Cocteau (tr. Hugo), 43–96.
41 TSE, 'The Post Georgians', 171–2.
42 TSE had reviewed *Cinnamon and Angelica: A Play* by John Middleton Murry, in the previous week's issue of the *Athenaeum*: 'The Poetic Drama', 635–6.
43 Unsigned, 'Paris A Poem by Hope Mirrlees', *Times Literary Supplement* (6 May 1920), 286.
44 Hope Mirrlees, 'The Mysterious Mr Eliot', BBC TV, 3 Jan. 1971, also 'Eliot's Life', *The Listener*, 85. 2181 (14 Jan. 1971), 50.
45 Virginia Woolf, 23 Nov. 1920, *VWD2*, 75.
46 Virginia Woolf, 18 May 1920, *VWD2*, 40.
47 KM–SW, [late Mar. 1921], *KMCL4*, 201–2.
48 KM–SS & VS, [10 May 1919], *KMCL4*, 9.
49 KM–SS & VS, 14 May 1920, *KMCL4*, 11.
50 EP–HLP, 20 May 1920, *EPLP*, 464; TSE–JQ, 10 May 1029, *TSEL1*, 464.
51 EP–ST, 1 June 1920, *EPLD*, 34.
52 James Joyce, 'A Memory of the Players in a Mirror at Midnight', *Dial*, LXIX. 1 (July 1920), 26.
53 ST–EP, 30 Apr. 1920, *EPLD*, 25.
54 EP–HLP, 20 May 1920, *EPLP*, 464.
55 ST–EP, 30 Apr. 1920, *EPLD*, 26.
56 W. C. Blum [James Sibley Watson], 422–3.
57 EP–ST, 14 Oct. 1920, *EPLD*, 164.
58 EP, 'Historical Survey', 41.
59 TSE–EP, 30 May 1920, *TSEL1*, 466.
60 EP–HLP, postmark 29 Apr. 1920, *EPLP*, 463.
61 EP–MMC, n.d. [*c.*1910], Kislak CGC, Kislak EPRC.
62 EP, 'Prologomena' [sic], 72; rep. *PD1918*, 103.
63 EP–JJ, 13 May 1920, *EPLJJ*, 165.
64 JJ–FB, 3 Jan. 1920, *JJL*, 134; *EPLJJ*, 163.
65 EP–HLP, 6 Apr. 1917, *EPLP*, 393; EP–HLP, 23 Aug. 1917, *EPLP*, 404.
66 EP, 'Books Current – Joyce', 161–3; 'In the Vortex: Joyce', *Instigations*, 207.
67 JJ–EP, [31 May 1920], *EPLJJ*, 167–9, as 5 June 1920, *JJL2*, 467–9.
68 EP–JJ, 2 June 1920, *EPLJJ*, 170–1.

69 JJ–HSW, 12 July 1920, *JLL*, 142.

70 EP, 'Canto LXXVI', *Sewanee Review*, LV. 1 (Jan./Mar. 1947), [56–67] 60; *Cantos*, 470 (476).

71 EP–JQ, 19 June 1920, *EPLJJ*, 178.

72 EP, 'Indiscretions; or, Une Revue de Deux Mondes – I', 56–7; rep. *PD1958*, 3–6.

73 *EPLP*, 465n.

74 EP, 'Indiscretions . . . VII', 156; *PD1958*, 29.

75 EP, 'Indiscretions . . . IX', 188; *PD1958*, 37.

76 Now 314 2nd Avenue S, Hailey, Idaho 83333.

77 EP, 'Indiscretions . . . III', 92, *PD1958*, 15–16.

78 Longfellow, 'Mezzo Cammin', *Selected Poems*, 356.

79 EP, 'Indiscretions . . . X', 204; *PD1958*, 41.

80 EP–DS, [25 Mar. 1914], *EPLS*, 337.

81 William Carlos Williams, *Autobiography*, 64.

82 Homer Pound, interviewed by Mary Dixon Thayer, Philadelphia *Evening Bulletin*, 20 Feb. 1928; see Norman, *Ezra Pound*, 15.

83 EP–TH, 31 Mar. 1921, see Davie, 46.

84 EP, 'Indiscretions . . . II', 77; *PD1958*, 8.

85 EP, 'Indiscretions . . . XII', 236; *PD1958*, 46.

86 EP, 'Canto 97', *HR*, IX. 3 (Autumn 1956), 387–98; *Cantos*, 687 (693).

87 EP in Hall, 'Ezra Pound', 40.

88 Wilhelm, *The American Roots of Ezra Pound*, 82.

89 Carlyle, 'Lecture I: The Hero as Divinity. Odin. Paganism: Scandinavian Mythology', *On Heroes, Hero-Worship, and the Heroic in History*, 2; 'Lecture III: The Hero as Poet. Dante: Shakespeare', 70.

90 Carlyle, 'Lecture II: The Hero as Prophet. Mahomet: Islam', 41.

91 Carlyle, 'Lecture III', 70; 'Lecture II', 41.

92 EP, 'Und Drang', *Canzoni*, 43.

93 EP, 'The New Sculpture', 67–8.

94 Ford Madox Ford, *Return to Yesterday*, 392 (409).

95 EP, 'De Gourmont', 7.

96 EP–JQ, 11 Aug. 1915, *EPLQ*, 37.

97 See EP–Amy Lowell, 26 Nov. 1913; EP–MA, [Sept.] 1917; EP–MA, [?Jan.] 1918; EP–WCW, 11 Sept. 1920; EP–Robert McAlmon, 2 Feb. 1934; all *EPSL*.

98 EP–JQ, 8 Nov. 1920, *EPLQ*, 203.

99 EP–JQ, 4 June 1920, Berg JQP; *TWL Facs*, xviii.

100 TSE–EP, [June? 1920], *TSEL1*, 468.

101 Unsigned, 'Hugh Selwyn Mauberley', *Times Literary Supplement*, 963 (1 July 1920), 427.

102 EP, 'The Fourth Canto', *Dial* (LXVIII. 6 (June 1920), 689–92, rep. from *FC*.

103 Edmund Wilson, 'Mr Pound's Patchwork', 323–3.

104 Muir, 'Recent Verse' (1922), 288.

105 Bodenheim, 87–91.

106 Leavis, 105, 115.

107 EP–R. P. Blackmur, 30 Nov. 1924, *EPSL*, 190 (261), *TSEL1*, 951.

108 EP, *SP1928*.

109 Muir, 'Recent Verse' (1920), 186–7.

110 TSE, 'The Perfect Critic, II', 102–4.

111 Sylvia Beach, 23.

112 Sylvia Beach, 35.

113 Sylvia Beach, 38.

114 Lewis, *Blasting and Bombardiering*, 294.

115 AH–BGB, 30 July 1920, *AHL*, 189; Virginia Woolf, 16 May 1919, *VWD2*, 272.

116 TSE–SS, [4 Aug. 1920], *TSEL1*, 483.

117 VHE–TSE, [16? Aug. 1920], *TSEL1*, 492.

118 VHE–TSE, 20 Aug. [1920], *TSEL1*, 493.

119 Lewis, *Blasting and Bombardiering*, 269–70.

120 Lewis, *Blasting and Bombardiering*, 290–5.

121 TSE–CWE, 20 Sept. 1920, *TSEL1*, 501.

122 TSE–HWE, 13 Sept. 1920, *TSEL1*, 499.

123 TSE–CWE, 20 Sept. 1920, *TSEL1*, 501–2.

124 Chesterton, 'Elegy in a Country Churchyard', *The Ballad of St Barbara*, 13.

125 TSE, 'G. K. Chesterton', 785.

126 EP–JQ, 21 Aug. 1917, *EPSL*, 116 (170).

127 TSE, 'In Memory of Henry James', 1–2; 'Observations', 69–70.

128 Chesterton, *Alarms and Discursions*, 57.

129 EP, 'The New Cake of Soap', *Blast*, 1 (20 June 1914), 49.

130 Chesterton, 'The New Jerusalem. The Crusade. Chapter XI', *Daily Telegraph* (10 Sept. 1920), *The New Jerusalem*, 219.

131 EP, 'The Crusades', 12.

132 TSE, 'G. K. Chesterton', 785.

133 TSE, *ASG*, 20.

134 TSE–JVH, 10 May 1940, *TSEL9*, 518.

135 TSE–IB, 9 Feb. 1952, *TSEL9*, xxx, 914n.

136 TSE–PG (*Fact Magazine*), 28 Apr. 1964, *TSEL9*, 518n.

137 EP, 'Mr Eliot's Quandaries', 558–9; TSE, 'Mr T. S. Eliot's Quandaries', 662–3.

138 TSE, 'The Use of Poetry', 215; rep. *TSEL7*, 232.

139 TSE–CWE, 6 Oct. 1920, *TSEL1*, 506.

140 VHE–OM, 27 Mar. [1926], *TSEL3*, 114.

141 VHE–EK, [21? Dec. 1925], *TSEL2*, 804.

142 VHE–MH, 29 Sept. 1928, *TSEL4*, 265–6.

143 TSE, *TWLF*, 127.

144 WS–TSE, 26 May 1932, *TSEL6*, 216n.

145 William Carlos Williams, *Autobiography*, 158.

146 WCW–DI, 9 Aug. 1948, *WCWSL*, 267.

147 William Carlos Williams, *I Wanted to Write a Poem* (30) 42; 'Prologue', 79, rep. *Kora in Hell*, 28.

148 William Carlos Williams, 'Prologue', 77, rep. *Kora in Hell*, 26; *I Wanted to Write a Poem* (30) 42.

149 EP–WCW, 11 Sept. 1920 [second letter], *EPSL*, 160 (225).
150 EP–WCW, 10 Nov. 1917, *EPSL*, 124 (181); *EPLW*, 31; quoted in Williams, *Kora in Hell*, 14.
151 William Carlos Williams, 'Prologue', 79; rep. *Kora in Hell*, 28.
152 EP–WCW, 11 Sept. 1920, *EPSL*, 156, 157 (221).
153 EP–WCW, 11 Sept. 1920, *EPSL*, 158 (223).
154 EP, 'Indiscretions . . . VII', 157.
155 TSE, 'The Possibility of a Poetic Drama', 441–7.
156 Aldington, 'The Sacred Wood', 191–3.
157 Frazer, I, 1–108.
158 TSE, *SW*, ii; Petronius, 'LXXXIII', *Satyricon* (tr. Heseltine), 167.
159 TSE, *SW*, vii; TSE would dedicate *P1925*, 5: 'To / Henry Ware Eliot / 1843–1919'.
160 *Tace et fac*, Be silent and act.
161 Marianne Moore, 'The Sacred Wood', 336–9.
162 Unsigned, 'Poetry and Criticism', *Times Literary Supplement*, 985 (2 Dec. 1920), 795.
163 Lynd, 359–60.
164 Aiken, 'The Scientific Critic', 593–4.
165 MacCarthy, 418–20.
166 EP, 'Londres et ses Environs', 2–3; 'London and its Environs' (tr. Henderson), 278.
167 TSE–PMJ, 19 Jan. 1927, *TSEL3*, 384.
168 L. W. [Leonard Woolf], 'Back to Aristotle', 834–5.
169 EP–ST, 25–6 Nov. 1920, *EPLD*, 184–5.
170 EP, 'The Island of Paris: A Letter, October 1920', 515–18.
171 EP–JQ [postmark 8 Nov. 1920], *EPLQ*, 201–3.
172 EP–JQ [postmark 8 Nov. 1920], *EPLQ*, 204.
173 'British Music Society: An "Unknown" Programme', *Times* (15 June 1921), 8.
174 Carson, 45.
175 EP ('William Atheling'), 'Music' (25 Nov. 1920), 44.
176 EP, 'The Island of Paris: A Letter, October 1920', 518.
177 EP, 'Vers Libre and Arnold Dolmetsch', 90–1; *PD1918*, 151; EP–FMF, 30 July 1920, *EPLF*, 35.
178 EP ('William Atheling'), 'Music' (23 Dec. 1920), 92–3.
179 Dunbar, 'Sympathy', *Lyrics of the Hearthside*, 40.
180 EP, 'The Island of Paris: A Letter, November 1920', 635–6.
181 VHE–MEB, 17 Nov. 1920, *TSEL1*, 520.
182 TSE–WL, 15 Oct. 1920, *TSEL1*, 508.
183 TSE–CWE, 3 Apr. 1921, *TSEL1*, 547.
184 *Daily Mail* (11 Nov. 1920).
185 'The Unknown Solider', produced by Simon Hollis and Jo Wheeler, BBC World Service, 6 Nov. 2018; Michael Gavaghan, *The Story of the British Unknown Warrior*, Preston: M&L Publications, 1995, Fourth Edition, Le Touquet, 2006.
186 TSE–CWE, 2 Dec. 1920, *TSEL1*, 524.

187 Pension Casaubon, 151 *bis* rue Saint-Jacques, Hôtel Louis XIV, Porte et Balcon,
Vème arr., Latin Quarter; JV–TSE, 5 Feb. 1912, *TSEL1*, 31; TSE–EHH, 26
Apr. [1911], *TSEL1*, 16; see also Hargrove, 10, 31–2, and George Watson, 468.
188 TSE, 6 Dec. 1920, *TSEL1*, 525.
189 TSE–CWE, 22 Jan. 1921, *TSEL1*, 536.
190 EP–HLP, 27 Dec. 1920, *EPLP*, 477.
191 EP, *FTS*; EP–HLP, 13 Dec. 1920, *EPLP*, 475.
192 A. R. Orage ('R.H.C.'), 'Readers and Writers', 126.
193 TSE–EP, [22 Dec. 1920], *TSEL1*, 527.
194 TSE–EP, [22 Dec. 1920], *TSEL1*, 528.
195 EP–HLP, 27 Dec. 1920, *EPLP*, 477.

PART II.

1 William Force Stead, 'Some Personal Impressions of T. S. Eliot', 63.

THE BURIAL OF THE DEAD.

1 TSE, 'Thomas Stearns Eliot' (1921), 107.
2 TSE–ST, 1 Jan. 1920 [i.e. 1921], Beinecke EPP, b. 31, f. 809; *TSEL1*,
529–31.
3 EP, 'Briefer Mention', 110.
4 VHE–CWE, 25 Jan. 1921, *TSEL1*, 538.
5 TSE–ST, 30 Jan. 1921, *TSEL1*, 539.
6 TSE–ST, 17 Oct. 1920, *TSEL1*, 509.
7 TSE–CWE, 22 Jan. 1921, *TSEL1*, 535; TSE–ST, 30 Jan. 1921, *TSEL1*, 539.
8 TSE, 'London Letter: March, 1921', 452.
9 Monro, *Some Contemporary Poets* (*1920*), 111, 119, 174, 180, 193.
10 Monro, *Some Contemporary Poets* (*1920*), 89.
11 TSE, 'London Letter: March, 1921', 449.
12 Unsigned, 'Obituary Verses', *SWG*, 2 Feb. 1921, 10.
13 TSE–ST, 30 Jan. 1921, *TSEL1*, 539.
14 ST–TSE, 10 Feb. 1921, *TSEL1*, 539n.
15 Virginia Woolf, 16 Feb. 1921, *VWD2*, 90.
16 EP, 'Briefer Mention', 110.
17 TSE–CWE, 2 Dec. 1920, *TSEL1*, 524; TSE–CWE, 31 Oct. 1920, *TSEL1*, 516;
TSE–CWE, 20 Sept. 1920, *TSEL1*, 502; TSE–HWE, 13 Sept. 1920, *TSEL1*,
499.
18 TSE–JQ, 5 Nov. 1919, *TSEL1*, 413.
19 TSE–CA, 10 Jan. 1916, *TSEL1*, 138.
20 WBY–MsF, 8 Feb. [1921], *WBYL*, 665; Aldous Huxley, 'Volpone', 6.
21 TSE, 'London Letter: May, 1921', 686.
22 WL–VS, 6 Feb. 1921, BL SP.
23 WL–SS, 7 Feb. 1921, BL SP.

24 TSE, 'I am the Resurrection and the Life', MS, Berg TSECP [Waste Land]; *TWLF*, 110–11.

25 'The Order for the Burial of the Dead', The Book of Common Prayer.

26 That Eliot was using a Corona at this time is evidenced by John Middleton Murry, who told Katherine Mansfield that he had sold his old typewriter for £5.10.0 to buy a Corona: 'the machine Aldous Huxley and Eliot have and swear by. It costs £15.15.0.' JMM–KM, *c*.25 Mar. 1920, *JMMLM*, 312n; TSE–HWE, 3 Oct. 1921, *TSEL1*, 585.

27 TSE–MB, 2 Jan. 1921, *TSEL1*, 532.

28 TSE, 'The Romantic Englishman', [4].

29 TSE, 'He Do the Police in Different Voices: Part I. The Burial of the Dead', TS, fo. [1], Berg TSECP [Waste Land]; *TWLF*, 4–5.

30 Valerie Eliot, Eliot Estate EVE, [1].

31 TSE, 'He Do the Police in Different Voices: Part I. The Burial of the Dead', TS, fo. 2, Berg TSECP [Waste Land]; *TWLF*, 6–7.

32 Geoffrey Chaucer, 'General Prologue', *The Canterbury Tales*, 1.

33 TSE, 'Conclusion', *UPUC*, 148.

34 TSE, 'The Romantic Englishman', [4].

35 TSE, 'Introduction', *Seneca his Tenne Tragedies*, x; rep. 'Seneca in Elizabethan Translation', *SE*, 69.

36 Stravinsky, 92.

37 Schwartz, 199.

38 Ezekiel 6:4.

39 TSE–EH, 3 Nov. 1930, Princeton EHL, b. 1, f. 1.

40 See Weston, 76; TSE, 'He Do the Police in Different Voices: Part I. The Burial of the Dead', TS, fo. 3, Berg TSECP [Waste Land]; *TWLF*, 8–9.

41 TSE, in Hall, 'T. S. Eliot', 59.

42 TSE–CA, 21 Aug. 1916, *TSEL1*, 158.

43 TSE–MC, 5 Dec. 1924, *TSEL2*, 550; TSE–HC, 8 Sept. 1927, *TSEL3*, 688.

44 TSE–MUC, 16 Dec. 1929, *TSEL4*, 714–15.

45 TSE–GC, 26 Feb. 1936, *TSEL8*, 86.

46 TSE–HWE, 30 Dec. 1936, *TSEL8*, 420.

47 TSE–ELM, 7 Mar. 1940, *TSEL9*, 442.

48 Gallup, 'The "Lost" Manuscripts of T. S. Eliot', 1238–9.

49 TSE–JQ, 21 Sept. 1922, *TSEL1*, 748.

50 TSE, in Hall, 'T. S. Eliot', 57.

51 Virginia Woolf, 16 Feb. 1921, *VWD2*, 90.

52 TSE–CWE, 13 Feb. 1921, *TSEL1*, 541.

53 Justice John J. McInerney, in 'Greenwich Village's Editoresses Fined', *NYH* (22 Feb. 1921), 8 (some contemporary sources give McInerney's 'unintelligible' as 'unintelligent').

54 James Joyce, 'Ulysses, Episode XIII (Continued)', 43.

55 'Improper Novel Costs Woman $50', *New York Times* (22 Feb. 1921), 6; 'Ulysses Adjudged Indecent; Review Editors are Fined', *NYH* (22 Feb. 1921), 8.

56 EP–JJ, [*c.* Oct.] 1920, *EPLJJ*, 185; also EP–JQ, 31 Oct. 1920, *EPLQ*, 199.

1 'Andrew Marvell', 26/7 Feb. or 5/6 Mar. 1921; 'Prose and Verse', ?19/20 Mar.
   1921; 'The Romantic Englishman', c.2 Feb.–c.26–7 Mar. 1921; 'The Lesson of
   Baudelaire', 'Song', ?26/7 Mar. 1921.

2 TSE, 'He Do the Police in Different Voices: Part II. ~~In the Cage~~ A Game of
   Chess', TSs ribbon and carbon, fo. [1], Berg TSECP [Waste Land]; *TWLF*,
   10–11, 16–17.

3 Petronius, *Trimalchio's Banquet*, 32 (Eliot's personal copy, with thanks to the
   Estate).

4 Petronius, *Satyricon*, §48; TSE, 'The Waste Land', TS title page, Berg TSECP
   [Waste Land]; *TWLF*, 2–3.

5 *Antony and Cleopatra*, 2.2.198.

6 TSE–BP, 17 Mar. [1921], *TSEL 1*, 546.

7 *The Tempest*, 1.2.488.

8 TSE, 'He Do the Police in Different Voices: Part II. ~~In the Cage~~ A Game of
   Chess', TSs ribbon and carbon, fo. 2, Berg TSECP [Waste Land]; *TWLF*,
   12–13, 18–19.

9 *The Tempest*, 1.2.401, 1.2.303.

10 *The Tempest*, 1.2.399–404.

11 TSE, 'He Do the Police in Different Voices: Part II. ~~In the Cage~~ A Game of
    Chess', TS ribbon, fo. 3, Berg TSECP [Waste Land]; *TWLF*, 14–15.

12 RA–HEM, 24 Oct. 1920, *RAAL*, 63.

13 TSE, 'Prose and Verse', 4.

14 Poe, 299.

15 Flint, 198; EP–HM, Jan. 1915, *EPSL*, 49 (91).

16 TSE, 'The Music of Poetry', *OPP*, 32.

17 TSE, 'Prose and Verse', 5.

18 TSE, 'Prose and Verse', 9.

19 Virginia Woolf, 22 Mar. 1921, *VWD2*, 103.

20 Aiken, 'The Scientific Critic', 593–4; TSE–CWE, 27 Apr. 1921, *TSEL 1*, 555.

21 Deutsch, 'Orchestral Poetry', 343, 345.

22 Deutsch, 'Another Impressionist', 89.

23 TSE–ST, 17 Oct. 1920, *TSEL 1*, 509–10.

24 CA–JF, 28 Sept. 1920, *CASL*, 56.

25 CA–RNL, 8 Nov. 1922, *CASL*, 72.

26 See Fred D. Crawford.

27 Aiken, *The Jig of Forslin* [V. 3], 91, cf. TSE, *TWL* [V] l. 384.

28 Aiken, *The Charnel Rose*, [III. 6], 46, cf. TSE, *TWL*, ll. 248, 250, 255.

29 Aiken, *The House of Dust*, [I. i] 12 and [IV. 7] 148, cf. TSE, *TWL*, ll. 65, 170.

30 Aiken, *The House of Dust*, [III. 8], 83, cf. TSE, *TWL*, ll. 382–3.

31 Aiken, *The House of Dust*, [IV. 3], 130, cf. TSE, *TWL*, ll. 113–14. Aiken, *The
    House of Dust*, [III. 3], 69 and [III. 11], 96, cf. TSE, *TWL*, ll. 133–4.

32 CA–RNL, 8 Nov. 1922, *CASL*, 72.

33 CA–RNL, 10 June 1925, *CASL*, 105.

34 TSE, 'The Romantic Englishman', [4].

35 TSE–DG, 25 July 1962, Beinecke DCGP, b. 23 (129).

36 TSE, 'Song. [For the Opherion]', TS, Berg TSECP [Waste Land]; *TWLF*, 98–9.

37 EP–TSE, 24 Saturnus An I [24 Jan. 1922], [28? Jan. 1922], Houghton TSECP, b. 3 (107, 108), *TSEL1*, 625, 630.

38 TSE, *TWL*, ll. 266–7; 'Doris's Dream Songs' [II ('The wind sprang up at four o'clock')], *Chapbook* ([Nov.] 1924), 36–7.

39 TSE, 'Song to the Opherian', *Tyro*, I (Apr. 1921), 6; also 'Song', TS, Berg TSECP [Waste Land], *TWLF*, 98–9.

40 WL–JQ, 14 June 1920, *WLL*, 120.

41 WL–AB, 14 Apr. 1921, *WLL*, 124.

42 Lewis, 'Note on Tyros', 2; 'The Children of the New Epoch', 3.

43 Lewis, 'Roger Fry's role of Continental Mediator', 3.

44 Lewis, 'Paris Versus the World', 25.

45 TSE, 'London Letter: May, 1921', 686–91.

46 WL, 'Vortices and Notes: Relativism and Picasso's Latest Work', 140.

47 EP–WL, 27 Apr. 1921, *EPLWL*, 127.

48 WL–AB, 14 Apr. 1921, *WLL*, 124.

49 TSE–RA, 7 Apr. 1921, *TSEL1*, 550.

50 TSE–JQ, 28 Sept. 1919, *TSEL1*, 401.

51 TSE, 'A French Romantic', 703.

52 TSE–RA, 7 Apr. 1921, *TSEL1*, 550.

53 TSE–JMM, 22 Apr. 1921, *TSEL1*, 554.

54 TSE–SS, 3 Apr. 1921, *TSEL1*, 549.

55 Sylvia Beach, 63–4.

56 JJ–HSW, 10 Apr. 1921, *JJL*, 162.

57 JJ–HSW, 24 June 1921, *JJL*, 165.

58 JJ–HSW, 3 Apr. 1921, *JJL*, 161.

59 TSE–DP, 22 May 1921, *TSEL1*, 564; EPP, 20 Apr. 1921, *EPLP*, 483.

60 EP–HLP, 20 Apr. 1921, *EPLP*, 483; EP–AB, Apr. 1921, *EPSL*, 166.

61 JJ–HSW, 23 Apr. 1921, *JJL3*, 41–2.

62 Joyce, *Ulysses* (§15.138), 565.

63 JJ–CL, 21 Sept. 1920, *JJSL*, 270, 271n. (trans.).

64 Sylvia Beach, 47.

65 TSE, 'London Letter: May, 1921', 686–91.

66 TSE–JQ, 9 May 1921, *TSEL1*, 557.

67 EP–MA, 22[?] Apr. 1921, *EPLLR*, 265; EP–AB, Apr. 1921, *EPSL*, 166 (230).

68 TSE, 'London Letter: May, 1921', 686–91.

69 TSE, 'He Do the Police in Different Voices: Part I. The Burial of the Dead', TS, fo. 3, Berg TSECP [Waste Land]; *TWLF*, 8–9.

70 TSE, 'Contemporanea', 84.

71 TSE, 'Ulysses, Order, and Myth', 483.

72 TSE–JQ, 9 May 1921, *TSEL1*, 558.

73 TSE–JJ, 21 May 1921, *TSEL1*, 561, 562.

74 TSE, 'The Romantic Englishman', [4].

75 Virginia Woolf, 19 Dec. 1923, *VWD2*, 278.

76 HWES–TLE, 7 Mar. 1914, *TSEL1*, 41.

77 Charlotte C. Eliot, *William Greenleaf Eliot*, 301–2.

78 Charlotte C. Eliot, *William Greenleaf Eliot*, 311.

79 TSE, 'Fragment of an Agon', *Criterion*, V. 1 (Jan. 1927), 74–80; rep. *SA*, 28.

80 TSE–DP, 22 May 1921, *TSEL1*, 564.

81 TSE–DP, 22 May 1921, *TSEL1*, 564.

82 TSE, 'He Do the Police in Different Voices: Part II. In the Cage A Game of
    Chess', TS ribbon, fo. [1], Berg TSECP [Waste Land]; *TWLF*, 10–11.

83 TSE, 'He Do the Police in Different Voices: Part II. In the Cage A Game of
    Chess', TS ribbon, fo. 2, Berg TSECP [Waste Land]; *TWLF*, 12–13; Gardner,
    '*The Waste Land*: Paris 1922', 76–7.

84 TSE, 'He Do the Police in Different Voices: Part II. In the Cage A Game of
    Chess', TSs ribbon and carbon, fo. 2, Berg TSECP [Waste Land]; *TWLF*,
    12–13, 18–19. In a letter of 20 June 1961 from Faber secretary Angela Milne to
    Valerie Eliot for the proofs for the Giovanni Mardersteig limited edition of *The
    Waste Land*, Eliot was asked whether the line 'HURRY UP PLEASE IT'S TIME'
    should read with or without the apostrophe; in an annotated of 20 June 1961, he
    underlined IT's and wrote in the margin 'Yes It's' (Eliot Estate, with thanks to
    John Haffenden).

85 TSE, 'The Death of the Duchess', TS, fos. [1–2], Berg TSECP [Waste Land],
    TWLF, 104–7; 'He Do the Police in Different Voices: Part II. In the Cage A
    Game of Chess', TSs ribbon and carbon, fo. 2, Berg TSECP [Waste Land];
    TWLF, 12–13, 18–19.

86 TSE, *FR*, II. ii, 102.

87 TSE–HRC (Ann Bowden), 11 May 1961, Texas TSEC, b. 3, f. 20.

88 Valerie Eliot, *TWLF*, 126n.

89 TSE, 'The Waste Land', Eliot Estate VOB1, 20r.

90 TSE–CA, 21 Aug. 1916, *TSEL1*, 157.

91 TSE, 'Petit Epître', TS, Berg TSECP [Poems]; pub. in *IMH*, 86–7.

92 TSE, 'Ode', TS, Berg TSECP [Poems], l. 12: 'Children singing in the or-
    chard' (*AVP*, 30); also, 'First Caprice in North Cambridge', MS, Berg TSECP
    [Notebook], [p.] 4, ll. 3–4: 'the distant strains / Of children's voices' (*IMH*, 13);
    'Prufrock's Pervigilium', MS, Berg TSECP [Notebook], [p.]. 32, l. 5: 'I heard
    the children whimpering in corners' (*IMH*, 43); 'The Burnt Dancer', TS, Berg
    TSECP [Poems], ll. 20–2: 'Children's voices in little corners / Whimper whim-
    per through the night / Of what disaster do you warn us' (*IMH*, 62).

93 TSE, 'Ash-Wednesday', [V] l. 25: 'For children at the gate' (*AW*, 19); 'A Song
    for Simeon', l. 13: 'where shall live my children's children' (*SS*, [2]); 'Marina',
    l. 20: 'Whispers and small laughter between leaves and hurrying feet' (*Marina*,
    [1]); 'The Rock: X', l. 37: 'We are children quickly tired: children who are up
    in the night' (*Rock*, 85); (*c*.1933); 'Landscapes: I. New Hampshire': 'Children's
    voices in the orchard' (*VQR*, X. 2 (Apr. 1934), 200, *WM*); 'Burnt Norton': 'the
    children in the apple-tree' m ll. [I] 40 and [V] 35–6: 'the leaves were full of

children', 'the hidden laughter / Of children in the foliage' (*CP1936*, 186, 191; *BN*, 10, 15); 'Little Gidding' [V], l. 35: 'the children in the apple-tree' (*LG*, 15).

94 Enid Faber, 'Recollections of Vivienne Eliot', 10 Nov. 1950, *TSEL2*, 593n., also Slater, [495–8] 496; VHE–MHW, 14 May 1936, Bodleian, MS Eng. lett. c. 383: 'that I never had children in my life, I thank God, and never wished to, since I was a little girl of about twelve' (my thanks to John Haffenden).

95 VHE, Bodleian AVHE/D2.

96 Enid Faber, 'Recollections of Vivienne Eliot', *TSEL2*, 593n., also Slater, 496.

97 The writer was the columnist and critic Charles Whibley.

98 TSE–TES [late Feb.? 1911], *TSEL1*, 15.

99 TSE–EP, 2 Feb. [1915], *TSEL1*, 93.

100 TSE–EH, 21 June 1932, Princeton EHL, b. 3, f. 3; 6 Aug. 1934, Princeton EHL, b. 5, f. 6; 9 Aug. 1932, Princeton EHL, b. 3, f. 5.

101 TSE–EH, 27 Aug. 1933, Princeton EHL, b. 4, f. 7.

102 TSE–EH, 6 Aug. 1931, Princeton EHL, b. 2, f. 1.

103 See Childs, 99–120.

104 TSE, 'The Rock', MSS, Bodleian WTSE, fos. 164–5.

105 TSE, 'He Do the Police in Different Voices: Part I. The Burial of the Dead', TS, fo. 2, Berg TSECP [Waste Land]; *TWLF*, 6–7.

106 VHE, on TSE, 'He Do the Police in Different Voices: Part II. ~~In the Cage~~ A Game of Chess', TS ribbon, fo. 3v, Berg TSECP [Waste Land], *TWLF1971*, 15n., *TWLF2022*, 137.

THE FIRE SERMON.

1 *White Star Line Famous Big 4*, New York: White Star Line / The International Mercantile Marine Company, 1909.

2 National Archives, Board of Trade: Commercial and Statistical Department and Successors: Inwards Passenger Lists, SS Adriatic, White Star Dominion Line, NA, BT 26/704/29.

3 TSE–RA, 23 June 1921, *TSEL1*, 568.

4 TSE–OM, 14 July 1921, *TSEL1*, 571.

5 TSE–RA, 23 June 1921, *TSEL1*, 568.

6 TSE, 'London Letter: September, 1921', 452–5.

7 Marianne Moore, 'The Sacred Wood', 339; TSE–MM, 3 Apr. 1921, *TSEL1*, 547.

8 MM–TSE, 17 Apr. 1921, *MMSL*, 152–3.

9 MM–Bryher, 7 July 1921, *MMSL*, 164.

10 MM–TSE, 15 July 1921, *MMSL*, 171.

11 MM–TSE, 18 Jan. 1934, *MMSL*, 317–18.

12 TSE–MM, 31 Jan. 1934, *TSEL7*, 54.

13 TSE, 'London Letter: July, 1921', 213–17.

14 MLH–TSE, 23 Aug. 1921, *TSEL1*, 577; TSE–RA, 4 July 1922, *TSEL1*, 691.

15 TSE, 'London Letter: July, 1921', 214; *The Tempest*, 1.2.404.

16 TSE, 'London Letter: July, 1921', 213.
17 EEC–E/RCC, samedi, 23 juillet [1921], *EEC[S]L*, 79.
18 Stein, 246.
19 ST–AG, [*c.* Aug. 1921], Beinecke DSTP, b. 33, f. 868–90.
20 Hemingway, *A Moveable Feast*, 28.
21 Huddleston, 82 (122), 121 (144).
22 Bowen, 48.
23 Crosby, 255 (New York: Ecco, 1979, 264–5).
24 EP, *GK*, 105.
25 See Josephson.
26 Lewis, *Blasting and Bombardiering*, 277.
27 TSE–RA, 6 July 1921, *TSEL1*, 569.
28 TSE–OM, 14 July 1921, *TSEL1*, 571.
29 VHE–ST, 20 July 1921, *TSEL1*, 571–2.
30 TSE, 'London Letter: September, 1921', 452.
31 VHE–ST, 20 July 1921, *TSEL1*, 571–2.
32 TSE, 'The Fire Sermon', TSs ribbon and carbon, fo. 2, Berg TSECP [Waste Land]; *TWLF*, 26–7, 40–1.
33 Hemingway, *A Moveable Feast*, 15.
34 *The Tempest*, 1.2.393–4.
35 TSE, 'Notes', *TWL 1922*, 57.
36 EP, 'A Communication', 97–8.
37 TSE, 'Introduction', *Seneca his Tenne Tragedies*, viii; *SE*, 67.
38 TSE–JE, 9 May 1939, *TSEL9*, 153.
39 EP, 'Three Cantos' ('The Fifth Canto', 'The Sixth Canto' [first two-thirds only], 'The Seventh Canto'), *Dial*, LXXI. 2 (Aug. 1921), 198–208.
40 EP–IWP, 18 Sept. [1921], *EPLP*, 489; DP–IWP, 20 Sept. 1921, *EPLP*, 489.
41 National Archives, Board of Trade: Commercial and Statistical Department and Successors: Outwards Passenger Lists, NA, BT 27/115354.
42 TSE–SS, 25 Aug. 1921, *TSEL1*, 578.
43 CWE–HWE, 14 Oct. 1921, *TSEL1*, 575n.
44 HWE–CWE, 30 Oct. 1921, *TSEL1*, 596.
45 CWE–HWE, 14 Oct. 1921, *TSEL1*, 575n.
46 VHE–HWE, 23 Aug. 1921, *TSEL1*, 576.
47 HWE–CWE, 30 Oct. 1921, *TSEL1*, 596.
48 VHE–HWE, Tuesday 23 [Aug. 1921], *TSEL1*, 577.
49 TSE–DP, 21 Aug. 1921, *TSEL1*, 574.
50 TSE–MH, 15 Aug. 1921, *TSEL1*, 573.
51 VHE–HWE, Tuesday 23 [Aug. 1921], *TSEL1*, 576.
52 TSE–RCS, 22 Aug. 1923, *TSEL2*, 189.
53 TSE–HWE, 3 Oct. 1921, *TSEL1*, 585.
54 VHE–HWE, 23 Aug. 1921, *TSEL1*, 576.
55 TSE–MH, 1 Sept. 1921, *TSEL1*, 579.
56 TSE–RA, Wednesday [7 Sept. 1921], *TSEL1*, 579–80.
57 TSE–RA, 16 Sept. 1921, *TSEL1*, 581.

58 TSE, 'The Metaphysical Poets', 669–70.

59 EP–ST, 9 & 10 Mars. [Mar.] 1922, *EPLD*, 236.

60 TSE–HWE, 3 Oct. 1921, *TSEL1*, 584.

61 EP, 'Canto XIX', 'Cantos XVII–XIX', *TQ*, I. 2 (Autumn/Winter 1925/1926), 5–16; *Cantos*, 85 (85).

62 EP–IWP, 22 Oct. [1921], *EPLP*, 489, 490.

63 TSE–HWE, 3 Oct. 1921, *TSEL1*, 584.

64 CWE–HWE, 14 Oct. 1921, *TSEL1*, 575n.

65 TSE–RA, [3? Oct. 1921], *TSEL1*, 586.

66 TSE–HWE, 3 Oct. 1921, *TSEL1*, 585.

67 TSE–RA, [13 Oct. 1921], *TSEL1*, 590.

68 TSE–HWE, 3 Oct. 1921, *TSEL1*, 585.

69 Met Office, *Monthly Weather Report*, 38. 10 (Oct. 1921).

70 *Keble's Penny Guide 1885*, Margate Museum.

71 Margate Museum.

72 *Thanet Advertiser and Echo* (15 Oct. 1921), 2.

73 TSE–RA, 13 Oct. 1921, *TSEL1*, 590.

74 VHE–ST, 13 Oct. 1921, *TSEL1*, 592.

75 Betjeman, 'Margate, 1940', *Listener* (24 Oct. 1940), rep. *New Bats in Old Belfries*, 29–30, both as 'Margate'.

76 Advertisement, Cliftonville Hydro, Margate, *c.*1905, quoting 'Opinions of the press', *Truth* publication.

77 Advertisement, the Albemarle, 47 Eastern Esplanade, Cliftonville, 1903.

78 *Chambers's Edinburgh Journal* (1834).

79 *Thanet Advertiser and Echo* (15 Oct. 1921), 2.

80 Advertisement, Parade Cinema, 21 Oct. 1921, rep. *Promenade*, 2018, 22.

81 TSE, 'Dramatis Personae', 303–6.

82 TSE–RCS, 9 Oct. 1921, *TSEL1*, 589.

83 VHE–VS, 26 Oct. 1921, *TSEL1*, 593.

84 TSE–JH, 26 Oct. 1921, *TSEL1*, 594.

85 VHE–MH, 28 Oct. 1921, *TSEL1*, 594.

86 Unsigned, *Times Literary Supplement*, 963 (1 July 1920), 427; TSE–RA, [postmark 29 Oct. 1921], *TSEL1*, 595.

87 TSE–Julian Huxley, 31 Oct. 1921, *TSEL1*, 598.

88 EP, 'The Little Review Calendar', 2; EP, *GK*, 96.

89 EP–HLM, 22 Mar. 1922, *EPSL*, 174 (240).

90 Albemarle receipts, Berg TSECP [Waste Land]; *TWLF2022*, 141–3.

91 TSE–HWE, [postmark] 1 Nov. 1921, *TSEL1*, 599.

92 TSE–RA, 6 Nov. 1921, *TSEL1*, 603.

93 Vittoz, 35 (tr. 25–6).

94 VHE–VS, 26 Oct. 1921, *TSEL1*, 593.

95 TSE, 'O City, City, I have heard + hear' ['The Fire Sermon'], MS, Berg TSECP [Waste Land] (my brackets and italics); see *TWLF*, 36–7.

96 TSE, 'London, the swarming life you kill + breed' ['The Fire Sermon'], MS, Berg TSECP [Waste Land] (my brackets and italics); *TWLF*, 36–7.

97 EP, on TSE, 'The Fire Sermon', TS ribbon, fo. 3, Berg TSECP [Waste Land]; *TWLF*, 30–1.

98 TSE, 'The river sweats' ['The Fire Sermon'], MS, Berg TSECP [Waste Land]; *TWLF*, 48–9.

99 TSE, ~~Highbury bore me. Highbury's children~~' ['The Fire Sermon'], MS, Berg TSECP [Waste Land]; *TWLF*, 50–1.

100 TSE–SS, Friday night [4? [i.e. 11] Nov. 1921], *TSEL 1*, 602.

101 TSE, ~~Highbury bore me. Highbury's children~~' ['The Fire Sermon'], MS verso, Berg TSECP [Waste Land]; *TWLF*, 52–3.

102 TSE, ~~Highbury bore me. Highbury's children~~' ['The Fire Sermon'], MS verso, Berg TSECP [Waste Land]; *TWLF*, 52–3 (full stop visible on 52 but not transcribed on 53).

103 *Tempest* 1.2.400–08.

104 *The Tempest*, 1.2.400–08; TSE, 'Dirge', MS (first draft), Berg TSECP [Waste Land], *TWLF*, 118–19, where the sheet is described as 'verso of "Elegy"' (119n.), however the tear of the page, which is similar to two other Margate leaves (*TWLF* 48 and 52/4), suggests that 'Dirge' is more likely to be the top or 'recto' sheet (and most likely written first), and 'Elegy' the verso (second).

105 TSE, 'Elegy', MS, Berg TSECP [Waste Land]; *TWLF*, 116–17.

106 TSE, 'Exequy', TS, Berg TSECP [Waste Land], *TWLF*, 100–1, 130n.; *Purgatorio*, 'XXVI', ll. 147, 143 (Oelsner, 330–1).

107 TSE–DG, 26 Nov. 1946, Beinecke DCGP, b. 23 (92).

108 TSE–SS, Friday night [4? [i.e. 11] Nov. 1921], *TSEL 1*, 601.

109 TSE–SS [16? Nov. 1921], *TSEL 1*, 604.

110 VHE–BR, 1 Nov. 1921, *TSEL 1*, 599.

111 Vittoz, 35 (tr. 26).

112 Vittoz, 37 (tr. 27).

113 Eliot's personal copy, with thanks to the Estate.

114 TSE–SS [16? Nov. 1921], *TSEL 1*, 604.

115 TSE–MH, [17 Nov. 1921], *TSEL 1*, 607.

116 TSE–GW, 16 Nov. 1921, *TSEL 1*, 605.

117 TSE–RA, 17 Nov. 1921, *TSEL 1*, 606.

DEATH BY WATER.

1 EP, 'Historical Survey', 39; EP–JH & MA, 21 May [1921], *EPLLR*, 277.

2 EP, 'Historical Survey', 39.

3 TSE–RA, 17 Nov. 1921, *TSEL 1*, 606.

4 TSE, 'The Lesson of Baudelaire', [4].

5 EP, 'Historical Survey', 39.

6 EP–HAMM (Secretary, Simon Guggenheim Foundation), 31 Mar. 1925, Beinecke EPP, b. 25, f. 1081–2; Gallup, *T. S. Eliot and Ezra Pound*, 28.

7 EP, 'Historical Survey', 39–40.

8 TSE–Woods, 21 Apr. 1919.

9 TSE, 'The Three Voices of Poetry', rep. *OP*, 89.

10 EP, 'Historical Survey', 42.

11 H. D., *Hymen*, New York: Henry Holt, 1921; TSE–RA, 17 Nov. 1921, *TSEL1*, 606.

12 RA, *TSEL1*, 601n.

13 TSE–RA, 17 Nov. 1921, *TSEL1*, 606.

14 Graves, 'Lawrence Vindicated', 16.

15 Aldington, *Ezra Pound and T. S. Eliot*, 11.

16 TSE, ['Richard Aldington'], 24–5.

17 Aldington, *Stepping Heavenward*, 57.

18 Aldington, *Stepping Heavenward*, 47–8.

19 GF–HRCW, 11 Nov. 1931, *TSEL5*, 733.

20 Aldington, *Ezra Pound and T. S. Eliot*, 17–18.

21 Aldington, *Ezra Pound and T. S. Eliot*, 19–20.

22 TSE, ['Richard Aldington'], 24–5.

23 EP–ST, 5 Dec. 1921, *EPLD*, 222; ST–TSE, 18 Dec. 1921, *TSEL1*, 616.

24 VHE–MH, Tuesday [20? [i.e. 13?] Dec. 1921], *TSEL1*, 619; a partially discernible postmark on the envelope at the Harry Ransom Center appears to read 13 15 [hrs] / 13 12 / 21', Texas MHP, b. 13, f. 1.

25 70 *bis* rue Notre-Dame-des-Champs, Paris.

26 VHE–MH, Tues. [20? [13?] Dec. 1921], *TSEL1*, 619.

27 EP–HLP, 3 Dec. [1921], *EPLP*, 490.

28 DP–IWP, 20 Sept. 1921, *EPLP*, 492.

29 EP–HLP, 3 Dec. [1921], *EPLP*, 491.

30 Joyce, in Sylvia Beach, 27.

31 See Mikriammos, 392; EP–JQ, 19 Dec. [1921], Berg JQP; see also Norman, 248; Stock, 299; Wilhelm, *Ezra Pound in London and Paris*, 288; Mikriammos, 387.

32 EP–HLP, 15 Oct. 1924, *EPLP*, 543.

33 Lewis, *Blasting and Bombardiering*, 277.

34 EMH–HGJ, 20 Mar. 1922, *EMHL1*, 335.

35 Hemingway, *A Moveable Feast*, 107.

36 EMH–EP, [8 Nov. 1922], *EMHL1*, 364; Hemingway, 'A Note on Ezra Pound', 151; 'Homage to Ezra', 74–6; TSE, 'Leadership and Letters', 7.

37 Swayne, 243.

38 Der Schweizerischen meterologischen Beobachtungen, *Annalen der Schweizerischen Meteorologischen Zentral-Anstalt*, Zürich: Buchdruckerei zur Alten Universität, 1921.

39 TSE–OM, 30 Nov. 1921, *TSEL1*, 608; Baedeker, *Switzerland* (1911), 300.

40 The Hôtel Pension Sainte-Luce was demolished in 1933 and replaced with Galerie Sainte-Luce, which still stands on its site. The neighbouring Hôtel Élite Lausanne was built at 1 Avenue Sainte-Luce in 1938.

41 Jean-Jacques Eggler, Archiviste Adjoint, Ville de Lausanne, correspondence with the author, 28 Oct. 2019: 'Called Cimerose (or Cime Rose), the house of Dr. Roger Vittoz, built in 1897, first bore the address Avenue d'Ouchy 67 until 1918, then was changed to avenue des Tilleuls 2. It still exists today at this address.'

42 Julian Huxley, 124; Morrell, *Early Memoirs*, 220–1.

43 OM–BR, 8, 10, 12, 13 Oct. 1911, McMaster BRA, b. 2.38; besides her visit of Oct. 1911, Morrell returned in Feb., June and Oct. 1912, and in Nov. 1913; she returned again, after Eliot's visit, in June 1921.

44 Morrell, Journal 1913, *Ottoline*, 237–8.

45 Julian Huxley, 124.

46 Vittoz, 31 (tr. 21).

47 The starting date of TSE's treatment is unknown, but given that his earliest arrival in Lausanne is Tue. 22 or 23 Nov. 1921, then it seems likely that the treatment doesn't begin before Thu. 24 Nov. and possibly later; letter to OM is Wed. 30 Nov. – therefore a week at most of treatment, which could be as little as three days if it began on Mon. 28 Nov.

48 TSE–OM, 30 Nov. 1921, *TSEL1*, 608.

49 TSE's copy, *Blick ins Chaos: drei Aufsätze*, Cambridge, GBR/0272/HB/B/16.

50 TSE–HH, 13 Mar. 1922, *TSEL1*, 645.

51 Hesse, 6 (tr. 610).

52 ST, 11 Dec. 1921, Dempsey, 100–1.

53 Hesse, 20 (tr. 618); TSE, 'Notes', *TWL1922*, 62.

54 EP–HLP, 3 Dec. 1921, *EPLP*, 490.

55 EP–ST, 5 Dec. 1921, Beinecke DSTP, b. 13, f. 581; *EPLD*, 222.

56 TSE–MH, [postmark 4 Dec. 1921], *TSEL1*, 609.

57 Today, the Payot Librairie Bookshop trades from Place Pépinet, in Lausanne.

58 TSE Estate copy, inscribed by Eliot, with the place and date, 1921.

59 TSE–WL, [postmark 3 Dec. 1921], *TSEL1*, 609.

60 TSE–NRF, 5 Dec. 1921, *TSEL1*, 609.

61 Vittoz, 31 (tr. 21).

62 TSE, 'Introduction', *Pascal's Pensées*, vii–xix.

63 TSE, '* From which, a Venus Anadyomene', MS, Berg TSECP [Waste Land]; *TWLF*, 28–9.

64 Arthur Rimbaud, 'Vénus Anadyomène', *Little Review*, V. 2 (Feb. 1918), 23; EP, *Instigations*, 30.

65 TSE, '* From which, a Venus Anadyomene', MS, Berg TSECP [Waste Land]; *TWLF*, 28–9.

66 TSE, 'Death by Water', MS, fo. [1], Berg TSEC [Waste Land]; *TWLF*, 54–5.

67 TSE, 'Death by Water', MS, fo. 3, Berg TSEC [Waste Land]; *TWLF*, 58–9.

68 TSE, 'Death by Water', MS, fo. 4, Berg TSEC [Waste Land]; *TWLF*, 60–1.

69 TSE, 'Dirge' MS fair copy, Berg TSECP [Waste Land]; *TWLF*, 120–1.

70 EP–HLP, [25 Dec. 1921], *EPLP*, 492.

71 Bodenheim, 87–91.

72 Bishop, 13–14.

73 Monroe, 'Ezra Pound', 90–7.

74 EP–HLP, [25 Dec. 1921], *EPLP*, 492.

75 TSE–APGG, 14 Dec. 1921, *TSEL1*, 616.

76 TSE–HWE, 13 Dec. 1921, *TSEL1*, 614.

77 HWE–CWE, 12 Dec. 1921, *TSEL1*, 613.

78 TSE–KA, 12 Nov. 1935, *TSEL7*, 825.

79 TSE, 'After the turning of ~~a thousand~~ the inspired days', MS, Berg TSECP [Waste Land]; *TWLF*, 108–9.

80 The Book of Common Prayer, 'The Order for the Burial of the Dead' ('though he were dead, yet ſhall he live' (John 11:25, 26)).

81 TSE–FMF, 14 Aug. 1923, *TSEL2*, 188; TSE, 'Notes', *TWL 1922*, 62.

82 TSE, '[What the Thunder Said]', MS, fo. 2, Berg TSECP [Waste Land]; *TWLF*, 72–3.

83 TSE, '[What the Thunder Said]', MS, fo. 3, Berg TSECP [Waste Land]; *TWLF*, 74–5.

84 EP, 'A Communication', 97–8.

85 Philippians 4:7; TSE, 'Notes', *TWL 1922*, 64.

86 TSE, '[What the Thunder Said]', MS, fo. 6, Berg TSECP [Waste Land]; *TWLF*, 80–1.

87 TSE–SW, 19 Dec. 1921, *TSEL1*, 617.

88 HWE–CWE, *TSEL1*, 620n.

WHAT THE THUNDER SAID.

1 HL–LL, 17 Dec. 1921, Dardis, 87.

2 HL–EP, 5 Apr. 1923, Egleston, 227; EP–JQ, 20 June 1920, Berg JQP, b. 34, f. 4.

3 EP–WL, 21 Jan. [1926], *EPLWL*, 163; EP–JRF, 5 Apr. 1922, Houghton JRF, b. 1 (4).

4 Djuna Barnes, *A Book.*

5 EP–JRF, 5 Apr. 1922, Houghton JRF, b. 1 (4).

6 Sherwood Anderson, 518.

7 Cerf, 40–1.

8 Albert Boni interview, 1972, Tamiment Library, New York University, Egleston, 28.

9 Lenin, 'Foreword', Reed, v.

10 Hicks, 353.

11 Trotzky, *The Bolsheviki and World Peace.*

12 EP, 'Canto LXXX', *Poetry* (Chicago), LXVIII. 6 (Sept. 1946), 310–21; *Cantos*, 519 (525).

13 VHE–MH, 12 Jan. 1922, *TSEL1*, 622.

14 TSE–EP, 1 June 1934, *TSEL7*, 210; Lewis, *Blasting and Bombardiering*, 267.

15 HL–JQ, 24 Mar. 1922, Egleston, 226.

16 Egleston, 225.

17 EP–JQ, 21 Feb. 1922, *EPLQ*, 206.

18 EP–TSE, [28? Jan. 1922], *TSEL1*, 631.

19 TSE, 'He Do the Police in Different Voices: Part I. The Burial of the Dead', TS, fo. 3, Berg TSECP [Waste Land]; *TWLF*, 8–9.

20 TSE, 'He Do the Police in Different Voices: Part II. ~~In the Cage~~ A Game of Chess', TS ribbon, fo. [1], Berg TSECP [Waste Land]; *TWLF*, 10–11.

21 TSE–EP [n.d.], Houghton TSEP, b. 3 (109), dated [26? Jan. 1922] in *TSEL1*, 628.

22 EP, annotation of TSE–EP, n.d., Houghton TSEP, b. 3 (109) (dated [26? Jan. 1922] in *TSEL1*, 628), returned with EP–TSE, n.d. ('Say early in 1922 TSE'), Houghton TSEP (108) and [28? Jan. 1922] in *TSEL1*, 630.

23 EP, annotation of TSE, 'The Fire Sermon', TS carbon, fo. [1], Berg TSECP [Waste Land]; *TWLF*, 38/9.

24 EP, annotation of TSE, 'The Fire Sermon', TS carbon, fos. 4–5, Berg TSECP [Waste Land]; *TWLF*, 44–7.

25 EP annotation of TSE, 'The Fire Sermon', TS ribbon, fo. 4, Berg TSECP [Waste Land]; *TWLF*, 32–3.

26 EP annotation of TSE, 'The Fire Sermon', TS ribbon, fo. 3, Berg TSECP [Waste Land]; *TWLF*, 30–1.

27 Hemingway, 'Wanderings: Mitrailliatrice', *Poetry* (Chicago), XXI. 4 (Jan. 1923): 193, rep. as 'Mitraigliatrice', *Three Stories & Ten Poems*, 49: 'Make this Corona / Their mitrailleuse.'

28 Corona Typewriter Company, *How to Use Corona, The Personal Writing Machine*, Groton, NY: Corona Typewriter Co. Inc., n.d. [*c.*1920], 10.

29 Eliot may have produced the pages as early as 5 January, but more likely on 9 January after visits to Jacques Rivière on 6th, an unsuccessful attempt to call upon André Gide on 7 January in Auteuil (he had left for Bruxelles), and after Pound had used it himself for correspondence on 8 January.

30 EP–IWP, 8 Jan. 1922, *EPLP*, 493.

31 TSE, 'Death by Water', TS, fo. [1], Berg TSECP [Waste Land]; *TWLF*, 62–3.

32 TSE, 'What the Thunder Said', TS, 4 fos., Berg TSECP [Waste Land]; *TWLF*, 82–9.

33 TSE–BR, 15 Oct. 1923, *TSEL2*, 257.

34 EP–ST, 23 Apr. 1922, *EPLD*, 237.

35 Edmund Spenser, 'Prothalamion', l. 110, 495.

36 TSE, 'The rivers tent is broken and the last fingers of leaf', MS, 'The Fire Sermon', TS ribbon, fo. [1]v, Berg TSECP [Waste Land]; *TWLF*, 24–5.

37 VHE–MH, 12 Jan. [1922], *TSEL1*, 622.

38 TSE, 'Death by Water', TS, fo. 4v, *TWLF1971*, 69n., *TWLF2022*, 138.

39 TSE–MH, [late Jan. 1922?], *TSEL1*, 633.

40 EP–TSE, [28? Jan. 1922], *TSEL1*, 631; TSE–EP, [26? Jan. 1922], *TSEL1*, 629.

41 EP–ST, 8 Feb. 1922, *EPLD*, 227.

42 EP–FMF, 13 Jan. 1922, *EPLF*, 63.

43 EP, 'Eighth Canto', *Dial*, LXXII. 5 (May 1922), 506–7; rep. as 'Canto II', *Cantos*, 7–8 (7–8).

44 EP, 'Eighth Canto', *Dial*, LXXII. 5 (May 1922), 508; rep. as 'Canto II', *Cantos*, 9 (9).

45 EP–JQ, 21 Feb. 1922, *EPLQ*, 206.

46 EP, 'Eighth Canto', *Dial*, LXXII. 5 (May 1922), 508; rep. as 'Canto II', *Cantos*, 9 (9).

47 EP–FMF, [21 Mar.] 1922, *EPLF*, 65–7.

48 WL–OM, 22 Jan. 1922, Texas OMC, b. 13, f. 4.

49 TSE–EP, 30 Aug. 1922, *TSEL1*, 736; TSE–AF, 22 Feb. 1928, *TSEL4*, 63; TSE–MLH, 12 Nov. 1927, *TSEL3*, 822.

50 Weston, 11.

51 Tennyson, 'Morte d'Arthur', ll. 200–3, *Poems*, II, 13.

52 Thomas Malory, *Le morte d'Arthur*, II, 240.

53 Madison Cawein, 'Waste Land', *Poetry* (Chicago), I. 4 (Jan. 1913), 104–5, rep. as 'Wasteland', *Minions of the Moon*, 122–3; it may have first appeared as 'Waste Land' in 1912 edition of the journal the *Revelator* (unverified); see Richard F. Patteson, 'An Additional Source for "The Waste Land"', *Notes and Queries* 23. 7, 300–1; Robert Ian Scott, 'The Waste Land Eliot Didn't Write', *Times Literary Supplement* (8 Dec. 1995), Christopher Hitchens, *Unacknowledged Legislation: Writers in the Public Sphere*, London: Verso, 2000, 297; Townsend, 82.

54 EP, *HSM*, 12.

55 Edmund Waller, 'Panegyric to Lord Protector', 41; Dryden, 'The Seventh Book of the Aeneid' (l. 310), *The Works of Virgil*, 723.

56 Conrad, 196 (56–7), 204 (70), 483 (108), 495 (129).

57 Conrad, 649 (168); quoted by TSE, 'The Waste Land', TS [title page], Berg TSECP [Waste Land]; *TWLF*, 2–3.

58 TSE, 'Death by Water', MS, fo. 3, Berg TSECP [Waste Land]; *TWLF*, 58–9.

59 TSE, '[The Death of St Narcissus]', MS, fo. [2], Berg TSECP [Waste Land]; *TWLF*, 92–3; TSE, 'Syllabus for a Tutorial Class in Modern English Literature'; TSE, 'Ben Jonson', 637–8.

60 TSE–RA, 7 Apr. 1921, *TSEL1*, 550.

61 HWE–CWE, 27 Apr. 1920, *TSEL1*, 467n.

62 TSE, 'Introduction', *Charles Baudelaire*, 23.

63 EP–TSE, 24 Saturnus An I [24 Jan. 1922], Houghton TSECP, b. 3 (107), *TSEL1*, 625.

64 TSE–ST, 20 Jan. 1922, *TSEL1*, 623.

65 EP–TSE, [28? Jan. 1922], Houghton TSECP, b. 3 (108), dated by TSE as 'Say – early in 1922'; *TSEL1*, 630.

66 TSE, 'Prose and Verse', 4.

67 HL–EP, 11 Jan. 1922, Beinecke WBEPP, 1, f. 5.

68 TSE–DG, 26 Nov. 1946, Beinecke DCGP, b. 23 (92).

69 EP–TSE, 24 Saturnus An I [24 Jan. 1922], Houghton TSECP, b. 3 (107), *TSEL1*, 625.

70 TSE–EP, [26? Jan. 1922], Houghton TSECP, b. 3 (109); *TSEL1*, 629.

71 EP–TSE, [28? Jan. 1922], Houghton TSECP, b. 3 (108); *TSEL1*, 630.

72 EP–TSE, 24 Saturnus, An I [24 Jan. 1922], Houghton TSEP, b. 3 (107); *TSEL1*, 626.

73 EP–TSE, 24 Saturnus, An I [24 Jan. 1922], Houghton TSEP, b. 3 (107); *TSEL1*, 625.

74 TSE–EP, [26? Jan. 1922], Houghton TSEP, b. 3 (108); *TSEL1*, 628.

75 TSE–ST, 20 Jan. 1922, *TSEL1*, 623.

76 T. S. Eliot, 'Ezra Pound', 326–38.

77 EP, 'A Communication', 97–8.

78 The thought is Helen Gardner's, see '*The Waste Land*: Paris 1922', 87–8.

79 TSE, 'On a Recent Piece of Criticism', 93.

80 EP, 'A Communication', 97–8.
81 TSE–JQ, 25 June 1922, *TSEL1*, 681.
82 EP–TSE, 24 Saturnus, An I [24 Jan. 1922], Houghton TSEP, b. 3 (107); *TSEL1*, 626.

LONDON 1960.

1   TSE–EP, 29 Jan. 1960, Beinecke EPP, b. 15, f. 674.
2   TSE–EP, 24 Aug. 1960, Beinecke EPP, b. 15, f. 674.
3   TSE–EP, 11 Nov. 1961, Beinecke EPP, b. 15, f. 674.
4   TSE–ST, 20 Jan. 1922, *TSEL1*, 623.
5   ST–TSE, 29 Jan. 1922, *TSEL1*, 632.
6   TSE–ST, 16 Mar. 1922, *TSEL1*, 651.
7   TSE–ST, 8 Mar. 1922, *TSEL1*, 639.
8   ST–TSE, 12 Mar. 1922, *TSEL1*, 644.
9   TSE–EP, 12 Mar. 1922, *TSEL1*, 641.
10 EP–ST, 9–10 Mar. 1922, *EPLD*, 236.
11 'Announcement', *Dial*, LXX. 6 (June 1921), 730–1; also, 'Comment', *Dial*, LXXIII. 6 (Dec. 1922), 685–7.
12 EP–ST, 9–10 Mar. 1922, *EPLD*, 236.
13 TSE–JR, [5? Feb. 1922], *TSEL1*, 634.
14 TSE–JMM, [21 Feb. 1922], *TSEL1*, 637.
15 TSE–EP, 12 Mar. 1922, *TSEL1*, 641.
16 TSE–MF, 26 Feb. 1922, *TSEL1*, 638.
17 MF–TSE, 11 Mar. 1922, *TSEL1*, 638n.
18 TSE–TSM, 3 Apr. 1922, *TSEL1*, 655.
19 TSE–RCS, 27 June 1922, *TSEL1*, 685; TSE–EP, 19 July 1922, *TSEL1*, 708; TSE–RA, 30 June 1922, *TSEL1*, 688.
20 Virginia Woolf, 12 Mar. 1922, *VWD2*, 171.
21 Virginia Woolf, 12 Mar. 1922, *VWD2*, 171.
22 Virginia Woolf, 12 Mar. 1922, *VWD2*, 171; 3 Aug. 1922, *VWD2*, 187; 27 Sept. 1922, *VWD2*, 204.
23 Virginia Woolf, 23 June 1922, *VWD2*, 178.
24 Virginia Woolf, 23 June 1922, *VWD2*, 178.
25 EP–MA, 14 Apr. 1922, *EPLLR*, 283.
26 Heap ('jh'), 'The "Art Season"', 60.
27 EP–HLP, 12 Apr. [1922], *EPLP*, 497–8; EP–WL, 14 July 1922, *EPLWL* 133.
28 EP, 'Credit and the Fine Arts', 285.
29 TSE–RA, 30 June 1922, *TSEL1*, 688.
30 TSE–SB, 4 Apr. 1922, *TSEL1*, 658.
31 TSE, '*Ulysses*, Order, and Myth', 483.
32 TSE–AAK, 3 Apr. 1922, *TSEL1*, 656.
33 TSE–AAK, 3 Apr. 1922, *TSEL1*, 656; TSE–AAK, 20 May 1922, *TSEL1*, 673: 'It is true that I am most anxious to publish my poem in America in the autumn, on account of copyright.'

34 AAK–TSE, 1 May 1922, *TSEL1*, 657n.
35 EP–JRF, 6 May 1922, Houghton JRF, b. 1 (7).
36 EP, 'Credit and the Fine Arts', 284–5; EP–WCW, 18 Mar. 1922, *EPSL*, 173 (239).
37 ST–GS, 9 Mar. 1922, Beinecke DSTP, b. 40, f. 1139.
38 GS– ST, 11 Mar. 1922, Beinecke DSTP, b. 40, f. 1139.
39 TSE–RA, 17 May 1922, *TSEL1*, 669; TSE–OM, [17? May 1922], *TSEL1*, 669.
40 TSE–RA, 4 July 1922, *TSEL1*, 690.
41 TS–RA, 13 July 1922, *TSEL1*, 699.
42 TSE–JQ, 25 June 1922, *TSEL1*, 681.
43 TSE–JQ, 19 July 1922, *TSEL1*, 707.
44 VHE–EP, 27 June 1922, *TSEL1*, 683–4.
45 TSE–EP, 19 July 1922, *TSEL1*, 708.
46 TSE–OM, [end July? 1922], *TSEL1*, 715.
47 Brother Savage, 'Books and Bookmen', *Liverpool Daily Post and Echo*, 16 Nov. 1922.
48 TSE–RA, 18 Nov. 1922, *TSEL1*, 790.
49 RA–TSE, 7 Dec. 1922, *TSEL1*, 802.
50 TSE–JQ, 19 July 1922, *TSEL1*, 707.
51 JQ–TSE, 1 Aug. 1922, *TSEL1*, 714n.
52 EP, 'T. S. Eliot' (1939), 24.
53 Clive Bell, 119; TSE–DHW, 26 June 1963, in Woodward, 260.
54 TSE, 'The Frontiers of Criticism', *OPP*, 109.
55 TSE–JQ, 19 July 1922, *TSEL1*, 706–7; JQ–TSE, 1 Aug. 1922, *TSEL1*, 714n.
56 GS–JSW, 31 Aug. 1922, *TSEL1*, 740; it seems likely that Eliot had included the notes in TSE–JQ, 21 Aug. 1922, *TSEL1*, 729.
57 EP, 'Communication', 97–8.
58 TSE–GZ, 10 Feb. 1937, *TSEL8*, 492.
59 TSE, 'The Frontiers of Criticism', *OPP*, 109–10.
60 EP–JSW, n.d. [? Aug. 1922], *EPLD*, 247.
61 JSW–ST, 12 Aug. [1922], *TSEL1*, 720; *EPLD*, 247.
62 TSE–JSW, 21 Aug. 1922, *TSEL1*, 731.
63 TSE–JQ, 21 Aug. 1922, *TSEL1*, 729.
64 TSE–JQ, 21 Sept. 1922, *TSEL1*, 748.
65 GS–HL, 7 Sept. 1922, Beinecke DSTP, b. 41, f. 1153.
66 *Dial*, LXXIII. 5 (Nov. 1922), 473n.: 'An edition of The Waste Land with annotations by Mr Eliot will presently be issued by Boni & Liveright.—The Editors.'
67 JQ–TSE, 7 Sept. 1922, *TSEL1*, 748n.; GS–HL, 7 Sept. 1922, Beinecke DSTP, b. 41, f. 1153.
68 VHE–SS, Monday [16 Oct. 1922], *TSEL1*, 765.
69 TSE–RA, 15 Nov. 1922, *TSEL1*, 786–7.
70 TSE–GS, 27 Dec. 1922, *TSEL1*, 813.
71 Texas EPL.
72 This account was told to me by Richard B. Watson, Head of Reference Services, University of Texas at Austin, 23 Apr. 2014, and subsequently verified in research by Exhibit A, Omar Pound Collection, Pound Library, Collection file, Item 165, LH 5955, Reg 8681, also King, 30–45.

73 Rachewiltz, 46.
74 TSE–OM, [?mid Apr. 1923], *TSEL2*, 107.
75 TSE–EP, 20 May 1923, *TSEL2*, 140.
76 VHE, 18 Nov. 1935, Bodleian AVHE/D4.
77 TSE–EH, 14 Feb. 1947, Princeton EHL, b. 13, f. 1.
78 TSE–EH, 3 Nov. 1930, Princeton EHL, b. 1, f. 1.
79 TSE–EH, 4 Feb. 1931, Princeton EHL, b. 1, f. 2.
80 TSE–EH, 21 Aug. 1931, Princeton EHL, b. 2, f. 1.
81 TSE–EH, 14 Feb. 1947, Princeton EHL, b. 13, f. 1.
82 TSE–EH, 3 Nov. 1930, Princeton EHL, b. 1, f. 1.
83 TSE–EH, 14 Feb. 1947, Princeton EHL, b. 13, f. 1.
84 TSE, 'Directions to my executors', 25 Nov. 1960, Houghton TSEP.
85 TSE–EH, 14 Feb. 1947, Princeton.
86 Nancy Cunard, Texas NCC/S2, 11v.
87 Unsigned, 'Medallions: III. Mr T. S. Eliot. The Exact Critic', *The Times* (13 June
    1922), Texas NCC/S2, 9v 'Sept. Hendaye': 'Nancy at Hendaye', 'Fuenterra Bia',
    'At Guadalupe', 'At Cap du Figuier', Texas NCC/S2, 13r.
88 Through June, July and August, the average temperature rarely crept above 12°C
    (53°F).
89 Nancy Cunard, 'Letter', Texas NCC, b. 6, f. 4; Cunard, *Selected Poems*, 226–9.
90 TSE–EH, 3 Nov. 1930, Princeton EHL, b. 1, f. 1.
91 NC–EP, 3 Oct. 1922, Wilhelm, 'Nancy Cunard', 209.
92 EP 'Canto LXXX', *Poetry* (Chicago), LXVIII. 6 (Sept. 1946), 310–21; *Cantos*,
    524 (530).
93 VHE–TSE, 5 Jan. [1926], *TSEL3*, 3.
94 TSE–EP, 13 Oct. 1925, *TSEL2*, 758.
95 T. S. Eliot, 'Ezra Pound', 326–38.
96 EP 'Canto LXXX', *Poetry* (Chicago), LXVIII. 6 (Sept. 1946), 310–21; *Cantos*,
    527 (533).
97 EP, draft letter to T. S. Eliot, n.d. [*c.*1959–60?], Toledo EPP, The Cantos (MSS-
    057), b. 1, f. 1.
98 EP, 'Canto CX', *DFC*, 11; EP's notebook has 'our ruins' ('Notebook 2', *DFFN*).
99 TSE–EP, 13 Aug. 1959, Beinecke EPP, b. 15, f. 673.
100 EP, 'From Canto CXV', *DFC*, 24.
101 EP–FES, 8–9 July 1922, *EPSL*, 180 (247).
102 Cory, 38–9.
103 EP, in Hall, 'Ezra Pound', 47; EP, 'Notes for CXVII et seq.', *DFC*, 32; *Cantos*,
    817 (823).
104 EP, 'From Canto CXV', *DFC*, 24; *Cantos*, 808 (814).
105 Reck, 'A Conversation', 29; EP, MS note in Olga Rudge Venice notebook,
    Beinecke ORP: 'That she wd. have save me / from idiocies in antisemitism.'
106 EP–MdR, 20 Aug. 1959, Beinecke EPP.
107 EP, 'Canto CXVI', *DFC*, 27; *Cantos*, 797 (803).
108 EP, comment to his French publisher Dominique de Roux, 1965, rep. *Time*, 5
    Nov. 1965.

109 EP, 'Notes from CXVII et seq.', *DFC*, 32; *Cantos*, 816 (822)
110 TSE–EP, telegram 30 Oct. 1959 (transmitted 31 Oct. 1959), Beinecke EPP, b. 15, f. 673, and Eliot Estate.
111 TSE–EP, 28 Dec. 1959, Beinecke EPP, b. 15, f. 673.
112 EP, quoted in Rachewiltz, 306.
113 TSE, 'Ezra Pound', 330; rep. 'Ezra Pound by T. S. Eliot', in Peter Russell, *Ezra Pound*, 28.
114 EP–JQ, 21 Feb. 1922, *EPLQ*, 205–6.

REVIEWS.

1 Unsigned, *Times Literary Supplement*, 1804 (26 Oct. 1922), 690.
2 Rascoe, 8.
3 Unsigned, 'The Sporting Spirit', *New York Evening Post Literary Review* (11 Nov. 1922), 1.
4 Unsigned, *New York Times Book Review* (26 Nov. 1922), 12.
5 Wilson, 'The Poetry of Drouth', 611–16.
6 Seldes, 614–16.
7 Untermeyer, 'Disillusion vs. Dogma', 453.
8 Wylie, 396.
9 Monro, 'Notes for a Study of *The Waste Land*', 20–4.
10 Aiken, 'The Anatomy of Melancholy', 294–5.
11 Drury, 15.
12 Unsigned, 'Shantih, Shantih, Shantih: Has the Reader Any Rights Before the Bar of Literature?', *Time*, 1.1 (3 Mar. 1923), 12.
13 Squire, 'Poetry', 655–7
14 Powell ['C.P.'], 7.

Permissions.

EZRA POUND

OTHER AUTHORS

Index.

Note: Page numbers in *italics* denote images. TSE is T. S. Eliot. EP is Ezra Pound.

London Library, 268
London Mercury, 96, 162, 163, 164, 165, 183, 221, 259, 276
Longfellow, Henry Wadsworth, 188
Louis IX of France, 39
Lowell, Amy, 18, 21, 70, 99
Lowell, Robert, 63; *Imitations*, 61–2
Loy, Mina, 197
Lutyens, Edwin, 97

McAlmon, Robert, 197
McCoy, Bill, 57–8
Macmillan, 21, 94, 96
Mahā-Vagga, 143, 280
Malleson, Constance, 44, 47, 48, 49, 307
Malory, Thomas, 355
Mansfield, Katherine, 59, 81, 123, 134, 162, 182–3
Margate, Kent, 101, 235, 277, 289–96, 297–8, 300–302, 306, 309, 310, 326, 344–6
Marlow, Buckinghamshire, 44, 48–9, 86, 117–18
Marsden, Dora, 69, 70, 71
Marsh, Edward, 168, 168
Marx, Karl, 38, 48
Mary Institute, St Louis, 39, 156, 157
Massine, Leonid, 102, 453 n. 51
Masters, Edgar Lee, 21
Mathews, Elkin, 23, 95, 100, 132, 195
Maurras, Charles, 255
Methuen, 137, 201
Mew, Charlotte, 'The Fête', 71
Millay, Edna St Vincent, 165
Milne, Angela, 470 n. 84
Mirrlees, Hope, 236; *Paris: A Poem*, 180–2
Mississippi River, 40, 42, 158, 160
Missouri State, 14, 15, 40, 42, 55
Missouri River, 39–40
Moffat, Curtis, 149
Mond, Alfred, 18, 81–2
Monnier, Adrienne, 197
Monro, Alida, 55
Monro, Harold, 16, 100, 169, 193, 223–4, 246, 310
Monroe, Harriet, 64, 65–6, 167, 246, 331
Montségur, 92–3, 117
Moore, George, 179, 368
Moore, Marianne, 6–7, 38–9, 66, 165, 209, 274–5; 'The Fish', 71
Moore, T. Sturge, 167–8
Morgan, Louise, 177
Morocco, xvii, 267, 268, 367

Morrell, Lady Ottoline, 46, 59, 86, 89, 90, 102, 198, 284, 291, 295, 297, 320, 321, 323, 476 n. 43
Mosley, Oswald, 163
Much Ado magazine, 161
Muir, Edwin, 194
Murry, John Middleton, 59, 60, 77, 83, 123, 133, 175, 182–3, 209, 259
Mussolini, Benito, 126, 162–3, 191, 379

The Nation, 210, 259
Nazism, 191, 203
Nesbitt, Catherine, 138
New Age, 58, 65, 73, 93, 101, 131, 132, 134, 151, 153, 154, 186, 193, 195, 202, 207, 212, 213, 217, 371
New China Restaurant, London, 17, 99, 442 n. 31
New English Weekly, 204
New Freewoman, 69–70
Newman, John Henry, 'The Dream of Gerontius', 105
New Republic, 167, 209
New Statesman, 162, 193, 209, 210
New York City, NY, 21, 55, 56, 195, 341, 370
New York Evening Post, 177
New York Public Library, 237
New York State, 58, 75
Nichols, Robert, 81, 167, 168; *The Assault*, 167; *Invocation and Peace Celebration*, 168
Noyes, Alfred, 168

objective correlative, 73, 130–1, 136
Observer, 60, 167, 168, 173, 175, 193
Okey, Thomas, 174
Olson, Charles, 5
Ophelia, 242, 245
Orage, A. R., 65, 151, 217
Others magazine, 23, 193
Outlook journal, 132, 177
Ovid Press, 18, 55, 93, 128, 135, 146, 166, 176, 183, 195, 235, 331, 341
Oxford Poetry Club, 26

Pach, Walter, 165
Pacy, May, 120
Palestine, 324
Paris: Eliot, 216–17, 225, 316, 327, 340, 350, 381–2; Joyce, 196–7, 199, 258, 340; Pound, 72, 120, 195, 222, 257, 277–9, 316–17, 325, 331, 338, 339
Paris Peace Conference, 32

THE WASTE LAND

Text of the First Edition

NEW YORK, BONI AND LIVERIGHT

1922

'Nam Sibyllam quidem Cumis ego ipse oculis meis
vidi in ampulla pendere, et cum illi pueri dicerent:
Σίβυλλα τί θέλεις; respondebat ilia: ἀποθανεῖν θέλω.'

I. THE BURIAL OF THE DEAD

APRIL is the cruellest month, breeding
Lilacs out of the dead land, mixing
Memory and desire, stirring
Dull roots with spring rain.
Winter kept us warm, covering
Earth in forgetful snow, feeding
A little life with dried tubers.
Summer surprised us, coming over the Starnbergersee
With a shower of rain; we stopped in the colonnade,
And went on in sunlight, into the Hofgarten,   10
And drank coffee, and talked for an hour.
Bin gar keine Russin, stamm' aus Litauen, echt deutsch.
And when we were children, staying at the archduke's,
My cousin's, he took me out on a sled,
And I was frightened. He said, Marie,
Marie, hold on tight. And down we went.
In the mountains, there you feel free.
I read, much of the night, and go south in the winter.

What are the roots that clutch, what branches grow
Out of this stony rubbish? Son of man,   20
You cannot say, or guess, for you know only
A heap of broken images, where the sun beats,
And the dead tree gives no shelter, the cricket no relief,
And the dry stone no sound of water. Only
There is shadow under this red rock,
(Come in under the shadow of this red rock),
And I will show you something different from either
Your shadow at morning striding behind you

Or your shadow at evening rising to meet you;
I will show you fear in a handful of dust.   30

> *Frisch weht der Wind*
> *Der Heimat zu.*
> *Mein Irisch Kind,*
> *Wo weilest du?*

'You gave me hyacinths first a year ago;
'They called me the hyacinth girl.'
—Yet when we came back, late, from the Hyacinth garden,
Your arms full, and your hair wet, I could not
Speak, and my eyes failed, I was neither
Living nor dead, and I knew nothing,   40
Looking into the heart of light, the silence.
Od' und leer das Meer.

Madame Sosostris, famous clairvoyante,
Had a bad cold, nevertheless
Is known to be the wisest woman in Europe,
With a wicked pack of cards. Here, said she,
Is your card, the drowned Phoenician Sailor,
(Those are pearls that were his eyes. Look!)
Here is Belladonna, the Lady of the Rocks,
The lady of situations.   50
Here is the man with three staves, and here the Wheel,
And here is the one-eyed merchant, and this card,
Which is blank, is something he carries on his back,
Which I am forbidden to see. I do not find
The Hanged Man. Fear death by water.
I see crowds of people, walking round in a ring.
Thank you. If you see dear Mrs. Equitone,
Tell her I bring the horoscope myself:
One must be so careful these days.

Unreal City,
Under the brown fog of a winter dawn,
A crowd flowed over London Bridge, so many,
I had not thought death had undone so many.
Sighs, short and infrequent, were exhaled,
And each man fixed his eyes before his feet.
Flowed up the hill and down King William Street,
To where Saint Mary Woolnoth kept the hours
With a dead sound on the final stroke of nine.
There I saw one I knew, and stopped him, crying: 'Stetson!
'You who were with me in the ships at Mylae!
'That corpse you planted last year in your garden,
'Has it begun to sprout? Will it bloom this year?
'Or has the sudden frost disturbed its bed?
'Oh keep the Dog far hence, that's friend to men,
'Or with his nails he'll dig it up again!
'You! hypocrite lecteur!—mon semblable,—mon frère!'

II. A GAME OF CHESS

THE Chair she sat in, like a burnished throne,
Glowed on the marble, where the glass
Held up by standards wrought with fruited vines
From which a golden Cupidon peeped out   80
(Another hid his eyes behind his wing)
Doubled the flames of sevenbranched candelabra
Reflecting light upon the table as
The glitter of her jewels rose to meet it,
From satin cases poured in rich profusion;
In vials of ivory and coloured glass
Unstoppered, lurked her strange synthetic perfumes,
Unguent, powdered, or liquid—troubled, confused
And drowned the sense in odours; stirred by the air
That freshened from the window, these ascended   90
In fattening the prolonged candle-flames,
Flung their smoke into the laquearia,
Stirring the pattern on the coffered ceiling.
Huge sea-wood fed with copper
Burned green and orange, framed by the coloured stone,
In which sad light a carvèd dolphin swam.
Above the antique mantel was displayed
As though a window gave upon the sylvan scene
The change of Philomel, by the barbarous king
So rudely forced; yet there the nightingale   100
Filled all the desert with inviolable voice
And still she cried, and still the world pursues,
'Jug Jug' to dirty ears.
And other withered stumps of time
Were told upon the walls; staring forms

Leaned out, leaning, hushing the room enclosed.
Footsteps shuffled on the stair.
Under the firelight, under the brush, her hair
Spread out in fiery points
Glowed into words, then would be savagely still.   110

'My nerves are bad tonight. Yes, bad. Stay with me.
'Speak to me. Why do you never speak. Speak.
'What are you thinking of? What thinking? What?
'I never know what you are thinking. Think.'

I think we are in rats' alley
Where the dead men lost their bones.

'What is that noise?'
                    The wind under the door.
'What is that noise now? What is the wind doing?'
                    Nothing again nothing.   120
                                        'Do
'You know nothing? Do you see nothing? Do you remember
'Nothing?'
        I remember
Those are pearls that were his eyes.
'Are you alive, or not? Is there nothing in your head?'
                                        But

O O O O that Shakespeherian Rag—
It's so elegant
So intelligent   130

'What shall I do now? What shall I do?'
'I shall rush out as I am, and walk the street
'With my hair down, so. What shall we do tomorrow?
'What shall we ever do?'

507

                    The hot water at ten.
And if it rains, a closed car at four.
And we shall play a game of chess,
Pressing lidless eyes and waiting for a knock upon the door.

When Lil's husband got demobbed, I said—
I didn't mince my words, I said to her myself,   140
HURRY UP PLEASE ITS TIME
Now Albert's coming back, make yourself a bit smart.
He'll want to know what you done with that money he gave you
To get yourself some teeth. He did, I was there.
You have them all out, Lil, and get a nice set,
He said, I swear, I can't bear to look at you.
And no more can't I, I said, and think of poor Albert,
He's been in the army four years, he wants a good time,
And if you dont give it him, there's others will, I said.
Oh is there, she said. Something o' that, I said.   150
Then I'll know who to thank, she said, and give me a straight look.
HURRY UP PLEASE ITS TIME
If you dont like it you can get on with it, I said,
Others can pick and choose if you can't.
But if Albert makes off, it won't be for lack of telling.
You ought to be ashamed, I said, to look so antique.
(And her only thirty-one.)
I can't help it, she said, pulling a long face,
It's them pills I took, to bring it off, she said.
(She's had five already, and nearly died of young George.)   160
The chemist said it would be alright, but I've never been the same.
You *are* a proper fool, I said.
Well, if Albert won't leave you alone, there it is, I said,
What you get married for if you dont want children?
HURRY UP PLEASE ITS TIME
Well, that Sunday Albert was home, they had a hot gammon,

And they asked me in to dinner, to get the beauty of it hot—
HURRY UP PLEASE ITS TIME
HURRY UP PLEASE ITS TIME
Goonight Bill. Goonight Lou. Goonight May. Goonight.   170
Ta ta. Goonight. Goonight.
Good night, ladies, good night, sweet ladies, good night, good night.

III. THE FIRE SERMON

THE river's tent is broken: the last fingers of leaf
Clutch and sink into the wet bank. The wind
Crosses the brown land, unheard. The nymphs are departed.
Sweet Thames, run softly, till I end my song.
The river bears no empty bottles, sandwich papers,
Silk handkerchiefs, cardboard boxes, cigarette ends
Or other testimony of summer nights. The nymphs are
    departed.
And their friends, the loitering heirs of city directors;   180
Departed, have left no addresses.
By the waters of Leman I sat down and wept . . .
Sweet Thames, run softly till I end my song,
Sweet Thames, run softly, for I speak not loud or long.
But at my back in a cold blast I hear
The rattle of the bones, and chuckle spread from ear to ear.

A rat crept softly through the vegetation
Dragging its slimy belly on the bank
While I was fishing in the dull canal
On a winter evening round behind the gashouse   190
Musing upon the king my brother's wreck
And on the king my father's death before him.
White bodies naked on the low damp ground
And bones cast in a little low dry garret,
Rattled by the rat's foot only, year to year.
But at my back from time to time I hear
The sound of horns and motors, which shall bring
Sweeney to Mrs. Porter in the spring.
O the moon shone bright on Mrs. Porter

And on her daughter   200
They wash their feet in soda water
Et, O ces voix d'enfants, chantant dans la coupole!

Twit twit twit
Jug jug jug jug jug jug
So rudely forc'd.
Tereu

Unreal City
Under the brown fog of a winter noon
Mr. Eugenides, the Smyrna merchant
Unshaven, with a pocket full of currants   210
C.i.f. London: documents at sight,
Asked me in demotic French
To luncheon at the Cannon Street Hotel
Followed by a weekend at the Metropole.

At the violet hour, when the eyes and back
Turn upward from the desk, when the human engine waits
Like a taxi throbbing waiting,
I Tiresias, though blind, throbbing between two lives,
Old man with wrinkled female breasts, can see
At the violet hour, the evening hour that strives   220
Homeward, and brings the sailor home from sea,
The typist home at teatime, clears her breakfast, lights
Her stove, and lays out food in tins.
Out of the window perilously spread
Her drying combinations touched by the sun's last rays,
On the divan are piled (at night her bed)
Stockings, slippers, camisoles, and stays.
I Tiresias, old man with wrinkled dugs
Perceived the scene, and foretold the rest—

I too awaited the expected guest. 230
He, the young man carbuncular, arrives,
A small house agent's clerk, with one bold stare,
One of the low on whom assurance sits
As a silk hat on a Bradford millionaire.
The time is now propitious, as he guesses,
The meal is ended, she is bored and tired,
Endeavours to engage her in caresses
Which still are unreproved, if undesired.
Flushed and decided, he assaults at once;
Exploring hands encounter no defence; 240
His vanity requires no response,
And makes a welcome of indifference.
(And I Tiresias have foresuffered all
Enacted on this same divan or bed;
I who have sat by Thebes below the wall
And walked among the lowest of the dead.)
Bestows one final patronising kiss,
And gropes his way, finding the stairs unlit . . .

She turns and looks a moment in the glass,
Hardly aware of her departed lover; 250
Her brain allows one half-formed thought to pass:
'Well now that's done: and I'm glad it's over.'
When lovely woman stoops to folly and
Paces about her room again, alone,
She smoothes her hair with automatic hand,
And puts a record on the gramophone.

'This music crept by me upon the waters'
And along the Strand, up Queen Victoria Street.
O City city, I can sometimes hear
Beside a public bar in Lower Thames Street, 260

The pleasant whining of a mandoline
And a clatter and a chatter from within
Where fishmen lounge at noon: where the walls
Of Magnus Martyr hold
Inexplicable splendour of Ionian white and gold.

The river sweats
Oil and tar
The barges drift
With the turning tide
Red sails   270
Wide
To leeward, swing on the heavy spar.
The barges wash
Drifting logs
Down Greenwich reach
Past the Isle of Dogs.
          Weialala leia
          Wallala leialala
Elizabeth and Leicester
Beating oars   280
The stern was formed
A gilded shell
Red and gold
The brisk swell
Rippled both shores
Southwest wind
Carried down stream
The peal of bells
White towers
          Weialala leia   290
          Wallala leialala

'Trams and dusty trees.
Highbury bore me. Richmond and Kew
Undid me. By Richmond I raised my knees
Supine on the floor of a narrow canoe.'

'My feet are at Moorgate, and my heart
Under my feet. After the event
He wept. He promised "a new start."
I made no comment. What should I resent?'

'On Margate Sands.   300
I can connect
Nothing with nothing.
The broken fingernails of dirty hands.
My people humble people who expect
Nothing.'
　　　　　la la

To Carthage then I came

Burning burning burning burning
O Lord Thou pluckest me out
O Lord Thou pluckest   310

burning

IV. DEATH BY WATER

PHLEBAS the Phoenician, a fortnight dead,
Forgot the cry of gulls, and the deep sea swell
And the profit and loss.
                              A current under sea
Picked his bones in whispers. As he rose and fell
He passed the stages of his age and youth
Entering the whirlpool.
                              Gentile or Jew
O you who turn the wheel and look to windward,   320
Consider Phlebas, who was once handsome and tall as you.

V. WHAT THE THUNDER SAID

AFTER the torchlight red on sweaty faces
After the frosty silence in the gardens
After the agony in stony places
The shouting and the crying
Prison and palace and reverberation
Of thunder of spring over distant mountains
He who was living is now dead
We who were living are now dying
With a little patience   330

Here is no water but only rock
Rock and no water and the sandy road
The road winding above among the mountains
Which are mountains of rock without water
If there were water we should stop and drink
Amongst the rock one cannot stop or think
Sweat is dry and feet are in the sand
If there were only water amongst the rock
Dead mountain mouth of carious teeth that cannot spit
Here one can neither stand nor lie nor sit   340
There is not even silence in the mountains
But dry sterile thunder without rain
There is not even solitude in the mountains
But red sullen faces sneer and snarl
From doors of mudcracked houses
                                        If there were water

    And no rock
    If there were rock
    And also water

And water
A spring
A pool among the rock
If there were the sound of water only
Not the cicada
And dry grass singing
But sound of water over a rock
Where the hermit-thrush sings in the pine trees
Drip drop drip drop drop drop drop
But there is no water

Who is the third who walks always beside you?
When I count, there are only you and I together
But when I look ahead up the white road
There is always another one walking beside you
Gliding wrapt in a brown mantle, hooded
I do not know whether a man or a woman
—But who is that on the other side of you?

What is that sound high in the air
Murmur of maternal lamentation
Who are those hooded hordes swarming
Over endless plains, stumbling in cracked earth
Ringed by the flat horizon only
What is the city over the mountains
Cracks and reforms and bursts in the violet air
Falling towers
Jerusalem Athens Alexandria
Vienna London
Unreal

A woman drew her long black hair out tight
And fiddled whisper music on those strings

And bats with baby faces in the violet light
Whistled, and beat their wings   380
And crawled head downward down a blackened wall
And upside down in air were towers
Tolling reminiscent bells, that kept the hours
And voices singing out of empty cisterns and exhausted wells.

In this decayed hole among the mountains
In the faint moonlight, the grass is singing
Over the tumbled graves, about the chapel
There is the empty chapel, only the wind's home.
It has no windows, and the door swings,
Dry bones can harm no one.   390
Only a cock stood on the rooftree
Co co rico co co rico
In a flash of lightning. Then a damp gust
Bringing rain

Ganga was sunken, and the limp leaves
Waited for rain, while the black clouds
Gathered far distant, over Himavant.
The jungle crouched, humped in silence.
Then spoke the thunder
Da   400
Datta: what have we given?
My friend, blood shaking my heart
The awful daring of a moment's surrender
Which an age of prudence can never retract
By this, and this only, we have existed
Which is not to be found in our obituaries
Or in memories draped by the beneficent spider
Or under seals broken by the lean solicitor
In our empty rooms

DA   410
Dayadhvam: I have heard the key
Turn in the door once and turn once only
We think of the key, each in his prison
Thinking of the key, each confirms a prison
Only at nightfall, aetherial rumours
Revive for a moment a broken Coriolanus
DA
Damyata: The boat responded
Gaily, to the hand expert with sail and oar
The sea was calm, your heart would have responded   420
Gaily, when invited, beating obedient
To controlling hands

                    I sat upon the shore
Fishing, with the arid plain behind me
Shall I at least set my lands in order?

London Bridge is falling down falling down falling down

Poi s'ascose nel foco che gli affina
Quando fiam ceu chelidon—O swallow swallow
Le Prince d'Aquitaine à la tour abolie
These fragments I have shored against my ruins   430
Why then Ile fit you. Hieronymo's mad againe.
Datta. Dayadhvam. Damyata.

          Shantih shantih shantih

NOTES

NOT only the title, but the plan and a good deal of the incidental symbolism of the poem were suggested by Miss Jessie L. Weston's book on the Grail legend: *From Ritual to Romance* (Macmillan). Indeed, so deeply am I indebted, Miss Weston's book will elucidate the difficulties of the poem much better than my notes can do; and I recommend it (apart from the great interest of the book itself) to any who think such elucidation of the poem worth the trouble. To another work of anthropology I am indebted in general, one which has influenced our generation profoundly; I mean *The Golden Bough*; I have used especially the two volumes *Atthis Adonis Osiris*. Anyone who is acquainted with these works will immediately recognise in the poem certain references to vegetation ceremonies.

I. THE BURIAL OF THE DEAD

Line 20. Cf. Ezekiel II, i.

    23. Cf. Ecclesiastes XII, v.

    31. V. *Tristan und Isolde*, I, verses 5–8.

    42. Id. III, verse 24.

    46. I am not familiar with the exact constitution of the Tarot pack of cards, from which I have obviously departed to suit my own convenience. The Hanged Man, a member of the traditional pack, fits my purpose in two ways: because he is associated in my mind with the Hanged God of Frazer, and because I associate him with the hooded figure in the passage of the disciples to Emmaus in Part V. The Phoenician Sailor and the Merchant appear later; also the 'crowds of people', and Death by Water is executed in Part IV. The Man with Three Staves (an authentic member of the Tarot pack) I associate, quite arbitrarily, with the Fisher King himself.

    60. Cf. Baudelaire:

> 'Fourmillante cité, cité pleine de rêves,
> 'Où le spectre en plein jour raccroche le passant.'

    63. Cf. *Inferno*, III, 55–7:

> 'sì lunga tratta
> di gente, ch'io non avrei mai creduto
> che morte tanta n'avesse disfatta.'

64. Cf. *Inferno*, IV, 25–7:
  'Quivi, secondo che per ascoltare,
  'non avea pianto, ma' che di sospiri,
  'che l'aura eterna facevan tremare.'
68. A phenomenon which I have often noticed.
74. Cf. the Dirge in Webster's *White Devil*.
76. V. Baudelaire, Preface to *Fleurs du Mal*.

II. A GAME OF CHESS

77. Cf. *Antony and Cleopatra*, II, ii, 190.
92. Laquearia. V. *Aeneid*, I, 726:
    dependent lychni laquearibus aureis
    incensi, et noctem flammis funalia vincunt.
98. Sylvan scene. V. Milton, *Paradise Lost*, IV, 140.
99. V. Ovid, *Metamorphoses*, VI, Philomela.
100. Cf. Part III, 204.
115. Cf. Part III, 195.
118. Cf. Webster: 'Is the wind in that door still?'
125. Cf. Part I, 39, 48.
137. Cf. the game of chess in Middleton's *Women beware Women*.

III. THE FIRE SERMON

176. V. Spenser, *Prothalamion*.
192. Cf. *The Tempest*, I, ii.
196. Cf. Marvell, *To His Coy Mistress*.
197. Cf. Day, *Parliament of Bees*:
    'When of the sudden, listening, you shall hear,
    'A noise of horns and hunting, which shall bring
    'Actaeon to Diana in the spring,
    'Where all shall see her naked skin . . .'
199. I do not know the origin of the ballad from which these lines are taken: it was reported to me from Sydney, Australia.
202. V. Verlaine, *Parsifal*.
210. The currants were quoted at a price 'carriage and insurance free to London'; and the Bill of Lading, etc., were to be handed to the buyer upon payment of the sight draft.
218. Tiresias, although a mere spectator and not indeed a 'character', is yet the most important personage in the poem, uniting all the rest. Just as the one-eyed merchant, seller of currants, melts into the Phoenician Sailor, and the latter is not wholly distinct from Ferdinand Prince of Naples, so

all the women are one woman, and the two sexes meet in Tiresias. What Tiresias *sees*, in fact, is the substance of the poem. The whole passage from Ovid is of great anthropological interest:

> ... Cum Iunone iocos et 'maior vestra profecto est
> Quam quae contingit maribus', dixisse, 'voluptas'.
> Illa negat; placuit quae sit sententia docti
> Quaerere Tiresiae: venus huic erat utraque nota.
> Nam duo magnorum viridi coeuntia silva
> Corpora serpentum baculi violaverat ictu
> Deque viro factus, mirabile, femina septem
> Egerat autumnos; octavo rursus eosdem
> Vidit et 'est vestrae si tanta potentia plagae',
> Dixit 'ut auctoris sortem in contraria mutet,
> Nunc quoque vos feriam!' percussis anguibus isdem
> Forma prior rediit genetivaque venit imago.
> Arbiter hic igitur sumptus de lite iocosa
> Dicta Iovis firmat; gravius Saturnia iusto
> Nec pro materia fertur doluisse suique
> Iudicis aeterna damnavit lumina nocte,
> At pater omnipotens (neque enim licet inrita cuiquam
> Facta dei fecisse deo) pro lumine adempto
> Scire futura dedit poenamque levavit honore.

221. This may not appear as exact as Sappho's lines, but I had in mind the 'longshore' or 'dory' fisherman, who returns at nightfall.

253. V. Goldsmith, the song in *The Vicar of Wakefield*.

257. V. *The Tempest*, as above.

264. The interior of St. Magnus Martyr is to my mind one of the finest among Wren's interiors. See *The Proposed Demolition of Nineteen City Churches* (P. S. King & Son, Ltd.).

266. The Song of the (three) Thames-daughters begins here. From line 292 to 305 inclusive they speak in turn. V. *Götterdämmerung*, III, i: the Rhine-daughters.

279. V. Froude, *Elizabeth*, Vol. I, ch. iv, letter of De Quadra to Philip of Spain: 'In the afternoon we were in a barge, watching the games on the river. (The Queen) was alone with Lord Robert and myself on the poop, when they began to talk nonsense, and went so far that Lord Robert at last said, as I was on the spot there was no reason why they should not be married if the queen pleased.'

293. Cf. *Purgatorio*, V, 133:

> 'Ricorditi di me, che son la Pia;
> 'Siena mi fe', disfecemi Maremma.'

307. V. St. Augustine's *Confessions*: 'to Carthage then I came, where a cauldron of unholy loves sang all about mine ears.'

308. The complete text of the Buddha's Fire Sermon (which corresponds in importance to the Sermon on the Mount) from which these words are taken, will be found translated in the late Henry Clarke Warren's *Buddhism in Translations* (Harvard Oriental Series). Mr. Warren was one of the great pioneers of Buddhist studies in the Occident.

309. From St. Augustine's *Confessions* again. The collocation of these two representatives of eastern and western asceticism, as the culmination of this part of the poem, is not an accident.

V. WHAT THE THUNDER SAID

In the first part of Part V three themes are employed: the journey to Emmaus, the approach to the Chapel Perilous (see Miss Weston's book) and the present decay of eastern Europe.

356. This is *Turdus aonalaschkae pallasii*, the hermit-thrush which I have heard in Quebec County. Chapman says (*Handbook of Birds of Eastern North America*) 'it is most at home in secluded woodland and thickety retreats ... Its notes are not remarkable for variety or volume, but in purity and sweetness of tone and exquisite modulation they are unequalled.' Its 'water-dripping song' is justly celebrated.

359. The following lines were stimulated by the account of one of the Antarctic expeditions (I forget which, but I think one of Shackleton's): it was related that the party of explorers, at the extremity of their strength, had the constant delusion that there was *one more member* than could actually be counted.

366–76. Cf. Hermann Hesse, *Blick ins Chaos*: 'Schon ist halb Europa, schon ist zumindest der halbe Osten Europas auf dem Wege zum Chaos, fährt betrunken im heiligen Wahn am Abgrund entlang und singt dazu, singt betrunken und hymnisch wie Dmitri Karamasoff sang. Ueber diese Lieder lacht der Bürger beleidigt, der Heilige und Seher hört sie mit Tränen.'

401. 'Datta, dayadhvam, damyata' (Give, sympathise, control). The fable of the meaning of the Thunder is found in the *Brihadaranyaka—Upanishad*, 5, 2. A translation is found in Deussen's *Sechzig Upanishads des Veda*, p. 489.

407. Cf. Webster, *The White Devil*, V, vi:

> '... they'll remarry
> Ere the worm pierce your winding-sheet, ere the spider
> Make a thin curtain for your epitaphs.'

411. Cf. *Inferno*, XXXIII, 46:
> 'ed io sentii chiavar l'uscio di sotto
> all'orribile torre.'

Also F. H. Bradley, *Appearance and Reality*, p. 346.

'My external sensations are no less private to myself than are my thoughts or my feelings. In either case my experience falls within my own circle, a circle closed on the outside; and, with all its elements alike, every sphere is opaque to the others which surround it . . . In brief, regarded as an existence which appears in a soul, the whole world for each is peculiar and private to that soul.'

424. V. Weston: *From Ritual to Romance*; chapter on the Fisher King.

427. V. *Purgatorio*, XXVI, 148.
> "'Ara vos prec, per aquella valor
> "que vos guida al som de l'escalina,
> "sovegna vos a temps de ma dolor."
> 'Poi s'ascose nel foco che gli affina.'

428. V. *Pervigilium Veneris*. Cf. Philomela in Parts II and III.

429. V. Gérard de Nerval, Sonnet *El Desdichado*.

431. V. Kyd's *Spanish Tragedy*.

433. Shantih. Repeated as here, a formal ending to an Upanishad. 'The Peace which passeth understanding' is a feeble translation of the content of this word.

EDITORIAL NOTES

The text of the poem and notes silently corrects typographical errors in Boni & Liveright's first edition, while preserving original wordings amended in later printings:

42 Od'] *Oed'* (amended in 1936)   161 alright] all right (1922)   415 aetherial] aethereal (1925)   428 *ceu*] *uti* (1936)   **Headnote** (Macmillan)] (Cambridge) (1925) **Headnote** *Atthis Adonis Osiris*] *Adonis, Attis, Osiris* (1936)   210 carriage and insurance free] cost insurance and freight (1963)   356 County] Province (1952)   433 a feeble translation of the content of] our equivalent to (1932).

In 1925, T. S. Eliot added a dedication: 'For Ezra Pound / *il miglior fabbro*'.